Grace Aguilar

LONDON: GROOMBRIDGE & SONS, PATERNOSTER ROW

Printed by Alfred Adlard.

THE
WOMEN OF ISRAEL,

OR

Characters and Sketches

FROM

THE HOLY SCRIPTURES AND JEWISH HISTORY.

BY

GRACE AGUILAR,

AUTHOR OF "HOME INFLUENCE," "THE MOTHER'S RECOMPENSE,"
"THE VALE OF CEDARS," ETC., ETC.

WITH PORTRAIT OF THE AUTHOR.

Fredonia Books
Amsterdam, The Netherlands

The Women of Israel:
Characters and Sketches from the Holy Scriptures
and Jewish History

by
Grace Aguilar

ISBN: 1-4101-0387-0

Copyright © 2003 by Fredonia Books

Reprinted from the 1886 edition

Fredonia Books
Amsterdam, The Netherlands
http://www.fredoniabooks.com

All rights reserved, including the right to reproduce this book, or portions thereof, in any form.

In order to make original editions of historical works available to scholars at an economical price, this facsimile of the original edition of 1886 is reproduced from the best available copy and has been digitally enhanced to improve legibility, but the text remains unaltered to retain historical authenticity.

CONTENTS.

	PAGE
INTRODUCTION	1

FIRST PERIOD.

Wives of Patriarchs.

EVE	11
SARAH	35
REBEKAH	67
LEAH AND RACHEL	97

SECOND PERIOD.

The Exodus and the Law.

EGYPTIAN CAPTIVITY AND JOCHEBED	124
THE EXODUS.—MOTHERS OF ISRAEL	139
LAWS FOR WIVES OF ISRAEL	147
LAWS FOR WIDOWS AND DAUGHTERS IN ISRAEL	162
MAID SERVANTS IN ISRAEL, AND SUNDRY OTHER LAWS	179

THIRD PERIOD.

The Delivery of the Law and the Monarchy.

MIRIAM	191
TABERNACLE WORKERS.—CALEB'S DAUGHTER	199
DEBORAH	205
WIFE OF MANOAH	215
NAOMI	223
HANNAH	241

FOURTH PERIOD.

The Monarchy.

	PAGE
MICHAL	258
ABIGAIL	272
WISE WOMAN OF TEKOAH — WOMAN OF ABEL — RIZPAH — PROPHET'S WIDOW	288
THE SHUNAMMITE	302
LITTLE ISRAELITISH MAID — HULDAH	317

FIFTH PERIOD.

The Babylonish Captivity.

THE CAPTIVITY — REVIEW OF BOOK OF EZRA	330
ESTHER	335
REVIEW OF EVENTS NARRATED BY EZRA AND NEHEMIAH	368

SIXTH PERIOD.

The Second Temple.

REVIEW OF THE JEWISH NATION, FROM THE RETURN FROM BABYLON TO THE APPEAL OF HYRCANUS AND ARISTOBULUS TO POMPEY	376
FROM THE APPEAL TO POMPEY TO THE DEATH OF HEROD	388
FROM THE DEATH OF HEROD TO THE WAR UNDER FLORUS	395
THE MARTYR-MOTHER	403
ALEXANDRA	415
MARIAMNE	435
HELENA	494
BERENICE	503
GENERAL HISTORY	514

SEVENTH PERIOD.

Women of Israel in the Present, as influenced by the Past.

THE WAR AND DISPERSION — THOUGHTS ON THE TALMUD	522
TALMUDIC ORDINANCES AND TALES	534
EFFECTS OF DISPERSION — GENERAL REMARKS	547

THE
WOMEN OF ISRAEL.

INTRODUCTION.

AMONG the many valuable works relative to woman's capabilities, influence, and missions, which in the present age are so continually appearing, one still seems wanting. The field has, indeed, been entered: detached notices of the women of Israel, the female biography of Scripture, have often formed interesting portions of those works where woman is the subject; but all the fruit has not been gathered: much yet remains, which, thrown together, would form a history as instructive as interesting, as full of warning as example, and tending to lead our female youth to the sacred volume, not only as their guide to duty, their support in toil, their comfort in affliction, but as a true and perfect mirror of themselves.

To desert the Bible for its commentators; never to peruse its pages without notes of explanation; to regard it as a work which of itself is incomprehensible; is, indeed, a practice as hurtful as injudicious. Sent as a message of love to our own souls, as written and addressed, not to nations alone, but as the voice of God to individuals—whispering to each of us that which we most need; thus it is we should first regard and venerate it. This accomplished, works tending to elucidate its glorious and consoling truths, to make manifest its simple lessons of character, as well as precept; to bring yet closer to the youthful and aspiring heart, the poetry, the beauty, the eloquence, the appealing tenderness of its sacred pages, may prove of essential service. In this hope, to bring clearly before the women of Israel all that they owe to the word of God, all that it may still be to them, the present task is undertaken.

We are far from asserting that this has not been attempted, and for the larger portion of the sex, accomplished before.

Religion is the foundation and mainspring of every work which has been written for the use and improvement of woman. Female biographers of Scripture have, we believe, often appeared; though the characters of the Old Testament are so briefly and imperfectly sketched, compared to those of the New, that but little pleasure or improvement could be derived from their perusal. Yet still, with the writings of Sandford, Ellis, and Hamilton before us, each exhibiting its author so earnest, so eloquent in her cause, with "woman's mission" marked so simply, yet so forcibly in the little volume of that name, has not woman of every race, and every creed, all sufficient to teach her her duty and herself?

We would say she had: yet for the women of Israel something still more is needed. The authors above mentioned are Christians themselves and write for the Christian world. Education and nationality compel them to believe that "Christianity is the sole source of female excellence;"—that to Christianity alone they owe their present station in the world, their influence, their equality with man, their spiritual provision in this life, and hopes of immortality in the next; —nay more, that the value and dignity of woman's character would never have been recognised, but for the religion of Jesus, that pure, loving, self-denying doctrines were unknown to woman: she knew not even her relation to the Eternal; dared not look upon him as her Father, Consoler, and Saviour till the advent of Christianity. We grant that the Gentiles knew it not, till the Bible became more generally read—till the Eternal, in His infinite mercy, permitted a partial knowledge of Himself to spread over the world—alike to prepare the Gentile for that day, when we shall all know Him as He is, and to render the trial of His people's faith and constancy yet more terribly severe. We feel neither anger nor uncharitableness towards those who would thus deny to Israel those very privileges which were ours ages before they became theirs; and which, in fact, have descended from us to them. Yet we cannot pass such assertion unanswered, lest from the very worth and popularity of those works in which it is promulgated, the young and thoughtless daughter of Israel may believe it really has foundation, and look no further than the page she reads.

How or whence originated the charge that the law of Moses sunk the Hebrew female to the lowest state of degradation, placed her on a level with slaves or heathens, and denied her all mental and spiritual enjoyment, we know not : yet certain it is, that this most extraordinary and unfounded idea obtains credence even in this enlightened age. The word of God at once proves its falsity ; for it is impossible to read the Mosaic law without the true and touching conviction, that the female Hebrew was even more an object of tender and soothing care of the Eternal than the male. The thanksgiving in the Israelitish morning prayer, on which so much stress is laid, as a proof how little woman is regarded, is but a false and foolish reasoning on the subject ; almost, in truth, too trivial for regard.

The very first consequence of woman's sin was to render her, in physical and mental strength, inferior to man ; to expose her to suffering more continued and more acute ; to prevent her obtaining those honours and emoluments of which man thinks so much ; to restrain her path to a more lowly and domestic, though not a less hallowed sphere ; and, all this considered, neither scorn towards the sex, nor too much haughtiness for themselves, actuate the thanksgiving which by our opponents is brought forward against us. It was but one of those blessings in which the pious Israelite thanks God for all things, demanding neither notice nor reproof.

To the Gentile assertion, that the Talmud has originated the above-mentioned blessing, and commanded or inculcated the moral and mental degradation of women, we reply, that even if it did so, which we do not believe it does, its commands are wholly disregarded, and its abolishment is not needed to raise the Hebrew female to that station assigned her in the word of God, and which through many centuries she has been permitted, without reproof or question, to enjoy. The Eternal's provision for her temporal and spiritual happiness is proved in His unalterable word ; and, therefore, no Hebrew can believe that He would issue another law for her degradation and abasement. If, indeed, there are such laws, they must have been compiled at a time when persecution had so brutalised and lowered the intellect of man, that he partook the savage barbarity of the nations around him, and of the age in which he lived ; when the law of his God had, as a natural consequence, become obscured, and the Hebrew female shared the same rude and savage treatment which was the lot of all the lower classes of women in the feudal ages. The protection, the glory, the civilising influence of chivalry extended, in its first establishment, only to the baronial classes.

We see no proofs of the humanising and elevating influence of Christianity, either on man or woman, till the Reformation opened the BIBLE, the whole BIBLE, to the nations at large; when civilisation gradually followed. If then, the situation of even Christian women was so uncertain, and but too often so degraded, for nearly fourteen centuries after the advent of Jesus, who his followers declare was the first to teach them their real position—was it very remarkable that the vilified and persecuted Hebrew should in a degree have forgotten his nationality, his immortal and glorious heritage, and shared in the barbarity around him? Granting, for the moment, that such was the case (but we by no means believe it was), if the degradation, mentally and morally, of the Hebrew female ever did become part of the Jewish law, it was when man was equally degraded, and the blessed word of God hid from him.

The situation of many of the Hebrews at the present day proves this. In but too many parts of the world, the Israelites are still the subjects of scorn, hatred, and persecution; and their condition is, in consequence, the lowest and most awfully degraded in the scale of man. But it is not to woman that degradation and slavery are confined; as, were it a portion of the law of Moses, would inevitably be the case. It is the consequence of cruelty, of abasement in social treatment; yet even here, where mind, principle, honour, all seem overthrown from such brutalising influence, the affections retain their power. Whatever of spiritual hope, of human privileges, the word of God bestows on man, and to which the mind, darkened and despairing from the horrors of persecution, may yet be open, is shared by the Hebrew wife, and imparted by the Hebrew mother.

Were it a portion of the law of Moses to enslave and degrade us, how is it that we do not see this law adhered to and obeyed, as well as others claiming the same divine origin? Neither Christianity nor civilisation would alter or improve our condition, were it indeed such as it has been represented. The Hebrew ever loves, protects, and reverences his female relative; and if, indeed, he do not—if he deny her all share in immortality, and, in consequence, thinks she has no need of religion now, nor hope hereafter, it is because the remnants of barbarism, ignorance, and superstition remain, to have blinded both his spiritual and mental eye; yet whatever he may be accused of believing, his acts deny the belief. Why is he so anxious that his wife and daughters should adhere to every law, attend to every precept which he believes to be the law of God? If they have no soul, no portion in the world to come, it surely cannot signify how they act, or what they believe in this? Why are they blotted from the minds and hearts of their relatives, if, as it may sometimes happen, they intermarry with the stranger? If they have no spiritual responsibility, no claim, no part in the law of God, why should they be blamed, and shunned, if they desert it for another? But it is idle to follow the argument further. The charge is either altogether false, or based on such contradictory and groundless report, as to render it of little consequence, save as it affects us in the eyes of those who uphold, that till Christianity was promulgated, woman knew not her own station, either towards God or man.

Simply to deny this assertion, to affirm, that instead of degrading and enslaving, the Jewish law exalted, protected, and provided for woman, teaching her to look up to God, not as a severe Master and awful Judge, but as her Father, her Defender, her Deliverer when oppressed, her Witness in times of false accusation, her Consoler and Protector when fatherless, widowed—aye, as the tender and loving Sovereign, who spared the young bride the anguish of separation from her beloved— merely to affirm, that with such laws woman was equally a subject of divine love as she is now, would not avail us much. The women of Israel must themselves arise, and prove the truth of what we urge—by their own conduct, their own belief, their own ever-acting and ever-influencing religion, prove without doubt or question that we need not Christianity to teach us our mission—prove that our duties, our privileges, were assigned us from the very beginning of the world, confirmed by that law to which we still adhere, and will adhere for ever, and manifested by the whole history of the Bible.

A new era is dawning for us. Persecution and intolerance have in so many lands ceased to predominate, that Israel may once more breathe in freedom; the law need no longer be preached in darkness, and obeyed in secret; the voice of man need no longer be the vehicle of instruction from father to son, unconsciously mingling with it human opinions, till those opinions could scarcely be severed from the word of God, and by degrees so dimmed its lustre as to render its comprehension an obscure and painful task. This need no longer be. The Bible may be perused in freedom; the law may be publicly explained and preached to all who will attend. A spirit of inquiry, of patriotism, of earnestness in seeking to know the

Lord, and obey Him according to His word, is springing up in lieu of the stagnating darkness, the appalling indifference, which had reigned so long. Persecution never decreased our numbers. As the bush, which burned without consuming, so was Israel in those blood-red ages of intolerance and butchery. In the very heart of the most catholic kingdom—amongst her senate, her warriors, her artisans—aye, even her monks and clergy—Judaism lurked unconsumed by the fires ever burning around. The spirit was ever awake and active, ready to endure martyrdom, but not to forswear that God whose witnesses they were. Persecution was a crisis in our History; prosperity the reaction; and from that reaction the natural consequence was the gradual rise, growth, and influence of indifference. Indifference, however, has but its appointed time; and Israel is springing up once more the stronger, nobler, more spiritually enlightened, from the long and waveless sleep. Free to assert their right as immortal children of the living God, let not the women of Israel be backward in proving they, too, have a Rock of Strength, a Refuge of Love; that they, too, have a station to uphold, and a "mission" to perform, not alone as daughters, wives, and mothers, but as witnesses of that faith which first raised, cherished, and defended them—witnesses of that God who has called them His, and who has so repeatedly sanctified the emotions peculiar to their sex, by graciously comparing the love He bears us, as yet deeper than a mother's for her child, a wife's for her husband, having compassion on His people, as on "a woman forsaken and grieved in spirit." "Can a woman forget her sucking child, that she should not have compassion on the son of her travail; yea, she may forget, yet will I not forget thee." "As a mother comforteth her children, so will I comfort thee."

Were not these relations holy and sanctified in the sight of the Lord, would He use them as figurative of His long-suffering love? Many terms similar to those above quoted, prove without a shadow of doubt, the tender compassion with which He regarded woman long before He used such terms to figure His compassionating love toward Israel, when sinfulness called forth His long-averted wrath.

Let us, then, endeavour to convince the nations of the high privileges we enjoy, in common with our fathers, brothers, and husbands, as the firstborn of the Lord, by the peculiar sanctity, spirituality, and inexpressible consolation of our belief. Let us not, as women of Israel, be content with the mere perform ance of domestic, social, and individual duties, but vivify and lighten them by the rays of eternal love and immortal hope which beam upon us from the pages of the Bible. A religion of love is indeed necessary to woman, yet more so than to man. Even in her happiest lot there must be a void in her heart, which ever-acting piety alone can fill; and to her whose portion is to suffer, whose lot is lonely, O what misery must be hers, unless she can lean upon her God, and draw from His word the blessed conviction that His love, His tenderness, are hers, far beyond the feeble conception of earth; and that whatever she may endure, however unknown to or scorned by man, it is known to Him who smites but in love, and has mercy even while He smites.

To realise this blessed conviction, the Bible must become indeed the book of life to the female descendants of that nation whose earliest history it so vividly records; and be regarded, not as a merely political or religious history, but as the voice of God speaking to each individual, giving strength to the weak, encouragement to the desponding, endurance to the patient, justice to the wronged, and consolation unspeakable as unmeasurable to the afflicted and the mourner. Do we need love ? We shall find innumerable verses telling us, that the Lord Himself proclaimed His attribute as "merciful and gracious, long-suffering, abundant in goodness and truth, keeping mercy for thousands, forgiving iniquity and sin;" that "as high as the Heaven is above the earth so great is His mercy, extending from everlasting to everlasting." We have but to read those appeals of the Eternal to Israel, alike in Jeremiah and Isaiah, and many of the minor prophets—and if our hearts be not stone, they must melt before such compassionating love, such appealing tenderness, and feel we cannot be lonely, cannot be unloved, while such deep, changeless love is ours. Do we need sympathy ? Shall we not find it in words similar to these, "In all their afflictions He was afflicted, and the Angel of His presence saved them. In His love and in His pity He redeemed them, and He bare them, and carried them all the days of old." Do we need patience and strength ? Shall we not exercise it when we have the precious promise, "*Wait* on the Lord, be of good courage, and He shall strengthen thine heart?" Shall we droop and grieve beneath the wrongs and false judgments of short-sighted man, when we are told the ways of God are not those of man —that He knoweth our frame, and readeth our thoughts—

that not a bodily or mental pang is ours which He does not know and compassionate—aye, and in His own good time will heal?

To throw together all those verses which confirm and prove the loving-tenderness borne towards us by the Eternal, would be an endless and a useless task. We can but point to that ever-flowing fount of healing waters, and assure those who have once really tasted, and will persevere in the heavenly draught, that it will never fail them, never change its properties, but each year sink deeper and deeper into their souls, till at length it becomes indeed all they need; and they themselves will cling to it, despite of occasional doubt and darkness, inseparable from our souls while denizens of earth.

Nor is it only the verses containing such gracious promises which will yield us comfort and assistance. We may glean the glad tidings of Eternal Love from the biographies and narratives with which the sacred book abounds—there may be some meek and lowly spirits amongst the female youth of Israel, who would gladly clasp the strength and guidance which we proffer them from the Bible, could they believe that God, the great, the almighty, the tremendous and awful Being (as which they have perhaps been accustomed to regard Him) can have love and pity for themselves, or give comfort and aid in trials, which appear even too trivial to ask or to excite the sympathy of man. We would lead them to look earnestly and believingly into the history of every woman in the Bible, and trace there the influence of God's holy and compassionating love. We are not indeed placed as the women of Israel before their dispersion, or as the wives of the patriarchs before the law was given; yet their God is our God. It was not to a race so perfect, so gifted, so hallowed, as to be free from all the present faults and failings of the sex that the Lord vouchsafed His love. No, it was to woman, even as she is now. The women of the Bible are but mirrors of ourselves. And if the Eternal, in His infinite mercy, extended love, compassion, forbearance, and forgiveness unto them, we may believe He extends them equally unto us, and draw comfort and encouragement and faith from the biographies we read.

In a work entitled "The Women of Israel," some apology, perhaps, is necessary for commencing with the wives of the Patriarchs, who may not lay claim to such holy appellation. Yet, as the chosen and beloved partners of those favoured of God, from whom Israel traces his descent, and for the sake of whose faith and righteousness, we were selected and chosen as a peculiar people, and the law given to be our guide through earth to heaven, we cannot consider our history complete without them; more particularly as their lives are so intimately blended with their husbands'; and that in them, even yet more vividly than at a later period, we may trace the Lord's dealings with His female children, and derive from them alike warning and support.

Eve, indeed, may not have such national claim; but if we believe that her history, as every other part of Genesis, was penned by the same inspired lawgiver—that Moses recorded only that which had been—we shall find much, indeed, to repay us for lingering awhile on her character and life. To the scepticism, the cavils, the doubts, and (but too often unhappily) the direct unbelief in the Mosaic account of the first disobedience of man, we give no heed whatever. We must either believe in the Pentateuch or deny it. There can be no intermediate path. The whole must be true or none. It is not because much may appear obscure, or even contradictory in the sacred narrative, that we are to pronounce it false, or mystify and poetise it as an allegory.

We are simply to believe, and endeavour to act on that belief. So much is there ever passing around us that we cannot solve; our thoughts, in their farthest flight, are so soon checked, can penetrate so little into the wonders of man and nature, that it appears extraordinary how man can doubt and deny, because he cannot understand. In this case, however—the history of Eve—truth is so simple and clear, that we know not how it can supply such an endless fund of argument and doubt. To remove this groundless disbelief, to endeavour to render the narrative clear and simple to the female youth of Israel, and, even through Eve's sad yet consoling history, to prove to them the deep love borne towards us from the very first of our creation by our gracious God, must be our apology, if apology be needed, for commencing a work entitled "The Women of Israel," with our general mother.

Beginning, then, from the very beginning, some degree of order is requisite in the arrangement of our subject. Our aim being to evince to the nations and to our own hearts, the privileges, alike temporal and eternal, which were ours from the very commencement—to prove that we have no need of Christianity, or the examples of the females in the Gospel, to raise us to an equality with man—to demonstrate our duties, and secure us consolation here, or salvation hereafter—the word of God must be alike our ground-work and our guide. From the past history which that unerring guide presents, our present duties and responsibilities, and our future destiny will alike be revealed. In a simple biography, each life is a sufficient division; but, with the exception of the wives of the patriarchs, and one or two more, we have scarcely sufficient notice of individuals to illustrate our design by regarding them separately There appear, therefore, seven periods in the history of the women of Israel, which demand our attention.

First Period — the Wives of the Patriarchs, including Eve, Sarah, Rebecca, Leah, and Rachel.

Second Period—the Exodus, and the law considered as affecting the condition, and establishing the privileges of women.

Third Period—Women of Israel between the establishment of the law and the authority of the Kings, comprising sketches of Miriam, Deborah, the wife of Manoah, Naomi, and Hannah.

Fourth Period—Women of Israel during the continuation of the Kingdom, comprising, among other sketches, Michal, Abigail, the Shunammite, and Huldah.

Fifth Period—Babylonish Captivity, including the life of Esther.

Sixth Period—the War and Dispersion, and their effects on the Condition and Privileges of Women in Israel.

Seventh Period—Women of Israel in the Present time, as influenced by the history of the Past.

For five of these periods, then, we perceive the Word of God can be our only guide; and this at once marks our history as sacred, not profane. If, therefore, there should be parts which resemble more a religious essay than female biography, we reply, that to inculcate religion, the vital spirit of religion, is the sole intention of these pages.

We wish to infuse the spirit of truth and patriotism, of nationality, and yet of universal love, into the hearts of the young daughters of Israel; and we know of no means more likely, under the Divine blessing, to accomplish this, than to bring before them, as vividly and engagingly as we can, the never-ending love, the compassionating tenderness, the unchanging sympathy, alike in our joys and in our sorrows manifested by the Eternal so touchingly and simply in the history of our female ancestors—to lead them to know Him and love Him, not only through the repeated promises, but through the narratives of His word, and to glory in those high privileges which, as children, retainers and promulgators of His holy law, are ours, over and above every other nation, past or present, in the history of the world!

FIRST PERIOD.

Wives of the Patriarchs.

EVE.

THE last and mightiest work of creation was completed. Man, in his angelic and immortal beauty, stood erect and perfect, fresh from the hand of his Creator; lord and possessor of the new formed world. Though formed of the dust, earth had not, as in the case of the inferior animals, brought him forth. Destined from the first to be made in the image of God, that is, to possess an emanation of the spiritual essence, and so become a living and immortal soul—the shrine of so glorious a possession was created by God himself. "And God created him," He did not "call him forth."

For man, the beautiful creation already wrought, was not sufficient; and "He planted a garden eastward in Eden, filling it with every tree that was pleasant for the sight, and good for food"—animate and inanimate creation brought together by the Eternal in one beautiful and perfect whole. Nor was this all: endowed with capabilities of love, happiness, and wisdom, as much above the other animals as the angelic nature is to man, still he needed more for the perfection of his felicity; and God in his infinite mercy provided for that want.

"It is not good for man to be alone," the Eternal said; "I will make him a help meet for him." And therefore woman was created, and brought unto man, who received her as the Eternal in His mercy had ordained, a being beloved above all others, whose gentler qualities and endearing sympathy should soften his rougher and prouder nature, and "help" him in all things "meet" for an immortal being.

The whole creation had had its origin in that Omnific Love which CREATED to ENJOY—called out of darkness and chaos a world teeming with life and beauty, that innumerable sources of happiness might spring forth from what had before been nought; but woman's creation was a still greater manifestation of love than all which had gone before it. She was created, not only to feel happiness herself, but to *make it for others;* and if that was the design of her existence in Eden, how deeply should we feel the solemn truth, that it is equally so now; and that woman has a higher and holier mission than the mere pursuit of pleasure and individual enjoyment; that to flutter through life without one serious thought or aim, without a dream beyond the present moment, without a feeling higher than temporal gratification, or an aspiration rising beyond this world, can never answer the purpose of her divine creation, or make her a help meet for man. Nor is it to wives only this privilege is accorded. Mother or sister, each has equally her appointed duty—to endeavour so to help and influence man, that her more spiritual and unselfish nature shall gradually be infused into him, and, raising him above mere worldly thought and sensual pleasures, compel him to feel that it is not indeed "good for man to be alone," but that woman may still fulfil the offices of help and love for which alone she was created.

Although the Mosaic record of man's residence in Paradise is mournfully brief, we have sufficient scriptural authority for lingering a little while on Eve's innocent career. Placed in a garden with every capability of felicity within herself—nature, meditation, commune with the Almighty in thanksgiving, or with Him direct, through the Voice which revealed the invisible presence, the sweet blessed intercourse of kindred spirits, springing from the love she bore to and received from, her husband,—simple and imperfect as such sources of enjoyment may appear, they were more exquisite, more perfect, than we can dream of now.

The spirit which God had breathed within man when he became a living soul, was the likeness or image of God in which "made He man;" and this spirit or essence, enabled both Adam and Eve to commune in close and beatified intercourse with the gloried Creator whence that essence sprung. No sin could fling its dark shade between the soul and its God: and so deaden spiritual joy. Nought of doubt could stagnate the love which must have been excited in their hearts towards their Father and their God. All *around* and *within* them bore such impress of His hand, as to excite nought but gratitude and devotion. If even now, when once we have realised the love of God and submission to His will—when once we can so put our trust in Him as to give Him, "all our heart," and come to Him in sorrow and in joy, convinced that he knows and loves us better than ourselves—we experience a peace, a blessedness no earthly tempests can remove; how thrice blessed must have been the felicity of Eve!

Apart from the spirit which the Eternal gave to lead man to Himself, was the MIND which opened to the creatures formed in His image the inexhaustible resources of wisdom, imagination, knowledge—all that could create the higher kind of happiness, which is synonymous with mental joy. Sources of what is now termed wisdom, that of books and man, were indeed unknown to our first parents; nor did they need them. In the wonders of creation the tree, the herb, the flower, the gushing rivers, the breezy winds; nay, from the mighty form of the largest beasts, to the structure of the tiniest leaf; the flow of the river to the globule of the dew, which watered the face of the whole earth, there was enough to excite and satisfy their mental powers; enough to excite emotions alike of wonder and adoration. Their commune with the angelic messengers of their benevolent Creator, their tidings of Heaven and its hosts, must have excited the highest and purest pleasures of imagination, and so diversified and lightened the mental exercises of wisdom, which the palpable and visible objects of creation so continually call forth.

Nor was spiritual and mental felicity the only portion of Eve—the affections, the impulses of the *heart*, fresh from the creating Hand of Love, had full play—created, as the perfecting finish to man's happiness, beholding him, the lord of all on which she gazed—earth formed to yield him her fruits—water and air, to unite for his refreshment—every animal obeying his authority—instinctively feeling, too, the mighty power of his intellect, the strength of his mind and frame, the deepest reverence must have mingled with, and so perfected, her love. Nor would this acknowledgment tend to degrade woman in the scale of creation. Formed, like man, in the immortal likeness of the Lord, she was his equal in his responsibilities towards God, and in the care of his creatures:

endowed *equally* with man, but *differently* as to the nature of those endowments. His mission was to protect, and guide, and have dominion—hers to soothe, bless, persuade to right, and " help " in all things " meet " for immortal beings.

The existence of Eve, then, in her innocence, was, in a word, an existence of love—love towards God, and nature, and man, which none of the infirmities of our present state could cloud or interrupt. Do we err, then, in saying that, even in the brief record of Scripture, we have sufficient authority for delineating the felicity of our first parents in Eden? And will it not demonstrate appealingly to us, those pleasures which God Himself ordained, and which even now, might so be cultivated as to bring us happiness, as infinitely superior to the amusements, so called, as innocence is to sin?

But beautiful as is this picture, we must turn from it to consider feelings and events of a sadly different nature. In the most conspicuous part of Paradise, the Eternal had called forth two trees, differing in their magnificence, perhaps in the halo with which they may have been encircled as peculiar witnesses of their Creator, from every other in the garden. They were the Tree of Life and the Tree of Knowledge. Of the first so little is known, that we are justified in supposing the intention of its existence was frustrated by the disobedience of man; a conjecture founded on the solemn fact, that as the Lord created not one thing in vain, that tree must also have had its use and intention, and from the words which follow at a later period, "Lest man put forth his hand, and take also of the tree of life, and eat and live for ever," we are quite authorised to suppose it possessed some qualities yet mightier than the Tree of Knowledge, with which its taste would have gifted man, had he not by rebellion frustrated the beneficent design of his Creator, and forfeited the privileges which might have been his own.

Of the Tree of Knowledge, its intention and its uses, we have sufficient information. The Eternal knew the nature of the creatures He had formed; that it was but an easy and slender trial of obedience and of love, if they had no temptation to rebel or disobey. Though subject to His sway, though deriving existence from His hand, and enjoying life and all its varied sources of felicity from the same infinite love, yet the Eternal in His wisdom and His justice, had endowed them with the power of free-will, of listening to and following, or struggling with and conquering, the seeds of corruption, which from their earthly shell were inherent, though as yet kept so completely under subjection from the divine and purifying nature of the soul, that, until he was tried, man himself was scarcely sensible of their existence. To have guarded jealously from every temptation—to have surrounded him with nought but sources of pleasure and enjoyment, and so called forth only the grateful and adoring faculties of the spirit, was not according to that divine and perfect economy of love and justice which characterised the dealings of the Creator with his creatures. It was deeper, dearer love, to permit man to win his immortality, his eternal innocence, than to bestow them upon him unsought, and, therefore, little valued. They could be guilty of no crime, in the world's parlance so termed. They were the sole possessors of the newly-created earth : in daily commune with their Creator, and therefore in neither idolatry, blasphemy, Sabbath-breaking, dishonouring of parents, murder, adultery, theft, false-witness, or covetousness, could they sin. God knew that all the crimes which *might* devastate the earth would spring from one alone, DISOBEDIENCE; and therefore was it that His infinite wisdom ordained that the trial of man's love, and faith, and virtue, should simply be, obedience to his will.

"And the Lord God commanded the man, saying, Of every tree of the garden thou mayst freely eat; but of the tree of the knowledge of the good and evil thou shalt not eat ; for in the day that thou eatest thereof, thou shalt surely die." Whether this threatened chastisement was robed in mystery, or that Adam had beheld death in the inferior animals (for Holy Writ gives no authority for believing that even they knew not death till after the fall), and so could have some idea of what he would become, even as a clod of the earth, if he disobeyed, we may not here determine ; suffice it, that the Eternal was too merciful, too just, to threaten his creature with a chastisement for disobedience which he could not comprehend.

Beautiful to look upon, and exquisite in its fragrance, we may imagine the Tree of Knowledge extending its rich foliage and tempting fruit in the most conspicuous part of the garden, no doubt frequently attracting the admiration of Adam and Eve, perhaps exciting wishes which the spirit within them had as yet power effectually to banish, or entirely to subdue.

Alone, unprotected by the sterner, firmer qualities of her husband, Eve had walked forth, secure in her innocence, in the consciousness of love lingering within, and all around her; —the young animals gamboling about her, calling forth her caresses and her smile—the little birds springing from tree to tree in joyous greeting, or nestling in her bosom without one touch of fear—the gorgeous flowers, in all their glowing robes and exquisite fragrance, clustering richly round her—the very buds seeming to look up into her sweet loving face, to reflect increase of beauty from the gaze, so may our fancy picture her, as she neared that tree under whose fair branches so much of misery lurked. Coiled at its root, or twisted in rainbow-coloured folds around its trunk, lay the serpent, "who was more subtle than any beast of the field, which the Lord God had made." And he said unto the woman, "Yea hath God said, Ye shall not eat of every tree in the garden? And the woman said, We may eat of the fruit of the trees of the garden, but of the fruit of the tree which is in the midst of the garden, God hath said, Ye shall not eat of it, neither shall ye touch it, lest ye die. And the serpent said unto the woman, Ye shall not surely die, for God doth know, that in the day ye eat thereof, then your eyes shall be opened, and ye shall be as gods, knowing good and evil. And when the woman saw that the tree was good for food, and it was pleasant to the eyes, and a tree to be desired to make one wise, she took of the fruit thereof, and did eat; and she gave also unto her husband with her, and he did eat."

Such are the brief, yet emphatic words, in which the inspired prophet of the Lord detailed those incidents on which the whole after-history of the world is founded—the mournful detail of that first sin, from which every other sprung, DISOBEDIENCE. Of the various speculations and opinions concerning the instrumentality of the serpent we shall take no heed, save the humble endeavour to reconcile the ways of the Lord. He *permitted* the trial, but He *commanded* not the evil interposition of the subtlest of His creatures, the serpent, any more than He *commanded* the subtlety of Jacob in obtaining his father's blessing. Both events were permitted to take place; but the evil means of their accomplishment were NOT of the Lord, and consequently their agents were both subject to His displeasure, and condemned to punishment and wrath.

In one brief hour, the whole nature of Eve was changed—the seeds of frailty, of whose very existence she had been scarcely conscious before, sprung up into influencing poison. Curiosity, presumption, an over-weening trust in her own strength, a desire to act alone, independent of all control, to become greater, wiser, higher than the scale of being, than the station in which God's love had placed her—discontent—scorn of the blessings which a moment before had seemed so precious, simply because imagination portrayed others more alluring, the attraction of novelty, beauty, those idol shrines at which woman so often sacrifices her better, her immortal self—such (and are they not the characteristics of woman, even as she is now?)—such were the emotions excited by the wily tempter, through whose baneful influence she fell. Where, at that moment, was the voice of the spirit, warning her of the God she disobeyed? Where the whisper of the mind, telling her that the sources of wisdom, of knowledge, already open, were the purest and the best? Where the fond tones of the heart, urging her to seek the protection, the counsel, the support, of her earthly lord? Hushed, drowned in the wild tumult of a new and terrible excitement of feelings, whose very novelty fascinated and held her chained. The voice of the tempter was in her ear. Sight and smell were filled with the exquisite fruit, the delicious fragrance; and if such were revealed, what must be its taste and touch, when to pluck and eat would make her "as gods, knowing good and evil"? Weak, frail, unguarded, for the still small voice of the soul was lost in that hour's tempest, was it a marvel that she fell? Could she have done otherwise? The bulwark of FAITH was shivered, her heart was open and defenceless—she was alone, alone—for even the guardian within, if not fled, was silent. The God of infinite love and compassion beheld, but approached not; and wherefore? If He permitted, ordained, why did He punish? O had the voice of His creature called on Him in that terrible hour; had but the faintest cry ascended for help, for strength, for mercy; had but the struggling murmur arisen, "Father, thy words are *truth*, let me but *believe*," strength, help, faith, would have poured their reviving rays into her sinking soul, and she had been saved, saved for immortality, saved to glorify her God! It was not that she had not the power so to pray. Free-will was her own—to obey, or disobey—to adhere, or to rebel. Of herself, indeed, she could not have resisted; but she had equal power to call upon the Lord, as to listen to the tempter. According to the path she chose, would have been the issue. Infinite, measureless, as is the love of the Eternal, yet how dare we believe He will grant us help and strength, unless they are implored? How dare we believe He will come forward to our aid, if we stand forth in our own strength, as if we needed nought; nay, through presumption, arrogance, self-righteousness, rebel against, and defy him? He had said, "Eat not of the tree of knowledge, for on the day that thou eatest thereof thou shalt surely die." He had not *commanded* only, though that should have been sufficient from a loving Father to his children; but the command was enforced with a warning, that love should be strengthened by reverential fear. He had given the power to resist temptation, by CALLING UPON HIM; but if that power were trampled upon and utterly disregarded; and the creature of His hand, whose whole existence, felicity, strength, wisdom, had their being but in Him, so depended upon *herself*, as to be satisfied with her own strength, believing it was in her power to become as a god, and so defying Him, is it contradiction to assert, that the All-wise, All-merciful, All-JUST, permitted, and yet punished? Surely, surely, there is not one portion of this mournful history, which, on mature consideration, will be found irreconcilable with the attributes of the Eternal, or with His dealings with His creatures.

"She took of the fruit thereof and did eat." For a brief interval, we may suppose, the tumult within, the struggle between virtue and vice, innocence and guilt, was stilled in a strange fearful intoxication of sinful joy. She had broken through the barrier, which, at the words of the serpent, seemed suddenly of iron, it so degraded her by its harshness and injustice. She was INDEPENDENT, had acted by herself, had shaken off all control; and the full tide of guilty pleasure so swept over her soul, as to permit, for the moment, no thought but of herself. But this lasted not long: the reaction came with the one thought—her husband. Terror of his anger was, in all probability, the first emotion—how might she evade it? Fear, notwithstanding her independence, deadened, banished, frustrated every feeling of remorse; repentance, sorrow—all would avail her nothing now; there was but one way to avert her husband's wrath—to make him disobedient as herself. The crime would appear less could another share it.

She recollected the influence she possessed; nay, that she had been created to be his help, to soften his sterner and less yielding nature, and would it fail her now? There was no pause, there could be none; guilt ever hurries on its victims. On her arguments, her persuasions, holy writ is silent. It was enough—"she gave also unto her husband with her and he did eat."

The crime was consummated. Love itself, the purest, noblest, most influencing of those spiritual blessings vouchsafed to man by his Creator—love deeper for the creature than the Creator, deeming the gift more precious than the Giver—love it was which to Adam was the tempter, and so converted the richest blessing to the direst curse. The specious offers, the dazzling allurements of the serpent, had, perhaps, to his stronger, more steadfast nature, been of no avail. He had no need of ambition, for he was lord over the whole created world. A glance from his eye, a stern rebuke from his lips, had awed even the subtlest of the beasts into silence, and banished him for ever; but strength and firmness fled before the endearing influence of the being whom, created to perfect his happiness, he loved better than himself. Excuse for his weakness, indeed, there is none; but if such may be the extent of woman's influence (and it is as powerful even now), how fearful is her responsibility, and how deep should be her humility, how fervent her petitions for grace to guide aright.

Not long might the triumph of guilt last. Day declined—the hour of evening came, which they were wont so joyfully to welcome, for it brought with it the voice of God. Remorse had come with all its horrors; and now for the first time the extent of their sin stood before them. Terror banished all of love, as all of joy; and when the first sound of the Eternal's voice reached them, they fled in anguish to hide themselves amid the trees of the garden. Vain hope; but proving how all of spirit and of mind was crushed and buried in this first and awful sway of guilt. "And the Lord God called unto Adam, and said unto him, Where art thou? And he said, I heard thy voice in the garden, and I was afraid, because I was naked; and I hid myself. And the Lord God said, Who told thee that thou wast naked? Hast thou eaten of the tree, whereof I commanded thee that thou shouldst not eat? And the man said, The woman thou gavest to be with me, she gave me of the fruit, and I did eat. And the Lord God said unto the woman, What is this that thou hast done ? And the woman said, The serpent beguiled me, and I did eat."

Though to him all was known, yet would not the beneficent, the ever-loving, aye, even at that moment, still *loving* God condemn without question, judge without permitting defence. And how unupbraiding, how loving the appeal, "What is this that thou hast done ?" breathing a Father's sorrowing mercy in the very midst of justly deserved punishment. There was no consuming wrath, no terrifying anger, nought to betray that mighty and awful being at whose first word might be annihilation.

The Eternal pronounced not sentence without requiring and *waiting* for reply : but what was that reply ? Accusation of another, not self-abhorrence and lowly repentance. How fearful was the change wrought in the *heart*, as well as in the spirit of man, by his sin. Where now was his deep love for Eve, that he could say, vainly hoping to exculpate himself, "The woman thou didst give me, she gave me of the fruit, and I did eat." She had led him by the power of his love into sin ; but from that moment her power was at an end, and he cared not to give her up to justice, so he excused himself. How terrible a commencement of her punishment must have been her husband's words to the still loving heart of Eve. It was true she had done as he had said ; but was he to be her accuser ? And to her were those words of sorrowing compassion said, "What is this that thou hast done ?" Hast thou indeed so used the power, the beauty, the influence with which I endowed thee, for so different a purpose ? She denied it not : she said not one word to justify her sin towards her husband ; his words had entered her heart with the first sharp pang which human affection knew, and there was no attempt at defence or evasion, —"The serpent beguiled me, and I did eat." If Adam had stooped to lay the blame of his own weakness upon one whom he had loved, instead of bewailing his own sin, it was no wonder Eve, not yet awakened to what she should have done to avert the temptation, conscious but of increasing misery, thought only of what might seem excuse, "The serpent beguiled me." The Eternal knew she had spoken truth ; and, still guided by that mercy and justice which in God alone are so perfectly united that there is no need of "man's ways" to reconcile them, proceeded to pronounce sentence according to the degrees of guilt.

This is not the place to enter into a dissertation on the punishment awarded to the serpent; suffice it that there seems no hidden or allegorical meaning in the inspired historian's simple words. The serpent, as a beast of the field, *beguiled*, and, as a beast of the field, was *punished*. Nor can an Israelite acknowledge any allusion to, or any necessity for a crucified and atoning Saviour, in the very simple words, "I will put enmity between thee and the woman, between thy seed and her seed; it shall bruise thy head, and thou shalt bruise his heel." For a Hebrew, the words can only be taken in their purely literal sense. We are particular on this point: because thus early, in the perusal of the sacred Scriptures, the Jewish and Gentile readings differ; and from childish readings of Bible histories by Gentile writers, we may find ourselves giving credence to an assertion, for which we have no Mosaic authority, and which in after years, we would gladly root out from the mystical and contradictory opinions with which it confuses our ideas.

Eve's chastisement was severer than her husband's, and it was just that so it was, for she was the first transgressor. Death, indeed,—that the dust of which the *frame* was composed should return to dust,—was the awful sentence pronounced on both: for such had been threatened from the first if they disobeyed: but during their sojourn upon earth, the sharper severer trial of pain, of multiplied sorrows, of sinking comparatively in the scale of strength and intellect, of becoming subject to her husband, not as before, from the sweet obedience of love, but from the sterner mandate of duty; of being exposed, as a mother, to a hundred sources of anguish of which man knows nothing; for his deepest dearest love for his offspring is not like a mother's, subject to the thousand anxieties and cares which, independent of severer maternal trials, fill her heart from the moment she hears the first faint cry of the new-born until death. And these trials *were* Eve's, and they *are* woman's. Man had, indeed, his work; the earth was cursed through his sin, and forbidden to yield her fruit without the severest labour; he was to go forth from the Paradise of innocence and love, to till the ground whence he was taken— banished and for ever.

The voice of their God, for the first time heard in reproachful though still forbearing enquiry, and then in fearful condemnation, removed the blackening veil of sin. The spirit burst from the chains of guilt and sin, and while it bowed in agony and remorse before the Father and the Judge, and acknowledged this awful sentence just, drew them once more to each other. Love was not given only for the happy : to the sorrowing, the repentant, it comes soothing while it softens, seeming, even while it deepens the heavy floods of grief, to banish all of harshness, of selfishness, and of despair. The Justice of the Eternal marked the woman as the greater sinner—Adam's further wrath was needless, remorse too told him that, as the stronger, the firmer, he should have resisted her persuasions, that his disobedience was his own sin, not her's ; and we may believe that, as weak, trembling, bowed to the very dust, not from the thoughts of her own chastisement so much as from the reflection of what she had hurled upon her husband, for such still is woman, Adam once more received her to his heart, the sharer of his future toils, the soother of his threatened cares, even as she had before been the help-meet of his joy.

And already Eve needed all of strength and comfort her earthly lord might give. Still remembering mercy, the Eternal clothed them for their departure, endowing them with those faculties of invention, alike for their personal comfort as for the tillage of the ground, for which they had no need in Eden ; but the very gift betrayed the bleak and desert world they were about to seek. Could they but remain in the home of their past innocence and joy, the anguish of the present might be sooner healed. Who that thinks a moment of what we now feel in turning from a beloved home, the scene of all our early hopes and joys and love, adorned with all of nature and of art, to seek another, impoverished, and fraught with toil and danger, apart from every object, animate, or inanimate which has twined round our hearts, and bound us there,—who, that pictures scenes like these, will refuse our general mother the meed of sympathy as she turned from Eden. A change perhaps her sin had wrought even there. The birds flew aloft, trembling to approach that gentle bosom which had before been their resting-place ; the young animals fled in terror from her step ; and there was that in the changed fierce aspects of the beasts of the field, which caused her heart to sicken with deadly fear. The very flowers hung their heads and drooped when gathered ; they could not bear the touch of sin. Yet to that woman's heart Eden was Eden still—her *home*, the receiver of all those varied channels of love which could be spared from her husband ; and to turn from it, never to approach it more, and from the consequences of her own act, how deep must have been her agony, how touching its remorse, and how necessary the support of love.

Though Moses, in his brief detail of past events, simply follows the expulsion from Eden by the birth of Cain, we have sufficient authority from the unchangeable attributes of the Eternal, to believe, that the same love which provided Adam and Eve with clothing, directed and blessed their wanderings; and though no longer revealing His gracious presence, as in Eden, yet still inspiring the power of prayer and belief in his constant omnipresence and protection. Their sin had indeed changed their earthly nature,—the *good* had been conquered by the *evil*. It was henceforth a difficult and weary task to subdue the evil inclinations, the proneness to disobedience and self-righteousness. It was a labour of toil and tears to bring the heavenly essence once more even to a faint and disfigured likeness of its God, the voice of the soul, once silenced as it had been, could only be heard after years of watching and prayer. The Eternal, in His prescience, knew this would be, not so much in Adam himself (for repentance and sorrow brought him back through his punishment to holiness and constant communion with his God), but in his offspring. Farther and farther, as the children of men advanced from their first father—as the tale of creation, of the Eternal's visible presence in Paradise, of all which his love had formed for his favoured creature, man, became fainter and fainter in the dim distance of the past,—so would the likeness of the Lord in which man was made, become more and more effaced, and sin become more and more ascendant. For this reason then it was, that the Eternal, alike in His wisdom and justice and MERCY, ordained death as the end of all, the righteous and the wicked : for Solomon himself telleth us "there is no man that sinneth not :" and we read in the narrative of Moses himself (Gen. vi. 6) that "every imagination of man's heart was only evil continually; and it repented the Lord that he had made man on the earth, and it grieved him at his heart ;" and again (Gen. viii.), "I will not curse the ground any more for man's sake; for the imagination of man's heart is evil from his youth."

But the Mosaic creed of love and perfect justice goes no further. To use the language of our own venerable sages :—
"Although the descendants of Adam inherited the body from

him, and with it the maledictions attached thereto, it is not because they received corporeal existence from him that the souls of all mankind are condemned, for *they had not existence from Adam, but are a direct emanation from God.* Therefore Noah, Shem, Abraham, Isaac, and Jacob, and all the other just, *did not* pay the *sin of Adam*, nor were their souls condemned."* And there is still more convincing proof from the Word of God; Pentateuch, History, Psalms, Proverbs, and Prophets, almost every page bears witness that *each man is responsible for his own individual acts.*—" See I have set before you this day LIFE and GOOD, DEATH and EVIL; therefore choose *life* that thou and thy seed may LIVE" (Deut. xxx. 15 and 19). "Then they that feared the Lord spake often one to another; and the Lord hearkened, and heard it: and a book of remembrances was written before Him for them that feared the Lord and thought upon His name. And they shall be mine, saith the Lord of hosts, in that day when I make up my jewels; and I will spare them, as a man spareth his own son that serveth him. Then shall ye return, and discern between the RIGHTEOUS and the WICKED; between him that *served God, and him that serveth him not*" (Mal. iii. 16, 17, 18). "*Repent*, and turn yourselves from all your transgressions; *so iniquity shall not be your ruin.* Cast away from you all your transgressions, whereby ye have transgressed; and make you a new heart and a new spirit: for why will ye die, O house of Israel? For I have no pleasure in the death of him that dieth, saith the Lord God: therefore turn yourselves, and live ye" (Eze. xviii. 30, 31, 32). "Turn ye unto me, saith the Lord of hosts, and I will turn unto you" (Zech. 1. 3).

It would be useless transcribing all the passages in the Bible similar to the above—and teeming with the doctrine of individual responsiblity and individual power to regain the favour of the Eternal—which is completely opposed to the Gentile creed. But while we reject wholly and utterly all belief in the Nazarene doctrine, that we are each and all, even the new-born babe, condemned to everlasting misery unless we acknowledge Jesus— we equally reject the mistaken and sceptical belief, that the disobedience of our first parents in no way affects us now. If its effects were only confined to them, where is the mercy, the justice of the Lord, in condemning *all*

---

* The Conciliator, vol. ii. page 214. Translated from the Spanish of Manasseh Ben Israel, by E. H. Lindo, Esq.

their seed to return to the dust? Who that looks into himself and knows the "plague of his own heart," the difficulty to realize spirituality and holiness—who that reads his Bible with faith and prayer, and marks the prevalence of evil even there, the failings and the weaknesses of the holiest men, even those hallowed by the appellations of the "friends of God," will still refuse belief that the disobedience of our first parents so far altered our nature, as to give the *body* more powerful dominion than the *soul;* and thus, by deadening the spiritual influence within us, exposing us to temptation of every kind, and, consequently, but too often to sin; and rendering it a difficult and often desponding task to give the *spiritual* dominion over the *corporeal*, and to devote our whole hearts—not alone in our closets, but in the duties and occupations of the world still to serve and love our God. What would have been the glorious nature of Adam and Eve if they had not sinned, we know not; for it is a subject far too holy for speculation or conjecture : but that their transgressions produced consequences which demanded that not only themselves, but their seed should return to dust, is a scriptural truth which no one who believes in Moses and the Prophets can, we think, have sufficient boldness to deny. But the SOUL it touched not.— An emanation from God Himself, it will return to Him untouched by any sin but those of the body in whom it was breathed : and there, at the bar of God, our own acts, purified by mercy, judged by the ways and thoughts of the Lord— which are not the ways and thoughts of man—guided by the law his mercy gave, hallowed by faith and justified by love— our own acts must be our witness or our condemnation. Nor is this an individual doctrine lightly and carelessly entered upon or produced from one particular class of reading. It has been the thought and study of long years, based on an earnest and prayerful study of the Holy Scriptures, and on the spirit pervading the writings of every Hebrew sage which are accessible to woman. We have brought it strongly forward; because unless we know exactly what we do believe, and what we do not believe, from the beginning of the Holy Scriptures our readings must always be attended with obscurity and pain, and the very attributes of the Eternal difficult to be realized amid the awful scenes of wickedness which the historical books present. We will now proceed with the more private history of Eve.

Years must have rolled over the heads of our first parents since their expulsion, ere the fearful event took place, which, although it mentions not their names, must recall our attention to them. Although, in comparison, they had become degraded, and the recollection of their sin must ever have remained with its stinging remorse,—still, repentance and real sorrow, meek submission to their chastisement and acknowledgment of its justice, raised them from their first abject misery, and permitted them once more, through prayer and thanksgiving and sacrifice, to commune with the Lord. Eve's exclamation on the birth of Cain—" I have gotten a man from the Lord," proves how closely and devoutly she still traced all blessing from His gracious hand:—hallowing her maternal joy by gratitude to Him. His love had bestowed on her a blessing unknown even in Eden— a child—a *possession* peculiarly her own and her husband's; and in the exultation of her grateful joy she called his name קַיִן Cain, from קָנָה, to possess or to acquire. In his early infancy, ere he became awake to right and wrong, his parents could but feel enjoyment to train him up so as to know no sin, to love and serve the Lord, and to give them love and reverence in return for the deep, endless fondness they lavished upon him. But by the name bestowed upon their second son, Abel, we may almost suppose that they had already felt the *vanity* of these hopes and wishes; that even in his boyhood Cain manifested those evil passions and that head strong will, which led in after years to such fearful consequences.

The effects of Eve's disobedience were now to be displayed in her own offspring—the child of exultation and joy—whom she had welcomed with such delight, that she almost felt as if no sorrow or suffering could assail her more, was the instrument in the Eternal hand to bring her back meekly and submissively to Him, in prayer for that beloved one; in recognition that her sin was working still. The passions and rebellion of her first-born brought all the agony of remorse fresh upon her heart; and deep as was the joy with which she had hailed his birth, was the anxiety, the suffering his dawning character called forth.

Actuated by such emotions, it was with sorrow, then, more than joy that the birth of her second boy was hailed. She had already felt the vanity, the transientness of her hopes:— and mournfully she called his name הֶבֶל Hebel—transientness or vanity, from הָבַל, which signifies to follow a vain thing, to cherish vain thoughts. But as is the case (how often even now!) the child of tears and anticipated sorrow, proved as dear and precious blessing, as the son of exultation was of grief. She saw him in the ascendency of the spiritual, the deathless part of their mingled nature, that evil could still be subdued, and man be still acceptable and worthy in the sight of his Creator. The compassionate love of the Eternal, while He chastised through Cain, gave hope and trust and comfort through Abel. He showed through these varying natures, that free-will to choose the good and eschew the evil was still given; and that though the latter to the eyes of the world might seem, nay, was the ascendant, He would yet preserve His witnesses among mankind, to keep alive the knowledge of the Lord, and prove the pre-eminence, the beauty, the glory, and the consolation of piety and virtue.

So years rolled on: the boys grew up to manhood. And though it is not specifically mentioned, it is evident that Eve must also have borne a daughter, who, as was absolutely necessary in the early stages of the world, became the wife of Cain. Some writers believe that Cain and Abel were both born with twin sisters. It may or may not be, as it must be only conjecture—though Cain's wife only is mentioned.

The words of Scripture, "and he (Adam) begat sons and daughters," are sufficient for our information. In all probability his family was a large one, that his seed might fulfil the intention of the Eternal in peopling the world; but how many daughters he had before the death of Abel does not appear, and is of little consequence.

During the growth of their elder children, the lives of our first parents differ little in feeling from those of the present day. Their employments, indeed, were as unlike, as patriarchal simplicity is from worldly interest and luxury—the peace of nature from the contention of the world. In reading the narratives of the Bible, we often blend *situation* with feeling, and believe that as the one is too antiquated for interest and example, so is the other for sympathy and love. But the Bible tells us of no character above human nature; and why not, then, in perusing the circumstances of their simple lives, try their feelings by the standard of their own? Who that is a mother does not feel anxiety, pleasure, grief, joy, despondency, and hope, almost at the same time. according to the different dispositions of her children? Who that is a parent does not acknowledge that maternal love may combine the intensest joy with the intensest grief? And will they not then sympathise in the feelings of Eve?—at one time bowed to the very dust in the anguish occasioned by the sinful inclinations and rude temper of her first-born, in self-accusation that she, perhaps, was the original cause, even as an affectionate mother very often accuses herself for the faults of her offspring—at another, weeping tears of sweet joy, and love, and consolation, on the gentle bosom of her Abel, whose whole life and thoughts were directed to piety and virtue to God and to his parents—whose very existence, as her own had been in Paradise, seemed bright with reverence and love.

But even this life of mingled grief and comfort might not last. Not yet had Eve sufficiently atoned for her disobedience, and proved her love and faith to pass through the awful portals of death, to the home prepared for her in heaven. Death, as concerned herself, her husband, her children, was still the dark shadow through which as yet no *certain* light had beamed. The Eternal, in His mercy, had prepared to reveal it, but through clouds of denser, more appalling blackness than had yet gathered round His creatures.

Wrought up to frenzy by the preference manifested towards the pious offering of his younger brother—refusing to acknowledge that it was the temper of his own mind at fault, and that he had himself trampled on, and defied the favour he yet coveted, when shewn to another—still sullenly and obstinately encouraging the evil, even when the Lord, in infinite mercy, condescended Himself to speak with his rebellious servant, and asking why he was wroth, informed him, that though sin was ever crouching beside him, he (Cain) *had the power to rule over and subdue it*, still disregarding even this, listening but to the fearful instigations of his own heart,—" it came to pass, when they were in the field together, that Cain rose up against his brother Abel, and slew him."

The dark terror of death was mysterious no longer. In its most fearful, most appalling shape, it had descended upon earth—the bright, the beautiful, the loving and the holy, there he lay before the eyes of his agonised parents, his life-blood dyeing the green-sward—that face, so fair, so sweet an index of the pure glorious soul—those limbs, so soft and round and graceful, whose every movement had brought joy to his mother's heart—they gazed upon them still, beautiful as if he slept, save that there was a stillness and a coldness as the earth on which he lay. This, then, was death, and it had been dealt by a *brother's* hand. Can any woman, much less a mother, reflect on Eve's immeasurable agony, and yet pass lightly and heedlessly over this first narration of Holy Writ, refusing sympathy, even interest, in the deep, dark floods of misery, with which, though her name is not mentioned, those few words of a brother's hate and wroth and murder teem? Not alone a mother's anguish, deprived of both her children in one fearful day—not, not alone the wild yearnings of affection towards the guilty and the exile, struggling with the passionate misery for her own bereavement, but more crushing, more agonising still—it was her work—she had disobeyed, to obtain the knowledge of good and evil—and how appalling had that forbidden knowledge poured back its stinging poison into her own heart! Her beautiful had fallen—she might never, never gaze upon him, list his sweet voice more—the dust had gone to its dust—sent to his grave in his youth, his sinlessness—the helpless and the innocent crushed by the strong hand of the guilty—and the Eternal had looked down from his awful throne, and interfered not. Why had the *only innocent*, the *only righteous*, been the first to pay the penalty of death, when his guilty parents, and yet more guilty brother were permitted still to live? Nay, the doom of Cain, which the hardened one himself declared "was greater than he could bear," was not to die, but to *live* as a wanderer whom none might slay. Why might such things be? Were they reconcilable with those attributes of justice and of love and long-suffering, which the Eternal had already proclaimed, through His conduct, to His creatures? They were : for in the death of the innocent IMMORTALITY was proclaimed!

The disobedient looked on the death their sin had brought—they felt in their own bosoms, the deepest agony of bereavement—they saw not the terror, only as the *end* of *existence;* but by the scythe cutting down the young in his first beautiful spring, and in the full prime of holiness and good, they learned what their own death, at the moment of disobedience, could not have taught—that the righteous must also be cut off, as well as the guilty—that death was not only chastisement for itself *alone*, but in the deep agony it inflicted upon the *living*, in the awful trial of separation and bereavement, and the utter loneliness of heart when a beloved one goes; and this learned, the world beyond death, the dwelling of the righteous, the reunion of the divine essence with its parent Fount—immortality—was revealed!

That the caviller, the sceptic, the thoughtless will deny this, because we can bring forward no *written proof* of its truth, we are perfectly aware : but we write for the believer, for the Israelite, who not only *reads* the words of the Bible, but *explains* them by one only unerring test—the ATTRIBUTES of God. The question is simply this—Do we believe in a God? That He is, as He proclaimed Himself, "merciful and gracious, long-suffering and abundant in goodness and truth, keeping mercy for *thousands*, forgiving iniquity and sin, yet clearing not the guilty," without repentance and amendment? Do we believe in him, as in every page of His Holy Word He is revealed, or do we not? If we do not—if we deny the existence of a just and merciful, though in many instances inscrutable, God, then indeed we may deny our immortality; but if we acknowledge there is a God, ay, and one whose justice and whose love are infinite and perfect as Himself, we must not only believe in our own immortality, but trace its doctrine running through the Holy Scriptures, alike from the death of Abel to the last verses of Malachi, pervading, vivifying, spiritualising its every portion, even as our mortal frame is pervaded, vivified, and spiritualised, by the *invisible*, yet everbreathing SOUL. We do not doubt and question that we have a soul, because we have nothing palpable and evident by which to *prove* it ; and even as the soul is the *essence*, the spirit of our being, so is immortality the essence and the spirit of the Bible.

Where was the mercy, nay, the *justice* of the Eternal, had he punished with *eternal* death the only righteous of His creatures? We can scarcely even dwell upon the idea for a moment without impiety. Abel was taken, that while death in his most fearful form was revealed, to manifest all the terrible evil and anguish Eve's sin had brought, the hope and promise of immortality might be given, and the agonised parents comforted. He was removed "from the evil to come," to that world, where "light had been sown for the righteous" from the beginning, and would be for ever.

But though this revelation must have brought with it comfort unspeakable, yet the heavy trial of Eve might not even through this beneficent assurance, be entirely assuaged. She could not now, as she had done in Eden, realise so blessedly the pre-eminence of the spirit over the feelings of the clay. Though comforted, the weakness of humanity must still have been too often in the ascendant, and taught her all the bitterness of grief. Even though the thought of Abel might, through the unselfishness of woman's love, be tranquilised by the idea, that however she might suffer, he was happy, as she had been in Eden, no such comfort could attend the thought of Cain. It is vain to measure maternal love by the worth or unworthiness of its objects. It was not only that he was exiled for ever from her sight, that her yearning heart might never seek to soothe him more; but she knew that he was, he must be, a wretched wanderer; and the mother felt his wretchedness, though she saw it not, in addition to her own. Mercy, indeed, had tempered his chastisement, for he had not been cut off in his sin—he had been doomed to length of days on earth, that he might repent and atone; but this to a weak and suffering parent, though she might struggle to lift up her heart in gratitude, could not afford consolation.

There is little more to narrate in the life of Eve, but that little, as every other incident in her life, proves forcibly the Eternal's still compassionating love. To remove all of utter bereavement from His first created, first beloved, when the first agony of Eve's heavy trial was over, God gave her another son. "And she called his name שֵׁת Seth, because she said, God has appointed me another seed instead of Abel, whom Cain slew." And as from Seth descended a line of venerable patriarchs, one of whom was taken up to heaven, without dying, for his righteousness; and from them came Noah, who alone was saved from universal destruction; then through him Abraham, the favoured servant and friend of the Eternal—Abraham, for whose sake Israel was the chosen, and is still the beloved of the Lord, we may quite believe that Eve was not only comforted by the gift of a son, but that even as Abel he was righteous, and that he was the comforter of his parents—that in beholding his opening manhood, the dawning virtue and graces of his spirit, the fiery trial of their early life was soothed, and they could trace the hand of the Lord bringing forth good out of the very midst of evil, and rest satisfied, that however the strong and the guilty might seem to prosper, He would never leave Himself without witnesses upon earth.

Although there is no mention of the death of Eve, the words of Holy Writ, recording that "Adam lived eight hundred years after he had begotten Seth, and had sons and daughters," would prove that she, too, lived that period, there being no mention whatever, as is often the case with other patriarchs, of Adam taking another wife. The former temptations, trials, and sorrows of our first parents, must, then, have been looked back to by them in their old age, as we should look on the events which may have befallen us before the age of twenty, when we have reached the venerable years of fourscore. That long life was evidently granted in mercy. Had they been cut off on the instant of their transgression, it must have been for eternity, or death would have been no punishment. Had they been taken sooner, we will suppose before the death of Abel, though they might have been spared that bitter sorrow, still darkness, and fear for themselves, and doubt as to the ways and attributes of the Eternal, must have crowded round them, and filled them with despair as to the probable effects of their sin on their offspring, and their offspring's seed. Long life, through the infinite mercy of the Eternal, removed such evils. While they felt, in all the bitterness of remorse, all the evil they had wrought, they were yet comforted by the revelation of immortality and the consequent incentive for the struggling after righteousness, which without such blessed incentive, man could never have achieved. They beheld, that though the likeness of God within them had been dulled in all, and in some would be almost entirely effaced, it might in heaven be regained, if while on earth it was sought with faith and works. They learned, that though discord and strife and oppression and labour and care, would reign tumultuously on earth, to the extinction, in *appearance*, of all that was spiritual and good, there was yet in heaven an omnipresent and ever-acting love, which would so over-rule the world, that even from "transitory evil" would spring forth "universal good," and every seemingly dark and contradictory event below, tend to the glory, the extension, and the perfection of the divine economy above.

To obtain this knowledge, our first parents were spared, and not cut off in their sin; and can we, their offspring, even at this length of time, peruse their eventful history, without feeling our hearts glow with grateful adoration of the love which guided and hallowed them throughout? The stream of time which divides us is indeed so wide, that we are apt to feel, that events so far distant can concern us so little. Yet while we trace in our mortal frame and painful infirmities, the *effects* of their *disobedience*, shall we not acknowledge with grateful and adoring faith, that the same love which guided, blest, and pardoned them, is still extended unto us?

To dwell in paradise, to be blessed with direct communings with the Eternal and His heavenly messengers, are indeed not ours; but many a home—ay, many a lot—is a sinless paradise to a young and gentle girl; and loving parents will so throng her path with care and blessings, that of evil she knows little, and temptation is afar off. And often, too often, like Eve, these blessings are undervalued and sacrificed, not through her sin and disobedience, but from woman's unfortunate desire to grasp *something more than is her allotted portion;*—her discontent with the lowlier station, which her weaker frame and less powerful mind mark imperatively as her own—her mistaken notion, that humility is degradation; and unless she *compels* man to concede to her rights, they will be trampled on and never acknowledged—her curiosity leading her too often to covet knowledge which she needs not for the continuance of her happiness. O let not women deny that such too often are her characteristics, and exclaim with scorn of Eve's weakness, that had she been in Eve's place, surrounded with felicity as she was, the forbidden tree might have remained for ever ere she would have touched it. She who thus thinks, commits unconsciously Eve's first sin, trusting too much in her own strength; and, in consequence, just as likely to fall beneath the very first temptation which assails her.

Let her not quiet such fears by the thought that Eve's particular temptation cannot be her's. No; but snares innumerable, and equally fearful, surround us. Each day brings its own temptations, each day calls upon us to pray against them; for we know not how, or in what shape they may arise, and how soon, if we trust in our own strength, they may triumph and lead us to perdition. Had Eve been truly *humble*, she had not sinned. And if in Eden HUMILITY was needed, if even there, without such panoply of proof, woman fell, how much more should we encourage it now. Humility is to woman her truest safeguard, her loveliest ornament, her noblest influence, her greatest strength. Teaching her true station in regard to man, it leads her ever to the footstool of her God, thence to derive firmness, devotedness, fortitude, consolation, hope, all that she needs. While such privilege is her's, let her not repine that God lowered Eve and made her less than man ; let her not look back with anger that the sin of one woman should thus punish her descendants. From the very first she was endowed differently to man ; had she not been the weaker, the serpent had not marked her as his easier prey. And as our own nature is even now as Eve's, let us rather thank God that his Love has granted us that lowly station where our natural qualities may best be proved, and our weaknesses and our failings have less power to work us harm. Let us cultivate, with all our heart and soul and might, the lovely flower of humility, which, by teaching us to think lowly of ourselves, will render us contented and thankful for the blessings around us, the gifts bestowed upon us, instead of urging us to covet more ;—the sweet flower on whose breath our souls are enabled more continually to ascend to God, and whose petals, seemingly so frail and tender, have yet more power to guard us from temptation and presumption than an unsheathed sword. Let us not pause till it is found and worn ; and if it make us invisible as itself, save to those who seek and value us, it will shed around us an atmosphere of love and peace and joy, with which no other flower can vie : and in death, as in life, we shall bless God for its possession, as for the dearest gift He has vouchsafed.

Would I, then, some may exclaim, deny all privileges to woman—refuse to acknowledge their equality with man— degrade them as the Jewish religion is falsely accused of doing? No! for in the sight of God, in their *spiritual* privileges, in their peculiar gifts and endowments, the power of performing their duties in their own sphere, in their *responsibility*, they are on a perfect equality with man. But I would conjure them to seek humility, simply from its magic power of keeping woman in her own beautiful sphere, without one wish, one ambitious whisper, to exchange it for another. *While there*, while satisfied and rejoicing in the infinite love and wisdom, which placed us there, we are not only in the privileges enumerated above man's equal, but,—however, in strength of frame, immense capability of physical and mental exertion, in might and grasp of intellect, his inferior—yet in the depth and faithfulness of love, in the capability of *feeling* and *enduring*, in devotedness and fortitude—alike in bodily and mental trial—we are unanswerably his superior. Then has not women enough to call for gratitude? Endowed with influence over the heart of man, O let her remember for what fearful end Eve used that influence, and keep a constant guard of watchfulness and prayer over her heart to preserve her from its similar abuse. Let her remember the employment of Eve in Eden, and so cultivate her intellectual faculties in the study of God and nature, both animate and inanimate, that her mind may be strengthened, and in the contemplation of the beauties of creation, she may learn the true value of the beauty which may be hers. How small is its *relative* proportion, and yet how blessedly it may be used, even, as the beauty of creation, for the glory of God, in its mild, soothing and benignant influence upon His creatures.

Above all, let the history of Eve impress this truth upon the hearts of her young descendants—that however weak and faulty and abased, however sorrowing and bereaved, however reaping in tears the effects of indiscretion or graver error,—yet still the compassion, the long suffering, the exhaustless love of their Father in heaven is theirs; that no circumstance in life can deprive them of that love, can throw a barrier between woman's yearning heart and the healing compassion of her God. No; not even departure from Him, neglect, or forgetfulness, will make Him forget or cease to compassionate, if she will but return in true repentance and clinging faithfulness to His deep love once more. We cannot weary that never-ceasing Mercy—for as far as the East is from the West, so far, when we return to Him, doth He remove our transgressions from us. And will woman, whose whole existence still is love—neglect or despise these thrice-blessed privileges; will the exile, the despised, the persecuted—for such has been, and is, the women of Israel—will she not receive with grateful adoration, the love vouchsafed, and come and make manifest the Sustainer, the Comforter, the Mainspring of her being? To woman of every creed, of every race, of every rank—life, though it may seem blessed, is a fearful desert without God. What then, without Him, is it to the woman of Israel, the exile and the mourner, who hath no land, no hope, no comforter, but Him?

SARAH.

So varied and so important are the incidents comprised in the life of Eve, that, on a mere superficial view, Sarah's biography appears somewhat deficient in interest. Yet, as the beloved partner of Abraham, she ought to be a subject of reverence and love to her female descendants; and we will endeavour to bring her history forward, that such she may become. Much of the Eternal's love and pity towards His female children is manifested in her simple life, and also in the life of her bondwoman, Hagar, which is too closely interwoven with hers to be omitted.

The real relationship between Abraham and Sarah, before marriage, has never yet been clearly or satisfactorily solved. Some commentators asserting she was his niece, the daughter of Haran his elder brother; and others that she was, as Abraham himself declares, his half-sister—" She is the daughter of my father, but not the daughter of my mother, and she became my wife." We believe the latter assertion much more likely to be the correct one, because, in the first place, there is no foundation whatever for the idea that she was Haran's daughter, except the supposition that Iscah means Sarah (Gen. xi. 29); and, in the second, it is not probable that, when questioned by Abimelech, Abraham would have condescended to utter a falsehood. The Bible mentions Lot only as the child of Haran; and Abraham himself says, Sarah was his half-sister. The latter relationship, as preventing marriage, is no proof in favour of her being his niece, as no laws of marriage had yet been issued; and, in the early stages of the world, such connections were not considered sin.

Leaving this difficult decision to more curious speculators we will proceed to subjects of greater interest. The first notice we have of Sarai is her accompanying her husband and Lot, from the home of her kindred, to a strange country, among all strange people, in simple obedience to the word of God. Holy writ is silent on the youth of Abram; but it is the opinion of our ancient fathers, that his earnest desire after divine knowledge—his pure and holy life—his affectionate and virtuous conduct, attracted towards him the blessing of the

Lord, and caused him to be selected as the promulgator of the Divine Revelation. That Abram was exposed to many dangers, on account of his loving obedience to the one sole invisible God, instead of acknowledging the idols of his race, is indeed very possible, and probably originated the first removal of his family to Charran, where also his father accompanied him. At Charran they seemed to have dwelt in peace and prosperity, secured from former persecutors, so that it must have been no little trial to go forth again, more particularly without any definite cause for the removal.

To Sarai the trial must have been more severe than to her husband. She was to go forth with him indeed; but it is woman's peculiar nature to cling to home, home ties, and home affections—to shrink from encountering a strange world, teeming with unknown trials and dangers. Rather than the parting from a husband, indeed, all other partings may seem light; but yet they are trials to a gentle woman : and the heart that can leave the home and friends of happy youth— the association of years—without regret, proves not that its affections are so centred on one object as to eschew all others ; but that it is too often wrapt in a chilling indifference, which prevents strong emotion on any subject whatever. We have enough of Sarai in the Bible to satisfy us that is not her character.

One cause for the love of home ties and associations, in the heart of a right feeling woman, originates in the belief that there she can do so much more good than elsewhere—that, unfitted by the weakness and infirmities of frame from active toil, and the pursuit of goodly service, as falls to the lot of man, she can yet benefit her friends, children, and domestics in the hallowed circle of home ; and better manifest the blessing of the Lord, and the love she bears Him, there than amongst strangers. And this was especially the case with Sarai. By one of our ancient fathers it is said, that as Abram and Lot were permitted to turn many of their own sex from idolatry to the knowledge of the one true God, so also was Sarai granted the hallowed privilege of leading many of her female friends and domestics to the same blessed Fount. It was, therefore, no doubt, a source of questioning and wonder in her mind, why the Eternal's mandate to go forth should be given. She had not even *experience* in the Eternal's glorious attributes, as displayed in His dealings with His creatures, and through His word, to comfort and be her guide. All was mental darkness in the world around her, except her husband and those few whom he had been enabled to teach a partial knowledge of his God. They stood alone in their peculiar faith; and how often, in such a case, do doubts and fears enter the breast of woman. Yet it was enough that her husband prepared, without question or hesitation, to obey his God—to leave his aged father, his kindred, and his friends; and, with simple and loving faith, she went with him where the Lord should lead. Well is it for us when we can do so likewise; when, in some of those bitterest trials that woman's heart can know, the change of home or land, be it with our parents, or husbands, or, more fearful still, *alone*, we can yet so stay upon our God that we can realise His presence, His loving mercy directing our weary way, and resting with us still. His direct communing, by voice or sign, or through angelic messengers, are indeed no longer ours; but those that seek to love and serve Him, may yet hear His still small voice breathing in the solemn whisper of their own hearts, and through the *individual* promises of His word.

Accompanied by Lot and their household—expressed in the term, "the souls they had gotten in Charran," who were probably those whom they had instructed in the true faith—and carrying with them the substance they possessed, Abram and Sarai "went forth into the land of Canaan," which was inhabited by a fierce people, and gave little hope of ever being possessed by the patriarch and his family, for, by their constant journeyings, it would seem as if they could not even obtain sufficient land to fix their home. Yet, there again the Lord appeared to the patriarch, and renewed His promise—thus proving His tender compassion for the human weakness of His creatures, and encouraging their faith, when without such encouragement, He knew it must have failed. To add to their numerous *human* discomforts and trials, a famine broke out in the land, so severe and grievous, that Abram sought the land of Egypt; and there, rendered fearful by the exceeding beauty of his wife, and the supposed barbarity of the land, he bade Sarai call herself his sister, not his wife.

In this first deception, however, Abram was much more to be excused than in the second. He had not yet had all the convincing proofs of the Eternal's tender watchfulness and care, as he had afterwards. He had gone to Egypt *without* the express command of the Lord, and this very fact, to one accustomed to divine guidance, and not yet perhaps feeling himself sufficiently strong spiritually to go alone, rendered him more fearful than he would otherwise have been. He might also have thought, that as he was destined for a great end, it was his duty to use any means to preserve the life so appointed, without sufficiently considering that life and death were equally in the hands of the Eternal, and that He would preserve His servant alive, without the intervention of human means. Spirtual advancement requires effort, perseverence and experience, as well as every other; and Abram himself, though the elect of the Eternal, could not obtain perfection and firmness in faith without some human tremblings, which it is enough for us to know, were over-ruled, compassionated, and forgiven. We perceive by the sacred narrative, that his intention was frustrated, and his words caused the very evil he dreaded;—which is sufficient warning for us to avoid all departure from the straight line of truth—while the continued care and favour of the Lord should check our presumptuous condemnation, and remind us that if His justice and mercy thought proper to over-rule and forgive, and continue, nay, increase His long tenderness towards Abram and his family, it is our part, instead of marvelling, to thank God that such weakness is recorded, that we may not feel it is human perfection *alone* which calls down His blessing, and so shrink back in terror and despair.

This part of Sarai's history gives us information generally very interesting to young female readers—that she was very beautiful. We are wont to imagine, that the charms of sixty-five could not be very remarkable; but, reckoning according to the age to which mortals then lived, she was not older than a woman of thirty or five and thirty would be now, consequently, in her prime: endowed, as her history gives us authority to suppose, with a quiet, retiring dignity, which greatly enhanced her beauty, and rendered it yet more interesting than that of girlhood.

Protected from this danger, his substance greatly increased by Pharaoh's gifts, Abram, his wife, and household, retraced their steps to where "his tent had been at first, between Bethel and Hai." The altar which he had originally erected was still there, and again he and his family "called on the name of the Lord." The command of Pharaoh—"Go thy way," was most probably regarded and acted on by the patriarch as a warning, that his safest and most hallowed home was in the land to which the Lord had originally guided him.

In the events which follow—the separation of Abram and Lot—the battle of the kings—the imprisonment and rescue of Lot—the blessing of Melchisedeck—Holy Writ makes no mention of Sarai. She was performing those duties of an affectionate wife and gentle mistress of her husband's immense establishment, which are nothing to write about, but which make up the sum of woman's life, create her dearest and purest sources of happiness, and bring her acceptably before God. Her home was still an unsettled one. The Lord had again appeared to renew His promises to Abram—comforting him in the sorrow which Lot's choice of a dwelling in the sinful Sodom had occasioned him, by the assurance that all the land which he saw, northward and southward, eastward and westward, would He give unto him and his seed, and his seed's seed for ever. That he was to "Arise, and walk through the land, in the breadth of it and in the length of it, for I will give it unto thee." In consequence of which, the tent of the patriarch was removed southward, to Mamre in Hebron, and an altar built, at once to claim the land in the name of the Lord, and give to Abram and his household a place where to worship. The extent of the patriarch's household may be imagined by the fact, that at his word, no less than three hundred and eighteen servants, born in his house and trained to arms, accompanied him to the rescue of his nephew. Those who were left to attend to his flocks and herds, which he possessed in great numbers, must have been in equal proportion; and over these, during his absence, Sarai, assisted by the steward, had unlimited dominion.

The beautiful confidence and true affection subsisting between Abram and Sarai, marks unanswerably their *equality;* that his wife was to Abram, friend as well as partner; and yet, that Sarai knew perfectly her own station, and never attempted to push herself forward in unseemly council, or use the influence which she so largely possessed for any weak or sinful purpose. Some, however, would have found it difficult to preserve their humility and meekness, situated as was Sarai. A coarser and narrower mind would have prided herself on the promises made her husband, imagining there must be some superlative merit, either in herself or Abram, to be so singled out by the Eternal. There is no pride so dangerous and subtle as spiritual pride, no sin more likely to gain dominion in the early stages of religion—none so disguised, and so difficult to be discovered and rooted out. But in Sarai there was none of this; not a particle of pride, even at a time when, of all others, she might have been *almost* justified in feeling it. She was, indeed, blessed in a husband whose exalted, yet domestic and affectionate character, must ever have strengthened, guided, and cherished her's; but it is not always the most blessed and distinguished woman who attends the most faithfully to her domestic duties, and preserves unharmed and untainted that meekness and integrity which is her greatest charm.

Abram's warlike expedition was the only one in which his wife did not accompany him. With what joy she must have welcomed her warrior lord! How gratefully must her loving heart have delighted to ponder on his magnanimity, in going instantly to the rescue of his weak and little grateful nephew; —on his courage—his success; and yet more on his noble refusal of all gifts from the king of Sodom, lest the glory should be taken from the Lord, and any mortal should say: " I have made Abram rich." We dwell with delight on the stirring records of chivalry; and it is right we should do so, for the study of all honourable, unselfish and unworldly deeds must do us good: but where shall we find, in the whole history of chivalry, an instance of such perfect nobility and magnanimity, unstained by one action from which mind or heart could revolt, as in the only warlike expedition of Abram? It was indeed enough for a woman to glory in: and, though nothing is said, for the record of Moses is too important to descend to the thoughts and feelings of woman, we may well imagine the grateful and rejoicing feelings of Sarai, as she welcomed her husband home—forgetting all the pangs of parting and loneliness of separation, in the triumph and delight of such a meeting.

It was after these things, that we have the first allusion to the patriarch's being childless. And by the words in which the Lord addressed him—" Fear not, Abram, I am thy shield, and exceeding great reward," we are led to suppose that some anxious thoughts, and perhaps doubts, natural to humanity, were occupying his mind. *We*, weak and frail as himself, might exclaim, What, still doubting, still fearing, when he has

had so many proofs of the Eternal's providence and care! But
God, whose "thoughts are not our thoughts," instead of
reproving, addresses him in terms of the tenderest love and
encouragement, for He knew the nature of His creatures, and
that faith could *not* be perfectly attained without years of
watchfulness and prayer: that if it were, man would cease to
be man, and this life be no longer what it was intended—a life
of trial. Abram's instant reply reveals the painful thoughts
which had engrossed him:—"Lord God, what wilt thou give
me? seeing I go childless, and the steward of my house is this
Eliezer of Damascus. Behold, to me thou hast given no seed,
and lo, one born in my house is mine heir." God had promised
that the land should be his and his *seed's*, but Abram in sorrow
beheld years pass, and still he had no child. Sarai had long
passed the age when, humanly speaking, she could be a mother.
It was much more natural—truly pious and faithful as he was
—that Abram should be harassed with contradictory fears and
doubts, than that he should have had none. God had promised,
but how was that promise to be fulfilled?—unless, indeed, not
his own child, but "one born in his house" was to be his
destined heir. This appeared perhaps the most probable,
though it was painfully disappointing; and to soothe his fear
and remove it, the Lord addressed him as we have said. The
gracious and most blessed promise directly followed—that not
one born in his house, but his own son should be his heir;
and, bidding him look up at the stars—as countless and
numberless they gemmed the clear, bright heavens—promised,
that "so shall his seed be." And then it was, that—all of
doubt and mist and fear dissolving in the heart of the patriarch,
before the words of the Lord, as snow before the sun—HE
BELIEVED: and that pure FAITH was accounted to him as
RIGHTEOUSNESS. How blessed are those words! In every
station of life, however tried and sad and mourning, and
deprived of all power to *serve* the Lord as our hearts dictate, we
may yet BELIEVE, and Faith is still accounted RIGHTEOUSNESS.

On the glorious prophetic vision which followed when the
sun went down, we may not linger, as it will take us too far
from the subject of our narrative.

Great must have been Sarai's joy when this gracious promise
was made known to her. If to Abram the being childless was
a source of deep regret, it must have been still more so to her.
Loving and domestic, as her whole history proves she was, how

often may she have yearned to list the welcome cry of infancy; to feel one being looked up to her for protection and love, and called her by that sweet name—Mother. But this joyful anticipation could only have been of short duration. Sarai, as in woman's nature, in all probability imagined the *fulfilment* would immediately follow the *promise*. The most difficult of all our spiritual attainments is to *wait* for the Lord : to believe still, through long months, perhaps years, of anticipation and disappointment, that as He has said it, so it *will be*, so it *must be*, though our finite wisdom cannot pronounce the *when*. Did the Eternal fulfil His gracious promises on the instant, where would be the trial of our faith, and of our confidence and constancy in prayer ?

Finding still there was no appearance of her becoming a mother, we are led to suppose, by the events which follow, that all Sarai's joyous anticipations turned into gloomy fears, not merely from the belief that she herself would not be blessed with a child, but that Abram might, as was and is the custom of Eastern nations, take another wife; an idea excited, perhaps, by the recollection that *her* name had not been mentioned as the destined mother of the promised seed, but precisely the most painful which could find entrance in a heart affectionate and faithful as her own. To prevent this misfortune, and yet to further (as she supposed) the will of the Eternal, Sarai, had recourse to human means.

All women in her position, and influenced as she was by the manners and customs of the East, would have both felt and acted as she did, but few, we think, would have waited so long. It was ten years after Abram had left Egypt to fix his residence in Canaan, before Hagar became his wife. The separation of himself and Lot appears to have taken place in the first year after their settlement in Canaan, the expedition against the kings in the second or third year following. And we are expressly told, that it was *soon after these occurrences* that the Lord appeared unto the patriarch, and promised him an heir in his own child; the Hebrew word, אחר (after), signifying, according to Rashi, that the event about to be related took place *soon after* the period of the former narration; but when a *long period* has intervened, the expression "אחרי is used.*

According to this reckoning, then, full five, or, at the very

* See "The Sacred Scriptures, Hebrew and English," translated by the Rev. D. A. De Sola, &c. Note to verse 1 of chapter xvi.

least, three years must have elapsed between the promise made to Abram and his taking Hagar, at Sarai's own request, to be his wife ; and few women would have beheld year after year pass, each year increasing the impossibility of her becoming a mother, and yet so believed as to adopt no human means for the furtherance of her wishes. In perusing and reflecting on the blessings promised, and revelations made to the favoured servants of the Lord, we are apt to suppose that their lives were preserved from all trouble, all trial of delay, from the fearful sickness of anticipation disappointed, and hope deferred: whereas, a more intimate study of the holy Scriptures would convince us, that though indeed most *spiritually* blessed, their *mortal* lives were not more exempt from labour, and all the sorrows proceeding from human emotions, than our own. We only see those periods on which the broad light of sunshine falls. The darker shades of human doubt, the often supposed blighting of hope, the struggles and terrors of the spirit alternating with the rest and confidence which it sometimes enjoys; these we see not, and, therefore, pronounce them unknown to our forefathers ; whereas, did we examine more closely, we should not find severer trials in our own lives than in theirs ; nor cease to believe, for a single moment, that the God who guided them through the dark shadows of human trials, and strengthened them with the light of His presence, does not equally guide and reveal Himself to us.

The first human evidence that Sarai's scheme would be productive of vexation and sorrow, as well as of joy, was her disappointment with regard to Hagar's continued humility and submission. Forgetful that it was to her mistress, humanly speaking, she owed the privileges now hers, the Egyptian so far forgot herself, as to feel and make manifest that Sarai " was despised in her eyes." Alas, how mournfully does that brief sentence breathe of woman's fallen nature ! How apt are we to exalt ourselves for imaginary superiority—to look down on those who have served us, when God has bestowed on us privileges of which they are deprived. We forget, often through thoughtlessness, that those very things of which we are so proud, come not from ourselves, but from Him who might equally have vouchsafed them to others. We may not indeed have the same incitement to pride and presumption as Hagar, but have we *never* despised others for the want of those accomplishments, those advantages, that beauty, and other gifts from God, which we ourselves may possess? Aye, sometimes, though we trust such emotions are rare as they are sad, the parents who have toiled and laboured to give us advantages of dress and education far above what they possessed themselves—the elder sister, who is contented and rejoiced to remain in the back ground, that younger and fairer ones, whom she loves almost with a mother's love, may come forward—the homely and older fashioned aunt, to whom, perhaps, a sister's orphan family owe their all—these are the beings whom the young and thoughtless but too often secretly despise, as if their superior advantages had come from themselves, not from God, through loving relatives and friends.

And this was the case with Hagar. A superficial reading of the Bible often causes Sarai to be most unjustly blamed for undue harshness. We think only of Hagar's wanderings in the wilderness, and pity her as cruelly treated, and suppose, that as the Most High relieved her through His angel, she had never been in any way to blame. Now, though to sympathise with the sorrowing and afflicted be one of our purest and best feelings, it must not so blind us as to prevent our doing justice to the inflicter of that affliction. We candidly avow, that until lately we too thought Sarai harsh and unjust, and rather turned from than admired her character : but we have seen the injustice of this decision, and, therefore, without the smallest remaining prejudice, retract it altogether : retract it, simply because the words of the angel are quite sufficient proof that Hagar had been *wrong*, and Sarai's chastisement *just*, or he would not have commanded her, as Sarai's *bondwoman,* to return and submit herself to her mistress' power, without any reservation whatever.

It must indeed have been a bitterly painful disappointment to Sarai, that instead of receiving increased gratitude and affection from one whom she had so raised and cherished, she was despised with an insolence that, unless checked, might bring discord and misery in a household which had before been so blessed with peace and love. Sarai's was not a character to submit tamely to ingratitude. There was neither coldness nor indifference about her. In no part of the Bible, either in character or precept, do we perceive the necessity or the merit of that species of cold indifference, which is by some well-meaning religious persons supposed to be the self-control and pious forgiveness of injuries most acceptable to God. The patriarchal and Jewish history alike prove that natural feelings were not to be trampled upon. The Hebrew code was formed by a God of love for the nature of *man*, not angels—formed so as to be *obeyed*, not to be laid aside as impracticable. The passions and feelings of the East were very different to those of the calmer and colder North; and nowhere in Holy Writ are we told that those feelings and emotions must be annihilated. *Subdued* and *guided* indeed, as must be the consequence of a true and strict adherence to the law of God, and impartial study of His word; but in the sight of a God of love, indifference can never be, and never was, religion.

Yet even this, an affair of feeling entirely between herself and Hagar, could not urge Sarai to any line of conduct unauthorised by her husband. Naturally indignant, she complained to him, perhaps, too, with some secret fear that Hagar, favoured so much above herself by the hope of her giving him a son, might be unduly justified and protected. But it was not so. Abram's answer at once convinced her that Hagar had not taken her place; nay, that though Abram could not do otherwise than feel tenderness and kindness towards her, he at once recognised Sarai's supremacy, both as his wife and Hagar's mistress, and bade her "do with her what seemeth good to thee." We have so many proofs of Abram's just, affectionate, and forgiving character, that we may fully believe he would never have said this, if he had not been convinced that it was no unjust accusation on the part of Sarai. He knew, too, that she was not likely to inflict more punishment than she deserved, particularly on a favourite slave; and, therefore, it was with his full consent "Sarai afflicted her, and she fled from her presence."

Whatever the nature of this affliction, it could not have been very severe—neither pain nor restraint—for Hagar had the power to fly. Reproof to an irritable and disdainful mind is often felt as intolerable, and given, too, as it no doubt was, with severity, and at a time when Hagar felt exalted and superior to all around her, even to her mistress, her proud spirit urged flight instead of submission, and not till addressed by the voice of the angel did those rebellious feelings subside.

There was no mistaking the angelic voice, and his first words destroyed the proud dreams which she had indulged. "Hagar, Sarai's bondwoman!" he said, and the term told her, in the sight of God she was still the same, "whence camest thou, and whither art thou going?" It was not because he knew not that he thus spoke. The messengers of the Lord need no enlightenment on the affairs of men, but their questions are adapted to the nature of men, to awaken them to consciousness, to still the tumult of human passion, and by clear and simple questioning *compel* a clear and true reply. Had his command to return been given without preparation, Hagar's obedience would have been the effect of fear, not conviction. But those simple questions, "Whence camest thou? whither art thou going?" startled her from the tumultuous emotions of rebellion and presumption. Whence had she come? From a happy loving home, where she had been the favourite of an indulgent and gentle mistress; a home which would speedily be to her yet dearer, as the birthplace of her child; that child who was to be the supposed heir to her master and all his sainted privileges; from friends, from companions, all whom she had loved: and she had left them! And whither was she going? How might she answer when she knew not? Was she about to resign all of affection, privilege, joy, to wander in the wilderness, helpless and alone? How idle and impotent now seemed her previous feelings. Those simple questions had flashed back light on her darkened heart, and humbled her at once; and simply and truthfully she answered, "I flee from the presence of my mistress Sarai;" thus meekly acknowledging that Sarai was still her mistress, and that her derision had indeed been wrong. Reproof, therefore, followed not; but the angel bade her, "Return to thy mistress, and submit thyself to her power." And, perceiving that her repentance was sincere, and would lead to obedience, he continued graciously to promise that her seed should be multiplied, so that it should not be numbered for the multitude; that her son should bear a name which would ever remind her that God had heard her affliction, with other promises concerning that son, *yet none* which might lead her to the deceitful belief that he would be Abram's promised seed.

Inexpressibly consoled, in the midst of her bitter self-reproach, and convinced, by his supernatural voice and disappearance, that it was indeed an angel direct from the Lord with whom she had spoken, it is evident from the context, although not there mentioned, that Hagar must have unhesitatingly obeyed, and returned to her mistress—convinced of her error—submissive and repentant, and been by Sarai received with returning confidence and full forgiveness.

In due course of time the promise was fulfilled, and Hagar, to the great joy of Abram, had a son, whom *Abram* called Ishmael, thus proving that Hagar must have imparted the visit of the angel, and his command as to the name of her son.

Before we proceed, we would entreat our younger readers to pause one moment on the simple facts we have related; and so take it to their hearts, that the first words of the angel may become theirs as well as Hagar's. We have not indeed the direct communings with the messengers of the Lord, as is recorded in the Bible; but we are not left unguided and unquestioned. We have still an angelic voice within us, that, would we but encourage it to speak—would we but listen to it—can, even as the angel's, still the wild torrent of passion, awaken us to our neglected duty, and lead us, repentant and sorrowing, to those whom we may have offended. God has not left us without His witness. The VOICE OF CONSCIENCE may be to us what angel visits were to our ancestors of old. There is no period of our lives in which it is wholly lost; but in youth it is strongest and most thrilling. In youth it is, that we awake from the (often) stagnant sleep of earlier years; —we awake to a consciousness of bright, glowing, beautiful existence;—we become conscious of a deep yearning after the *good*, and at the same time sorrowfully feel, that it is not quite as easy to attain as we believed it. As our emotions and feelings spring into life, so does conscience. We become aware of a peculiar thrilling sense of joy, when we have accomplished good, either in conquering ourselves—in giving up a selfish inclination—or in shewing kindness, affection, and respect to others. There is a glowing sense of joy, when conscience tells us that we have done well, unlike the joy proceeding from any other cause; and as it approves, with an angel voice that *will* be heard, so does it disapprove. We may stifle it—we may refuse to listen to its still small tones—yet we cannot shake off the depression and the sadness which it leaves. We may *refuse* to know wherefore we thus feel; but it is *conscience* still. How much better then to permit its having voice and power, and, as it dictates, do—to encourage it at times to speak, and ever keep its silent watch, for we need it, O how powerfully we need it! How fearful is our responsibility if we permit it to lie unused; for more strongly than aught else does it breathe our approval, or our condemnation, in the sight of the Lord. Is there one amongst us that has not felt, at one time or other, emotions similar to those of Hagar—anger at reproof, scorn of those who reprove, rebellion against their dictates; and we would fly from their presence with wrath at our hearts, and rebellion on our lips; and, at such times, does the voice of conscience never steal over us with questions similar to these? "Whence comest thou? Whither wouldst thou flee? What wouldst thou do?" Startling us from wrath, often and often into a burst of passionate and self-reproachful, though, as yet, only half-repentant tears. And when that passion in a degree is stilled—when affection and reason, softly and pleadingly resume their sway, does not the angel voice bid us also "return" unto those whom we have offended? It is wisest, best, though our wayward spirits shrink from it, proud of their own will, desirous of undue freedom. And at such times, O well it is for us, now and hereafter, if, even as Hagar, we return and submit, and thus acknowledge the power of that inward voice! Its angelic whisper will come to us again; we need not fear then, nor shrink from a lonely path—we have within us the "angel of the Lord." But those who hear yet refuse to heed, drowning that heavenly whisper by plunging anew into gaiety and pleasure, or stifling it by unwonted industry, are exposing themselves to distant but untold of sorrows. It will, indeed, be long ere conscience becomes so silenced as not to intrude, but she will at length; and then, when, in agony of spirit, we wake from our vain dream, and would give worlds, if we had them, to feel as we have felt—to hear once more the voice of conscience thrilling and directing as in happier years—to be awake to the consciousness of our faults, that we might correct and subdue them—and feel once more the glowing approval of our strivings after good, O how agonising must be the conviction—it is we who have spurned, neglected, and so silenced the angel of the Lord, that it must be a long, long, and weary interval of pain and toil, and watching, ere we may list those sweet low spiritual tones again. Better, far better, the momentary pain and humility of acknowledgment and submission. Better, far better, the too tender conscience, giving pain, in some cases apparently unnecessarily, than its silence and stagnation; for it MUST one day awake, and dreadful will be that waking. To obtain that blessed influence—to feel that to us is sent, as to our ancestors, "the angel of the Lord"—we have but to study the word of God and ourselves. It may cost us at first many sad and weary hours—many bitter tears —and many a secret pang; for it is hard so to know ourselves as to see faults and failings which others see not. It is hard to restrain the too frequent indulgence of favourite pleasures, because *we* know they will do us harm. It is hard sometimes to perform a disagreeable, nay a painful duty, *only* because we feel we ought, even though our friends see not the necessity;— hard, when friends approve, for our hearts to disapprove; and all this we must encounter, would we study ourselves and God's word, till our hearts become shrines for His guiding angel. But O, sad, depressing as all this may seem, it is but a grain in the balance compared to the deep thrilling joy which is its accompaniment. Those who have once felt the glow of approving conscience—the strength, encouragement, consolation, hope, which it gives when all around is desolate and dark, who feel that, hand-in-hand with faith and prayer, it is leading us safely and blessedly through the stony paths of earth, even through the dark valley of death, up to the glowing and immortal light of heaven, will welcome even its severest pang to call it theirs, and hail it as, indeed, the angel of the Lord.

It may be that Sarai's correction of Hagar was unduly harsh, although we have no warrant in Scripture for so believing; but it is evident, that there is no further mention of contention and disagreement between them, that she received her submission with gentleness, and restored her to favour. It is well when forgiveness is thus recorded: many and many a young meek spirit would obey the voice of the angel and return, in humility and love, could they but be sure that submission would be gently and lovingly received; and shrink from it only because the chilling reception, the *uttered* but not *felt* reconciliation, falls upon their still quivering hearts with a pang and degradation which they feel that as yet they cannot bear. The spirit of that healing and consoling love, which has its birth in religion, must guide both the offended and the offender, or reconciliation never can be complete; nor the latter be securely and convincingly led back to that better path to which the angel points. The pang of unrequited confidence, chilled affection, and all the bitterness of unnecessary degradation, will be stronger at first than the approving glow of conscience; while a contrary reception, even though it may heighten the pang of self-reproach, will soothe and encourage, for the inward voice whispers—we have done well; and from that moment, the heavenly messenger assumes her mild dominion in the heart, never to be lured thence again.

For thirteen years Abram and Sarai must have looked upon Ishmael as the promised seed; for, though not actually so said, there was neither spiritual sign nor human hope of the patriarch having any other child. At the end of that period, however, the Most High again appeared unto Abram, proclaiming Himself as the ALMIGHTY,—a fit introduction to the event He was about to foretell; and bidding His favoured servant, "Walk before me, and be thou perfect," perfect in trust, in faith, without any regard to human probabilities, for, as Almighty God, all things were possible with Him. The name of the patriarch was then changed, as a sign of the many nations over whom he was appointed father—the land again promised him—and the covenant appointed which was to mark his descendants as the chosen of the Lord, the everlasting inheritors of Canaan ; and bear witness, to untold-of ages, of the truth of the Lord's word, and the election of His people. This proclaimed and commanded, the Eternal commenced His information of the miracle He was about to perform, by desiring Abraham to call his wife no longer Sarai שָׂרַי but Sarah שָׂרָה—a change which our ancient fathers suppose to mean the same as from Abram to Abraham. "Sarai, signifying a lady or princess in a restricted sense, imported that she was a lady, or princess, to Abram only; whereas the latter name signifies princess or lady absolutely, indicating that she would thus be acknowledged by many, even as Abraham was to become the father of many nations."* A meaning perfectly reconcilable with the verse which follows : "And I will bless her, and give thee a son also of her : yea, I will bless her, so that she shall be a *mother of nations; kings of people* shall be of her." She was, therefore, no longer a princess over Abraham's household, but a princess in royal rank, from whom *kings* should descend. Joy must have been the first emotion of Abraham's heart at this miraculous announcement, mingled with a feeling of wonder, and astonishment how such a thing could be ; but then, in his peculiarly affectionate heart, came the thought of his first-born Ishmael, and with earnestness he prayed, "O that Ishmael might live before thee !" And

* See note to Gen. xvii. 15, in the Rev. D. A. De Sola's translation of the Bible.

though the Eternal could not grant this prayer, for the seed of Abraham, from whom His chosen people would spring, must be of pure and unmixed birth, He yet, with compassionating tenderness, soothed the father's anxious love, by the gracious promise that, though Sarah's child must be the seed with whom His covenant should be established, yet Ishmael also should be blessed and multiplied exceedingly, and become, even as Isaac, the father of a great nation. "And for Ishmael I have also heard thee." How blessed an encouragement for us to pour forth our prayers unto the Lord, proving, how consolingly, that no prayer is offered in vain; for if He cannot grant as our infinite wishes would dictate, He will yet hear us—yet fulfil our prayer far better for our welfare, and the welfare of our beloved ones, than our own wishes could have accomplished, had they been granted to the full.

The acceptance of the covenant throughout Abraham's household, and the change in her own name, must, of course, have been imparted by Abraham to his wife, with the addition of the startling promise, that she too, even at her advanced age, should bear a son. Yet by her behaviour, when the promise was repeated in the following chapter, it would appear that, though informed of it, she had dismissed it from her mind as a thing impossible. Accustomed to regard Ishmael as the only seed of Abraham—to suppose her scheme had been blessed, more particularly as she had never been named before as the mother of the chosen seed—the hope of being so had long since entirely faded; and, not having attained the simple questionless faith of her husband, she, in all probability, dismissed the thought, as recalling too painfully those ardent hopes and wishes, which she had with such difficulty previously subdued. Engaged, as was her wont, in her domestic duties, she was one day interrupted by the hasty entrance of her husband, requiring her "quickly to prepare three measures of fine meal, knead it, and make it into cakes." Patriarchal hospitality was never satisfied by committing to hirelings only the fit preparations for a hearty welcome. We see either Sarah herself making the desired cakes, or closely superintending her domestics in doing so; and the patriarch hastening, in the warmth of his hospitality, himself to fetch a calf from the herd, to give it to a young man to dress it, though he had abundance of servants around him to save him the exertion. Yet both Abraham and Sarah were of the nobility of the Eternal's creating. He had raised them above their fellows, and bestowed on them the patent of an aristocracy, with which not one of the nations could vie, for it came from God Himself. He had changed their names to signify their royal claims—to make them regarded, in future ages, as noble ancestors of a long line of prophets, kings, princes, and nobles; and there was a refinement, a nobleness, a magnanimity of character in both the patriarch and his wife, which, breathing through their very simplicity, betrayed their native aristocracy, and marked them of that princely race which has its origin in the favour and election of the King of kings. The primitive simplicity of our first fathers, generally imbues the mind with the mistaken idea of their being simply farmers or agriculturists, both of which they certainly were, but not these alone, as supposed in the present acceptation of the term. They were princes and nobles, not only in their mental superiority but in their immense possessions—in their large and well-ordered households, in the power they possessed both in their own establishments and in the adjoining lands, and in the respect and submission ever paid them by the nations with whom they might have held intercourse. Abraham was never addressed save as "My Lord," either by his own domestics or other nations; thus acknowledged as superior, and of noble if not royal rank, by those who could scarcely be supposed to understand why he was so, save by the outward signs of landed possession and large establishment. Those who think so much of noble descent, and princely connection, would do well to remember this—that impoverished, scattered, chastised for a "little moment," as we are—yet, that if we are children and descendants of Abraham—ISRAELITES not only in seeming but in heart—we are descended from the aristocracy of the Lord—from a higher and nobler race than even Gentile kings may boast; a privilege and glory of which no circumstance, no affliction, no persecution can deprive us—ours, through all and every event of life, unless we cast it from us by the dark deed of forsaking, for ambition, or gold or power, the banner of our blessed faith—the religion of our God.

Yet noble, even princely, as were Abraham and Sarah, it was no sign of rank, with them, to be cold, and restrained by false artificial laws. In the Bible, nobility was nature and *heart*, simplicity and benevolence, cordiality and warmth; no coldness, no indifference, no folding up the affections and the impulse of feeling in the icy garment of pride and fashion, which so often turns to selfishness, and so utterly prevents all of benevolence and social good. Abraham knew not, at his first invitation, the rank or mission of his visitors. His address was one of the *heart's respect*, not the mere politeness of the lip; and the warmth of his welcome would not permit his sitting idly down while hirelings prepared their meal—nay, we find that, even while they sat down to partake of it, their host stood,—a mark of profound respect, which a further consideration of their majestic aspect prompted, by the supposition that they were more than ordinary mortals.

Sarah joined not her husband or his guests. The modest and dignified customs of the East prevented all intrusion, or even the wish to intrude. Unless particularly asked for, the place of the Eastern, and Jewish wife, was in the retirement of home; not from any inferiority of rank, or servitude of station, but simply because their inclination so prompted. The strangers might have business with Abraham, which, if indeed, he would impart to her; there was no occasion for her to come forward. But, while seated in the inner tent, engaged in her usual avocations, she had heard her own name, "where is Sarah, thy wife?" and her husband's reply, "she is in the tent," followed by words that must indeed have sounded strange and improbable, "Sarah, thy wife, shall bear a son:" yet, improbable as they might have seemed, there is no excuse for the laugh of incredulity with which they were received. Already prepared, by the previous promise of the Lord, the words should at once have revealed the heavenly nature of those who spake, and been heard with faith and thankfulness; but Sarah thought only of the human impossibility. Strange as it is, that such unbelief should be found in the beloved partner of Abraham, yet her laugh proves that even she was not exempt from the natural feelings of mortality—the looking to human means and human possibilities alone; forgetting that with God all things are possible. Yet, to us, the whole of this incident is consoling. It proves that even Sarah was not utterly free from human infirmities; and yet that the Eternal, through His angel, deigned graciously to *reprove*, not to *chastise*. It proves that God has compassion on the nature of His erring children; for He knows their weakness. *Man* would have been wroth with the laugh of scorn, and withdrawn his intended favour; but "the Lord said unto Abraham, Wherefore did Sarah laugh, saying, Shall I, who am old, indeed bear a child? Is anything too mighty for the Lord? At the time appointed I will return unto thee, and Sarah shall indeed have a son." The gracious mildness of the rebuke— the blessed repetition of the promise—must, to one so affectionate as Sarah, have caused the bitterest reproach, but, weakly listening to fear instead of repentance, she denied her fault, seeking thus mistakenly to extenuate it. But he said, "Nay, but thou didst laugh," proving that her innermost thoughts were known; and, silenced at once, left to the solitude of her own tent, for Abraham accompanied his guests on the road to Sodom, we know quite enough of Sarah's character, to rest satisfied that repentance and self-abasement for unbelief, mingled with, and hallowed, the burst of rejoicing thankfulness with which she must have looked forward to an event so full of bliss to her individually, and so blessed a revelation of the Lord's deep love for Abraham and herself. Nearly twenty years had passed since the first promise of an heir in his own child had been given. Years, long, full of incident and feeling, seeming in their passing an interval long enough for the utter forgetfulness of the promise, save as it was supposed fulfilled in the birth of Ishmael; but now, in the retrospect, the promise flashed back with a vividness, a brightness, as if scarce a single year had passed ere it had been given: and Sarah must have felt self-reproach in the midst of her joy, that she had not waited, had not trusted, had not believed unto the end. And many a one, ere life has closed, will feel as she did; not, indeed, from the same cause, —but often and often a prayer has been offered up, a promise given from the word of God, and both have been forgotten, neglected, mistrusted, through long weary years—as vainly prayed and vainly answered—and yet, ere life has closed, recalled as by a flash of sudden light, by the divine answer to the one, and gracious fulfilment of the other.

Before the birth of Isaac, however, Abraham and his family once more removed their dwelling, partly, it may be supposed, to fulfil the words of the Lord previously spoken:—" Arise, walk through the land, in the length of it and the breadth of it, for I will give it unto thee;"—and partly from the desolate appearance and poisonous vapours of the once beautiful vale of Sodom, and in consequence of the cessation of travellers, to whom Abraham had so delighted to show hospitality. We shall pass lightly over the next event in the life of Sarah, having already made our remarks on a similar occurrence. The fault of the patriarch in again passing his wife for his sister, was indeed much greater than it had been at the first. He had now no longer the excuse of not sufficiently knowing the ways of the Lord, to trust in Him, even in the midst of those dangers incidental to mankind, yet seeming too trivial for the interference of the Most High. He had had nearly thirty years' experience, that he was in truth the chosen servant, and the well-beloved of the Lord—that there was not an event in his life which had not been ordered and guided by a special providence; and he ought to have known, that this danger, as every other, would be overruled. Yet, while we *regret* that this incomprehensible weakness should overshadow the beautiful character of our great ancestor, we may not condemn; for, at this distance of time, and complete change in manners and customs, it is impossible for us to know the temptation he may have had to act as he did, or the extent of danger to which he was exposed. The most truly pious, the most experienced in religion, have often to mourn their "iniquities in holy things." The painful struggle is always to realise faith, to trust without one doubt, and more particularly in the smaller trials of life, which they may deem too trivial for the notice, compassion, or interference of the Eternal. Nor can even *proofs* of a superintending providence always conquer the weakness of human nature. In this world, the likeness of God will at times be completely hidden in the earthly shell, however it may stand forth at others, as if nought of clay could dull it more. And this was the case with Abraham, who, though the beloved of the Lord, was yet *human*, and liable to all the weaknesses and frailties of human nature. We are not, therefore, to condemn, and so withdraw our admiration of his great and most consolingly beautiful character, because in two instances he falls short of our ideas of perfection,—but rather thank God that in His Word human nature is recorded as *it is*, simply that we may not despair. It is enough for us, in this part of our narrative, to notice that our gracious God demands no more of His creatures than He knows they can perform; that Abraham's faulty weakness in this one instance, could not blot from the recollection of the Lord his pure and simple faith in every other; and that He permitted all that occurred in the kingdom of Gerar, to make manifest, alike to Abraham and the nations,

His continued watchfulness and miraculous interposition in favour of those whom he loves—His power to protect them from all harm, and also, that nothing was too wonderful for Him. Sarah had imagined she was too old to enjoy the felicity of becoming a mother—too old in any way to excite admiration, save to the beloved husband of her youth ; and, ignorant that her beauty had been supernaturally renewed, neglected to assume the veil, which was worn by all eastern women dwelling in towns. This explains Abimelech's present of "a covering for the eyes," and the words—"thus she was reproved," or warned, that her beauty subjected her to as much danger as had been the case in her youth.

Miraculously protected by the Eternal, and publicly vindicated from all dishonour by the king of Gerar, Sarah and her husband continued to dwell in Abimelech's dominions, some few miles to the south of Gerar; a place afterwards called Beer-Shebang, or Well of the Oath, from the covenant of peace there made between the patriarch and the king. Here it was, that at the appointed time, "God visited Sarah as He had said ;" and the promised seed—the child of rejoicing—Isaac was born. What must have been the emotions of Sarah on beholding him ? Not alone the bliss of a mother; but that in him, the infant claimer of a love and joy which she had never so felt before, she beheld a visible and palpable manifestation of the wonderful power and unchanging love of the Most High God. Devoted, as Sarah had been, to the service and love of the Lord, how inexpressibly must these emotions have been heightened as she gazed upon her babe, and held him to her bosom as her *own*, her granted child. To those who really love the Lord, joy is as dear, as bright, as close a link between the heart and its God, as grief is to more fallen natures. We find the hymn of rejoicing, the song of thanksgiving, always the vehicle in which the favoured servants of the Lord poured forth their grateful adoration, thus proving that the thought of the beneficent Giver ever hallowed and sanctified the gift ; and therefore we believe, with our ancient fathers, that though *not translated metrically*, Sarah expressed her joy in a short hymn of thanksgiving. The peculiar idiom of the Hebrew text confirms this supposition,[*] and we adopt it as most natural to the occasion. Her age had no power, even before she became a mother, to dull her feelings, and her

[*] See the Rev. D. A. De Sola's translation and note thereon.

song of thanksgiving well expresses every emotion natural, not alone to the occasion, but to her peculiar situation. As a young mother, full of life, of sentiment, of affection, she felt towards her babe—giving him his natural food from her own bosom—tending his infant years—guiding him from boyhood to youth—from youth to manhood, and lavishing on him the full tide of love which had been pent up so long. The very character of Isaac, as is afterwards displayed—meek, yielding, affectionate, almost as a woman's—disinclined to enterprise—satisfied with his heritage—all prove the influence which his mother had possessed, and that his disposition was more the work of her hand than of his father's.

"The child grew and was weaned," Holy Writ proceeds to inform us, "And Abraham made a great feast the day Isaac was weaned,"—a feast of rejoicing, that the Eternal had mercifully preserved him through the first epoch of his young existence. He was now three years old, if not more—for the women of the East, even now, do not wean their children till that age. The feast, however, which commenced in joy, was, for the patriarch, dashed with sorrow ere it closed. Educated with the full idea that he was his father's heir —though the words of the angel before his birth gave no warrant for the supposition—to Ishmael and his mother, the birth of Isaac must have been a grievous disappointment. And we find the son committing the same fault as his mother previously had done—deriding, speaking disrespectfully of Sarah and her child. The youth of Ishmael, and Sarah's request, that the bond-woman might also be expelled, would lead to the supposition, that it was Hagar who had instigated the affront. The age of Sarah, and the decidedly super-human birth of Isaac, must, to all but the patriarch's own household, have naturally given rise to many strange, and perhaps calumniating reports. In the common events of life, all that is incomprehensible, is either ridiculed, disbelieved, or made matter of scandal; and, therefore, in a case so uncommon as this, it is more than probable, reports very discreditable both to Sarah and Abraham, were promulgated all around them. Hagar, indeed, and Ishmael must have known differently :—that it was the hand of God which worked, and therefore all things were possible; but it was to Ishmael's interest to dispute or deny the legitimacy of Isaac; and, therefore, it was not in human nature to neglect the opportunity. No other offence would have so worked on Sarah. We are apt to think more poetically than justly of this part of the Bible. Hagar and her young son, expelled from their luxurious and happy home, almost perishing in the desert from thirst, are infinitely more interesting objects of consideration and sympathy, than the harsh and jealous Sarah, who, for seemingly such trifling offence, demanded and obtained such severe retribution.

We generally rest satisfied with one or two verses; whereas, did we look further and think deeper, our judgment would be different. In a mere superficial reading, we acknowledge Sarah does appear in rather an unfavourable light; as if her love for Isaac had suddenly narrowed and stagnated every other feeling; and, jealous of Ishmael's influence over his father, she had determined on seizing the first opportunity for his expulsion. That this, however, is a wrong judgment, is proved by the fact, that the Eternal Himself desires Abraham to hearken to the voice of Sarah in all that she shall say; for in Isaac was to be the promised seed, though of Ishmael also would He make a nation, because he was Abraham's son. That Sarah's advice was not to be displeasing to him, because of the lad and his mother.

Now, had Sarah's advice proceeded from an undue harshness, a mean and jealous motive, the Most High would, in His divine justice, have taken other means for the fulfilment of His decrees. He would not have desired His good and faithful servant to be so guided by an evil and suspicious tongue. There are times when we feel urged and impelled to speak that which we are yet conscious will be productive of pain and suffering to ourselves. All such impulses are of God; and it must have been some such feeling which actuated Sarah, and compelled her to continue her solicitation for the expulsion of Hagar and Ishmael, even after the moment of anger was passed. We know that Hagar had ever been her favourite slave;—it was impossible for one affectionate as was Sarah, to have regarded Ishmael as her son for thirteen or fourteen years, and yet not have loved him, though, of course, with less intensity than his father. The birth of Isaac naturally revealed yet stronger emotions; still Ishmael could not have been so excluded from her affections as to render her separation from him void of pain. And still she spoke, still urged the necessity, conscious all the time she was inflicting pain, not only on her husband but on herself. This appears like contradiction; but each one who has attentively studied the workings of his own heart, will not only feel, but pronounce it *truth*. Anger caused the demand: "Expel this bondwoman and her son; for the son of this bondwoman shall not inherit with my son, even with Isaac;" and calmer reflection continued to see the necessity. Abraham's possessions were sufficient for the heritage of both his sons; but as the course of nature was changed, and the younger, not the elder, was to be the heir of promise, confusion and discord would have ensued, and the brothers continually have been at war. Sarah's penetration appears to have discovered this; and as it was necessary for Ishmael to form a separate establishment, it was an act of kindness, not of harshness, to let him depart with Hagar, instead of going forth alone. From her own feelings, she now knew the whole extent of a mother's love; and, therefore, though Ishmael had been the sole offender, and the only one whose claims were likely to clash with Isaac's, she would not separate the mother from the son, and so urged Abraham to separate from both.

There is something touchingly beautiful in the patriarch's love for his elder son, and yet his instant conquest of self at the word of the Lord. His deep affection had blinded him to the probable discomforts which might ensue from his sons remaining together. His gentle and affectionate nature shrunk from the pang of separation, causing even displeasure against Sarah, for the first time in their long and faithful intercourse. Yet when God spake, there was neither complaint nor murmur, nor one word of supplication that the heavy trial might be averted from him. It was enough that the Most High had spoken; and, though all was dark before his son, to the fond anxious gaze of paternal affection, he knew even from that darkness God *could* bring forth light, and *would* do so, for He had promised.

We are sometimes surprised at the small provision with which Abraham endowed his son at his departure. The riches of the patriarchs consisted of land, flocks, herds, and servants; nothing which could easily be bestowed. Besides which, Ishmael was to become the ancestor of a nation, through *the direct agency of the Lord*, not from any provision made him by his earthly father. Had Abraham endowed him, the interposition of the Eternal would not have been so clearly and unanswerably demonstrated. There would have been many to have traced his riches and the princely rank of his descendants from the gifts and power of Abraham, and denied altogether any interposition of the Lord; whereas, sent forth as he was, with nothing but sufficient provision to sustain him till he reached his appointed resting, it was impossible even for the greatest sceptic to trace his future prosperity and wealth to any earthly power alone. The bread and water must not be supposed as meaning only what we now regard them. In the language of the Bible bread is used indiscriminately for every kind of food, and the bottle of water signifies a skinful, such being used by Eastern travellers even now, and containing much more than we imagine is comprised by the term "bottle." Yet even these were to fail, that the miraculous power and compassionate love of the Eternal might still more startlingly be proved. It was as easy for the Most High to have guided Ishmael and his mother at once to their destined dwelling, as to try them as He did in the ordeal of alike physical and mental suffering. But he chose the latter, at once to prove His love to them and to give to future ages, through His unerring word, comfort in their darkest hours; for as He relieved Hagar, so will He them. The God of the bondwoman is ours still; no time, no change can part us from Him.

The narrative of Hagar's wanderings in the wilderness, her maternal suffering, and miraculous relief, is one of the most beautiful and most touching amongst the many beauties of the Bible. Hagar was not of Abraham's race, but one of a heathen and benighted nation, a bondwoman and a wanderer, a weak and lonely female, exiled from a home of love, overwhelmed with anxious fears for her child, perhaps, too, with self-reproaches for the unguarded words which she encouraged her boy to speak, and which she regarded as the sole cause of her banishment; yet was this poor sufferer the peculiar care of the great and mighty God. He caused the clouds of densest darkness to close around her, from them to bring forth the brightest, most enduring light. He deigned, by His angel, to speak comfort and hope, and even for her human wants provided the necessary aid. He did not guard from sorrow; for it was not until "the water was spent in the bottle, and she cast the child under one of the shrubs, and she went and sat down over against him, a good way off, for she said, Let me not see the death of the child; and she sat over against him, and lifted up her voice and wept"—not till her trial was thus at its height, that the angelic voice descended from heaven in such pitying and sympathising accents: "What aileth thee, O Hagar? Fear not, for God hath heard the voice of the lad whence he is. Arise, lift up the lad, and hold him in thine hand, for I will make him a great nation." And the promise was fulfilled.

The whole history of Hagar is fraught with the deepest comfort. She was one of the many in individual character; possessing alike woman's engaging and faulty characteristics: feeling and affectionate at one time, overbearing and insolent at another—loving Ishmael with impetuous and clinging love, which could not bear to see his supposed heritage become the property of another, though she knew it was the decree of God—reverencing and loving Abraham, alike as her master and the father of her child, but unable always to preserve the submission and respect due to Sarah as her mistress and indulgent friend; for, though the mother of Abraham's child, she was still Sarah's maid;—such was Hagar. Neither in character superior, nor in station equal, to the daughters of Israel now; yet was she the peculiar charge of the Most High, and twice did He deign, in closest communion, to instruct and console. Her life had its trials, in no way inferior in severity or in deep suffering to the trials of the present day. Yet God was with her in them all; and, in His own appointed time, permitted them to give place to prosperity and joy. And as He worked then, so He worketh now. It is no proof of His dearest love, when life passes by without a cloud—when sorrow and trial are strangers to our path. His word reveals that those whom He loved the *best*, alike male or female, endured the severest trials—that His love, His guiding words, were not given to the children of joy. To become His servant, His beloved, His chosen, was to suffer and to labour. We see this throughout His word; and shall we, dare we, except their exemption now? O no, no! Would we love the Lord, would we truly be loved by Him, would we pray for and seek His paths, would we struggle on to the goal of immortal love and bliss, we must nerve both heart and frame to *bear*; strengthen and arouse every faculty to *endure* and *suffer*; for so did His chosen, His best beloved, and so too must we. We have still His word to be to us as the angelic whisper was to our ancestors. Their hope is ours, and their *reward*.

Few other events mark the life of Sarah. The Most High had brought her forth from the trials, anxieties, and doubts of previous years. He had, in His infinite mercy, fulfilled His word, and bestowed on her the blessed gift for which, in the midst of happiness, she had pined. Continuing His loving kindness, He lengthened her days much beyond the usual sum of mortality, that she might rear her child to manhood, and receive all the blessed fruit of her maternal care in Isaac's deep love and reverence for herself. In a mere superficial perusal of the life of Sarah, as read in our Sabbath portions, we are likely to overlook much of the consoling proofs of the Eternal's compassionating love for His female children, which it so powerfully reveals. Sarah was ninety years of age when Isaac was born. In the course of nature, ten or twelve years more would either have closed her mortal career, or rendered it, from the infirmities of so great an age, a burden to herself and all around her. There was no need of her preservation to forward the decrees of the Lord. In giving birth to the child of promise, her part was fulfilled, and at the age of ten or twelve the boy might have done without her. But God is LOVE, and the affections of His children are, in their strength and purity, peculiarly acceptable to Him. He never bestoweth happiness to withdraw it; and, therefore, to perfect the felicity of Sarah and her child, His tenderness preserved her in life and vigour seven and thirty years after she had given him birth. In this simple fact we trace the beneficent and tender Father, sympathising not alone in every grief and pang, but in every joy and affection of His creatures. We feel to our heart's core the truth of the words of Moses, "Who hath God so near to him" as Israel? What nation can so trace, so claim the love of the Eternal?

Nor was the preservation of Sarah the *only* proof of our Father's loving tenderness towards her, and of His condescending sympathy with the love she bore her child. The trial of faith, in the sacrifice of his son, was given to the *father;* but the *mother* was spared the consuming agony which must have been her portion, even had her faith continued strong. God had compassion on the feebler, weaker nature of His female servant. He demanded not from her that which He knew the mother could not bear. He spared her, in His immeasurable love, the suffering which it pleased Him to inflict upon the father,—suffering and temptation *not* to satisfy the Lord, for His omniscience knew that His faithful servant would not fail; but to prove in future ages the mighty power of spiritual faith and love, even while in the mortal clay.

In the early part of his spiritual career, even Abraham's faith would in all probability have failed. He was *not* supernaturally endowed with divine grace and strength. All through his life we can trace his gradual advance and improvement, till his faith and love arrived at the climax which permitted even the offered and unmurmuring sacrifice of his dearly beloved and now only child. Even in this we trace the guiding and fostering love of the Lord—demanding not more than He knew *could* be given, and measuring the trial of faith according to the advancing strength of His servant, each one more than the last. But this consideration has more to do with Abraham individually and Israel at large. It is his loving kindness manifested towards Sarah that we, her female descendants, must take to our hearts, thence to derive alike strength and consolation. The conviction of the Eternal's love for us *individually*, is necessary for woman's happiness, and peculiarly adapted to its bestowal.

It is woman's *nature* to yearn and droop for love—to shrink in agony from a lonely path—to long for some supporting arm on which to rest her weakness; and it is woman's *doom*, too often, to find *on earth* no loving rest, and therefore is her lot so sad. But when she can once realise that she is the subject of a love as immeasurably superior, in consolation, strength, and changeless sympathy, to that of man as the heaven is above the earth :—when she can once feel she has a friend who will never " leave her nor forsake "—in whose pitying ear she may pour forth her trials and griefs, either petty or great which she would not, even if she might, confide to man, secure not only of pity but of *healing*—when she is conscious that she is never lonely—never left to her own weakness, but in her every need will have strength *infused*—then, then is she so blessed, that she is no more lonely, no more sad ! And the word of God will give us this thrice blessed consolation, not in His gracious promises alone, though they in themselves would be sufficient, but in His dealings with His creatures.

As the ancestor of His beloved, we find Sarah's death and age particularly recorded ; being the first woman of the Bible whose death and burial are mentioned. The deep grief of her husband and son, are simply but touchingly betrayed in the brief words, "And Abraham came to mourn for Sarah, and to weep for her;" and at a later period, not till his marriage with Rebekah, "and Isaac was comforted after his mother's death." Words that pourtray the beauty and affection of Sarah's domestic character, and confirm our belief that, although perhaps possessing many of the failings of her sex, she was yet a help meet for Abraham—a tender and judicious parent to her son—and a kind indulgent friend to the large household of which she was the mistress. Her noble, or rather princely, rank, received as it had been direct from the Lord, is still more strongly proved by the intercourse between Abraham and the sons of Heth, when seeking from them a place to bury his dead: "Hear us, my Lord," is their reply; "thou art a *mighty prince of God* amongst us: in the choicest of our sepulchres bury thy dead;" and it was with difficulty Abraham could elude the offered gift, and procure the cave as a purchase. His princely rank, however, and in consequence that of his wife, we see at once acknowledged, even by strangers; and the promise of the Lord, expressed in changing the name of *Sarai* into *Sarah*, clearly fulfilled.

The grief of Isaac appears to have lasted yet longer than that of his father, and beautifully illustrates the love between the mother and son. Abraham, advanced in years and spiritual experience, felt less keenly the mere emotions of humanity; he was convinced that Sarah had only gone before him to that world, in which, from his great age, he would, no doubt, speedily join her. His many duties—his close communion with the Eternal—enabled him to rouse himself sooner from the grief, which, at first, was equally severe; but Isaac was, according to the patriarchal reckoning of time, still a very young man, at the age when feeling is keener, less controlled than at any other; and when, though spiritual comfort is great, human emotions will have full vent. Except the three days' journey to Mount Moriah with his father, Isaac does not appear to have been separated a single day from his mother; and her care, her guiding and fostering love, had so entwined her round his heart, that for three years after her death her son could find no comfort. How exalted and lovely must have been that mother's character to demand such a term of mourning from her son; whose youth and sex would, in some, have speedily roused him from sorrow, or urged its forgetfulness in scenes of pleasure.

F

We have little more to add on the spiritual lesson and divine consolation, which Sarah's life presents to her female descendants, than those hints already given. Differently situated as we are, with regard to station, land, and customs, we may yet imitate her faithfulness in all her household duties—her love and reverence to her husband—her tenderness to her child—her quiet, unpretending, domestic, yet dignified fulfilment of all which she was called upon to do. We may learn from her to set no value on personal charms, save as they may enhance the gratification of those who love us best; or of rank and station, save as they demand from us yet deeper gratitude towards God, and more extended usefulness towards man. We may learn, too, from her history, that it is better to wait for the Lord—to leave in His hands the fulfilment of our ardent wishes—than to seek to compass them by human means. We may trace and feel that nothing, in truth, is too wonderful for the Lord; that He will do what pleaseth Him, however we may deem it hopeless and in vain. Direct revelations as vouchsafed to Sarah, indeed, we have not; but God has, in His deep mercy, granted us His word—the record of all HE HAS DONE—that we may feel that He is still OUR God; and though He worketh now in *secret*—for our sins have hid from us His ways—yet He worketh for us still, and hath compassion and mercy and love for each of us individually, even as He had for Sarah, and her bond-woman Hagar. All these to us, as women, her history reveals; as women of Israel, O yet more. It is of no stranger in race and clime and faith we read. It is of OUR OWN—of one from whom Israel has descended in a direct unshadowed line—of one—the beloved and cherished partner of that chosen servant and beloved friend of the Eternal, for whose sake revelation was given to mankind—Israel made not alone the nation, but the FIRST-BORN of the Lord; and that law bestowed, which revealed a God of "love, long-suffering and gracious, plenteous in mercy and truth;"—instructed us how to tread our earthly path, so as to give happiness to ourselves and fellow-creatures to be acceptable to Him;—and pointed with an angel-finger to that immortal goal, where man shall live for ever!

Is it nothing to be the lineal descendants of one so favoured—nothing to hold in our hands and shrine in our hearts, the record of her life from whom the race of promise sprung? Nothing, to peruse the wonderful manifestations of the Lord's love to her—to feel that from Him direct, was Sarah's patent of nobility, and yet possess the privilege of being her descendant? Will the women of Israel feel this as nothing—will they disdain their princely birth—their heavenly heritage? Will they scorn to look back on Sarah as their ancestor, and yet long for earthly distinctions, earthly rank? No! O no! Let us but think of these things—of those from whom we have descended, and our minds will be ennobled, our hearts enlarged. We shall scorn the false shame which would descend to petty meanness to hide our faith, and so exalt us in the sight of a Gentile world. Humbled, cast off for a little moment as we are—liable to persecution, scorn, contumely—to be "despised and rejected" of men—to bear the burden of affliction from all who choose to afflict—still, still, we cannot lose our blessed heritage unless we cast it off;—we cannot be deprived of our birthright, unless, like Esau, we exchange it for mere worldly pelf, and momentary (because *earthly*) gratification. We are still Israelites—still the chosen, the beloved, the ARISTOCRACY of the Lord.

REBEKAH.

IN the same beautiful country whence, nearly seventy years previous, the son of Terah had been called by the divine command, still dwelt the children of his brother Nahor. Contrary to the long period of childlessness which had been the portion of Abraham, eight sons were born unto Nahor. And when tidings of his family again reached the patriarch, just after the offered sacrifice of his son, he heard that his brother was also a grandfather—Bethuel, one of his sons, having married, and possessing sons and one fair daughter. The many wanderings of Abraham, the distance to which he had removed, and the almost impossibility of obtaining reciprocal intelligence, had, of course, prevented family intercourse. Yet, by the notice taken of Abraham's having unexpectedly received intelligence of his kindred, and also by the momentous events recorded in the XXIV. chapter, it is evident that both Abraham and Nahor retained a vivid recollection of, and continued affection towards, each other—an affecting illustration of the doctrine we so earnestly uphold: that Holy

Writ never fails to inculcate—alike by precept, character and narrative—the *ascendancy, necessity*, and *beauty* of the natural affections. Though elected to know and serve the Lord, and to promulgate the knowledge of the true religion throughout the world, still, no forgetfulness, no contempt of the less favoured of his father's house actuated Abraham. In simple, questionless obedience to his God, he had departed from all the haunts, the friends of his youth; but to a disposition so strongly affectionate as his own, often and often must the yearnings have returned, to learn somewhat of the brother of his love. The characters of the Bible are all *human*: though we are but too apt to judge them by any and every other test than that of humanity. Religion, instead of *deadening*, ever deepens and strengthens mere human feelings. No one has ever yet truly and devotedly loved God, without feeling every natural affection heightened and more precious. Indifference in any one single point is utterly banished. It *cannot* exist with true spirituality; and therefore do we always find in the Bible, the strongest, most affectionate feelings, actuating the chosen servants of the Lord.

From a careful consideration of this portion of Bible history, and of Laban's family in the sequel, it appears probable, that Abraham had other reasons besides those of kindred, for wishing his son to choose a wife from the daughters of Mesopotamia, instead of those of Canaan. Had the patriarch's kindred been merely idolatrous as the other families of the earth, it is not likely that the mere recital of the steward should have called forth Laban and Bethuel's answering exclamation—" The thing proceedeth from the LORD, we cannot speak unto thee bad or good!"—nor many years afterward, in Laban's intercourse with his nephew, his entreaty, "Tarry with me, for I have learned by experience that the LORD hath blessed me for thy sake." It would seem from these simply recorded facts, that though they worshipped images, which are referred to more than once in the sequel, their religion was certainly purer than that of the Canaanites. It was from his father's house Abraham had been elected and called by the Almighty. His firm rejection and abhorrence of idols, his meek and gentle un-upbraiding conduct, his departure in simple obedience to an unknown Being—all this was probably remembered, and so commented upon by his kindred, that his memory had more influence than his presence; and **vague** notions of the religion and the God whom he had followed and preached, mingled with the image-worship which they still retained. These notions, very possibly strengthened by the rumours of Abraham's continued communings with this mysterious God, and the manifestations of a superhuman agency vouchsafed to him, which, by slow degrees, reached even Mesopotamia, prepared them to acknowledge and even believe in Him ; though, from ignorance as to the manner of worship which could be acceptable to a Being so awful and invisible, they adhered to the worship of their fathers.

Abraham no doubt felt that it would be easy to impart to the daughter of such a race, the true and spiritual religion, of which the Patriarch's own family was the only witness. There would be no fear of her retaining and secretly promulgating the impure and idolatrous notions which would undoubtedly have been the case with the daughters of Canaan ; and this, acting powerfully on the affecting recollections of kindred and home, appears to me the real cause of Abraham's intense anxiety to take a wife for his son Isaac from the daughters of his father's house.

Meanwhile the daughter of Bethuel had grown into beautiful womanhood, beloved and cherished alike by her parents and brothers, and pursuing with cheerful content and affection, the simple routine of domestic life. There is no mention in Scripture, of her having ever been sought in marriage, before the offer of Isaac. We are rather to suppose, that she was scarcely seen or known beyond the precincts of her father's establishment; and, as this was the case also with the daughters of Laban, some years afterwards, the supposition of their superiority to the other heathen nations is confirmed.

The daily employments of the young females of the East, appear to have been completely domestic ; and, in obedience to these daily duties, we find Rebekah, one evening, going as usual to the well with her pitcher on her shoulder to draw water. The group of strangers beside the well, must have struck her as something remarkable, but we do not find that she in any way loitered, or wavered in the steady performance of her task.

"And the damsel was very fair to look upon, a virgin ; *and she went down to the well, and filled her pitcher and came up.* And the servant ran to meet her, and said, Let me, I pray thee, drink a little water of thy pitcher. And she said, Drink, my lord : and she let down her pitcher upon her hand, and gave him drink. And when she had done giving him drink, she said, I will draw water for thy camels also, until they have done drinking. And she hasted, and emptied her pitcher into the trough, and ran again unto the well to draw water, and drew for all his camels."

Among the many little exquisite touches of artless and gentle nature, with which the Bible abounds, none surpasses this for truth and beauty. The same unsophisticated nature that led her quietly to pursue her duty, without turning to the right hand or to the left, also prompted the active and cordial kindness to the stranger, when he addressed her, and the respectful deference to his age and sex, which the words, "Drink, my lord," imply. It was the quiet self-possession, the modest ease and frankness, the total disregard of self, alike with regard to personal trouble as to the impression her own beautiful face and form might make, which ever proceed from a proper self-esteem, without which no woman, however situated, can happily, or with propriety, pass through life. She not only gave refreshment to the steward, but filled the trough for the weary camels to drink also. Many times must she have ascended and descended to the well, burdened with a weighty pitcher—a fair and gentle girl, while so many strong men were standing round—but they were strangers and travellers, and she was in her own land.

Well might Eliezer, "wondering at her, hold his peace, to wit whether the Lord had made his journey prosperous or not." It was difficult to believe that the prayer he had scarcely concluded before Rebekah appeared, should so speedily be answered ; and it was, no doubt, with some little trembling he asked, "Whose daughter art thou ? Tell me, I pray thee, is there room in thy father's house for us to lodge in ?" and how must his heart have bounded with returning confidence at the artless reply, "I am the daughter of Bethuel, the son of Milcah, which she bare unto Nahor. She said moreover to him, we have both straw and provender enough, and room to lodge in." Our ancient fathers, with much justice, suppose that the splendid presents of the steward *followed* this announcement, and were not given, as we might imagine from the general translations of the Bible, *before* he knew her name. They had been entrusted to him for the bride of Isaac ; and therefore, it was not likely he should bestow them on any one, however beautiful and hospitable, unless perfectly convinced that she was the maiden destined so to be. The little conversation between them, and even the steward's fervent ejaculation of thanksgiving, probably took place while the camels were drinking; and it was when they had done, "that the man took a golden earring of half a shekel weight, and the bracelets for her hands of ten shekels weight of gold." Greatly must the maiden have marvelled, not only at the richness of the presents, but that they should be offered at all; and, true to the almost childish nature which the whole narration displays, "she ran and told them of her mother's house these things."

It is by some commentators considered strange, I believe, that in all which follows, Laban, not Bethuel, should be the principal actor. The Bible appears to tell us, that Laban was decidedly the head of his father's house; and as there is no mention whatever of Rebekah's father, no reference to any relation but her mother and brother, it does not seem probable that she had a father living, the Bethuel, who is mentioned, being possibly a younger brother, and one of very inferior consequence.

We have already perceived, that Rebekah "told them of her *mother's* house." And now, without any notice whatever of a father, we read—that "Rebekah had a brother, whose name was Laban." And when he saw the earring and bracelets on his sister's hands, and when he heard her words, he came unto the man who still stood with his camels beside the well, and accosted him, not only as one who was master, with independent authority, but with an exclamation which confirms our previous suggestion, that some vague notions of Abraham's God had reached even Mesopotamia. The hurried narration of his sister would not have been sufficient incentive for such greeting;—"Come in, thou BLESSED OF THE LORD; wherefore standest thou without? for I have prepared the house, and room for the camels. And the man came into the house, and he ungirded his camels. And they gave straw and provender for the camels, and water to wash his feet, and the men's feet who were with him. And they set meat before him to eat: but he said, I will not eat, till I have said mine errand. And he [Laban] said, Speak on."

Laban, as the generous, unsuspicious host, had performed his part. And now the servant of Abraham failed not to perform his. Earnest in his master's cause, his mission occupying alike heart and mind—convinced that he was in the Lord's hands, he would not wait till hunger was appeased and weariness subdued, but at once spoke; his first words refusing all honor to himself by the simple declaration עֶבֶד אַבְרָהָם אָנֹכִי "Servant of Abraham am I." It was, indeed, a a wondrous tale to which the family of Bethuel listened. By the words of Laban, at its conclusion, "Behold, Rebekah is *before* thee," we may infer, that the maiden and her mother were both present; though, by no word or exclamation did the former interrupt a narrative which concerned her so deeply; yet, as a woman, and a very young one, how many feelings must have stirred within her, as the steward spoke!

Eliezer told how his venerable master had grown rich and great by the blessing of the Lord, who had also granted him, in his old age, a son, to whom Abraham had given all that he had; how anxious he was to guard his son from a connection with the Canaanites, and to take him a wife from his own kindred — overruling Eliezer's objection, "Peradventure, the woman will not follow me," by the solemn assurance that, "the Lord, before whom I walk, will send His angel before thee, and prosper thy way;" how, in obedience he had set forth, and arriving that day at the well, had prayed to the Lord God of his master Abraham, to grant that the virgin who when he wished for a little water from her pitcher, should reply, "Drink thou, and I will draw for the camels also," should be the maiden, whom the Lord had appointed for his master's son; how his prayer had been heard and answered, by the appearance and kindly courtesy of Rebekah; and he concluded, "I bowed down my head, and worshipped the Lord God of my master Abraham, who had led me in the right way, to take my master's brother's daughter for his son. And now, if you will deal kindly and truly with my master, tell me; and if not, tell me; that I may turn to the right hand, or the left."

Deeply indeed must the simple tale have affected its hearers. The rich, the princely Abraham had remembered and yearned towards his father's house; even those who, perchance, in his youth had reviled and persecuted him for his rejection of their idols. Seeking from them, in preference to every other, a wife for his son. "The thing proceedeth from the Lord," was their instant answer. "We cannot speak unto thee bad or good.

Behold, Rebekah is before thee, take her, and go, and let her be thy master's son's wife, as the Lord hath spoken."

Blessed thus far, the richest jewels of gold and silver were presented by the steward to the youthful bride, her mother and brother. Surely, if her father had still been living, he would here have been mentioned: but neither here, nor in the 55th and 60th verses following, which are important, as relating to her influential kindred, is there any notice taken of his existence.

One night only, the steward accepted the lavish hospitality of his hosts. Anxious to report the success of his mission, he entreated, "Send me away to my master." But natural ties could not be so quickly severed without pain. How could they so suddenly part with the cherished darling of their house —in all probability never to look upon her again? "Let the damsel abide with us a few days," her mother and brother said; "at least ten, after that she shall go." But the steward entreated them to "hinder him not," believing that to loiter, would be "displeasing to the Lord who had prospered his way." And they said, "We will call the damsel, and enquire at her mouth." Young, and retiring as she was, her own voice was to decide the matter. They would neither retain nor send her away without her own consent; thus proving, that even family authority in the Bible, was an authority of love. "And calling her, they said, Wilt thou go with this man? And she said, I will go;"—a brief and simple answer, yet suited alike to her character and the occasion. No doubt, there will be some to exclaim against the reply as abrupt and unmaidenly; but have they quite considered all the circumstances of the case? Rebekah's character, at this period of her life, was a beautiful blending of simplicity and truth. Sought by Abraham for his son, of whom, most likely she had already favourably heard; selected by God himself, every *natural* feeling of woman, was satisfied and soothed. Perhaps, now, in this period of ultra refinement, such simplicity will scarcely be understood. Yet, *then* her meek assent was in perfect accordance with all that had passed before. Is it not ordained, even by God himself— that woman, even as man, should leave father, mother, and home, to cleave unto her husband? Besides, this was no engagement of mere human devising. She was, unconsciously, the instrument in the Eternal's hand to further His decrees. And her brief assent was His inspiration, as certainly as all the previous incidents. Nor can we doubt for a moment, even while she declared her willingness to go, that natural affections were busy within her. Have not our readers themselves felt, at times, two completely opposing feelings filling their hearts at once? And O how blessed would it be at such times, if we could but realise that the words, fraught with a pain and anxiety unknown, unthought of, when we spoke them, proceed alone, as Rebekah's "I will go," from the guidance of the Lord, and that therefore, spite of all the sufferings which may gather round us, they will in the end be blessed.

Rebekah had accepted the presents of betrothal, and was, therefore, already of the family of Abraham. How then might his steward go without her? It was not her part to detain him on his way. We may imagine the tears of affection with which the fond blessing was pronounced by her brothers. The mother, though still present, is not mentioned; for her prayers were in her heart. And they blessed Rebekah, and said unto her, Thou art our sister; be thou the mother of thousands of millions, and let thy seed possess the gates of those which hate them." And Rebekah arose (probably from the detaining arms of her kindred) and with her nurse, and attendant damsels, sought their camels, and accompanied the steward on his homeward way.

How many thoughts must have crowded the heart and mind of the young daughter of Bethuel during this journey—the home she had left, and the home she was about to seek—the friends of her childhood, and those unknown; yet, towards whom she turned with the yearning to love and be beloved; probably hearing from the lips of the steward so much of his young master, as to render him in her mind no longer a stranger.

Simply and beautifully is the last touch to this portion of her history, given by the inspired historian. Canaan was reached; the tents of the patriarch in sight. And lifting up her eyes, Rebekah beheld a man walking forth in the fertile fields; bearing in his pensive mind and measured tread, the aspect of one in holy meditation. It was eventide, that still solemn hour of holy musing, sought only by those, who have no thought from which to shrink, who can call up sweet dreamy visions of the past—sad, yet how inexpressibly soothing. That holy hour, when the soul of the departed comes back to the spirit of the bereaved, holding such commune as *must* proclaim our union with the invisible world, and confirm our immortality. The maiden probably guessed who it was on whom she gazed.

But when the question was asked and answered by her guide, modesty, refinement, simplicity, and that respect which ever springs from the heart, all impelled her to "light off her camel," and "to take a veil and cover herself."

This was true humility, for she knew her own dignity. She demanded no more respect than she paid herself. She waited no ceremonious introduction, but alighting from the camel, completely shrouded in her veil, she proved by the one action, the respect due to the son of Abraham, her destined husband; and by the other retained her own gentle dignity, by concealing every charm, till the servant's tale was told, and Isaac claimed her as his bride. Personal beauty was in this case as nothing, though she possessed it in no ordinary degree. Her conduct proceeded from an artless unsophisticated nature, timidly shrinking from the eyes of him whom she most wished to please—a desire to conceal the very beauty which she must have yet ardently hoped that he might prize; and her hope was fulfilled, for "Isaac brought her into his mother Sarah's tent, and he took Rebekah, and she became his wife, and he loved her, and Isaac was comforted after his mother's death." How beautifully do those few words illustrate the extent of his love both towards his mother and wife. Though three years had passed since the death of his mother, he yet mourned for her. Not even the affections of his father could satisfy that painful yearning—not even religion, with her host of soothing thoughts and blessed images, could wholly *comfort* him, though she gave him strength to endure, and spiritual love to bless the hand which smote. Nor is this a contradictory assertion. Religion leads us to Him who alone can heal, in deep and most fervid prayer—that prayer brings, from Him whose deep mercy hears and answers, support and consolation, by the conviction that we are not lonely—that we shall meet again those whom we love in His presence, who is love itself; and this is comfort. The comfort here alluded to was for the mortal; the *immortal* could realise consolation, the *mortal* could not. Though it be in very truth the *invisible soul* we love, yet we become so knit with the *mortal* habitation of that soul, that we cannot feel it has perished from our sight for ever, without an agony of heart that time and prayer, and constant communings with the *invisible* Spirit alone, can in any way assuage. Nor is there one portion in the Holy Bible which would tell us, that God condemns such grief. If with the whole fervour of our-immortal being, we can bow in such submission, faith, and love, unto His will, He condemns not, nay, feels compassionate, and in His own good time heals the agony which our *human* nature feels through the human agency of wife, or friend, or child. And so it was with Isaac. Wedded as he was to the memory of his mother, no ordinary woman could have so gained his love as to give him comfort, and fill up the aching void which had existed three long years. He must have seen in Rebekah, when she first became his wife, a reflection of Sarah's endearing qualities; and united as these were to youth and beauty, inspired still deeper and dearer emotions than he had ever experienced before.

To some dispositions, this sudden elevation in a social and domestic position would have been a dangerous ordeal; but neither presumption, arrogance, nor pride, appear to have marked the conduct of Rebekah. The same steady performance of household duty manifested in her girlhood, probably continued in her higher and more responsible station; and year after year found her calmly following the quiet routine of daily duty happily to herself, and to her household. And here, for a brief while, we would pause to gather the sweet blossoms of instruction and guidance proffered by a Father's love, which Rebekah's history, thus far considered, can impart. We would linger a moment on the past ere we go forward, for the picture must be changed. Yet it is no marvellous and incomprehensible change—it is no history of woman in an era so long past that we wonder, and scarce believe—the picture is too perfect even now; it is woman *then*, and woman *now*, as we shall see hereafter.

Although from the wide distinction between patriarchal and modern times, our position and duties as daughters of Israel can never resemble those of Rebekah, we have, like her, domestic duties to perform, and a station not only to fulfil, but to adorn, so as to excite towards us respect and love. The women of the Bible are forcibly portrayed, not for us to follow them exactly, for that we could not do, but from their conduct in their respective spheres to guide us in ours; from the approval or reproof, bestowed directly or indirectly upon them, to teach their descendants what is acceptable in the sight of our heavenly Father, and what is not; and of this we may rest assured, there is no contradiction to puzzle us in the Word of God. The *precepts* of His law are proved by the *practice* of His servants. "Whatsoever thy hand findeth to do, do it with all thy might," was said centuries after by the sage monarch, who in obedience to the command of God relating to Kings, must have been acquainted with the whole of His law ; and that precept was exemplified in Rebekah's conduct at the well. She had every temptation to turn aside for a few moments in her simple task. Had she ever accustomed herself to encourage wandering thoughts in her different employments, to turn from them for every frivolous pretence, she would never have withstood the temptation of idling away her time with the goodly looking strangers, and thus demonstrated a character totally unfit to be the ancestress of God's chosen race. But as she went down to the well, and filled her pitcher, and came up, "neither turning to the right nor to the left," so it behoves us to follow our daily duties, would we, like her, receive the blessing of the Lord. It is said to be woman's nature ever to be unsteady—to be caught by the glare of every new object, every new face—to become frivolous, from allowing herself in youth to flutter from one employment to another, seeking but sweets, and terrified at the first sight of all that may seem harsh or stern. But such frivolity is incompatible with the regenerate and spiritual woman, whose guidance is her Bible, whose sustainer is her God. She feels too deeply responsible to Him for every hour of her time, to squander its smallest portion needlessly away. She seeks to love him too earnestly, too continually, not to associate the hope of His approval with her every employment, and so associated, it is impossible for them to be frivolously followed, or lightly interrupted ; and if domestic duties were thus performed by the young daughter of a house who knew not by direct revelation the Lord, how much more devolves upon us, her descendants, to whom the Lord himself has vouchsafed, through His holy Word, both guidance and example ! O let us then, in our every pursuit, first ponder well if we may lay it before our God, and upon it ask His blessing ; and if we truly can, let us pursue it with all our heart, and soul, and might, if we would, indeed, seek the loving tenderness of our God, the respect of the world, and of ourselves.

Nor is her steadiness the only portion of Rebekah's early character demanding our admiration. The winning and obliging gentleness with which she met the stranger's address, proceeded from the genuine kindness, the real politeness of an utterly unselfish heart. The request was not only granted, but granted with such sweetness of manner, and respectful words, as threefold to enhance the kindness of the deed. The beautiful laws contained in the 32nd, 33rd, and 34th verses of the 19th chapter of Leviticus, had not then been issued, yet the conduct of Rebekah was a practical illustration of the *spirit* which they teach. She paid respect to age, and did unto the stranger even as if he had been one born in the land; and this we may all do. It is not enough that we *act kindly*, and *mean kindly*, in our intercourse either with friends or strangers. We must make manifest kindly *feeling* by a kindly and conciliating *manner*. At a period when the drift of education sometimes appears to comdemn, conquer, and entirely annihilate feeling, this will be difficult, for widely different is the manner which is *taught*, however perfect may be its propriety, its gentleness, its suavity, to that which springs from the heart, and has its origin in overflowing and unselfish feeling. But has the heart—has feeling any thing to do with our behaviour to a perfect stranger, and acquaintance of the hour, whom in the whole of our life we may never meet again? It has, and it may be productive of good, both to ourselves and others. The great, the good, the mighty and most merciful Creator of heaven and earth, disdained not, even in the midst of this stupendous creation, to bid the earth bring forth her *flowers*, not to serve as food, or shelter, or absolute use, in the common meaning of the word, but simply to beautify, to enliven, to rejoice, to fling a gladness and a sunshine on the desert waste, and weary wilderness, and add beauty and rejoicing even where all around is joy; and as flowers to the earth, so is kindliness to man. It will not remove grief, nor give him what perchance he needs, but it may cause a flower to spring up in the lonely recess, or careworn furrow of his heart, whose memory may linger long after the flower itself has perished. And shall we scorn the power that will do this? Shall we think a flower of half an hour's growth too worthless to be given, too trifling to be gathered? O let us not encourage such a thought. We may know, indeed, nothing of the stranger with whom, for a brief hour, we may be thrown; but that very ignorance should urge us to courtesy and kindliness. His course may have been one of care, his present lot a waste, and a gentle tone and kind manner may be to him as the flower in the desert, wiling him a brief while from his own sad thoughts. Or it may be his lot has been and is all joy; and yet will kindliness be sweet, even as the flower in the festive hall, or in the pathway of the bride; its form scarce noticed at the time, yet so blending with its associated images, as in memory to be called up again and yet again. We are not placed here to live for ourselves alone, and more powerfully than aught else, *if it spring from the heart, and has its birth in feeling*, will a kind and gentle manner rivet the links of brotherhood, bid us feel we are all children of our common Father, and so strengthen our love in Him, and for each other.

On us more especially, aliens and exiles from our own land, is manner, as the mirror of the heart, incumbent. There was a time, but lately passed away, when to perform this duty was impossible, and therefore supposed to be unnecessary. When scorned, persecuted, condemned as the very scum of the earth, hated and reproached, it was as utterly impossible for us to manifest courtesy and kindness, as to receive them. Hatred begets hatred, as scorn begets scorn, more especially when neither emotion may be avowed. What did the cringing manner, the abject tone of the persecuted, tortured Jew conceal? Was it marvel it should be hatred as strong, if not stronger, because utterly powerless, than that of his cruel, his tyrannical oppressor? But now that in some enlightened and blessed realms these fearful times are past, and the right hand of fellowship extended to us, shall the exile and oppressed refuse to meet in amity and confidence, the sons of the land which gives them protection and home? We were commanded to show kindness to a stranger, as to one born amongst us. That blessed privilege is no longer ours, for we are strangers in a strange land; yet may we still obey the *spirit* of the law, and in the cultivation of a kindly heart, and manifestation of a kindly feeling, let us remember we have not only an *individual*, but a *national* character to support—that a brief half hour's intercourse with a stranger is endowed with power to *exalt* or to *lower* the cause of Israel; and as Rebekah's kindly cordiality was blessed to her, by making her the wife of Isaac, and so revealing to her the glorious tidings of a God of love, so may the kindly manner of the youngest daughter of Israel be blessed to her, by making her the unconscious instrument, in God's hand, to exalt His holy faith, and proclaim His truth in the heart and mind of the Gentiles amongst whom she dwells.

Yet, Rebekah's courtesy to the steward demonstrates neither presumption nor forwardness incompatible with her age or sex. We find her, directly her brother Laban comes forth, retiring to her own modest station in her mother's tent, and claiming no further notice. We see, therefore, that to act kindly demands not the forsaking of our own natural sphere. We are not to *look abroad* for opportunities to act as Rebekah did; but, like her, we shall find them without leaving our home, in the domestic and social intercourse of daily life. Let us ponder well upon these things and, as daughters of Israel, make it our glory and our pride, to do our simplest duty "with all our might;" our pleasure, to scatter flowers on the path of all with whom we may be thrown; and dwelling with meek and loving contentment in our appointed sphere, remember that the cause of Israel is our own, and it is in our power to exalt or degrade it.

For twenty years, the lives of Rebekah and Isaac appear to have passed in all the quiet felicity of domestic love and peace. Abraham was still living, happy in the happiness of his son Isaac; for to his other sons "Abraham gave gifts, and sent them away from Isaac his son, while he yet lived, eastward unto the east country." He gave them, in all probability, a knowledge of the Lord, enough to recognise and worship Him; but in Isaac, Abraham knew was the promised seed, and therefore by him was the aged patriarch's home. Anxiously he, too, must have anticipated the birth that would prolong his line, but from his personal experience in "waiting for the Lord," his feelings must have been less anxious than those of Isaac. In these twenty years, we hear of no temporal disturbance, nor divine interference, as in the earlier life of Abraham; but that spiritual communing with the Lord, and improvement in knowledge of and faith in Him, in no ways slackened or diminished, we are called upon to believe by the simple fact of Isaac going to " entreat the Lord for his wife," and the instant answer to his prayer. Again we see divine interference, not what is called *natural causes*, operating for the fulfilment of the Eternal's promise of a chosen seed. Jacob the father of the twelve tribes, from one or other of whom the wandering Hebrew can still trace descent, and claim the promises vouchsafed unto his fathers—Jacob, even as Isaac, was the child, not alone of promise, but of PRAYER.

Those twenty years saw Rebekah as we last beheld her, only

matured in the graces of womanhood, and so grafted on the house of Abraham, as like him to worship and know the great God alone. She had had, as yet, no temptation to swerve aside from the straight path of duty. A beloved and cherished wife, daughter and mistress, her life passed by so smoothly, her affection so devoted to one first object, and thence calmly emanating on all under her influence, that she was, as every other woman in a similar position must have been, still entirely ignorant of the shoals and quicksands in her heart, which might lead to sin, and end in sorrow.

Yet, her first action, after proof was given of the Eternal's gracious answer to her husband's prayer, was one of such childlike simple confidence in the power and wisdom of the Lord to answer all of doubt and fear, that to reconcile her conduct afterwards becomes more difficult. Unusual and incomprehensible suffering, so oppressed her, as to raise a doubt of the promise being then about to be fulfilled. "If it be so," she thought, "why am I thus?"—and without pause or hesitation, went directly "to enquire of the Lord." She asked no advice, demanded no human aid; but, in heartfelt prayer—for in prayer only could she so enquire—laid before Him her every emotion, and from Him implored reply. We would humbly ask those, if indeed there can be such, who deny to woman an immortal soul, refuse her the blessed privilege and secret commune with her Creator, and believe man's prayer alone omnipotent, how they would interpret this very simple narration? They may assert, as I believe some commentators do, that it was through Abraham she enquired of the Lord, and received reply—but, as we have no warrant whatever in Scripture, by direct word or implied inference, to confirm this assertion, we must reject it altogether. The long years which Rebekah had passed in the household of Abraham, had not flown by unused, and spiritually unimproved. She had seen the Great and Invisible Being acknowledged and adored. She had been taught by example; and we may be scripturally certain, though the fact itself is not mentioned, by precept also. The natural impulse of humanity, under all difficulties and suffering, is to pray—and, in the beautiful simplicity of the patriarchal ages, no artificial coldness, no appalling scepticism, no disheartening doubt, could have crowded round her, whispering that the prayer was vain, that the Creator of heaven and earth was a Being too far removed from woman's petty griefs to listen and give reply. In the simple trusting confidence of a child, she sought the Parent whose love was omnipotent not only to understand the doubt and pain, but to give relief—and her confidence was answered. How that gracious answer was vouchsafed, whether through Abraham, or directly to herself is, I believe, an argument—but Scripture bids us believe, without hesitation, the latter—"And the Lord said *unto her*," clear simple words, banishing at once all necessity for mediation, either of man or angel; words almost impossible, even wilfully to be misunderstood. The *how* she received this answer—whether through the medium of the ear, or by an impression on the mind—can be of very little consequence; and is one of those cavilling enquiries, which we could wish banished, ere formed into words; tending as they do to fill up the mind with vain and idle speculations, instead of the pure simple truths of Scripture. It is enough, and a most blessed enough for us, that the "Lord said unto her,"the direct answer to her enquiring prayer. The words were mysterious—that she was already the mother of two opposing nations, one of whom should be stronger than the other—and the "elder should serve the younger." Yet, mysterious as they must have been, they came from the Lord. He had graciously vouchsafed to explain the cause of her unusual sufferings—and Rebekah was satisfied; for we find not another word from her, of either wonderment or complaint.

And O what a blessed incentive have we from this simple narrative, in all our griefs and sufferings, bodily or mental, to enquire of the Lord—to come to him as our ancestress, in guileless faith, and simple minded prayer. He is our God as. He was hers—yea, ours—exiles, wanderers—WOMEN as we are—and who, with the holy Word of God within his hand, shall dare to refuse to us, as women, as Israelitish women, the power, the purity, the privilege of prayer? Who shall dare assert that we are powerless to pray, or need the mediation of man, to bear up our petitions to the throne of grace? Mothers, wives, daughters of Israel, you alone must prove the utter falsity of this charge! Before the law, under the law, during the captivity we shall still find the Hebrew woman seeking her God in prayer; and receiving from Him direct reply. O shall we not thus prove, that we have a soul immortal as that of man —that the very breath of our being, the light of our path, the support of strength, is prayer—that prayer which brings us daily, nay hourly, in commune with a loving Father, whose tender sympathy is endless as His love. Let us prove we need not Christianity either to teach, or direct us how to pray—but, turning to the blessed pages of our own Bible, make manifest, that to look further is not needed; that there we have indeed sufficient for encouragement and hope; for confidence and faith. As Rebekah prayed, so too may we; and as our Father answered her, so will He us. Not indeed, with word direct, but with that blessed calm and hope, and faith, which prayer only can bestow; and with that heavenly patience, which will enable us to "wait for the Lord," in the firm belief that whatever He may will is best. It is worthy of remark, that Rebekah is the first recorded instance of woman's immediate appeal to God, and the condescending reply.

At the appointed time, Isaac and Rebekah became parents of twin sons, who grew and flourished; and in early youth displayed a contrariety of disposition and pursuits—which must have appeared strange, in such nearly allied relations, had it not been rendered clearly intelligible, at least to their mother, by the previous words of the Lord. But yet these words do not appear to me sufficient for Rebekah always to have regarded Jacob as the promised seed. The promise, or rather explanation, given in answer to her prayer was simply, "the one people shall be stronger than the other, and the elder shall serve the younger." Not as was the case with Abraham, when the promised seed was specifically *named*. And in the very next revelation which was vouchsafed to Isaac, a few years afterwards, we read, "Sojourn in this land, and I will be with thee, and will bless thee; for unto thee, and unto *thy seed* will I give all these countries, and I will perform the oath which I sware unto Abraham thy father. And I will make *thy seed* to multiply as the stars of heaven, and will give unto *thy seed* all the countries; and in *thy seed* shall all the nations of the earth be blessed;" and again, the last verse of this same xxvii. chapter—the Lord appeared unto him the same night, and said, "I am the God of Abraham, thy father; fear not, for I am with thee, and will bless thee, and multiply *thy seed* for my servant Abraham's sake."

The Eternal expressly says "thy seed." Isaac might be justified in supposing that *both* his sons were concerned in the promises, until Esau's reckless disregard of his birthright, and other spiritual blessings, in addition to his intermarrying with the daugnters of Canaan, must have convinced his father, that not from him could spring the chosen seed. The revelation that "the elder should serve the younger," must have occasioned Rebekah many mental enquiries—but even if she herself supposed that Jacob was the destined inheritor of Abraham's line, it is evident that she did not impart it to her husband.

Isaac's love for the reckless and able hunter, Esau, is one of those contradictions of the heart, unaccountable indeed, but very often found. He loved Esau best, because in every respect he was completely his opposite. Isaac was meek, affectionate, faithful, quietly and contentedly dwelling in one spot, moving thence only at the command of the Lord; satisfied with the temporal blessings around him; and the spiritual blessings of promise. Esau was bold, enterprising, ever roving in search of active pursuit; heeding nought but the present; scorning his home and home ties; rude and rough, yet, when excited, deeply and warmly affectionate to his aged father. And Isaac loved him better than his younger son, who, more like himself, "was a plain or upright man, dwelling in tents." But Rebekah loved Jacob. Sacred history does not say why —and we are therefore permitted to infer, that it was simply because it is woman's nature to love him best who is least loved by his father. But Rebekah's favouritism, as we shall see in the sequel, was stronger and more culpable than that of Isaac. All such emotions are stronger in woman's heart than in man's—because with the former, *feeling* is the most powerful, and with the latter *reason*. Partiality must always occasion injustice, and more particularly in a parent; for no task demands more control and feeling, more complete conquest of self, than that of parental affection. The dispositions, the characters of the divers members of one family are so varied, that it is impossible to guide all by one and the same training. An impartial mother will know every light and shadow of every disposition, and guide and act accordingly. A partial mother sees but the virtues and qualities of *one*, and from want of sympathy and proper management of the other in early years, makes him in reality, all that she believed him. Jacob was domestic, because a mother's doting love made his home one of enjoyment, and administered to every want.

It was not till after Sarah's death that Isaac even sought a wife, and not till he was parted from his mother that Jacob loved, proofs all convincing of the strength, the beauty, the fulness of the love which in those simple ages united the mother and the son.

To Esau this soothing and blessed love was not given as it was to Jacob, and while his hasty and inconsiderate marriage with the daughters of the Hittite was a grief of mind to Isaac and Rebekah, the latter's neglect might have been in part their cause. Esau had no kindly woman's heart to turn to, as had his brother, yet we have proof that his affections were as strong—perchance, from his ruder character, yet stronger—and the very want of female love at home might have first urged him to seek it from the stranger. Oh it is sad when partiality, and its concomitant, injustice, obtains entrance into a mother's heart. It steals in so silently, so disguisedly, that unless every avenue be guarded, its advances are utterly unknown, till it has gained a strength and substance which hold us chained. Mere human love, omnipotent as in a mother's breast it is, is not sufficient to guard us from such weakness—no, nor former strength and stability of character. Rebekah had all this, and yet as a mother she fell. It can only be that close communing with the universal Father, who alone knows and feels every secret throbbing of a mother's heart, and from whose hand alone can come the strength, not only to *guide* aright her treasures, but to *feel* aright herself.

During the growth of his sons, Isaac's temporal riches were greatly increased. Abraham's death did not take place till his grandsons were fifteen. He who had believed it next to impossible in his old age to have a son, lived not only to bless his son, but his son's seed. A famine had sent Isaac and his family, by direction of the Eternal, to Gerar, and there he dwelt, until he became so rich and great, that the "Philistines envied him;" and their king, Abimelech, said unto him, "Depart from us, for thou art much mightier than we." And he did so, and after some wanderings, fixed his tent at Beersheba; and there again the Lord appeared unto him, bidding him "fear not, for he was with him." Beersheba, therefore, appears to have been the scene of all the domestic events which followed—Esau selling his unvalued birthright—his subsequent marriage—the vexations thence proceeding to Isaac and Rebekah—and those bodily infirmities of the former, which occasioned his anxious desire to "bless his son before he died."

Rebekah heard the words of her husband. She had seen him call his first-born to his couch, and bid him seek venison, and bring the savoury meat that he loved, that his soul might bless him before he died; and her heart swelled tremblingly within her. Esau? Was Esau to have his father's blessing? He who had sold his birthright, and so spurned his privileges as heir; and if he had it, how could the Lord's words be fulfilled, and the "elder serve the younger"? Why could she not prevent it, and secure to him, whom the Lord before his birth had chosen as the mightiest, the blessing of his father? It was easy to be accomplished; and surely as the Lord had said it, she was justified in using any means to bring it to pass. Such was weak, finite reasoning—such the baneful whisper of our earthly nature, urged on by the rushing torrent of human affections. In that dread moment of temptation, how might she realise the unquestioning faith, which would bid her feel, "The Lord hath spoken and will he not do it?" That His will needed no human aid for its fulfilment—that He would do His pleasure in the very face of those contradictory events, which human will and finite wisdom might so weave, as to render its fulfilment seemingly impossible. If Rebekah had but "enquired of the Lord" in this perplexity, as in a former one, the whole train of deceit, and its subsequent suffering would have been averted. But she was still a woman, weak, wavering, a very reed in her mortal nature, and liable, as every child of Adam, to temptation and to sin.

Had she even waited but one brief hour, all would have been well—the evil impulse would have been conquered in her pious heart, by a train of thought as above, but there was no time either to wait or think again; and, acting on the impulse, she called Jacob, and after informing him of his father's directions to his brother, continued in a strain that would lead us to believe, that even at that moment she feared Jacob's upright nature would shrink from the task she imposed. "Now, therefore, my son, OBEY my voice, according to that which I command thee." She claimed his unquestioning obedience, ere imparting that which she desired, and then proceeded. Surely her heart must have reproached her, when her own son ventured to suggest, though guardedly and respectfully, that it was a fraud, and might bring upon him a curse instead of blessing. Yet still she enforces the command, "Upon me be the curse, my son, only obey my voice." And he did obey her, weakly and mistakenly; for had he resisted, had he submissively, yet firmly braved her momentary wrath, the evil temptation must have been subdued, and the mother saved by the unscrupulous honesty of the son.

But this was not to be. To make manifest His ways, that suffering *must* attend deceit, however for the moment it may seem to succeed, the Eternal permitted the plans of finite forming uninterruptedly to proceed, working out indeed His will through them, but punishing even in success. The kid was procured and dressed—the very hands and neck of Jacob disguised, lest their smoothness should betray him; and thus attired by a mother to deceive, he approached the bed-side of his blind father. How fearfully must the heart of Rebekah have throbbed at every word uttered by her husband and son. How terrified at the words of the unsuspecting, yet half doubting Isaac. "Come near, I pray thee, that I may feel thee, my son, whether thou be my very son Esau or not." And Jacob went near unto Isaac his father, and he felt him, and said, "The voice is Jacob's voice, but the hands are the hands of Esau." And, again, as doubting still, he asks, "Art thou my very son Esau? and Jacob answered, I am." The inspired historian might not interrupt his brief, yet how deeply impressive detail, to dilate on a woman's feelings; yet we, her descendants, are surely justified in judging for a moment of Rebekah's emotions during this interview, by what our own would be. She could have had no support, no stay, for she had wilfully banished TRUTH, and how, then, might she PRAY? Her whole heart and mind must have been troubled and tossed by every trifling word; discovery, and shame, perhaps the very loss or estrangement of her husband's love, were as likely as the longed for success. How often, during that interim, must she have longed once more to tread the path of truth, for Rebekah was a mere novice in deceit. Her nature, as we have seen, was guileless and open as the day; the mere temptation of the moment, and its consequent anxious and impelling feelings, could not have so changed that nature, as to make her an unmoved witness of that which followed—the very falsehood repeated and insisted upon by those lips which she had taught from infancy to lisp forth truth. But when the blessing was obtained, when she saw her plan had in truth succeeded, we may suppose, judging still by human nature, that these agonising doubts and fears were for the moment calmed in the triumph of success—conscience was hushed again, in the thought that she had compassed by stratagem that which she believed impossible to have been obtained else—that it must have been right and good so to have acted, or it would not have been permitted to succeed. Alas! how often do we so deceive ourselves! Could we but glance a little, a very little, further on, we should know, and feel (how bitterly!) that the very deceit we believed innocent, because it brought success, has been our first step in the paths of woe.

And so it was with Rebekah, though as yet she knew it not. Her feelings of triumph could not, however, have lasted long: "And it came to pass, as soon as Isaac had made an end of blessing Jacob, and Jacob was yet scarce gone out from the presence of his father, that Esau, his brother, came in from hunting;" and that interview followed, which, for simple and touching pathos, is not surpassed by any incident in the Bible.

Rebekah was a partial, but not a weak or unkind mother. She loved Jacob better than his brother, but Esau was still her son, her first-born, and O how painfully must her heart have yearned towards him, when she heard his "great and exceeding bitter cry!"—"Hast thou but one blessing, my father? bless me, even me also, O my father. And Esau lifted up his voice and wept." Esau, the rude, the careless hunter, who had seemed to care for nought but his own pleasures; the chase, the field, the wild! He bowed down by his blind father like an infant and wept; beseeching the blessing, of which a mother's and a brother's subtlety had deprived him. Could Rebekah have been a witness, or even hearer of this scene, without losing all the triumph of success, in sympathy with the anguish of her first-born? It is impossible to ponder on her previous character, without being convinced of this. It is not from one act, one unresisted temptation, that we ought to pronounce judgment on a fellow-creature: yet from our unhappy proneness to condemn, we generally do so. The character of Rebekah is thus too often supposed to be evil alone, and her unfortunate deception in favour of her best beloved son is the only part of her life brought strongly forward; whereas, if we look and think on all that sacred history has recorded of her, that there is also perfect silence as to any other fault (which, had she committed, we may be sure would have been told for our warning)—it becomes evident that this guilty action proceeded, not from *forethought*, which would have manifested a naturally evil disposition, but from *impulse*; the thought, the temptation of a moment, overbalancing by its force the rectitude of years. As forethought, we must condemn both the sin and the sinner. As impulse, we must abhor the sin—but only grief and trembling for the weakness of human nature must attend our reflections on the sinner. Nor are we justified in denying her those emotions of grief and doubt, which must have succeeded the triumphant success of her momentarily formed plan.

But self-accusation was not to be her only punishment. Did the blessed word of the All-Just relate the deception alone, we might well hesitate to affirm that her conscience brought reproach, and believe that the deed was not as guilty as it seems. But we are not thus left to our own imaginations. The events which followed, so prove, without doubt or question, the displeasure of the Eternal against the deed, that we can have no hesitation whatever in believing that conscience, " the angel of the Lord," was busy within her, ere the bolt of justice fell.

" And Esau hated Jacob, because of the blessing wherewith his father blessed him. And Esau said in his heart, The days of mourning for my father are at hand ; then will I slay my brother Jacob. And these words of Esau her elder son were told to Rebekah." What fearful tidings for a mother ! How must her thought have returned, with agonising forebodings, to the *first death* which marred this beautiful world. Had not that been *fratricide* and for envy, the same feeling which now actuated Esau ? And was not she, as Eve had been, the cause ? Still nearer cause; for she it was, who, by leading Jacob to deceive, had armed a brother's hand against him. How Esau's intentions could have been revealed to her when the sacred historian expressly tells us that Esau but spake them *in his heart*, must remain unsolved, unless, as appears most probable, it was Rebekah's own fears which betrayed them ; confirmed by the manner of Esau towards his brother, and by her own knowledge of his character. His strong love for his father, which to me is the redeeming beauty of Esau's character, might restrain him awhile—but were the death which Isaac himself appeared to anticipate, speedily to take place, the mother's forebodings well imagined that the haughty Esau would never submit to bow to his brother, and call him heir. Painfully she must have felt, that not for her would

Esau restrain his purpose, though the wildest ebullition of his natural anger was subdued by the deep loving reverence he bore his father. Might not she too have claimed that love, had she lavished on his youthful years the same affection she had given to his brother? Was it not her own fault, that in this wild wish for vengeance, the death of the offender, he thought not of the suffering, which such a deed would inflict on her? That such thoughts were ascendant, and the voice of self-reproach, more loud and thrilling than any anger against Esau for his fearful design, is proved by her council to Jacob— when, calling him to her, she said, "Behold thy brother Esau, as touching thee, doth comfort himself, purposing to kill thee. Now, therefore, my son, obey my voice and arise, and flee thou to my brother Laban, in Haran. And tarry with him a few days, until thy brother's fury turn away, and he forget that which thou hast done to him; then I will send, and fetch thee from thence. Why should I also be deprived of you both in one day?"

There is not one word of invective against Esau. If she still supposed that her act was justified, inasmuch as it seemed to further the designs of the Eternal, Esau's intention to slay his brother must have seemed too sinful, too horrible, to be passed without some comment either of anger or fear. But far otherwise is the spirit of her words. They breathe but a mother's anxious agony—a consciousness that Esau's wrath was but too just. Jacob had no defence to plead, and so avert the threatened wrath. Nothing could save him but flight, till the hasty but not placable Esau was appeased; and from *her* lips the mandate of exile went forth—"Why should I also be deprived of you both in one day?" How affectingly do those simple words betray, not alone the love she bore to *both* her sons, but that her thoughts turned to the history of the past—foreboding Eve's awful trial for herself. There is no wailing, no complaint, but in those brief words, what a volume of woman's deepest feeling is revealed!

Her real emotions having thus had vent to Jacob, Rebekah was better able to control them before her husband; and she said unto him, "I am weary of my life, because of the daughters of Heth. If Jacob take a wife of the daughters of Heth, such as these which are of the daughters of the land, what good shall my life do me?"

It would have been the extreme of cruelty to have increased

the grief of the infirm Isaac, by a narration of Esau's evil intentions towards his brother—when Esau himself had controlled his fierce passion for his father's sake. Nor could Rebekah's confession of her fault, now in any way redeem it. It would but have excited against her the anger of her husband, as being the primary cause of the dissensions between his sons—and have occasioned him increased affliction. It was in this instance, wiser and better to hide from Isaac the sad cause of Jacob's departure; and urge him to do that for *his son* of promise, which Abraham had done for him; and the mother's fearful anxiety was calmed by the paternal command, coupled with a reiterated blessing, for her younger son " to go to Padan-Aram, the house of Bethuel, thy mother's father, and take thee a wife from one of the daughters of Laban, thy mother's brother." "And Isaac sent away Jacob."

And thus was the mother parted from her son, for whose beloved sake she had been tempted to turn aside from the straight line of probity and truth which in such guilelessness and beauty she had trodden so changelessly before. And is it not ever thus? When we once turn from one straight path, can we say, thus far shall we go and no farther? Can we set a boundary to the rushing flood of pain and sorrow which, when we have removed the barrier of truth, obtains dominion, dashing our fairest dreams to earth, and bringing misery in the very garments of success? And well is it for those whom the Lord so graciously compassionates as to reveal these fatal companions of deception ere it be too late, and the charmed path be trodden till there is no turning back.

Who can peruse the history of Rebekah, and yet believe she was not punished for her sin? Wherefore had she pursued such fatal measures for the obtaining of the blessing for her favourite Jacob, save to keep him for ever by her side, even as Isaac had never quitted the tents of his father? As a younger son, his lot would in all probability have been to seek his own fortune. As the inheritor of the blessings vouchsafed to Abraham, there could be no need for him to leave her: and what was the issue? Banishment from his mother's home, or exposure to his brother's wrath—the sword of vengeance ever hanging above his head. Was this nothing to a fond mother's heart? Let a parent ponder for one moment on the idea of one beloved child falling by the hand of another, and his heart will give the answer. Parting itself was preferable to such ever dread, yet what agony must have been that parting?

Not then, as now, might the absent one be united by mutual intelligence. Neither post nor traveller passed between Beersheba and Padan-Aram. Long weary wastes of country stretched between, and though Rebekah's command was, "Tarry there a *few days*," she knew it must be long months ere they met again. Nor will the vague thought of the hour of meeting ever lessen the pang of parting. It is the pang itself which is felt, the looking in vain for the beloved form in its accustomed haunts, the wild yearning to list once more the voice which sounds in memory alone, to feel the fond pressure of the hand, the kiss which welcomed morning and evening, without which day seemed scarce begun, and night come unobserved. The pictured hardships of the lonely wanderer which no mother's hand may soften, the woe unsoothed, the pain unhealed, the tired frame untended—these, and a hundred other fears, and thoughts of suffering, haunt a mother's waking dreams, and nightly pillow —felt not, dreamed not by the wanderer, yet clinging to woman's breast with a tenacity and anguish time only can dispel. And because Rebekah lived so many thousand years ago, shall we deny to her these feelings when the hour came, and her beloved one departed—departed and alone, with no manifestation of the fruit of that blessing which she had lured him to obtain?

With the departure of Jacob, the history of Rebekah concludes, for her name is no more mentioned. Even on her death Holy Writ is silent. We only know that she was buried in the cave of Macpelah, by the words of Jacob in Gen. xlix. 31. And from there being no mention whatever of her on Jacob's return to Hebron, we must infer that she died before his arrival, and never had the happiness of folding him to her heart again. How sad and lonely must her declining years have seemed without him who had been so long her stay; even though her long dormant affection for Esau may have been aroused from the injustice she had done him—and he evidently sought, with a softened spirit, to gratify his parents, by a union with a daughter of his uncle Ishmael—he could never have been to her like Jacob; and painfully and sadly must she have yearned for the absent, as the "few days," which she had pictured, widened into long months and yet longer years. How changed must her life have seemed, and changed from the impulse of the moment; and as death neared—as she felt it might no longer be averted, and she had waited and prayed in vain to behold her son on earth once more—must she not have felt to the full, that, though the deception had been successful, though the blessing had been given, the *means* of its bestowal could not have been "acceptable to the Lord?" and had she, as we are privileged to do, beheld the life of trial and disappointment, and *retributive deception*, which marked the earthly course of her favourite son, this solemn truth would have been impressed still more.

Yet the death of Rebekah was in all probability one of peace, and calm holy reliance on the infinite mercy of her God. He had chastised, but in the midst of chastisement had mercy; the fury of Esau had been turned aside, Jacob been saved, and peace preserved in the household of Isaac. Her earthly idol removed from her sight, we may well believe that Rebekah returned to her domestic duties with that singleness of purpose and uprightness of heart which had marked her earlier years. The temptation to turn aside, the loving mercy of the Eternal had removed, and the mother, even while her heart bled, must have pronounced the mandate just. If in her youth, before the knowledge of the God of Abraham had been imparted, she had felt with her brother, "It is the Lord, we cannot speak unto thee bad or good," would she not—now that long years had been passed in His service—have felt even in her affliction, "it is the Lord," and, without murmur or complaint, submit herself to His will?

Are we then, it may be asked, to give Rebekah the meed of unmixed admiration? to rest only on the good points of her character? No, like all human nature, it was a blending of the good and evil. Had Rebekah been told that, ere her life closed, she should have acted as she did, she would in all probability have felt it impossible; nay, ere her children were born, would have shrunk with horror from the idea of loving one more than the other. All we would urge is simply, that we are not to condemn her, as if the unfortunate propensity of woman, "to compass by stratagem," were the marked failing of her character, and that therefore the *evil* not the *good* was ever the ascendant. This is the common error into which superficial thinkers fall; and from such have arisen questions as to the morality of the Bible, that its holiness would be more confirmed were there no such faults recorded. If indeed those of whom it so impartially writes, were thus faultless, it would be destined for the use of angels, not of man. But not such was the design of the Eternal. He inspired holy men to write that which would comfort and sustain man, when His immediate presence and guidance were veiled from mortal eyes; and His faithful servants alike, male and female, were depicted in their virtues and their failures, with an impartiality and truth which were to be our hope in our lowly efforts after virtue, and our consolation in our weakness and our sin. Rebekah's fault was one, her virtues many; and therefore, while we abhor and pray against her *sin*, we can only grieve and lament that human weakness which triumphed in one moment of strong temptation over the virtuous strength of years. We dare not condemn and scorn that weakness; for did we so, we scorn, and condemn, and pronounce judgment on ourselves. How may we assert that, had we been placed as Rebekah in that dread moment, we too should not have done as she did? Can we assert that the promise of the Eternal would have been so strongly impressed within us, that we could have left its fulfilment in His hands, without one effort by our own agency to forward it? Can we say that we should have gone to Him in prayer, beseeching Him to counteract the design of Isaac in favour of his first-born, and rest contented that the prayer would be heard and answered?

There may be some, too, loudly and reproachfully to condemn that weak partiality which was the real origin of the evil—yet let such take heed lest they too should fall by the same weakness, for they know not how their affections may equally be tried. O, not in *condemnation* of our meek and gentle ancestress shall we reap the benefit of her example, and turn aside from her faults. If, even in her, the weakness of human nature once triumphed over the immortal spirit, what may save us from the same fault? Will the purity of youth, the piety of early womanhood, the truth and virtue of long years? Will these obtain such sway as always to be our safeguard and our strength? Alas, not these: it must be the grace of God alone, sought by constant prayer and utter dependence upon Him—the constant watch over ourselves—the knowledge of our own weakness—that which most exposes us to fall beneath temptation—the consciousness that there is not a domestic duty—not a home affection—not an hour's employment—not a daily path or nightly thought in which sin may not creep in and obtain dominion, unless effectually guarded against by unceasing watchfulness and prayer. And to us, yet more than any other nation in the world, is this watchful care and daily petition needed. To ISRAEL IS ENTRUSTED THE HONOR OF THE LORD; His chosen—His beloved—His witnesses; the recorders of His ways unto man—the promulgators of His eternal love. How may we be luke-warm in His cause, when we are so called upon to exalt His Glory? We are scattered among the nations as witnesses of the PAST and pledges of the FUTURE, and shall we with indifference permit others to claim the privileges which are ours, and assert that, until the epoch of Christianity, God had no witnesses upon earth? No, O no! Surely, individually and nationally, we shall use our every effort to proclaim our high and glorious descent amid the nations!

One point more, and we must conclude this memoir, already so much longer than we intended. It has been said, that as the Eternal ordained that Jacob was to receive the promised blessing, and that the "elder should serve the younger," it must have been obtained in some way; and therefore the *means* of its accomplishment were of little consequence, thus endeavouring to remove all that was reprehensible in the conduct of Jacob and his mother. Nay, some commentators try to make her conduct proceed from a belief that her course of "acting was in such conformity with the divine prediction, that she determined at all risks, and by any means, to secure the blessing for her younger and more worthy son."*

This species of reasoning appears as mistaken as the too violent condemnation of Rebekah, and so completely at variance with the simple, trusting piety of the patriarchs and their families, that we cannot at all suppose it actuating the mother's feelings. Besides which, to think thus, supposes a *pre-determination* to deceive her husband, whereas the narrative of the Bible clearly marks it the *impulse* of the moment.

Isaac, before his birth, was the child of promise to Abraham: the Lord had promised he should be the father of a multitude, and in him and his seed all nations should be blessed. Yet that very child, Abraham was commanded to sacrifice; and without hesitation he prepared to obey, feeling convinced, that though to him the means of accomplishing the divine promise were plunged in darkest mystery—if indeed his child must die —yet still that the promise *would* be fulfilled without any intervention of man; his duty was simply to obey,—and the promised *was* fulfilled.

As the command of the Lord to slay his son was the trial of

* Philippson:—see Notes to Mr. De Sola's Bible.

Abraham's faith, so were the words of Isaac to Esau the trial of Rebekah's. She ought to have known from that very incident in the early life of her husband, that whatever the Lord has once said, HE WILL perform, however mysterious may seem the means of its accomplishment—that though Isaac might intend to give the blessing to his first-born, his words would have been overruled, and the blessing reserved for Jacob, without any strife between the brothers or their consequent separation. But her *faith* was not strong enough for that most difficult duty—to "wait for the Lord." Woman-like, *feeling* was her *weakness, impulse* her guide—faith succumbed before these, and so left her unguarded, when its invulnerable defence was more needed than it had ever been before.

Rebekah had, perhaps, some excuse for her momentary fancy that her course of acting was, from its *success*, acceptable to the Lord: but we have NONE. The idea that human means are necessary to forward any intention of the Most High, cannot be entertained a single moment without verging on impiety, when we have the whole Word of God to prove by precept and example that He is as omnipotent to *do* as to *will*. Man is a free agent. Rebekah had equal power "to wait for the Lord" as to urge her son to deception. That she chose the latter was human frailty—no pre-ordainment. He indeed permitted the fraud in appearance to succeed, because He had already ordained that Jacob should be the promised seed, and His changeless and allwise decree might not be turned aside even to annul, and so punish the designs of sin. But that in no ways exculpates the fraud. Had no deceit whatever been practised, the blessing would still have been Jacob's. It matters not how: it is enough to know that the ways of the Eternal are not our ways, and that His decrees require no aid of man.

That human designs, however sinful, however contrary to the pleasure of the Lord, are over-ruled to further His divine economy—no one who attentively studies and believes God's Word can for a single moment doubt; but this truth in not one tittle, renders us less responsible beings. That the Eternal ever bringeth forth and worketh universal good from partial evil, proves His loving-kindness, His beneficence, His all-wise, ever-acting mercy alone. Not that man is in any point acquitted, or that evil is a necessary adjunct to the bringing forth of good. The workers and the designers of evil are, individually, objects of displeasure, and will suffer the burden of their guilt. The *doers* of evil the God of Love abhors, even while his compassion over-rules the *deeds*, and turns them in His hand to the furtherance of good.

We are earnestly and heartily anxious to impress this important truth on the minds of our younger readers, who, in their early perusal of God's Holy Word, may and will feel startled, that human weakness should not only be recorded, but its actions be permitted to succeed. Success is not always a proof of the Eternal's approbation. The history of both Rebekah and Jacob, prove the displeasure of the Lord *towards themselves individually*, though their action was over-ruled to the accomplishment of His previous will. Rebekah never saw her son again; and Jacob, though *spiritually blessed*, was, in his earthly career, more unfortunate than any of his family before or after him.

This narrative alone, then, ought to bid us eschew all wandering from the one straight path of single-hearted truth; that we can never do so without exciting the displeasure of our Heavenly Father, even though our plans may seem crowned with unmerited success. The attribute of our God is TRUTH; how then dare we believe that He smiles upon those who depart from it, or requires human deception to forward His almighty will? As His children, His own, His first-born, O let our watch-word be TRUTH! Let our upright, single-minded, straightforward adherence to truth, in every thought, word, and deed, proclaim WHOSE WITNESSES we are, and compel the nations to acknowledge that we are "Israelites indeed!"

LEAH AND RACHEL.

IT was on the same spot, in the land of the East, where nearly a century previous Abraham's steward had bowed himself to the earth in prayer, that several shepherds and their flocks were assembled, grouped by the side of a well, from whose mouth the great stone covering had not yet been rolled aside. It was high noon, when a stranger approached, and courteously addressing the shepherds, enquired: "My brethren, whence be ye? And they said Of Haran are we. And he said unto them, Know ye Laban, the son of Nahor? And they said,

We know him. And he said unto them, Is he well? And they said, He is well, and behold Rachel his daughter cometh with the sheep. And while he yet spake with them, Rachel came with her father's sheep, for she kept them. And it came to pass when Jacob saw Rachel, the daughter of Laban, his mother's brother, and the sheep of Laban, his mother's brother, that Jacob went near, and rolled the stone from the well's mouth and watered the sheep; and Jacob kissed Rachel, and lifted up his voice and wept, and Jacob told Rachel that he was her father's brother, and that he was Rebekah's son. And she ran and told her father."

Such, in the simple yet impressive language of Holy Writ, was the first meeting of Jacob and his beautiful cousin.

Lonely and sad the exiled Jacob had turned from the home of his childhood and the parents of his love. The child of promise and of prayer—the inheritor of God's especial blessing—the ancestor of kings—was compelled to make his bed on the cold earth, with nothing but stones for his pillow. How must his thoughts have clung to his mother and his home! That his heart was once more fitted for the reception and comprehension of holy things, is proved by the dream which Infinite wisdom vouchsafed, to strengthen and encourage him. The promise would not have been revealed to one unworthy to receive it. Though human weakness may sully and darken even the choicest servants of the Lord, yet not unto the impure, the unholy, the unrepentant, would the Holy One impart the blessing of His spirit and His guidance. Acknowledgment of his fault must have brought Jacob once more to the feet of his Heavenly Father, or the confirmation of the blessed promise would have still been delayed.

On the beautiful, the most consoling vision vouchsafed to Jacob, consoling, not only to him but to us, we may not linger. Yet, though so spiritually consoled, strengthened and refreshed, the mortal nature of the wanderer must often have obtained ascendency during his journey, and have rendered it at the very least dreary and sad. Jacob had never been tried till his departure from his father's house; and, therefore, though awe-struck and " afraid " at the glorious revelation when its impression was vividly before him; his very vow supposes a slight degree of doubt, natural to one only just called upon to believe; "If the Lord will be with me, and will keep me in this way that I go, *give me bread to eat and raiment to put on*, so that I come again to my father's house in peace, then the LORD shall be my God." "Bread to eat and raiment to put on." Even for these petty cares and trials he was dependent on the Lord alone; yet that he did not possess even these—that he had literally left the tent of his father with his staff for his sole possession, may give us some idea of the *human trials* of our forefathers, even of those whom the Lord most blessed. Their greatness, their influence, their riches were to come *from God alone*, not from man; their *lives* were to bear witness to His providence, even as their descendants are witnesses of the fulfilment of His word.

As Jacob was subject to all the inconveniences, fatigue, and suffering of travelling through a strange and often hostile country, as any other wanderer, his feelings, on nearing the abode of his uncle, may more easily be imagined than described. In his conversation with the shepherds, and then in his actively rolling aside the stone and watering the sheep, we may read the manly effort to restrain emotion, which, however, spurned all control when, in the simple and beautiful affection of the patriarchal age, "he kissed Rachel, and lifted up his voice and wept." Wept, that God had, in his loving mercy guided him thus far, and seemed to promise that newly known, yet instinctively loved, relations should fill up the aching void in his heart, which the sudden separation from his mother must have caused.

"And it came to pass when Laban heard the tidings of Jacob, his sister's son, that he ran to meet him, and embraced him, and kissed him, and brought him to his house. And he told Laban all these things. And Laban said, Surely thou art my bone and my flesh. And he abode with him the space of a month." Again is family affection vividly brought before us. If the reckoning of some commentators be true, and Jacob was seventy-six when he entered the household of Laban, nearly one hundred years must have elapsed since Rebekah had quitted her maiden home. Yet how closely and fondly must her memory have been enshrined in the heart of her brother, and, through him, cherished by his children, that Jacob was thus so warmly and delightedly welcomed, simply because he was "Rebekah's son."

Youth in Laban had changed to manhood, manhood to age. He had nearer and dearer calls upon his heart in his character of husband and father; yet still the memory of the "hand in hand companion of his childhood" remained pure, and beautiful and strong, as if absence had never come between them. Will not this fact reveal how acceptable in the Lord's sight is the encouragement of those affections which His love has given to his children? And how sad, how wrong it is to permit coldness and indifference to steal in between the members of one family. Would Laban have entertained such fond recollections of Rebekah, had their early youth been passed in that utter want of cordiality and confidence, faithfulness and affection, which but too often mar the unity and beauty of modern and fashionable homes? O, not to be expended only on the stranger, hath the God of love stored our hearts with affection, with reverence, with all that can make home an earthly heaven! Would we truly love and seek to please Him, our first duty must be, to love and make those happy with whom our daily lot is cast.

Two daughters blessed the house of Laban; the elder Leah, the younger Rachel. Now "Leah was tender-eyed, and Rachel beautiful and well-favoured." As the sacred historian disdains not to mention this, we may be permitted to pause one moment upon the characteristics of the two sisters. That Leah was much less beautiful than her sister, is evident from the words of the text, but it does not appear that she was as plain and homely as some commentators declare her. The Hebrew word translated "tender," "And the eyes of Leah were tender (וְעֵינֵי לֵאָה רַכּוֹת)," does not signify *weak* only, as is generally supposed, but soft and delicate, and leads me to suppose that the soft and tender eyes of Leah were her only good feature, whereas her younger sister was "very beautiful and of exceeding beauty," which is the literal meaning of the Hebrew expression וְרָחֵל הָיְתָה יְפַת תֹּאַר וִיפַת מַרְאֶה, though even such translation is far from possessing the force of the original. This difference of appearance occasioned, as would appear by the sequel, a complete difference of character.

One month Jacob abode with his uncle, evidently doing him active service in return for the hospitality which he had received. That he did so, tells well for the real character of the wanderer; for in his father's house Jacob had never been accustomed to active service, and it must have demanded some little exertion of will over inclination, to have permitted its steady and active performance. Laban, however, at this period of their intimacy, felt too kindly and generously towards his nephew to permit him to work without wages. " And he said unto him, Because thou art my brother, shouldst thou therefore serve me for nought ? Tell me what shall thy wages be ? And Jacob loved Rachel, and said, I will serve thee seven years for Rachel thy younger daughter. And Laban said, It is better I give her unto thee than to another man. Abide with me. And Jacob served seven years for Rachel ; *and they seemed unto him but a few days, for the love he had to her.*"

We think much of those tales of chivalry where man performs some great and striking deed—conquers his own passions—becomes a voluntary wanderer—all to win the smile and love of woman. And we do right, for the motive is pure and the moral good. But such high wrought volumes should not blind our hearts and eyes to this exquisite narration, wherein the same truth, the same moral is impressed, with equal force and beauty, only in the simple language of the Bible. Jacob's servitude was a more convincing proof of his love and constancy than those exciting deeds of heroism which chivalry records. His was no service to call upon distant lands and far-off ages to admire. Nothing for FAME, that brilliant meteor, which, equally with love, divided the warrior's heart in the middle ages. Nothing to vary the routine of seven year's domestic duty, the wearisome nature of which we find in the 38th and 39th verses of chapter xxxi. Yet these seven years " seemed but as *a few days for the love he had to her.*" A brief yet most emphatic sentence, revealing the purest, the holiest, the most unselfish love, unrestrained by one fleeting thought of worldly aggrandisement, or a hope beyond making that beloved one his own. " Consumed by the drought by day, chilled by the frost at night," still he never wavered. Love was his upholder—his sustainer. And it was for this end love was so mercifully given.

As the word of God disdains not to pourtray the extent of love borne by one mortal for another, we trust we may be pardoned if we linger a moment on that emotion, the very name of which is generally banished from the education of young females, as if to feel or excite it were a crime, forgetting that, in banishing all idea of its *influence*, we banish also the proper means of regulating that influence, and subject our young charge unguarded to the very evil that we dread.

God gave not love to bind to earth, but to raise to heaven :

not to make us earthly idols, but, on the very love we bear each other, to lift up the soul to Him; to lighten toil and soften grief, to heighten joy and bless our earthly sojourn with a bright ray from that exhaustless fount of love which waits for us above. Without some emotion powerful enough to draw us out of ourselves for an earthly brother, how could we ever subject our selfish hearts to the will of our God? how perform those self-sacrifices most acceptable to Him? Stronger than pain and toil, and even death, it is the very essence of our being, the spiritual essence, which marks more powerfully than aught else our immortal destiny; and from the reflection of that destiny lends a glow to earth. "Thou shalt love the Lord thy God with all thy heart, and soul, and might," is the command of the Eternal—an important command—yet not given till after His word had revealed to us that it was possible, nay, that it was a necessary consequence, for those who served and loved Him best, to love and cleave unto each other. Had not the heart been created with full capacity to love, this command would not have been given; and He, who has placed us in a world of beauty, who has gathered around us objects to excite every feeling, demands not that those feelings are to be devoted to Him alone, in utter neglect of our fellows.

It is not passion to which we allude, though but too often the words are deemed synonymous. Nor do we mean passion, when we say that love is the handmaid of religion. No, it is a spiritual, not an earthly feeling; spiritual even when it relates to man, not God. And if, indeed, it be so, and the more we reflect upon it the more we feel it is, or *ought to be*, why should it be a subject, as it too often is, of jest, of scorn, and those under its influence deemed not far removed from folly and romance? Why should education never allude to it save as a dreadful and unlikely thing, and the sage lesson, so often conned, that *reason*, not affection, is to be our guide? Were the word *religion* substituted for reason in such educational codes, the young heart would be so trained as to eschew all fear of mere earthly love; it would know itself, its own impulses, its own feelings, and so set a strong guard upon those most likely to lead to error, while it encouraged all that would urge to good. It would feel that love was of God, and therefore not a subject for levity or jest—that it was sent to lift up the spirit to Him, and therefore not so to expend its force on an earthly idol as to lead to extravagance and folly—that it was to last for ever, not unto *death, but beyond it,* and therefore not to be given to one whose future was of earth, and who sought in its possession but the gratification of a few fleeting years—that it was to endure through sorrow and sickness, and trial and woe, not to be the mere harbinger of gaiety and joy, to shine in a ball-room and glitter in a bridal robe—but to bear with occasional irritability or even with unkindness and apparent neglect, with faults which we must never breathe, with intervals of an utter want of sympathy, even of depreciation, which we must endure, solace, and forgive—not to suppose, that we shall ever be as when that love is first called forth, our wishes granted ere told, our every feeling answered, our every virtue appreciated, our very failings loved. And to be prepared for this—to love thus, with a strength, a purity, that will bear all this, aye, and more painful still, the very sacrifices of self which love impels, unfelt, unknown, uncared for, or if seen, but deemed our duty, and coldly passed uncheered—will aught but that love which is spiritual sustain us? and will such emotion come to the young heart without some preparatory training? O, not while love is deemed romance, not while it is made a jest, or shunned as something guilty or derogatory, will it, can it, ever be as the God of love ordained, the purest, dearest blessing earth can know, the loveliest type of heaven.

Something more than Rachel's beauty, marvellous as that was, must have so retained Jacob's love for her in those seven years of domestic intercourse as to make the time appear but a few days. Beauty may attract, and win, if the time of courtship be too brief to require no other charm, but it is not sufficient of itself to *retain* affection. Gift from God, as it is, how may it be abused, and how may it be wasted, in caring only for the lovely shape *without,* and leaving the rich invisible gems *within* uncared for and unused. O if there be one among my youthful readers, of beauty exceeding as that of Rachel, who holdeth in her possession this rich gift of God, let her remember that He will demand of her how she hath used it—that its abuse, its *pretended* neglect, yet, in reality, proud value, will pass not unnoticed by its beneficent Giver. It has been granted for some end—for if to look on a beautiful flower will excite emotions of admiration and love, and consequently enjoyment, how much more deeply would such feelings be called forth by a beautiful face, could we but behold it as the hands of God had formed it, unshaded by the impress of those emotions of pride, contempt, or self sufficiency, or that utter void of intellect, which are but too often its concomitants, from the mistaken notion that outward beauty is omnipotent and needs no help within.

To hide from a young girl that she is beautiful, is the extreme of folly, for her mirror will tell her that she is being deceived, and the influence of such informers will be lost at once. No, let the real value and consequent *responsibility* of beauty be inculcated, and there will be no fear of its abuse.

That Rachel had many most endearing qualities, we may quite infer from Jacob's devoted love to her, even to her death. The spirit most impatient under contradiction, and loving its own will, is often united to a manner so engaging and qualities so calculated to win regard, that trivial faults of temper and will are literally engendered from the difficulty it is to reprove a being so beautiful and so beloved ; and this would seem the case with Rachel. Young, joyous, and loving, we may fancy her the very star of her father's home, valuing her beauty as it gave her power to obtain whatever she willed uncontradicted, but using it only in the sphere of home.

But though Jacob's affections were devoted to one alone, those seven years of intimate association must have been fraught with suffering and sadness to Laban's elder daughter, whose strong affection for Jacob the sequel will reveal. Her compelled agency in her father's fraud must have been fraught with absolute horror to a heart that loved secretly and unreturned, as herself, and heightened the trial of unrequited affection in no ordinary degree.

We will not linger on the affairs narrated in Genesis xxix., from the 21st to the 30th verse, because they belong so strictly to the manners and customs of the Eastern nations that it is quite impossible to comment upon them with any justice, prejudiced, as birth and education cannot fail to make us, in favour of the manners and customs of modern Europe. Yet the customs of the East have undergone little or no change ; and repeatedly we find that, which in the narrative of the Bible may startle our modern European notions as strange or improbable, confirmed by events passing in the East at this very day, so that those very narratives would there scarcely be considered a history of the past.

Though beguiled into another seven years' servitude for his much-loved Rachel, it is evident that she had become his wife *first*, Jacob honourably performing the word he had pledged, *after* the wished-for prize had been obtained; and not till those seven years were completed do we hear him utter one word of complaint, or one wish to provide for "his own house also."

"And when the Lord saw that Leah was hated [lit. less loved], He gave her children, but Rachel had none. And she called the name of her eldest son Reuben: for she said, Surely the Lord hath looked upon my affliction; now therefore my husband will love me." What a volume of woman's deepest feelings, and the compassionating love of the Eternal do these brief lines reveal! He who had in his inscrutable wisdom ordained that Leah should be tried in the fiery ordeal of woman's saddest loneliness, unrequited affection, yet deigned to grant a compensating blessing in all the sweet pure feelings of a mother's love. Who that reads but this one verse can uphold, that woman is less an object of tender love and compassion to her God than man? Who can say that the Mosaic records are silent on this head? The words of *man*, to point out the proper station and value of woman, we need not, for the children of Israel have the WORD OF THEIR GOD. And do we not still recognize the God of Leah? His ear has not become heavy that it cannot hear, nor His arm shortened that it cannot save. And though he may not bestow on us a *visible* and audible manifestation of His tender compassion, as on Leah, yet we may be certain, that He will grant us some compensating blessing for every joy of which he may think fit to deprive us. And even for those bitter griefs, which, from their nature, their seeming selfishness, woman shrinks in trembling from bringing before her God, and buries them in her own heart till it bleeds at every pore—Leah's history proves that He will grant peace and healing. It may be that a wiser and kinder will than her own has flung an insuperable barrier between woman's heart and its dearest object; and impelled her, by all that is refined and delicate in her character, to hide deep from every eye the anguish which is her burden. How blessed then, that even for such a grief there is the fount of healing waters still in the word of God—that she may come there and read, not only the abundance, the fulness of His love, but that He has especial tenderness for those by earth *unloved.* And, as He gave Leah children because she was not loved, so will He grant such sufferers a peace and calm, and joy in the consciousness of His unfailing tenderness, far surpassing even the rich and glowing, but too transient, happiness of sympathy on earth.

Leah must have known and loved the Lord long before the event recorded, else she had not thus welcomed the birth of her first child. Eight years of Jacob's sojourn in her father's household would scarcely have been sufficient for her to know and love her cousin's invisible God, had she not had some vague yet true notions of Him before.

That Jacob should often have alluded to the God of his fathers, and narrated the wonderful manifestations of His providence, and that such solemn themes should have fallen with peculiar impressiveness on the heart of Leah, and but lightly on the buoyant impetuous Rachel, may be inferred from the history of both. After the gods of her father, Leah has no hankering whatever; her reference, in both her griefs and joys, is to Jacob's God alone.

By her exclamation at the birth of her second son, we may suppose that the fond hope expressed the year previous, "Now therefore my husband will love me," was still not realised. "Because the Lord hath heard that I am not loved, He hath therefore given me this son also." To many the repetition of a blessing renders it invaluable, and, in the imperfection of our earthly nature, the continued disappointment of our dearest wishes would have rendered the heart callous, perhaps repining, at the very blessing which had before brought joy. But not thus was it with Leah: gratefully she received a second little treasure from the hand of her God; and, bearing again the pang of ever-blighted hope, she utters no wish of an earthly kind, but simply feels she has still the love of God. Another year, and another son is granted; and we may trace a ray beaming even through her earthly darkness, in the new upspringing of buoyant hope—"Now will my husband be joined unto me, for I have borne him three sons."

Whether, indeed, the fond wish was realised, and Jacob's heart was softened towards her, must be but conjecture; yet it would almost appear so, for, at the birth of her fourth son, her pious heart is satisfied with the fervent ejaculation, "Now will I praise the Lord." Drawn closer and closer unto her God, with His every precious gift, she, who gave her first-born a name signifying "the son of affliction," gave her fourth the beautiful appellation of "praise unto the Lord." It was not, then, only a gift of children His love bestowed. He had brought light from darkness, He had turned her mourning into praise, and returned with ten-fold blessing her meek enduring confidence in Him. Shall we then, who may be in the darkness of sorrow and heavy care, shrink from walking in her steps, and dwell only on the *affliction* which is ours? Shall we not also look and strive for some blessing which can bid us too " praise the Lord," and lead us to behold *light* where all was heaviness? There is no lot so desolate which, if we seek Him, the Lord will not bless; not, perhaps, by the removal of our present sorrow, but by some compensating mercy. We must not suppose that seeking Him and loving Him will exempt us from affliction. No; for, if it did, where would be that heavenly exercise which alone can fit us for heaven? Nor are we, as some enthusiasts would urge, to regard *trials* as *joys*, and welcome them with gladness. When a tender loving parent chastises a beloved child to keep him from the paths of sin, would he feel that the chastisement had done its work if the little being received it with smiles and rejoicing? Surely the parent would be more hopeful if the child were serious, and even sad. And is it not so with the afflictions sent from our eternal and most tender Father? We may think that we surely need them not; and our lives may even be, in the sight of man, as we ourselves suppose them. Nay, they may be numbered amongst those whom the Bible gives us promise shall be accounted the righteous in the sight of God; yet how know we, what we might have been *without* such affliction? How know we but those very sorrows, lasting but a *time*, are preparing us to be of those whom the Lord writeth in His book for eternity, who shall be His when He maketh up His jewels? Of this only are we certain, that the Lord *loveth* whom He correcteth. Then, while like Leah we *feel* affliction, let us hope on, pray on, with undoubting faith, that one day we too shall cry aloud, " Now will I praise the Lord."

Very different to the meek submissiveness and gentle disposition of her elder sister, is the impetuous temper and sinful feeling of envy which urged Rachel angrily to exclaim, even to her doting husband, "Give me children or else I die. And Jacob's anger was kindled against Rachel: and he said, Am I in God's stead, who hath withheld children from thee?"

We have been previously told—" And when Rachel saw

that she bare Jacob no children, she envied her sister." Envied whom? Even the homely, the unloved Leah. It was not enough that God had endowed her with most surpassing beauty, and given her the perfect love of a husband who had proved, was still proving his devoted attachment to herself alone, by fourteen years' hard servitude. It signified little that Leah *had but her children*, and that her own cup of blessings was filled to flowing over.

In glancing over the history of the two sisters, must we not feel, that Rachel *ought* to be the happier, as she was the more blessed? Yet it was not so. Leah, with her heavy burden of affliction, was the happier, for she neither envied nor complained, but leaned upon her God—and in consequence, from Him received consolation. Rachel could have had no such stay. "Give me children, or else I die!" was the exclamation of a querulous self-willed spirit, looking only to man, and depending upon him. Yet the knowledge of the Lord must have been equally revealed to Rachel as to her sister. Daughters of the same household, cousins of the same witness of God—Jacob's religious education and experience must have been imparted to her also. She may have even listened during the time for Jacob's sake, banishing its recollection entirely afterwards, as a theme much too solemn and grave for her present joyous days. And are there not such even now, deeming religion and her rich train of holy and blessed thoughts, quite incompatible with youth and beauty, and who believe age is time enough to think of such serious things?

That her feeling and its expression were both wrong, we perceive by Jacob's anger and reproof. Loving Rachel as he did, it must have been something very blameable to call severity from his lips. Ignorance may excite our pity but not our blame. Had Rachel been ignorant who had blessed her sister with children, Jacob would have answered differently—but her impatient words caused his "anger to be kindled against her," because he felt and knew that they must have come from a spirit as impatient as rebellious, and were therefore likely to excite the displeasure of the Lord. "Am I in God's stead?" meaning, can I give you children if God hath withheld them. Words brief, but impressively proving Jacob's individual dependence on and trust in his God, and which ought to have subdued and humbled the discontent and envy of his wife. But though they checked the querulous *words*, they had no power to change the inward *feelings*, and determined at all risks, all sacrifices, to obtain children also, she followed the example of Sarah, and forced her husband, by increasing the number of his wives, to undergo all the miseries of a divided household.

Yet, when Bilhah had a son, we find Rachel welcoming him with such a joyful thanksgiving, and as a gift from God —that we might wonder at her former impatience—did we not know, that there are many who trace the hand of the Lord, and think they love and serve Him, when all of life is smooth and smiling, yet act, at the first trial, the first cross, as if they knew Him not at all, and denied His power to help and save. "God hath judged me, and hath also heard my voice, and hath given me a son." Had she then prayed—and did she recognise in thoughtfulness the answer *to her prayer?* Or was her exclamation at the birth of Dan but a presumptuous supposition from a presumptuous spirit—believing without due authority that she had prevailed with God? We have not sufficient authority in Scripture to pronounce judgment one way or the other on this point, and must therefore leave it to the consideration of our readers.

Once only do words of sorrowing reproach escape Leah's lips towards her sister. "Is it a small matter that thou has taken my husband?" Words simply expressive of the natural pang which must sometimes have entered her heart—when year after year passed, and still beheld her deep affections less valued than the lighter love of Rachel.

Two other sons were born unto the elder sister; and one daughter, a blessing which had never before been vouchsafed the patriarchs. Then it was, "that God remembered Rachel; and God hearkened to her and gave her children." "God remembered Rachel." Had He forgotten? no, neither forgetfulness nor memory dwelleth with God—for He is omniscient as omnipotent, knowing and perceiving all. But when speaking of Him, His dealings with His children must be expressed in language, and by images suited to their finite conception— not according to the adorable and glorious, but unfathomable infinity surrounding Him. He *thought* upon and *hearkened* to her—for such is, equally with *remember*, the meaning of the term ויזכר אלהים את־רחל וישמע אליה אלהים—words, how full of consolation and encouragement to Rachel's female descendants! Man would have condemned, and sentenced her to a chastisement of perpetual childlessness—for the tenderest mercies of humanity are cruel compared to the tender mercies of the Most High! but He whom she had offended by mistrust, forgetfulness, impatience, angry emotions towards her sister, had compassion, and not only "remembered" that she was a weak and yearning woman, but "hearkened" to her supplications, and gave reply.

"God hath taken away my reproach," Rachel gratefully exclaimed. "And she called his name Joseph and said, the Lord shall add unto me another son." Could she have penetrated futurity—well indeed might she have felt that God had removed her reproach; for who that reflects on the angelic beauty and faultlessness of Joseph, can recall his mother without bestowing on her a portion of the love and veneration we lavish on her son.

It is when bowed down by inward remorse for a consciousness of innate sinfulness, by the impossibility of realising that perfect holiness which would guard us from approach to wrong either in act and thought towards our fellow-creatures, or in mistrust and forgetfulness of God, that we should remember the history of Rachel and take comfort. There are some, who, unable to bear the sting of an awakened conscience, drown it altogether, by fleeing from every holy exercise of prayer and self-examination, and believe that, as in this life, we must be liable to occasional faults, it is perfectly useless striving, much less praying against them, as such prayer can be of no service, and is but a mockery before God. Some minds may bear this awful state; to others, the young, the deeper feeling, and more yearning heart, it is a period of absolute anguish, which, without some spiritual help, is impossible to be sustained; and so religion is cast off as a subject of terror, of suffering, and the world and the world's panaceas substituted in its place. To such, more especially if they be women, we would say, Come but to the word of God—and even for such griefs there is all we need. There the Eternal not only proclaims "Himself a God full of compassion, long suffering, abundant in goodness and mercy, forgiving iniquity, transgression, and sin," but *proves* these consoling and most blessed attributes, not only *after*, but *before* they were proclaimed. Rachel was more faulty than many of her sex yet, her prayers were heard, her affliction compassionated, her wish fulfilled. How may we then despair, or think that the infirmities of our mortal frame, and the sinfulness they bring, can throw a barrier between us and our God. It is not to the righteous alone He awardeth mercy and love, but to the contrite and humble spirit, with whom the "High and Holy One who inhabiteth eternity delighteth to dwell." With such proofs we may not despair, we *dare not* doubt, but we are called to Him as little children sorrowing to be *forgiven*, in the full consciousness how deeply we are *loved*.

It was after the birth of Joseph, that Jacob's fourteen years of servitude being completed, he said unto Laban, "Send me away unto my own place, and to my country. Give me my wives and children for whom I have served thee, and let me go, for thou knowest the service which I have done thee. And Laban said unto him, I pray thee, if I have found favor in thine eyes, tarry; for I have learned by experience, that the Lord hath blessed me for thy sake: and he said, Appoint me thy wages, and I will give it. And he said unto him, Thou knowest how I have served thee, and how thy cattle was with me—for it was little before I came, and now it is increased into a multitude, and the Lord has blessed thee since my coming; now when shall I provide for mine own house also. And he said, What shall I give thee? And Jacob said, Thou shalt not give me any thing."

And that agreement followed which has most unjustly exposed Jacob to the accusation of duplicity and fraud. It is supposed, that his plan of placing the peeled rods in the drinking troughs, occasioned the greater number of the cattle to be "ring-straked, speckled, and spotted;" and in that manner Laban was defrauded, and Jacob received much more than his due. That Jacob refused all *gifts* from Laban, appears to me to originate in the same feeling which actuated Abraham to refuse gifts from the king of Sodom, "lest he should say, I have made Abraham rich." Depending upon him who had promised, "I will not leave thee until I have done that which I have spoken to thee of." Jacob neither could nor would accept gifts from man, preferring to work himself, and leave the issue in the hands of God. And this he did, and God blessed him with riches sufficient for his need.

Can it be supposed for one moment, after mature consideration, that the cattle could have become ring-straked, speckled and spotted, without the immediate agency of God, who had determined thus to provide for His believing servant? Can it be believed that it was in the power of man, by however subtle a scheme in appearance, to create a variety in the cattle, unless the Lord also had so willed it? Laban had not behaved as generously, or even as fairly by his nephew as his first affectionate welcome might lead us to suppose. We know from the words of Jacob himself, which Laban *does not contradict*, that, "except the God of my fathers had been with me, surely thou hadst now sent me away empty." And we may, therefore, rest perfectly content, that in the affair of the cattle no blame can be attached to Jacob. He was but a secondary cause, whose scheme would have been entirely vain had it not been blessed by the Eternal.

Increasing exceedingly in much cattle, and maid-servants, and men-servants, and camels, and asses, the wrath and envy of Laban's sons were excited towards him. And he saw that Laban's own countenance was not towards him as before—circumstances which must have excited much human anxiety and fear. And then it was, the Lord said unto him, "Return unto the land of thy fathers and thy kindred, and I will be with thee." "And Jacob sent and called Rachel and Leah to the field unto his flock." And in the perfect confidence of love and respect, imparted all to them. "I see your father's countenance is not towards me as before; but the God of my fathers has been with me. And ye know that with all my power I have served your father; and your father has deceived me, and changed my wages ten times; but God suffered him not to hurt me. If he said thus, The speckled shall be thy wages, then all the cattle bare speckled; and if he said thus, The ring-straked shall be thy hire, then all the cattle bare ring-straked. *Thus God hath taken away the cattle of your father, and given them to me.*"

There is something to me peculiarly beautiful in this simple address of Jacob, spoken as it is to his wives. Not a word of reproach on their father, but the simple truth—infinitely more expressive of the wrong he has suffered than any violence or invective. All that has blessed him, he traces unfailingly to God. The whole of his address, from the 5th to the 13th verse of Gen. xxxi., demands attention from its revealing so much more concerning Laban's real conduct to his nephew, and in what manner that conduct was regarded and overruled by the Eternal, than we can learn by the bare narration of the previous chapter. Our present subject forbids our lingering on it, except to say, it completely absolves Jacob from all fraudulent dealings with his uncle, while it reveals that he himself was the victim of deceit.

The mandate of God was in Jacob's ear, and every emotion of humanity was urging him to tarry not, but to flee at once. He had dominion over all his household, yet he waits to impart his wishes and his fears to his wives : he will make no step in advance without their concurrence ; thus at once proving his love and their equality. And, without a moment's hesitation, Rachel and Leah answered and said unto him, " Is there yet any portion or inheritance for us in our father's house ? Are we not accounted of him as strangers ? for he hath sold us, and has quite devoured our money. For all the riches which God has taken from our father, that is our's and our children's. Now then, whatsoever God hath said unto thee do."

Different as the sisters were in disposition, and placed in a situation most likely to create discord and disunion, yet when the interests of a beloved husband are at stake they act in perfect unity and love. There is no "mine and thine"—words how often fraught with discord—but simply "*ours* and *our* children's." Seeking even to reconcile him yet more to his flight—enriched as he was—by stating the simple fact, that Laban had failed in his duty towards them, by giving them neither portion nor inheritance ; and by having *sold* them to Jacob for fourteen years of labour. That which God then had marked as Jacob's share of the flocks and herds, was but their right and their children's.

Yet it must have been a trial to both sisters to remove so hastily and unexpectedly with their young children from the home of their earliest years, without even bidding farewell to the parent they had loved so long, to their brothers and their friends, to venture on a strange and dangerous track to a land they knew not, save that it was far away from their childhood's home. We already know where Leah's affliction always led her, and are, therefore, justified in believing that now, as before, prayer was the soother of her natural sorrows, and her confidence, that even if her father pursued them, he would not be permitted to work them harm. But Rachel could not thus realise the ever present, ever protecting arm of the Eternal ; and, as before she had sought human means to further her impatient wishes, so now does she bear away with her secretly "the images which were her father's ;" superstitiously believing, according to some commentators, that by consulting them, Laban would discover their route, and so be enabled to follow and arrest them. It is scarcely possible to peruse the history of these two sisters without being struck with the beautiful unity and harmony displayed in their two characters —distinct from first to last, and each preserving her individual peculiarities. Thrown back upon herself, from wanting the attractions of beauty and vivacity granted to her younger sister, Leah's graces expanded inwardly and spiritually; her yearning affections always strongest from never finding vent by being called for and appreciated by man. Rejoicingly and gratefully acknowledging and believing, the blessed religion which told her of an unchanging Friend and most tender loving Father, she found in such belief enough, and could realise content in the midst of trial, happiness in the midst of grief. Such a character as Leah's, from the time she is revealed to us, so perfectly free from all wrong feelings in a situation so likely to excite them, is not natural to woman; and we may, therefore, infer that her youth had had its trials, which the grace of God had blessed, in making her rise from them the gentle, enduring, lovable being which His word reveals.

The faults of Rachel originated in the very cause which had been a chastening to her sister. Her own surpassing loveliness, while ever the theme of admiration to her fellows, so raised her in her own estimation, that it was difficult to look beyond this world, where she reigned pre-eminent, to another, where she, in all her beauty, was but an atom—a creature of the dust. What to her was the love and protection of an Invisible being, when she was so surrounded by the love and care of man? What to her needed the tale of future happiness? Was she not joyous and laughter-loving the live-long day? With power in herself to bend all hearts, and direct all circumstances to the furtherance of her own impetuous will? Such we must believe the youth of Rachel, when we see her repining that children were granted to her sister and not to her. We behold her secretly bearing away the gods of her father—whether from the reason mentioned above, or from her own lingering belief in their efficacy and power, still equally reprehensible in the wife of Jacob.

If, indeed, Rachel supposed that in removing the images she prevented her father from discovering their route, she very speedily found herself mistaken. Jacob had stolen "away unawares from Laban the Syrian, in that he told him not that he fled; so he fled with all that he had, and he rose up, and passed over the river, and set his face toward the mount Gilead." And there, seven days after their hasty flight, Laban overtook him with all his kindred, and sufficient followers "to do them hurt," "Had not the God of your father," he said, "spake unto me yesternight, saying, Take thou heed that thou speak not to Jacob good or bad."

Anxiously and fearfully, according to their different characters, must Leah and Rachel have awaited the issue of the conference. The number of followers argued ill; yet the words of Laban were at first but mild reproach. "Wherefore didst thou flee away secretly, and steal away from me, and didst not tell me, that I might have sent thee away with mirth and with songs, with tabret and with harp: and hast not suffered me to kiss my sons and daughters? Thou hast done foolishly in so doing."

We may well suppose words such as these being fraught with self-reproach to affectionate daughters, that they had indeed so left their father. To Leah his next words, alluding to the " God of thy father," must have been particularly and gratefully soothing. He to whom she prayed was indeed ever round them, turning aside the wrath of men, forbidding him to arouse wrath by "speaking either bad or good." Holy writ does not indeed tell us, that Leah prayed in this instance; but she who welcomed the birth of every child with prayer and thanksgiving —who in no instance had recourse to her father's gods—was not likely to forget her husband's God when his protection was so needed. We may be permitted to believe she prayed; and can we not imagine the fervour of her grateful thanksgiving when she heard such words from her father? And we may all experience this. There is not one who has addressed the Lord in prayer, the daily prayer for all things, who can say he has had no answer. And O, who would not realise the glowing of the heart—the burst of thanksgiving which fills it—when we trace his hand in the daily events of life, and feel that that which we have asked for He has given? But to realise this, we must come to him in all things. We must pray to Him in our hearts as well as with our lips; we must *think* individual prayer as well as those public petitions framed for us. We must be in the constant habit of tracing all things to His almighty hand, and believe that His love is as deep, as pitying, for us individually, as His bounty is shown throughout the world. We must so commune with Him, that the hours of prayer will feel but the *continuation*, not the commencement and end of devotion. Did we but do this—bring before Him every care, and thought, and grief, and joy, and doubt, and thankfulness —how many many instances of *answered* prayer would the briefest life recall. Then, oh! how can we keep Him far from us, by withholding from Him the wishes which He alone has power to grant, the sorrows which He alone has compassion sufficient to heal?

On Rachel's ear the words which filled her sister's heart with deepest thankfulness must have fallen little heeded, while those which followed them, utterly meaningless to Leah, must have been fraught to her with the wildest terror, fearfully increased by the instant answer of her husband:—"And now, though thou wouldst needs be gone, because thou sore longedst after thy father's house, yet wherefore hast thou stolen my gods? And Jacob answered and said [in reply to Laban's previous words of reproach], Because I was afraid, for I said, peradventure thou wouldst take by force thy daughters from me." And then, with regard to the last accusation: "With whomsoever thou findest thy gods let him not live. Before our brethren discover what is thine and take it to thee. For Jacob knew not that Rachel had stolen them."

That she had concealed the theft from her husband proves at once that she knew the feelings dictating it were wrong, yet had not sufficient moral courage to resist them. And now what must have been her terrors? Not only was the plan which she had adopted to prevent a hostile meeting between her father and husband apparently about to be the very means of dissension, but if discovered, Jacob's own lips had pronounced her death doom. We know not if in the patriarchal times death was usually the punishment awarded to criminals convicted of theft; but it is evident that Jacob fully intended the criminal in his household to suffer even death for his offence, by the sacred historian so expressly declaring that "Jacob knew not that Rachel had stolen them." How could he suspect the wife of his bosom—his best beloved—of such theft as might almost convict her of idolatry.

Little did he dream whom he was condemning, or the misery he would have drawn upon himself, had not the God who had promised to bring him to his father's home in peace, here interposed, and saved both him, and for his sake, and the sake of His own great name, the faulty Rachel.

Yet during the period of Laban's search for the images, till the danger of discovery was quite past, how terrible must have been her alarm, and how painful her emotions? How different from the meek quietude of a holy spirit, at peace with itself and its God, which throughout this interview was Leah's? Yet no doubt, true to the contrarieties of imperfect humanity, when discovery was averted, and Laban found not the gods, Rachel only felt penetrated with pious gratitude, and resolved to keep her fault more strictly secret from her husband than ever. Some commentators, I believe, accuse her of an inclination to, if not of direct, idolatry; but we do not think that Holy Writ sufficiently authorises such a charge. Superstition, the remains of childhood's tales, which urged her to the course of acting with regard to the images already dilated upon, is not in the least incompatible with her recognition of, and belief in, Jacob's God, even though the images remained with her until Jacob bade them "put away the strange gods that were amongst them," nearly seven years afterwards. As his household consisted only of those who had lived with Laban, he might easily have supposed the strange gods theirs, and Rachel had thus an opportunity of resigning them, without causing her husband the suffering it would have been, to suspect her of having either stolen them at first, or harboured them so long.

There is something very beautiful in Laban's parting care of his daughters, when the somewhat warm recrimination between himself and Jacob was at an end. The heap of stones was raised by all who had met in wrath, proving their reunion by their united labour, and the feast which all shared in harmony when the work was concluded. "And Laban said, This heap is a witness between me and thee. Therefore was the name of it called Gilead and Mizpah, for he said, The LORD watch between me and thee, when we are absent one from another. *If thou shalt afflict my daughters, or if thou shalt take wives beside my daughters* (though no man is with us), see God is witness betwixt me and thee. This heap be my witness, and this pillar be my witness, that I will not pass over this heap to thee, and thou shalt not pass over this heap and this pillar unto me for harm. The God of Abraham, and the God of Nahor, and the God of thy father judge betwixt us. And Jacob swore by the fear of his father Isaac. And Jacob offered sacrifices on the mount, and called his brethren to eat bread; and they did eat bread, and tarried all night in the mount. And early in the morning Laban rose up, and kissed his sons (i.e. grandsons) and daughters, and blessed them; and Laban departed, and returned unto his place."

Thus were angry feelings calmed and soothed by a mutual covenant of love. While to the wives of the one, and the daughters of the other, how thrice blessed must have been the reconciliation which gave them again the dear privilege of a father's loving kiss and parting blessing. We learn too, from this simple narrative, that even in the East a multiplicity of wives was decidedly *not* lawful, and that Laban considered the rights of his daughters would be infringed, and so call upon him to come forward in their defence, even to break the covenant of peace, did Jacob take any other wives. Human nature is indeed the same in all ages—for as Laban spake to Jacob thousands and thousands of years ago, so would a father now. As truly as the Bible reveals the truth, the beneficence, the tenderness of God—so truly does it reveal and answer every emotion of the human heart.

As our task is a record only of Leah the wife of Jacob, we must pass lightly over the events of the xxxii. and xxxiii. chapters of Genesis, which belong exclusively to the history of the patriarch himself. The wrath of man was again turned aside, and the blessing of the Lord made Jacob at peace even with his brother Esau. His doubts and fears which must have extended painfully to the weaker nature of his wives, at news of Esau's armed approach were subdued by the influence of his prayer, and the long separated brothers met in mutual tenderness and love. They did not, however, long remain together. Jacob and his family proceeded to Succoth, and then to Shechem, where he "bought a parcel of a field," after erecting his tents, and "built there an altar," and there remained, till commanded by the Lord to "arise and go to Bethel."

The period of these sojournings between his departure from Padan-Aram, to his proceeding to Bethel, must have been full seven years. The then tender ages of his younger children, and the number of his flocks and herds, in all probability prompted him to settle his residence in the first convenient spot in the land of Canaan. It appears strange that he did not pursue his way without any pause to his father's house; but it is one of those subjects on which the word of God gives us no information, and, therefore, may be dismissed without wasting time and thought on what can be only speculation. At Shechem, Leah must have encountered indeed a fiery trial in the insult offered to her daughter, and the guilty conduct of her sons—Simeon and Levi. Here, as elsewhere, Jacob was punished by *deception*, causing fear and trouble, as he justly says : " Ye have troubled me to make me to stink among the inhabitants of the land, among the Canaanites and Perizzites, and I being few in number, they shall gather themselves against me, and slay me, and I shall be destroyed, I and my household."

But though, punished for the sin of his youth by mortal anxieties and fears continually darkening around him—the God of his father Abraham, mindful of his gracious promise to that holy man, still watched over Jacob, and relieved him from threatening danger by commanding him to go to Bethel and build an altar there. The patriarch without hesitation obeyed—first purifying his household of all strange gods ; and when " they journeyed, the terror of God was upon the cities that were round about them, and they did not pursue after the sons of Jacob." Then, as now, punishment fell not at once upon the sinning ones. They were preserved to work out their own chastisement in furthering the will of their God.

At Bethel, God again appeared unto the patriarch, and not only reiterated the promise made to his fathers and himself, but confirmed the change of name from Jacob to Israel ; that holy and blessed name which was to descend through thousands and thousands of ages, associated for ever with the mercy and the love and the glory of the Lord—given by the Eternal ; a mark of especial favor from the King of kings, expressing that as a Prince our father Jacob had power with God and with man, and had prevailed. Is there, can there be one amongst the descendants of this prince of God's creating, ashamed of the name he bears. Should it not be our glory, our pride— of which no persecution, no injury, no wrong can rob us ? Does not its very sound teem with the wondrous mercies of the past—with the truth, the unanswerable truth of revelation ? What scorner, what sceptic can point the finger of doubt or denial at the Bible—while that name is yet heard in every corner of the globe, borne by the very descendants of him, to whom by God Himself it was bestowed. The watchword, the banner of our cause, recognised as such in every nation, every land—the man or woman who feels shame to call himself of ISRAEL, flings scorn upon his God. Cheered and consoled by this renewed blessing of God, Jacob proceeded on his journey, advancing southward in the direction of Mamre, where Isaac his father then was.

Ephrah was nearly reached, when the sudden illness of Rachel compelled the whole cavalcade to halt—and Jacob must have beheld with inexpressible anguish, his best beloved wife torn from him, at the very moment she had increased his joy and her own by giving birth to a second son. When in the midst of bodily and mental anguish, she called his name Benoni, son of my sorrow, did she think of her own impatient words— " Give me children, or else I die !" and feel that it would have been better for her to have waited for the Lord ? How may we answer ? Enough for us to benefit by the record vouchsafed, and feel His will is better than our own—and in impatient restless longings for blessings granted to another, we may know, that even in the very fufilment of the wish, the punishment may fall.

Rachel committed no fault in wishing for a child—her fault had been envy and its subsequent discontent. Years had passed, the very recollection of her restless discontent may have faded from her mind, but not from His whom she had by want of faith and gratitude offended. In His infinite mercy He forgave, He blessed, for He called her to Himself ere the evil days came, and her beloved one was sold by his brethren, and reported for long long years as dead. He saved the mother this deep suffering, but, in His justice towards her and love to her descendants, He chastised by an early and painful death, the most trying separation of soul and body which human nature (so to speak) may know. Her husband, her Joseph, her new-born ! suddenly and fearfully the silver links of love, binding her to all these, were snapt asunder, and she might know her place on earth no more. " Give me children, or else I die." Alas! the too impatient cry was heard and answered; children *were* bestowed, and with them death. How little knew she what she asked ! In all her surpassing loveliness, in the full possession of most faithful love, the destroying angel came and snatched her from this world. O ! will not this teach us to be content with what God has given, and restrain us from looking with secret envy on the richer (in seeming) blessings of another? Will it not bid us beware of seeking aught of good only because it belongs to a companion, or because we fancy we have equal right to its possession, by the lesson that, even were it ours, we might have no power to enjoy it? Death, indeed, may not come between us and its enjoyment; but that which we have coveted loses its value the moment we possess it. Will not the warm young heart shrink from the very anticipation of the sin towards God and man which discontent may bring? Let us think *more* of our sorrowing and afflicted fellow-creatures, and *less* of those more blessed in outward seeming. Did we think on the bereaved, the physically afflicted, the poor, how could we still retain discontent of our own lot, or envy of our fellow-creatures! And O! if no other reasoning will avail, let us remember, our God is not only a merciful tender father, but a just and jealous God, who will one day, we know not when or how, call upon us to render an account of the blessings He has given; and if we know them not, how may we answer? Long years had passed since Rachel's offence, yet He who slumbereth not nor sleepeth, chastised it in the very hour that the wish which caused it was fulfilled.

It may be asked (as in similar cases of bereavement it, alas, too often is), "Why, granting that the lot of the departed is blessedness, does the God of love so afflict the survivors? Why did He cause such deep grief to his favoured servant Jacob? Because God loved him; because His omniscience had seen, that Rachel might come between Jacob's heart and his God; because he would demonstrate to futurity that to possess His favour, His blessing, does not in any manner emancipate us from trial and suffering in this world; because He would lift up our affections from the narrow limits of this world, He would make His heaven a dearer home than our earth, He would people it with the immortal spirits of those we have loved on earth, that we may look upon it no longer as a strange land; but as the beautiful country where our beloved are gone, and where we shall follow. This is wherefore He bereaves, and therefore even in bereavement there is love.

There is no mention of Jacob's grief; yet in the very silence of Scripture, in some points, there is eloquence, borne out, as in this case it is, by the deep love he bore towards Joseph and Benjamin. What can more exquisitely express the intensity of that love, than when entreated by his sons to let Benjamin accompany them to Egypt, he answered, "My son shall not go down with you : for his brother is dead, and he is left alone : if mischief befall him in the way which ye go, then shall ye bring my grey hairs with sorrow to the grave." "He is left alone," and yet ye had ten brethren—alone of his mother, the patriarch felt—sole record of that beloved one whom he had lost, and how might he let him depart? It is impossible to reflect on Jacob's intense love for Joseph and Benjamin, without fully imagining the suffering of their mother's loss. Silent he was, for who might question the decrees of the Most High ; but faith and love for our Father in heaven does not forbid us to mourn. We are placed here to love each other ; and if we love not those with whom we are in daily, hourly intercourse, how may we love God? Without love, earth would be a desert and heaven a void.

The death of Leah is not recorded ; we only know that she did not accompany the patriarch and his family to Egypt, and that she was buried with Abraham and Sarah, Isaac and Rebekah, in the cave of Machpelah. Left dependant on her tenderness and love, the extent of which we know, Jacob no doubt lavished warmer affection upon her, after the death of Rachel than before. How gratefully her pious heart must have traced this tranquil calm, which probably closed her days, to her God, we may infer from the thanksgiving with which every previous blessing had been received. But, as her future life can only be suggestion, much as imagination may love to dwell upon it, our present task must be concluded. We have dilated already at so much length upon the characters of the sisters, and the instruction and consolation therein developed, that we need add little further now, except to notice what has always appeared a remarkable manifestation of the perfect equality of the sisters in their position as mothers of that race which is to last for ever. Ten tribes are lost—not to be discovered till the day which will behold the glorious and stupendous miracle of our restoration. The two which remain to bear witness to the mercy and justice of the Eternal, and the truth of His word, are JUDAH, the descendants of LEAH, and BENJAMIN the descendants of RACHEL, from one or other of which every Israelite (except the representatives of the Levites, who were accounted the priests of the Lord, not of the twelve tribes) traces his descent.

Shall we then dismiss the beautiful record of Leah and

Rachel, which the word of God contains, as a mere relation, concerning an age so long past as to appear almost fabulous and obsolete? Shall we not rather take it to our hearts, and, as women of Israel, feel it is of *our own ancestry* we read? Shall we not emulate the much enduring piety of Leah; and in all our afflictions—even in that of a lone and unloved heart —turn to her God, and emulate her rejoicing acknowledgment of blessings at his hand? Shall we not take warning of the loved and lovely Rachel, and feel that neither beauty nor love —the dearest love of man—can afford us happiness and joy, unless both are traced to, and held from, the grace of God? That not in outward attraction—not even in human love—can blessedness exist, unless the vital spark, to give them rest and life and continuance, hath dwelling *within*, to lift up the whole soul to God. O better—far better—homeliness of form and face, with a guileless contented heart. Better—far better—a heart desolate of earthly sympathy, with the love of our Father in heaven, than beauty and grace and human love the fullest, dearest, combined with every worldly blessing—if these be sufficient for our need, and we pass through life without one thought of God.

SECOND PERIOD.

The Exodus and the Law Considered.

EGYPTIAN CAPTIVITY AND JOCHEBED.

We are now to commence the second period of our history—an interval, differing materially from that which went before, and from that which will succeed it, yet of vital importance to the women of Israel. Their station is no longer to depend upon the changes of time and states. The protection, tenderness, reverence, and support, which, in their varied relations of life, they so imperatively need, no longer rest on the will of man alone: the God of Abraham proclaims Himself their Guardian and their Father, and, by innumerable statutes in His Holy Law, provides for their temporal and eternal welfare equally with that of man.

The mother, the wife, the daughter, the maid-servant, the widow, and the fatherless—for each and all, His love and mercy so provided, that every social and domestic duty became obedience unto Him, and woman was thus raised to that rank in the scale of intellectual and immortal beings, by the ordinance of God, from which her weakness of frame and gentle delicacy of mind would, had she depended on man's judgment alone, have entirely deprived her.

For the women of Israel were those laws issued which were to guard the innocence, purity, honour, and well-doing of woman in general throughout the world; for, however other revelations may profess to be the first and purest, however the smile of scorn and unbelief may attend the mention of the Jewish dispensation in conjunction with woman, the truth remains the same, that as from that law every other sprung, so from that law does woman in every age, clime, rank, and race, receive her guardianship on earth, and hope of heaven.

That this assertion will meet with scorn and denial on all sides, we believe—perchance even from those whom nationality and duty both, should arouse to its defence. Yet firmly and unhesitatingly we retain the position we have advanced, prepared to defend it from the same blessed Book on which it is founded—the Word of God. Much has been said of the wide distinction between ancient and modern Judaism, of Talmudical perversions of Holy Writ, of Jewish degradation of woman, and a melancholy list of similar accusations. With them we neither have nor intend to have anything to do, save boldly to assert, that IF there be this wide distinction between ancient and modern Judaism—IF customs and laws derogatory to God's changeless truth, and contrary to His holy Word, have crept in amongst us—the dark and bloody eras of persecution are at fault, not the ancient fathers, who knew how to *die* for their faith, but not to sully or degrade it. And it behoves us, in this blessed age of peace and this land of freedom, to prove the falsity of the charge, to awake and manifest to all men, that the religion of the Jew is the religion of Moses, as given by the Lord; and that *if* laws have crept in *contrary* to the spirit and the ordinances of His word, they are *not* Judaism, but the remnants of an age of barbarism and darkness, when that Pure and holy word was almost death to read. Oh! why has not Israel joined heart and hand in this holy cause? Why has he not borne, in charity and patience, with those who differ from him in minor points, and thought only how, by union, harmony, and love, he could exalt his nation and his faith in the sight of the Gentile world, and *prove* that, however close and binding may be the casket, the jewel it enshrines is still the revelation of the Lord, the religion of the Bible?

But our present task has not to do with the nation and Judaism at large; it is simply to prove to the women of Israel their position in the sight of God, and their duties towards man. The intricacies of the law, as commented upon and explained by our ancient fathers, are not for us. Woman needs only comfort, strength, and guidance, so simply yet so clearly given, that a little child may read and understand them; and these are ours, alike in the records of our female ancestors and in the precepts of the Lord.

Hitherto we have been regarding His love, mercy, and justice, as manifested to individuals; deriving lessons from example, and guidance from the Eternal's dealings with his creatures. Recorded in His book, we know that their lives are now intended for our instruction and benefit, or they would not have been written. But God knew that something yet more was needed, for the religious training and well-doing of His elected people; something more than the mere history of the past, bright as that was with the wonderful manifestations of His presence in direct communings with His saints; —and for the love He bore His faithful servant Abraham, it pleased Him to bring from the deepest darkness the purest light, and vouchsafed a law which was to last for ever, and through which, not alone His chosen, but every nation should be blessed.

From the death of Joseph to a short time preceding the birth of Moses, Holy Writ is silent as to the history of the Israelites, both individually and nationally, except the important truth that "they were fruitful and increased abundantly, and multiplied and waxed exceeding mighty, and the land was filled with them." Though no law had been given, they were still, it is evident, a completely distinct people, retaining a pure religion in the midst of barbarous idolatry. With no ordained worship—no revealed ordinances—no appointed sacrifice, or priest; still they were the elect and beloved of the Lord, requiring no mediator, either angelic or human, to bring up their prayers before God, and render them acceptable. Yet God not only "heard their cry, but had respect unto them." This is a point in our history too important to be overlooked, though it concerns Israel generally, not the women of Israel alone. It is very often brought forward as a proof that we must now be wholly rejected by the Lord, because the daily sacrifice has ceased, and many parts of the law, obligatory upon us in Judæa, are scarcely possible to be observed in our captivity—the cessation of sacrifices and atonement-offerings especially are perpetually insisted upon, as proving that unless we acknowledge the atoning sacrifice of Jesus, and regard him as our High Priest, we are lost temporally and eternally.

The single fact that the Israelites in Egypt had neither sacrifice nor high priest, though the former was already ordained, yet were still a distinct people, still the first-born of the Lord, and had power to lift up their cry to Him, and be heard, compassionated, and answered, is a sufficiently convincing answer. Israel is now, and has been for eighteen hundred years, as he was in Egypt, with the sole difference that there we were not the captives of the Lord as we are now; nor had we then a law to guide us, and by obedience prove repentance. We are now fulfilling the prophecy, that "Israel shall abide many days without priest or sacrifice," etc. (Hosea iii. 4); but the same blessed word which foretells this, says not one word of our being utterly cast off, but repeatedly enforces the divine consolation, that we have but to cry unto the Lord, even from the lands of our captivity, to be heard and compassionated as we were in Egypt. We have no need of sacrifice, when God Himself ordained that it should cease; nor can we have the head of the nation, alike of its religious, civil, and even military divisions, while scattered in every quarter of the globe. Were we to accept Jesus in his blended character of sacrifice, atoner, and high priest, the prophecies would all remain *un*fulfilled; as we should still possess all these, instead of being, as the prophet so expressly declared, deprived during our captivity of "king, prince, sacrifice, image, ephod, and teraphim" (Hosea iii. 4).

To Israel in Egypt they were not given; to Israel in her lengthened captivity they have ceased, until she be purified and chastened sufficiently to receive once again the visible manifestation of the Lord's acceptance, their constant attendant, and which was forfeited by our rebellion. Yet still, even as in Egypt, we are the first-born of the Lord, and have, nationally and individually, equal access to His compassionating love.

A new king had arisen in Egypt; one who knew not Joseph, and saw only in the Israelites, a people harmless indeed in employments and pursuits, but sufficiently mighty in numbers to arouse the jealous fears of tyranny: and the commandment went forth to afflict them, by weighty tasks and heavy burdens. But the more they afflicted them, the more they multiplied and grew; and in consequence, heavier and heavier grew their afflictions, till at length the fatal command was given to destroy every male child at its birth. Yet even this was overruled by a merciful God. The hearts of the women designed for this barbarous office were in His hand, and He so softened them into tenderness and compassion that the innocent babes were saved by the very means adopted for their destruction. Finding this scheme unavailing, Pharoah issued another command, more fatal than the first, for it seemed not in the power of man to evade or counteract it. And in the power of man it was not; God alone could bring forth delivery; and therefore did He permit the deepest darkness to close around His people, that both they and the Egyptians might know the power to redeem, and the love to accomplish it, were in Him alone.

The situation of the women of Israel, at this period, must have been terrible indeed. Their infants, born in the midst of sorrow, yet hailed, perhaps, as the sole blessing which they could call their own, snatched from them by ruthless murderers, and flung into the Nile. And where were they to look for redress—for pity? Where but to their God—and "He heard their groaning;" and from this very desolation raised up His own.

The family of Amram, a son of Levi, already consisted of himself, his wife, a little son of three years' old, and an elder daughter. The birth of Aaron must have been attended with heavy sorrow from the tyrannical oppression under which his father and the other Israelites laboured; but dark as was that hour, it must have been almost joyous compared with the awful trial awaiting his mother now. About to add another little one to their family, how agonisingly must the shriek of torture, wrung from her sisters in Israel—marking every fresh assault of the Egyptians within their houses, in search of their babes—have sounded in her ears? Day after day, night after night, one or other dwelling of the miserable Hebrews was searched: and ransacked, if no child were found. Voices of cursing and mockery mingled with the wild entreaties for mercy—the scream of agony—the wailing moan of impotent suffering—the feeble wail of helpless infancy—the sullen splash, that told the work of butchery done! such must have been the sight and sounds around the home of Jochebed, as she awaited in trembling horror that day which must expose her to the same. It came at length, and a fair lovely babe was born—a boy—whose first wailing cry, if it reached the ears of the Egyptian butchers, would be his death-knell. But the prayers of the mother had not been in vain. Her God was with her, endowing her with wisdom and energy sufficiently effectual to conceal her boy three months. But then danger once more approached. Suspicions had either been excited or the increasing age and size of the child rendered the task of concealment no longer possible. Fearful must have been the struggle of natural terrors and spiritual confidence, filling the mother's mind, ere the plan she eventually followed was matured and executed. Faith alone in a God of infinite compassion could have inspired a mode of proceeding apparently so fraught with danger, as herself to expose her babe to the deep and dangerous current of the river; but even while faith impelled, and at times soothed by the firm conviction that her God would save, natural affections and human fears must often have had the ascendant, breathing but of danger and of death. The future was veiled in impenetrable darkness. The fate of her child, even if his slender ark bore him in safety on the waters, must be one of suffering, or perhaps of starvation—for who would give him food? Did she do right to expose him thus? If he were to be saved, would not the Eternal equally accomplish it without this fearful venture? Such would be mere human reasoning in woman's feeble heart. But prayer gave her the needful grace and strength to listen only to the immortal spirit, and trust undoubtedly in God. Can we not picture the anxious throbbings of maternal affection as her own hand weaved the ark or basket of bulrushes, in which her babe was to be exposed? Would not merely earthly natures have smiled in scorn on this feeble invention, and pronounced it futile? But the mother of Moses had not such to increase the difficulty of her task. Her husband's name is never mentioned in this proceeding; for Amram, as the remainder of his miserable brethren, was in all probability too much weighed down, and spirit-broken by their multiplied afflictions, to think of the inmates of his home, save with increased affliction and despondency; nay, had perchance closed his heart against all love for his new-born, believing it was destined, as every other, for immediate death. He could have had no time to watch over it, and share his wife's anxieties. To his mother alone, therefore, under the especial providence of God, did Moses owe his preservation.

The ark was completed. Gifted with unusual foresight and wisdom for the task, Jochebed carefully daubed it with slime and pitch, that no water should penetrate within; and with trembling yet still trusting spirit, placed her babe therein, and laid it on the flags by the river's brink. To watch what would be done with it—whether it would rest there till some compassionate passer-by should behold and save him, or be indeed launched on the waters and carried from her sight—was indeed a task too fearful for maternal love. We may picture, with perfect truth and justice, her last lingering kiss pressed upon the lips, cheek, and brow of the unconscious babe; her waiting till sleep closed those beauteous eyes, which, in their pleading gaze, seemed to her fond heart, beseeching her not so cruelly to abandon him—waiting till slumber, light, pure, beautiful, as only infancy can know, lay upon those sweet features, those rounded limbs, making them seem like some folded flower, waiting but the return of day to brighten into renewed and still lovelier existence. Would that day ever dawn on earth for that sweet unconscious slumberer? Alas! now may she answer? Her look deepens in its silent anguish—its immeasurable love. Faith seems departing in that intensity of human feeling; she will look no more, lest indeed it fail. The light lid closes softly over the sleeping babe. She lays it amidst the flowering flags—looks once, once more. Does the infant moan or weep? How may she leave it, if it does? No; all is silent, voiceless—the boy still sleeps—and she hurries from the spot—bids Miriam stand "afar off," yet near enough "to know what would be done with him." And for herself—where, where shall she find rest, from the anxiety and suffering of that fearful hour? Where, but at the footstool of her God, in whose gracious hand she has placed her babe? What could calm that heart but prayer! And how can we doubt one moment that to the MOTHER of MOSES prayer was her sole support, strength, and life!

Holy Writ is silent as to the length of time which elapsed ere Pharaoh's daughter "came down to wash at the river; and her maidens walked along by the river's side, and when she saw the ark among the flags, she sent her maid to fetch it. And when she had opened it, she saw the child: and, behold, the babe wept. And she had compassion on him, and said, This is one of the Hebrew's children." How exquisitely true and touching is this picture of human nature! The simple words, "and, behold, the babe wept," even in reading, seem to fill woman's heart with a gush of tears. The utter helplessness, the innocence, the beauty of the poor babe, seem to cling to our affections, as if he were entwined with them by stronger ties than mere narration. And is he not? What woman of Israel can read this touching narrative unmoved? "The babe wept;" and, true to nature, Pharoah's daughter had compassion on him. Cold, terrified, hungry, the poor infant might have been weeping long in his bulrush prison; but those tears, sad as they were to him, obtained his human preservation.

The compassion of the princess emboldened Miriam to go forward, and respectfully to ask, "Shall I go and call to thee a nurse of the Hebrew women, that she may nurse the child for thee?" An address which would almost make us believe that the compassionate and gentle character of the tyrant's daughter must have been known to the Hebrews, or the young Miriam would scarcely have had sufficient courage so to have spoken. This, however, must be suggestion; the inspired narrative only enforces upon us the hand of God throughout. The same God who inspired Rebekah unconsciously to speak those words which answered the steward's prayer, and elected her for Isaac's wife, also inspired the youthful daughter of Amram to come forward and speak such words to the princess of Egypt, as, at another time, she would have trembled to utter even in thought.

"And Pharaoh's daughter said to her, Go. And the maid went and called the child's mother. And Pharaoh's daughter said unto her, Take this child away, and nurse it for me, and I will give thee thy wages. And the woman took the child and nursed it."

What must have been the emotions of Jochebed, thus to clasp again to her heart her rescued treasure? Not alone saved from present death, but future suffering and labour—restored to her maternal bosom, to receive thence not only his necessary infant nourishment, but such lessons of his father's God and his brethren's faith as would render him invulnerable to the temptations and idolatry of the Egyptian Court. Her emotions in parting from her child we might try to picture; but on those which must have attended his rescue, his restoration, silence is most eloquent. How had not her simple trusting faith been rewarded? How clearly, how startlingly had the hand of the Eternal been displayed? And how could she prove the grateful devotedness of her overflowing heart, save by devoting the child His love had saved unto His service? Not even poverty and privation had she to encounter. While her brethren were enduring the heaviest burdens from cruel taskmasters, she was receiving wages from the princess of Egypt for the nurture of her own child; and well may we believe those wages were devoted to the needy and the suffering—from her who in the midst of natural sorrow must have felt herself individually so blessed.

"And the child grew, and she brought him unto Pharoah's daughter, and he became her son." But it was in those years he had passed with his own mother his character had been formed; his principles were fixed; his religion obtained living and breathing, and ever actuating influence. We know not the age at which he left his mother, but we must infer, from all that is narrated of him, that *her* influence, not that of his adopted parent, made him what he was. No lessons of Pharoah's daughter could have endowed him with that feeling of patriotism which bade him rise up against the Egyptian who was smiting an Israelite, or interfere between the two Israelites, endeavouring meekly to restore peace. Had his early instruction been confined to Pharoah's palace, his very birth and race would have been unknown; he would have imbibed only such principles as actuated the Egyptians, and could not fail to have bowed down to their idols. Some very powerful influence must have been at work counteracting these evils; and what influence is so great over the susceptible age of infancy as that of mother or nurse? and Jochebed combined both these endearing relations. Even after the actual task of nursing was accomplished, "and the child grew, and she brought him unto Pharoah's daughter," it appears to me more than probable that she was still retained near the person of her child, tending him even after he was called the princess's son; and thus had frequent opportunities of inculcating those divine truths which, though no law was yet given, the past history of his people so vividly revealed.

That Moses makes no further mention of his parents is no proof of such idea being but fancy. Of everything concerning himself he writes so slightly, so evidently imagining his personal history of no possible consequence compared with the mighty and solemn matters intrusted to him, that it was not likely the days of his childhood should be recalled and dwelt upon. Nay, he himself might have been perfectly unconscious to what influence he actually owed his peculiar feelings as an Israelite, his gentle, lovely virtues as a man. The work of a mother is silent and unseen as dew upon the earth—the seed must be planted, watched, watered, but unless spared to behold it springing into flower, the hand of the planter may for ever rest unknown. Jochebed was parted from her son years before this blessed reward was given; his *childhood* alone was hers. His youth, his manhood, when the seed she had sown might have repaid her with abundant harvest, were passed, the one in all the temptations, the luxuries of an Egyptian court; the other in exile—the lowly shepherd of his father-in-law, a priest of Midian—apart even from his countrymen. It does not appear that his parents were among those who left Egypt, or their names would have been mentioned with the other relatives of Moses. Jochebed had not the privilege of beholding the spiritual and temporal greatness of her rescued boy; but had the seed of her sowing withered? Were her counsels vain? Can we not trace in the peculiarly gentle, much-forgiving character of our lawgiver, the moulding of a *woman's* hand? Is there ought to prove the minion of a court, the favorite of a princess? No, O no. The whole character of Moses displays a mother's guidance. A mother's love watching over childhood, and inculcating those high and glowing principles of virtue and patriotism, which the blessing of the Eternal ripened into such a beautiful maturity, as to render Moses a fit instrument in His hand to lead His chosen people from the land of bondage, and to reveal His changeless law.

And what will not this beautiful narrative teach us? As Jochebed, we too are in a land of bondage; indeed, in free and happy England, not a bondage of suffering and persecution, but yet as exiles from our own land; and, alas! too often, exiles from our God. We too are in a land of strangers, whose faith is not ours; a faith which, though it be not idolatry, is fraught with yet more temptation and danger. In this blessed land, no cruel taskmaster afflicts us with heavy burdens; yet there are some to look upon us with scorn and hate, who would strew our daily path with the thorns and briars of contempt, calumny, and abuse; and others again who, with kindly yet mistaken zeal, would appal us by the vivid recital of the fearful precipice on which we stand, telling us that but one escape is left us, one only way, or we are temporally and eternally lost; and that way no Israelite can recognize. Yet fearful are the temptations to seek it, and few, too few, his weapons of defence. Worldly rank and worldly honours are closed to the believing Hebrew, and wherever he turns he feels himself a stranger.

Blest in this land with peace and freedom, yet, ever and anon, the low growl of the tempest of persecution reaches him from distant shores; sometimes sinking into silence ere more than the heart's quick throbbing is aroused; at others waxing louder and more loud, till the wailing of thousands, and the shrieks of torture, are borne on the heavy air, breathing that Israel is afflicted still. And wherefore? To bid us still feel we are the captives of the Lord—that Jerusalem lieth desolate and waste for our sins—that the awful prophecy of the twenty-eighth chapter of Deuteronomy has been, and in many lands still is, in actual fulfilment—that we are now, as we were in Egypt, afflicted and oppressed—" despised and rejected of men—a man of sorrows and acquainted with grief "—" as one that gropeth at noon-day as the blind gropeth in darkness, that shall not prosper in his ways, that shall only be spoiled and oppressed evermore, and whom no man shall save." And if it be so (and who shall say it is not?), O does it not devolve on the mothers of Israel to do even as Jochebed, and so influence the childhood of their sons as to render them indeed faithful to their God, meek and forgiving towards man, and invulnerable to every temptation held forth by the opposers of their faith?

The very safety we enjoy, the habits of friendly intimacy which it is right and happy we should cultivate, all call upon the Hebrew mother to instil those principles in the heart of her son which shall guide him through life, and, while they raise him in the estimation of the nations around him, inspire him individually to glory in his own.

We have enlarged, in a former work, on the duty of mothers regarding religion generally. We would here conjure them to follow the example of the mother of Moses, and make their sons the receivers, and in their turn the promulgators, of that holy law which is their glorious inheritance. Their faith, in England, may not be tried as that of Jochebed—they may not be called upon to expose their innocent babes to the dangers of the river to save them from the cruelties of man—but they are called upon to provide a suit of defence for riper years. They must so instruct, so guide, the first ten or twelve years of boyhood, that, even then, they may leave their maternal homes as Israelites rejoicing in their faith. They must infuse some balsam to heal, or some invulnerable shield to eject, the arrows of contempt or pity which, ere they pass through life, they must encounter. They must so lead that graver years may conduct them to that only study, the blessed word of God, which alone can give peace to their spirits, rest to their minds, and convictions to their hearts—alike in their private hours and their communings with the Nazarene world. This is now the Hebrew mothers' task, which may be blessed to their offspring as Jochebed's was to Moses. It is for this they must have faith, must trust that God will perfect that which is imperfect, fill up every deficiency, and bring the seed to flower, or vain and hopeless will be their task. They must impress upon their offspring their SPIRITUAL ARISTOCRACY, and so not only remove all temptation to barter their heavenly heritage for earthly rank, but infuse their minds and hearts with that nobility of thought, word, and action, which should be the heirloom, the glory of every Hebrew, be he of what rank, profession, or even trade, he may. Persecution and barbarity in our opposers, and their consequent ignorance and superstition in ourselves, have for long ages so crushed and trampled on this innate nobility, that in all but a very few instances, it seems, and has long seemed, departed from us; its banishment stigmatising us as degraded to the lowest and vilest of mankind. Can we now then, in those blessed lands where the Jew may walk in freedom, with "none to molest or make him afraid," permit this stigma to remain. Shall we not rather wake every energy, string every nerve, to prove that it is not Judaism, but persecution, at fault; and that wherever the Hebrew is FREE, he is NOBLE? That the princely blood of Abraham, Moses, and David still flows within his veins, and incites him to thoughts and deeds as far removed from ignorance and degradation as the sun is from the earth?

But not when arrived at manhood can this nobility be infused. It must be imbibed with the mother's milk, and form the very atmosphere of childhood and youth. Let every mother in Israel look upon her infant treasure as direct from the hand of God, and believe that He saith to her as the princess of Egypt said to Jochebed—"Nurse this child for ME, and I will give thee thy wages;" for HIM, for the LORD, who in every age, clime, and position, calleth Israel HIS CHILDREN. And let her indeed so nurse him, that whenever he may be called to his Father in Heaven he may be fit to go. Let her, weak and feeble of herself as she is, remember that with the Lord all things are possible, and that, as He blessed Jochebed in the preservation and nurture of her child, so, if we will but blend effort with prayer, perseverance with faith, He will equally bless us; and though it may not be ours to rear a deliverer from Egyptian bondage, yet how will the mothers Israel rejoice and glory to receive "their wages" in the elevation of their nation by their sons?

To do this, they must be NOBLE; and to become so let the Hebrew mother teach her boy, from his earliest years, to think of his heavenly heritage, his spiritual election, his eternal life, and leave the interests and ambition of earth till riper years, when even these dull sordid cares shall become ennobled and spiritualised by the purer atmosphere which he has in his boyhood breathed. We are not indeed, while denizens of earth, to think so exclusively of heaven as to unfit us for the life of trial and temptation which, in our mortal career, we are commanded to tread; but we are to infuse earth with Heaven, time with Eternity, the soul with GOD. As Israelites we *cannot* sever our temporal from our eternal interests, we *cannot* fling off the memory of, and obedience to, the Eternal; for with every single relation, duty, ordinance, and habit of daily life His commands are blended. We *are* not Israelites if we think to live apart from Him or to do aught in which we cannot associate Him by the entreaty for His blessing, and the looking to Him throughout. We are not Israelites if we do not feel our every domestic duty and loving tie sanctified by Him, and bringing us nearer, closer, more lovingly to Him with every passing month. This is to be an Israelite—this is to be the aristocracy of the Lord; for did we so associate our religion with our lives, we must be NOBLE. But how can we attain this, how dare we hope it, if the pursuit of gold, the vain longing for wealth, the idle dream of worldly aggrandisement, the empty rivalship with those richer and higher than ourselves, be the sole end, aim, and being of the Israelite? We look with loud condemnation and scorn on the worshippers of the golden calf—we contemn the worshippers more than we tremble at the awful chastisement from the hand of the Lord—yet let us beware lest our sons too bow before the golden idol. It may take no form, we may not approach it with forms of worship, and priests, and incense, but if it fill up our hearts to the exclusion of all other and nobler thoughts, if its pursuit drag us from the house of God, from our own hearths, deaden us to the love of home ties, prevent the spiritual and enlarged education of our children, what is it to us but as the golden calf to the Israelites of old? And how dare *we* hope to be exempt from the chastisement of God, when it fell upon our brethren?

Oh let us not case up our hearts, and pursue our way in confident security because it is deferred. God works not now as He did then. Israel, in his redemption from Egypt, needed constant, visible, and palpable evidences of the providence and the justice of the Lord. *We* have them not to guide us now, but their *record* is ours, in which to learn our duty and the effects of its neglect or disobedience. That which was displeasing to Him *then*, is displeasing to Him *now;* but, scattered as we are among the nations, deprived through our iniquities of the visible manifestation of His presence, His approval, and His wrath, not on earth may our judgment be known; nor can we "discern between him that serveth God, and him that serveth Him not," till that day when "the Lord shall make up His jewels, and spare those that love Him, as a man spareth his own son that serveth him."

That the long dark ages of persecution originated that fearful indifference to all ennobling pursuits, of which the Hebrew is accused, we quite acknowledge. Deprived of all honourable and elevating employment, of every profession, of every trade, which, bringing them into friendly contact with their fellow-men, would have enlarged their minds and awakened social affections; cowed, crushed, hunted down, and often persecuted for the sake of their wealth; deadened, stupefied to all spiritual elevation, even as the Israelites in Egypt; was it marvel they should cling to gold, and seek its increase, as their sole rank and privilege? For them God had compassion, for He knew how they were tried. It was natural, too, that, even when in lands of comparative freedom and peace, the habits and associations of past years should cling pertinaciously to them still. But their encouragement is no longer guiltless—prosperity, peace, friendly intercourse with some of the nations, are granted us, that we may come back with heart and soul unto our holy law, and strive with all our might against every idol which comes between us and our God. In England, France, Belgium, and America, it is no longer persecution and intolerance that degrade and pronounce us vile. If such feelings do find entrance, it is the prejudice arising from what we *were*. They, as is natural, see not the *cause* of that past degradation; but let *us* make it manifest—let us evince more and more that gold is no longer our sole pursuit—that fraud and cunning, which to the ignorant Gentile are synonymous with the word Jew, are as far from us as from them—that when free we too are noble, honorable, and spiritual to an extent that, if we adhere to our blessed law, only Israelites can be—and prejudice *must* pass away, and Israel be acknowledged the witnesses of the Lord.

It is this noble, this spiritual feeling of independence we would beseech every Hebrew mother to instil into her boy; and which we now humbly, yet earnestly, prayerfully, and heartfully conjure every Hebrew father to aid and confirm. Let not the ears of the infant Israelite be polluted by reference to earthly gain and worldly rivalship, but let him hear often from his father's lips those sweet lessons of heaven and God—of self-denial and its blessed reward—of those purer pleasures of intellect and heart, which, if not infused into his infancy, can never find entrance and dominion in after years. Ably and delightfully would such paternal lessons assist the mother's task, and lighten the blessed yet exquisitely anxious labour of teaching their offspring their proper station in the sight of God and man, and so ennoble, purify, and spiritualise heart and mind, as to render them fit descendants of the princes, priests, and prophets from whom they spring.

And let not such parents fear for their sons' earthly welfare. Such training will not unfit them for the necessary cares and toils of life. It will but render them less engrossing, less worldly, and annihilate every feeling which they would blush to acknowledge before God and man. It will take from life its dross, its stagnating care, teaching them that their duty indeed is to work and persevere alike for their families and themselves, but that in the hand of the Lord is their portion, and that He will order their daily lot as will be most fitted for their eternal welfare. It will remove every temptation to turn aside, for lucre or ambition, from their fathers' faith. It will open heart and hand towards the suffering and the poor; and, removing every selfish feeling and grovelling thought, prepare them for that day when the Lord again shall call them His, and bid them resume that kingly station in the sight of the nations, of which for a "little moment" only, they are deprived.

The suffering Israelites, under the terrible oppression of Pharoah, imagined not the rank to which they would be called by the word of the Lord. While groaning under their heavy burdens, toiling day and night with neither relief or relaxation, could they have imagined that, in their persecuted offspring, princes should arise—that, in a brief interval, Chiefs of their tribes, Heads of families, Captains of well-appointed squadrons

—Priests, sacred in the sight of all the people, and acknowledged by the Eternal—Workers in every elegant art which was needed in the building and embellishment of the Tabernacle—Warriors, dauntless in bravery and skilful in the art of war—Judges, gifted to decide causes, award sentences, and keep civil peace and order amid a disorderly multitude—Princes, of such wealth and consequence as to make the splendid offerings enumerated in the seventh chapter of Numbers—could they have imagined that such would be? Yet such WAS, and such WILL BE. We know not when, we know not how—we only know that the word of God has said it, and that He is a God of truth. Shall we not remember this in the education of our sons, and infuse such feeling as will render them indeed but sojourners in the land of the captivity, watchers, as it were, on the frontiers, prepared to arise and fall into their appointed stations the moment the Lord shall call? Let us welcome in them the inclination for the liberal professions, all that will enlarge the mind and ennoble the heart, and bid them prove, in the sight of the whole Gentile world, that where the Hebrew is FREE, he is brave, enterprising, self-denying, gifted, wise, magnanimous, as the noblest of the nations around him. Let the Hebrew mother give her boy the solid foundation of his glorious faith, and he may go forth in the Nazarene world unharmed; and in other professions, other lines than that of merchant, in which alone till now the Jew has been known, he will honour the name of Israelite.

And if such be the fruit of nursing her child for God, O will not every Hebrew mother feel that she has indeed received "her wages"!

THE EXODUS.

LAWS FOR THE MOTHERS OF ISRAEL.

WE have seen quoted in a Jewish periodical, that "it was for the sake of the righteous women the Lord delivered our ancestors from Egypt." Scriptural authority for this assertion we certainly cannot find, as it is expressly said, "the Lord remembered the promises which He had made to Abraham, Isaac, and Jacob." We only quote it as a proof that the ancient fathers, from whom we believe it taken, could not have had the low idea of women with which they are charged, to have put such an opinion forth, even in suggestion; but must have imagined the righteousness of women of no little importance towards the well-doing of the state. That so, in fact, it is, we have direct scriptural authority to believe; as not only a review of the law will make manifest, but the consequences of the sins of the women in a more distant period. Were not woman an equally responsible agent in the sight of God—were He not in His infinite mercy tenderly careful of her innocence, her honour, her well-doing, her protection by man—no laws for her in particular need have been issued, nor such especial care taken to cleanse her from impurity and guilt, to free her from false charges and an unjust husband, to permit and sanctify her singular vow, and give her every incentive for a chaste, virtuous, and modest life. This need not have been— would not have been—if the Eternal had not, in His compassionating love, regarded His frailer, weaker children with even more tenderness than He looked on man, and resolved on fixing her station and her privileges, and so bringing her forward as an object at once of tenderness and respect—of cherishing, as a wife and daughter—of the deepest veneration as a mother—the especial object of national as well as individual love and protection, as widowed and fatherless—and of the kindest, most fatherly care and gentleness, as the maid-servant. Nay, even the female captive was marked out for fostering and healing kindness, and allowed time for mourning, instead of, as in the case of other nations—aye, even those in later days who call themselves followers of Jesus—being hurried to the bed of the brutal conqueror, who was often still reeking with the blood of her relations. How then can it be said, that in every other religion, save that of the Nazarene, woman's station is degraded, even as the heathen and the slave?

With a mighty arm the Lord had brought forth Israel from the land of bondage, enriched by the spoil, which they did not *borrow* from the Egyptians, as the usual translation renders it, but had *demanded*, as their right from weary years of unpaid labour, and which, terrified at the awful plagues which had befallen them, were granted them at once. "The Lord gave the people favour in the sight of the Egyptians," are words twice repeated, thus doing away at once all idea of the Eternal having favoured fraud, even against his enemies and the enemies of His people. They demanded the long arrears of payment, and they were given, in jewels of silver, and jewels of gold : and so, not by deceit, but in justice, they, to use the Bible language, "spoiled the Egyptians."

The powers of Nature herself succumbed before the mighty will of her Creator. Fire, earth, air, and water, had departed from what is called their natural course, to bring forth Israel from bondage, and to falsify at once the awful denial of a God, in the vain dream of necessity and nature. The sea itself—as the final seal to the stupendous manifestations of Almighty Power displayed in the ten plagues—divided at the word of its Creator, and the host of Israel—men, women, and little children—passed through on dry land, with a watery wall, seeming to unite earth to heaven, on either side. And when the unbelieving scoffers followed—when, denying still the sanctity of Israel, the wonders of Israel's God, the chariots and hosts of Pharaoh dashed on in vain defiance of the Lord— down tumbled the overwhelming mass of mighty waters, and the proud hosts of Pharaoh lay dead before their slaves. And when the song of thanksgiving, of adoration, rose from the hearts and lips of the redeemed, the voice not only of man but of *woman* prolonged the strain. "And Miriam the prophetess, the sister of Aaron, took a timbrel in her hand ; and all the women went after her with timbrels and with dances. And Miriam answered them, Sing ye to the Lord ! for He hath triumphed gloriously. The horse and his rider hath He thrown into the sea."

Woman is not gifted with a silvery voice and an ear for harmony, to devote to the pleasure of man alone. Let her devote them sometimes to the praises of the Lord, and bid the psalm of thanksgiving filling the sanctuary of the Lord be answered from her lips ; and the sweet sanctuary of home, at morning and evening prayer, behold her, leading infant lips to tune their first song in thanksgiving to their Father and their God !

As a general view of the beautiful laws constituting the Mosaic religion does not enter into the plan of this work, we shall throw together those portions on which, as they regard woman, we shall somewhat lengthily treat, without any reference to their probable dates. We know that all the laws forming our religion were given between the departure from Egypt and arrival in the promised land, and are contained principally in chapters 19, 20, 21, 22, 23, and 29 of Exodus—in the whole book of Leviticus—in chapters 5, 6, 8, 9, 15, 16, 17, 27, 28, 29, 30, 35 and 36 of Numbers—and in the whole book of Deuteronomy. From these we shall select and examine all that can give weight to, and throw light upon, the six divisions of our present subject.

As the first and most beautiful relationship in which woman is undeniably necessary to man—the object of his first affections, to whom he owes all of cherishing, happiness, and health, from infancy to boyhood, and often from boyhood to youth ; and who, in consequence, must be entwined with every fond remembrance of childhood, the recollection of which is often the only soother, the only light, in the darker heart of man—it is but just that we should examine, first, how the holy relationship of a MOTHER in Israel is guarded and noticed by our law.

The very first command relative to the duties of man towards man, marks out the position of children with regard to their parents, male and *female*, the representatives of God on earth. It was not enough that such position should be left to the natural impulses of gratitude and affection—not enough that the love and reverence of a child to his parent should be left to his own heart, although in the cases of both Isaac and Jacob such had been so distinctly manifested. No; the same tremendous voice which bade the very earth quake, and the fast rooted mountain reel—which spoke in the midst of thunders and lightnings, "Thou shalt have no other gods but me" —also said, "Honour thy father and thy MOTHER," and added unto its obedience a promise of reward, the only command to which recompense is annexed, that its obedience might indeed be an obedience of love. And lest there should be some natures so stubborn and obtuse that the fear of punishment only could affect, we read in the repetition, and, as it were, enlargement on the ten commandments, "He that smiteth his father or his MOTHER shall surely be put to death, and he that curseth or revileth his father or his MOTHER shall surely be put to death" (Exodus xxi. 15—17). "Ye shall *fear* every man his MOTHER and his father, and keep my sabbaths; I am the Lord" (Levit. xix. 3). "For every one that curseth his father or his MOTHER, shall surely be put to death. He hath cursed his father or his MOTHER, his blood shall be upon him." And again, in Deuteronomy v. 16, we have the repetition of the fifth commandment, the reward attending its obedience still more vividly enforced : " Honour thy father and thy MOTHER, as the Lord thy God hath commanded thee, that thy days may be prolonged, and that it go well with thee in the land which the Lord thy God giveth thee."

With laws like these, bearing on every one of them the stamp of divine truth, of a sacred solemnity which could come from God alone, how can any one believe in, much less assert, the Jewish degradation of woman, or call that JUDAISM which upholds it!

How could these solemn and often reiterated commands be obeyed, if the son of Israel beheld his mother merely the ignorant bond-slave of his father? How could he honour her? What could have such influence upon his moments of passion as to restrain him, when so tempted, from smiting, reviling, or cursing her? How could he *fear* her, when he beheld her trembling before his father, not as her husband, but as her master? But such he saw not. Weaker in frame, from her position and her duties; less mighty in mental powers, yet possessing every attribute to make home blessed, and her children holy followers of God, virtuous and patriotic citizens of their land; shrined in his heart with every memory of his infancy—such was the Hebrew mother to her son. Were the laws obeyed, there could be no neglectful or sinning mother. Not even suspicion could attack her. The law guarded her even from her own relatives, if they falsely wronged her—compelled her, even under the fear of death, to be chaste, holy, virtuous, and faithful in every duty of domestic and public life; and, therefore, it was a labour of love for her children to obey their God in honouring her, and crime worthy of death, if indeed there could be found any sufficiently hardened and rebellious as to disobey.

Again, we find in Deut. xxi. 18, " If a man have a stubborn and rebellious son, which will not obey the voice of his father or the voice of his MOTHER, and who, when they have chastened him, will not hearken unto them, then shall his father and his MOTHER lay hold of him, and bring him to the elders of the city, and unto the gate of his place. And they shall say unto the elders of the city, This our son is stubborn and rebellious; he will not obey our voice. And all the men of his city shall stone him with stones that he die. So shalt thou put away evil from among you, that all Israel shall hear and fear."

We here find at length a practical commentary or example as it were, of the briefer laws on the same subject, given previously. To modern ears, and present notions of false refinement, such commands seem unnaturally harsh and terrible. In those times, they must have been needed, or they would not have been given. And beautifully, even in their harshness, do they demonstrate the reverential duty of Israelitish children to their parents. Still more powerfully do they illustrate the perfect equality of father and mother in respect to their children. It was not only that disobedience to the latter was equally punishable as to the former, but that the voice of the MOTHER was also to condemn her son, or he could not be proved guilty; a peculiarly just law in a nation where more than one wife was allowed. Without it, how often might the more favoured work upon the husband to believe false tales of the offspring of her rival! How often might innocence have been condemned, injustice and cruelty permitted, in a man's own household! Evils effectually prevented by the father's witness being unavailable without that of the accuser's own mother—one, we must feel, not at all likely to come forward against her own child, unless his crimes had been so heinous as to prevent the possibility of her shielding him any longer. We have no recorded instances of such a fearful evil in Israel; but the severe law given in case of such, should never be forgotten by us, marking, as it does, the wrath and justice of the Lord against all those of His chosen people who could forget, neglect, or wilfully abuse, in any one point, their duty to their earthly parents.

Although mothers are not individually commanded to instruct their children in the knowledge of God and His Law, they are certainly joined with the fathers in the performance of that sacred duty. Every statute, every ordinance, given by the Lord to Moses, was always introduced by the command, "Speak ye to the *children of Israel;*" "Say ye to the children of Israel;" or, "Hear, O Israel;" words including the *whole* congregation, male and FEMALE. Had *man* only been included, Moses would have addressed them as sons, or as fathers of tribes, as we find Aaron and his sons, and the priests or Levites, in some few instances particularly specified. That woman is intimately joined with man in the religious instruction of her children, is also proved by the fact that the *mothers* of the kings of Israel and Judah are always mentioned by name, as if to them, yet more than to their fathers, they owed their early impressions of good or evil which their after lives displayed. The very commands regarding parents are strong confirmation. A son could not honour, and fear, and love his mother, if he only owed her his first nourishment, and received nothing at her hand but the same instinctive care as the brute creation display towards their young. The immortal mind and soul of man must have something more to reverence and fear, even if the natural links binding mother and son were sufficient (which we much doubt) to call for love. In commanding reverence and obedience from children, God knew that He had so gifted the Hebrew mother, and so marked her duties and position, as to render such emotions merely her due. To her, then, as well as to the father, are those important injunctions contained in Deut. vi. 20—25, emphatically addressed; and according to the measure of her obedience to them, so will be the measure of her children's reverence and love.

The same chapter, but a few verses previous, had solemnly commanded Israel to love the Lord his God with heart, and soul, and might—to lay his words upon his own heart, and teach them diligently to his children. And, after demanding obedience and righteousness in other statutes, proceeds: "And when thy son asketh thee in time to come, saying, What mean these testimonies, and statutes, and judgments which the Lord our God hath commanded you? Then thou shalt say unto thy son, We were Pharaoh's bondmen in Egypt, and the Lord brought us out of Egypt with a mighty hand; and the Lord shewed signs and wonders, great and sore, upon Egypt, upon Pharaoh, and upon all his household before our eyes; and He brought us out from thence that He might bring us in, to give us the land which He sware unto our fathers. And the Lord commanded us to do all these statutes, to fear the Lord our God, for our good always, that He might preserve us alive, as it is at this day. And it is our righteousness if we observe to do all these commandments before the Lord our God, as He hath commanded us."

On the weighty *all*, which to Hebrew parents is comprised in these emphatic verses, we must not at present linger, save to observe, that much as was required from parents, when the law was given, and in Jerusalem, still more is needed now. We have to add to the history of our bondage and redemption, that of our glory and our sins—of our first captivity and our partial restoration—our renewed and increased iniquities—of the long suffering, long forbearance of an infinitely merciful God—of His averted, yet at length falling wrath—of our exile, our persecution, and misery—all which Moses himself foretold; and yet our never-dying hope, our incentive for constancy, even through the flames of martyrdom, or the more lingering martyrdom of a crushed spirit and broken heart; the imperative necessity of a return unto the Lord through humility and righteousness, trusting in Him to purify and save.

All this must now be added to the parental instruction enforced by Moses: and all this is equally demanded from the mother as from the father, would they receive to its full extent the reverence ordained by God himself. For not by *precept* alone must this instruction be given. The young spirit must be led by example as well as exhortation. Let him see that the instructions of his parents come from the heart as well as lips—influence their thoughts, words, and actions—nay, their very being—and never need they despair. However long it may be before the fruit they have sown appear, it will spring into beautiful maturity at last, and shed its purest fragrance in that hour when the faithful mother watches the rapid approach of that last struggle which shall wing her spirit to the footstool of her God.

Will, then, the Hebrew mother rest content with the station assigned her by the ignorant and the prejudiced, and not strain every nerve, rouse every energy, to make the command of the Eternal for her children to honour and fear her, easy, and joyous to obey.

She has done, and she does this! Not a slur, not a stigma, not a shadow can be flung upon the conduct of Hebrew mothers to their offspring. Neglect, injustice, partiality, want of affection, harshness, coldness flung by fashion between mother and child, that littleness and jealousy which would keep back youthful loveliness for a longer individual reign,— such things may be known—may be common, among other nations, but to the Hebrew they are utterly unknown. It is easy to assert that the woman of Israel is degraded and a slave; but did such false accusers visit a domestic circle—did they but see a Hebrew mother and her children—they would find it difficult to *prove* it. Then letevery son of Israel receive such religious training from his mother, in addition, or rather closely twined, to the moral and intellectual education she has so long given, that he may be ready, from his very boyhood, indignantly to repudiate the charge, and prove, by his whole conduct—alike in public career, as well as his domestic reverence and love—that his mother is as free in the sight of man, as responsible in the sight of God, and as much the possessor of an immortal spirit, as his father and himself.

To the Mosaic religion, then, and to no other, does not only Israel, but every other nation by whom the Bible is acknowledged divine, owe the elevation, the dignity, the holiness of woman as a MOTHER, a position marked out by God himself, and proclaimed and held sacred, not only by the awful threat of punishment, but by the solemn promise of divine reward. How sacred then to every son and daughter of Israel must be their duty to their parents! Disobedience, neglect, scorn, are no longer capital offences according to the justice of man; but, oh! let us not for one moment forget, that the same God who commanded that such they should be, is watching over Israel still, will demand from every child if His command has been obeyed—from every parent if they have done their duty, and taught their children from earliest years, that *disobedience to them is disobedience to their God, and in His eyes, and in His law, a capital offence*. Were this truth more constantly, more impressively enforced, the reciprocal duties of parent and child would be more easily and more happily fulfilled; and the heart-burnings, the anguish, occasioned to parents by neglect and unkindness, and the rebellion and constant struggles of their offspring to fling off an authority which has never been exerted in infancy, and so must gall in youth, alike be at an end, and Israel's homes, as well as Israel's law, proclaim the guiding spirit and loving mercy of the Lord.

THE EXODUS (Continued).

LAWS FOR THE WIVES OF ISRAEL.

THE laws instituted for the protection, the position, the duties, of the wives of Israel, were more peculiar to the manners and customs of the East only than those relative to mothers, which can be obeyed and attended to in every age and clime. Still much was instituted, even with regard to wives, which marked and fixed their position, and decidedly elevated woman in the scale of being, and proved that though, as was just and wise, "her desires must bow to her husband, and he should rule over her," yet that this rule was to be one of perfect confidence and love.

It has always appeared a mystery how any person, even among the Gentiles, who has seriously reflected on and studied the word of God, can assert that it was *only* through the preaching of Jesus and his apostles that woman took her proper station, and those ordinances were given which restrained the passions of men and made marriage a pure and holy tie. Centuries before the advent of Christianity those laws were given which, regarding and prohibiting too near consanguinity in marriage, are acknowledged and obeyed by the whole civilised world. Where do we find, amid the Gentile nations, the purity, the chastity, the stainless virtue of woman, to the extent which is still the glory of Israel, and which owes its origin simply to the laws which were issued by the Lord through Moses; seeming indeed, most terribly severe, but blessed in their very severity by the beautiful purity in Israel which they wrought? Were the law of Moses universally received, how different would be the aspect of the world!

Polygamy was permitted in Israel at the period of the delivery of the law simply because the Eternal's mercy would not interfere with an immemorial usage which his wisdom knew, from local customs and long-indulged habit, would demand violence to be relinquished. The laws he instituted in no way interfered with those habits of His people which custom had endeared; His prescience leaving to time that improvement and greater refinement of the human race which demands ages to accomplish, but which would at length fling aside of itself every fetter that once had linked it to the customs of less enlightened nations. The Eternal never works by superhuman agency when His gracious plans can be accomplished without it. "A thousand years in His sight are but as yesterday when passed, and as a watch in the night;" but His infinite wisdom knew that, to finite man, that period is ever fraught with progression, and His omniscience leaves to time, according to the reckoning of humanity, the effect of His law in the amelioration and improvement of the human race. Our very banishment amid the nations—a banishment occasioned by Israel's sinful abuse of the tender mercies of the Lord—by his *retrogression*, instead of *advancement*, in the glorious career to which he was destined—by his indulgence of every guilty passion, and utter forgetfulness of his father's God to bow down before the idols of his idolatrous wives—this very banishment will purify Israel from the grosser part of his Eastern nature, and render him fitted, by increase of purity and refinement, to become once more the first-born of the Lord, from whose beautiful land those laws shall issue once again to emanate in reviving light and gladness over the whole world.

But, though *permitted* by the Mosaic law, polygamy was so restricted, that the protection, happiness, and well-doing of both wives were provided for; no partiality could permit injustice; the man that did so was punishable by law. "If a man have two wives, the one beloved and the other hated, and they have borne him children both the beloved and the hated, and if the first-born son be hers that is hated, then it shall be when he maketh his sons to inherit all that he hath, that he may not make the son of the beloved first-born before the son of the hated, which is indeed the first-born, but he shall acknowledge the son of the hated for the first-born by giving him a double portion of all that he hath."

The Hebrew term translated *hated* here, as in the case of Leah, does not signify so strong a feeling, but simply the one *less beloved* than the other. And as had already, been practically illustrated in the wives of the Patriarch Jacob, this law provides for, and fixes the perfect equality of both; guarding the less beloved from all the evil effects of indiscriminate partiality, and utterly preventing the father from doing injustice to her offspring. The care taken of every member of a Jewish family—from the strongest to the weakest—by the law of God, would, had that law been obeyed, have effectually prevented that fearful abuse of the Lord's mercy in not interfering with the ancient customs of His people, which in the time of the monarchy so disgraced and desecrated Israel. But let not the scoffer cast the odium of such abuse on the Jewish law. That law was pure—infused with the love, the compassion, the fostering care, the justice, and the severity of the God from whom it came. Its OBEDIENCE would have wrought "the days of heaven upon the earth." Its DISOBEDIENCE, springing from the innate sinfulness of man, wrought evil from the good, and plunged the whole nation of Israel into that fearful abyss of crime which could only be expiated by ages of misery and blood.

But though *allowed* to exist without being considered a crime at the period of the redemption from Egypt, for the reasons stated above, the laws of Moses, relating to conjugal duties, provided for *one wife alone*, thus proving the superior and holier purity of such unions in the sight of God, and thus forcibly marking the distinction between those customs which were to last for ever, through every age, and race, and clime, and those which were merely nationalised from previous habit and association.

The *oneness* of heart and feeling, of purpose and obedience, which was ordained by God himself from the very beginning to exist between husband and wife, and which could only spring from perfect equality, is most beautifully *infused* throughout the law. Inferred from the simple fact that in every recorded instance of enumeration at festivals, eating of holy meats, obedience to commandments, &c., the wife is *not* distinctly mentioned, although every other domestic relation is expressly stated. As *one* with her husband, the wife was included in the emphatic *thou*, to whom the command or ordinance was addressed. The children and servants of a household might have rebelliously turned aside from the precepts of the Lord, but the wife's duty and happiness were *one* with her husband's. Her will was his when that will was guided and sanctified by the will of God. That she could require the divine command individually to keep holy the Sabbath day, to share the feast of the offerings, &c., was a supposition too utterly at variance with her duty as a daughter and wife in Israel, to demand a distinct law—being counted amongst those to whom Moses proclaimed, "When *all* Israel is come to appear before the Lord thy God, in the place which He shall choose, thou shalt read this law before *all* Israel in their hearing; Gather the people together, men, *women*, and children, and the stranger that is within thy gates, that they may hear, and that they may learn, and fear the Lord your God, and observe to do all the words of this law," no Hebrew wife could have needed more, for she, as well as her husband—*one* with him—was the recipient, the obeyer, and the promulgator of every law in which there was no specified distinction of individual duties.

That the omission of wife in the commandments and ordinances which specify other members of the family, cannot be taken in any other light, is proved by the fact that wherever there was a possibility of her occupying a distinct position, or being engaged in any devices or employments contrary to the will of her husband, she is expressly named.

"Thou shalt not covet thy neighbour's *wife*," is emphatically commanded by the same Divine Voice which omitted her, or, rather, included her in the "*thou*" to whom the fourth of the same precepts, whence the line we have quoted was the tenth, was given. Thus guarding her safety and prohibiting the very first thought towards her which could have led to sin.

Again, "If thy brother, the son of thy mother, or thy son, or thy daughter, or the *wife of thy bosom*, or the friend whom thou lovest as thine own soul, entice thee secretly, saying, Let us go and serve other gods, whom thou hast not known, thou and thy fathers, &c., thou shalt not consent unto him, nor hearken unto him; neither shalt thine eye pity, neither shalt thou spare, neither shalt thou conceal him." Here, in intimate conjunction with the preceding commandment, is a positive mention of the wife, supposing her to be actuated by feelings and principles so distinct from her husband as to tempt him to sin. The omission of wives in ordinances where every other member of the household is named is not, then, in any way whatever to suppose her a nonentity, a mere name in Israel, but simply to mark her *oneness* with her husband in every duty to her God and in every command and restriction of His law, addressed to the CHILDREN of Israel and, therefore, binding on them BOTH.

"When a man has taken a wife he shall not go out to war; neither shall he be charged with any business, but he shall be free at home for one year." Were this the whole law, we might justly suppose that the happiness of *man* was alone regarded: but it is not so. Why was this year of release granted him? For his own enjoyment—his own pleasure? No! but to "cheer up"—or, in other words, to make happy—the wife which he had taken. Words how exquisitely descriptive of the Eternal's tender sympathy in the *earthly* happiness of His children. He condescended to enter into the minute details of domestic life; He guarded even their earthly happiness from all contingencies, and proved that He demanded not His love to be realised *only* in sorrow, but that joy—chastened, spiritualised, by gratitude and love—was equally acceptable and blessed.

Man might find happiness apart from his wife, even in the first year of his marriage. The exciting call of war, or the grosser and more engrossing claims of business, might easily obtain such dominion as to render him less careful of his home, less anxious for the happiness of his wife, than were he free. Woman has no such claims to share her heart with her husband. Almost more than any other time in her young existence does she need the protecting care and fostering tenderness of man in the first year of her wedded life. She has left the home of her youth, the fond parents who had lavished on her such love and care, that it seems strange how she can possibly exist without them. She has turned from the occupations, the amusements of her early years—dear from long association—to enter into an entirely new scene, new feelings, new duties, new responsibilities; and for guidance and support, under her God, looks with justice to her husband alone. She may be called upon to battle with sickness and with pain, and she has no mother beside her to give her the fond cares of a tender nurse and take from her all household duties. She has turned from all for the love of one. And how may she be happy if that one be torn from her by the call to war, perhaps never to return; or by civil duties, which, though the lesser evil, might yet check the daily intercourse of mutual love and confidence for which she pines?

But, left "free for one year," how much of felicity, not only for the present, but the future, would that single ordinance bring to both. And must not we, the lineal descendants of those to whom such a revelation of God's love was given, feel, to our heart's core, that God is indeed the God of love which He proclaimed Himself to Moses? Surely no woman of Israel can fear to approach Him, deeming Him a being too awfully holy to look on such as her, when that unapproachable holiness is veiled by such a flood of irradiating love towards her individually, that she is more than weak, is guilty, if she keep aloof, and refuse, under the mistaken plea of too great unworthiness, to clasp the mercy proffered, and fold its healing balsam to her heart. God would not bid us love Him, if we were too unworthy so to do. He would not in His every law, His every promise, demonstrate His compassionating care, His appealing love, His long-suffering mercy, did He deem us too unworthy to receive them. Can the flower that gems the grass give back the loving care that there hath placed, guards, and will renew it? Can the bird give back the fostering love which guards its fragile form, teaches the construction of its tiny nest, and guards its helpless young? Can the insect know and return the Father's love that guards its gossamer life, blesses it with acute sensation, and endows it with such wisdom in the construction of its web, nest, or cell, as to excite man's envy? Yet, has not the Eternal care for these? and will not therefore all Nature confirm His precious word, and tell us He has equal care and equal love for us? True, we have sinned—we do sin—and, alas! will sin again, till that blessed day when the "stony heart shall be replaced with a heart of flesh," which will, unsullied by mortal frailties, cleave unto the Lord. Yet God has given us power to struggle with and resist the evil, if we cannot in this world wholly conquer it. He has told us, that "His ways are not our ways," and, therefore, however incomprehensible to finite man, "in HIM shall the SEED of ISRAEL be justified, and shall glory." He has taught us, in infinite compassion, what we must DO, and how FEEL, to be acceptable in His sight; not in the law alone—for if we study only that in our captivity, we shall be appalled by the ordinances we cannot now perform—but in His prophets and the Psalms, which, as rules of conduct and of feeling, will give us all we need.

As a statute of the Israelitish state, the law we have been considering is no longer obeyed; it cannot be, for we are not now in our own land; but it is the spirit of the ordinance which so nearly concerns us, more especially as women.

To recognise to its full extent the distinction between the ways of God and the ways of man, so beautifully displayed in this our law, let us think one moment on the policy actuating leaders and lawgivers of more modern times, men professing to be guided by the spirit of love and peace. Where, in feudal times, do we find provision thus made for the newly wedded? A stigma, never to be blotted out, would have clung round the name and reputation of that man who would not turn from his home and young wife, even on his marriage day, at the first rude call to lawless, and often most unnecessary war. Where do we find lawgivers, princes and nobles, ever taking into consideration the comfort and peace, we will not even say happiness, of their female followers? Where were laws ever issued for her, to guard with fostering tenderness her gentle virtues, her clinging affections, her domestic charms? Where, save in the law of God? To attract attention, to win respect, to obtain protection, she was compelled to be more *great* than *good*, to leave her natural sphere, and manifest fortitude, bravery, and devotedness, qualities indeed excellent in themselves, but, as proved in the middle ages, only valued for their near relation to the qualities of the warrior, and departure from woman's ordinary habits and home. And by what thousands of suffering women, of all ages, must these characteristics have been unattainable, and in consequence how many thousands left to all the misery of deserted homes, crushed affections, and the countless nameless tortures borne by woman in a lonely unprotected path? And much later than the feudal times, a period but very little removed into the past—shall we say the horrible conscription which devastated France, and every conquered territory owning Buonaparte as master, manifested that care of woman, that tender sympathy in her every feeling, which we are told is only found with the believers in the gospel? We must judge of the divinity of laws by the spirit which, from their observance, emanates over those to whom they are binding. The Jewish law is, on many points, during our captivity, impossible to be observed. Yet we see the spirit of its ancient ordinances still guiding our homesteads, impelling the gentlest and most confiding spirit towards woman in every relation in life. The Hebrew may scarcely be conscious what actuates his tenderness towards his wife and children, but it comes from the spirit of that law, given to his fathers, in which woman was marked as the especial care and protection of the Lord. The law, in form, like the human frame, may die for a time, but the spirit of the ordinances, like the soul of the body, is immortal, and will revive again the shell from which awhile it may have flown.

The Law of Vows is considered by some derogatory to the dignity of woman, by rendering her liable to the will of her husband, and subject to his approval, even in her devoting herself to her God. We will endeavour to prove that the supposition is mistaken. Equally acceptable and responsible as man in the sight of God, still, as we have said before, "her desires were to bow to her husband." She neglected her conjugal duty if she pursued any course, even under the pretence of religious motives, contrary to his will. A singular vow demanded a voluntary relinquishment of domestic duties and enjoyments to devote herself in some way to His service. It is generally supposed in some employments of the Tabernacle, or in the service of His poor, or in the "binding oath to afflict the soul," giving herself up for a certain time to individual fast and prayer. Now few women in Israel, except orphaned single women, and childless widows, could be so independently situated as to make and follow up these vows, without interfering with some nearer domestic duty. Woman's sphere in the law of God, without doubt, is HOME; her noblest attraction, devotedness to those with whom she is there thrown in daily intercourse. Some women there are, who find not only duty, but pleasure there—not only love but safety. Others again, restless and discontented, fancy they should be happier, and better, and more useful, any where but where they are, and gladly seize the first pretence to turn aside.

Spiritual devotedness is too often a worldly snare, and the pride of holiness the most dangerous temptation which can possibly assail us. We have often heard (amongst the Gentiles indeed, not amongst ourselves, for we have unhappily too few enthusiasts of any kind) of what is termed a saint (we abhor the falsity of the term, but we are using now the language of the world). One avowedly devoted to the cause of religion; passing hours in her closet, surrounded by religious books, all, we may observe, *commentaries*, but not the *Word of Life* itself; or, with religious friends, wearing a peculiar dress, and most peculiar manners; visiting the poor, more often with tracts than food; censuring every innocent amusement as profane, and temptations of Satan; bearing words of humility on the lips, but of pride in heart; outwardly condemning and abhorring her own sins, but inwardly thanking God that she is so much holier than others: robing religion in such dark and terrible colours, that the young spirit shrinks from it, and plunges in the world with renewed zest, to escape from the faintest semblance of its acceptance.

If there be such, mistaken they certainly are; but their judgment rests with Him whom they seek after their own thoughts to serve, not with their brother man, who, without some more true and sacred guide, might equally be led astray. We have merely alluded to this class of religious enthusiasts, more clearly to manifest the evil which the law of vows effectually excluded, but which, without such law, might, from the holiness pervading God's people, have been more than likely to ensue.

Man did not need such restraint upon his "singular vows;" because, in the first place, he was more independent than woman ; in the next *reason*, not *feeling*, being his guide, he was not likely to fall into the temptation of ill-regulated enthusiasm, even in his holiest and dearest duty. Woman's guide in general is feeling; she is a creature of impulse, ever likely, unless strongly yet tenderly restrained, to turn aside from the safer and less excitable path of daily duty, wherever the affections, or the enthusiasm of the moment may lead. More especially is she likely to fall into this temptation when first awakened to the claims, and beauty, and comfort of religion. The simple duties of home then seem little worth, compared to the service of heaven. Herself, her parents and brothers, husband and children, appear of slender consequence compared to the state of her affections and faith towards God. The perfect compatibility of her duties towards God and towards man is unperceived. She cannot realise that the unfatiguing, unexciting duties of domestic usefulness, infused with thoughts of God and of His word, is the path most acceptable to Him. And severing, instead of uniting, she neglects what she deems the lesser, to pursue the greater duty.

Many avenues were open to the wives of Israel to tempt the taking "singular vows." The birth of children, the recovery from illness, escape from danger, receipt of some unexpected blessing, dread of impending sorrow, or misfortune extraordinarily averted, and sin repented of, all these might, in the close links which, when the law was given, bound Israel to the Lord, and in the warm passionate emotions of Eastern women, have impelled either the vow of service, to make manifest their thanksgiving, or the vow of affliction by fasting and prayer, to propitiate the Lord and turn away his wrath. And this vow might be taken in a moment of strong feeling, without sufficient thought as to the possibility of its performance, without interfering with the comforts of her husband and children, or her duties to her household. Was it not, then, just and wise, that the impetuous feeling of woman should be guided and tenderly restrained by the calmer, stronger reason and foresight of man?

But that this dependence on her husband in no way subjected her to his *caprice*, is proved by the law which we will extract at length. "If a woman shall vow a vow unto the Lord, and bind herself by a bond . . . And if she had at all a husband when she vowed or uttered aught out of her lips wherewith she bound her soul; and her husband heard it, and held his peace at her in the day that he heard it, then her vows shall stand, and her bonds wherewith she bound her soul shall stand. But if her husband disallowed her on the day that he heard, then he shall make her vows which she vowed, and that which she uttered with her lips, wherewith she bound her soul, of none effect, and the Lord shall forgive her. . . . . Every vow, and every binding oath to afflict the soul, her husband may establish it, or her husband may make it void. *But if her husband hold his peace at her from day to day, then he establisheth all her vows, or all her bonds which are upon her. He confirmeth them, because he held his peace at her in the day that he heard them. And if he shall any ways make them void, after that he hath heard them,* THEN HE SHALL BEAR HER INIQUITY" (Numbers xxx. 3, 6, 7, 8, 13, 14, 15).

We here find most particular care taken to shield woman from that indecision and caprice from which she is so often the innocent sufferer.

The honour, respect, and deference which should characterise a wife's conduct and feelings towards her husband, is first enforced, for the unperformed vow, or the breaking the vows of the lips, the Lord will forgive her, because they have been disallowed by her husband. But they must be disallowed *when taken.* If from indecision, or weakness, or unkindness, in the determination to thwart the wishes of his wife, he neither forbids nor confirms, but remains silent, that silence, in the sight of God and to his wife, is CONFIRMATION. He has no power capriciously to prevent the fulfilment of her bond or vow by declaring that silence is not consent, and he does not choose that her vow shall be performed. He cannot do this. His very caprice is effectually prevented, for, if he acts thus, the woman's breach of vows will indeed be forgiven to her, but HE SHALL BEAR ITS INIQUITY—a law whose beautiful justice marks its divine origin more forcibly than almost any other guiding the conduct of husband and wife.

No human legislator could have enacted it, for what lawgiver of earth could have gone so deeply into the very heart of man, and guarded the domestic relations of life from such petty yet constant misery as caprice?

One most consoling truth we learn by this law: it is in itself a direct and positive refutation of the charge brought against us, that Jewish women have no access to God—no right whatever to interfere with the requirements and ordinances of religion. Were woman the creature of a day, passing hence to be no more, with neither hope of reward nor liability to wrath, beyond this world, why should she have the power of making vows at all ; and so solemnly, that did man interfere with their due performance, he should bear her iniquity, and woman—aye the despised and degraded woman—should be forgiven ?

The candid and unprejudiced reader of the word of life, be his faith what it may, must perceive how mistaken is such a charge ; and let not, then, our young sisters be tempted to quit their native fold for another, where they are told greater privileges await them, both as women and as immortal beings. Let them not be terrified by the charge that, as Jewish women, they are soulless slaves. But let them come to the word of God, and prove that *there* is their shield, *there* is their defence. That there their God Himself has revealed a love and care for His weaker children, too deeply, too nearly, too blessedly for them to need aught else ; that there is their hope, as there is their consolation.

Yet more to protect his feebler creation from the fierce passions and unjust accusations of Eastern natures, the Most High, in His infinite mercy, instituted the law of jealousy, an awful and most terrible law, yet one which every *innocent* woman must have hailed with thankfulness, and which every *guilty* woman must have died ere she could have faced. The various sins prohibited by the voice of God Himself, in His Ten Commandments, are all in His sight of equal magnitude, and, therefore, without any reservation whatever, were all punishable with death. And well had it been for the purity, virtue, and happiness of man, had this blessed law continued in force as it was given, and thence had emanated over the whole world. It has been called a law of fire and blood, given but to destroy and be destroyed. But the charge is false. The Eternal knew the natures of those to whom it was given —that severity was needed for the time ; and had that severity been used, and the law literally and purely OBEYED, even as it was intended, each generation would have been purer and more spiritual than the former, till that holiness was at length universally attained, which would indeed have brought " the days of heaven on the earth ;" and Israel would not now have been persecuted and tortured in some lands, and an exile and a wanderer, houseless and priestless, in them all!

Adultery, even as idolatry, sabbath-breaking, murder, &c., was punishable by death. In Israel, the ruthless spoiler of man's dearest shrine—his home—sacrificed not only his honour (which, however high-sounding, to such characters must be but a name), not only his standing and his wealth, but his LIFE. Aye, and not the tempter only, but his wife, the mother, who could fling misery upon a tortured husband, and undying shame upon her helpless babes. Yet amid a people irascible and fierce, too liable to jealousy to examine calmly and justly, as we know is the case at this very day with every Eastern nation, a law was imperatively needed to protect the helpless and innocent, alike from false charges and a husband's unjust hate. No man could take justice into his own hands. He dared not injure the reputation, or take the life of his wife, without having her guilt proved by God Himself. A false accusation had no power to fling shame upon her, or render her station doubtful, as it would now. The Most High Himself interfered in her defence, and proved in the face of the whole people, her innocence and honour; as, where she guilty, He took into His own hands her punishment, and the manifestation of her guilt.

The law of jealousy is not in general regarded by the women of Israel as it ought to be. False refinement shrinks from it as a thing perfectly unnecessary and antiquated now. Nay, perhaps, as a law so horrible, so indelicate, that they wonder that it is not expunged from the Bible. By us it is welcomed as another most consoling and unanswerable proof of the Eternal's tender mercy towards us. The full extent of its use and justice can only be realised by contrasting it with the statutes of the southern and eastern nations, with those quick passions and excitability, Israel, when the law was given, had more in common than with the cooler and more dispassioned north.

With the followers of Mahomet does not a mere thought, a mere suspicion, unaided by the very shadow of proof, commit the helpless woman to a watery grave, with none to interfere in her behalf, or mourn her when at rest—none to clear her name, or bring the false and cruel husband to justice and to shame? And amidst those bearing the Christian name, do not the Italian and Spaniard make as murderous use of the stiletto or the drugged cup, as the Moslem of the sack? That such misery is seldom heard of in Protestant countries, comes not from actual law, but from that greater civilisation and refinement, which must spring from public and private communion with the BIBLE. This is the safeguard of Protestant women, and this they owe to the spirit of that law given to us by God Himself. Some among the Gentiles there are, honest and spiritual enough to acknowledge this; and from our very heart we honour such honest lovers of truth. But others, and unhappily the greater number, there are who fling shame and dishonour upon the women of the very people for whose safety those blessed laws were framed, the spirit of which is now guiding the Protestants themselves.

By contrasting the laws vouchsafed to us with those guiding the Gentiles of all denominations, we learn to know the true value of the blessed faith which we possess, and are armed against all insidious efforts to turn us from it. But this can never be whilst the women of Israel regard the laws of Moses only in a national and local, not in an individual, view, believing that, because they are no longer in actual use, they only relate to them in their several positions in Jerusalem, and do not in the least concern them now.

They do concern us, most nearly and most consolingly. He whose infinite mercy gave them has not cast us from His love, though, for a time, compelled for our sins to bear witness to the nations of His justice and His wrath. Yet for us, as a people, and each of us individually, He bears the same infinite long-suffering love which He bore to our ancestors in Egypt. We learn this from every prophet, who never spoke of sin without holding forth forgiveness, who never prophesied dispersion and banishment without comforting with the promise of restoration; and we know the extent of our Father's love towards us by every statute of His law.

The interference of the Most High in cases similar to those calling for the law of jealousy, the wives of Israel may no longer need; but are there none in minor circumstances wrongfully accused? None needing a Father who knoweth every secret thought and inward struggle, to whom to look when man may wilfully wrong, or blindly misappreciate? None who struggle on in the petty, but how sadly wearying, trials of daily life, to do what seems the best, to act the kindest, to banish every throb of self, and sacrifice all of individual comfort and enjoyment to further the comfort and the wishes of another, yet finds her every effort turned against herself, and armed with acutest woe? In such cases, and who shall say there are none such, where can woman turn, but to her God? Where find consolation, save in the belief that her innocence, her efforts, rest with Him, and He will one day make them known? Where shall her heart, bleeding and torn from its earthly rest, find peace save in His love? O what woman, bearing the name of Israel, can hesitate one moment to pour forth her every grief to Him, and feel she is individually His care, and He will plead her cause?

The express commands relating to the marriages of the priests is another beautiful proof of woman's perfect equality in Israel, and compatibility to be holy unto the Lord, by sharing the holiness of His elected servants; a proof also that in His service the Eternal demanded no sacrifice of human affections. They were, indeed, to be sanctified to Him, to be infused with His spirit, and so to become a blessing and a joy to His servants; but never to be annihilated and so give temptation for the most awful abuses and crimes, as in the monastic seclusions of the Roman church. The sanctity, the purity, which was to attend the wife of the priest, was a further incentive to the purity and holiness of the women in Israel. Superiority of actual ranks there was none, but superiority in virtue there was, and to gain that superiority was in the power of all women under the guidance of the law. The priests were the very highest and noblest in the sight of the people, being the elect of the Lord, and the ministers of His will. How pure then and holy must have been the ambition to become worthy of selection as the priests' wives, and how beautifully is the superior holiness and sanctity of the women of Israel brought forward by the simple fact that the priests of the Lord might only choose a wife from "their own people!"

It is evident then, from every law we have regarded, that, instead of being degraded and enslaved, the wives in Israel were peculiarly and especially objects of the Eternal's love. For their safety, their honour, those laws were issued, now recognised by the greater part of the civilised world; and all those who deny this shake the very foundations of the whole system of morality, under whatever creed it may be found. The Gentile is in very truth "debtor to the Jew" for far more than he acknowledges; for every law unconsciously guiding and sanctifying his domestic relations, refining his own conduct, elevating his own mind—for every law blessing his home with a faithful wife, respected mother, and duteous child. That, therefore, any woman can fling odium on the Jewish law, can only excite our pity towards her. The innocence, honour, and purity, and domestic, social, and religious duties of wives, being more clearly and unanswerably developed in the sacred canon of the Mosaic law than in any other, from the very simple fact that every other is founded upon them.

THE EXODUS (CONTINUED).

LAWS RELATING TO THE WIDOWS AND DAUGHTERS OF ISRAEL.

BEFORE regarding the laws instituted for the widows of Israel, let us pause one moment on the full tide of anguish and unprotected isolation comprised to woman in that one word "widow," that we may comprehend our Father's love to the full extent. What woman's heart, awake to kind and generous feelings, can look upon a widow without sympathy—without the yearning prayer that consolation may be granted her and her fatherless babes find friends to guide them through a stormy world ? We know no description so thrillingly powerful of this, the heart's desolation, as the lines we subjoin.

> "Lone sharer of a widowed lot,
> Where is the language, though a Seraph hymned
> The poetry of heaven, to picture thee,
> Wrecked as thou art, *whose life has now become*
> *Affliction's martyrdom ? for such is love*
> *Doomed to remain on desolation's rock*
> *And look for ever where the past lies dead.*
> What is the world to thy benighted soul ?
> *A dungeon !* Save that where thy children's tones
> Can ring with gladness its sepulchral gloom.
> Placid and cold, and spiritually pale
> Art thou. The lustre of thy youth is dimmed,
> The verdure of thy spirit o'er. In vain
> The beaming eloquence of day attracts
> Thy heart's communion with creation's joy.
> *Like twilight imaged on a bank of snow*
> *The smile that waneth o'er thy marble cheek.*"
>
> ROBERT MONTGOMERY.

Such, indeed, is the earthly sadness of the widow. *One with him who has departed*, how may she tread the earth's dark vales alone? Where look for love to supply the place of that now gone? Where find a father for those babes, clinging to her for that support, that love, which in her first bereavement she feels utterly unable to bestow? Where but in Him, who in His law so especially provides for her and for her fatherless children? And, by his prophets, reinforces the statutes already given, and brings forward their *neglect* as one of the manifold sins, which called down His displeasure.

We find in His gracious word not alone the command, but the severe penalty attached to its disobedience, first in Exodus xxii. 22, 23, 24—" Ye shall not afflict any widow or fatherless child. If thou afflict them in any wise, and they cry at all unto ME, I will surely hear their cry, and my wrath shall wax hot, and I will kill you with the sword; and your wives shall be widows, your children fatherless."

Can any language more emphatically and forcibly denote the tender mercy of the Eternal? His love made their sorrows His own. As a positive sin against Himself, He threatened to afflict all those who dared afflict them by the infliction of similar suffering. He knew that, left to man's mercy, the widow and the fatherless would often meet with oppression, fraud, and injustice; be defrauded of their natural rights, and afflicted by hard creditors. Not only as a widow, called upon to bear "affliction's martyrdom," but, as a mother, to behold her children a prey to suffering and want. In Israel this could not be. The widow and the fatherless were God's own, for He knew that not alone the wife, but the mother must be cared for.

"Leave thy fatherless children to ME," He said by His prophet Jeremiah at a time when misery, desolation, and destruction were falling on Judæa and her sons for their awful iniquity. "Leave them to ME, and I will keep them alive. And let Thy widows trust in ME." Even then, when disobedience and idolatry had so cursed the land that His wrath could no longer be withheld, He reiterated the gracious promise given in His law. Sunk into the lowest depth of iniquity, how could the widow and orphan be protected if left to the care of man? Where might they look at such a season but to their God, who for them alone had mercy and long suffering still?

The ruin and worldly misfortunes and trials, so often now the portion of the widow, could not exist in Israel. The nation at large was commanded to provide for them, and in every feast of offerings or of festivals, and in the ingathering of their corn, and oils, and fruits, to include the widow and the fatherless: laws not once, but several times repeated. "When thou cuttest down thy harvest in thy field, and hast forgotten the sheaf in the field, thou shalt not go again to fetch it, but it shall be for the stranger, the FATHERLESS, and the WIDOW. When thou gatherest the grapes of thy vineyard thou shalt not glean it again, it shall be for the stranger, the FATHERLESS, and the WIDOW."

Nor was this all. The tithes of wine, corn, and oil, the firstlings of herds and flocks, all of which were devoted to the service of the Lord, that all worldliness and niggardliness should be banished from Israel, and "they should learn to fear the Lord their God always." The feast of Weeks and of the Tabernacles, when the families of Israel rejoiced before the Lord in the place which He chose, the WIDOW and the FATHERLESS were included. There was to be no affliction, no dependence, no sorrow in Israel (though the poor were not to cease out of the land) at these times. *All* were to rejoice before the Lord. And yet more in addition: "At the end of three years thou shalt bring forth the tithe of thine increase the same year, and lay it up within the gates. And the Levite, because he hath no part or inheritance with thee, and the stranger, and the FATHERLESS, and the WIDOW, which are within thy gates, shall come, and shall eat and be satisfied, that the Lord thy God may bless thee in all the work of thine hand which thou doest." And so important was obedience to this statute that its profession was necessary in the confession of him who came to offer the basket of first-fruits as a sign of his having come unto the land of his inheritance. "Then shalt thou say," proceeded the instruction of the priest, "before the Lord thy God, I have brought away the hallowed things out of mine house, and also have given them to the Levite, and the stranger, and the FATHERLESS, and the WIDOW, according to all thy commandments which thou hast commanded. I have not transgressed thy commandments, neither have I forgotten them" (Deut. xxvi. 12, 13).

Again, in Deut. xxiv. 17, it is not enough that we have already heard, "thou shalt not afflict them," under the awful penalty of similar affliction from the hand of God, but prohibition as to the manner of that affliction is expressly pointed out. "Thou shalt not pervert the judgment of the stranger, nor of the FATHERLESS, nor take a WIDOW'S raiment to pledge." Why? Because they had no earthly friend to redeem the latter, or plead for the former. Weak and unguarded, they were exposed to all these evils had not the Eternal, in His tender compassion, taken them under His own especial care, and, instead of compelling them to depend on the insecure tenure of man's compassion, or even justice, instituting laws for their benefit, the disobedience of which was *sin* unto Himself.

Had these laws been obeyed, it was impossible for the widow and the fatherless, however destitute they might have been left, to suffer mere worldly ills. The agony of the widowed wife could not be increased by the thought of how she was to provide for her fatherless little ones. The Lord was their guardian, and He gave her and her children the gentle care and affection of their brethren in Israel; bidding her cry unto Him in sorrow and affliction, for He would assuredly hear her cry, and punish those who called it forth.

What nation then, what code, however just, however perfect, ever framed such laws as these? "What nation," in truth, "has God so near to them as Israel in all we call upon Him for?" Were no other laws relative to woman instituted, these alone would be sufficient to mark that their very weakness rendered them objects, even more than man, of compassion and love, for where has God provided for man as for woman in the desolation of her widowhood?

That modern Judaism cannot obey these laws now, as when they were given, interferes not with the fact of their institution itself. This very charge, reiterated, enforced, as it is, elevates woman and excites towards her not alone the humanity and tenderness, but the *respect* of man. How could he feel otherwise towards those whom God Himself has promised to protect? What stronger incentive could he have to be forbearing and gentle towards her, and in no way to afflict her, than that if he failed in kindness, his wife should be widowed, his children fatherless? Where shall we find a law to disannul this, proceeding, as it does, from the mouth of God?

To the women of Israel at the present day how inexpressibly consoling are these laws. In form they can no longer be obeyed, but, as in the case of the statutes relating to wives, it is the spirit pervading them which we must take to our hearts, till they swell in grateful thankfulness to Him who from His throne in heaven condescends to make widows His especial care. And He does so *now* as then. God is immutable—a Spirit of Truth, knowing not the shadow of a change; and, therefore, do we know and feel that the same love from which issued those beautiful laws actuates His dealings with His people now. It is vain, utterly vain, to say we are cast off, and therefore cannot claim it. The Bible teems with passages relating to our banishment alone, and to the Eternal's deep love borne towards us while in captivity, and consequently towards us now. We could multiply passages on passages from the Pentateuch, Psalms, and Prophets, to prove this. But the very words already quoted from Jeremiah would be almost sufficient. When they were pronounced, the sins of Jerusalem were far more heinous than those of Israel in her captivity. Yet even then God took the fatherless and the widow under His fostering care; separating them, for the innocence of the one, and the unprotected weakness of the other, from the mass of iniquity which desecrated Judea.

As concerns His compassion towards us now, we shall find them so distinctly, so clearly enforced in Leviticus xxiv., particularly from verse 40 to the end, and in the whole of Deuteronomy xxx., that to doubt and keep back, from a supposition of our inability to approach our God, and claim His love in our captivity, becomes actual guilt, and is likely not only to throw a wider and wider barrier between Him and ourselves, but to expose us more dangerously than any other temptation to the sophisms of the Nazarene, who in mistaken kindness, would terrify us from our sole rock of refuge and strength, by insisting that, cast out from the Lord's favour as we are, nothing can save us from eternal perdition but the acceptance of their faith. The more solid sense and unimpassioned reason of man may, and do, effectually guard him from such danger; but woman's quicker feeling, and more easily blinded judgment, need all the defence and rest in a divine love which the study of her own faith, and its manifold manifestations of the Eternal as a God of truth and love, alone can give. No argument is more likely to weigh with a strong-feeling, unguarded woman, knowing little or nothing but the mere formula of her own religion, than the idea, if pressed at a right moment, that the law of Moses is a law of fire and blood given only to destroy, and that the religion of Jesus is one of love; that Jewish women can have no comfort in adversity, but that as Christians they will find all they need : that in the one Faith they must feel themselves degraded, as in the other exalted and secure.

Now, without affecting actual *creed* at all, temptations like these, unless fully and faithfully convinced that we, as women of Israel, have privileges still higher, must on some dispositions fall with sufficient weight as so to confuse and entangle, that even belief is adopted ere we are at all aware of what we are about. We allude not to those whom reason only guides —who, cold, unimaginative, passionless themselves, laugh at feeling, because they know it not—who find philosophy always sufficient for their need. But the larger portion of women— creatures of mere feeling and impulse—we would beseech to come to the Word of God, and derive thence, in the days of youth and happiness, that peace, love, and consolation, which if unknown till "the evil days come, and the years when thou shalt say, I have no pleasure in them," may be sought, from very blindness and wilfulness, in a stranger fold. The arguments we have quoted would fall to the ground by the simple answer, that as women of Israel we *have* ALL we need ; that God revealed His deep love to us ages before He became known to our Gentile sisters ; that while we possess His blessed Word, we can never feel too unworthy to claim the tenderness He so proffers. He Himself has given us privileges in every relation and position in life which no other nation has, except as derived from us, and that, instead of fire and blood, the whole Jewish law to woman teems with LOVE.

These feelings, inculcated in childhood, felt and experienced in riper years, will be sufficient for woman, and enable her to realise all the blessed consolation which every law relating to her so spiritually bestows. Not to widows only, but to all who are in affliction, the Divine spirit infusing every law *must* bring comfort, by evincing how closely, how consolingly, she is drawn to God.

Can the widow and the fatherless in Israel recall this truth, yet not bless God that the record of His law is still our own, granted that in times of dispersion and banishment we might not despair, even though the form of the law must be, till our restoration, at an end ? O let the afflicted take comfort. She has but to believe and obey, and the deep compassion of her God will perfect both, and render them acceptable. Let her but think on the magnitude of that love which has provided

for her both as widow and mother. That by *name* she is
singled out as especially the object of Divine solicitude, and,
therefore, that the Eternal knew, and knows, the heaviness of
her trial, the extent of her deep sorrow, the pressure of her
cares. Let her recall every law given for the widow and the
fatherless, and remember that He who gave them knows not
the shadow of a change, and, therefore, feels for her now as
tenderly as He did for her ancestors of old. What is time to
Him? We look back with our finite gaze, and think there is
such a wide distinction between past and present, that the
laws given for the one can in no way concern the other.
Customs, manners, all of *earth may* change, but not the
nature of the immortal soul, nor of the human heart. From
the beginning of the world, until the end, these *were, are,* and
will be the same. And so is HE from whom they spring, and
who guides and cares for them now as when He first grafted
them into man. What, then, is time to Him? Can frail
finite humanity believe that *time* has changed His tenderness
towards His afflicted children? O who would throw such
scorn, such disrespect on that word which repeats and enforces
in every manner of expression, "I, even I, am He, that
changeth not; therefore ye sons of Israel are not consumed?"
Let the widows of Israel take to their hearts every law which
manifests His love towards them as widows. They are as
much theirs *now* as at the moment they were given. Let
them not believe, for a single moment, that the superior holiness of their ancestors, gave them greater favour in the sight
of their God. He saith, "Not for your own sakes will I do
this, O Israel, for ye are a perverse and rebellious generation,
but for the sake of the covenant I swore unto your fathers,
Abraham, Isaac, and Jacob." And again in strong confirmation, "For mine own sake, even for mine own sake, will I do
it; for how should my name be polluted: and I will not give
my glory to another" (Isaiah xlviii). With such words, how
may we hesitate? Come unto Him, ye widows of Israel, for
ye are HIS. Clasp to your hearts His love. Think not ye
can weary it, for "God is not man, that He should lie, nor
the son of man, that He should repent." Let no thought of
unworthiness keep us back, for not in our own righteousness,
but in His must we trust. And O believe in Him—trust in
Him; and, as the widows of old, in our very affliction we
shall be comforted, and to the Gentiles show forth His glory.

Our next section, the Daughters of Israel, while it principally relates to the duties of our younger sisters as inferred from the laws concerning them, also brings much important matter to light, regarding the equality of women.

In every command and ordinance relative to obedience to parents, to the eating of holy things (Levit. xi. 14; Deut. xii. and xvi.) to appearing and rejoicing at the various festivals (Deut. xvi.) daughters, equally with the sons, are so emphatically specified, that it is impossible to believe that the religious as well as the moral duties of the law are not equally incumbent on *woman* as well as man. It is useless to transcribe the verses which point this out, as they will be found, in their own simple force of expression, in the chapters of the Lord's own Word quoted above. Were the maidens of Israel to keep aloof from all religious observances, to be bound to household duties and frivolous employments, become authorised to leave all the concerns of an immortal soul and of eternity to the care of fathers, husbands, or brothers, we should find no mention of such a class of beings. Nay, had the Eternal even intended that their fitness or unfitness for His service should depend on the judgment of man, we should still find only the sons mentioned. But to remove this entirely, the attendance of the maidens of Israel at every rejoicing, etc., becomes an *absolute command* from God, and its disobedience, neglect, or change, was sin against Himself. Such laws as those of Mezuzzot or Tephilim were given in an indeterminate manner, requiring the aid of the priest to decide who should wear the latter, and how use the former; but the obedience of the daughters of Israel, with their brothers, unto every ordinance, is so clearly and simply put, that the mind must indeed be perverted who would seek to deprive them of such blessed privileges, and insist that religion is too deep a thing for woman.

God bade woman as well as man love Him with heart, and soul, and might; knowing that to all who did so, the comprehension of His will, His attributes, was comparatively easy, and obedience to His every statute a labour of rejoicing and love. To learn and to feel this in youth, woman, equally with man must be *taught* to know and love the Lord, not left to the mere practice of forms; must be taught, that to appear at His festivals, to keep His ordinances, to obey His commandments, are privileges of joy, granted to them in the fulness of

God's love, and mark the distinction between His rule and that
of every other. They would be led to compare their station
and their privileges as maidens of Israel, with those of the
women of Greece and Rome, and every contemporary nation,
and, in more modern times, with the women of many a
Gentile land. Civilisation, and a study and practice of
the moral laws of the Bible, are doing their work, and pervading
the customs and feelings of the Nazarene world; but their
guiding law breathes not the Eternal's especial care for woman,
in her every relation of life, more forcibly than ours does.

That the daughters of Israel must have had the power to
obtain influence over their fathers, even to persuade them to
evil, is proved by their being specially named in the law already
quoted, regarding the punishment of all those, be they brother,
son, DAUGHTER, wife, or friend who enticed to idolatry.

Again, we are told in Deut. vii. 2, 4, alluding to the care
needed to preserve the Israelites a holy people, and prevent all
communion with the idolatrous nations around: "Thou shalt
make no covenant with them, nor show mercy to them; neither
shalt thou make marriages with them; thy DAUGHTER thou
shalt not give unto his son, nor his daughter shalt thou take
unto thy son. For they will turn away thy son from following
ME, that they may serve other gods, etc. For thou art an holy
people unto the Lord thy God. The Lord thy God hath chosen
thee to be a special people unto Himself, above all the people
that are upon the face of the earth."

"Son," in the sentence "for they will turn away thy son,"
etc., evidently signifies both son and daughter, as both are
specifically named in the preceding verse, and the Hebrew
word בֵּן, though always translated *son*, is equivalent to the
English noun *child*, for which there is no distinct Hebrew term,
" Children of Israel," is written in Hebrew exactly as if it were
translated, "sons of Israel" (בְּנֵי יִשְׂרָאֵל), but it evidently
and unanswerably includes both sexes, by the words already
quoted: "Gather the people together, men, women, and
children," and other verses of similar import. As Israel had
been already warned against giving his daughter in marriage to
a son of Canaan, she is, of course, included in the danger thence
ensuing, although only "son" is mentioned; the plural meaning
of that "son" being evident from the pronoun following it
being *they* instead of *he*. "For they will turn aside thy child
from following ME, that THEY may serve other gods."

Now if nothing depended on women in Israel to uphold and make manifest the glory of their God, in obedience to His law and in serving Him, what necessity was there for this law? If her soul was of less moment than that of man, why should it have been so carefully guarded from pollution? This law of itself would be sufficient to prove to the daughters of Israel their solemn responsibility, not only individually, but *nationally;* and we shall find still more.

In Numbers xxvii., we read that the daughters of Zelophehad came "before Moses, and all the princes of the congregation," and, boldly stating the death of their father without sons, enquired, " why should the name of our father be done away from among his family because he had no sons? Give us therefore," they continued, " a possession among the brethren of our fathers. And Moses brought their cause before the Lord. And the Lord spake unto Moses, saying, The daughters of Zelophehad speak right. Thou shalt surely give them a possession of an inheritance among their father's brethren, and thou shalt cause the inheritance of their father to pass unto them. And thou shalt speak unto the children of Israel, saying, If a man die, and have no son, then shall ye cause his inheritance to pass unto his daughter."

Now this simple narration very clearly proves that the civil, as well as religious, privileges were protected and ensured. Here are five unmarried women, most probably young, and acting on no guidance but their own sense of right and justice, as inculcated by the whole law of Moses, unhesitatingly addressing their great Lawgiver, in presence of all the heads of Israel, and fearlessly stating their case. Their position must have been one of perfect freedom, or they could not so have sought Moses, and not only been heard, but, because he did not feel himself adequate to pronounce a decision on a case never before occurring, their cause was brought by him before the Lord, and God Himself deigned to reply. They had spoken right, the Eternal said: the inheritance should be as they said, not only to them, but ever after, as a law in Israel.

We see here, not only the daughters of Israel protected and established in their birthrights, but the practical illustration of the Eternal's gracious promise repeated in Deut. x. 17, 18, " For the Lord your God is a God of gods and Lord of lords, a mighty and a terrible who regardeth not persons, nor taketh reward, but does execute the judgment of the FATHERLESS and the widow." The daughters of Zelophehad were *fatherless;* perchance (for such is human nature), surrounded by those who disputed their right, deeming that woman could have no civil privileges; compelled to do violence to their feminine nature, and make an appeal; whereupon God, not man, took their judgment in His own hands and gave them right. The supposition of their having to encounter human opposition, is further confirmed by the event of the thirty-sixth chapter of Numbers. The chief fathers of the tribe of Manasseh, to which Zelophehad belonged, came before Moses and the heads of Israel, stating the inconvenience of female inheritance, as being likely to be lost by marriage with some other tribe; and in the jubilee, when every man returned to the inheritance of his fathers, the portion inherited by daughters would be amalgamated with the inheritance of the tribe whereunto they were received. This difficulty, to mere human reasoning, would have seemed so to interfere with the statute already given, that man would have been at a loss how to overcome it. But that which God has once said, He altereth not; and He bade Moses inform the children of Israel, that "the tribe of the sons of Joseph had said well. This is the thing which the Lord doth command concerning the daughters of Zelophehad, saying, LET THEM MARRY TO WHOM THEY THINK BEST; only to the tribe of the family of their father shall they marry. And every daughter that possesseth an inheritance in any tribe of the children of Israel, shall be wife unto one of the families of the tribe of her father, that the children of Israel may enjoy every man the inheritance of his fathers."

Even in this law, so important for the peace and harmony of the tribes of Israel, the Eternal disdained not to care also for the temporal happiness of His weaker children, by expressly stating, that their choice was to be he *whom they think best;* bounded, indeed, by the tribe of their father, amongst whom as they principally associated it was most natural their choice should fall. No arbitrary law interfered with domestic happiness. Neither consanguinity, fortune, nor any of the modern reasons, impelling unions of convenience, of ambition, or of any kind but of the heart, interfered with woman's choice of happiness. Heiress in her own right, with none daring to interfere with the judgment of God Himself, she might select whom she thought best to share the possessions accorded to her. No human judgment, no thought of man, would have so cared for woman. The law, indeed, might have been given, but those impressive words, "Let them marry whom they think best," speak but of the omniscient care and infinite love of God.

The law of vows we have already enlarged upon in our second section, the wives of Israel, yet, as its ordinance concerns the daughters of Israel also, we must briefly recur to it. The nature of those vows and in what manner they are liable to abuse, we have already seen. A daughter might, perhaps, more easily than a wife, devote herself by a singular vow to the service of the Lord, but more easily also be led into its abuse. A young woman (for it is to such the laws refer—see Numbers xxx. 16), while in her father's house, performs her duty to her God, and proves her zeal in His service to greatest perfection, while evincing her obedience to the fifth commandment, and devoting herself as much as possible to the comfort and happiness of her parents, and to all the unobtrusive claims of home. This, as we have said before, is often neglected during the early enthusiasm of first religious impressions, and the wish to do something great and striking, to evince the fervour of her professions, occupies the mind to the exclusion of all else. This, in Israel, is effectually guarded against, by rendering the daughter dependent in some measure on the will of her father, and by so doing increasing the veneration, love, and submission which, did she obey the fifth commandment, she could not fail to bear him, at the same time guarded, like the wife in Israel, from all capriciousness, or indecision, and the petty trials thence proceeding.

That she had the power, even when in her youth in her father's house, of devoting herself by a vow unto the Lord, clearly evinces that even young women had access to the Eternal, and their prayers and service were graciously accepted by Him, without any interference of man.

This is the spirit of the law concerning us most nearly now, and which every young daughter in Israel should lovingly remember, that young, lowly, weak as she is, and dependent as she may be, she has yet the glorious privilege of devoting herself to the service of her God. No longer, indeed, by a singular vow, calling upon her to depart from home duties, and affections, for outward service, nor by a binding oath to afflict the soul by departure from her usual food and innocent amusements, but simply by associating the love of God and hope of His approval with all her thoughts, and the meek and unpretending effort to make manifest spirituality and holiness in every action, every trial, every blessing of her life. This will be less difficult to accomplish if she do but study, heartfully and prayerfully, His precious word, and read there, borne out by the whole beautiful world of nature, the blessed record of God's unfailing love; if she will but persevere in trust and prayer, and not despair if many many times she turns seemingly unanswered from the Fount of living waters, and her earthly nature tempt her to put her whole trust in "cisterns, broken cisterns that will hold no water." This was Israel's sin, which more powerfully than any other, at length hurled on her the Eternal's long averted wrath; and, knowing this, we shall sin threefold now if we strain not every nerve to resist all such specious colouring of earth, and cleave under every difficulty, spite of disappointment, of despondency, of doubt, unwaveringly to the Lord.

But let not the young daughter of Israel, rejoicing in her fond enthusiasm that she is so specially designated in His law, believe that to do His work is easy and all joy, as at first it seems. There must come a time, if she truly seek and pray to love Him, that He will try that love; not, it may be, with the afflictions publicly acknowledged as such, but with the coldness, deadness, utter stagnation of the spirit, as if all of religion, or even interest, in religious things, had entirely departed. This is the most fearful period in the religious experience of the young. They doubt every feeling of piety which had been theirs before. They mentally ask, why should they be different to their more worldly companions, who are ever happy, ever gay? Why should they voluntarily resign such pleasures for a service that, instead of bringing comfort, does but make them miserable? Were they not over presumptuous to have supposed for a moment that God should care for such as they, and would it not be wiser and better to join the multitude, who, living but for earth and time, never cast a thought on heaven and eternity; for to whom can they express feelings so impossible to be relieved or understood?

O let not such periods of trial turn the daughter of Israel from that better path which an earlier age has chosen. Come indeed they *must*, for God thus tries the extent of his children's love. The truly, sincerely, spiritually religious of every creed, of every class, have experienced all that they may feel. It is the dread "phantom of the threshold," which must be resisted by its only all-subduing foe—that faith which can ascend on the wings of prayer, and trust in God to give comfort, hope, and joy. It is no proof of superior holiness, of more rapid advancement in the one straight path, where these emotions are unknown. It is rather an unanswerable evidence that the spirit yet sleeps, unawakened to its weakness, its dependence. It does not yet know the workings of the Lord within; or that its fancied strength may be broken as a reed. O let not the young daughter of Israel, when bowed and sorrowing beneath the strange despondency of heart and thought, envy these. God hath not departed from her. He doth but try the strength of her faith and love. If comfort, if spiritual joy always attended on religious service, where would be that necessity for faithfulness and constancy? where the *trial* of love, if ever coupled with reward? Where its strength, its durability, if the first moment the object of its aspirings *appear* to forsake, to darken His countenance towards them, it takes wing to some more rewarding God? Would we love a mortal thus? And shall we do less for God, whose love we know to be so unending, so infinite, so exhaustless, and who never in reality withdraws it, though to try us He permits the human infirmities of frame to produce the darkness under which we pine?

Would we, in truth, follow the example of our ancestors, and devote ourselves to our God, we must endure this meekly and trustingly, as we would any more tangible evil, or more visible affliction. And even when this is removed, through His loving mercy, and again our souls spring up rejoicing, though more chastened, let us still "remember the days of darkness, for they shall be many." Religion in no way saves us from afflictions, but it supports us under them. It gives us what nothing else can give, the unvarying comfort of a Father's love, and an unfailing hope in heaven.

As in former ages a young woman could not devote herself by a singular vow without the approval of her father, although with her *spiritual feelings* he had no power to interfere, so now let every daughter of Israel abstain from every public or presumptuous evidence of religious profession which can interfere with the prejudices of her parents. The spirit of that beautiful religion which *was* granted to us, and which *will* again be ours, was "to turn the heart of the fathers to their children, and the hearts of the children to their fathers;"

not to sow dissension and disunion. Whatever a young woman may feel, however grieve at what she may think is wanting in the theoretical or practical religion of her parents, it is her duty to *pray* and *wait*. God will answer in His own time, but it is no part of her duty either to condemn or cease to love. No parent will interfere with a child's religion, if, instead of being obtruded upon him, it does but guide alike conduct and feeling, impel obedience and cheerfulness, and strengthen to endure. The *motive* of these superior characteristics an irreligious and unbelieving parent may not, indeed, for long years perceive; but, almost unconsciously, he will learn to respect the prejudices of such a child; and if, indeed, it may please God to permit such earthly recompense, she may be the blessed means of leading him to the same immortal goal.

But this can never be if she obtrude religion, or in the slightest degree evince a supposition of her own superior holiness. It is indeed one of the hardest trials in life, to see any one of those whom we most love perseveringly reject all we feel the dearest, most important. But if we bring it before God, He will give us strength to continue constant in prayer for them, and lesson the evil we deplore. The case of a parent refusing to let his child serve God, and make religion her first object, is utterly unknown in Israel; but should it be, in this instance only a child is imperatively called upon to disobey. The commands of an earthly parent must be disregarded, if they interfere with and compel disobedience to the commands of God. Leviticus xix. 29 authorises our upholding this. Although the case itself, in which there is a daughter guarded from an unnatural father, be different in details, yet it is equally protective in the present instance; and a child may be fully assured, if the command of her father compel disobedience to her God in any one of His commandments (for all are of equal sanctity to the one alluded to in the verse quoted), her painful duty must be to disobey.

But a state of things so fearful can never be in Israel, if a daughter's religion be practised as we have hinted above.

There may be indifference, there may be the apparent absence of all spiritual religion; but no man who wishes to be thought an Israelite, ever neglects the peculiar forms of his faith, and his daughter, therefore, has no cause for dividing herself from him, however more earnest, more spiritual, may be her individual views. She may have to bear with the neglect or disregard of some ordinances which her heart tells her are sacred, but if she have the will, she has the power to keep her own way undefiled; and if she be truly and sincerely a daughter of Israel, every parental disregard of holy things will bring her to her God yet more earnestly in prayer.

One other point we would urge ere we quit the subject. Let not Israel's young daughters fancy, that to devote heart, mind, and soul to God, demands the relinquishment of those innocent pleasures and enjoyments for which God Himself has framed our hearts. There are many among the Gentiles who believe religion wholly incompatible with recreation and amusement; that all social pleasures must be resigned; only certain books perused, and even some accomplishments forbidden, as likely to lead to sin. The religion of God is, on the contrary, so consistent with man's capabilities and yearnings, that we never can believe these things incumbent upon us. The first grand object of our lives, in truth, it must be; and that gained—which, if we inculcate the immortal spirit of religion as well as its more perishable form unto our children, it will be—we need not fear, that enjoyment either of social intercourse or of intellectual resources will turn us from it. God has framed us to give and to receive pleasure. He has stored our hearts with sweet emotions, our minds with inexhaustible resources. We best make manifest our deep and grateful sense of His loving-kindness by its enjoyment. "God loveth a cheerful giver," we have somewhere read. And in no religion is this sentiment so truly, practically illustrated as in ours, coming, as it does, from God Himself. A knowledge of ourselves, which, if we are accustomed in youth to examine our hearts by the standard of God's Word, we shall undoubtedly obtain, will warn us of those weaknesses and failings most likely to lead us into temptation; and we shall guard against these, and either conquer them through His infused grace, or shun them till the strength we implored is granted. There is no need to become different in seeming from our fellows, and tacitly condemn and chide every innocent amusement and resource by our refusal to join in them. The idea that no amusement is innocent, that nothing we do, think, or feel is free from sin, is not—blessed be God!—the creed of Israel. He hath appointed our religious and moral duties; He hath laid down our earthly path; He hath taught us how to look to Him, and how by faith we shall be justified, and through His infinite mercy be received with Him. He hath stored our souls and minds with exhaustless capabilities of happiness, even upon earth. He hath gathered around us in His beautiful world a thousand objects to call forth love, gratitude, and joy; and He who is truth and justice would not have done these things, were we so incapable of righteousness, as from our birth to be blackened with such sin as only blood can wash away.

Let me not be misunderstood, or accused of contradicting my own theory, so to speak, for my theory is the theory of the Bible. Liable to every weakness—more inclined to the evil than the good—we are; but such is inherent from the time that our heavenly origin was changed and marred by the dominion of the passions, infirmities, and weakness of earth. And it was for such beings the law was given, to aid them to subdue natural corruption, to give them opportunities to exercise righteousness, virtue, and faith; to awaken the immortal part of our nature; to arouse all those better, higher, and purer feelings, which, however *dormant*, cannot *die*, for they have been breathed into us by the spirit of the Lord; and for which, if we neglect and let them ever sleep, because we fancy we either possess them not, or are too closely bound to arouse them, we shall be called to a fearful account. Not one single point of the Eternal's precious word—the Bible which we acknowledge—authorises a belief in the Gentile creed.

The particular mention of the superior sanctity of the priests' daughters, evinces that the holiness of the fathers was shared by the daughters. They were to partake of the holy meats, not only in their youth; but if widows, or divorced, without children, had the power of returning to their father's house. As further proof of the holiness incumbent on her as the daughter of the Eternal's appointed servant, and one who had power by her conduct either to exalt or "profane her father," we find, in Levit. xxi. 9, a different and more awful death appointed for her, if she became sinful, than the usual mode of Hebrew executions. These laws, of course, cannot concern us now (though would that they could, our priests being, as they ought to be, the first in rank and consequence of our nation), but the spirit of them, as of every other relative to the women of Israel, tends to mark their equality, their elevation, and their immortal responsibility, so forcibly as to prevent all possible rejoinder. Were the prayers of man sufficient for the welfare of woman—had she no individual soul to render account of—there would be less necessity to notice the wives and the daughters of the priests than any other. The superior sanctity of their husbands and fathers would surely be more than sufficient for them. We trust, however, we have said enough to convince our young sisters that, as Daughters of Israel, they have higher and nobler privileges than the daughters of any other race; that their God Himself has deigned to give laws and ordinances for their especial guidance and protection, which cannot be gainsaid without verging on impiety. And that, therefore, much, very much, depends on them, one and all, to uphold His glory through their own religious and moral dignity, and give evidence, alike to their own hearts and to those nations, by word, thought, and deed, that they need nothing more than their own beautiful religion to guide them through earth and time and fit them for eternity and heaven. They *can* do this, and will they fail?

THE EXODUS (Continued).

MAID SERVANTS IN ISRAEL, AND SUNDRY OTHER LAWS.

Our fifth section alludes to a class which (we say it with grief) no longer exists amongst us, and, therefore, can only be looked upon as a still farther proof of the Eternal's loving care for His female children. It cannot guide us till once more we have maid-servants of our own faith amongst us. How often, how constantly, this subject has engrossed the thoughts and wishes of the writer, that by any possible means, the daughters of our poorer and dependent brethren could be received as domestics in our families, and so enable us to adhere to the laws framed for them, can be known but to the Searcher of all hearts; for when spoken to man, the idea is received but as high-flown folly, impossible to be realised. If so considered by the mass, there is no help for it, and so it must remain till it please God to put His spirit once more within us, and enlighten the darkness whicn, in some instances, has gathered around us, rich and poor.

That it is only the rich and influential who can bring about reform in our poorer classes, we quite acknowledge. Their religious education must be carried on on a different basis. The spirit and meaning of every form must be inculcated, or they can never rise from the ignorance and superstition in which, through long ages of fearful persecution, they are plunged. The mind and heart alike must be enlarged; their own dignity, their own responsibility inculcated; the distinction between essential and local laws; the superior, the unchangeable sanctity of the law of God, combined with reverence and love for the fence which good, and wise, and holy men have raised around it. Were these things inculcated, there would be many eager to accept the offers of service in Jewish families, and find there obedience to their God quite compatible with their duty to their employers. Of course we allude not to those establishments in which but one or two servants only are kept. We simply mean those classes where there are upper and lower domestics—where one day in the week the former may not be called upon either for servile work, or to break through any of the forms which hallowed the Sabbath day. There are such things, we have heard, as head nurses, who, even though Gentiles, have nothing to do with the servile work of their nursery kingdoms. Ladies' maids, who have nothing to do but needle work, dress hair, and attend to their mistress and young ladies. Housekeepers, even housemaids, where there are upper and lower. All these situations might, were they properly educated for it, be filled by the maid-servants in Israel, without interfering one tittle with their adherence and obedience to their Faith. There must, indeed, be a WILL on both sides, the employers and the employed, but were that WILL found, the WAY would be easy.

Every law instituted in Israel for the safety, happiness, and welfare of the man-servant, mentioned by name the maid-servant also. In obedience to the fourth commandment, in the protection of the tenth, in every festival and fast, every ordinance binding on Jewish families as individuals, we find the maid-servant expressly named; thus proving that, though her actual rank was subordinate, though her duties were distinct, she was as carefully and tenderly provided for as the daughters of a family themselves. Even in the eating of holy things, which some might suppose a privilege only granted to the heirs of households, she was associated. No man could rejoice before the Lord by himself; sons, daughters, widows, fatherless, men-servants, and MAID-SERVANTS, all were included, and so distinctly enumerated, that not one could be omitted without a decided breach of law. The twenty-first chapter of Exodus and fifteenth chapter of Deuteronomy treat powerfully on the protection and kindness demanded towards male and *female* domestics. The simple words, "they shall not go out as men-servants do," reveal the loving care for their protection, that they should not be exposed to all the rougher labour of the field and out-door service incumbent on the males. To sell her to a strange nation, which would be the natural desire of the injurer and the deceiver to conceal his sin, no man had power; for, if he did so, she could regain her freedom at the end of seven years, and be restored to her family, as was the law in Israel. If he betrothed her to his son, she was to become even as a daughter; and if, as was the custom of the East, another wife were taken, her food, her raiment, her duty of marriage, he had no power to diminish. If he failed in either, she was free and spotless, alike in the sight of God and man. These beautiful laws appear, not only pretty convincing of the equality of female servants with their male brethren in the same class, but rather a startling manifestation of the falsity of the charge, that *wives* in Israel are degraded and abased. If even a female slave, when raised to become the wife of her master's son, was to be regarded as a daughter, to retain her every privilege as first-selected wife, however the capricious heart of her husband might select another of his own rank, we rather imagine that every grade of Hebrew wives was equally protected by the Lord, and that no man whatever had power to degrade them.

All injury committed on a female servant exposed her master to punishment of equal severity as the injury of a male. He dared do her no hurt, for if he did, whether through predetermination, or momentary passion, she was his slave no longer. She had power to appeal from him to the representatives of her God, His priests, and she knew justice would be done her, for to do it was the ordinance of God. And, even without injury, the term of servitude was over in the seventh year. The extremity of destitution might have compelled a parent to sell, or rather to devote, his child to servitude; or reasons less imperative might urge his doing so, knowing that his children, even though they worked, would be better provided for, and perhaps more easily enabled to keep every ordinance of the Lord, in the family of their master, than struggling on for a scanty subsistence, nominally free. The poor were not to cease out of the land, that the people might obey the words of their God, in which He bade them, "Open thine hand *wide* unto thy poor brother, to thy poor and to thy needy in thy land;" and then, as a practical illustration of how the hand is to be opened *wide*, we are told that when our brother a Hebrew man, or a Hebrew *woman*, has been sold, and served in a family six years, we were not only to let him, or her, go free, which did we act according to the finite judgment of man, there would be many to think sufficient; but they were to be furnished liberally out of the flock and the floor (*i.e.* barn, meaning corn), and out of the wine-press; of all wherewith the Lord had blessed us we were to give unto them. And not satisfied with having already mentioned the Hebrew woman, as included with the Hebrew man, in these laws, the law again enforces the equal rights of both, by repeating, "and also unto thy maid-servant thou shalt do likewise;" adding, with that exquisite spirit of love infused through every law, "It shall not seem hard unto thee, when thou sendest him away free from thee, for he has been worth a doubled hired servant, in serving thee six years, and the Lord thy God shall bless thee in all thou doest." Now, had there been no other mention of woman, these beautiful laws would have been sufficient to prove her equality with man in the sight of the Eternal. The *illustration* of these laws was given *before* the *precept*, in the Most High's dealings with Hagar, as we have already seen; as a bond-slave, and one not even of his chosen, He had compassion and love for her; and that His people should endeavour as strongly as lay in their power to follow in His own paths, He laid down statutes, the obedience to which would make every maid-servant as much the object of her master's care, tenderness, and liberality, as Hagar had been to Him.

The command relative to the maid-servant's attendance at the feast of holy things, on every sabbath, festival, etc., is rather convincing of religion being as incumbent on her as on man; nay, that her master himself was liable to punishment if he neglected to associate her, as well as every other of his household, in his religious exercises.

LAWS FOR SERVANTS.

Some over-refined natures are horrified at the idea of being sold to service—of the very term *slave* (the Hebrew word עֶבֶד, by the way, signifies *servant* or *domestic* also); and taking up the position that the law of Moses countenanced similar traffic as the slave trade in all its modern horrors, make it the grand objection to regarding the religion as the revelation of God. Yet no one who really studies the Word of God, can entertain an idea so erroneous for a moment. Perpetual slavery—that awful sacrifice of all home affections, all human emotions, that horrible system which permitted man to regard his brother man as a beast of the field, to be bought and sold, live and die at his will—was utterly unknown in Israel. The term "selling" a son or daughter, simply signified the receiving *beforehand* the price of six years' labour, in which six years the slave (so called) was equal to his master in everything except actual labour. He was to share in every feast, every rejoicing, sit at his master's table, listen to the law, accept every covenant of God, be clothed, fed, and cared for, and at the term of his release be so liberally treated individually, as to enable him, if he pleased, to quit service, and enter into independent business for himself, or remain, from *pure affection or voluntary relinquishment* of freedom, for ever with his master. This was the actual state of slavery in Israel, productive of a threefold good. It saved many a parent from beholding the utter destitution of his children ; gave him the means of working for himself by the price received for their six years' labour, assured him of their temporal and spiritual welfare, and of their being cared for, on their release, far better than he could for them, much as he loved them ; prevented all those horrible incentives to crime and misery produced by the abject destitution of many a Gentile land; united master and servant in the sweet and holy ties of brotherhood, alike of religion, tribe, and land ; subject to one law, worshipping one God, caring for the helpless and the weak, and making every household where the laws of God were obeyed one of heavenly harmony and love. In Israel there was no surplus of hands for work; none of those fearful temptations to sin in being thrown out of employ, in the inability to meet the heavy taxes and other drains upon the poor. The law in its every item spoke of God, and revealed Him as a God of love. He alone could have framed statutes entering into every man's household, guiding his conduct from his parents to his very servants ; shielding, compassionating, loving every individual in Israel, from the high priest to the lowest slave.

Having now regarded all the laws instituted expressly for woman, in her several positions of mother, wife, widow, daughter, and maid-servant, we have but to throw together all the remaining statutes relating to her generally. In every offering, be it of trespass, of thanksgiving, of purification, we find in Leviticus, Numbers, and Deuteronomy, woman was so emphatically included as to be the subject of laws set apart for herself. The ordinances were binding on both man and woman, and care expressly taken to mark the guiding line of obedience for both. There was nothing left for inference, but all which was necessary distinctly laid down. In the very particular law for lepers, *woman* was named as well as *man*. Nothing was left to human judgment; every item concerning its treatment, its cure, and its purification, precisely written down. In the laws for the Nazarite (Numbers vi.), woman is specified so clearly, that it is utterly impossible to retain a doubt of her service being equally acceptable, or that she had not the same power as man, to separate herself by a vow unto the Lord. That which was to guide man in this devotion, must equally have been given to guide her, or we should not see it so expressly stated, " when man or WOMAN shall separate themselves to vow the vow of a Nazarite," etc. A woman who could wish to devote herself, appears to us to have been an independent single woman, and, therefore, not one of the daughters and wives specified in the latter law regarding vows, which, judging from the beautiful precision of the laws of God, would, had it alluded to the Nazarites, have been so expressed. The singular vow mentioned in Leviticus xxvii., including, as every other ordinance, woman as well as man, may or may not relate to the same kind of vows as mentioned in Numbers xxx. But whether it be or not, the law for the respective valuation of male and female service, proves that woman could make a singular vow, and either fulfil or redeem it with equal freedom and acceptance as man. That her service was valued at a less rate is no proof of her inequality, but simply that the service she could render the Temple was, from the weakness of her frame, and the retiring nature of her sex, of less use and importance than man's. Compare the work and capability of a man from the age of twenty to sixty, to those of a woman during the same period. There would be full the worth of " twenty shekels" difference. After the age of sixty, or in early childhood, the difference of valuation was much less, because the capabilities of both drew nearer each other. We see, then, the real meaning of these differing estimations. The law of God, while it elevates and spiritualises woman to an equal share of immortality and responsibility before Him, in no way permits or encourages her coming unduly forward or exalting herself above man. Her weaker frame, her less mighty mind, her more easily excited emotions, all mark the necessity of a more retiring and dependent station. She may contend for equal earthly rights, she may deem our assertion of her inferior capabilities of frame and mind an unfounded aspersion cast upon her, she may say she is equally independent, equally strong, in reason and power, yet to *prove* this, we fear she will not find quite so easy. Certainly not by the word of God, her only sure test of reason and feeling. And how much more just and graceful is her voluntary adherence to her own allotted path, and her determination to adorn that path with all the winning qualities, the devotedness, the affections, peculiar to her own sex, than the vain struggle to be in all things as man; a struggle in which she can but make manifest her weakness, and finally be so vanquished, that even her natural claims are denied her, or conceded as a favour, not as a right.

The equality which we contend for (and which we uphold is so clearly demonstrated, in not only our holy law itself, but in the mention of every female of the Bible), is not, in our capability, our station, humanly considered, but simply as immortal children of the Most High; having equal access to His gracious ear, equal power to win His condescending reply, equal responsibility in the performance of our every duty, in the just exercise of our several faculties; which faculties, so peculiarly adapted by our merciful Father to our wants, happiness, and duties, are of equal valuation in His sight as those of man. This is woman's equality, proved by the very law which, by some misguided spirits, may be twisted into her abasement. What would be the need of marking her human valuation, if she had not the power of devoting herself by a singular vow unto the Lord, in any period of her life, from a month old to above sixty? Or, if she have no access to God, save through man, what could be the use of her vow? Were she to be degraded morally and mentally, where would be even her inclination for this spiritual service?

Surely there need not have been any reference to her in this law, if the women of Israel were to be considered slaves and heathens.

By this twenty-seventh chapter of Leviticus, we see too that *female* infants might be devoted by their parents to the Lord, another beautiful and unanswerable manifestation of their perfect equality with their brothers from their birth, and must entirely do away with the idea that has been so idly brought forward, that the festival attending the naming of male children in Israel, compared with the quiet reception of the female, at once proves in what an inferior light the latter is regarded. The festivity which hails the entrance of the new-born son of Israel into the holy covenant of his fathers, is an immemorial national usage, descending to us from " the time that Abraham made a great feast, the day that Isaac was weaned," and has nothing whatever to do with the claims of one sex over the other. To my own heart, the different reception of male and female children is an exquisite illustration and type of their respective paths. The world and man must be the theatre and the fellow-actor of the *boy;* he must go forth armed with a religious heart and unbending spirit to meet the temptations of pleasure, ambition, and a host of other passions and emotions which must assail his more public path. But, to the *girl,* home is her theatre, her God her only stay. Why should festivity and idle revelry hail the birth of one, in whose own heart must be her purest pleasures, distinct from every pleasure (so called) of the world ; whose path must be one of quiet and unostentatious retirement and usefulness? Her name is given in the house of God, and by one of His elected servants. Taken to the most holy place, which, in our captive and desolate state, His house presents, by that ceremony to be received into the congregation of His people, does the female babe need more ? Cannot the Hebrew mother thus realise the devoting her child to the faith and service of her God, more powerfully, more solemnly, than in even the festive circle which gathers round to hail the naming of her boy ? We think, were these several rites more seriously considered, the idle charge we have quoted above, merely to disprove it, would find little resting in the heart of our fellows.

The express prohibition relating to woman's adopting, on any pretence whatever, the garments of the male, is another beautiful ordinance marking her natural sphere, and proving that any departure from it was not acceptable to the Lord. It was not only the act itself which is so forcibly brought forward, that Deut. xxii. 5, tells us, "All that do so are *abomination unto the Lord thy God,*" but the thoughts and feelings included in such an act, the temptation to depart from the retirement, the modesty, the purity of that home station which woman should so quietly fulfil. Were she not an equally responsible moral and religious agent as man, why need this law have been given?

Again, we find that *women* who have wrought wickedness, *women* who have a familiar spirit (that is, sought to deceive by pretended spells and enchantments), *women* who have enticed to idolatry—all these, as well as similar sinners among the males, were to be stoned to death on the evidence of two witnesses. Now the very power to work such wickedness, supposes a perfect freedom of thought and will, wholly distinct from the power of man. Were woman so entirely the slave of man that her very prayers must be guided by his, and could only be acceptable through him, there could be no justice in condemning her as a free agent; her sins must be the sins of her father or husband, not her own, if her merit were only acceptable through his. She could not possibly be bound to obey the law, or punished for its disobedience, if it were only given to, and incumbent on, man. If she were to be made a slave and heathen, how does it happen that, wherever there can be a doubt as to both sexes being included, either in religious observances, or prohibiting of customs which were abomination unto the Lord, WOMAN is expressly mentioned in conjunction with man? The very wrath threatened in case of her transgression proves her equality quite as powerfully as the rewards promised to obedience, and the laws instituted for her adherence.

Three times a year it was a *positive enjoinment* for every *male* to appear before the Lord, in the place appointed for His temple. That woman was not included by name, was, instead of being a proof of her lesser importance and responsibility, a beautiful manifestation of that divine tenderness and justice, which, in their perfection and prescience, God only could display. A nameless variety of causes might intervene to prevent woman's leaving her home in the distant provinces of Judea to accompany her father and husband to Jerusalem. Many a man might be enabled to obey the law himself, who would have been prevented doing so, had he been under a *positive command* to bring with him wife and children.

Locomotion is man's native element, and he can more often indulge in it without interfering with home duties than woman. It was right and just, that he who so frequently travelled for pleasure should do so three times a year in obedience to the will of God. But many causes, in her own physical inability or maternal anxiety, in the illness of some member of her family, might occur to prevent woman, and therefore the law was not made *binding* upon her, as it was on man.

That this distinct mention of "all thy males" in no way degraded her, however, is clearly proved by the simple fact of her being required, when it was possible, and in all her positions in life, to rejoice before the Lord in His appointed festivals, to listen to the reading of His law at the Feast of Tabernacles, to attend to the offerings instituted expressly for her, to abstain from all wickedness and idolatry, and to come unto the Lord in every event, thought, act, desire, public or private, of her life. "Ye stand this day all of you before the Lord your God," Moses exclaims in the twenty-ninth chapter of Deuteronomy; "your captains of your tribes, your elders, and your officers, with all the men of Israel, your little ones, your WIVES, and the stranger that is in thy camp, from the hewer of wood to the drawer of water, that thou shouldst enter into covenant with the Lord thy God, and into His oath, that He may establish thee to-day for a people unto Himself, and that He may be unto thee a God, as He hath said unto thee, and as He hath sworn unto thy fathers, to Abraham, to Isaac, and to Jacob. Neither with you only do I make this covenant and this oath, but with him that standeth here with us this day before the Lord our God, and *also* with *him who is not here with* us this day, lest there should be among you any *man, woman,* family, or tribe, whose heart turneth away this day to go and serve the gods of these nations."

In these few verses, and yet more powerfully in the whole chapter, to which we entreat our readers to turn, we have all which, as women of Israel, we need to seal the scriptural truth and basis of the position which we have adopted and set forth. Every class, grade, and condition of women, as of men, must have been present when Moses spoke these emphatic words—all included in the terms, "little ones and WIVES." And they heard, that Moses addressed not only *them*, but their *descendants*, lest any man, WOMAN, family, or tribe, should, by their idolatry, or other transgression, hurl down on the whole nation the awful curses which he proceeds to enumerate. Would he, need he, have been thus particular, were the women of Israel destined to be but slaves to man, nonentities before God? Alas! whatever the falsely accusing Gentile, or mistaken Hebrew, may assert, we have but fearful evidence in the monarch of Israel of the influence of woman, manifesting too terribly the prophet's prescience in including her, as leading herself and man to sin, and so hastening the great and terrible wrath of the Lord.

We have now drawn to the conclusion of our Second Period, the women of Israel's most momentous era; the delivery and establishment of that law, which, in the very midst of revolutions, changes, new creeds, and their awful persecutions—in the very midst of denial, abuse, and heavy darkness—yet remains the hope, the guide, the protection, the defence, the elevation of woman, whatever her station, whatever her country, aye, and whatever her creed may be—more especially the blessed inheritance of the females of that people on whom our God Himself bestowed it, and one, therefore, which should be their glory, their privilege, their delight, to render so exalted, by their individual and national conduct, in the sight of a Gentile world, that none dare fling odium on the female Jewish name, or seek to heathenise and degrade them.

We have sought to bring together every law relative to woman; but the subject is so momentous, the field so wide, we can scarce hope we have accomplished it as fully as we could wish. We can only hope and pray, that a perusal of these pages may lead our sisters in Israel to seek their *foundation* yet more earnestly than the *frail superstructure*, and find for themselves, in their Bibles, all that we may have omitted, or failed to treat as largely as we might. The more our beautiful law is studied, the more must we feel, that, as women, we are especially objects of the Eternal's loving protection and care; that we are privileged in every feeling as well as every act to come to Him, alike in thanksgiving and prayer; that we have no need whatever, in obtaining our eternal welfare, for the aid and interference of man. The more we study, the more we must feel that we have, as women of Israel, a station to uphold alike before God and man; that as the first, the only people to whom God Himself deigned to provide a law, we should be the very first in holiness, purity, spirituality, and divine love, amid the nations. We may be captives, we may be awhile under the Eternal's wrath, but that truth in no way lessens our responsibility, or diminishes the necessity for our firmly upholding our heavenly heritage and guiding law. We may be captives, but, and O! let the blessed truth be remembered and clasped to our hearts, we are NOT CAST OFF. Our chastisement is not the sign of divine wrath alone, but of that DEEP LOVE which punisheth to save, to amend, to bring back to the blessed paths which we have deserted, NOT to annihilate, as in the case of so many other nations. Our very existence through so many centuries of darkness would alone prove this, even had we not the whole word of God to assert that so it would be. Every prophet abounds in the divine entreaty, so fraught with forbearing love, "O Israel, return unto the Lord thy God; why hast thou fallen by thine iniquity?" And shall we, as women, reject these gracious proffers? Oh, let us indeed ever come unto the Lord our God, and make manifest to the Gentiles, to ourselves, how deeply, how earnestly we feel, that alike our protection, innocence, honour, purity, elevation, all that can make life dear and holy, all that is provided to lighten our temporal toil, with eternal hope to strengthen our weakness, to guide our daily path, and bless our daily work, is of the Lord, not man. That every pure throb of love, every sweet tie of life, every aspiring prayer and grateful thanksgiving, comes from and is hallowed by Him, who, in His deep love, entered into the heart and home of woman, and so fenced them round with just and beautiful laws, that it was impossible to perform a single duty, social or domestic, parental, filial, conjugal, or fraternal, without being holy unto the Lord? Can we think on this important and most blessed truth without lifting up our yearning hearts in the fervent prayer for that guidance, that blessing, which will enable us to remember our solemn responsibility, our heavenly heritage; and, in the midst of captivity, and its varied ordeals of adversity, stagnation, and prosperity, that we may still join heart to heart and hand to hand in the persevering effort to make manifest to our God, that we would indeed be once more His own, and to the nations, that, cast off for a "little moment" as we are, WE ARE STILL, and SHALL EVER BE, the CHOSEN PEOPLE of the LORD.

THIRD PERIOD.

Women of Israel, between the Establishment of the Law and the Authority of the Kings.

MIRIAM.

HAVING now considered the law of God under all its various bearings relative to woman, it only remains to prove, from the female characters of Scripture, in what manner that law was obeyed; and whether it be possible to discover any trace of statutes, which, in direct contradistinction to the changeless law of the Eternal, tend to degrade, instead of to elevate, the female character; or whether we cannot bring forward some sufficiently convincing arguments in favour of our deeply studied theory, that the law of the Eternal is explained, by its practical illustration, through the whole history of the Bible.

To the oralist, or non-oralist, this consideration ought to be of equal weight. Keeping aloof entirely from the discussion which has of late too painfully agitated the whole Jewish nation, we would yet present to both parties the simple fact, that the supposed degradation of the women of Israel can have no existence whatever in the Oral Law, or we must find some trace of this abasement in this and the succeeding periods of our history. If both were given at the same time, the women of Israel whom we are about to bring forward, must have lived under the jurisdiction of both; and as their lives, feelings, and actions, are all in exact accordance with the spirit and the form of the written law, it is clearly evident, that the modern accusation against us can have *no* foundation whatever in the Oral Law, or we must have discovered it in the female characters of Scripture. Nor will the groundless assertion of our individual inferiority and social abasement find confirmation in the writings of our ancient fathers, whose beautiful parables and tales all tend to illustrate alike the spirit of our law, and the axiom of our wise man, "Who can find a virtuous woman, for her price is far above rubies?"

We will proceed, then, without further introduction, to our history, convinced that were the word of the Eternal more deeply studied, the love and peace it breathes must infuse themselves unconsciously in every human heart, and strife and discord melt away before the inspired transcript of the love and mercy of our God.

The character of Miriam is one of the most perfect delineations of woman in her mixed nature of good and evil which the Bible gives. Her first introduction we have already noticed—a young girl, watching, at the command of her mother, the fate of the ark which held her baby brother, and boldly addressing the princess of Egypt in the child's behalf.

Her next mention is her sharing the holy triumph of that brother, and responding, with apparently her whole heart, to the song of praise bursting forth from the assembled Israelites on the shores of the Red Sea. "And Miriam the prophetess, the sister of Aaron, took a timbrel in her hand, and all the women went out after her, with timbrels, and with dances. And Miriam answered them, Sing, sing ye to the Lord, for He hath triumphed gloriously, the horse and his rider hath He thrown into the sea."

The Hebrew word, הנביאה, here used, and translated prophetess, means also a *poetess*, and the wife of a prophet, and is applied sometimes to a singer of hymns. In this latter meaning, and perhaps also as a poetess, it must be applied to Miriam, as she was neither the wife of a prophet, nor, as in the case of Deborah, and afterwards Huldah, endowed by the Eternal with the power of prophecy itself. She appears to have been one of those gifted beings, from whom the words of sacred song flow spontaneously. The miracles performed in their very sight were sufficient to excite enthusiasm in a woman's heart, and awaken the burst of thanksgiving; and Miriam might have fancied herself at that moment as zealous and earnest in the cause of God as she appeared to be. But for true piety, something more is wanted than the mere enthusiasm of the moment, or the high-sounding religion of flowing verse. By Miriam not being permitted to enter the promised land, it is evident that she "had not followed the Lord fully," but had probably joined in the rebellions and murmurings which characterised almost the whole body of the Israelites during their wanderings in the wilderness. The very next mention of her after her song of praise, is her presumptuous attack upon Moses, and daring insult to the power of the Lord, contained in the twelfth chapter of Numbers. Some chronologists believe this incident occurred only one year after the passage of the Red Sea, a period not sufficiently long for circumstances to have changed the character of Miriam so completely, had not jealousy and presumption been secretly inmates of her heart before; unknown, perhaps, even to herself; for how few of us know our "secret sins," until they are roused into action, by some unlooked-for temptation in an unguarded moment, and we are startled at ourselves.

The feelings of Miriam, recorded in this chapter, are so perfectly accordant with woman's nature, that surely no woman of Israel will turn from it, believing the length of time which has elapsed removes all the warning which it should inculcate. One of the most prominent of female failings is secret jealousy, quite distinct, however, from the fearful passion so called. We allude simply to that species of secret and unconfessed jealousy, which is the real origin of *detraction*, so often, unhappily, practised by woman upon woman. We are not now writing of any class, or creed, or people, in particular, but of women in general. There never yet was gossip, without some species of detraction spoken or implied; and never yet has detraction been probed candidly and fairly (disregarding the pain of so doing) to its root, without being traced to either jealousy or envy of some quality, or possession, of the more favoured being so unkindly judged.

Women, and single women more especially, are more liable to petty failings than men, simply because they have less to engross their minds, and less of consequence to employ their hands. Unless taught from earliest years to find and take pleasure in resources *within*, they must look *without*, and busy themselves with the characters, and conduct, and concerns of their neighbours. Now acknowledged merit to such characters gives very little food for cosy chat; it wants *esprit*, and so they are never content, till something doubtful or suspicious is discovered, or supposed to be, and then the lovers of gossip may be found in full conclave, marvelling, and wondering, and turning, and twisting, and blaming, and pitying, till the very object of such animadversion might find it difficult to trace of whom they speak, and know infinitely less of her own concerns, intentions, and feelings, than her reporters.

As Miriam acted, so would most women, unenlightened by that pure spirit of religious love, which alone can conquer the natural inclination towards detraction, and subdue secret jealousy, by making us aware of its existence. "And Miriam and Aaron spake against Moses, *because of the Ethiopian woman whom he had married.*" The very thing to arouse jealousy and disturbance in an unenlightened woman's mind.

Miriam had never been thrown in contact with her sister-in-law till within the last few months; Moses having sent his wife for safety, with his two sons, to her father Jethro, during the troubles in Egypt and their subsequent redemption. From the silence with regard to Zipporah, we are led to infer that she was a woman of meek and retiring habits, but of course, as the wife of their great leader Moses, held in higher repute by the people than his sister. And this, trifling as it seems, is now, as it always has been, a trial to some of our sex. Few single women there are who can look upon the elevation of a brother's wife without some secret feelings of pain, which will be subdued and changed into warmest affection or gain ascendancy and violence, finding vent in petty malice or half-concealed detraction, according as religion, and candour, and self-knowledge are, or are not, predominant in the sister's character. Perhaps it is hard, in some cases, to see one younger and fairer, and only known but a few years or months, as the case may be, usurp entire possession of a beloved brother's heart; wherein we, who have been his hand-in-hand companion from earliest infancy, must now be content with but a very secondary place; but such is one of the many trials peculiarly woman's—permitted, that from her very loneliness below, she may look above for that fulness of love and tenderness for which she yearns. And thrice happy is that woman who, conscious of this, can yet be content with, and value as before, the love her brother has still to spare for her; who will so subdue natural feeling as to find in very truth a friend and sister in a brother's wife, and subjects of deepest interest in her children.

Miriam, as we may infer from her punishment, was not one

of these. That an Ethiopian should be raised above herself, who was a daughter of Israel, was to one of her evidently proud spirit, unendurable. Unable, however, to discover ought in Zipporah herself for a publicly-avowed scorn, she sought to lessen the holiness and greatness of her brother, by daring to declare that the Lord had spoken through her and Aaron also. That this jealousy arose because of the "Ethiopian woman whom he had married," Holy Writ itself informs us, and from Miriam's name being mentioned before that of Aaron, and yet more, from the wrath of the Lord being manifested towards her alone, it is evident that hers was the greater sin. Her individual assumption of prophetic power, she knew, would avail her nothing; but, uniting Aaron in the declaration, she sought to make it appear, that God had breathed His spirit into every member of Amram's family. She had too much policy to endeavour to deprive Moses of all his granted and allowed privileges. Her only wish was, to decrease the value and spirituality of those privileges to him individually, and elevate herself and Aaron on his descent; emboldened so to do by the excessive meekness and forbearance of Moses, which she knew would shield her from all *human* reproof. She might, perhaps, have so dwelt upon her own imaginary importance, as really to believe what she asserted, and so feel more and more galled at the little account in which she was held.

It is quite possible for woman so to feel and so to act, and for all to proceed from the petty feelings of jealousy and malice, first excited by the higher grade and more considered position of a brother's wife. "Hath the Lord indeed spoken only by Moses? hath he not spoken also by us?" were the words they said; brief, and perchance of little weight considered by themselves, but in a people ever ready to revolt and murmur, more than likely to kindle sedition and disturbance. "And the Lord heard it, and the Lord spake suddenly unto Moses, and unto Aaron, and unto Miriam, Come out ye three unto the tabernacle of the congregation: and they three came out, and the Lord came down in the pillar of the cloud, and stood in the door of the tabernacle, and called Aaron and Miriam; and they both came forth."

Where now could have been the presumptuous self-importance of Miriam, called thus by Him at whose word might be annihilation? With what fearful terror must she have heard that summons, and listened to the reproving words of the Eternal! exalting Moses above even His inspired prophets; for to them He declared He would make Himself known in a vision, and speak unto them in a dream, "but my servant Moses is not so, who is faithful in all mine house. With him will I speak mouth to mouth, even apparently, and not in dark speeches; and the similitude of the Lord shall he behold: wherefore then were ye not afraid to speak against my servant Moses? And the anger of the Lord was kindled against them; and He departed. And the cloud departed from off the tabernacle; and, behold, Miriam was leprous, as snow: and Aaron looked upon Miriam, and, behold, she was leprous."

It is from this awful chastisement, inflicted by the Lord Himself, that we must judge of the heinousness of her sin; that presumption and arrogancy are no small crimes in His sight, and that God Himself was insulted in the insult offered to His chosen servant. "My servant Moses," He ever designates him; implying the severest reproof in those simple words. Even were they endowed with prophetic power, He tells them they would be less than Moses; for to Moses alone would He deign to speak mouth to mouth. Had Miriam's sin been but the impulse of the moment, the reproof would have been sufficient, as we see in other cases in Scripture; but, effectually to root out the sinful presumption which probably had lain dormant for months, the Eternal, in His perfect justice, inflicted such chastisement as would cause her to be shunned and loathed by the very people whom she had sought to impress with her individual importance. Human reproof, indeed, she had not; for Moses, "meek above all the men which were on the face of the earth," had not even answered the detracting words, conscious that his power was not his own, and that He who gave it, would, if needed, appear in his defence. Had Miriam's heart been perfect towards God, neither her sin nor her punishment would have taken place. Pride and presumption *cannot* exist with true piety; and we are therefore justified in supposing, that the awful infliction was not only a chastisement for present sin, but to awaken her to all the neglectfulness and presumption dividing her from the Lord in years long past. She was now not only to feel His stupendous power, but the true forgiving meekness and piety of the brother she had scorned and spoken against, only "because of his Ethiopian wife."

Stunned and appalled with the suddenness of the infliction, and dumb perhaps from awakening shame, Miriam herself stood silent before Moses; and Aaron therefore appealed for her.

"Alas, my lord, I beseech thee, lay not the sin upon us, wherein we have done foolishly, and wherein we have sinned. Let her not be as one dead, of whom the flesh is half consumed as in the moment of his birth." And Moses, without pause, without one word of reproof, or just indignation at being thus appealed to by the very persons who had sought to injure him, lifted up his voice in earnest prayer unto the Lord, saying, "Heal her now, O God, I beseech thee." And God heard the prayer, and in His infinite goodness so answered it, as to temper justice with mercy, promising to withdraw His hand after seven days, during which time, in obedience to the already instituted laws for lepers, she was to be shut out from the camp. "And the people journeyed not till she was healed."

As there is no further mention of Miriam, except her death, in Numbers xx., we may infer that her chastisement had its effect, and that her haughty and seditious spirit was sufficiently subdued. We learn, from her brief history, much to guide us as women in general, and much to support our position as women of Israel. In the former, we see in what light presumption is regarded by the Lord—that would we retain his favour we must be content with our own position, and in no way interfere, or seek to depreciate those whom, even in our own families, it may have pleased Him to set above us; that even from so small a beginning as jealousy of a brother's wife, simply because she was the daughter of a stranger, sin gained such powerful ascendancy, as to demand the most awful punishment for its subjection. We learn, that according to the nature of our transgression, so will be its chastisement. Miriam sought to raise herself not only above her brother's wife, but to an equality with that brother himself: and, by the infliction of a loathsome disease, she sunk at once below the lowest of her people. No one dared approach her; she was cut off even from employment, from every former object of interest, banished from the camp; and she would have thus remained till her death, had not Moses interfered to beseech and obtain forgiveness.

The direct interposition of the Lord in punishing sin, and rewarding virtue, is no longer visible; but few who study His word, their own hearts, and the face of the world, both past and present, will not acknowledge that He is still the same, retributing and rewarding as when His ways were made manifest to all. By the example of Scripture characters, He reveals to us now that which is still acceptable or unacceptable to Him. Presumption, jealousy, the scorn of individual blessings, in the coveting others, may no longer be punished by leprosy, but "the Lord's arm is not shortened," and He may afflict us in a variety of ways, and through the very feelings which we so sinfully encourage. Let us beware, then, of detraction, of jealousy, of presumption; for our Father in Heaven abhors these things. Let us look only for the blessings granted us individually, in our inward and outward lot, and comparing them with the sorrowing and afflicted, bless God for what he has given us; not insult Him, by looking with an eye of envy only on those to whom His wisdom has given more. There is not a thought, not a feeling, unknown to him; and O let us so guard our hearts, that we may be aware of the first whispering of sin, and banish it, even if it be in seeming but a thought.

As women of Israel, the history of Miriam is fraught with particular interest, from its so undeniably proving that woman must be quite as responsible a being as man before the Lord, or He certainly would not have deigned to appear Himself as her judge. Were woman unable of herself to eschew sin, Miriam's punishment would have been undoubtedly unjust. Nay, were she not responsible for *feelings*, as well as acts, God would not thus have stretched forth His avenging hand. Her feelings had only been formed into words, *not* yet into *action;* still the Lord punished. And would he have done so, did He not wish to make manifest, in the sight of the whole people, that both sexes were alike before Him? Were woman in a degraded position, Miriam, in the first place, would not have had sufficient power for her seditious words to be of any consequence; and, in the next, it would have been incumbent on man to chastise—there needed no interference of the Lord. We see therefore the very sinfulness of Jewish women, as recorded in the Bible, is undeniable evidence of their equality, alike in their power to subdue sin, and in its responsibility before God.

That the Eternal graciously pardoned at the word of Moses, is no proof that Miriam *needed* the supplication of man to bring her cause before the Lord, but simply that forgiveness and intercession from the *injured* for the *injurer*, are peculiarly acceptable to Him, and will ever bring reply. Miriam had equal power to pray and be heard, as Rebekah, Hannah, and other female characters of Scripture; but her punishment was no doubt to be increased by the painful feelings which, if she were not quite hardened, must have been excited, by the appeal of Moses in her favor, and in receiving the remission of her sentence through him. It at once proclaimed his power with the Lord, which she had sought to depreciate, and his still continued affection for herself. That the whole camp of Israel should halt in its march seven days for her alone—that she should suffer less than were she shut out from her fellows in the act of travelling—argues pretty strongly, that her being a woman in no degree lessened her importance, or rendered the men of Israel less careful for her comfort. They could not have done more, had the chastised been Aaron in her stead.

FEMALE WORKERS OF THE TABERNACLE.—CALEB'S DAUGHTER.

IN a history of the women of Israel, we must not forget those who are mentioned as aiding the holy work of the tabernacle. Proclamation was made throughout the camp, that every man and woman who had a *willing heart* should bring an offering unto the Lord, either of gold, silver, or brass, blue, purple, or scarlet, and fine linen, and goats' hair, and oil, and spices, and sweet incense, and onyx stones, and stones of all kinds; and that every one who was *wise-hearted* among them should come and make all that the Lord had commanded, which Moses proceeds to enumerate (see Exod. xxxv, and xxxvi). The congregation then departed to their several tents, but speedily came every one *whose heart stirred him up*, and every one whom his *spirit made willing*. "And they came, both men and WOMEN, as many as were willing-hearted, and brought bracelets, and earrings, and rings, and tablets of gold," &c. "And all *the women* who were *wise-hearted* did spin with their hands, and brought that which they had spun, both of blue, and of purple, and of scarlet, and of fine linen. And all the women *whose heart stirred them up in wisdom*, spun goats' hair. The children of Israel brought a willing offering unto the Lord, every man and *woman*, whose heart made them willing." In such quantities were these free offerings, that another proclamation was soon made; for " they spake unto Moses, saying, The people bring *much more than enough* for the service of the work, which the Lord commanded to make. And Moses gave commandment, and they caused it to be proclaimed throughout the camp, saying, Let neither man nor *woman* make any more work for the offering of the sanctuary. And the people were restrained from bringing."

We have quoted all these verses, at the risk of being thought tedious, on account of the very important truths they contain. In the first place we see that, notwithstanding the innumerable rebellions, seditions, and murmurings of the Israelites, there was still a vast multitude, whose hearts so stirred them up for the service of the Lord, as to bring more valuable offerings than could all be used. In the text, by the constant allusion to the *willing hearted*, and to those whose spirits made them willing, we read, that only those gifts were acceptable which were offered from the *heart*. No mere formal profession could here avail. The *spirit* within was to be the prompter, not the outward appearance. In the third, the frequent mention of the wise-hearted, or those whose hearts stirred them up in wisdom, we learn, from the context, specified more especially those whom God Himself had gifted for the work; and that all those arts of engraving, of embroidery, of weaving, of cunning work, of spinning, nay, every kind of male and female work, came originally as much from His inspiration, as every other higher branch usually denominated " natural gifts," " talents," or " genius." Spinning, weaving, engraving, and embroidery, are now so common, that we have quite forgotten from whose inspiration they originally came; and were we told that these very resources of the mind and fingers should be amongst the innumerable daily blessings for which we should thank God, we might be accused of enthusiasm and religious romance; yet who can read this chapter of Exodus, without feeling the truth of our position, and bidding the heart glow with thanksgiving for the innocent and happy resources of daily life?

In the fourth place, by both proclamations being addressed to WOMAN, as well as man, we have another unanswerable proof of their equality, not only in the power and freedom to bring offerings, but in their being equally gifted by the Eternal for the work. We peruse with admiration the self-devotion of the women of Carthage, when bringing together all their gold and silver ornaments to form arms for the defence of their city, even cutting off their hair to make strings for bows and other weapons; and our admiration is just: but how much more strongly should it be excited towards the women of Israel of old, who, from pure love of God, and zeal in His holy service, brought all their ornaments, bracelets, earrings, tablets, rings, jewels of gold and silver, every article of value which they could collect, and set themselves, heart and hand, to spin, weave, embroider, and use all their talents in His service by whom they had been bestowed. The women of Carthage were roused by a sense of rapidly approaching danger, by the excitement of war, by that pure love of home and land which God has implanted in every breast. The women of Israel were under no excitement; nay, they were wandering in a wilderness fraught with much to exhaust and weary mere *human nature*, however the immortal spirit might be sustained by the presence and revelation of the Lord. Their goal was in *perspective*. The voice of murmuring, of disbelief, was constantly sounding around them. "Wherefore is it, that thou hast brought us up out of Egypt, to kill us and our children?" were words, not once or twice, but countless times repeated, with every new trial of their faith. And what is so infectious in a "mixed multitude" as unbelief—aye, even in the very face of miracles performed in their behalf? Yet, at the first call, there were still very many wise and willing-hearted to come forward. The women of Carthage were actuated by the mere feelings of humanity, by *palpable* danger, by the clearly traced issue of their efforts. The women of Israel worked through FAITH. Hoping for no earthly reward, seeking no worldly glory, sacrificing ornaments most prized (for dress, as we shall presently see, was considered rather too much than too little by our ancestors), knowing that once given they could not be recalled, keeping neither time nor talent back, but using both perseveringly and indiscriminately, and all simply and solely out of pure love to God.

There is something both beautiful and consoling in this portion of our history. It informs us, that in the very midst of constant rebellions and constant fallings away, there were, and will always be found, many to love and serve their God. That

He will never leave Himself without witnesses upon earth; and that, therefore, however we may mourn the lack of energy and spirituality in Israel—however we may grieve and deplore the cases of infidelity or indifference, or even direct departures from His most Holy Law—still God is with us to retain many an unsuspected one in fidelity and zeal. Despondency, even in His cause, is more than wrong; it is sinful, for it doubts Him who is so strong to save; whose word is passed, that "Israel shall *never* cease to be a nation before Him;" and who even, from the deepest darkness, can and will bring forth light. It causes feelings towards our fellows, both of injustice and pain; and in ourselves deadens every effort after holiness and righteousness, by the supposition, that the struggles of one individual must be all in vain. Despondency treads so closely upon indifference, that every effort should be put in force to prevent its ascendancy. We cannot have faith either in God or man if we despond, and thus we are gradually led into sin, alike against our Father in Heaven, our brother man, and ourselves.

To us as women, the particular mention of our female ancestors, as bringing offerings and working for the tabernacle, is inexpressibly consoling. It assures us that, lowly as we are, retired as is our natural sphere, incapable as is our weaker frame for the exertions of man in the Lord's service, that still we are acceptable—still He will graciously look down on our "willing hearts," and the humble work of our hand, and bless them with such love, as will give us peace even upon earth. It tells us, that from Him comes every employment and resource, alike of mind and hand; and that, in consequence, all should be used to His glory; not, indeed, for the service of the tabernacle, for we are not now so called upon to work, but in the happiness which His gifts should bestow upon ourselves and our fellow-creatures. Had we but these two chapters in our Holy Law, we should have sufficient to confirm our spiritual privileges—that our Father asks but a willing spirit, a heart that is stirred within us to do His service, whatever it may be, to resign whatever He may call; but it MUST BE a willing heart: mere lip-service is mockery and sin. Let it not be said that the Jewish religion is a religion of mere form, incumbent only on the males, and therefore debarring woman from all religious exercises, all access to God. Bid those who throw such foul wrong on Israel, come hither to the pure unadulterated fount of the Living God, and then say, if the religion of the Nazarene were the *first*, and *only one*, to teach woman her holy privileges, and to preach that pure spiritual piety of the heart, that simple working through faith, which is revealed so blessedly in our Law, and confirmed by every inspired prophet of the Lord. And that religion of the heart is ours still. We need no other to replace it.

The age of chivalry is generally supposed to be a powerful proof of the respect and consideration with which women were regarded amongst the Gentile nations during the middle ages. Their position was marked; their love, their hand—the greatest reward, the most powerful incentive for the young warriors to distinguish themselves. Marvellous deeds were done, and dangers dared, all for the smiles of woman; nay, evil passions were often subdued: generosity, magnanimity, kindness, and many other virtues, were called into play by woman's influence, without which, those ages would have been dark indeed. Her individual position might have been too elevated; but still that elevation was far more often used for good than evil. Chivalry *did* bring forth good with regard to woman's influence on man, and no one assuredly will deny, but that to have been held up as the rewarder of valour, the incentive of virtue, must have made her a subject of consideration, respect, and love, very different to slavery and degradation.

Now, the very instance of chivalry which history records, is found in the Bible, and in the history of that very people to whose women similar privileges are denied. "And Caleb said, He that smiteth Kirjathsepher [also called Debir], and taketh it, to him will I give Achsah my daughter to wife. And Othniel, the son of Kenaz, Caleb's younger brother, took it: and he gave him Achsah his daughter to wife. And it came to pass, as she came unto him, she moved him to ask of her father a field: and she lighted off her ass; and Caleb said unto her, What wouldst thou? and she said unto him, Give me a blessing: for thou hast given me a south land; give me also springs of water. And Caleb gave her also the upper springs, and the nether springs." We find all these verses, first in Joshua xv. 16—19, and repeated without any variation in Judges i. 12—15. Caleb was a prince of the tribe of Judah (Numbers xiii. 6), so high in favour with the Lord, as to be joined with Joshua in being permitted to enter the promised land, and designated by the Eternal as "My servant Caleb, who hath followed me fully."

Caleb seems to have been, like Joshua, a prince and warrior of high repute, dauntless, and faithful before God and before man. His daughter (though not an only child, for we read in 1 Chron. iv. 15, that he had also three sons) shared the consideration proffered to her father. Caleb must have seen the high respect and admiration in which she was held, or he never would have dreamed of offering her as the reward of valour. That which is of no value, lightly won, and lightly held, and, when obtained, to sink merely into a household slave, was not at all likely to excite young men to the arduous task of smiting and taking a fortified city, defended as it was by the sons of Anak, whose immense stature, and extraordinary prowess, had formerly caused them to be considered as "giants," in whose sight the children of Israel were but as "grasshoppers." Nor can we regard this as merely a solitary instance : it is a proof of the *general condition* of Hebrew women at that period ; and also that Othniel was not Achsah's only admirer.

"He that smiteth and taketh it, to him will I give Achsah my daughter to wife," is a general appeal, supposing her hand to be a sufficient incentive to all the young men of the tribe ; and that His Law, regarding the inheritance of daughters, should not be transgressed, the Eternal blessed the valiant efforts of Othniel, Caleb's own nephew, with success ; and the coveted maiden became his wife.

That it was solely Achsah herself who was sought and won, with no idea of her wealth, is clearly proved by the simple words " she moved him [her husband] to ask of her father, a field or piece of land ;" the wish for possession came from her, not from Othniel, who was in all probability fully satisfied with the recompense he had gained ; and when Caleb had granted this request, as we know by the words in which she afterwards addresses him, she approached him herself, and lighting off her ass, a token of the respect natural to Israel, Caleb asked her, " What wilt thou ?" and she answered him, "Give me a blessing :" meaning, possibly, a further token of his love for her ; " for thou hast given me a south land, [alluding to that already given at Othniel's request,] give me also springs of water : and Caleb gave her the upper and the nether springs."

Without springs, land, in so hot a country as Judea, was of little value ; and therefore is it that Achsah craves this boon in addition to that already granted. The affectionate confidence subsisting between the father and daughter is beautifully illustrated in this simple little incident. Though Achsah held her father in such respect as not to prefer her request while *sitting* on her ass before him, yet she feared not to make her wishes known, fully conscious that, were they in his power, he would grant them unhesitatingly; and his instant reply proves how much reason she had for her confidence.

We learn too from this, that woman must undoubtedly have had the power of possessing landed property in her own right, and in a degree exclusive of her husband;[*] else Caleb would have made over the portion intended for her to Othniel on his marriage, instead of waiting for Achsah to ask, and granting it to her alone.

The beautiful law of our God was then in full force among every rank and condition of man; and surely we can find no trace in the history of Achsah to confirm the false position of our being degraded. Does it not rather elevate us to a perfect equality with our brother man, and prove undeniably that the Israelites were the very first nation in the world to hold forth the love and hand of woman as the pure and holy incentive to deeds of manliness and valour?

DEBORAH.

THE promised land was gained: deeds of extraordinary valour and military skill and prowess marked its conquest and subdivision; but God's express command was disobeyed: and, in consequence, the tribes, even after they had settled in their respective territories, were continually, "doing evil in the sight of the Lord," and at war, as a chastisement, with their idolatrous neighbours. God had ordained the extermination of the former inhabitants of Palestine, because of their fearful state of idolatry, and various abominations. He had deferred bringing in the seed of Abraham to their appointed land,

---

[*] And exclusive also of her brothers; for if landed inheritance were to be man's only, she could have had no claim to any portion. The above was written originally, under the impression that Achsah was Caleb's only child: a further study of the genealogies in Chronicles, proves that she was not.

because "the iniquity of the Amorites was not yet full." He might in His wisdom have exterminated them by fire, water, or disease; but he appointed the swords of the Israelites as the instruments of His wrath, simply to try their faith, and obedience, and bid them *earn* the rest, peace, spiritual and temporal glory, which he had held forth as the recompense of perfect obedience.

This fact is very frequently disregarded in a mere superficial reading of the history of Canaan. There are those even to doubt and cavil at the ways of their God, because He commanded His people to obtain possession of the promised land by the edge of the sword; forgetting that so doing was at once a punishment for those who had insulted Him by their awful iniquities (having full power to subdue sin, and keep in the straight path, as did the inhabitants of Mesopotamia even without direct revelation), and also to try the obedience of His people. Disease, fire, or flood, would have accomplished the first of these designs equally with the plan adopted; but not the second. Yet the former would at once have been recognised as the hand of God; no one questioning the agency of either the deluge, the destruction of Sodom, or the earthquake and the plague, punishing the rebellion of Korah. Why then should not the sword of slaughter be traced to the same Divine ordination, whence alone in fact it proceeded?

The Israelites, however, failed in their commanded obedience. Instead of exterminating, they entered into friendly leagues with the enemies and insulters of their God; and the Eternal, in His just anger, permitted them, in consequence, to remain as "thorns, and pricks in their sides, and their false gods as a snare unto them." And so it was: "They took their daughters to be their wives, and gave their daughters to their sons, and served their gods. And the children of Israel did evil in the sight of God, and forgat the Lord their God, and served Baalim and the groves." And this fearful state of things occurred repeatedly; rousing the anger of the Lord each time to sell them into the hands of their enemies; and yet whenever they cried unto Him in returning faith and repentance, His infinite mercy raised up deliverers in whom He put His spirit, and saved them.

Othniel, the nephew and son-in-law of Caleb, Ehud, and Shamgar, had each in his turn been thus selected by the Lord; and during their respective sways Israel was at rest and obedient. But between each, they had relapsed into idolatry and rebellion; and after the deaths of Ehud and Shamgar, who appeared contemporaries, falling anew into evil, the Eternal sold them into the hands of Jabin king of Hazor, who mightily oppressed them twenty years, and caused them again to cry unto the Lord.

But even in these periods of anarchy and rebellion, all were not idolatrous. There must still have been many "seven thousands who had not bowed the knee to Baal," else would not the Lord have thus repeatedly compassionated and relieved them. Amongst these faithful few, the law was of course followed, and the people judged according to the statutes given through Moses. Had there been the very least foundation for the supposition of the degrading and heathenising the Hebrew female, we should not find the offices of prophet, judge, military instructor, poet, and sacred singer, all *combined* and all *perfected* in the person of a woman; a fact clearly and almost startlingly illustrative of what must have been their high and intellectual training, as well as natural aptitude for guiding and enforcing the statutes of their God, to which at that time woman could attain.

"And Deborah, a prophetess, the wife of Lapidoth, she judged Israel at that time. And she dwelt under the palm tree of Deborah between Ramah and Bethel, in Mount Ephraim: and the children of Israel came unto her for judgment." This simple description evinces that the greatness of Deborah consisted not at all in outward state, in semblance of high rank, or in any particular respect or homage outwardly paid her; but simply in her vast superiority of mental and spiritual acquirements which were acknowledged by her countrymen, and consequently revered. The office of judge in Israel was not hereditary. It only devolved on those gifted to perform it; and, by the example before us, might be held by either sex, rather an *unsatisfactory* proof of the degradation of Jewish women. We are expressly told that Deborah was a prophetess, and "the wife of Lapidoth." Now, by the arrangement of the sentence, confirmed by the context, it is very evident that Deborah was a prophetess in her own person, wholly and entirely distinct from her husband, who was a mere cypher in public concerns. The Eternal had inspired her, a WOMAN and a WIFE in Israel, with His spirit expressly to do His will, and make manifest to her countrymen how little is He the respector of persons ; judging only by hearts perfect in His service, and spirits willing for the work : heeding neither the weakness nor apparent inability of one sex, compared with the greater natural powers of the other.

Yet so naturally are her public position and personal gifts described, that we cannot possibly believe her elevation to be an extraordinary occurrence, or that her position as a wife forbade her rising above mere conjugal and household duties. We never hear of a slave, or leper, or heathen, being entrusted with the prophetic spirit of the Eternal, simply because the social condition of such persons would and must prevent their obtaining either the respect, obedience, or even attention of the people. For the same reason, had woman really been on a par with these, as she is by some declared to be, she would never have been entrusted with gifts spiritual and mental, which Deborah so richly possessed. She never could have been a prophetess, for her words would only have been regarded as idle raving. She could never have been a judge, from the want of opportunities to train and perfect her intellect, and to obtain the necessary experience. Now it is clear that instead of this, her natural position must have been so high, that there needed not even adventitious state and splendour to make it acknowledged ; and her intellect and judgment so cultivated, as not only to bring the people flocking to her for judgment, but to occasion Barak's refusal to set out on a warlike expedition unless she accompanied them.

We find the first recorded instance of her using her prophetic power in Judges iv. 6 : " And she sent and called Barak the son of Abinoam out of Kedesh Naphtali, and said unto him, Hath not the Lord God of Israel commanded, saying, Go and draw towards Mount Tabor, and take with thee ten thousand men of the children of Naphtali and the children of Zebulun ? And I will draw unto thee Sisera, the captain of Jabin's army, and his chariots and his multitudes ; and I will deliver him into thine hand. And Barak said unto her, *If thou wilt go with me*, then I will go : but if thou wilt not go with me, then will I not go. And she said, I will surely go with thee : notwithstanding the journey shall not be for thine honour ; for the Lord will sell Sisera into the hand of a woman."

We should be at a loss to understand the feeling in Barak, which impelled his reply, might we not infer it from Deborah's rejoinder. It would appear that, like many of his countrymen, while he obeyed, he was still wanting in the perfect faith which would have given him a glorious triumph in his own person. The presence of Deborah could in no way give him greater increase of safety and glory, than had he gone without her. She was but the instrument of the Lord, making His will known to her fellows. The words were not hers, but God's; and Barak should have acted on them without either reservation or doubt. Instead of which we find him making a *condition* to his obedience; and refusing to obey, if that condition were not complied with. What could the presence of a woman avail him? Her being a prophetess gave him no more assurance of conquest than the word of the Lord had already done; and *because he trusted more in the woman than in her God* the journey would not be to his honour; a *woman's* hand should accomplish that complete downfall of Sisera, which would otherwise have accrued to his individual glory. It is evident that this is the real rendering of this rather obscure sentence, else we should not have it so expressly stated that the "journey would not be for his honour."

Deborah however arose, and went with Barak, first to collect the necessary troops from Zebulun and Naphtali, and then to Mount Tabor, where Sisera and his immense armament of nine hundred chariots of iron, besides infantry, marched to meet them. Still we find Barak but secondary, doing nothing without the word of the Lord through Deborah. And Deborah said, "Up! for this is the day in which the Lord hath delivered Sisera into thine hand: is not the Lord gone out before thee? So Barak went down from Mount Tabor, and ten thousand men after them;" and the Lord gave them such complete victory, that but Sisera escaped, to receive his death at the hand of a woman, according to the Eternal's word. Nor was it a single victory, for "the hand of the children of Israel prospered and prevailed against Jabin, king of Canaan."

We next find Deborah exercising that glorious talent of extempore poetry only found amongst the Hebrews; and by her, a woman and a wife in Israel, possessed to an almost equal degree with the Psalmist and prophets, who followed at a later period. Her song is considered one of the most beautiful specimens of Hebrew poetry, whether read in the original, or in the English version. We find her taking no glory whatever to herself, but calling upon the princes, and governors, and people of Israel, to join with her in "blessing the Lord for the avenging of Israel." In the fourth and fifth verses, she alludes, by a most beautiful figure, to the power of the Eternal. That before Him "the earth trembled, and the heavens dropped, and the clouds dropped water. And the mountains trembled, even Sinai, before the Lord God of Israel," thus manifesting that His power, not man's, had brought delivery to Israel. Then in the sixth and eighth verses she describes the condition of the people before she arose a mother in Israel; that they were compelled to travel in by-paths, because of the high roads all being occupied by their foes; and from the villages all the inhabitants had ceased, from their being continually exposed undefended to the enemy. Nor was there a shield or spear seen in the forty thousand of Israel. The simplicity and lowliness of the prophetess' natural position, is beautifully illustrated by the term she applies to herself—neither princess, nor governor, nor judge, nor prophetess, though both the last offices she fulfilled—"until that I, Deborah, arose, until I arose a MOTHER in Israel." She asked no greater honour or privilege for herself individually, than the being recognised as the mother of the people whom the Lord alone had endowed her with power to judge. "My heart is towards the governors of Israel," she continues, "that offered themselves willingly among the people. Bless ye the Lord," meaning those who, rising from the idolatry and sloth which had encompassed the people, offered themselves willingly for the service of the Lord. She bids them speak—all classes of people—from those princes who rode on white asses, and those who sat in judgment, and those who walked by the way, to even the drawers of water who had before been harassed by the noise of the archers coming forcibly to disturb their domestic employments; and all were to rehearse the righteous acts of the Lord, for to Him alone they owed their preservation. "The Lord made ME have dominion over the mighty," she says, in verse thirteen, thus retaining her own dignity and power in Israel, yet tracing it to the Eternal, not to herself. The poetry describing the downfall of their foes, calling forth the imagery of nature to give it force and life: the death of Sisera, and the waiting and watching of his mother at her lattice—"Why is his chariot so long in coming? why tarry the wheels of his chariots?" and the answer, alike from her ladies, and her own heart, "Have they not sped? have they not divided the prey; to every man a damsel or two; to Sisera a prey of divers colours, a prey of divers colours of needle work, meet for the necks of them that take the spoil?" as if to fail with his mighty armament were impossible; and thus sung by the lips of the conquerors, infused with a species of satire, giving indescribable poignancy to the strain; and then the glorious conclusion, "So let all thine enemies perish, O Lord: but let them that love thee be as the sun when he goeth forth in his might;" form altogether one of the sublimest strains of spiritual fervour in the Bible; and mark forcibly, by her conduct, both as prophetess and judge, that in Deborah, even as in Gideon, David, and the prophets of later years, God disdained not to breathe His spirit, but made a WOMAN His instrument to judge, to prophecy, to teach, and to redeem.

"And the land had rest forty years," we are told at the conclusion of Deborah's song; words which, as no other judge is mentioned, would lead us to infer that Deborah continued "a mother in Israel" all that time, retaining the people in fidelity, and consequently in temporal and spiritual peace. Even if she did not live herself to govern all those years, it is evident that her influence and instructions were remembered and acted upon, for it was not till *after* these forty years that "Israel again did evil in the sight of the Lord," and so again required a redeemer, which was granted in the person of Gideon.

The silence preserved regarding the subsequent life and death of Deborah, is a simple confirmation of the meekness and humility with which we found her judging Israel under her own palm-tree, before being called to a more stirring scene. The land was at peace, the power of prophecy and foresight in military matters was no longer needed, and Deborah resumed her personally humble station, evidently without any ambitious wish, or attempt to elevate her rank or prospects. It was enough that she was useful to her countrymen; that she was a lowly instrument in the Eternal's hand to work them good. What, now, did she need to satisfy the *woman nature*, which she still so evidently retained? Her judgments, her works, are covered with the veil of silence, but we learn their effects by the simple phrase, that "the land had rest forty years"—the land, the whole land, not merely that which was under her direct superintendence. Virtue, holiness, and wisdom, though the gifts of but one lowly individual, are not confined to one place, when used, as were Deborah's, to the glory of God, and the good of her people. Silently, and perhaps unperceived, they spread over space and time ; and O how glorious must be the destiny of that woman, who, without one moment quitting her natural sphere, can yet by precept, example, and labour, produce such blessed effects as to give the land peace, and bring a whole people unto God !

In a *practical* view, perhaps, the character of Deborah cannot now be brought home to the conduct of her descendants, for woman can no longer occupy a position of such trust and wisdom in Israel ; but, *theoretically*, we may take the history of Deborah to our hearts, both *nationally* and individually. With such an example in the Word of our God, it is unanswerably evident that neither the Written nor the Oral Law could have contained one syllable to the disparagement of woman.

Men were in no condition to have permitted the influence of woman, had they not been accustomed, by the constant and emphatic enjoinments of the law, to look on her with respect, consideration, and tenderness. Mentally and spiritually, Deborah was gifted in an extraordinary degree, leading us to infer that the women of Israel must have had the power to cultivate both mind and spirit, and to delight in their resources, for we have the whole Bible to prove that the Eternal never selected for the instruments of His will, any but those whose hearts were inclined towards Him, even before He called them —witness the history of Abraham, Joseph, Moses, David, and others. All and every talent comes from God, but will not work and influence by His sole gift alone. They are given to be improved, persevered in, perfected, by those to whom they are entrusted, and then used in the service of their Giver. It is evident, then, that Deborah had the *inclination* and the *power* to cultivate, perfect, and use the gifts of her God ; and this would have been quite impossible, had her social condition been such as the enemies of *scriptural* and *spiritual* Judaism declare. With the history of Deborah in their hands, the young daughters of Israel need little other defence or argument to convince their adversaries that they require no other creed, nor even a denial of the Oral Law, to teach them their proper position, alike to themselves and their fellows, and in their relative duties towards God and man.

Deborah being a wife, confirms this yet more strongly. There must not only have been perfect freedom of *position*, but of *action;* even more than is found in the history of any modern nation, for we do not find a single instance of a wife being elected to any public office requiring intellect and spirituality, secular and religious knowledge, so completely distinct from her husband. Yet the history of Deborah in no way infers that she was neglectful of her conjugal and domestic duties. There is an unpretending simplicity about her very greatness. The very fact of those she judged coming to her under her own palm tree, supposes her quiet and retired mode of living. She never leaves her home, except at the earnest entreaty of Barak, which urges her to sacrifice domestic retirement for public good. To a really great mind, domestic and public duties are so perfectly compatible, that the first need never be sacrificed for the last. And that Lapidoth in no manner interfered with the public offices of his wife, called as she was to them by God Himself through His gifts, infers a noble confidence and respectful consideration towards her, evidently springing at once from the national equality and freedom tendered to Jewish women : and from a mind great enough to appreciate and value such talents even in a woman; a greatness not very often found in modern times.

To follow in the steps of our great ancestress is not possible now that the prophetic spirit is removed from Israel, and the few public offices left us fall naturally to the guardianship of man; yet many and many a Jewish woman is entrusted with one or more talents direct from God; and if she can stretch forth a helping hand to the less enlightened of her people, let her not hold back, from the false and unscriptural belief that woman cannot aid the cause of God, or in any way attain to religious knowledge. His word is open to her, as to man. In Moses' command to read and explain the Law to all people, woman was included by name. And now the whole Bible, Law, Historical books, Psalms, and Prophets, are open to her daily commune, and shall it be said that she has neither the right nor the understanding to make use of such blessed privilege? Shame, shame, on those who would thus cramp the power of the Lord, in denying to any one of His creatures the power of addressing and comprehending Him through the inexhaustible treasure of His gracious word!

Every married woman is judge and guardian of her own

household. She may have to encounter the prejudices of a husband, not yet thinking with her on all points; but if she have really a great mind, she will know how to *influence* without in any way *interfering*. She will know how to serve the Lord in her household, without neglecting her duty and affection towards her husband; and by domestic conduct influence society at large, secretly and unsuspectedly indeed, but more powerfully than she herself can in the least degree suppose.

To unmarried women, even as to wives, some talent is entrusted which may be used to the glory of its Giver. Life is not lent us to be frittered away in an unmeaning, little satisfactory run of amusements, or often in their mere fruitless search. There surely is some period in a single woman's existence, when the hopes, ambition, and even favorite amusements of girlhood must come to an end. Because unmarried, is woman still to believe herself a girl, hoping for, and looking for, a change in her existence, which will in reality never come? Would it not be wiser and better, aye, and incalculably happier, if woman herself withdrew from the sphere of exciting hopes and pleasures which she had occupied in girlhood? If she sought, perseveringly and prayerfully, some new objects of interest, affection, and employment, which she might justly hope would become a stay and support in rapidly advancing years, and thus entirely prevent the ennui, and its attendants, love of gossip, frivolity, and often sourness and irritability, which are too generally believed to be the sole characteristics of single (and so of course supposed, disappointed) women? Have we not all some precious talent lent us by our God, and for the use of which He will demand an account? Is there not the whole human family from which to select some few objects of interest, on whom to expend some of our leisure time, and draw our thoughts from all engrossing self? Were there but one object on whom we have lavished kindness, and taught to look up to God and heaven, and to walk this earth virtuously and meekly—but one or two whom, had we the pecuniary means, we have clothed and fed—a sick or dying bed that we have soothed—a sorrowing one consoled—an erring one turned from the guilty path—the repentant, or the weak, strengthened and encouraged—we shall not have lived in vain; or, when we come to die, look shudderingly back on a useless life and wasted gifts; on existence lost in the vain struggle to arrest the flight of time, and still seek hope and pleasure in thoughts and scenes whose sweetness has been too long extracted for ought to remain but bitterness and gall. Deborahs in truth we cannot be; but each and all have talents given, and a sphere assigned them, and, like her, all have it in their power, in the good performed towards man, to use the one, and consecrate the other to the service of their God.

WIFE OF MANOAH.

SEVERAL years passed since the death of Deborah. Gideon, Tola, Jair, Jephthah, Ibzan, Elon, and Abdan, had successively judged Israel, often with interregnums of rebellion, apostasy, and anarchy. After the death of the last mentioned judge, "the children of Israel again did evil in the sight of the Lord, and He delivered them into the hands of the Philistines forty years." We now come to another incident in the history of the women of Israel demanding our attention. In the tribe of Dan was a certain man of the city of Zorah, named Manoah, whose wife had no children, always a source of grief in the families of Israel; *not*, as the Christians believe, from the idea of becoming the mother of the promised Messiah (who is scarcely mentioned till the time of the prophets, when the awfully threatened chastisements of the Eternal needed such consolatory promises), but because children were always considered proofs of the Lord's love, a privilege granted from Him as the recompense of faithful service; as we read in the words of David, "Lo, children are an heritage of the Lord: and the fruit of the womb IS HIS REWARD" (Psalm cxxvii.). And, again, "Thy wife shall be as a fruitful vine by the sides of thine house: and thy children like olive plants around thy table. Behold, *thus shall* the man *be blessed* that feareth the Lord. Thou shalt see thy children's children, and peace on Israel" (Psalm cxxviii.). To go down childless to the grave, and so prevent the name from being "built up," in Israel, was deemed a heavy affliction, inferring, for some secret sin or public transgression, the anger of the Lord.

Sacred Writ is silent as to the reason of the Eternal's selection falling on the family of Manoah for a deliverer in part from the Philistines, but we are justified in inferring from the context, that they were one of the few faithful followers of

Israel, by whom the Law was in all points obeyed. Be that, however, as it may, this is certain, that it was to the WOMAN, not to the man, the Most High deigned to send His angelic messenger, with not only the blessed revelation that He would grant her a son, but deigning to instruct her as to the food and drink she was to refrain from taking herself, and to the devoting her babe as a Nazarite to the Lord, even from his infancy; thus making the direct commands of the Immutable agree in all points with the Law which His wisdom and mercy had already given.

Naturally astonished, for such revelations were not even then common in Israel, we find " the woman" following the impulse of her confiding nature, hastening on the instant to her husband, and informing him that a man of God had come unto her, and his countenance was very terrible (signifying, not actually terrible, but grand and imposing), like the countenance of an angel of the Lord; but "I asked him not whence he was, neither told me his name." From this description of the heavenly messenger, it appears that the woman did not consider him in reality an angel, supposing him a man of God or prophet, bearing a message from the Most High, as was usual in Israel, yet still struck by the imposing beauty of his countenance, and feeling it possessed something beyond mortality.

Equally astonished, but *believing*, Manoah lost no time in idle speculation, but betook himself instantly to prayer; thus confirming our idea of his faithfulness and piety, and proving one grand and important national truth, that the Israelites needed no *mediator* whatever, be he man or angel, to bring up their prayers before God, and obtain His gracious reply. Here was Manoah, living on his own estates, in his own tribe, far removed from the priests of the Lord and the tabernacle, through the first of whom alone it is declared, by our opponents, that the prayers of Israel could be acceptably offered up. No priest near, of whom he could either ask or obtain counsel; no wise man or judge, of whom he might demand advice or explanation. Yet the law was then in force all over Israel, and if it had been illegal and derogatory to the dignity of the Lord to address Him in prayer from any place, or at any time, we should have found Manoah hastening without a moment's delay to the appointed spot, and offering sacrifices to obtain the mediation of the anointed priest, knowing that through him only he could obtain reply.

Instead of which, we find him, without even pause or hesitation, believing the words of his wife so implicitly, as to offer up a prayer of such simple construction that it clearly proves how little the Most High regards mere formula in prayer, when springing, as did Manoah's, from humility and faith. "Then Manoah entreated the Lord, and said, O my Lord, let the man of God which thou didst send come again to us, and teach us what we shall do unto the child that shall be born." Here is no doubt expressed as to the reality of the blessing proffered: "The child that shall be born," reveals how fully he believed in the promise; but, as was natural to humanity, he entreated a confirmation of the instructions vouchsafed, not knowing how far the imagination and the fears of his wife might have tinctured her relation.

"And God hearkened to the voice of Manoah." Did we need any further incentive to "entreat the Lord" in all things, surely we have it here. Manoah had simply spoken the thoughts of his heart in words, which would be their natural vehicle of expression. He had prayed through the merits of neither dead nor living, man nor angel, but in lowly trusting faith, and God hearkened and answered. Again His messenger appeared unto the woman as she sat in the field, Manoah not being with her, and she ran to inform her husband, saying that the man had again appeared unto her, the same who had come previously; and Manoah, no doubt in secret adoring the Beneficent God who had thus deigned to answer his prayer, went with his wife, and demanded of the messenger, if he were indeed the man who had visited them before. And being answered in the affirmative, he besought a repetition of how to "order the child;" and the angel condescended a full reply, reiterating all his previous instructions. Still believing him a man, as himself, only gifted with the spirit of the Lord, Manoah, with the hospitality peculiar to the Hebrew, besought him to remain until "we shall have made ready a kid for thee." And the angel of the Lord said unto Manoah, "Though thou detain me, I will not eat of thy bread. And if thou wilt offer a burnt offering thou must offer it unto the Lord; *for Manoah knew not that he was an angel of the Lord.* And Manoah said, "What is thy name? that when thy sayings come to pass, we may do thee honour. And the angel of the Lord said unto him, Wherefore askest thou thus after my name, seeing it is secret? So Manoah took a kid with a meat-offering, and offered it upon a rock unto the Lord. And it came to pass, when the flame went up towards heaven from off the altar, the angel of the Lord ascended in the flame of the altar, and Manoah and his wife looked on it, and fell with their faces to the ground. And the angel of the Lord did no more appear unto Manoah and his wife; then Manoah knew he was an angel of the Lord. And Manoah said, We shall surely die, for we have seen God [i.e. a messenger direct from God]. But his wife said unto him, If the Lord were pleased to kill us, He would not have received a burnt-offering and a meat-offering at our hands, neither would He have showed us all these things, nor would at this [second] time have told us such things as these" (Judges xiii).

We have quoted this chapter almost at length, because it contains so much which is almost imperative for us to consider in a national point of view, before we can come to regard it in its bearings on our history as women. Any elucidation or defence of our national belief will not, we trust, be deemed out of place in a Jewish work, however little it may be pronounced to have to do with the main point of its subject. In an age when so much of controversy is going on, when even the intimate association, and often friendships, between Hebrew and Gentile may bring forward peculiar points of belief, to inquire their differences or varying modes of interpretation—it becomes imperatively necessary for the young Hebrew of either sex to be provided with such defence as will, at least, satisfy his own heart and conscience, and render him invulnerable to the peculiar expositions proffered to his attention, however little such defence may weigh with the hereditary prejudices of his opponents. There is a wide difference between an argument seeking the conversion of another, and that merely defending our own belief, on the same sacred authority as gives a supposed foundation for the belief of an opponent. As long as the Christian confines his arguments and quotations to the New Testament, the Israelite feels perfectly secure, from his entire rejection of such authority as Divine. But when the words of the Old Testament are so explained as to bear almost startlingly upon the creed of our adversaries, then it is we need careful, though perfectly simple, training, to provide us both with reply and with defence. To be kept in ignorance of the Nazarine readings of the Bible does no good whatever; for there are very few who can hope to pass through life, particularly now that social intercourse is so unrestrained, without some approach to the differences of belief, and their causes. Much better is it to know clearly the danger we are not unlikely to encounter, and how to avert it, than to come upon it wholly unprepared. Not in childhood indeed, for it would be folly to perplex the young mind with the tenets of *two* beliefs: then it is simply necessary to impress and explain the essentials of their own creed; but in maturer years, when the opening mind is not only capable of understanding, but feels itself restless and anxious for something more than the mere education of childhood, then let them compare their belief with that of others; let them know what and why their opponents so believe, through the enlarged and liberal views of a spiritually Jewish instructor; let the light of reason and revelation be their guide, and we shall find both male and female of the Hebrew youth so confirmed in their own blessed faith, as to live and die for it, yet eschewing all of illiberality, uncharitableness, and scorn, towards those of other and less enlightened creeds.

The chapter under consideration is one of those much regarded by the Nazarene, and always brought forward in controversial discussion. From Manoah's simple words "We have seen God," they believe, that wherever the "angel of the Lord" is mentioned, it signifies the second person of the Godhead; and that as He took visible form to our ancestors of old, so we might equally believe in His taking the form of Jesus to save the world.

To a mere superficial thinker this argument might prove dangerous; and we are therefore anxious to explain this chapter according to the Israelite's belief. In the first place, we refuse to see in this messenger any thing more than the Word of God declares, "an angel of the Lord," simply because the Eternal said unto Moses, in answer to his earnest entreaty, "Shew me thy glory, THOU CANST NOT SEE MY FACE: FOR THERE SHALL NO MAN SEE ME, AND LIVE." And we therefore know, that no man has or ever can see His face, and live; for God is a God of truth, and knows not the very shadow of a change. That which He has once said is immutable, unwavering, changeless as Himself. That there may be, even in the books of Moses, one or two verses seeming to contradict this assertion, as in Exodus xxiv, verses 10 and 11, and in verse 11 of chapter xxxiii., is of no importance, being either a wrong translation, or the mere manner of writing, to bring down the solemn appearance of the glory of God to the comprehensions of the mixed multitude, and impossible to be weighed a single moment with the words of the Most High Himself. Would He declare the solemn truth in one part of His Holy Word, confirming it by every prophet, and in another part command His people, as a condition of their salvation, to believe in His appearing on earth, and conversing face to face with man, first as an angel, and then in human form? The very words of Manoah confirm this belief, and prove it was entertained as strongly by the ancient as the modern Jews. The Nazarenes take only the last member of this sentence, forgetting the important fact, "*We shall surely die, if, indeed, we have seen God,*" for such is the real meaning of his words, and that he did not die; and the simple truth of his wife's suggestion convinced him, no doubt, as it convinces us, that it was not God whom he had seen, but one of those angelic messengers whom it sometimes pleased the Lord to employ to deliver His missions unto man. The nature of such beings it needs not now to inquire; but the belief in the existence of angels is so twined with the belief in the Bible, that if we disbelieve the one, we must disbelieve the other. The very word מַלְאָךְ, derived from the Arabic לאך, *to send,* or *employ,* signifies merely a messenger, a legate, used indiscriminately for one employed by a king as ambassador, or by the Lord as an angel, prophet, or priest; and sometimes also applied to whatever is sent by the Eternal to execute His will, even as winds and plagues.

The grand and imposing aspect of the angelic countenance, as we have seen, struck Manoah's wife; but that neither she nor her husband supposed him any thing more than a prophet or priest, is evident by their manner of addressing him, and their entreating him to tarry for refreshment. The angel's reply is strong confirmation of what we have already stated concerning his real office. To eat of their bread would be confirming their idea that he was but a man; to accept their burnt-offering would be arrogating to himself what was due only to his Heavenly Master. "If thou offer a burnt-offering thou must offer it unto the Lord;" not to him, who, though of an angelic nature, was still nothing but a messeng Still ignorant that he was an angel, Manoah asks his name, to do him honour; and *because he knew how liable were even believing Israelites to turn aside from the worship of the im-*

mutable God to worship others, and jealous for the glory of His Master, the angel refused to tell his name, declaring it was secret—that when his words came to pass, Manoah or his wife might not have even a *name* to turn aside their thoughts from the one sole God ; still, to convince them that he was not a mere mortal, but came direct from the Lord, he ascended, or disappeared, in the flame of the altar, as had been the sign of the divine acceptance of the offering, from the sacrifice of Abel downward. And it was knowing this, and recognising the immediate agency of the Most High, in thus sending one of His own messengers, that so overwhelmed Manoah and his wife with religious awe, as to cause them to fall with their faces to the ground, not daring to look even upon the semblance of His glory.

A layman, and a lowly individual of his father's tribe, it was not unnatural that Manoah should even be more awe-struck, than rejoiced, at the revelation so graciously vouchsafed ; and whilst the mistaken idea engrossed him, if, indeed, it ever did, that he had conversed with God, he could not do otherwise than fear instant death, for, like all his brethren, he knew the God of Israel was a God of truth ; and, therefore, if he had seen him, he must cease to live. The ready answer of his wife removed these groundless fears ; and while it told him, that if it had pleased the Lord to kill them, He would not have accepted offerings at their hands, or so revealed His will, it must have equally have convinced him, as a believer in the revelation of the Lord through Moses, that it was *not* God, but His messenger whom he had seen.

Such is the simple rendering of this very simple chapter ; while the second commandment, and the words already quoted, " No man can see me, and live," with the firm belief that God is TRUTH, are all sufficient wherewith satisfactorily to explain, both to our own hearts and those of our children, every verse that may seem to read slightly contradictory, and supply us with an impenetrable shield, against which the reasonings of our opponents must fall blunted and harmless to the ground.

Regarding this narrative in its bearings on our history as Women of Israel, it is confirmation strong of our always attested declaration, that neither Written nor Oral Law interfered with the perfect equality of man and wife. The chapter before us displays a simple and natural picture of conjugal confidence and equality, and of the respective peculiarities of man and woman. It is impossible to read this chapter, without perceiving that Manoah's wife was a perfectly free agent, only bound by the links of love and confidence which the marriage-law enjoins. As the mother of the child selected to deliver Israel in part from the Philistines, she was even of more importance in the sight of God than her husband, a fact inferred from the angel appearing both times to *her*, and only addressing Manoah when addressed by him. We find, too, Manoah including her alike in all he said and did. "Let *us* detain thee, until *we* have prepared a kid," &c. In the religious observance of the burnt-offering, and in the lowly prostration acknowledging the divine power, Manoah and his *wife* are separately named, proving her perfect equality in all religious observances, and her *right* to partake of them. That the angel never again appeared either to Manoah or his *wife*, is the proof to them that he was a messenger from the Lord. The words, "we shall surely die," included her in the penalty supposed to have been incurred, and marks the female as equally a responsible agent as the male. Still more clearly demonstrative that the Hebrew wife really occupied the free and equal position which the laws of God Himself assigned her, is the fact that it was her ready wit, and quickness of intellect, which re-assured her husband. She had been awe-struck like himself, but yet, perfectly in accordance with woman's nature, was the first to comprehend the real intention of the revelation. Man's more solid nature and deeper thought, requires time for mature judgment—woman's quicker fancy, and often more easily excited feeling, gives her the advantage in the rapidity of comprehension, and, very often, in the correctness of judgment, which man's greater solidity strengthens and matures.

But that Manoah's wife could thus comprehend, and thus correctly judge, implies a domestic and social position which not only permitted, but exercised these peculiar faculties. In an enslaved and degraded position, their possession was practically and theoretically impossible.

We find, then, much even in this brief chapter to interest and instruct us, alike as Hebrew women, and as women taken generally. In the latter, we shall do well to reflect on the simple trusting confidence of Manoah's wife, seeming the more tender and deferential from the greater correctness of judgment manifested afterwards. And so it should always be. However woman may be naturally endowed with superior attain ments, with, perhaps, even a greater share of strength and firmness, and a quicker aptitude for intellectual acquirements, still it is her bounden duty so to guide and use these gifts, that they shall never in any way jar upon the feelings of the one chosen as her husband; and check mutual confidence and love by that assumption of superiority, even granted it exist, of all things most irritating to man's nature. It is woman's province to *influence*, never to *dictate;* to conceal, rather than assume, superiority. She may find many and many an opportunity to use it for the good of her husband and children, as was the case with the wife of Manoah; but never let her display it—never let her permit her husband to feel his inferiority—never let her withhold confidence, from the mistaken notion that as her judgment is as good, if not better than his, she cannot need his advice or interference—for if she does, she may rest assured, that from that instant her influence is at an end for ever.

NAOMI.

WE now come to a portion of our history as Women of Israel, which, from the loveliness of female character that it displays, has in neither history or romance been equalled. In the Bible it is termed the book of Ruth; but as Ruth does not properly belong, by birth and ancestry, to the women of Israel, Naomi must be the subject of our consideration. With her history, however, Ruth is so entwined, that we cannot reflect on the one without also pausing on the touching beauty of the other.

The country of Moab, situated in the north-east part of Arabia Petræa, was separated from Judæa by the desolate tract of the Dead Sea, and the river Arnon. It could not probably be said ever to have formed part of the land of Canaan; but was one of those nations which the Eternal expressly commanded His people to spare: see Deut. ii. 9.

The Dead Sea was also the boundary of the tribe of Judah; and it is rather a remarkable fact, that Judah and Simeon are the only tribes of Israel who appear to have driven out all the previous Canaanitish possessors. Judah was the first appointed by the Most High to go up against the land; and, accompanied by his brother Simeon, evinced not only more obedience, but more valour and military skill. We do not read of them, as of Benjamin, Manasseh, Ephraim, Zebulun, Asher, Naphtali, and Dan, who, with scarcely any fighting, entered into peaceful covenants with the Canaanites, and permitted them to dwell with them even in their cities. Nor, in consequence, do we find recorded of the tribe of Judah those awful crimes and wilful idolatries practised by his brethren. In the early part of Jewish history, Judah was undoubtedly the most faithful tribe, else had he not been the chosen branch, from which, in God's own time, will spring our Restorer and Messiah.

Elimelech was a man of this valiant tribe, and, in consequence of a severe famine which devastated Judæa (the punishment, in all probability, of national sin), he removed his family, consisting of a wife and two sons, to the country of Moab, not far distant from their native city, Bethlehem-Judah or Ephratah. Elimelech died in Moab not very long after he sojourned there; and his two sons, Chilion and Mahlon, took them wives of the women of Moab, and dwelled there about ten years. Such unions were contrary to the given law of God; and we may infer that, notwithstanding the virtue and attractions of those selected, the act itself as disobedience was displeasing in the sight of the Lord, from the early deaths, without leaving children, of Elimelech's two sons. This, however, is a mere suggestion which may or may not be, and does not infer Divine displeasure against either Orpah or Ruth; as those not under the Law were not bound by its instructions.

During the lifetime of her husband and sons, we hear nothing of Naomi ; but it is by her conduct and sentiments in adversity, and the strong affection borne towards her by her daughters-in-law, that we may judge of her previous character.

A faithful wife, an affectionate mother—gentle, meek, trusting—manifesting a simple, guileless piety in every relation, every circumstance of life; such she must have been, or we should not find her in affliction the character which the Word of God displays.

It is not always in prosperity that we discover the true graces of a spiritual character. The quiet unostentatious discharge of domestic duty—the fond, unwavering affections of domestic life—these strike us not: nay, we often pass them by, wondering at the simplicity and tame-spiritedness which can rest content in such unexciting scenes. But when adversity comes, and strength and piety is to an extraordinary degree displayed, then it is we learn that it *is* in unexciting scenes woman's character is best matured; and we may chance to envy those whom we had before almost despised.

The heart of the Hebrew widow yearned towards that lovely land, from which she had been so long a willing exile for her husband's and children's sake—yearned towards it, for it was the land of her brethren, where the Lord had set up His only Tabernacle; where His law had assured her of His especial protection, for she was a *widow* in Israel: where her full heart could pour itself before Him in the congregation of her people—could worship Him in all points according to His law. In Moab she was alone of her race and faith. No wonder she yearned once more to rest in her native land; or that, lonely and aged as she was, she should yet set forth on the weary way. Another reason, also, might thus have urged her: she heard that "the Lord had visited His people with bread," and, therefore, she was no longer guiltless in continuing to sojourn in a heathen land.

Accompanied by her daughters, she departed from "the place where she was;" but, after going some little way together, she tenderly besought them to return, each to her mother's house, praying that the Lord might deal kindly with them, even as they had dealt with the dead and with her; and grant them each rest and peace, with a husband of their own people. Then she kissed them, and they lifted up their voices and wept, saying, "We will surely return with thee unto thine own people." They had lived with her ten years— a long period for the character and conduct to have been tried —and we see what Naomi's must have been, by the grief of her two daughters—unable to part with her, even to return to their own parents. To Naomi, such separation must also have been a heavy trial; but she was too unselfish to wish them to accompany her to a land of strangers. With renewed tenderness, then, she sought to turn them from their purpose, telling them she might no longer give them husbands; thus alluding to the law of her people, which commands the brother or nearest kinsman of the deceased to take unto himself the childless wife; and then only do we hear this meek and pious mother in Israel revert to her heavy affliction. "It grieveth me much, for your sakes, that the hand of the Lord has gone out against me." She recognised the hand of the Lord, and met her individual sorrows not only with uncomplaining resignation, but feeling yet more deeply for her daughters than for herself, and seeking to console them—leaving her own consolation to Him who had smitten and would heal. No wonder that her fond words increased their grief and bade them weep again: but the effect on the sisters was different. Orpah was one of the many, feeling painfully at the moment, passionately desirous to evince that she felt, but liable to be easily diverted from her purpose. Penetrating no deeper than the surface, she, perhaps, believed Naomi's words as neither desiring nor requiring her farther company; and, therefore, repeatedly she kissed her mother-in-law and wept, but at length turned back to her own home. Much as she loved the aged Naomi, earnestly as she wished to serve her, she had not sufficient firmness and steadiness of character to *act of herself*, and set at nought the persuasions of affection. Gentle and yielding, it was easier for her to *grieve* than to *act*; and is not this the nature of many women? They fear to abide by their own judgment when two alternatives are presented to them. They hesitate and linger, fearing to commit themselves by decision, and so are guided by a breath. Accustomed to express all their own impulses and feelings without regarding others, such natures cannot possibly understand those firmer and less selfish ones, who would do violence to their own wishes, to secure what may seem the greater share of happiness for another. That Orpah was one of these, solves her conduct far more justly and agreeably than to suppose her, as many do, merely *professing* a love and regret which she could not really feel—else, she too would have followed Naomi. Orpah was woman in her *weakness*; Ruth, woman in her *strength*; and both are as beautifully true to woman's nature now as then.

Ruth's own unselfish character gave her the clue to her mother-in-law's words. She could understand that Naomi might persuade them to return home, and yet cling to them as her last ties on earth. To Ruth, action was better than passive grief—deeds, than the tenderest words; and, therefore, when Naomi besought her to follow her sister-in-law, and return to her own people, Ruth's sole answer was couched in words exquisitely illustrative of the deep tenderness, the firm devotion, the beautiful difference of her individual character:—
"Entreat me not to leave thee, or to return from following thee. Whither thou goest, I will go; and where thou lodgest, I will lodge. Thy people shall be my people, and thy God

my God. Where thou diest, I will die, and there will I be buried. The Lord do so to me, and more also, if aught but death part me and thee!"

Not the most carefully studied oration could breathe more undying, changeless, self-submitting devotion, than these few and simple words. Naomi was evidently poor. The riches of the Hebrews did not consist then of such wealth as would provide for their families after their death—land and its produce constituted their possessions; and these, where there were no males to cultivate, could not prevent the female survivors from being poor as well as bereaved. Naomi's return to her own land would, of course, according to the law of God, secure her provision; but in the constant rebellion and disobedience of the people, it was precarious and uncertain—she might not even be recognised by her countrymen, so long a time had elapsed since she had left Ephratah. By her earnest entreaties for her daughters to return, it is evident that sufficiency and comfort marked their own homes. Yet Ruth unhesitatingly resigned them all to share her mother-in-law's fate, whatever it might be. Bidding farewell to the friends, scenes, and associations of her youth, not for a time but for a life, some cause for this pure devoted love there must have been. Ruth's simple words not only reveal the beauty of her own character, but that of the aged Naomi. Affection is ever the impulse to devotion and unselfishness. The human heart ever needs something to which so to cling as to be drawn out from self—and Ruth was not a character to devote her affection and energies to an unworthy object. We know what the character of Naomi must have been in those ten or twelve years of which we hear nothing, by the simple devotedness of Ruth in her adversity.

And what a comfort to that lone heart must have been the soothing words, and "steadfast mindedness," of the Moabitish damsel. Must not she who we shall find, under every circumstance of joy or grief, looking to the Lord alone, and tracing all things from His Almighty hand, have felt this comfort came from Him—and that even then she had not trusted in vain. In the midst of affliction He sent consolation; in her deepest loneliness raised up an earthly friend. Here, as we have already seen in the love of Isaac for Rebekah, we find the tender compassion of the Eternal for His creatures manifested in giving human comfort; He not only pours spiritual balm into the bleeding heart, but provides some being on whom its quivering affections may again find rest, and whose faithful love shall fill the aching void. To the bereaved wife and mother, left in her old age alone, a withered tree from which every leaf and flower has gone, with no hope of ever bearing more, Ruth's affection must have been indeed a precious balm. Without her Naomi had been *alone*, and O at all times how fearful is the suffering included in that word! Yet more in the adversity of bereavement and old age!

We do not hear how long the travellers journeyed, but Holy Writ simply yet forcibly brings before us the wonder and sympathy excited by the Bethlehemites on Naomi's return, "and it came to pass when they were come to Bethlehem, that all the city was moved about them, and they said, " Is this Naomi?' Can we not fancy the whole city flocking to look upon the travellers, to discover if indeed the rumour of Naomi's return could be correct—and anxious, if it were, to give her kindly welcome? Struck by her look of years and sorrow, remembering her only as the fair and pleasant-looking wife of Elimelech then in her freshest prime, marvelling one to another, Can this indeed be Naomi? It is a complete picture of that primitive union of family and tribe, peculiar to early Judaism. Men were not then so engrossed with self as to feel no sympathy, no interest, out of their own confined circle. They could spare both time and feeling to "be moved" at the return of a country-woman who had been absent so long ; and to grieve with her at those heavy afflictions which caused her to reply to their eager greetings, " Call me not Naomi, call me Mara, for the Almighty hath dealt very bitterly with me—I went out full, and the Lord hath brought me home again empty. Why then call ye me Naomi, seeing that the Lord hath testified against me, and the Almighty hath afflicted me?"

Again we find Naomi in meek submission referring all the events of her life to her God, yet uttering no complaint. She alludes to her heavy afflictions indeed—alludes to them *as afflictions*, as God Himself ordained ; not as some enthusiasts would seek to persuade us, that all bereavements are to be considered joys, and so received with thanksgiving and praise ; that pain is not to be pain if sent by the hand of the Lord. This is not the spirit of the Jewish religion as taught and practised in the Bible. Our Father demands not such violence done to the heart which He hath so mercifully and so wisely stored with such vast capabilities of pleasure and of pain. He demands not that sorrow is to be looked on as joy—and joy to be despised as leading us far from Him. When He tries us in affliction, where would be its spiritual improvement in faith and submission, if we are to welcome it as joy? Where would be the trial of pain, if it be not pain? No, God loves us too well to forbid the healing and saving influence of that holy grief, which, without detaching us from the sweet and lovely links of earth that He Himself vouchsafed, will yet lead us to Him, convinced that He afflicts for our eternal good; that He acts, even in bereavement, through His changeless love, and that He who smote, in His own time will heal. No sorrow has yet been soothed by the vain philosophy which would seek to lessen either its pang or its extent. The sufferer must weep and mourn awhile; but if it be in the spirit of Naomi there will still be comfort found.

Naomi makes no complaint: but how deeply she feels the contrast between her return to, and her departure from, Bethlehem, we read in her shrinking from the name of her youth, which, signifying pleasantness, sweetness, and grace, too painfully recalled the days when those terms were applicable, not only to the charms of her personal character, but the pleasantness and sweetness of her daily life. Bitterness and sadness were more applicable to her present lot, than the sweetness and joyance which had characterised it heretofore; and therefore she bids them call her Marah—but it is not complaint: it is but the natural shrinking of humanity from the memory of the past, contrasted with the suffering of the present.

It was at the beginning of the barley harvest Naomi and her daughter-in-law arrived at Bethlehem. There, it appears from the context, the former sought a retired and very humble dwelling. Notwithstanding that she had a wealthy kinsman, of the family of Elimelech, who, had she applied to him, was bound by the law to give her all the relief she needed, the gentle, unassuming nature of the widow preferred retirement and lowliness to *claiming* the attention of her wealthy kinsman. The contrast between their respective positions was too great; —and how beautifully does this shrinking from making herself known to Boaz, or even from revealing his existence to Ruth, betray her gentle dignity and that self-esteem ever proceeding from true piety! The character of Naomi is consistent in all its parts, forcibly marking one who, from youth to age, was found true to herself and to her God.

The holy narration tells us that "it was *Ruth's hap* to light on a part of the field belonging to Boaz." Had she known his near connection, her refinement and delicacy of feeling would have led her to any other field in preference. The whole scene which follows is a most beautiful illustration of the domestic manners and customs of the early Jews, and all in exact accordance with the given law. The kind and conciliatory manner of Boaz, " the mighty man of wealth," to his dependants ; his salutation, and their reply; evince how completely the thought and recollection of the God of Israel was entwined with the daily work of His people. The intimate acquaintance which Boaz must have had with all his household, male and female, from his instant discovery of the youthful stranger, and the reply of the reapers, all breathe a refinement and civilisation of feeling and action, found at this period only amidst the people of the Lord.

Boaz confirmed the kindness of his dependants by addressing Ruth in words of most gentle courtesy, peculiarly adapted to re-assure and soothe her. He not only tells her to glean in his field alone—there was no need for her to go farther—but to abide by his maidens, thus removing unconsciously all painful feelings on her being a Moabitish stranger, which would keep her aloof. He told her too to follow close after the reapers, that she should receive neither harshness nor insult, and when she was athirst, to drink freely from that which the young men had drawn.

With the respect ever proffered to real goodness, and astonished at such unexpected kindness, Ruth replied in words the meekness and humility of which increased Boaz's prepossession in her favour, and confirmed all which rumour had already proclaimed concerning her. "Why have I found grace in thy eyes," she said, "that thou shouldst take this knowledge of me, seeing I am a stranger?" And how must her heart have throbbed with natural pleasure at Boaz's rejoinder, "It hath been fully shewed me all that thou hast done unto thy mother-in-law, since the death of thine husband : how thou hast left father and mother, and the land of thy nativity, and art come unto a people which thou knewest not heretofore. The Lord recompense thy work, and a full reward be given thee of the Lord God of Israel, under whose wings thou art come to trust." Deserved approbation *is* sweet, however some stern Stoics may say that virtue is its own reward ; and if conscience approves we need no more. Ruth must at once have felt that it was not the mere kindness springing from a good heart which dictated Boaz's conduct to her, but that she was known and appreciated, stranger as she was. A coarser and more worldly nature than that of Boaz, even while it equally benefited, would have *exalted itself*, not the being it served ; would have manifested kindness only because it would obtain personal praise, and care little for the feeling of the person served. Boaz, on the contrary, removed the idea of obligation to himself by elevating Ruth, and making her believe that to her own virtue, not to his kindness, she owed the attention she received. "Let me still find favour in thy sight, my Lord," was her grateful reply; "for thou hast comforted me, and hast spoken friendly to thine handmaid, though I be not like one of thine own handmaidens." We never find Ruth forgetting her origin, nor in any way assuming the privileges which her acceptance of and belief in Naomi's God might naturally have assigned her; a lowliness which secured her, unasked, the privileges which, from a contrary conduct, would, no doubt, have been refused.

Not content with desiring her freely to share the meal provided for his reapers, Boaz himself reached her the "parched corn"—seeing that she ate till she was sufficed; and when she rose up again to glean, he gave orders to let her glean amid the sheaves, and reproach her not, and also "to let fall some handfuls on purpose for her." His generosity and her own perseverance enabled her to take home an ephah of barley. And Naomi, eager to bring her child refreshment, not knowing how she might have fared during the day, "brought forth and gave to her the food which she had reserved for her," affectionately asking from her, at the same time, where and what she had gleaned, and fervently blessing him who had thus taken knowledge of her. Ruth's reply elicited a burst of thanksgiving from Naomi. "Blessed be the Lord, who hath not left off his kindness to the living and the dead." She felt it was no chance, but her God, who had guided Ruth to the field of their kinsman, and infused his heart with kindness towards her. Convinced now that their restoration to their rights would be brought about by the direct agency of her God, she no longer scrupled to impart to Ruth the near relationship of Boaz; and when Ruth repeated his injunctions to keep fast by his young men until they had ended all his harvest, Naomi, still tracing divine agency, gladly replied, "It is good, my daughter, that thou go out with his maidens, that they meet thee not in any other field." And Ruth, in unquestioning obedience, "kept fast by the maidens of Boaz, to glean unto the end of the barley and wheat harvest, and dwelt with her mother-in-law." Not all that was in all probability reported of her devotion and beauty, could tempt her to turn aside from her lowly path of usefulness and good. Novelty and change could have had no glare for her, or she might have restlessly longed to join the gleaners of other fields. She was too grateful for the friendly kindness of Boaz, too devoted to her mother-in-law, to wish to go beyond the field of the former, or the humble house of the latter. "Where thou lodgest I will lodge," she had said, and her words were but the index of her actions.

But the time had now come when her earthly lot was to undergo a material change. Naomi, who had, in all probability, passed the intervening days in thought and prayer, determined on seeking the rest and prosperity of her devoted daughter, according to the dictates of the law. She therefore gave Ruth the necessary directions—directions which to us may appear strange, and even revolting, but which seem, in the time of Naomi, to have been authorised by custom, and therefore containing nothing whatever indelicate or forward. To Ruth, as a Moabitess, the whole proceedings might have felt unusual, and perhaps even painful; but we have neither remark nor hesitation. She asks not, wherefore, but simply says, "All that thou sayest unto me I will do." She had *proved* the affection and wisdom of her mother-in-law much too long to doubt them now, however her own feelings and judgment might shrink from the course of action proposed. Naomi's influence had ever been that of *love*, not of authority, and therefore was she ever sure of unquestioning obedience.

Human means Naomi refused not to adopt, but still she left the entire *end* of these means to the justice and mercy of her God. She knew that in His hand was the heart of Boaz, and therefore she merely told Ruth how to obtain his attention, leaving it to him "to tell thee what thou shalt do;" convinced that the Lord, in whom she trusted, would order the end aright.

All took place as she had anticipated.

Waking in terror at midnight—a terror not a little increased by finding some one lying at his feet—Boaz demanded, "Who art thou?" and received such a reply as at once calmed his affright, and roused him to a renewal of all the nobleness and generosity of his character. Some of our Hebrew translators of this book suppose Ruth's words, "Spread, therefore, thy skirt over thine handmaid, for thou art a near kinsman," to signify, "Give me thy protection as a husband;" and, as such, was in exact accordance with the law, we rather incline towards the opinion.

The reply of Boaz reassured the trembling suppliant; for steadily she had adhered to the straight path of duty, "followed neither young men, neither rich nor poor," so that the whole city "knew that she was a virtuous woman." He proceeded to inform her that he was indeed their near kinsman, but there was one still nearer, whose duty it was to perform the husband's part; but that if he refused, even he, Boaz, pledged himself to do so, as the Lord liveth, bidding her lie down till morning; but ere the day broke so that one could recognize another, Ruth rose to depart, encouraged so to do by him with whom she had so fearlessly trusted herself, and whose care for her reputation was tender and thoughtful as a brother's. Nor did he send her away empty. Fearful lest she and her mother-in-law might be in want ere the business could be settled, he filled her veil with six measures of barley, with which she returned to her home; and Naomi bid her sit calmly down until they knew how the matter would fall.

There is no need to transcribe the events detailed in the fourth chapter, from the 1st to the 12th verse. A reference to the word of God itself is all that is needed on the part of our readers, to impress them forcibly with the beautiful picture of the manners and customs of our ancestors which it presents. The gate of the city was always the place of public judgment, that all the people might be aware of what was going on, and give their suffrages, and witness for or against. Thither Boaz repaired the very next morning after his interview with Ruth, and sat him down, waiting the appearance of the person he had named as the nearer of kin than himself. He hailed him on his approach, and the man willingly turned aside from his intended path, and sat down by the gate. Boaz next assembled ten elders, and stated his business. The field which Naomi wished disposed of, the kinsman seemed willing to redeem: but the remainder of his duty, to raise up the name of the dead to his inheritance, he refused, on the plea that to do so would interfere with his own inheritance; requiring Boaz, in consequence to redeem the right for himself, as he, the nearest kinsman, could not ; loosening at the same time his shoe or glove as some commentators believe—and giving it to his neighbour, as confirmation of his words. Boaz then addressed the elders and the people, bidding them be witness that he had purchased of the hand of Naomi all that was Elimelech's, Chilion's, and Mahlon's, and Ruth, the wife of Mahlon, to be his wife, that he might raise up the name of the dead, and so let it not be cut off from his brethren, or the gate of his place. And the elders of the people bore witness joyfully, coupled with earnest aspirations that the LORD might make the woman he had chosen, like Rachel and like Leah, who had built up the house of Israel ; and that he himself might "do worthily in Ephratah, and be famous in Bethlehem."

And so he was ; for as the great-grandfather of David, the name of Boaz must indeed be still famous in Judah, and dear to Israel. The uncomplaining submission and lowly trust of Naomi, and the filial obedience and devotion of Ruth, were both alike rewarded ; for the latter not only became the wife of the generous and noble-minded Boaz, but, in due course of time, God granted her a son ; and Naomi, who had believed herself but a withered branch, to which neither joy nor fruitfulness might ever return, "took the child, and laid it on her bosom, and became nurse to it." We may read in the lively greetings of the women of Bethlehem, the joy which this event occasioned, and their affectionate sympathy in Naomi's previous affliction. "Blessed be the Lord," they said, "who hath not left thee this day without a kinsman, that his name may be famous in Israel. And he shall be unto thee a restorer of life, and a nourisher of thine old age, for thy daughter-in-law, who loveth thee, and who is *better to thee than seven sons*, hath borne him."

How beautifully do these words express the women of Israel's appreciation and love of the gentle Moabitess ! The babe would be a restorer of Naomi's life, and a cherisher of her old age, *for he was Ruth's son*. She who had been to Naomi better than seven sons (in the Hebrew the number is unlimited), would not fail to rear up her child in such virtue and holiness as would make his name indeed precious in Israel, and a blessing to his grandmother. Nor can we doubt that the affection and devotedness marking their mutual intercourse in adversity, was lessened in prosperity. The love which had been so mutually proved, was not likely to decrease, but would rather deepen with every passing year.

With the genealogy of Boaz, down to David, this most interesting book concludes; and before we proceed to notice the beautiful lessons of domestic life which it inculcates, we would endeavour to prove how mistaken is the objection, sometimes brought forward, that Ruth, a Moabitess, should have been the ancestress of David the elected servant of the Lord. When Ruth resigned alike, home, parents, and the gods of her youth, she voluntarily engrafted herself upon the children of God; and we know that such engrafting was permitted, not only from the Law, but from its after-explanation by the prophets. In the Law we repeatedly find the command to save the *virgins alive*, even of those nations whom they were commanded to exterminate, that they might be brought to the worship of the One true God, and multiply Israel. In the Prophets we read, that those of the stranger, whether male or female, who voluntarily accepted the covenants of the Lord, and kept His sabbaths and appointed feasts and ordinances, even had they been only eunuchs before, were (see Isaiah, chap. lxvi, 3-8), instead of being despised, to receive a place and a name in His house, better even than sons and daughters, an everlasting name which shall not be cut off, to be brought to the holy mountain, and made joyful in His house of prayer; and their burnt offerings and sacrifices, the essential privilege of the Holy People, accepted on God's altar. In the Law, too, we find repeated injunctions,—"love ye the stranger, for ye were strangers in the land of Egypt;" and by the whole history of Ruth, we see how precisely this law was obeyed. She was one of those coming under the denomination of "the stranger," and who yet, from her acceptance of the Lord's sabbaths, covenants, &c., all of which is implied in her own words, "thy God shall be my God," deserved and received the privileges enumerated above.

She was yet more than a daughter in His sight, because her acceptance of, and obedience to, the Law, were entirely *voluntary;* not merely received from education and as heritage. That God is no respecter of persons, we read throughout the whole of His changeless word. Faithfulness and virtue, the *heart*—but neither birth nor appearance—are valued by Him. And when, therefore, Ruth turns from all the associations and scenes of her youth, to adopt and accept the religion of Naomi, and faithfully serve her God, she is in act no longer a Moabitess (and is only called so to designate her as a stranger amidst Israel), but as worthy, if not even more so, to be the ancestress of David, than the lineal descendants of Abraham, who were Israelites, because God had selected them so to be; *not* for their own sakes, or their own worth, but simply for the love He bore, and the promise He made, unto His favoured servants. Ruth became an Israelite from *voluntary adoption*. Her filial devotion and reverence was the most exquisite illustration of *how* she not only accepted, but obeyed the Law; and, from the character of David, still more than even his selection, we may easily infer, how faithfully she not only obeyed the Law herself, but transmitted it to her descendants. That the Eternal should have selected a king whose great-grandmother was of Moabitish descent, cannot, then, we think, with any justice be brought forward as matter either of wonder or objection. If it were unlawful for any stranger to be engrafted upon Israel we should not find so many laws regarding "the stranger" in the Mosaic code itself, nor their *practical commentary* in Isaiah, as quoted above. Her virtue and goodness gave her favour in the sight alike of God and man, and rendered her worthy of being the ancestress of that holy line whence the Messiah himself will spring—while her voluntary acceptance of the God, and of course the faith, of Naomi, removed from her own Moabitish birth all reproach, and gave her yet a dearer name in the eyes of God and of his people than even that of daughter.

To us, as women of Israel, the whole book of Ruth teems with unspeakable consolation and support. It is a picture so vivid of the manners, customs, aye, and even feelings of Israel at that period, that even Gentile writers are struck by it, and refer to it with high eulogiums on its touching beauty, and impressive truth. Shall we then value it less, and refuse to draw from it the strong confirmation which it contains of our contested point—the refined and elevated position of the women of Israel themselves, and the tender yet respectful consideration with which they were regarded by their brethren? Will any one point of Naomi's character permit us to suppose, that during her husband's lifetime she was merely a slave, with neither religious, moral, nor intellectual training? Had she been such in Elimelech's lifetime, such she must have remained. Instead of which, from her determination to return to her own land, and worship her God once more amongst her own people, we perceive that she was a woman of strong mind and unfailing energy; while from the affection of both her sons' wives, and the devotion of one, we must equally infer that she possessed, and in her domestic duties must have displayed, such winning and amiable qualities, as to call such affection forth; these characteristics, and all which follow—the refined and retiring dignity, the correct judgment, and also the patient faith in her God—all were quite incompatible with a degraded position either individually or socially. It is very clear, then, that not in any received Law of Israel could the position of the women of Israel have been that which our enemies so ignorantly report. If *two* Laws were in action at this period, one must have been an exact repetition of the other, or in a book like that of Ruth, so strikingly illustrative of the national character and customs, some difference must have been discernible.

If, then, the charge on modern Judaism be really founded on apparent truth, it must be a state of things brought about by the awful horrors of persecution, and their natural effect in narrowing and brutalising the human mind. In all that relates to Ruth too, we see the real light in which the Hebrew woman was regarded, very clearly. We should not find her filial devotion and individual goodness so appreciated by all the Bethlehemites, female as well as male, were not virtue and goodness in woman subjects of admiration, of cherishing, and respect. It was not only in obedience to the Law, which commanded love and kindness to be shown towards the stranger, that Boaz so encouraged and cherished her when first gleaning in his field. He expressly states the wherefore, *because of* her devotion to her mother-in-law, and her having given up her father's gods to accept Him under whose wings she had come to trust. "A full reward shall be given thee from the Lord," he says; thus marking her as accepted and cherished by God as well as man. The most reverential yet fatherly care marks the whole of his conduct towards her; and here we see very strongly marked the obedience to the law instituted for the benefit of the stranger; he not only "showed kindness," but literally left for her the "gleanings of his field."

The third chapter of the sacred story most emphatically proves the superiority of morality and civilisation in Israel, over the known world. In what other nation could Ruth have so trusted herself, as she did to the honour and justice of

Boaz? How fully must Naomi have been assured of the safety of her child, or how could she have counselled such a mode of proceeding? and how completely she was justified in her confidence, we read in Boaz's anxiety to save Ruth from all insulting remarks, by letting it "not be known that a woman had been to the floor."

Again, in Boaz's instant pursuance of Ruth's suit, we very clearly perceive that women must have been considered of some account; and also another important point in a national view, Boaz's exact obedience to the formula of the Law, in calling the nearest kinsman to give his attention to the subject, and decide—notwithstanding his own evident anxiety to obtain Ruth as his wife—unquestionably proves that as the Law was so strictly kept in *one point*, so it would be in *all*; and consequently there could have been, neither practically nor theoretically, any one single statute to the disparagement of woman.

The very joy of the whole people in Boaz's decision to make Ruth his wife; their hearty congratulations, and earnest wishes for his welfare, and hers, that she might be as Leah and Rachel; the delight of the women, and their joyous sympathy with Naomi at the unexpected issue to all her misfortunes; all prove the beautiful unity and love marking the people of the Lord. All seemed to vie with each other in making their respective tribes as one affectionate family, bound by the same ties, hoping the same hope, trusting the same God, weeping with those that wept, and rejoicing with those that joyed.

Such a state of things could never have existed if the women of Israel had not been, morally, spiritually, and intellectually, on a perfect equality with man.

Regarding the book of Ruth in its final bearings—that is, as it concerns women in general—we are particularly struck with the exquisite lesson of maternal and filial affection which it teaches. The beauty of Ruth's words and actions sometimes occupies attention alone, to the exclusion of the tenderness characterising Naomi, which, to our feelings, is equally touching and impressive. Ruth's determination to quit her own land, her parents, and their gods, was indeed one of beautiful self-devotion; but it was evidently Love, not duty, which impelled it, and that love must have been called forth by the tenderness she had originally received. Seldom is the love of the young excited to such an extent towards an elder, unless by affection and appreciation from that elder invited so to love; and not

only *invited* but *retained* by unwavering kindness and regard.
That such feelings had always actuated Naomi towards her
daughter-in-law, we infer, from the caressing tenderness with
which, in all that passes between them, she invariably addressed
her. We never can find either coldness or indifference, much
less the harsh mistrust, breathing often more in *tone* than
actual words, which sometimes characterises the manner of an
elder towards a younger. All she says, either in persuasion to
return, or in advice or inquiry, is with the same caressing love.
In her bringing forth on Ruth's return the remains of the day's
meal, which she had been compelled to take while Ruth was
absent, how touchingly we read of the love lingering with her
absent child, the thought of saving for her the evening meal,
and bringing it with eager haste the moment Ruth appeared,
not knowing how she might have fared during the hot and
weary day.

Oh! while we would have our young sisters imitate, as they
cannot fail to love, the conduct of Ruth, will not their elders
do well to ponder on, and imitate, the tenderness of Naomi?
Youth will not, *cannot* love, a pure unselfish love, unless invited so to do; no, not even in the sanctuary of home, not
even parents, unless love, not only *felt* but *displayed* in confidence and caressing kindness, marks the parental conduct.
Duty done on either side is not enough; for it is not according
to the spirit of the Lord, and of His word. There love predominates, and so should it predominate in the homes of His
children. We do not deny that it does, but we would have it
displayed as well as felt, by every member of that hallowed
temple, HOME. Brothers and sisters, parents and children,
twined together in that sacred silvery link, unbroken even by
death; for they know it is immortal. Love not only felt, but
breathing in every tone, and actuating every deed; confidence
and trust—mutually given, mutually felt. How thrice blest
would such things make home! The parental heart would not
then bleed in secret, at what seems like neglect and unkindness,
if not an utter want of love. Nor would the young spirit
shrink within itself, chilled and sad—yearning for affection
spoken, as well as felt; and utterly unconscious how truly and
how deeply they may still be loved. How different is that
home where no gentle word is heard—no caress asked for, or
voluntarily bestowed—no interchange of mutual thought; but
each member walks alone, seeking no sympathy save from the

stranger, caring not to shed one flower on the parental hearth, and believing they have no place in the parental heart *save as a child*, words of which, until they are parents themselves, they know not, guess not, the unutterable meaning. How different is such a home to that where love is *visible*. Where parents and, as its natural consequence, children vie with each other, as to who can *prove* it most; and by the words and manner of daily life, throw such a beautiful halo even over its cares and sorrows, as inexpressibly heighten its sweetest joys.

There are some who doubt the love that dwells in caressing words and a loving manner. Yet why should it be doubted, till its absence has been proved? Why should the gentle power be despised, which will make daily life happier, and so inexpressibly soothe the sickness and sorrow which ask but love alone. No! It is the icy surface we must doubt, for never yet were there warm and unselfish loving hearts, who could think it necessary to suppress such fond emotions in the sweet sanctuary of *home*. It is the cold at heart who never give *domestic* affections vent, and can therefore never hope so to attract the young as to rouse them to evince the love they could have felt, or proffer more than the cold dull routine of daily duty. *We must love to be loved*—we must evince that love, would we so unite young hearts to our own, as, if needed, to sacrifice all of self for us, or to devote life, energy, hope, all to our service. Would we have our daughters Ruths, we must be Naomis; we have no right, no pretence, to demand more than we *evince*, as well as give. Reserve, coldness, command, may win us duty; but duty in the domestic circle is a poor substitute for love. Even kindness *in act* is often undervalued, nay, absolutely unknown, if it be not hallowed by the kindness of manner and of word. In the *world*, words and manner may be deceiving, but not in the temple of home; for the love which would there dictate kindness of manner, must equally incite kind deeds. The latter may exist without the former, and if only one may have existence, we may grant the superiority of good deeds, though there are some griefs, some trials, which kind *words* may soothe, where *action* has no power. O let us unite the two like Ruth and Naomi—and however dark and troubled our earthly course, a light will shine within our homes, which no sorrow, nor care, nor even death, will have power to darken or remove. God is Love—the spirit of His word is Love; and would we indeed walk according to His dictates, Love, proved alike in *word* and *deed*, must be the Guardian Angel of our homes!

HANNAH.

In the history of the Jews, by Josephus, the story of Hannan is mentioned as taking place before that of Ruth. We prefer following the arrangements of the Bible, although it is not improbable that Ruth and Hannah lived much at the same time; for we find the son of Hannah, when a very old man, visiting the grandson of Ruth, then in his prime, to choose from his household his youngest born as the anointed of the Lord. The period of the existence of these two beautiful female characters is in itself of little importance; but it is interesting to trace the intimate connection of their descendants, thrown together as they were so closely in after life.

There was a certain man living in the city of Rama Sophim of Mount Ephraim, an Ephrathite by descent, named Elkanah, who had two wives, Hannah and Peninnah. It is a remakable fact, that this is the very first mention of a man having two wives, since the days of Jacob. Joseph, Moses, Aaron and his sons, Caleb, Othniel, Lapidoth, Manoah, Elimelech, Chilion, and Mahlon, all had but one wife; a striking confirmation of our former assertion, that though polygamy was permitted, from its being an immemorial usage, *it was not*, in the early days of Israel, considered a necessary part of their domestic policy; and that almost every great and good man selected by the Eternal to work His will, before the monarchy, had but the one wife for whom the Laws were given; and so evinced in their own persons, the incipient dawnings of that more refined and elevated state of being and society, which in the natural progression of humanity would undoubtedly ensue.

The abuse of the permission to have more than one wife without transgressing the Law, which grew to such an awful height during the continuance of the monarchy, is no evidence of the degrading nature of the Law, but it is the literal fulfilment of the threatened wrath of the Eternal, when the people insisted upon having an earthly king to rule over them, like other nations. That he would not only take unto himself their store and their fields, and their olive-yards and vineyards, but even their sons and their daughters to minister to his service and his pleasures ; and, of course, the licentious conduct of the sovereign would be followed by equal licence in his subjects.

But before the monarchy, though the people were ever in rebellion and disobedience, still no such domestic abuses had existence. Even when there were two wives, as in the case we are about to consider, we find the beautiful laws, instituted for domestic equity and peace, entering and guiding a man's household, as the Eternal had intended in their bestowal. Yet even these, while they prevented all injustice on the part of the husband, could not entirely do away with the evils of a divided household, which Sacred Writ never fails to record for our warning.

"And Elkanah, with his wives and household, went up out of his city yearly to worship and sacrifice unto the Lord in Shiloh"—then the residence of God's holy ark, and of his priests—a *practical* confirmation of the law so to do, which we have already noticed. At these times, " he gave to Peninnah his wife, and to all her sons and daughters, portions, but unto Hannah he gave a double portion ; for he loved Hannah: though the Lord had not granted her any children"—loved her for herself, even above Peninnah, though she had given him a goodly progeny, and Hannah had but her own gentle virtues, which were sufficient for her husband.

But in Israel the denial of children was considered too sad a reproach, too painfully a proof of individual unworthiness in the sight of God, for the meek spirit of Hannah to endure it without bitter grief ; a grief painfully aggravated by the provocations of her more favoured rival, whose unkind reproaches increased with every year that diminished Hannah's hope. Still, Holy Writ tells us of no complaint on the part of Hannah against Peninnah. As the more beloved by her husband, had she told him of the continual provocations she received, she might have been sure of such interference as would have effectually shielded her from them in future, though at the expense of alienating Peninnah from her husband, and causing domestic strife. But such a course of acting was not according to Hannah's character. It was easier far to suffer than to complain ; sweeter far to endure herself than seek revenge upon another.

Each visit to Shiloh excited anew the reproaches of Peninnah; and as this took place some years before Elkanah noticed the deep grief of his favourite wife, we may in a degree suppose the extent of Hannah's gentle forbearance. Hers was no trial of a day, or even a month, but of years; and can we imagine anything more trying to the heart and temper, than to live with one whose tongue was ever bitter with reproach? because it is not likely that it was *only* during their visits to Shiloh that "Peninnah provoked her sore, to make her fret," and provoked her for no fault; for nothing which Hannah herself could remedy, but simply for being less favoured by the Lord. And yet, how many are there like her! How many love to reproach instead of soothe? as if sorrow and disappointment were the *fault* of the sufferers, not the loving sentence of the Lord. How many there are who thus make daily life bitter to their fellows, instead of, as they might do, rendering grief less sad, and inexpressibly heightening joy!

Their visits to Shiloh must have been fraught with deep suffering to Hannah. It was not only the signal of Peninnah's aggravated unkindness; but the very sight of all her fellow-countrymen flocking to the temple of the Lord* with their goodly show of sons and daughters, must have made her pious heart shrink deeper and deeper within itself in its own unspoken woe: and it is shown in her spirit's sad but unmurmuring enquiry, "Why had the Lord whom she loved and sought to serve, so reproached and forsaken her?" That this was really the case, and her grief was never spoken, never found vent in reproachful words, we know by Elkanah's gently reproving address. "Hannah, why weepest thou?" he said, "why eatest thou not? and why is thy heart grieved? Am not I better to thee than ten sons?" Here there is no reference to anything but Hannah's visible sorrow, and to Elkanah's natural supposition as to the cause of her grief; and in perfect accordance with the meek enduring beauty of her true womanly character, she makes no complaining answer. It would have been easy for her to exculpate herself for too repining sorrow by invectives against her happier rival; but she who had borne so much and so long, was far too spiritual

* Though that the House of God which we are accustomed to regard as the Temple was not built till the reign of Solomon, the residence of the Ark of God was always called the Temple.— See 1 Sam. i. 9.

for such petty revenge. Answer to man, save such as affection would dictate, the struggle to smile and be happy for a loved one's sake, she made none ; but sought relief, where alone it might be found, at the footstool of her God—woman's best and surest refuge. For how may man, even when most loving, most beloved, so know the secret nature of a woman's heart, as to bring the balm it seeks, and give the strength it needs ? Elkanah's words reveal the extent and truth of his love ; and had it not been for the daily provocations of Peninnah, he might indeed have been to Hannah "better than ten sons :" but she had griefs and trials of which he knew nothing— peculiarly her own, as what woman has not ?—and these, in childlike faith and voiceless prayer, she brought unto her God.

The condition of married women amongst the Jews, in the time of the Judges, must have been perfectly free and unrestrained. We find her rising up after they had eaten and drank in Shiloh, and without even imparting her intentions to her husband, much less asking his consent, going perfectly unattended and unrebuked to the temple of the Lord. There, in bitterness of soul weeping, she prayed unto the Lord of Hosts; and, in perfect accordance with the Mosaic Law, which expressly provided for such emergencies, she vowed a vow, that if the Eternal would in His infinite mercy remember His handmaid, and grant her a male child, she would devote him unto the Lord all the days of his life, and not a razor should come near his head.

But she prayed not aloud, nor in any stated formula of prayer ; she prayed merely as the heart dictated : "she spoke in her heart," as we have it in the touching language of Scripture—only her lips moved, but her voice was not heard ; and Eli, the high priest, who sat beside one of the posts of the temple, marked her mouth, and hearing no word, combined with the agitated figure before him, believed she was drunken, and reproaching her bade her put her wine from her.

It must have been an aggravation of her sorrow to find herself so misunderstood by one, who, as high priest, she might with some justice believe would have required no explanation on her part, but in the name of the Eternal, have proffered her relief at once. Still we find nothing in her touchingly beautiful reply, to evince a failing in the firm faith which brought her there. "No, my lord," she answered, "I am a woman of a sorrowful spirit ; I have drunk neither wine nor strong drink, but have poured out my soul before the Lord. Count not thine handmaid for a daughter of Belial; for out of the abundance of my grief and complaint have I spoken hitherto. Then Eli answered and said, Go in peace, and the God of Israel grant thee thy petition that thou hast asked of Him :" and, without doubt, without question, Hannah simply answered, "Let thine handmaid find grace in thy sight"—meaning, to remember her in his prayers—and then " she went her way, and did eat, and her countenance was no more sad."

The exquisite lesson and consolation which these verses contain (1 Sam. i. 9—19) we will defer to our concluding observations, now merely narrating the history itself. At the conclusion of the festival, Elkanah and his family returned to Ramah, where the Eternal in His mercy remembered His faithful servant, and taking from her her reproach, in due course of time granted her the son for which she had so earnestly prayed; and in joyful acknowledgment that it was in answer to her prayer he had been given, she called him Samuel, or "asked of the Lord."

The time again came round for Elkanah and his family to make their yearly offerings in Shiloh; and by the allusion to a vow of Elkanah's (see verse 21) we may infer that Hannah had of course imparted to him her vow, and received not only his unqualified sanction, but that he was anxious, in his next visit to the temple of the Eternal, himself to confirm it. We find, too, as we ought previously to have noticed, the day after Hannah had been to the temple, that *they* (probably herself and her husband) rose up in the morning early, and "worshipped before the Lord;" a worship, possibly, of thanksgiving and rejoicing on the part of both; on Elkanah's that his beloved wife was no longer sad, on Hannah's that her prayer was heard; for that it *was* heard, it is evident she never entertained a doubt, long before she could have had proof that it really was so. That this early worship had to do with the vow is, however, of course a mere suggestion: the Word of God is open to all; we would not compel the adoption of any suggestion, to which both reason and feeling cannot give reply.

Hannah, however, when the time of the yearly sacrifice arrived, refused to go up, saying to her husband, "I will not go up till the child is weaned; and then I will bring him, that he may appear before the Lord, and there abide for ever :" a resolution freely approved of by Elkanah. "Do what seemeth thee good," he replied, "tarry until thou hast weaned him." This incident is a striking confirmation of all which we brought forward in the Second Period of our history, regarding the appearance and the non-appearance of the female part of a Jewish household in the Temple at the times appointed.

The history of Elkanah and his family illustrates this law exactly. That women as well as men were to appear in the house of the Lord, and join in His worship, is proved by both Hannah and Peninnah, with the latter's children, attending their husband to Shiloh ; and that the law to go up thrice a year was only *binding* upon males from the many causes which might prevent females, particularly mothers, from so doing, we perceive by Hannah's tarrying till the child was weaned, and having her husband's free permission so to do.

The time at length came, when, in obedience to her voluntary vow, Hannah must part from her boy, and deliver him up to the service of the God whose mercy had bestowed him to her prayer. Her only one, precious beyond all price ! yet we find no hesitation, no thought of delay, no idea of forgetting that which she had vowed, though the nature of her vow, nay, that she had vowed at all, was unknown to all, even to the high priest, who had promised that her prayer should be granted without knowing what it was. Without listening to the maternal anxieties that must have engrossed her, we find her, directly the child was weaned, taking him with her to Shiloh, and three bullocks, and one ephah of flour, and a bottle of wine—offerings from the store, and the field, and the vineyard—all in exact accordance with the written Law, and came unto the house of the Lord, and they slew a bullock there, and brought the child to Eli. "And she said, O my lord, as thy soul liveth, my lord, I am the woman that stood by thee here praying unto the Lord. For this child I prayed, and the Lord hath given me my petition which I asked of Him, and therefore also have I lent him to the Lord : as long as he liveth he shall be lent to the Lord. And he worshipped the Lord there"—rather an obscure phrase, but probably signifying that Eli worshipped the Lord, in acknowledgment of His divine goodness, in thus permitting his words to come to pass, and giving the woman that which she desired.

The prayer, or rather hymn, of thanksgiving in which Hannah poured forth her gratitude to her God in a strain of the sublimest poetry and vivid conception of the power and goodness of Him whom she addressed, is a forcible illustration of the *intellectual* as well as the spiritual piety which characterised the women of Israel, and which in its very existence denies the possibility of degradation applying to women, either individually, socially, or domestically. Their intellect must have been of a very superior grade ; while the facility of throwing the aspirations of the spirit into the sublimest poetry, evinces constant practice in so doing, and proves how completely prayer and thanksgiving impregnated their vital breath. It is useless quoting this beautiful song of praise, when the blessed Word which contains it is open to all classes and ages of readers ; but we would beseech our young friends not to be satisfied with this uninspired notice, but to turn to the Word themselves, and mark the soul-felt clinging piety throughout. It is as exact a transcript of the swelling gratitude of a truly pious heart, as her prayer before had breathed its bitterness of grief. Some there are who gladly come to their God in sorrow, but quite forget that the seasons of joy should be devoted to Him as well. Hannah was evidently not of these, but one of the most perfectly spirituously pious characters of the Bible. There was no self-exaltation in her song of praise ; no supposition that for any individual worth her reproach had been removed ; or even that any peculiar meritorious fervour in her prayer had wrought reply. No ; all was of the LORD. All came from His exceeding mercy—His omnipotent power. It was He who had made bare his holy arm, and to the barren given children—He who gave strength to those that stumbled, while the arms of mighty men were broken—He who maketh poor and maketh rich—He who bringeth low, and lifteth up—He who killeth and maketh alive—for " by strength no man shall prevail."

Nor was it only because she was permitted thus to rejoice, and behold the power she exalted, that Hannah so magnified the Lord, and believed in His wisdom and love to do all that He willed. She must have known and felt all her hymn expressed in her time of grief, else we should not have seen her in lowly supplication, prostrate in the court of the Lord's house—beseeching His relief. She must have *believed*, else she could not thus have prayed.

Lonely and sad must have been the feelings of this true Hebrew mother, when she returned to her house at Ramah, leaving her beautiful boy with the high priest, and knowing that but three times in the year might she behold him; and then not to receive from him the service and caresses of a son, but only to look on him as one devoted to his God and to His service! How must her heart have yearned for the engaging prattle, the caressing playfulness, the lovely looks of clinging love, which had so blessed her since his birth! What a blank in her existence must have been his absence! and what but spiritual trust and devoted love to her God, could have brought her consolation? The feelings alike of her human and spiritual nature are so exquisitely portrayed by that beautiful delineator of woman's spiritual character, Mrs. Hemans, that we can but refer our readers to her pages, convinced that it will aid them to enter into the full beauty of Hannah's character, and the extent of her trial in parting from her boy.*

Licentiousness and sin had crept into the very bosom of the Temple, through the conduct of the high priest's sons. Yet, in the midst of impurity, under the too indulgent control of an aged man, whose laxity of parental discipline exposed him to the anger of the Lord—still was the child Samuel kept pure and undefiled even as he left his mother's roof, and, while yet a child, ministered before the Lord. His so doing explains and confirms the law of the Nazarite, and the singular vow, to which we alluded in our Second Period, as implying devotion to the Lord's service, which even children might perform (see Lev. xxvii. 6) by some personal service. It is thus we so repeatedly find the Hagiography, or historical parts of the Bible, containing the *practical illustration* of the *theoretical* statutes, exactly as Moses gave them, and so rendering the holy Scriptures in very truth the verified transcript of the Eternal will. Moses' instructions to the elders regarding the practical obedience to the law, must have been in exact accordance with that which, being written, was, and is still, open to our perusal: or we should have found some traces of its difference in the manners and customs of our ancestors. All, therefore, in Modern Judaism, which is accused of contradicting the spirit of the eternal holy word, cannot have had its origin in either of the laws, oral or written, transmitted by Moses. We are anxious always to

* See Mrs. Hemans's Poems, vol. iv. p. 169.

notice, as forcibly as may be, those portions of the Bible containing the *practical* confirmation of the written laws of Moses, because we have heard (though we can scarcely believe it) that the written word of the Eternal is pronounced by some as imperfect and incomplete. The promulgators of such a fearful doctrine are not perhaps aware that by so doing, and so depriving our females and youth of both sexes of their only stay, and strength, and consolation, they are opening a wider avenue and offering a greater temptation to embrace Christianity, than was ever proffered by our opponents. To guard the women of Israel from such insidious danger, we are tempted to wander from our main subject, whenever the opportunity offers, to give them refuge and strength by the conviction that for *them*, at least, the Word of the Most High is all-sufficient, containing, as it does, in the historical books, the *practical illustration*, and in the prophets the *spiritual explanation*, of the whole Mosaic system, whether imparted by word of month or dash of pen. Of the delivery or non-delivery by the Eternal of an oral law, we write not at all, as it is a subject much too learned and too weighty for a woman ; and we are ready and willing to submit our opinions on all points to the wisdom and piety of our venerable sages. We only affirm, what we think no Hebrew will contradict, that as the God of Israel is a God of changeless truth and wisdom, He would not have desired Moses to *write* that which *speech* was to deny ; in other words, that each law must be so perfect and so exact a counterpart of the other, that in our present captive state, the Bible, provided through the eternal mercy for this very emergency, must be the key to both laws, and so perfect in itself.

Though the evil conduct of the sons of Eli was well known, Hannah does not appear to have entertained a fear as to the effect of their example upon the tender years of her child. It was not likely that she who, in all her individual joys and sorrows, came to her God in prayer, should neglect that holy duty for the welfare of her boy. She had experienced too consolingly the effect of faith and prayer, to doubt them now ; and as a mother, a Hebrew mother—one whose whole heart was love and praise to God—we may quite believe that, day and night, her meek and humble orisons arose for her boy, that he might become all that would make him indeed a faithful servant of his God; for in being such, he would be all her heart could wish.

Some mothers, indeed, there may be, who, when they send their children from them, and provide them with all things needful for temporal welfare, think they have done sufficient, and only remember them with mere human, and consequently perishable, affections; rejoicing in their prosperity, anxious when ill, desirous for them to "get on,"—an emphatic though not elegant phrase for the world's success. And if they do all they can to forward this "getting-on," in the way of education and lavish expenditure, what more could be required of them? Some will answer, "Nothing." Others may feel as Hannah *must have* felt, that though their children may no longer be beneath their roof—though all of human means is done to further their advancement, what will it all avail without the blessing of the Lord? And how may such blessing be attained, save with faithful and unceasing PRAYER—prayer that unites us in spirit alike with our beloved ones, and with our God. Oh, is there one who really *loves*, be it as parent, wife, child, betrothed, or friend, and can yet rest secure and happy without prayer? If we have never prayed before, we *must* when we feel love. Can we love in any single relation of life, and yet not feel the craving, the desire, the absolute necessity to pour out our hearts to our God for our beloved ones, and *in them* for ourselves? Can we rest quiet, incapacitated, perhaps from active *service* by circumstances, and not at least seek to serve by fervent prayer? And if in every relation of life this must be the effect of love, O more than any other must we find it in a mother for a child! What love can be like hers, so watchful, so changeless, so unwearied? And how may she still the anxious throbbings of her heart, when divided from its earthly treasures, save by simple trust and fervent prayer?

And when we look back on the character of Hannah, as it has already been displayed, can we doubt that such were her feelings, that she could have supposed merely to leave her child with the high priest was sufficient—that nothing more depended on herself? She who in all things had prayed? No; prayer must have sanctified her offering, not only when offered, but when apart from him. She had nought but prayer for him on which to rest. And might it not have been, nay, was it not, that mother's prayer, which retained her boy in such pure and lowly piety, in such singleness of purpose, and faithfulness of heart, in the very midst of the licentiousness reigning around? Long before Samuel could have prayed for himself, must

Hannah's prayers have ascended for him, and in his favour—both with the Lord and with men—she had her answer.

Every time of her visit to Shiloh, we find Hannah bringing a little coat, or robe, for her child, the work of her own hands, which had fondly lingered on the task from month to month, in the periods of absence; and Eli blessed Elkanah and his wife, and said "the Lord give thee seed of this woman, for the loan which is lent to the Lord." Now, though not put till several verses after the narration of Hannah's address to the high priest, when leaving Samuel with him, these words were most probably spoken when he first accepted the offering of the child; and the Lord did visit Hannah, and granted her three more sons, and two daughters, thus powerfully proving, that the Eternal ever returns double, and more than double, that which we devote to Him; be it the affections, the intellect, the will, or that more active service, charity and good works. Hannah devoted to Him her all, her only one, caring not for the conquest of self, which this resignation of her treasure must have demanded; and the Eternal, in His infinite mercy, granted her five in the place of one. And what was it which had originally turned aside her reproach, and inclined the Lord towards her! No great work—no mighty sacrifice—no wealthy offering; it was none of these, but simple faith and heartfelt prayer.

With the information that she became the mother of five children, Holy Writ concludes the history of Hannah; but knowing the longevity of Scriptual characters, we are justified in inferring that she was spared to feel to the full, all the happiness which her first-born's matured character must have excited.

We hear of not one failing from his earliest childhood. We read of his unvarying integrity and single-minded obedience to the word of his God, from his first repetition to Eli of the Eternal's awful sentence, to the conclusion of his career; interfering as that obedience so repeatedly did, with his own private feelings, alike towards Eli, in the selection of a king, and in all his conduct towards Saul. If Hannah lived until the monarchy she must indeed have been blessed in the innate goodness and love, and in the popularity of her child, and have felt that in nursing him for the Lord, she had indeed received "her wages."

The history we have been regarding, though brief in itself,

is yet so fraught with importance to us as women of Israel, and as women in general, that we trust we shall be pardoned for dwelling upon it in all its bearings at some length. Forcibly as the stories of Naomi and Deborah marked the real position of the Israelitish women, and proved their powers alike of intellect, judgment, and spirituality, as well as the deferential light in which they were regarded by their countrymen, the history of Hannah brings their perfect freedom and equality, even in the marriage state, yet more distinctly forward. Deborah was inspired to do the will of the Lord; gifted, extraordinarily and expressly to judge and deliver her countrymen. Naomi was a widow, unshackled by either conjugal or household duties, and with no relation whatever to interfere with her proceedings. Hannah was one of two wives, her husband living, and the head of a wealthy household; consequently, she must have had all her part of the domestic economy to look after and perform; yet there could not have been the very smallest restraint upon either her temporal proceedings, or spiritual feelings. She does not even ask her husband's acquiescence, much less depend upon his consent to seek the house of God. Her very going to pray, must have excited remark, and even scandal, if such had not been the common custom of the nation. And if women were not permitted to pray for themselves, Eli would have rebuked her presumption, and desired her to send her husband, as the only chance of her wishes being granted; instead of which, when once convinced she was praying with earnestness and in sorrow, he bids her "go in peace," for God would hearken to her.

Again, had she not possessed perfect freedom of will and action, she could not have vowed her child to God. Unless she had been perfectly sure that her husband reposed sufficient confidence in her, to abide by her decision, she could not have so devoted him, without, as it were, mocking the majesty of the Lord, by making a promise which she had not the power to perform.

That her vow was subject to the approbation of her husband, we believe, because such deference was commanded in our law. But Elkanah's full acquiescence throughout, clearly proves the high esteem in which he held her. She does not ask even *his permission* to remain at home, till her child were old enough to be left with the priest.

In all relating to Samuel, Elkanah was completely secondary. Even in the bullocks, flour, and wine, provided for the offering, it was Hannah who brought and offered them; Hannah who addressed Eli; Hannah who chaunted the song of thanksgiving to her God; and Hannah who devoted her child. The husband and father had no more to do with it, than the simple acts of acquiescence and approval, which he would not have so unhesitatingly bestowed, had he not possessed the most perfect confidence in the judgment and actions of his wife.

That no severe restrictions as to the time, form or words of prayer, existed in the time of Hannah, is proved by her seeking the Temple to pray when it was *not* the appointed time of service, when there was no one there but the high priest and herself; by her *speaking in her heart* the words which sorrow and entreaty dictated, without any regard whatever to instituted forms, which, though *indispensable* for public service and national interests, will not give all that is needed to individuals. Eli marked the lips of Hannah move, but he heard no voice, for she *spake in her heart, and as her heart dictated*. And in her song of thanksgiving, though she prayed aloud, still it was from the heart alone.

That forms of prayer were not needed in the time of Hannah, as they are now, we acknowledge; and also with all our heart and soul do we reverence their institution, and acknowledge their full value, both nationally and individually. Many, and many a one, from incapacity to frame words of prayer, would be fearfully and painfully bereft, did they not possess the invaluable treasure of words of prayer, framed by good and learned men expressly for their use, and hallowed by long years. We are no advocate for the abolishment of established forms; for fully and heartfully we feel their sanctity and value. We would only beseech our young sisters to accustom themselves sometimes in their private hours, to pray and to praise from the *heart*, not always to depend on printed words; not, indeed, to neglect the latter, but to hallow and add to them, by individual petitions from individual hearts. Self-knowledge must be their first step to such secret prayers; for by self-knowledge alone can they discover their natural sins, their greatest temptations, their most secret weaknesses, their favourite faults. Self-knowledge alone can teach them where they are most likely to fail, and where to be unduly elevated; and display broadly and unsoftened, the *true motives* of their every action. Self-knowledge alone can teach them their true position with regard to eternity and God, and for all these things it is, that every individual needs individual prayer, wholly and utterly distinct from established forms; not, as we said above, to take the latter's place, but so to be added to them, as to give them life and breath.

The history of Hannah is all-sufficient for us to be convinced, that such individual and heartfelt prayers are not only *legal*, according to the laws, but *acceptable* to the Lord. No restrictions of man can alter or interfere with that which is *divine;* and, therefore, nothing which may be told concerning the inefficacy of individual prayer, unless guided by certain rules, forms, and words, can do away with the consolation and example afforded us by the history of our sweet and gentle ancestress, alike in the manner of her prayer and its reply, and in her unhesitating, unquestioning, and all-confiding FAITH.

We are thus particular, because we would at once remove the foul stigma flung by scoffers on our blessed faith, that her female children have no power to pray, and are, consequently, soulless nonentities before their God; and bring forward, from the Word of God itself, the unanswerable assurance, that woman's prayers *are* heard, and *are* acceptable to Him, needing nothing more than childlike faith in His power to hear and answer, and a loving heart to dictate the imploring words. It is idle for us to say that we cannot pray, for we know not how appropriately to address the Supreme, His awful attributes appal us, and prevent all connected words. Such may be the sentiments of those who keep the Eternal far from them; but not of Israel, His firstborn, first beloved, whose very sins have no power to separate him from his God, if he will but repent and believe. "What nation hath God so near them as Israel, in all we call upon Him for?" were the precious words of Moses, confirmed by the whole after-records of the Bible. Hagiography, Psalms, Proverbs, Prophets, all and every one teem with the same consoling truth, proclaim our God as LOVE, the hearer and answerer of prayer, its gracious receiver, whenever it comes from the *heart*, and is offered up in *faith*. "Call upon me, and I will deliver thee," is the blessed assurance repeated again and again, in different modes of expression, in every part of the Bible. It is folly, it is guilt, to keep away from prayer, under the misleading plea, that God is a being too pre-eminently holy to be approached. Did we but really love Him as He commands, with heart, and soul, and might; did we but trust in Him, as Abraham did, when "his faith was accounted righteousness;" we should find words enough wherewith to pray and praise. Love would bring us to Him, believing and rejoicing in that inexhaustible love which would in such infinite mercy bend down its reviving rays on us, and lift up the wearied spirit, till it found rest on the healing sympathy of its all-compassionating God.

It was thus that Hannah came to Him, loving Him, trusting Him, yet more than she loved and confided in her husband, the nearest and dearest tie on earth. She did not think herself too unworthy to approach and beseech Him, because she knew that the Law which she obeyed, and the whole history of her people, teemed with his invitations so to do, and His promises to answer. She came to Him, because she knew He loved her, and would have compassion; and because she so loved Him, that it was far easier to pour into His gracious ears her silent sorrows than breathe them unto man. She came to Him, because she not only *loved*, but *believed* with such a pure and child-like faith, that when the high-priest bade her "Go in peace, and God grant thee thy petition," she returned to her own home so calmly, so trustingly, that she "did eat, and her countenance was no more sad"—words that convince us how fully she must have *believed* when she prayed, and not only then, but through her lifetime, for faith is of no instantaneous growth. It is a plant so foreign to this cold, sceptical, questioning world, that it must be nursed and tended into life; it must be a *habit*, not a *feeling;* it must attend our every prayer, our every spiritual aspiration, or when most needed, it will fail us, and plunge us into gloom.

But it may be asked, in what need we have such perfect and constant faith? Hannah's position will not bear upon us now, as we have neither high priest nor Temple, nor any visible manifestations of the Eternal's interference in human affairs. We have not, indeed; but we have still HIS WORD, the BIBLE, wherein so to learn His attributes, His promises, that during our captivity we need no more; for if we disbelieve that Word, no priest, no temple, no apparently visible reply, would give us the faith *we* need, and which Hannah *proved*.

We need faith to believe that God is love, and our souls immortal; that every precious promise in His word is addressed as emphatically to us *individually* as to us *nationally;* to feel that there is another and a brighter World, where " eye hath not seen, neither hath ear heard, what He hath prepared for those that love Him "—faith to know that we are individually objects of His love and care, as surely as that every blade of grass and invisible insect are alike the work of His hand, and the constant renewal of that power which at a word called forth creation. We need faith to discern the workings of an eternal Love and infinite Goodness in the History of Man, Past and Present; to mark through the evil which is often alone visible, the furtherance of that Divine Will and Perfect Good, which runs as a silver thread through the darkest web, and links this world with heaven—man with God.

It is for all these things we need Faith: that faith which, instead of banishing *Reason,* welcomes and rejoices in her as her companion and handmaid. Faith may exist without reason; but let reason attempt to exclude faith altogether, let the materialist and scoffer laugh and mock at all things which cannot be substantially proved, and on his bed of death what shall support him? Let him explain, if he can, birth and death, the beginning and the end; and then, and not till then, may he contemn and deride those who, contented to be less wise and less inquiring, walk calmly and happily through this dark valley of earth with the angel, Faith, at their side; sending up their lowly petitions on His aspiring wings ; and calmly sinking, when the tale of life is done, secure, through faith's simple readings of the word of God, of that everlasting bliss which awaits him in another and purer world.

With the history of Hannah, our Third Period concludes; and from the length with which we have treated each separate notice, we have little further to add, save the earnest hope that an *impartial* and unprejudiced study of all that we have brought forward, will convince our readers that no law for the degradation and heathenising the Women of Israel could have had existence from the Exodus to the monarchy; that, therefore, all statutes to that effect, which may be quoted, must be Human, not Divine, and cannot be charged to the Law of God, or regarded as characteristic of the manners and customs of His people.

To us, as women, the whole of the Third Period teems with guidance and consolation; and, as Women of Israel, must satisfy us with the confirmation of our equality and elevation. Shall we, then, feel ashamed of the faith which provides such laws, and the lineage which counts such characters as Deborah, Naomi, and Hannah amongst our ancestry? Shall we prefer listening to the mistaken zeal which would persuade us that, as Hebrew females, we are lowered and degraded, and can only become spiritually free by deserting the faith of our ancestors, to looking through the Word of God, and, tracing our privileges there, make it our glory to reveal them, through our faith and conduct, to the whole Gentile world? Oh, will not every woman nerve her heart to prove that her religion comes from that God of Love and Truth, whose words once spoken will last for ever, whose Law once given will know no change; that she has in that faith enough to give her strength to live, and hope to die; aye, and to glory in that blessed Law which cared for woman first, and will care for her for ever.

FOURTH PERIOD.

Women of Israel during the Continuance of the Monarchy.

ESTABLISHMENT OF THE MONARCHY.—PATRIOTISM OF THE WOMEN OF ISRAEL.—MICHAL.

We are now come to an important change in the history of Israel; the first step to her downfall, and the first opening for the fearful flood of misery and crime which nationally and individually deluged Judea. We allude to the election of an earthly king, and the establishment of a temporal monarchy. In vain the prophet Samuel reasoned and implored, beseeching them to rest contented with the government already established; and in the deepest humility of spirit prayed unto the Lord. "Hearken unto the voice of the people, in all that they say unto thee," was the gracious answer, "for they have not rejected thee, but they have rejected ME, that *I* should not reign over them." Awful words, and most awfully fulfilled! The infinite mercy of Israel's God would not reject His people, though they had rejected Him; but in the very gratification of their desire to have a king they received their chastisement; a chastisement not of a year's, or a century's continuance, but lasting through ages and ages, of crime, misery, expulsion, persecution, and working against unhappy Israel even at this present day.

But the Eternal would not expose them to these terrible effects of their own choice without warning; and by the mouth of Samuel He told them of all the evils they would experience under earthly kings, and that they would cry out in their distress unto the Lord, and then He would not hear them; but still they persisted in the very face of that prophetical word. God granted indeed their request. The people with the wildest rejoicings received the king, and beheld a monarchy established; but the awful effects thence ensuing ought to convince us, that the granting our requests is not always the evidence of the Lord's love and approbation. Better, far better, to rest in Him, and submit to His will, however it may interfere with our own short-sighted wishes, than persist in their accomplishment, and so weary our Father in heaven with repinings and complaints, as to make Him grant that in anger, which in love He would refuse. We should, indeed, bring before Him all our wishes, through the blessed medium of prayer; but such prayers should ever be coupled with the entreaty for grace to meet His will, whatever it may be; to submit unmurmuringly to His decision; and still to realise His love, however he may ordain disappointment. To such prayers we are assured, through the promises of His Word, that he will deign to reply; but for the mere entreaty for the gratification of earthly wishes, the proneness to complain and repine at the faintest semblance of denial, O let us remember the misery hurled upon Israel by the granting their request for a king, and take warning. It is thus that, even in our history, the Word of God may instruct and guide us, and give us lessons for daily life and individual petitions from national examples.

The monarchy of Israel lasted for the period of four hundred and fifty years, and thus presents us with a fourth division of our subject; the social and domestic condition of the Women of Israel during its continuance being a remarkable proof for or against our argument, that no law transmitted to us by Moses commanded our degradation. By a careful study of their positions, as displayed in the various sketches of female character found in the historic books, we shall be able at least to discover if indeed there were any human laws or customs at work counteracting the elevating and spiritualising influence of the statutes for woman's benefit enjoined by Moses. The fearful crimes, and awful state of anarchy and rebellion, during the kingdom, will not indeed allow us either the variety or the completeness of female characters, as displayed in our first and third periods; nor shall we find such beautiful lessons guiding us individually; still, in the brief sketches brought before us, there is sufficient for our conviction that, as women of Israel, we are as elevated and spiritualised as the most exacting nations can require; and that *if* we *are* degraded, socially and individually, in the mind of any man bearing the honoured name of Jew, it is in direct contradiction to the laws of God, and completely opposed to the practice of Judaism, even in that period when her followers were sunk to the lowest ebb of misery and sin.

The establishment of the kingdom had in all probability less influence on the social position of the Hebrew women than on any other class, until the universal wickedness spread even to them, and caused the prophetical denunciations against their sins, as distinct from those of man. The first mention of women in this period, is their coming forth from all the cities of Israel, singing and dancing, to meet King Saul, after the destruction of Goliath by David, with tabrets, with joy, and with instruments of music; evidently a voluntary act, and marking their social position to have been one of perfect freedom, and also of some influence, else their ascribing to David the glory of slaying his ten thousands, and Saul only his thousands, would not have caused the king so much disturbance. We learn, too, from this account, that the gifts of song, and the dance, and playing upon divers instruments, had not at all degenerated in the Israelitish women since the time of Miriam, when they echoed back Moses' song of praise. The skill in these accomplishments argues an education both polished and refined, very superior to the instruction accorded to the women of contemporary nations. Examples of intellect and judgment we have had already, and shall have again; therefore it is also clear that their education was not confined to mere superficial accomplishments, which is often supposed the only instruction necessary for woman. The song, and dance, and knowledge of musical instruments, were but a small portion of the female Hebrew's acquirements; but that they are expressly named more than once in the Word of God, should encourage us alike in their cultivation and in their *enjoyment*, granted as sources of recreation, of innocent pleasure, and yet more as the means of sacred rejoicing. To abuse them, by making them sources of envy and display, and all kinds of ill-feeling, or to undervalue and despise them as snares and foolishness, must both alike be wrong, and prevent the perfection of the heart towards God. He endowed us not with talents to lie unused, but to make others happy, and to increase our own innocent and healthful resources, and create an ever-gushing spring of gratitude towards him.

Nor did the women of Israel refrain from *national rejoicing*. They were not confined to their own narrow spheres, feeling no interest beyond. They did not smile to scorn the holy feeling of patriotism, which should awaken every female heart to the joys and griefs, triumphs and defeats of her country, as if they were her own. They encouraged, they rejoiced in it; and its very possession and display proves their equality with man as citizens of Israel, and children of the Lord. We never find patriotism in a degraded position—the slave knows not even its name, much less the glow, the enthusiam with which it lights up our being. It is in itself a refining and spiritual principle, intimately connected with our higher selves. To the Israelites it must have been yet more powerful than to any other nation, for their beautiful land was the direct gift of God: and bearing every sabbatical year miraculous witness of His unceasing love, in permitting the sanctified earth to give forth of itself sufficient for the holy people, that they might not have the temptation of *necessity* to disobey their law. Israel in captivity may not indeed be enabled to realise the same feeling of *amor patriæ* as Israel in Judea; yet let us not forget that we are exiles, and sometimes cast a longing look of lingering love to that land which is still ours, and which will once again, at the mandate of the Lord, spring up in renewed and renovated loveliness, to welcome home the weary wanderers "from the north, and from the south, and from the east, and from the west." Did we sometimes think of Judea as our own land, we should not regard our destined return to Jerusalem either with direct unbelief, or as a change from the creature comforts which we may be enjoying in our captivity, not at all to be desired. Daily is the prayer for the rebuilding of Jerusalem offered up; yet how very many of those who, while they would think the omission of that petition almost sin, yet so little enter into its spirit, as to shrink from even the thought of returning unto our own most holy land.

Nor does this feeling towards Jerusalem interfere with the emotions which we all ought to experience towards the lands of our adoption—" Seek the peace of the city [or land] whither I have caused you to be carried away captives," the Lord Himself proclaimed through His prophet Jeremiah, "and pray unto the Lord for it; for in the peace thereof shall ye have peace." What injunction can be stronger or more solemn than these words, directing even our prayers, and thus at once reproving the scoffers who scorn the idea of individual petitions benefiting a nation? That Israel is deeply susceptible of love of country distinct from the love borne towards Judea, is beautifully and forcibly exemplified in the history of her expulsion from Spain, and of her secret existence there in the very midst of danger, and death if discovered, when so many other lands offered a secure retreat. And shall not we, respected and at peace as we are, in free and happy England, encourage this refined and holy feeling, and "pray unto the Lord for it," as for our own bright land? By woman, even more than man, should this emotion be experienced—for how heavy would be her burthen, if the peace of home were liable to be disturbed. Let us then remember our privileges and duties as women of Israel, and bid our own hearts to glow with patriotism, alike in mourning fondness for Judea, as in grateful and prayerful affection for the lands blessing the exile with liberty and rest; that we may unconsciously imbue the hearts of our sons with the same elevating and purifying emotions, and behold them, while glorying in the sacred name they bear, as heritors and future denizens of the land of promise, ever ready to stand forward as able citizens and valiant defenders of their adopted homes.

In confirmation of our theory, that in the earlier history of Israel one wife was the natural and legal position of woman, we find that Saul had no more—or more than the one would have been specified, as in the case of the other kings. He had two daughters, Merab and Michal. Of the former little is mentioned; except that she it was, who was the first offered to David as an excitement to fight for Saul; who, already envious and malignant, thought to slay the valiant youth by the hands of the Philistines, and thus save himself all shame. But the Lord was with David, and had departed from Saul, and the young man must evidently have won the promised reward, for we read in Holy Writ, "It came to pass at the time when Merab should have been given to David, that she was given unto Adriel the Meholathite to wife;" a course of acting exactly such as we should expect from the capricious tyrant which Saul had become. Still David, with a single-mindedness and simple confidence, only found in early youth, and in a youth of virtue, seems to have trusted and fought again; and this time evidently with so much settled foresight and determination, that we might almost infer that the love which Michal, Saul's second daughter, bore towards David was fully returned, and so inspired the dangerous expedition on which he ventured.

We have not very much of Michal, nor any particularly pleasing portraiture of character, yet our history will not be complete without noticing all that is recorded concerning her. The deep love that in her youth she appears to have borne David, must have exposed her many times to an intensity of suffering which throws a degree of interest around her, and enlists us more warmly in her favour than we otherwise could have been. Jonathan's faithful friendship for David always receives the meed of our admiration, the more so from his being the son of his deadliest foe. The love borne towards him by the daughter of Saul, must have been a yet stronger emotion; and in consequence subjected Michal to still deeper suffering. It does not appear that Merab loved David; and therefore Michal's first suffering must have been excited by beholding him destined for another who loved him not; while she who had given him the first freshness and fervour of her affections was set aside and disregarded. Even when this sorrow was removed by the union of Merab with Adriel, and her love being reported to her father, it pleased him as the means of ensnaring David, how little confidence could she have placed in her father's promise, when she remembered how he had already deceived. Her fears of Saul's caprice were, however, at this time without foundation. She became the wife of David, whom, we are told, she continued to love as fondly after marriage as before. In her case it was not " because the current of true love never will run smooth" that she loved him, and consequently that, when the desired happiness was obtained, its glow dissolved. Peace indeed, and rest from anxiety, she had not, even when the wife of David. The love she bore him must continually have exposed her to terror for his safety, for her father " grew yet the more afraid of David," and repeatedly gave orders that he should be slain; fortunately, he had taken his son Jonathan into his confidence, and the young man boldly and firmly stood forward in his friend's defence, venturing even to call the king's desired deed a sin against David, who had ever done his duty alike to Saul and to his country. For a time his pleadings succeeded, and as David was again with Saul, as in times past, Michal's terror might have in a degree subsided, and the heart alike of the daughter and the wife been a brief while at peace. But, again, there was war with the Philistines; and David, true to his heroic character, went out and fought with them, and slew them with such great slaughter that they fled from him: yet how might Michal rejoice in the glorious heroism of her husband, when his deeds of valour ever recalled the king's deadly hatred, and exposed him to renewed peril? Even in the very act of charming, by his exquisite skill on the harp, the evil spirit from the monarch's heart, Saul flung the javelin which he had in his hand with such fierce and deadly aim that David only escaped instant death by starting aside, and the instrument struck the wall. He fled from the royal presence to his own home, revealing by his sudden return the danger he had incurred, and recalling all Michal's fears. Nor was the danger over. Messengers sent to David's house to watch and slay him in the morning, at once roused the terror and the energy of his devoted wife. David was so universally beloved, that information of the king's intentions towards him had in all probability been transmitted to Michal by the messengers themselves, or through the agency of Jonathan, who, like his sister, was ever on the alert for David's preservation. In whatever way she received tidings of his danger, it is certain that she it was whose energy and judgment saved him; arousing him "to save thy life to-night, else to-morrow thou wilt be slain."

We find neither complaint nor bewailing on the part of Michal, though she was parting from her husband for an indefinite period, during which time suffering and horror of every description might assail both him and her; that she felt, even to anguish, we must believe, for we have been twice told that she "loved David." And those who love, can alone have an adequate idea of all that parting must have been; yet Feeling itself succumbed before the energy of Will, which only sought his preservation, scarcely allowing time even for words of kindness or one farewell embrace. "She let him down through the window, and he went, and fled, and escaped;" and Michal, not daring to give way to emotion, busied herself in carrying out her stratagem to obtain sufficient time for his escape, ere he was pursued. She laid an image in David's bed, and put a pillow of goat's hair for his bolster, and covered it with a cloth; and when the morning came, and Saul's messengers demanded David, she calmly told them he was sick;

and with that information they evidently returned to their sovereign, probably not at all sorry that David was unable to accompany them. The wrath of the king, however, was not to be turned aside; he commanded them—"Bring him up to me in the bed, that I may slay him." And, again proceeding to his house, the deceit was discovered, and Michal herself brought before her father.

"Wherefore hath thou deceived me so," he demanded, "and sent away mine enemy that he has escaped?" And Michal answered Saul, "He said unto me, Let me go; why should I kill thee?" an answer which, though by the previous narrative not strictly true, was perhaps allowable from the dangerous and difficult position in which Michal was placed. To avow the share she had had in his escape, would only have aggravated her father's anger; and though the enemy and persecutor of her innocent husband, yet Saul was still her father: and Michal, who had, no doubt, been brought up in the peculiarly strict and reverential feelings of Hebrew children to their parents, might not have felt justified in exciting her father's wrath towards herself, more than David's escape had already done. The answer appears to have satisfied Saul so far as his daughter was concerned; but the search and pursuit after David continued unabated.

During the immediate pressure of danger, the mind and heart are supported by their own energy; and we know not how fearfully the nerves have been overstrained, till the period of *action* is passed, and we can only *be still and endure*. How sadly this must have been the case with Michal we may well imagine, when we remember that, from the hour of his escape by her means until he was established in the sovereignty of Israel, an interval of five or six years, she never looked on the husband of her love again. Month after month, year after year, if she heard of him at all, it must have been still as a wanderer flying from place to place, at the imminent risk of his life, either from the emissaries of Saul, or from the treachery and spite of the various courts in which he was compelled to take a refuge. At one time even the inmate of caves and deserts—at another forced to feign madness—often in want of actual food and other necessaries of daily life; and yet more than these;—Michal was a woman, and a loving woman; and though the custom of marrying many wives was not illegal in Judea, and not felt as it would be now, we have already seen that it was sometimes productive of sorrow and vexation; and to the absent and the loving Michal, the thought that David had found others to supply her place, and that therefore he could not need or think of her as she did of him, must have been fraught with no little degree of bitterness, greatly aggravating the pang of separation.

Nor was this all. We are told (1 Sam. xxv. 4), "that Saul had given Michal, his daughter, David's wife, to Phalti, the son of Laish," an act of capricious tyranny in direct disobedience to the laws of Israel. A divorce might permit a woman to become the wife of another man, but no divorce whatever had taken place between David and Michal; and consequently Saul's action must only have proceeded from that determined persecution of the Lord's Anointed, which urged him to annoy him in every possible way, even if to do so occasioned disobedience to the law. That Michal herself could ever have voluntarily acquiesced, when we know how "she loved David," is neither possible nor probable. Saul had become a tyrant even to his own family; and the same man who could cast a javelin at his noble son Jonathan, with the hope to slay him, after heaping on him all manner of abuse, only because of his love for, and defence of, David, would not scruple to outrage every feeling of his daughter, and compel her, by the most iniquitous force, to annul her brief period of connection with David, and become the wife of another.

That Michal was the unhappy *sufferer*, not the *agent*, in these nefarious and most illegal proceedings, is clearly evident from two circumstances. In the first place we are expressly told, "that *Saul* gave Michal, his daughter," &c. Her name, as agent, is not mentioned, whence we infer that it was her father's tyranny, against which a weak and defenceless woman had no power to rebel. In the second, it is clearly demonstrable that she herself was blameless, else David would not have made her restoration to himself one of the very first proceedings of his regal power. Had there been even the semblance of a divorce, he could not have done this, the law expressly forbidding it; but the iniquitous tyranny of Saul, in this outrage to his child, completely justified David's after-proceedings. He would not visit on a blameless child the sins of a guilty father, by leaving her in the position to which parental tyranny had assigned her; but recalled her to his heart, and to his home, at the very time, when, had his noble spirit retained any spark of emnity towards the house of Saul, he might, and with some appearance of justice, have permitted her to remain neglected and uncared for, in the equivocal station which, as no divorce had taken place between her and himself, she must unavoidably have occupied in Phalti's house.

The next mention we have of Michal after her restoration to David, is indicative of a feeling very contrary to that which at first attracted us towards her, and displays an imperfection of character which we might perhaps expect from the daughter of Saul, but certainly not from the wife of David.

For the last twenty years, the ark of God had remained in Kirjath Jearim, in the house of Abinadab, whose son, Eleazer, had been sanctified to keep it. Through all the troubles of the reign of Saul it had quietly remained there; no inclination having been demonstrated by either king or subjects to remove it, and so arguing an indifference to its sacred presence, only too fully borne out by the many illegal acts of Saul. David could not feel this indifference. The ark of God was to him so inexpressibly sacred, that his heart yearned for its holy influence in the city where he dwelt; and therefore every preparation was made for conducting it to Hebron with all befitting sanctity and honour. The fear, however, excited by the smiting of Uzzah for his irreverence, urged his turning it aside from the direct road to the city, and bringing it into the house of Obed-edom, the Gittite. There it abode three months; and the Lord so blessed Obed-edom, and all his household, that David again coveted its presence in his own city, believing with a child-like and loving faith, that the presence of the Lord dwelt there, and would bless all those who sought to do him reverence and honour. "So David went and brought up the ark of God from the house of Obed-edom, to the city of David, with gladness."

It was a very jubilee of rejoicing to the inmates of Hebron. Trumpets and holy songs marked its progress, and every six paces sacrifices of oxen and fatlings were offered to the Lord; and the king himself, disrobed of all regal ornaments, and attired simply in a linen ephod as one of the inferior priests, joined with his whole heart in the solemn rejoicing, by leaping and dancing before the Lord. The *mode* of this holy rejoicing may read strangely to our refined ears; but the song and the dance were ever the natural symbols of rejoicing in Israel. Amusements, which are by many deemed so profane as to be excluded from all professors of religion, were, in Judea and by the chosen people of God, not only allowed, but sanctified and hallowed, by their intimate association with the service of the Lord.

"And as the ark came into the city of David, Michal, Saul's daughter, looked through a window, and saw the king rejoicing . . . . And she *despised him* in her heart." Despised him! she who had once so loved him? How could contempt exist with love? Michal was a very woman; it was not the leaping and dancing she despised, but that King David should, without any semblance of royalty or state, clothed in the lowly garments of an inferior priest, mingle with the crowd, and become for the time as one of them. We know that such were her feelings by her scornful address to the king, when on the conclusion of the burnt-offerings and peace-offerings David returned to bless his household, and was met by Michal, eager to give vent to her contempt. "How glorious was the king of Israel to-day, who uncovered himself [meaning removed the insignia of royalty] in the eyes of the lowest of his servants, even as one of the vain fellows shamelessly uncovereth himself," alluding to the lowest class of the people, who were often compelled to remove their long upper garment, lest it should hinder them in their work. "And David said unto Michal, It was before the Lord, which chose me before thy father, and before all his house, to appoint me ruler over the people of the Lord, over Israel: and therefore will I rejoice before the Lord. And I will yet be more vile than this, and be base in my own sight: and (yet more) of the maidservants of which thou hast spoken, shall I be had in honour;" a calm, yet emphatic reproof, bringing forcibly before her the folly of her contempt. What were the trappings of state, the distinction of ranks, before the Eternal? In His sight king and serf, prince and peasant were the same, judged only by the rendering of the heart towards Him, by their zeal or indifference in His service. It was the Lord who had made David what he was, and therefore what was he more in His sight than the lowest of His subjects? Nor did he rejoice merely from individual thanksgiving. It was the purest joy to a heart like David's, that to him the blessed privilege was granted of bringing the ark of the Lord into his city; a proof that the Eternal deigned to bless the city of David with His immediate presence, and must in itself have created not only individual, but national rejoicing.

The allusion to his having been chosen in lieu of Michal's father, and all his house, cannot in any way be regarded as an unkind and uncalled-for reproach from David to his wife. The extent of the love he bore her, we infer not only from the fact of his recalling her, but from his making her restoration an absolute condition with Abner ere he would accept that warrior's allegiance. Abner was a person of the greatest consequence in Israel, alike from his near connection with the family of Saul, his great influence with the people, and his skill and courage as a warrior. To obtain his subjection and allegiance was of almost vital importance to the popularity of David; yet did that monarch refuse to receive him, even at the risk of sacrificing his offered submission, unless he would bring him back his wife.

No feeling, therefore, actuated him towards Michal as Saul's daughter. Nor would a syllable of reproach have escaped his lips concerning her parentage, had he not been roused to just indignation, by her reproaching him with his zeal in the service of his God. Nothing is more painful, or more difficult to be borne with patience, than a contemptuous attack on our zeal in devotion, or in our ardent wish to serve the Lord, either in glorifying him, or doing good to our fellow-creatures; and the nearer and dearer the person who utters such reproach, the more exquisitely painful is it to bear. Michal does not appear to have been a religious woman. In no part of her history can we trace the workings of that secret, yet ever-acting piety, which characterised so many of her countrywomen. Her very love for David would seem to have been excited, not so much from his beautiful and unwavering piety, but from the dazzling beauty and chivalric qualities which had so distinguished him. Had she been religious, her joy and thanksgiving that the ark of her God was permitted to abide in her husband's city would have occupied her mind to the exclusion of every petty and contemptuous feeling. Had she loved David for those spiritual qualities which had so gained him the loving favour of the Lord—delight and admiration, that to him this privilege was accorded, must utterly have prevented all thought and emotion but veneration and rejoicing; but that it was merely exterior beauty and brilliant qualities which had attracted her, is clearly evident from the scornful contempt with which she regarded him, when these were laid aside for the moment, and nought could find entrance into the heart of David, but rejoicing, thankfulness, and holy zeal.

David was satisfied with administering a just reproof; but the Lord was not: and from the punishment which befel Michal, we must infer that her sin was greater than at a first perusal it may seem. That it was not contempt of *David* only which she felt, but contempt of the holy service in which he was engaged; and therefore was it "that Michal the daughter of Saul had no child unto the day of her death:" not only debarred from having children of her own, but even deprived by a subsequent act of the Eternal's justice of the five she had acquired by adoption. In 2 Sam. xxi. we find mention of a famine in Israel, which was to arouse David to the fact that all the awful actions of Saul and his bloody house were not yet atoned, and reparation to the Gibeonites still to be made. Seven of Saul's nearest descendants they demanded should be delivered up to them, in lieu of either gold or silver, or even execution on the part of Israel's king. David, guided by the Lord, delivered up, in consequence, two of Saul's remaining sons, and his five grandsons, which Merab his eldest daughter had borne to her husband Adriel, and whom Holy Writ informs us, "Michal had brought up for Adriel the son of Barzillai the Meholathite."

Thus was she doubly childless, and by a bereavement most awful in its kind; yet the very choice of these might not only be for justice done to the Gibeonites, but to work out still more fully the Eternal's anger against Michal. The same spirit which had incited her to scorn His holy service, might have prompted the very adoption of these children in proud defiance to His almighty will. Children of her own she might be restrained from having, but who or what was to prevent her adopting the children of her sister, and making them in every respect her own? If such were in truth her incitement to their adoption (and we only suppose it from an impartial consideration of her character), how fearfully must she have been taught the sinful and miserable vanity of striving with the Lord. How much better it would have been to have humbled herself in penitence and prayer before Him, acknowledge the justice of his first sentence of childlessness, and endeavour so to reform her heart and life, as not only to become more worthy of her husband's love, but to regain the loving mercy of the Lord; not by a change in His decree, for that was immutable as Himself, but by the spiritual calm and blessedness which He grants to all who love Him. Had she done so, she might have been happier, notwithstanding her having no child, than she had ever been before; but of such conduct we have no trace. She looked only to human means for the acquirement of happiness, and those proved indeed "the reed whereon if a man lean, it will go into his hand and pierce it."

The mention of her having brought up the sons of Adriel, is the last notice which we have of Michal. Her character is not one to linger on, with either pleasure or admiration; and therefore we cannot regret that we have reached its close. The only pleasing trait about her is, her love for David; and that he truly loved her, endows her with an interest scarcely her own. Nor can we find any part of either her history or character to hold up as an example. A warning indeed it presents us, and one which, alas! but too many of us need. How often does silent and avowed, yet still *realised* contempt, fill the human heart, when we witness an outpouring of zeal, to which our own cold unexcitable natures never can attain. How frequently do we condemn enthusiasm as romantic folly, only because to us it is incomprehensible; and, an evil still worse, how often do we secretly scorn the religion of those whose outward forms may appear to us childish, or unounded, and not needed to bring up our prayers before the Lord. How many times do we contemn those who in the merest trifle differ from that standard of holiness which we may have set up for ourselves, and refuse to believe in their sincerity, because its semblance is unlike our own. And in scorn and disdain towards those who serve the Lord with those orms which their conscience approves and dictates. O let us beware, lest contempt extend to the *service*, as well as to the *servers*—to the religion, as well as to the forms. This was the sin of Michal. For this the Lord Himself chastised her; and that she *was* chastised, is an unerring proof to us how deeply displeasing in the sight of the Eternal is contempt for holy things. Let us then look with more charity on the mere outward forms of our brethren, however they may differ from our own preconceived opinions. Let us not condemn their zeal, or be too hasty in pronouncing enthusiasm to be the service of the lip and not of the heart. If we look well within ourselves to know what may be lurking there, what may need rooting out (even if to do so painfully severs the habits and prejudices of years), to discover if our own hearts and spirits be perfect with our God, we shall have little time for contempt towards the religious observances of others, and be thus effectually shielded from following in the mistaken steps of Michal, and like her incurring the wrath and chastisement of the Lord.

ABIGAIL.

BEFORE commencing our next biographical sketch, we would call our readers' attention to one verse contained in the history we have just completed, as it so strikingly confirms our often-repeated assertion, that in the religion of God, the women of Israel were privileged to join in all religious ceremonies, and to receive the blessings of king or priest equally with men.

We have already noticed the procession of the Ark into Hebron, the sacrifices and shoutings and soundings of the trumpets; and that when they had brought in the Ark of the Lord, and set it in its place in the midst of the Tabernacle that David had pitched for it—and David had sacrificed burnt offerings and peace-offerings before the Lord—as soon as he had made an end of the offerings, he blessed the people in the name of the Lord of Hosts. And he dealt among all the people, even among the whole multitude of Israel, as well to the WOMEN as to the men, "to every one a cake of bread, a good piece of flesh, and a flagon of wine; so all the people departed, every one to his house."

In most public rejoicings, it is generally thought sufficient to provide for *families*, not for individuals. In Israel, we find every one sent away, with the means of not only feasting for the day, but for some days afterwards. And by the particular mention of women as well as men, we see that they were not only *witnesses* of the sacred procession and of the sacrifices, but were singled out by the king as receivers, alike of his blessing and his bounty. This is but a trifling circumstance in itself: yet every verse in the Word of God tending to make manifest the equality of the Hebrew females, their peculiar and glorious privileges as women of Israel, is of no small importance. According even to the ultra orthodox, the law and its traditionary explanation must have been in force, both in theory and practice, during the monarchy of Israel; and if we can find no evidence there of the slavery and ignorance of women, it is clear that the laws which are said to command these things have no foundation in Judaism.

We come now, to a character which proves the dignity and elevation of the Israelitish woman most completely. There was a man in Maon, whose possessions were in Carmel; and the man was very great, and he had three thousand sheep, and a thousand goats. His name was Nabal, of the house of Caleb, churlish in his disposition, and evil in his doings. He had a wife named Abigail, of whom we are expressly told by the Sacred Historian, that "she was a woman of good understanding, and of a beautiful countenance." How such a superior person could ever have become the wife of the churlish Nabal, we might be at a loss to discover, did we not feel with a quaint old chronicler, that love of wealth was as likely to be found in ancient Israel as in other nations, and that Nabal's wealth had in consequence been a greater attraction in the eyes of Abigail's father, than the domestic happiness of his child, which happiness an evil temper must inevitably have destroyed; the beauty and the very gifts of Abigail were likely to have won Nabal's love; for affection and even kindness may be found in churlish dispositions, though neither can be pleasantly demonstrated. Perfect freedom and equality Abigail evidently enjoyed in her husband's house; but the want of companionship for her superior understanding, the constant annoyances which Nabal's temper must have occasioned her, even if not shown to herself, displayed broadly in her household and to all who sought favors or even common courtesy at his hand, must have painfully embittered her domestic life. Still we do not find that either her energy or happy temper sunk under it, as would have been the case with any but a very superior mind. Nothing is so infectious as an evil temper. The strongest control, the most enduring and ever-acting piety, the most determined resolution to bear and forbear, to love and forgive, however pained or annoyed—all these must be experienced or practised by a wife, if the evil temper of her husband really fails to sour hers. Some meek, gentle dispositions, and unwavering sweetness of temper, may indeed stand the torrent of churlishness uninjured; but in these, though the temper does not fail, health and energy both succumb, and the most lasting misery is the consequence. Abigail evidently did not belong to this latter class, or she could not have acted in an emergency of terror as we find she did.

The confusion and misery reigning in Judea, from the Lord's rejection of Saul, until his death, do not appear to have penetrated as far as Carmel, so as to interfere with the usual rural employments of the Israelites. Rumours of the contest between Saul and David, of the cruelties of the former and troubles of the latter, had no doubt spread far and near, and had enlisted the popular feelings in favor of the noble and persecuted David. It was sheep-shearing time, and all Nabal's flocks were gathered together; while feasting and merry-making diversified the pleasant labour in the household, and displayed the plenteousness of Nabal's stores. Feeling his safety still less secure since the recent death of Samuel, David, with his men, had retreated into the wilderness of Paran, in the vicinity of Carmel, where Nabal's flocks were fed. Scorning to appropriate to himself the smallest portion of the wealth of another, however sorely pressed by hunger and privation, David waited till the sheep-shearing, a time when most men's hearts were open towards their poorer brethren, and sent messengers to Nabal, bidding them greet him in his [David's] name, and with a winning courtesy which spoke well for the gentle and lowly character of the Lord's anointed, ask the food and drink he so imperatively needed. "Peace be both to thee, and peace be to thine house, and peace unto all that thou hast. And now I have heard that thou hast shearers: now thy shepherds which were with us, we hurt them not, neither was there ought missing unto them, all the while they were in Carmel. Ask thy young men, and they will shew thee. Wherefore let the young men find favor in thine eyes; for we come in a good day: give, I pray thee, whatsoever cometh to thine hand unto thy servants, and to thy son David."

Could any address have been more gentle and respectful, or more calculated to have found an equally conciliating reply? Instead of which, we find Nabal, true to his churlish character, peremptorily refusing, and scornfully demanding, "Who is David? And who is the son of Jesse? There be many servants now-a-days that break away every man from his master.

Shall I then take my bread, and my water, and my flesh, that I have killed for my shearers, and give it unto men whom I know not whence they be?"

He might easily have known, by any inquiry of his own young men, to whom David, as a warrant of his truth, had so unhesitatingly referred him; but to do so would have inferred a softening spirit; and their information, perhaps, might have compelled him to comply with David's request; therefore he listened only to the dictates of his own ill-temper, caring not for the consequences, or indeed thinking of any thing but the peculiar pleasure it was to be disobliging and ungrateful; for from the after-words of David, it would seem that he had not only *restrained* his needy followers from taking any part of Nabal's property, but absolutely *protected* them from the bands of marauders which, from the fearful state of the kingdom, prowled about Judea.

The indignation of the young warrior was roused by this surly refusal, perhaps to somewhat too great an extent; but David, though so truly holy and pious, and perfect in his heart towards God, as to be spiritually favoured by Him above all his fellows, is never portrayed in Holy Writ as any thing but a mortal, with all the infirmities and feelings of humanity. He was roused not only by this ill return for his courtesy, but by the requital of evil for good; and in a moment of anger, he commanded all his young men to gird on their swords, and with a troop of four hundred equally indignant as himself, marched from the wilderness in the direction of Nabal's dwelling, resolved utterly to exterminate all that belonged to him; and no doubt he would have done so, had not his wrath been turned aside, and his better spirit recalled, by the energy and judgment of a beautiful and noble-minded woman.

The high opinion which the superior understanding, and unwavering temper of Abigail, had won her in the minds and hearts of her household, is clearly evident from all which followed her husband's speech. One of the young men to whom David had referred as witnesses of his truth, hastened to his mistress, and informed her of all that had occurred. "Behold, David sent messengers out of the wilderness to salute our master; and he railed on them [a forcible description, in a few words, of the request and the reply]. But the men were very good unto us, and we were not hurt, neither missed we any thing, as long as we were conversant with them in the fields: they were a wall unto us both by night and by day, all the while we were with them keeping the sheep. Now therefore know and consider what thou wilt do; for evil is determined against our master, and against all his household: for he is such a man of Belial, that a man cannot speak to him."

From these words we are led to suppose that the young man who spoke had seen enough of David, when in the wilderness together, to feel well assured that such ungraciousness would be severely punished. To attempt to speak to his master he knew was impossible, for his words would either have been wholly disregarded, or not even allowed to be spoken. We see, too, that he was ready and willing to bear witness to David's truth, but his master was such a man of Belial, that he dared not speak to him; yet he was too faithful to allow such a danger to fall upon his churlish master unawares, and so sought his mistress, whose gentleness and wisdom were in all probability the real source of his fidelity, and of that of all his companions.

Abigail lost no time in either lamentations on their hovering danger, or in aspersions on her churlish husband. Her active and energetic character is clearly displayed in the promptness and judgment of her proceedings. She asked no advice, demanded no assistance, requiring only the willing help of her domestics, and acting on the impulse of the moment, as judiciously and quietly, as if she had had months to think and to prepare. No woman could have done this unless her understanding was ever in exercise, her mind well trained, and her *principles* so regulated as ever to guide her *impulses* aright. It is only when the mind and principles are unregulated that impulses are dangerous, and peculiarly liable to mislead. The habit of *thinking* when life is smooth, prepares us for *acting* promptly on an emergency; and the impulse that we follow springs scarcely so much from the feelings of the moment, as from the habit of steady thought to which we have long subjected our minds before.

Such must have been the character and habits of the wife of Nabal, for we read that she "made haste, and took two hundred loaves, two bottles of wine, five sheep ready dressed, five measures of parched corn, a hundred clusters of raisins, and two hundred cakes of figs, and laid them on asses. And she said to her servants, Go on before me; and behold, I come after you. *But she told not* her husband Nabal." She knew it was useless so to do, for she might not hope for his permission, and all depended on speed and decision. His safety, her own, and that of her whole household were at stake. It was no time for deference to one who would oppose for the very sake of opposition, even if his life were the sacrifice of his foolishness ; and so mounting her ass, she speedily followed her servants. She could not have gone very far, when David and his armed men, in alarming fulfilment of her servant's fears, "came down against her, and she met them." Dismounting from her ass, she hastened to pay him the reverential homage due to him, alike as the anointed of the Lord and the destined king of Israel ; and kneeling at his feet, addressed him in a strain so fraught with the spirit of wisdom and piety, so truly deferential, without one spark of cringing servility, rising, as she proceeded, almost into prophecy, that we can but wonder and admire.

"Upon me, my lord, upon me let this iniquity be :" she answered, wisely seeking to turn David's anger on herself, that by her speedy submission it might be averted ; " yet let thine handmaid, I pray thee, speak in thine ears, and hear the words of thine handmaid. Let not my lord, I pray thee, regard this man of Belial, even Nabal : for as his name is, so is he ; Nabal is his name, and folly is with him : but I thine handmaid saw not the young men of my lord, whom thou didst send. Now therefore, my lord, as the LORD liveth, and as thy soul liveth, seeing the LORD hath withholden thee from coming to shed blood, and from avenging thyself with thine own hand, now let thine enemies, and those that seek evil to my lord, be as Nabal. And now this blessing [or gift] which thine handmaid hath brought unto my lord, let it be even given unto the young men that follow my lord. I pray thee forgive the trespass of thine handmaid ; for the LORD will certainly make my lord a sure house ; because my lord fighteth the battles of the LORD, and evil hath not been found in thee all thy days. Yet a man is risen to pursue thee, and to seek thy soul : but the soul of my lord shall be bound up in the bundle of life with the LORD thy God ; and the souls of thine enemies, them shall He sling out as from the middle of a sling. And it shall come to pass, when the LORD shall have done to my lord according to all the good that He hath spoken concerning thee, and shall have appointed thee ruler over Israel ; that this shall be no grief unto thee, nor offence of heart unto my lord, either that thou hast shed blood causeless, or that my lord hath avenged himself; but when the Lord shall have dealt well with my lord, then remember thine handmaid."

In not one word of this beautiful address do we find Abigail forgetting her own dignity, by that fulsome adulation with which a mind of a less elevated grade would have thought to disarm David's wrath. She does not say one word which grates upon the mind as flattery. All of greatness, of victory, of life which was to befall David, she attributes to the one only source, the ordainment and the blessing of the Lord; and that victory only obtained, because it was not his own, but the Lord's battles which he fought. She speaks of his becoming king of Israel, of the Eternal accomplishing all that He had spoken concerning David as *things assured*, although at the very time she spoke, David was a persecuted exile, with not a place but the wild desert in which to lay his head; and all those who loved or showed him kindness, exposed to wrath and even massacre at the hand of Saul. What but faith, the unquestioning faith springing from the piety of the heart towards God, and the intimate knowledge of His ways, could have dictated these words? and could Abigail have attained these things, if in any part of the Mosaic law she was denied the privilege of praying to the Lord, and studying His words? No. If woman were refused the spiritual privileges granted to her brother man in the law of God, there would be no such character as Abigail.

Not only does she, with prudence and ready wit, deprecate the anger of David by taking the trespass against him on herself, and asking his forgiveness as if she it was who had offended, but she contrives to lessen the offence of Nabal by attributing it not to malice or determined enmity, but only to folly, which prevented his being answerable for his own actions, and therefore not worthy of David's further regard.

There is something singularly noble in Abigail thus taking on herself the trespass, and so voluntarily offering herself to bear its penalty. It was woman in her noblest and purest character. The temper and other evil habits of Nabal must not only have prevented all affection towards him, but repeatedly exposed her to those petty yet incurable sufferings springing from the surliness and moroseness of a churlish husband; yet of these things she thinks nothing, only remembering that, as her husband, Nabal demanded every exertion and even sacrifice on her part, and these without a moment's hesitation she makes.

Had not her appeal struck David, even as it strikes us, it would not have so turned aside his purpose. Unselfishness and piety, uprightness and honour, he himself so richly possessed, that to such in another his heart was literally compelled to respond, and wrath vanished before them "Blessed be the Lord God of Israel, which sent thee this day to meet me," he exclaims, with that true unquestioning piety which never knows chance, but attributes every event of daily life to the loving guidance of the Most High God; "and blessed be thy advice, and blessed be thou, which hast kept me this day from coming to shed blood, and from avenging myself with mine own hand. For in very deed, as the Lord God of Israel liveth, which hath kept me back from hurting thee, except thou hadst hasted and come to meet me, surely by the morning light there had not been one left to Nabal."

How must the noble heart of Abigail have rejoiced within her, that her energy of purpose and promptness of act had, under the blessing of God, been permitted to save so many innocent lives, and also checked David in the commission of a great sin. The whole of this scene is so vividly described in Holy Writ, that it is rather remarkable that it should never have been taken as the subject of a picture, by some of the many illustrators of Scripture. A rocky defile of Carmel winding round the side of a hill, down which the four hundred armed followers of David in their glittering armour might be scattered in and out the rocks, except the few which, close beside their leader and the kneeling Abigail, marked the fore ground. The servants and led asses of the wife of Nabal gracefully grouped on the opposite side to the armed men, forming a beautiful contrast, by their peaceful habiliments and alarmed looks, to the fierce and eager countenances of the warriors. The extreme beauty of Abigail, the pleading look and posture of the suppliant, blending with the modest dignity of the woman; the superb countenance and form of the still youthful David, varying from indignation to softening admiration, all might form a combination not unworthy of first-rate talent in an artist, more especially when that artist may be found at this very day amid the ranks of Israel.

Courteously and kindly David accepted the proffered gifts of Abigail, bidding her "go up in peace to her house, for he had hearkened to her voice and accepted her person." Meaning that he had accepted her as the person who had committed the trespass, and so forgiven it. She need be under no farther alarm on account of her husband.

Her business thus blessedly accomplished, Abigail loitered not on her way, and without further parley returned to her house, evidently not having been missed by her husband; who, while death was hovering over his head, was holding a great feast in his house like the feast of a king. "And his heart was merry within him," in all the imbecile and sinful mirth of drunkenness. What a contrast to the dignified and exalted character of Abigail! How inexpressibly trying to her mind must have been the degraded brutish habits of such a husband! How strong must have been her innate dignity, her self-possession and enduring temper, to have so acquired and preserved the respect and faithfulness of her household, whom the example of their master might have rendered rude and sottish as himself, and who, were woman lowered in Israel, could have had no restraint whatever.

Wisely, though no doubt with a sorrowful heart, she left Nabal undisturbed in his inebriety till the morning's light, although the news of the danger which he had so narrowly escaped would effectually have roused him from his idle mirth. When told, its effect seems extraordinary, "his heart died within him, and he became as stone;" only explained by the supposition of his utter want of manliness and trust, which prevented all belief in David's assurances, and occasioned such vivid horror of his vengeance as literally to cause the death he dreaded; for "ten days after, the Lord smote Nabal that he died." An awful chastisement for his churlish insult to the young warrior known throughout all Israel as the Anointed of the Eternal. He had grudged the smallest particle of his immense stores to one who, with such winning courtesy, had asked it at his hand; and the Eternal's justice, by one stroke, deprived him of them all, and compelled him, naked and bare, to appear before His awful throne in judgment for his crimes. And those crimes came not under the denomination of great delinquencies; they were those petty sins of stingy selfishness, and an aggravating disobliging temper, which (how often!) grow upon us unconsciously; and we scarcely know their influence until some awful stroke of judgment awakens us to what *what we might have been*, and to *what we are*. His wife's narrative was this awakening stroke to Nabal. He had sunk too low, too enervatingly, in the fathomless abyss of selfish indulgence to rouse himself to a better course of life, so that deadly fear of vengeance took possession of him; and, combined with a torturing recollection of an abused and wasted existence, rendered him as feelingless and senseless as the stone to which he is compared.

How, completely the appeal of Abigail had awakened David to the sin which his immoderate anger prompted him to commit, we read by his pious and thankful exclamation, when he heard of Nabal's death, "Blessed be the Lord that hath pleaded the cause of my reproach from the hand of Nabal, and *hath kept His servant from evil*, for the Lord hath returned the wickedness of Nabal, on his own head;" words not only illustrative of his rejoicing thankfulness of his own restraint from sin, but also of his firm belief that all the changes of the heart are of *God* not of man, and that would we keep ourselves from evil we must pray to Him to do so; not imagine we can keep pure, *only* by efforts of our own.

It was now David's turn to plead, and to her who had so lately knelt to him as a supplicant. When the usual term of mourning for a husband was over, "he sent and communed with Abigail to become his wife." Her answer is strikingly illustrative of that beautiful humility of character which is so perfectly compatible with true dignity and modest self-esteem. "Behold, let thine handmaid be a servant, to wash the feet of the servants of my Lord." When she was in the character of a *petitioner*, we find no such expressions; for in entreaty they would have been servile and degrading; but as the *petitioned*, they did but express the deep sense she entertained of her own individual unworthiness, as little suiting her to be the wife of one whom the Lord God of Israel had so singled out above his fellows. In worldly state and earthly possessions, David could not compare with her former husband. Destined to the kingdom he was indeed; but as we have previously stated, there was no *human* semblance that such he would be, or any apparent end to the troubles, the privations, the wanderings to which he was still so mercilessly exposed. Yet he was the beloved, the chosen of the Lord; and in comparison with the holiness—the virtue which must have originally gained him these appellations in the hearts of his countrymen — Abigail might well have deemed herself unworthy. She became his wife, however; and though in doing so, she exchanged the wealth, the security, the luxuries of such an establishment as had been Nabal's, for an anxious and wandering life, continually exposed to danger from the enmity of Saul and his followers, and to captivity from the neighbouring nations; yet still the love and sympathy of such a mind as David's, the rest from the weary annoyances of a diseased temper, the indulgence of pious emotions and obedience to all the observances of religion without the sneering scorn of a churlish and uncongenial disposition, must indeed have marked the exchange as a blessed one, and rendered her after-life as happy as it had previously been sad.

We have one more mention of Abigail, and in the very situation of suffering and peril to which, as we have said, that she was, as the wife of David, continually exposed. About two years after his marriage, David took refuge in the kingdom of Gath; and besought and obtained from Achish, their king, the town of Ziklag, which though situated in the territory of Simeon, had till then belonged to the Philistines. In that city, David and his companions, with their wives and children, composed a faithful little Hebrew colony; and the town formed a quiet residence for the females and children, while their husbands were engaged in war. On the many valiant acts of David we must not linger. Two years after he had received the gift of Ziklag, the Philistines gathered together all their armies in Aphek, and the Israelites pitched by a fountain in Jezreel. David and his men were with the rere-ward of the army of Achish; but, distrusted by the princes and lords of the Philistines, because of their being Israelites, they were disbanded from the army; and in consequence returned to Ziklag. Only three days had elapsed since they had left it; but what a change awaited their return! The city was a heap of smoking ruins, and their wives, and their sons, and their daughters, all had been carried off; the Amalekites had made an invasion in the south, and without tarrying to slay, had marked their path with fire, and carried off every woman and child. Few lengthy descriptions of grief have the force and beauty of the scriptural relation, "Then David, and the people that were with him, lifted up their voices and wept, until they *had no more power to weep.*" And David himself had not only to mourn the loss of his two wives, but was "greatly distressed, for the people spake of stoning him, because the soul of all the people was grieved, every man for his sons and for his daughters." Stoning him, the Lord's Anointed! How fearfully must grief have disordered the minds and hearts of his followers; and how painful the position of David. To feel distress was no weakness in Israel. Human nature is never described in the Bible as other than deeply susceptible of all human and gentle emotions. Religion in Israel was never intended to render the heart insensible to the sweet charities of life and all their subsequent afflictions. It was no sin to weep—no weakness to feel distressed—but as "David encouraged himself in the Lord his God," so too must we, when the deep waters of affliction flow over us; and like him we shall receive the guidance and encouragement we need. But even in this emergency, when every human feeling must have been striving within him, urging instant action, we find him in meekness and humility *inquiring of the Lord.* And to him God vouchsafed reply, and bade him pursue, "for thou shalt surely overtake them, and without fail recover all."

To enter into the detail of this chivalrous expedition we have not space, as it relates more to David than to his wife, whose history we are recording. Our readers will find the whole far more emphatically told than could be by an uninspired pen, in the thirtieth chapter of the First Book of Samuel. Suffice it here to state, "that David recovered all that the Amalekites had carried away; and he rescued his two wives, and there was nothing lacking to him, neither small nor great, neither sons nor daughters, nor anything that they had taken to them; David recovered all."

The whole of this stirring tale reminds us of those narratives of the middle ages, on which the youthful lovers of chivalry delight to linger; why should they not then feel equal pleasure in the inspired story of their immediate ancestors? We have quite enough of Abigail's character and sentiments revealed, to give us all sufficient for a just conception of what not only her feelings but her conduct must have been, when she saw the city of her husband burned and sacked, and herself and all her female companions, with their helpless children, carried off by their lawless foes—exposed to every horror which the mind could frame or the heart could dread. The wild attack; the hurried flight; the agony of those days of capture which could have no hopeful future, for David and his men were with Achish, and the time of their return to Ziklag so uncertain, that traces of the Amalekite spoilers might be lost ere their capture was even known; and then the wild rekindling of hope at the sudden descent of David and his men; the awful strife lasting from even unto even; the glorious conquest; and the re-union of husbands and wives, children and fathers; are so completely all the elements of romance, that we need little of imagination to give it life and breath, or turn to the records of fiction for events to stir the very heart's blood with the recital of chivalric deeds.

But not to record it merely in its romantic bearings, have we brought this portion of Scripture forward. It is to remark how truly and beautifully both the grief and the exertions of David and his men demonstrate the extent of love, conjugal and parental, which reigned in the Hebrew households. It is a beautiful illustration of the spirit of those Mosaic laws, which, penetrating the very homes of the first-born of the Lord, guided and sanctified the conduct of husbands and wives, children and parents. LOVE was the watchword of Israel, alike in their relations to their Father in heaven and to each other. That the law was severe in its justice, is no contradiction to this assertion. Its perfection of justice was far purer, deeper, more influencing Love, than the modern codes which are pronounced so much more merciful.

The social and domestic position of the wife of Nabal must have been as perfectly free, independent, and influencing, as that of any woman of the present day, be the laws which guide her what they may. We perceive the counsel and wisdom of their mistress, sought and followed by the servants of Nabal without the smallest regard to their master. Compare this liberty of will and action, this exercise of judgment displayed in the history of Abigail, with the position and the characters of the Eastern females of the present day, under the laws of Mahomet, and then let truth pronounce which are the degraded? Again, we are expressly told that Abigail was not merely a beautiful woman, but of *good understanding*, which her whole story proves; and yet more, every word of her address to David evinces an almost remarkable knowledge of the *ways* and the words of the Lord. She is even called by the Ancient Fathers, a prophetess. "There were seven women of Israel," they say, "who were prophetesses—Sarah,

Miriam, Deborah, Hannah, *Abigail*, Huldah and Esther."
We know not on what authority our venerable sages have
honoured by the term prophetess, those whom the Bible does
not so distinguish; but it is a forcible proof of the deep
learning and profound knowledge of the Word of God which
must have been possessed by Abigail, and which she could not
have acquired without study. The study of religion, then,
was evidently *not* prohibited to the women of Israel; and
therefore we know not by what authority such blessed study
can be denied to us now.

Nor is it only religious knowledge which Abigail's character
develops. It is a perfect acquaintance with *human nature*,
else she had not so soon turned aside the wrath of David.
Judgment, intellect, and talent, all breathe in her eloquent
appeal, and evince an elevation of intelligence impossible to be
obtained were the social position of woman confined to household work. The more we study the story of Abigail, the more
deeply we must feel how valuable it is to us as women of
Israel; how impressively it marks out our privileges in every
relation of life, and how unanswerably it proves, that Jewish
women need no other creed to give them either spiritual or
temporal advantages.

As women, the character of Abigail equally concerns us.
We have frequently insisted that the *narratives*, as well as the
precepts, of the Bible are written for our guidance; and therefore are we so anxious to bring forward all that can aid our
young sisters in making their Bibles their daily guide. Many
would do so, but they know not how, from the sad scarcity of
religious books amongst us, in modern tongues. The more we
daily study the Bible, the more easy in truth shall we find it;
but then we must not confine our readings to the five books
of Moses. One chapter every morning, one every night, and
three on the Sabbath, complete the whole Bible—Pentateuch,
Hagiography, and Prophets—all, with the sole exception of
the Psalms, in the three hundred and sixty-five days forming
the Nazarene year; and this formed into a habit, not done
one year and laid aside, but persevered in for a life, would, in
process of time, and without either labour or weariness, give
the comfort and the knowledge that we seek. Nor need we
fear that we shall grow weary of the task: each year it would
become lighter and more blessed, each year we should discover
something we knew not before, and in the valley of the shadow

of death feel, to our heart's core, that the word of our God is in truth "the rod and the staff, they comfort me," of which the Monarch-Psalmist spake.

We have already noticed the little power which Nabal's churlish temper, and all the discomforts thence ensuing, had over the pious and energetic character of Abigail. From her wise forbearance towards him, both in acting without his knowledge in seeking David, and in not mentioning the effect of that interview till he was in a state to hear it, we can quite infer, that she not only bore with a churlish temper, but well knew how to manage it—a task not a little difficult, and which none but an unselfish and well-controlled temper ever can attempt. Many women, instead of acting on such an emergency, would have lost all the proper time of action in vain lamentations, and in bitter reproaches of the churlish folly which had caused it; or, if they acted as Abigail did, many would have *displayed triumph*, would have vaunted of their own skill in turning wrath aside, and taunted Nabal with what might have befallen him. But Abigail, with true womanly dignity, did neither. That she had been permitted to save her household from an imminent danger was enough for her—and if the kind providence of the Eternal had not ordained it otherwise, she would have returned to all her usual quiet duties and silent endurance, never dreaming that her conduct had evinced any thing worthy of reward.

Let us then, as women, not only admire, but imitate the piety, the forbearance, and the energy of our gentle ancestress, assured that such virtues are acceptable to our God. Many and many a one have a Nabal in their households in one or other relation of life. Temper, thought of so little, encouraged because it is no palpable vice, so blinding the eyes of its possessor as to fling its black shadow on all his associates, till *they* are thought the churlish, *not* himself; temper, the severer of so many gentle ties, the rude breaker of so many loving hearts, the baleful spirit of so many otherwise richly favoured homes, —Oh what but a character, a piety, an energy like Abigail's, can enable us to sustain its trials, in a manner acceptable to the Lord, and not overwhelming to ourselves? As women, as women of Israel more especially, let us endeavour to cultivate these noble qualities, and feel that even for the sufferings of a churlish temper, we have sympathy, comfort, and guidance in the Bible. We may not all have either the beauty, or the good understanding of Abigail; but we may all have piety and energy and influence if we so will, the one springs from the other; for the want of energy, the absence of all influence, arises from a listless indifference which never can exist with true piety. The service of God demands constant watchfulness, constant activity, aye, and constant thought; nor can we serve Him, apart from serving our fellow-creatures. To bear and forbear is peculiarly woman's duty—in every station of life, and more especially towards a husband; and every religious and justly feeling woman will rouse her every energy to conceal, or at least prevent, the evil consequences of temper and ill-judgment spreading over her household, and lowering the character of a husband in the minds of his inferiors. Abigail's constant superiority of judgment and action we learn by her servants going to her without hesitation. They must have frequently confided in her judgment before, else they could not have demonstrated such implicit trust in a moment of danger.

Her influence we as clearly perceive in the success of her appeal to David; a quick judgment and few well chosen words saved herself and household from destruction, and David from the committal of a great sin. And if by the cultivation of *mind* and *manner* woman can achieve such things, who shall deny her the privilege of being an instrument of good, or seek to confine her to a false and degraded position, and so compel either vacuity and idleness, or frivolity and folly? We may not be called upon to exert our influence in a matter of life or death, but few are the women who pass through this life without some opportunity to use their natural influence for good, either in the encouragement of worth, or the wise and gentle guidance from the paths of sin. If there are some who will deny this, who will assert that in their isolated position they have influence on none, and have no power to do good, we would say, it is because they *seek it not*, not because *they have it not;* and beseech them to rouse their dormant energy to find and use it, and by the superiority of their mental resources, their spiritual piety, their noble energy, and pure meek womanly influence, alike in their domestic and social position, make manifest to the nations how deeply they feel and glory in the privileges accorded to, and in the duties demanded from them, as the female children of the Lord.

WISE WOMAN OF TEKOAH.—WOMAN OF ABEL.—RIZPAH.—JUDGMENT OF SOLOMON.—WIDOW OF ONE OF THE SONS OF THE PROPHETS.

The period of our history which we are now regarding, will not supply us with such regular biographies as the preceding ones. Between Abigail and the Shunammite, in the time of Elisha, there is no female character which we can look upon as a whole, and derive thence individual benefit; but in the years of the monarchy stretching between the two above mentioned, there are some notices of women peculiarly valuable to us in a national sense, as portraying our position, both social and intellectual.

The first of these is the wise woman of Tekoah, suborned by Joab to incline the king's heart towards Absalom. In what sense the epithet "a wise woman" was regarded, we cannot exactly determine; but from Joab sending at once to Tekoah, we are led to suppose her a person noted for her wisdom, and selected for that reason. Her story is, of course, a feigned one, and therefore does not command our commiseration; but it is valuable, as it so undeniably manifests how easy it was for the *women* of Israel to obtain the ear of the monarch, and receive justice and protection at his hand, even against the opinions of the people. She tells David that she is a woman who had two sons, one of whom, in striving with the other, had smitten and slain him. That the whole family had risen against the widow, commanding her to deliver up the survivor, that they might revenge his brother's death by also slaying him; and so, in the beautiful language of Scripture, "quench my coal which is left, and not leave to my husband either name or remainder upon the earth." David, in answer, desires her to return to her home in peace; and that he would give charge concerning her. Still she lingers, and he reiterates, "Whosoever saith ought unto thee, bring him unto me, and he shall not touch thee any more. Then said she, I pray thee, let the king remember the Lord thy God, that thou wouldst not suffer the revengers of blood to destroy any more, lest they destroy my son. And he said, As the Lord liveth, there shall not one hair of thy son fall to the ground."

By this we are led to believe, that the supposed crime of the one brother against the other came under the accidental murders, where the slayer was permitted to seek the cities of refuge. It is, as we know, a fictitious tale of grief; still it is important to mark how exactly it tallies with obedience to the laws. The woman asserts herself to be a widow, and consequently the peculiar care of her brethren. Her position is sanctified, and therefore is it that David not only hears her, and promises that he will take her in charge, but pledges himself to yet greater leniency than the law allows. In his own case, one exactly similar, David had done such violence to his own parental feelings, that three years had elapsed since he had looked on his darling Absalom, towards whom we are expressly told *his soul longed to go forth*. The laws of his country might not be transgressed for him, though a sovereign; and yet for a mourning widow his kind heart yielded. This does not evince disregard to woman's feelings, or that they were less objects of care in the state than man, but rather the complete contrary: the *king's* son was to remain in exile and ignominy, the *widow's* son was to be protected and pardoned.

Not content with the favour granted the supposed widow, she proceeds to entreat the king, " Let thine handmaid speak, I pray thee, one word unto my lord the king. And the king said, Say on." And then boldly and unhesitatingly the suppliant turns reprover; and, making her own case the king's, pronounces it a faulty judgment, else why does he not fetch home his banished? We need not transcribe the whole of her well-judged appeal (see 2 Sam. xiv.) The king's penetration at once discovered the real mover of this scene, and addressing the woman as his equal, instead of demanding the truth from her as some might imagine due to his royal prerogative, he asks, " Hide not from me, I pray thee, the thing that I shall ask thee. And the woman said, Let my lord the king now speak. And the king said, Is not the hand of Joab with thee in all this?" The whole is consequently revealed; but no anger at the deception followed. The king's word had passed, and though it was to a supposed case, he would not withdraw it. The young man Absalom was recalled from his grandfather's court, and brought by Joab to Jerusalem; but still, true to his paternal severity, David would not listen to his feelings; and for two years, though dwelling in the same town, the father and son never saw each other's face; whereas, had the widow's story been true, he would have permitted her the rich blessing of her son's continued presence and full pardon.

The incident is not an important one in itself; but by Joab's seeking a *woman* to bring the king to his wishes; by the little difficulty she had to obtain a hearing; by the kindness and feeling which dictated the monarch's manner and words towards her, we cannot entertain a doubt of the real position of women in Judea;—that she was thought of, felt for, and protected, infinitely more in the state of Israel, than in any contemporary or even in any more modern nation; that even warriors and courtiers disdain not to ask and use her aid; and that the king himself listened, not only when she was a supplicant on her own affairs, but when the strain was changed and she ventured to address him on his own.

Nor is she the only "wise woman" whose instrumentality is mentioned in Holy Writ. Soon after the death of Absalom other confusions arose; and a quarrel took place between the men of Israel and the tribe of Judah, as to who should have the greater influence over the aged king, " and the words of the men of Judah were fiercer than the words of the men of Israel;" in consequence of which, a man of Belial (the scriptural term for a seditious and rebellious spirit) named Sheba, a Benjamite, blew a trumpet, and proclaimed, "We have no part in David, neither have we inheritance in the son of Jesse; every man to his tents, O Israel"—the usual war cry of the Jews. "So every man of Israel went up from David, and followed Sheba, the son of Bichri: but the men of Judah clave unto their king." A war of course ensued, seeming likely to be yet more injurious to Judea, than even Absalom's rebellion. And Joab with a large army "went from Jerusalem to pursue Sheba." His appearance and proclamation, "He that is for David let him go after Joab," recalled the wavering Israelites, and Sheba was compelled to take refuge in the city of Abel of Beth-maachah. There Joab besieged him, casting up a bank against the city, and rearing battering engines against the wall, so that destruction and slaughter were inevitable; for no possibility or inclination for resistance appeared from within. Not one *man* had the necessary courage and wisdom to come forward, either to pacify Joab or to meet him in battle. A hesitation no doubt occasioned by the fear of Sheba, the natural reluctance to the delivering up of one who had taken refuge in their city, and the yet greater reluctance to rise against David. Between these conflicting emotions the downfall of the city was inevitable; but there was one within its walls, not only a wise, but a patriotic woman, who, boldly taking on herself all risk of personal danger, alike from the battering rams of Joab without, and the rage of Sheba's adherents within, suddenly appeared upon the walls and called aloud, "Hear, hear; say, I pray thee, unto Joab, Come near hither, that I may speak with thee."

The noise of attack on the part of the besiegers involuntarily ceased, and soldiers and general must have gazed with some astonishment on the vision appearing thus boldly before them. And Joab approaching, she bade him "hear the words of thine handmaid. And he said, I do hear. Then she spake, saying, They were wont to speak in old time, saying, They shall surely ask council at Abel, and so they ended the matter;" rather obscure words, yet, as appears to us from the succeeding verse, meaning that, in former years, the councils held by the inhabitants of Abel ended all difficult matters; but that Joab coming upon them in determined hostility had prevented any amicable treaty, and had in consequence checked the interference of all these who, like herself, were "peaceable and faithful in Israel."

The address also appears to allude to, and in fact to illustrate, the law contained in Deut. xx. 10—12. "When thou comest nigh unto a city to fight against it, then proclaim peace unto it. And it shall be, if it make thee answer of peace, and open unto thee, then it shall be, that all the people that is found therein shall be tributaries unto thee, and they shall serve thee. And if it will make no peace with thee, but will make war against thee, then thou shall besiege it." Joab's impetuous zeal seems to have neglected this merciful ordinance and therefore no council as in ancient times could be held in Abel, and no decision made, either for peace or war. And this was the more blameable on the part of Joab because the city belonged to David; the inhabitants were his own subjects. The speaker feels this in her concluding words, "Thou seekest to destroy a city and a mother in Israel: why wilt thou swallow up the inheritance of the Lord?"

All she says is so essentially feminine, so moderate and gentle, that it at once satisfies us that her boldness and wisdom in no way mark her a masculine character. She was still a mother in Israel; her endowments were evidently common to her sex and country, proving that they knew well how to unite the wisdom of the patriot with all the graces of the woman. Her very first words to Joab, "Hear the words of thine handmaid," mark her perfect consciousness of her own position, and pay that respect due alike to the rank and generalship of the person she addressed. An assumption of wisdom and, consequently, of authority, would have lost her the ear of Joab at once. A man may be *influenced* by woman, but not *dictated* to, however superior may be her wisdom. We cannot discover the wisdom of this mother in Israel in her actual *words*, so much as in her *actions*. The address was indeed well chosen, for it appealed directly to the best and holiest feelings of Joab, and could only have proceeded from a mind long accustomed to well-regulated thought; but from sole plea was, that she was "a mother in Israel," a character and station to which the rudest and hardest nature never refused reverence.

"Far be it, far be it from me," was Joab's earnest answer, "to swallow up or destroy—the matter is not so, but a man of Mount Ephraim, Sheba the son of Bichri by name, hath lifted up his hand against the king, even against David. Deliver him only, and I will depart from the city. And the woman said, Behold, his head shall be thrown to thee over the wall. Then the woman went unto all the people in her wisdom; and they cut off the head of Sheba the son of Bichri, and cast it out to Joab; and he blew a trumpet, and they retired from the city every man to his tent. And Joab returned to Jerusalem and to the king" (2 Sam. xx).

There will be, no doubt, some fair affectors of refinement, horror-stricken at the idea of a woman being influential in the execution of a criminal, and condemn the age in which such deeds were done as something too barbarous to be regarded without a shudder. Now there are few of our countrywomen, we think, more painfully affected by scenes and thoughts of blood than ourself; but it is the *necessity* for such fearful punishments we feel and mourn, more than the punishment itself. The Eternal ordained capital punishments for capital crimes: and if His infinite wisdom and His immeasurable mercy saw that it was good so to do, surely we poor weak finite creatures of a day, can have neither right nor wisdom to deem such acts of justice cruel, or loathe them as remnants of barbarity. Joab's demand was unanswerably just. The man whose seditious and rebellious spirit sought to light the flame of discord all over Judæa, and dared to arm his countrymen against the Lord's Anointed, was deserving of death; and his own execution saved the lives of hundreds.

Was it not then an act of far greater mercy to demand the head of Sheba, than, by the weak shrinking from a duty so painfully repugnant to woman's nature, expose men, women, and children, in countless numbers, to the destroying sword? Yet from the latter few would shrink as they do from the former, only because there is something so dreadful in the idea of a woman seeking the life of a fellow-creature. She sought, in fact, to *save life*, not to take it; and her efforts were successful. Enviable must have been that "wise woman's" feelings as the trumpet sounded, and the fierce warriors under command of Joab struck their tents, withdrew their battering-rams, and in goodly array marched away from the pre-doomed city; leaving freedom and rejoicing gladness behind them, in a people saved alike from the destroying sword, and from the sin of strife and rebellion against the Lord's Anointed.

Now, it is not at all likely that these wise counsels were the impulse of the moment. The women of Israel must have had a voice even in the senate of their several cities. Their position must have been alike elevated and intellectual. In a state like Israel, composed as it was of so many unruly members and constantly seditious spirits, wisdom could no more have obtained ascendancy without cultivation, *then*, than it can *now*. Had there been any law confining woman to any particular sphere, prohibiting her interference in any religious or secular matters, wisdom and judgment would not only have been *publicly* useless in a woman, but *privately* uncultivated, and we should find no such instances as the two we have recorded. A little attentive thought on the conditions of the beleaguered city, the multitude of diverse opinions with which at such a time it must have been agitated, moved as it was by the presence and pleadings of the arch rebel himself, the fierce troops without, the noise of the siege, and all its concomitant terrors; and remember, that out of these multitudes it was a woman who came forward, a *mother in Israel* (how sacred is the term!) who in her wisdom obtained not only the hearing of Joab, but, a more difficult matter of the warring people, and bent them like a reed, only from the superiority of MIND—must we not feel to our heart's core the real position of the women of Israel in the PAST? That she, even as man, enjoyed, not alone the spiritual, but the intellectual and refining privileges of being one of the chosen of God; and must we not long for that FUTURE, when we shall again be blessed and influential in our own most holy land, doing the will of God, and being in very truth spiritually and temporally *helps meet* for His sons? Oh, shall not the thought of the past, and of the future, influence Israel's PRESENT, and waken her daughters to their immortal heritage, in being of the first-born children of the Lord; who holdeth them so inexpressibly dear, that the individual or nation who injureth them injureth the apple of HIS eye? Is not the thought that we are of a nation so beloved, a sufficient incentive for the cultivation of spirituality, virtue, intellect, wisdom, affection, devotedness to God and man, all that could make the days of this life even "as the days of heaven on the earth"?

The devotion of Rizpah is another exquisitely beautiful trait of female character. Its mention does not contain a *lesson*, but a *picture*. It does not tell us what woman *should be* but what *she is*, and is valuable as proving that the women of the Bible are but portraits of woman's nature now. The stern mandate of the Lord against the bloody house of Saul had not all been fulfilled; and justice, that inscrutable justice which man dare not hope to explain, demanded the execution of the last remaining scions of the family of Saul. The narrative contained in the first nine verses of 2 Sam. xxi., is one on which it is better not to linger, lest it arouse doubts and questions verging on impiety. It is enough that it was the ordinance of the Eternal, and that He ever tempereth justice with mercy; and though to finite minds, in this instance, mercy may seem hidden in blood, it is enough for us to know that "God's ways are not our ways, nor His thoughts our thoughts," and calmly resting on this blessed truth, dismiss the subject as one to be explained hereafter, when the immortal likeness of God in which He made man, purified from the corrupting clay, will be permitted to trace the secret of His ways; and all that in His word seemed dark and terrible, bear witness to the perfect justice and the perfect mercy of Him, with whom "is the fountain of life, and in whose light we shall see light."

Day and night, from the beginning of the barley harvest, till the rain came down from heaven, a period of many weeks, did Rizpah, the daughter of Aiah, keep solitary watch beside the mouldering bodies of the last remnants of the house of Saul. "She took sackcloth and spread it for her upon the rock, and suffered neither the birds of the air to rest upon them by day, nor the beasts of the field by night." What a volume of woman's heart is told in that brief verse! The devotedness to the beloved dead which would guard the poor remnants of mortality from all insult of bird or beast—that lingering beside all which was spared her, alas, for that mournful "all"! Scorched by the sun of day, and chilled by the dews of night, yet moved she not from the stony rock, nor cared she for aught besides. Mourning, yet not repining; guarding the hallowed dead, yet breathing not her anguish, save through the tears that fell on the impenetrable rock, and the sighs that mingled with the breeze. Who might feel for her, sole remnant of that bloody house? Who might lament dreadful retributive deaths? None. And the mourner asked nought of man. Her world was by the dead, and there the mocking sun and the pitying moon gazed down upon her in her sad and solitary watch. And O is not this woman?—Is not this the love, the devotedness, which are the natural dwellers of woman's heart, when nought but nature speaks? And not entirely unsympathised was her affliction. It reached the ear, and penetrated the heart, of the feeling and affectionate king; and the bones of Saul and Jonathan, and of them that were hanged, were gathered by David's express command, and buried with due honours in the sepulchre of Kish the father of Saul, which was in the country of his tribe; and thus that fearful ignominy, so revolting to an Israelite, the denying burial to the dead, was removed from the house of Saul by the devotion of a woman. Who, then, will assert that the purest and best feelings of our nature find no place in the Word of God? Who can seek to make religion trample on the most sacred feelings of humanity, by asserting that, if we truly love the Lord, we can never grieve, nor be afflicted? How painfully mistaken are those who would thus instruct, and how sadly deceived those who would banish all *feeling* from woman's nature! Who would guide her by rule and measure? Who would check every enthusiastic impulse, every kind sentiment, every sympathising emotion, every imaginative glow, all because it is so unfitted for this unromantic world; and therefore destines its possessor to more pain than pleasure? Oh, if we believe the Word of the Lord divine, let us come there, and we shall find guides for *feeling* as well as for action! There we find the emotions which God in His mercy gave, encouraged not subdued; feeling, devotedness, affection, enthusiasm, all that can lift us up from the mere petty concerns and thoughts of a day, are there brought forward; and why then should the sweet emotions of the Israelite in the past, be deemed folly and romance, and so unworthy of the Israelite in the *present?* Oh, as women, women of Israel, let us cultivate every emotion which can refine and elevate and prepare us for that Future which has been so long our promised heritage? We are but strangers and sojourners in the land of our captivity; but our destiny is laid up with our God for that day when, in the face of the whole world, we shall be acknowledged as his own.

The next striking evidence of woman's social position in our present Period, is found in the far-famed, often-quoted judgment of Solomon. The wisdom of the monarch's sentence is the point generally insisted upon, to the exclusion of all the other topics of interest which this remarkable incident presents.

The term *harlot*, more than once applied to women in the Bible, had a very different meaning to that in which it is alone used now. It is generally supposed to signify, indiscriminately, an innkeeper or hostess, as in the case of Rahab, or women in the servile classes, independent of servitude in households, but occupying some trades in Jerusalem peculiar to themselves. They had in consequence, neither rank, wealth, nor any of the usual accessories to the royal favour. Yet we find that the very first persons who obtained access to Solomon, after the offerings with which he sanctified his entrance into Jerusalem, were two women of this class. It was not that there were no inferior courts of justice in the Mosaic Law, no order or division of ranks in the Jewish State. There were all these. Yet, if the woman of Israel demanded the judgment of their monarch himself, the very lowest classes had access to him, and their cases were heard and judged. Certainly a very different mode of proceeding to the customs of other nations, either then or now.

Surrounded by his officers and court, in the magnificent array which marked all the proceedings of King Solomon, the monarch himself listened with patient and sympathising attention to the tale of affliction boldly spoken before him. It was a sad and a strange one, and seemingly so difficult for a just decision on the part of the youthful judge, that interest was in no slight degree excited. Two women dwelt in the same house, to each of whom a child was born, the one within three days of the other. They were alone within the house, and the child of the one woman died; and she arose at midnight and changed the dead for the living; and when her companion awoke in the morning, to nurse her child, behold it was dead; but when she had looked on it attentively, it was not her child which she did bear. And when the complainant narrated this tale, her opponent denied that it was so, saying, "Nay, but the living is my son, and the dead is thy son! And this said, No, but the dead is thy son, and the living is my son; and thus they spake before the king." In a modern court of justice we think a similar case would be found somewhat difficult to solve. Solomon made no pause; repeating the charge and its denial, so as to make it clear to all who heard, he continued, "Bring me a sword," and when obeyed, pronounced that memorable sentence which first revealed his godlike wisdom to his subjects;—"Divide the living child in two, give half to the one, and half to the other. Then spake the woman whose the living child was unto the king, for her bowels yearned unto her son, O my lord, give her the living child, and in no wise slay it. But the other said, Let it be neither mine or thine, but divide it. And the king answered and said, Give her [the first speaker] the living child, and in no wise slay it : she is the mother thereof." And if all Israel, when they heard of this judgment, feared the king, for they saw that the wisdom of God was in him, how deeply, how gratefully, must the real mother have rejoiced in the courage which brought her before the monarch, and, through his sentence, received back her son!

Solomon's wisdom, in this instance, proceeded simply from a profound knowledge of human nature. He tested the truth or falsehood of the relation by an appeal to the heart, and decided according to its unguarded witness, demanding nothing more for his own satisfaction or that of his hearers. The incident is a trifling one; but it is valuable in demonstrating the social position of the women of Israel at the period. We have already seen that to obtain the monarch's ear was quite accessible to woman, in the narration of David and the widow of Tekoah; but the present instance is, if possible, still more convincing, from the fact of the women being of the lowest classes, and having no friendly influence to bring them forward; nothing in fact to plead in their favour, but their privileges as women of Israel, which of course gave them admission to their earthly sovereign, who was but the vice-regent of Him by whom all Israel, men, women, and children, were heard, judged, and answered: and when the law of the land permitted, nay, commanded, impartial judgment on all who claimed it, *women* as well as men, it surely cannot be accused of either degrading or enslaving; many an afflicted and oppressed one of the Gentile lands might be found to wish it were in action still.

And how beautifully does this simple narrative display the power of nature! It was far easier to resign her babe than see him die, even at the risk of her previous recital being disbelieved. She could feel nothing but the fatal command of the king to slay the child; little could she think those agonised words of entreaty were expressly called for by the king, for the discovery of the truth; and that the burst of natural feeling would be the means of giving her back her child. How forcibly does this little anecdote confirm our reiterated assertion that the Word of our God guides and portrays *feeling* as well as action, and that all our purest, best, and noblest affections will always find their reflection there. And this is one of the widest distinctions between the Bible and Profane History. The latter narrates *events*, actions; the palpable and striking parts of man, if we may so express it, but touches not that immaterial and subtle essence of thought and feeling, whence alone all that is palpable and striking comes. The Bible in a few brief words will give the key to actions, will simply portray a feeling, an impulse which flashes on the heart, awakening, as by electricity, the links of nature which unite the present with the past in the history of humanity; and we know such record is divine, else the darkly hidden, rarely penetrated, mysteries of the human heart could not have been so forcibly revealed.

Nor are they the only illustrations of feeling. How touchingly illustrative of that affection is Elisha's first address to Elijah! When the latter threw his mantle upon him, as symbolical of his elevation to the prophetical calling, a rush of strange yet ecstatic feeling must have taken possession of him; perhaps the aspirings of many years, the heart's hopes and longings for such spiritual election, unknown to any but his own heart, were gratified. It must have been some extraordinary and incomprehensible impulse, actuating the resignation of all early employments and associations, simply to follow Elijah—feelings probably overwhelming in their suddenness; yet we find him in the midst of them thinking of his parents. "Let me, I pray thee, kiss my father and my mother, and then I will follow thee."

It is in truth only a feeling, not any momentous incident or striking illustration, which these simple words betray: but it is often from little things like these, that we may form an estimate of the social condition and feelings of a people. The Jewish law, as we have seen, peculiarly and affectingly touches on the conduct and even emotions of children for their parents, and parents for their children. Elisha, we may feel sure, both from his being the anointed prophet of the Lord, and from the whole course of his after-life, had been brought up strictly as an Israelite. He had, as is often the case, received an education which, in the very midst of idolatry and misery, preserved him undefiled and fitted to supply Elijah's place. His exclamation strongly proves how completely the *affections* were blended with spiritual gifts: while from his lingering yearning towards his parents, we feel what they must have been to him—his *mother* as well as his father. There is no such thing as filial reverence and love in nations where woman is degraded. In the Jewish nation, on the contrary, we find repeated instances of both reverence and love—such could not fail to have been the case when "Honour thy father and thy mother" was one of the first commands of God Himself.

We trace, too, much of a mother's nurture and influence in the peculiarly sweet and loving character of Elisha during his prophetical career. His mission was almost all of love; and the feeling and sympathy which he manifested to all who sought him, especially towards women, as we shall see in more than one instance, display a manly character formed by a *woman's* hand.

One of the first miracles performed by Elisha was for a woman, evincing the tender kindness of his disposition, and proving that woman was not considered unworthy to receive relief, through him, from the hand of her gracious God. She was a poor widow, whose only claim to the compassion of the prophet appeared to be, that he knew that her husband, "thy servant did fear the Lord." But he died poor, and in debt, and, in exact illustration of the law, the creditor came to demand the service of his two sons, in lieu of the sum that was owing,—a hard trial for the poor woman, left in her bereavement with but two sons, from whom the justice of the law compelled her to part, unless she could raise money sufficient to discharge her debt; and so without fear she approached the prophet and stated her case. "What shall I do for thee?" was the commiserating reply; "tell me what thou hast in thy house." And what a picture of uncomplaining poverty does her answer bring! "Thine handmaid hath nothing in the house but a pot of oil." The prophet felt for and relieved her; but how much of childlike and trusting faith must she have needed, in her obedience to his strange command,—"Borrow thee vessels of all thy neighbours, even empty vessels, borrow not a few. And when thou art come in, thou shalt shut the door upon thee, and upon thy sons, and shalt pour out into all those vessels, and thou shalt set aside that which is full." Borrow vessels to fill with oil, when she had but one pot of oil in the house! How could this be? Was not the prophet playing with her distress? How could such a strange command avail her? Such questions would only have been natural; but we do not find that they entered her mind, or prompted doubt and speculation. She might, perhaps, have heard of the widow of Zarephath, whose cruise of oil had miraculously lasted during the famine; but more probably her instant obedience originated in that simple and guileless trust wnich should characterise every feeling of our hearts towards God. "So she went from him, and shut the door upon her and upon her sons, who had brought the vessels to her, and poured out. And it came to pass when the vessels were full, that she said unto her son, Bring me yet another; and he said, There is not a vessel more; and the oil stayed. Then she came and told the man of God, and he said, Go, sell the oil, and pay thy debt, and live, thou and thy children, on the rest." It was not enough to give her *present* relief—the merciful kindness of the man of God provided also for the future, and gave her the blessed relief of retaining her children beside her. Now if woman were of no accouut in Israel, it would have been a greater kindness to take her sons from her, than leave them to her training. As a widow in Israel, she herself would have been provided for: there was no *need* for this great mercy to have been shewn her: nor in her retired, simple mode of living, could the performance of the miracle for her have increased Elisha's prophetical reputation.

She was a poor afflicted individual—of no more consequence amongst her countrymen either in life or death, joy or sorrow, than were we to remove one grain of sand from the sea-shore. Yet she was as much an object of pitying mercy in the sight of her God and of His prophet, as the highest and most important in the land. And what was her sole plea for hearing and acceptance? "Thou knowest my husband, thy servant, did fear the Lord;"—meaning not only the departed, but herself and her whole household. There was no long list of high-sounding deeds, of sublime projects, and seemingly important services. The sons of the prophets, as they were called, appeared to have passed their quiet lives in holy meditation on the law and the works of God, and in serving Him by such deeds of unostentatious kindness and social benevolence as very often to die poor. They asked nothing but a bare sufficiency of board and lodging, blessed with family love. They were never heard of out of their own retired sphere; but they feared the Lord, and taught their wives and children to do so likewise. And this was the poor widow's plea; and it was accepted. And shall we then say the women of Israel have no access to God? Do we need more than our own blessed faith and its vivid illustrations in the Eternal's own word, to give us not only consolation but encouragement? Can we not all feel as that poor widow did—a guileless faith, which asked no question, but obeyed—which came at once to the man of God, and, though his words were strange, yet trusted and was relieved?

True we have no man of God to whom to seek . we may not look to miracles for our relief ; but we may all come to God's word, and, through it, to God Himself. There is no barrier between us and Him. Our holy faith gives us the blessed consolation of coming to Him direct, and of feeling that, if we do but seek to fear, and love, and serve Him, we shall be accepted and beloved. Lowliness of station, of intellect, of service, is of no account with Him. The poor widow is an evidence that the poorest, and the humblest, the merest atom of His stupendous creation, is not unworthy of His regard, ay, even to the performance of a miracle in her behalf; and her sole plea was, "she feared the Lord." O let not the false idea of too great unworthiness to approach Him, of incapacity to address Him in words fit for His acceptance, obtain a moment's resting in the female Jewish heart! We are His—His own—and every expression in His Holy Word proves that we are so, and that now, ay, even now, every women who bears the glorious name of Israel, be she rich or poor—full of good deeds and pious thoughts, or bereft of all but a childlike faith and guileless love of God—still she has spiritual privileges; a closer, dearer, more blessed connection with her Father in heaven, than is the lot of any woman. She cannot read her Bible without feeling this. O let her *prove* it in the sight of the whole world!

THE SHUNAMMITE.

THE poor widow so mercifully relieved and blessed, marks the social and spiritual condition of the humbler classes of Israelitish women. We are now about to consider a Jewish female in a much higher station.

In the town of Shunem dwelt one, designated in the Bible as a "great woman," meaning a woman of rank and consequence, to whose hospitable house the prophet Elisha ever turned when he passed through the town. It was not the custom of the prophets to enter the houses of the great and eat at their luxurious tables, preferring the humble meal and lowly roof as more accordant with their heavenly mission than the good things of earth. Not that they resembled the self-mortifying ascetics of some Gentile creeds, and imagined that their merit in the sight of God was weighed according to the extent of their self-inflicted penances; but simply, that the mind might be kept clearer, the spirit poorer, and the body healthier, by moderation in all things. Their mission of love, too, was to all classes, and the poor could not have come to them with such confidence, as in the case of the widow, if their luxurious style of living placed them with the nobles of the land.

That to lodge and eat amid the wealthy was contrary to their usual habits, we learn from the forcible expression, "she *constrained* him to eat bread [bread in Hebrew comprising all sorts of food, of course signifies regular meals]. And so it was, that as oft as he passed by, he turned in thither to eat bread;" and in so doing, it is evident that he found the Shunammite, one of "the seven thousand who had not bowed the knee to Baal nor kissed him," and accepted her hospitality in the same spirit of piety and kindly love with which it was proffered.

Once he had been *constrained*, for the prophet might have feared that the wealth and luxury, which marked the abode, was impregnated with the same awful seeds of vice and impiety which desecrated the wealthy of the capital; but the second time he needed not constraint, for one interview sufficed to mark the spiritual elevation of his hosts, and that they were indeed those with whom a prophet of the Lord might enjoy the delights of social intercourse in innocence and peace.

Not contented with proffering the mere hospitality of rest and food, we find the Shunammite saying to her husband, "Behold now, I know this is a holy man of God, which passeth by us continually. Let us make him a little chamber, I pray thee, in the wall; and let us set for him there a bed, and a table, and a stool, and a candlestick: and it shall be, when he cometh to us, that he shall turn in thither." And we know that her husband's acquiescence was instantly obtained, and her plan accomplished; for the very next verse we read, "And it fell on a day that he came thither, and he turned into the chamber and slept there."

Briefly as this is related, how beautifully it illustrates the character of woman—the eager desire to show kindness, and so to show it as best to harmonise with the feelings and habits of its object. The establishment was probably the highest and most influential in Shunem. The Shunammite was an independent mistress of her own household, possessed of power to ask whom, and do what she willed; she is the prime mover in the whole narration; and she it is to whom the reward is given, as the one from whose pure mind, and noble heart, the hospitable kindness originally came.

That she did not at first know Elisha as a prophet does but enhance the mild benevolence of her character. There was nothing in his appearance to mark superior rank, or superior endowments; nothing probably but a gentle courtesy of manners which marked him worthy of kindness and attention. That they would ever be returned, she could not for a moment suppose; for the stranger was evidently a wanderer, with no settled home or calling. But true benevolence never thinks of further recompense than *the act* of showing kindness brings. It is wrong to suppose that benevolence is but synonymous with acts of charity to the poor and needy. It finds space for its encouragement in every social and domestic duty of life. Benevolence to equals appears almost a paradox; yet it is not: for were such more often proved, in the earnest search after one another's social happiness, in acts of daily kindness, and every active fellow feeling, how much happier might this life be!

It was this rare and beautiful benevolence which the Shunammite so richly possessed, and which is still more forcibly displayed in building a chamber for the man of God, than in her first hospitality. A very few interviews probably convinced her that he was something beyond that which he appeared, and the prophet's own lips might have told the rest, or at least have imparted that his mission was of God. The bustle and varied scenes of a large establishment were no fit home for one who, when not employed in the service of his fellow-creatures, passed his time in meditation and prayer. Even a chamber to himself within the house would not have permitted him the privacy he desired, besides causing him to diverge from the plan of moderation and retirement, demanded from him as a prophet and a reprover, by *act* as well as word, of the far-spreading vices of the time.

To remedy this, and silently tempt his sojourning a longer time with them than the mere acceptance of a meal, the Shunammite's ready mind conceived the idea of erecting a chamber expressly for him, with an egress and ingress of its own, and furnished with that kindly regard to all, which might make him look upon it as his own. Her plan was, of course, imparted to her husband, and how clearly does her simple expression, "Let *us make* a little chamber, I pray thee," evince the affectionate confidence, only found when husband and wife are equals; even though, by a succeeding verse, we are led to suppose that her husband was very much older than herself.

The chamber was built and furnished; and greatly must Elisha have been surprised and affected by this proof of regard. We find him in truth, making no remark; but how deeply he felt it, we learn by his desiring his servant the following morning to "call the Shunammite." Call her? Why, had she not been in the chamber to give him welcome, and bid him look on all around him as his own? No. Her truly refined and feminine nature shrunk back from obtruding herself upon the prophet, and so compelling thanks and approbation. She wished him to *feel* the comfort of a retired and private home, but *not* that he owed her obligation; and so she kept aloof, demanding no more than her own heart gave, in the delightful thought that it was in her power to add to the comfort of a man of God.

And in this eager desire to reverence and serve the *prophet*, can we not read the love she bore to *God?* To mere earthly natures Elisha would have been nothing more than any other man,—except perhaps exciting the emotions of dislike and dread with which those persons are ever regarded, whose lives and even characters are the reprovers of our own; but to those who truly and earnestly seek to love God, His ministers are especial objects of reverence and care; and such was the feeling of the Shunammite.

"Behold! thou hast been careful for us with all this care," was the address of Gehazi, by his master's command; "what is to be done for thee? Wouldest thou be spoken for to the king, or to the captain of the host? And she answered, I dwell among mine own people."

And what a volume of feeling is contained in these brief words. Not only a perfect contentment with her lot, but a meek and sorrowful reproach, that they could think she had shown this care in the hope of reward. Nothing can be more painful to a delicately feeling mind, than the idea of receiving return for aught of kindness; the heart glowing with its own warmth, with the peculiar pleasure of serving another, shrinks chilled into itself, feeling how completely it is misunderstood; how little its pure motives can be appreciated. Some natures would have been indignant at the supposition, that she could not do a kind deed without reward; but the character of the Shunammite permitted not the *expression* of the feeling. Her lip was closed, but her heart was full. Expostulation with Gehazi at the injustice of the motive attributed to her, or acceptance of the offer, were alike contrary to the retiring dignity of her character; and simply saying, "I dwell among mine own people," she retreated hastily, as desirous the conference should be closed; but Elisha was not satisfied. He himself, probably, did full justice to the pious motives which had actuated her; but he wished to make publicly manifest, that no action engaged in out of pure love of God and reverence to His ministers, should pass without reward; and on hearing from Gehazi that her husband was old and she had no child, he again summoned her, and this time into his immediate presence.

It was, no doubt, with some little repugnance, she obeyed; fearing that her sensitive feelings might again be wounded by a proffer of service which she had so fully resolved not to accept. And "when he had called her, she stood at the door" —how impressively betraying her reluctance! She could not refuse to speak with her guest; but, with that mixture of humility and real dignity which the true-feeling woman knows so well how to blend, she waited his commands on the threshold of his apartment.

This time, however, no *offer* of reward chilled and saddened her. The prophet asked not, sought not, the expression of her wishes; but at once promised, "Thou shalt embrace a son"—a child, a son! Should she indeed possess that for which, as a woman of Israel in the olden time, she must so often have longed, though the wish was never uttered! and, in the fulness of her sudden joy, the promise seemed too precious for belief, "Nay, my lord, thou man of God, do not lie unto thy handmaid!" Still, even in that moment, we trace the same gentle self-possession which had characterised her answer to Gehazi. No burst of rapture, no triumph, as would have been had she looked to her hospitality to bring reward. No; while her whole heart must have so trembled with the suddenly awakened hope and joy, that steady thought was impossible, she yet spoke calmly, seeking to strengthen her faith in the promise, by the recollection it was in truth "a man of God who spoke," even while she besought him not to deceive her—the very entreaty proving how earnestly and how long she had yearned for such a blessing.

Doubt of the power of the Eternal to bring the promise to pass, it is evident never assailed her. Her words to the prophet sprung merely from a too sudden thought of joy, and the anticipation was fulfilled; for at the proper season, exactly in accordance with Elisha's promise, she embraced a son.

Can we not picture the increase of domestic love and happiness which this infant treasure must have created in the Shunammite's happy household? All we read of her, marks her the very character to enjoy to the full the intense happiness of maternal love, in its highest and most spiritual sense—one whose years passed in *deeds*, not merely words; who would enshrine deeply in her own heart those pure emotions and high feelings from which the simplest action sprung—one whose best resources had ever been independent of all outward excitement, and who, "dwelling among her own people," had not a thought or ambition beyond. Her home was the shrine which knew her best, and from which the mild light of kindness and benevolence emanated many roods around. To such a one, life, even when childless, could never have been sad; yet how many a lonely moment, a yearning thought unspoken, uncomplained of, yet still her own, must have been filled with the irrepressible gush of tenderness called forth by her child. How inexpressibly sweet must have been the holy task of leading that infant heart to God, and in the very midst of national sin and misery training him for heaven. Can we not fancy her strong affections concentrating their force and intensity around her boy, and lifting up her whole soul in increased adoration to her God.

Nine or ten years might have thus passed: and her love and care seemed blessed in the growth and improvement of her child. He was now old enough to leave his mother's side, and sometimes accompany his father in his agricultural employments. We can imagine him in his innocent glee, running from field to field, and eagerly sharing every rural occupation. A sudden stroke, either from the burning heat of the sun or some other cause, arrested his boyish joys, and, clinging to his father, he could only utter, "My head! my head!" Imagining it only a slight pain, which would soon pass, his father desired one of his men to carry him to his mother; "and when they had taken him and brought him to his mother he sat on her knees till noon and died."

What a sudden and awful change! A few brief hours previous, the fond mother had parted with her darling in full health and glee, and he was brought back to her pale, suffering, powerless—only sufficiently sensible to cling to her neck and lay his burning head upon her bosom. And she sate still, calm—apparently unmoved—lest the faintest display of her uncontrollable agony should increase his suffering, or disturb him as he lay—that every aid possible to be obtained to alleviate the disease was sought, we cannot doubt: but the mother moved not, nor would she have her child removed, whilst life remained. And when we read this, shall we say the narratives of the Bible enter not into the emotions of the present day; that the characters there represented are of a nature utterly distinct from ours? What mother, more especially of an only child, can read the brief record of "they brought him to his mother and he sat on her knees and died," without sympathy; and as she pictures the sad scene in her fancy, without feeling that human nature, alike in sorrow or joy, is in all ages the same; and that, therefore, the Bible records do indeed concern her, for they speak of characters in all their strength and weakness, faults and virtues, like her own.

No sound of wailing, nor murmur of complaint, escaped the mother's lips, as the breath of life passed from that loved form, as those sweet eyes still fixed on her, became dim and lustreless, and even the faint moan of infant suffering no longer met her ear. "She rose and went up, and laid him on the bed of the man of God, and shut the door upon him, and went out. And she called to her husband, and said, Send me, I pray thee, one of the young men and one of the asses, that I may run to the man of God and come again. And he said, Wherefore wilt thou go to him to day? it is neither new moon, nor Sabbath. And she said, It shall be well."

Here, again, is woman brought before us in her highest and loveliest nature. A weak mind would have only *felt*, not acted; would have been so overwhelmed with agony, as to have been incapable of any thought but the affliction which had befallen her. Not so the Shunammite—sustained by that noble energy, that perfect self-control, which had characterised her whole life, this trial cannot disturb the beautiful harmony of her character. Even to her husband she is silent as to their heavy affliction, and she evades his question; whilst there is hope—ay, and to her faithful heart there is hope even now, though the child is dead—she will not afflict her husband. The full tide of grief is laid up in her own breast, aside from herself. Till she has *acted*, she has no time to sit down and weep, though her throat is dry and her breath impeded. We read the unutterable agony in her movements, not her words— "she saddled an ass, and said to her servant, Drive on, and go forward, slack not thy riding for me, except I bid thee." What was to her the heat, the fatigue of this unusual journey? She had but one thought, the man of God. He alone who had promised her "a child from the Lord," could have the power, by prayer, to restore him even from the dead. One recollection only mingles with the thought, Elijah and the widow of Zarephath. Had not her child been restored from the dead? And had not Elisha equal power with the gracious Lord? Without this thought, this *faith*, the mother must have sunk; for minds like hers ever prostrate the *frame*. Tears and complaints give relief: it is the heart which never breathes its grief that bows the body to the dust. And not alone the *power of Elisha* was uppermost in her mind; she must have known—have perfectly realised—the attributes of Elisha's God, or the thought of the prophet would have been no comfort. She must have felt that God was love, had compassion and sympathy even for *her individually*, a woman, a mere speck in this creation, or how could she have believed that He would grant His prophet the power to relieve her? She knew, as all believing Israel did, that prophets were mere instruments in His Almighty hand, of themselves powerless, spiritless, as their less favoured brethren. And, therefore, that the Shunammite had a man of God through whom to seek, does not, in any way, prevent the example from bearing upon us. We have not Elisha, but we have still Elisha's God.

The way was not very long; but O the interminable period it must have felt to that poor mother's heart, till Mount Carmel was reached! And how could she know the holy man was there? for he was a wanderer through Judea. But the impulse leading in that direction was of the Lord; and even before her dim eyes discovered the Prophet, he had recognised her afar off; and, surprised, bade Gehazi run to meet her, and ask if it were well with her, and her husband and child; thus demonstrating how kindly and lovingly the human emotions were ever at work in the heart of the holy man. But to Gehazi she could give no reply, save as she had said before to her husband, "It is well;" hers was no grief to speak to indifferent ears. None but Elisha could assist her, and her heart was too closely wrapt in its own anguish to open to any but to him. Yet what stern command must she have had over her woman's nature to retain her calmness during this journey! Control never failed her, till she beheld the man of God, and sunk almost powerless at his feet. She had reached him, indeed; but the energy which had sustained her throughout, seemed deserting her. She had no power to utter the entreaty with which her heart was filled. She could only clasp his knees, and gaze on his face in agony, till roused by the kindly gentleness with which the prophet reproved Gehazi for seeking to thrust her aside. "Let her alone," he said, "for her soul is vexed within her; and the Lord has hid it from me, and has not told me." Then she said, "Did I desire a son of my lord? Did I not say, Do not deceive me?" The mother could not say her boy was dead. Faith was strong within her that he would be saved; and how powerfully does the very form of her address to the prophet betray the depth, the intensity of her feelings; refusing, even to him, to give vent to the torrent of grief and lamentation, and even of reproach, which would have burst forth unrestrainedly from a weaker and less superior mind.

Elisha needed no further information; and promptly he desired Gehazi to take his staff, and neither loiter nor speak by the way, till he had laid it on the face of the child. But this was not sufficient for the poor mother. "As the Lord liveth, and as thy soul liveth," she implored, "I will not leave thee." None could be to her as Elisha, and he rebuked her not, nor denied her; his heart was too full of kindly emotions, and he arose and followed her.

But not to Gehazi was such a miracle vouchsafed; his coming to meet his master with the information, "the child is not awake," probably first convinced Elisha the event was of the Lord, and that the necessary power would be granted him. The restoring the dead was a greater miracle than he had yet performed; and as we find him saying, "the Lord hath hid it from me, and hath not told me," he perhaps at first supposed that the child was merely in a stupor, resembling death, and the virtue of the prophetic staff would revive him. But Gehazi's words proved to him that the child was really dead: and he quickened his steps, and hastened to his own chamber, where the child lay, "and shut the door upon them twain, and *prayed unto the Lord.*" Words, how full of important meaning! In every other action of the prophet we find the prophetic spirit acting, as it were, instantaneously. The power intrusted to him for the good of the Eternal's chosen, as for the punishment of the unrighteous and disobedient, had seemed ready at his word. In this it was no consequence of his superhuman endowments, but simply the effect of *prayer unto the Lord.* He might foretell events, might multiply oil, render poison harmless; so feed a hundred men with twenty loaves, and a few baskets of first fruits, that they were not only satisfied, but left thereof; might bid iron swim, and know what the king said in his bed-chamber, though hundreds of miles away; but life and death were laid up with the Lord, and prayer only gave him power over the human frame.*

What a tumult of contending emotions must have oppressed the Shunammite during that awful interval. Let any anxious mother recall the time when the darling of her heart has been pronounced sick unto death—that there is *no* hope—death is fast approaching, when, in the wild agony of her despair, she has refused belief in the skill of him who has thus spoken, and sent or flown for the first physician of the age, and led him to the chamber of her child, and left him there, without the power of waiting for his decisive mandate, and then sunk prostrate in her own closet before her God, seeking to pray, but finding her words trembling, fearing, hoping, and only conscious that life and death are with the Lord, and, if He willed, the skill she had so wildly sought might save her darling still. Let any mother recall such periods of her life, and she may enter into the feelings of the Shunammite, as she sat alone in that interval of suspense, for her husband, still out in his agricultural employment, knew not of the suffering at home; and she had now none to look to in her agony, save her God.

Time passed; how long she knew not, save that she felt as if an age was passing over heart and head. Hush! Is it the prophet's voice? The mother started from her prostrate prayer, her head flung back, her very breathing ceased. "Call this Shunammite," seemed to have rung in her ears; but it might be only fancy, only the mocking torture of her bewildered brain. No! Gehazi is at her door—he calls her to his master, though he says not wherefore, and she dares not look upon his face to read his tidings there. She stood within the prophet's chamber—she glanced upon the bed—her boy lived, breathed, smiled, stretched out his arms to her once more, and the voice of the prophet spake, "Take up thy son." And she sought to obey: but the spirit which had sustained her in sorrow, in suspense, departed now, and she fell at his feet powerless, voiceless, conscious only that her child lived—that the prayer of Elisha, and the compassionate love of Elisha's God, had given her back the dead.

And even when she recovered sufficiently to bow herself to

* As is further displayed very strikingly in 2 Kings vi. 17, 18.

the very ground, in silent acknowledgment of the power of Elisha, the mercy of her God, and, with her living child clasped to her bosom, retired from the chamber, leaving the man of God to the adoration and meditation which this great mercy called for, still no word broke from that heart, so swelling in thankfulness and love that only tears might relieve it; and beautifully does this stillness continue to illustrate the character of this sweet and gentle woman, so controlled, so energetic in affliction—so calm, so still in joy—so full of deep, of intense feeling, sensibility, affection, yet so restrained within, that though all around her felt its blessed effects, alike in deed, and word, and manner, none knew its *extent*, save her God.

Blessed as must have been the little domestic circle of the Shunammite before, it must have been thrice blessed from the restoration of her child. What must have been the feelings of the husband and the father on his return, when told that, in so short a space, his treasured child had been snatched from him by death, and been restored? How must his heart have glowed in increased love and veneration for the gentle woman, who, rather than expose him to the agony of such intelligence, had buried it all in her own breast; and sought the prophet alone, and unsoothed, and, through that energetic promptness, had been a lowly instrument in the hands of the Lord for the restoration of her child! Had she lingered in unavailing, and probably complaining sorrow—had she permitted herself to fail in faith and prayer—she had not sought the prophet, nor would her child have been restored, for she would have been no fit receiver for such manifestation of almighty love.

The character of the Shunammite was not one to change or waver. We find her, at a later period, displaying the same retiring gentleness, yet dignified self-possession and energetic will. Some years must have passed; and from there being no mention of the Shunammite's husband in affairs which, had he been living, would have devolved upon him, not on her, we infer that she had become a widow, an inference confirmed by the previous statement, that, " her husband was old."

Elisha had never lost sight of her, but had probably continued to occupy the "little chamber," whenever he passed through Shunem. He advised a removal, which must have been both irksome and painful to one whose house had always been on one spot, and whose richest possessions consisted of the land,

and flocks, and herds around it, which she could not carry away with her, nor for the safety of which provide. However, she had too much faith and trust to hesitate in obedience; and when the mandate of the prophet came, "Arise, and go thou and thine household, and sojourn wheresoever thou canst sojourn: for the Lord hath called for a famine; and it shall also come upon the land seven years," she unhesitatingly "arose, and did after the saying of the man of God: and she went with her household, and sojourned in the land of the Philistines seven years." A sojourn which would have been inexpressibly sad to such a true follower of Israel, had she not been cheered by the blessed thought of the Eternal's continued care for her. What was she in His sight? and yet, even by His prophet, he had deigned to warn her of the evil about to ensue, and provide for her safety, by permission to sojourn wheresoever she would. In those seven years of exile, how much must have devolved on her to keep her son and her household faithful, and live as if they were still in their own land, and still guided by the councils of the man of God. Can we not fancy the morning and evening prayer arising daily from that little circle of faithful hearts led by a woman's voice, and the Sabbaths and the festivals marking that lowly home a sanctuary before the Lord? O if the heart be but true to its God, it matters little where its home is cast. The magnet points unfailingly to its answering star, whithersoever the vessel glides. In tempest or calm, in cold or heat, it wavers not, or fails to guide aright; and so is it with the man whose heart, like the magnet to the pole, is fixed upon its God.

At the end of the seven years, the Shunammite and her household returned to Judæa; but her home and land had been seized during her absence, and apparent ruin and privation in consequence was her welcome home. Some would have been ready to accuse Elisha as the cause of this evil, as having advised her removal. Others, again, would have demanded, or, at least, depended on, the prophet's influence with the king. The Shunammite felt and did neither. With calm self-possession she went herself to make her complaint before the king, and demanded her house and land. This was no service in which Elisha's spiritual ministry was needed. It was no favour for herself, no advancement for her boy. The heart which had once answered, "I dwell among mine own people," to offers of reward, had not changed. As a woman and a widow in Israel, her sole plea was the justice of her cause.

But though with true feminine delicacy she had shrunk from appealing to Elisha in this emergency, the Eternal had so ordered events, that the prophet was in fact the true cause of the king's instant attention to her suit. It so chanced that the king was talking to Gehazi, and demanding a recital of the great things Elisha had done; and at the very time the young man was relating the restoration of the dead child, the Shunammite herself appeared before the king, led into his presence by that very beloved child, now grown into manhood, of whom Gehazi spoke. "Behold, my lord, O king," he exclaimed, "this is the woman, and this is her son, whom Elisha restored to life. And when the king asked the woman, she told him." And so strong an impression did the narrative make, that without hesitation he appointed unto her a certain officer, saying, "Restore all that was hers, and all the fruits of the field since the day that she left the land, even until now."

Gratefully must the Shunammite have recognised the hand of God in this instant judgment from one whose character was noted for impotence and indecision—one whose very justice was ever likely to be sullied by caprice; for though we are expressly told in Holy Writ that Jehoram's character was not of the actively evil, as his father and his mother, Ahab and Jezebel, his whole history marks him one of those *fainéants*, whose indolence and weakness wrought almost as much evil in Israel as wickedness itself.

The energy which had urged the prosecution of her suit was indeed rewarded. Not only were all her possessions restored, but their full value during her seven years of absence. Through *her* exertions, her boy received his inheritance; and, from his non-interference, though he must have been quite of an age to assert his own right, what a powerful proof have we of the deep veneration in which the mothers of Israel were regarded by their sons. We hear no more of the Shunammite; but we have become sufficiently intimate with her sweet character to picture her declining years, full of piety, of that calm and beautiful dignity, which, if woman's in her youth, will never forsake her in her age. Full of love to God and man, of good deeds and blessed thoughts, it was for her, and for seven thousand such as her, who had not bowed the knee to Baal, that the Eternal, in His loving mercy, still restrained His avenging wrath.

The peculiar charm of the Shunammite's character is its

unity, its harmonious blending of parts. In every position, adversity or prosperity, or that period of often greater trial than either—the uninterrupted routine of daily life—still we see her in the same calm and beautiful light, never turning aside from the beaten path of duty, never seeking more than the day may bring, and finding enough there, not only to occupy her, but to give her grace and favour in the sight of God. But though never apparently disturbed, her calmness was not indifference. All that we read of her betrays an undercurrent of intense feeling, which, while it caused her to suffer deeply, also endowed her with the purest susceptibility to joy. Feeling it was, that inspired that constantly working energy which never permitted her to sit down and weep when she could act, or remain satisfied with the mere expression of kindness when she could manifest it in deed: and of that intensity of feeling piety was the spring. No heart can rest indifferent when once awaked to a love of God, and, as must follow, a love of man. It was with no thought of reward she showed such warm hospitality to Elisha, yet from that one deed all her after-happiness sprung. He was the chosen servant of the Eternal, and a service done to him was an offering to his God. From first to last, the character of the Shunammite offers the beautiful lesson of *example*. Her good use of wealth and greatness—her moderation in all circumstances—her firmness in affliction—her absolute control of every emotion till her child was restored—her unselfish endurance of anxiety and anguish rather than impart them to her husband—her calm, yet energetic, prosecution of her son's rights—all these are points which every young daughter of Israel may admire and imitate, even though her position in life be different. We must exercise energy and self-control in little things, even in daily employments, or we shall never find them when most needed. We must set out in life with a conviction that we are destined for something worthier and nobler than the mere routine of frivolous employments and unmeaning recreations—that we are endowed with a heart and mind, for the proper use of which an account will be demanded; and sad will it be if we then feel that the impulses and usefulness of both have been neglected, and opportunities, alike of virtuous deeds and beneficial feeling, have long passed us by unused.

And, as women of Israel, even more powerfully should the history of the Shunammite affect us; her elevated character—

her domestic and social influence—nay, the very mention of her as a "great woman"—the mention of her, instead of her husband or son, as the one principally concerned in the whole narration—all convince us that, even in such an era of national anarchy and discord, the women of Israel were in the full enjoyment of all the liberty and privileges, spiritual and temporal, granted them in the law of God. Her very piety, which obtained her such favour in the sight of God and of His prophet, is unspeakable comfort to us now. She had, indeed, the friendship and counsel of a prophet, which we cannot have; but her piety had life and influence at a period of much darker misery and sin, and rebellion and idolatry, than we have to encounter now. To retain purity and faithfulness, to walk firmly in the very midst of vast multitudes who so derided all true piety and adherence to the law of God as to endanger even personal safety, was a position of infinitely harder trial than is ours now. The Shunammite's being blessed with Elisha, raises no barrier between us. What the prophets were to the faithful in the olden time, the word of the Lord is now to us. We cannot too often dwell upon the truth that the same gracious God who manifested Himself through prophets and miracles to our ancestors is ours still, and has granted us a record of His words and works, to give us strength, and hope, and comfort, till that glorious day when we shall be restored to our own land, and His almighty presence be again revealed.

The natural powers and endowments of the Shunammite were not superior to woman's capabilities now; and, therefore, that she found such grace and favour in the sight of God, as for Him in His infinite mercy, to restore her child from the dead, should encourage us to follow in the same holy and rejoicing path. Events so marked as those in the Shunammite's history, may never be ours, but piety of thought and deed is never passed unheeded by our God. The Shunammite was one of the seven thousand who alone remained faithful amid millions. Let each of Israel's daughters determine to prove herself one of the faithful, who in every age are found, unseen, unrecognised, perhaps, by man, when mourning over *apparent* universal indifference, and falling away from the rock of righteousness; but known, recognised, ay, and upheld by God. Let her not think that, as a woman, her prayers and deeds are unavailing, save perchance unto herself. No! as a woman of Israel, she is one of the supporters of a temple which will last for ever; nationally, as well as individually, she is bound to forward the holy cause; and she may rest assured that her piety and faithfulness, even as those of man, will hasten "the great and glorious day of the Lord."

THE LITTLE ISRAELITISH MAID.—HULDAH.—INFLUENCE OF WOMEN DURING THE MONARCHY.

THAT the Eternal often chooses the weakest and the feeblest, through whose unconscious influence to spread a knowledge of His ways and works amid the Gentiles, is proved by the mention of the little Israelitish maid (see 2 Kings v. 2, 3, &c). In one of the predatory incursions of the Syrians into the north of Judea, they had carried off, amongst other booty, a little maid, who became the property of Naaman's wife. Naaman was the captain of the host of the king of Syria, a man of high rank and great valour, who had frequently been the means of deliverance to Syria; but he had become a leper, and was, of course, incapacitated from all public duties and domestic enjoyments. It must have been a sad change to the little maid of Israel; torn from the bosom of her affectionate family, and sold as a slave in the service of a heathen. But it is clear, from her recollection of Elisha, and her earnest wish that her master would go to him to be cured of his leprosy, that she was a child of one of the seven thousand faithful, and one who had been tenderly and spiritually brought up in the religion of her God; and, consequently, with firm faith in the power of His prophets. We can picture her child-like orisons, rising morning and evening in the language of her country to Israel's God, undisturbed by the heathen worship with which she was surrounded; lingering with fond affection on the memory of her parents, cherishing their instructions in her heart of hearts, and praying to God, as they had taught her, to keep her undefiled, that she might bear witness to His glory.

The effects of *true piety* never fails to obtain the love and kindness of our fellow-creatures. The respectful deference of the young slave, her quiet discharge of her duties, her uncomplaining gentleness, though often visible sadness, had no doubt attracted the attention of her mistress, and called forth, not only kindness towards the child, but led her to confide in her own affliction from her husband's disease. A peculiar sanctity ever surrounded the Hebrew, in the eyes even of many ignorant and heathen nations. They were not only the first-born of the Lord in spiritual privileges; but, in arts and sciences, and all that marked them, almost an age in advance, both in refinement and intellect. It is not improbable that the wife of Naaman was questioning her young slave as to the treatment of lepers in Judea, of which the child could give her but little information; but all she had heard of Elisha, we may imagine, flashing on her mind, the power he had received from the Eternal, the miracles he had done, the tender kindness his character had so often evinced, caused the instant exclamation, "Would God my lord were with the prophet who is in Samaria; for he would recover him of his leprosy." There is no hesitation, no doubt —the very faith of a child satisfied that it was in his power, and he would do it. And so completely did that simple faith enter into the hearts of those who heard, that we find, not only Naaman's domestics and Naaman himself, but the king of Syria acting upon it, the very instant that it was reported, "Thus, and thus, saith the maid, who is of the land of Israel."

The story of Naaman's visit to Judea, and miraculous cure, does not enter into the plan of this history, much as we should delight in dwelling upon it, as so strikingly illustrative of the Eternal's loving-mercy over *all* His creatures. Naaman was a heathen, and often an enemy to Judea; yet when *he sought* the prophet of the Lord, even he was accepted, and a miracle performed in his behalf. How powerfully should this rebuke us, when inclined to pronounce harsh judgment on the religion of a fellow-creature, or arrogate to ourselves alone, or to those who think exactly with us, the sole care and love of our Creator.

How happy must the little Maid of Israel have felt, when she beheld her master perfectly cured; and the God of her fathers acknowledged and worshipped, as the sole and only one, by those who had so lately been heathens and idolaters— "Thy servant will henceforth offer neither burnt-offering, nor sacrifice, unto other gods, but unto the LORD," Naaman had declared unto Elisha: and when she saw this change, how must the Hebrew child have rejoiced! That all had originated in her confident reference to the prophet, she probably never knew; but we see that she was the direct instrument in the Lord's hand, to bring about the revelation of His power; she had glorified Him by trusting in His prophet, and so made both her God and His servant venerated in a Gentile land. But this would not have been had she been ashamed to confess her religion and her country before men. A solitary exile in the household of Naaman, young, and undirected by man, holier associations must have been powerful within her, to have prevented the adoption of the forms and customs, and even worship, of those around her. The childish faith which caused the exclamation and its consequences, as we have recorded, did not spring from the mere impulse of the *moment*, but from the education and subsequent thought of early years. That which springs from mere impulse would have been startled and terrified at the instant acting on the words; but to the child of Israel there was no fear or doubt.

If then even a child, a female child, was permitted to be the means of bringing a heathen household to a knowledge of the only God, shall we not do all we can to make the education of our children subservient to the same great end? Amongst heathens and idolaters, indeed, we do not dwell; but thrown, as we are so often, into terms of intimacy and kindness with those who worship God, though not as we do, it is more necessary than ever to infuse a national spirit amongst us; to inculcate into the very youngest of our families, who and what they are—that a solemn charge is entrusted to them, as *witnesses* of the Eternal—and that a denial or concealment of our true faith, and sacrifice of its ordinances, to assimilate with the world, is a denial of God Himself. Let us teach our children from earliest infancy to venerate and glory in their faith; and that faith will be respected in them by every Gentile with whom they associate. The law of God makes no distinction between the education of sons and daughters, and let us make none; but equally children of Israel—and both equally heirs of all the spiritual and temporal privileges which that holy name includes. Let our daughters then feel and glory in their nationality; and by making the religion of their fathers the mainspring of their being, so serve the cause of God, and so elevate the character of Israel, that their very exile may hasten the day of our restoration, by bringing all the nations to a knowledge of the Lord. The youngest child may, like the little Maid of Israel, bear witness to the truth of her religion, and the power of her God. An infant of six years once had the moral courage, in the midst of an assemblage of Gentile children (and her mother was not present) to refuse touching some forbidden food, and with childish and most touching artlessness to say aloud that they were not allowed to eat it. And that infant upheld the sanctity of her religious ordinances, and inspired a feeling of respect and admiration, not only towards herself, but towards the religion she professed: and this is the practical nationality we should inculcate. Teach a child from the first that she is the depository of a solemn office—that she can, in her own proper person, either elevate or degrade the religion which her Father in Heaven Himself deigned to give—that she is not like the children of the soil, for whom it is enough to follow the multitude, and who have advantages of all kinds to teach them their religious duty, but one of a peculiar and holy faith, scattered in every land, exiled and often oppressed, yet still the firstborn of the Lord ; and, therefore, that it depends upon her, even as if she stood alone, to do all she can to raise her faith, and its blessed ordinances, in the estimation of the whole Gentile world.

We have now come to a very important character in our present period, with little to concern us as women generally, but much to encourage us as women of Israel ; and sufficient in itself to give a direct denial to the accusation, that the Jewish religion utterly prohibits all spiritual and intellectual privileges; and that for a woman to attempt the study of, or instruction in, religion, is little less than folly. We have already seen a female judge and prophetess in the person of Deborah ; but still, if she were the only female so mentioned, we might incline to the idea that women were thus sanctified only in the very first selection of Israel. Such however, is not the fact ; several hundred years had passed away—the kingdom of Israel was sinking deeper into the abyss of sin. Had there been any single portion of the law derogatory to women, or confining her to mere household sphere, with neither liberty nor inclination to employ her intellect and influence, now would have been the very time for such laws to obtain ascendancy; the state of society must effectually have prevented her rising against it. If, however, we refer to 2 Kings xxii. 11—20, also 2 Chron. xxiv. 20—29, we shall find a very different picture of women in Israel.

The wicked kings Manasseh and Amon had been succeeded by the youthful Josiah, at the early age of eight years. His mother's name, we are expressly told, was Jedidah, and her influence it probably was which so guided and instructed his youthful years as to make him very different from his predecessors. "He did that which was right in the sight of the Lord, and walked in all the ways of David his father, and turned not aside to the right nor to the left." In the eighteenth year of his reign he gave orders for the repairing and beautifying of the house of the Lord; and it was when obeying this order that Hilkiah the high priest found the book of the law, which he gave to Shaphan the scribe, who, after reading it, brought it unto the king. What an awful picture do these verses present of the national apostacy; that the very high priest should have been ignorant of the existence of the book of the law in the house of God, and its enactments, and prohibitions, of course, never read, as was so imperatively commanded, before the people—men, women, and children! The mere formula of high priests, scribes, and other officers of the temple, appeared still filled; but what a fearful mockery must it have been before the Lord: the mere empty shell, whence all of obedience, and love, and spirituality, had departed.

That the ordinances of the law were utterly disregarded, is evident from the effect which the hearing of the law produced upon Josiah. He rent his clothes (always a sign of intense affliction), and sent instantly the priest, and other superior officers, to "enquire of the Lord for me, and for all Judah, concerning the words of the book that is found, for great is the wrath of the Lord that is kindled against us, because our fathers have not hearkened unto the words of this book, to do according unto all that which is written concerning us." And to whom did these high officers go? To a mighty man of wisdom? To a holy man of God, whose sanctity and influence gave him courage to threaten and to warn, to risk personal danger from the anger of the populace, whom his denunciations might enrage? No; it was to a WOMAN that they came—a woman and a WIFE in Israel—and yet an inspired prophetess of the Eternal, the chosen medium between him and his people, the bold denouncer of his wrath, and the truthful reporter of his love.

"And Hilkiah the priest, and Ahikam and Achbor, and Shaphan, and Asaiah, went unto Huldah the prophetess, the wife of Shallum, the son of the keeper of the wardrobe (now she dwelt in Jerusalem in the college), and they communed with her."—Now, if the women of Israel were confined entirely to their household duties, it is strange that Huldah could have obtained admission within the college, which was probably an establishment devoted to the study of the law. Her being a prophetess, does not make an exception in her favour, or render her dwelling in the college a necessary consequence. We have seen, in the case of Elijah and Elisha, that the prophets had no appointed residence, but were generally wanderers and mere sojourners in the various cities of Judea. Deborah judged and prophesied under her own palm tree, between Ramah and Bethel. Huldah, on the contrary, dwelt in the college; and from the officers of Josiah seeking her without any hesitation, as the only one of whom they could enquire of the Lord, we are justified in inferring that her wisdom and piety had long been known and acknowledged in Jerusalem.

The prophetic power was never intrusted to the undeserving, man or woman; it was always some superior piety and virtue, which originally attracted towards them the loving mercy of the Lord, and rendered them worthy to become His messengers. No effort after righteousness and virtue, however lowly, passes unnoticed in His sight; and His love will ever increase the desire after good, and the power to accomplish it. But virtue and righteousness were not the only requisites for a prophet; they needed intellect, a profound knowledge of the law and of man, and a strong perception of the ways and works of the Eternal. Huldah's dwelling in the college supposes a mind anxious and enquiring after the study of the law, and a heart yearning to obey every statute therein commanded, while her very selection as a prophetess proves that her spiritual privileges and intellectual powers were on a perfect equality with those of man.

Yet from the very circumstance of her only being mentioned once in the sacred record, we may be convinced that her solemn office interfered not at all with her domestic and conjugal duties, or that in any one instance she came unduly forward. Woman's natural sphere is to influence, not to command; to entreat, not to threaten; to lead far more by example than by precept; and every woman, conscious of her own weakness, will rejoice that such are the kind of duties assigned her. In the awful condition of Judæa, a mind like Huldah's must have shrunk from coming forward. The state of restraint, and subsequent depression, which must attend the intercourse of pious and believing hearts, with those to whom all of piety and spirituality are utter strangers, was probably the original cause of Huldah's religious retirement. Seeking to conquer the suffering which the public and private condition of her country occasioned, by quietly following the daily routine of domestic duty, and spending every leisure hour in learning to know that merciful and gracious God, whom Judea seemed to have forgotten.

Possessed, as she was, of unusual spiritual gifts, her mind must have been of no ordinary cast to allow her remaining contented in a retired sphere without the restless desire to become of public service; her very consciousness of responsibility would urge this without any failing of woman's native modesty. But Huldah *waits for the Lord.* He who had reposed in her a gift so precious would vouchsafe her some sign when to use it, and meanwhile her duty was to pray, and meditate, and beseech the Eternal to have mercy on His people. And this we can all do, though we are not prophetesses; and we have His whole word to prove how much intercessory prayer prevaileth.

The sign, for which the prophetess awaited, came. The highest officers of the state suddenly approached her, and with humility and deference reported the sovereign's message, enquiring through her the mandate of the Lord. There is neither pause nor doubt, as there must have been had she been a mere pretender in the prophetic art ; the rushing spirit of prophecy was poured within her by Him whose instrument she was, and with fearless dignity she answered, "Thus saith the Lord God of Israel, Tell the man that sent you to me, Thus saith the Lord, Behold I will bring evil upon this place, and upon the inhabitants thereof; even all the words of the book which the king of Judah hath read ; because they have forsaken me, and have burned incense unto other gods, that they might provoke me to anger with all the works of their hands, therefore my wrath shall be kindled against this place, and shall not be quenched." Then, softening into the tenderest compassion, still inspired by Him who ever tempereth justice with mercy, she continued, "But to the king of Judah who sent you to enquire of the Lord, thus shall ye say to him, Thus said the Lord God of Israel, As touching the words which thou hast heard; Because thy heart was tender, and thou hast humbled thyself before the Lord, when thou heardest what I spake against this place, and against the inhabitants thereof, that they should become a desolation and a curse, and hast rent thy clothes and wept before me; I also have heard thee, saith the Lord. Behold, therefore, I will gather thee unto thy fathers, and thou shalt be gathered into thy grave in peace; and thine eyes shall not see all the evil which I will bring upon this place. And they brought the king word again."

Although this prophecy does not properly belong to a history of the women of Israel, we have transcribed the whole, that our readers may better judge the full extent of prophetic power vouchsafed to Huldah; and the bold disregard of all, except of her mission, which it evinced. "Tell ye the man who sent you," she says; yet she has no disrespect for the Lord's anointed, she was simply uttering the words of the Eternal. The persecution of Elijah and Elisha marked the prophetic office as one of danger; but Huldah felt nothing but the spirit which inspired her; feared nothing but to fail in the calm and dignified boldness required of her as the prophetess of the Lord. The high regard in which her words were held is proved by the messengers of Josiah "bringing the king word again," and by his continuing his endeavours to render himself worthy of the promised forbearance of the Eternal, though the threatened evil to his country and his people he knew could not be averted.

We have no further mention of Huldah; nor do we need more for the confirmation of our assertion, that the women of Israel enjoyed higher and nobler privileges, in the sight alike of God and man, than any other women in the world. Every former argument which we advanced in our notice of Deborah, is still more strongly applicable to Huldah. One great difference there was, which, however, only marks the national elevation of women still more forcibly. Deborah lived, and exercised her prophetic power, at a time when Israel was under the *direct guidance* of the Lord. Huldah flourished, not thirty years before the first captivity; and some centuries *after* the nation had, by their sins, thrown a dark cloud between them and their God. The laws and customs, which, according to our opponents, have crept in and sullied, if not entirely altered, the pure Judaism inculcated by Moses, *must* have been ascendant during the period of which we are writing. And in consequence, if they degraded women, it follows that the domestic and social position of the women of Israel must, during the monarchy, have given positive evidence of such degradation; and we certainly should not find a woman dwelling in the college, which is synonymous with devoting herself to the study of the law, and also as the only one, in the whole nation of Judah, who was entrusted with the prophetic power.

To such a height in spiritual privileges, the women of Israel cannot now hope to attain; but the example of Huldah is sufficient for them to rest content that the study of the law, and all religious observances, as well as the piety of the heart, are now equally incumbent on them as on men, and equally acceptable before God: and that Israel is the only nation in the whole world in which women sufficiently gifted to perform the offices of Prophetess and Judge have been found.

These truths ought to be enough for us; and the very names of Deborah and Huldah serve as shields to guard us against all arguments tempting us from the Rock of Ages. We have said this often; but we cannot too often or too forcibly impress it on the female Hebrew heart. It depends on woman, not alone to *feel*, but to *prove* its truth: to shake off all of stagnating apathy, all of cold indifference: not to rest satisfied with a due performance of their duties as women—even as pious women,—but to feel and glory in being women of Israel, and infuse the same national spirit within the hearts and minds of their children.

Prophetesses, in our present captive state, we cannot have, nor do we need them, till the spirit of our God rests upon us in our own fair land once more; but we need the same bold uncompromising spirit, the same religious zeal and pious fervour which actuated Huldah. Did every woman in Israel determine to elevate her faith, and to glorify her God in her own proper person, apathy, and that fearful want of nationality too often discoverable amongst us, would vanish altogether. We should not be content with mere amalgamation with the Gentiles in society; but, without relinquishing the social position which an age of superior civilisation and refinement has assigned us, we should still retain our nationality—still, before man and before God, remain Israelites indeed; and thus compel respect towards our faith, and remove not only the prejudices excited by ignorance, but check the zealous efforts of conversionists by convincing them, that our constancy, as our religion, must be indeed of God, and therefore no effort of man can turn us from it.

Nor was it to an unmarried, and therefore more independent woman, the prophetic power was granted. We are expressly told that Huldah was the wife of Shallum, the keeper of the robes; and we must therefore feel convinced that the marriage state in Israel was far from being one of slavery or dependence. How she contrived to unite her domestic duties with her divine office, holy writ does not inform us; but there is no doubt that both were fully accomplished; for the chosen messengers of the Eternal were ever those actuated by the tenderest human emotions, and the earnest desire to serve *all* the human family. We read Huldah's feminine nature in the fact of *her being sought* in her own dwelling. The condition of Judea must have filled her with the deepest suffering; but she left it in the hands of her God, content to perform his mission, when called upon so to do, but never forgetting, even in the furtherance of His service, the modest and retiring dignity of the woman.

And this is the union we should so strenuously endeavour to obtain. More than the females of every other nation, are the women of Israel called upon to cultivate their intellect, that they may be enabled to comprehend the religion of their fathers; that *reason* and *conviction*, as well as love and long associations, should bind it on their hearts. Yet that intellect must never be obtruded; never tempt them to quit their own holy and beautiful sphere. Woman may have opportunities for the study—aye and the practice—of religion, which man has not; such study will never be in vain: opportunities of usefulness, of influence, will come to her: she need never seek them by the sacrifice of feminine gentleness and retirement; and man will thankfully seek that comfort and even guidance from her, which, had they been obtruded on him, he would condemn and scorn.

Oh that the history of the past would influence the present; that the women of Israel would feel to their heart's core, that they are still the same in the sight of their God, as their ancestors of old; that they have it in their power *individually* to hasten that day when "the earth shall be covered with the knowledge of the Lord as the waters cover the sea!" Piety must come from the *mind* as well as the heart; and the more the intellect is cultivated, the better will it enter into the mysteries alike of Creation and Revelation, of the works and the Word of God; and the clearer these become, the purer, higher, more deeply spiritual, will be the emotions of adoring love, uniting the soul with God. We must not rest content with mere accomplishment, we must rise superior to the frivolity and excitements which form the existence of some women; or how can we become worthy, or make our souls worthy, to be once more the favoured of the Lord? Women of Israel! the very name should impress our hearts with a solemn conviction of our individual responsibility, and urge us on to such spiritual and intellectual improvement as will mark us, in the eyes of the whole world, as worthy descendants of the first-born of the Lord.

We have now completed our review of the female characters contained in the Fourth Period of Jewish History. Our readers will, we think, universally agree that it does not contain a single passage, much less a single character or incident, which demonstrates the social, domestic, intellectual, and spiritual position and endowments of women as enslaved and degraded. There is not a hint or allusion to any second law opposed to the written one of Moses; for if there had been, the monarchy lasted sufficiently long for it to have obtained such dominion as to make manifest its existence.

That man's evil and licentious passions had increased to an extent so fearful as to demand the captivity of the whole nation, is no proof of the imperfection of the law, but only of the imperfection of human nature. That the sins of the women increased the burden of Israel's guilt we do not deny, because the prophets so inform us. We merely affirm, that the *social condition* of women had not degenerated—that there were no laws then degrading and enslaving her; and, therefore, that as there were none then, there can be *none now*, as we acknowledge no other law of sufficient power to annul or contradict those given by the Eternal to Moses, and by him transmitted to man.

This important fact is strongly confirmed by the fearful wickedness of Jezebel and Athaliah. The former was the daughter of a notorious idolatrous king, and the mother of Athaliah; consequently we may indulge the comfort of the belief that neither was of Israel, and that such awful crimes stained not the women whom the Lord so blessed. There is no occasion to bring forward their histories, subjects from which no good can be obtained, except that, in the creeping horror of the evil and the sin to which woman can attain, the prayer for help and strength, and freedom from temptation, may arise more frequently from our hearts. The fact of their influence is all we need, as confirming the assertion, that woman had both power and freedom in the land. Ahab's natural wickedness was fearfully increased, and made productive of still more horrible evil, by the counsels of his wife, as we must perceive by a very casual glance over his history: and of Athaliah we are expressly told, when speaking of her husband Jehoram, "that he walked in the ways of the kings of Israel, for he had the *daughter of Ahab to wife, so he wrought that which was evil in the eyes of the Lord.*" And, again, of her son Ahaziah, "he also walked in the ways of the house of Ahab, *for his mother was his counsellor to do wickedly.*" What can more forcibly illustrate the power and influence which woman could obtain and exercise in Judea? Had there been any law confining them to one particular sphere and debasing employments, not even the idolatrous wives and mothers of the kings could have obtained such ascendancy. Nor was it only *through* kings, female authority was exercised. Athaliah reigned six years sole mistress of Judea; and we may be certain, that however low the nation had fallen, however the laws of Moses had sunk into neglect and abuse, still, had there ever been any portion of this law degrading to woman, Athaliah never would have had either the means of making herself queen, or supporting so high a dignity, even for the short space of six years.

The very fact, then, of there being such characters as Jezebel and Athaliah, is unanswerable confirmation of the freedom and equality of woman, because, though they were *not women of Israel*, their union with the Hebrew kings subjected them to all the restrictions of the Mosaic law; and had that law made them slaves, they would not have exchanged their liberty in their own idolatrous countries for conjugal thraldom in Judea, the social and domestic position of the Hebrew females being sufficiently well known to them, from the immediate vicinity of the land, to prevent any misconception on a subject so *i*mportant.

And whilst we shudder at this picture of awful wickedness, and feel inexpressibly thankful that our merciful God has vouchsafed us a law, which, if obeyed, must effectually prevent the dominion of such evil, let us not turn from it as an overcharged portrait, and believe that human nature is incapable of such heinous crimes. Alas! we have only to look into the annals of modern history, and even amidst those very nations who proclaim themselves so much more enlightened and spiritual than the blinded Jew—ay, and within the last four centuries we shall find woman tempted to follow the same awful path, and instigating husbands and sons to the commission of crimes and massacres, from which the heart turns with loathing sickness, and the vain longing to realise disbelief in the story that it reads. And if so lately, comparatively speaking, such things have been even in enlightened nations, can we continue to think the Bible-picture of woman's depravity overcharged? O we know not, we cannot know, the awful effects of unlimited authority and unrestrained passions on the weak human heart. We can only pray God to guard us from positions in which feelings may be aroused of whose very existence we dream not now; to bind closer and closer still His blessed law upon our hearts, His spirit on our souls; to remove from us all those evil inclinations and embryo passions which His eye may trace, but of which we are unconscious; to enable us to cling closer and closer unto Him in prayer and praise; and we shall be guarded, as by an angel's wing, from every evil thought and evil deed.

FIFTH PERIOD.

The Babylonish Captivity, including the Life of Esther.

THE CAPTIVITY.—REVIEW OF CHAPTERS ONE TO SEVEN OF THE BOOK OF EZRA.

A GREAT and melancholy change had taken place in the condition of the Israelites. Their continued disobedience and idolatry had, at length, called down upon them the long-averted chastisement; and in the land of their foemen were now their mournful dwellings. The great armies of Nebuchadnezzar had overrun Judea; and, carrying off kings, priests, and people to Babylon, left their beautiful land to desolation.

But even in their captivity, a captivity which their sinfulness compelled, God had not forsaken them. All were not sinful, all were not disobedient, though all alike were exiled, and captives in a strange land. Even then the Lord raised up His witnesses. The firm constancy of the youthful Daniel and his companions, gave them examples of exalted righteousness in the very midst of darkness. The glorious visions of Ezekiel, yet more bold and sublime in imagery than the visions of any who had gone before him, inspired them with hope for the Future, and consolation for the Present. While, when the period for action came, such men as Ezra, Nehemiah, Zerubbabel, Haggai, and others equally earnest, were not found wanting in the furtherance of their holy cause.

The condition of the exiled Hebrews appears more that of colonists than slaves. Allowed to dwell together in large bodies, they became at length possessed of considerable property;[*] so that many of them refused to return to their

[*] Milman's History of the Jews, vol. ii. p. 4.

THE CAPTIVITY. 331

own land, even when the mandate of Cyrus gave them permission so to do. It seemed a strange and painful contradiction, this refusal to quit the land of their captivity, when, during that captivity, so many had yearned and wept when they "remembered Zion." Yet, that it was so, and that the return to Judea was by no means general, is a convincing proof to us that the *universal restoration*, of which every prophet speaks, *is still to be fulfilled*.

The chronology, nay, the very personages of the events we are about to regard, as identified with those flourishing at the same period in Profane History, are so entangled and confused, that a clear elucidation is impossible. Not only do Jewish and Christian chronology differ as to national dates, but also amongst themselves. Josephus, following the arrangements of the Bible, places the history of Esther *after* the books of Ezra and Nehemiah. In the Jewish calendar,[*] Esther's being made queen and saving her people takes place six years after Cyrus's decree for the return of the Jews; sixteen or eighteen before the building of the second temple and the departure of Ezra; and thirty before the rebuilding of the walls by Nehemiah. The chronology at the end of Bagster's Comprehensive Bible rather favours this opinion—only differing in regard to the departure of Ezra, which he states to have taken place only one year after Esther's accession, five before Haman's plot, and thirteen before the petition of Nehemiah. Milman, in his History of the Jews, and Gleig, in his History of the Bible, again differ; the former agreeing with the authorities already quoted, in placing the migration of the Jews under Ezra, *after* the accession of Esther; and the latter agreeing with Josephus, in placing him *before* it.

Now, in alluding to these differing authorities, let it be remembered, that we do not interfere at all with the grand question at issue between Jews and Christians, viz.: the correct data of the creation of the world; the one placing it 3760, the other 4004 before the Christian era.[†] The Jew has demonstration of his correctness quite sufficient to satisfy himself, and prevent all adoption of the Christian supposition.

---

[*] By E. H. Lindo, Esq.

[†] Even these are disputed: The Samaritan Pentateuch asserts the date of the creation to be 4700 B.C.; the Septuagint, 5372; Scaliger, 3950; Petavius, 3984; Dr. Hales, 5411; the Talmudists, 5344 (?) See note to Bagster's Comprehensive Bible, p. 1339.

All we wish to do, is to make the Book of Esther clearer as to time and characters, and more connected with the books of Ezra and Nehemiah than is generally supposed. As on a very careful consideration of the subject, both in itself, and in connection with Profane History, our own opinion differs from all the authorities above mentioned : we will state it openly, as also our reasons for holding it—not at all compelling others to adopt it, nor as supposing it positively correct, but merely a suggestion founded on a careful study of the time. To bring it clearly forward, we must throw a cursory glance on the first six chapters of the book of Ezra.

The first chapter contains the celebrated proclamation of Cyrus; who, we are expressly told, was "stirred up by the spirit of the Lord," that is, the Lord put it into his heart to have mercy on the Jews; informing us also that the heads of the tribes of Judah and Benjamin, Priests and Levites, all whose spirit "God had raised," gladly hastened their return, bearing with them all the vessels of gold and silver of which Nebuchadnezzar had spoiled the temple, but which Cyrus now restored. In the second, we learn the number that return, their names, substance, and offerings: in the third, the exertions of Jeshua, Zerubbabel, and their brethren the high priests, in preparing for the work of the temple, setting up first an altar on which to offer the usual evening and morning burnt-offerings; the celebration of the feast of the tabernacle, new moons, and all the feasts of the Lord; in the second year of their return to Judea, and the second month, the solemn foundation of the temple with shouting and with joy, mingled with the mourning of those who yet remembered the first house of the Lord, "so that the people could not discern the noise of the shout of joy from the noise of the weeping of the people." In the fourth, we have the painful hindrance of the building by the adversaries of the Jews—their letter to Ahasuerus, king of Persia—and the royal prohibition to continue the building of the temple, believing it detrimental to the Persian power, by giving too much sway into the hands of the Jews. The Ahasuerus of the sixth verse of this fourth chapter, is evidently Cambyses, son and successor of Cyrus—not the Ahasuerus of the time of Esther. In profane history, we are told that he did not openly revoke the edict of his father Cyrus; but greatly frustrated its execution, by many annoyances levelled against the Jews. This underhand kind of working is implied in the verse before us, which merely mentions the writing to the king an accusation against the inhabitants of Judah and Jerusalem.

The Artaxerxes of the next verse is not the same sovereign, but the Smerdis of profane history, the brother and successor of Cambyses; who, not satisfied with secretly frustrating the building of the temple, openly revoked the degree of Cyrus, and sent such letters to the adversaries of the Jews, as to make them "go up in haste to Jerusalem, and the Jews, and made them to cease by force and power." "Then ceased the work of the house of God, which is in Jerusalem; so it ceased until the second year of the reign of Darius king of Persia."

This tallies exactly with the dates and names of profane history. Smerdis, suspected to be an imposter, was dethroned and murdered, and Darius Hystaspes elected in his room.

In the reign of Darius, we find, by the fifth chapter of Ezra, the prophets, Haggai, Zechariah, and Iddo, prophesying to the Jews that were in Judah and Jerusalem; and encouraged by this manifestation that the spirit of the God of Israel was still at work, Zerubbabel and Jeshua urged and helped the people again to set forward the work, disregarding even the threatening questions of Tatnai and Shethar-boznai; and "the eye of their God was upon the elders of the Jews, that they should not cease till the matter came before Darius." A letter was consequently written to the king by Tatnia and his companions, stating all that had passed between them and the Jews, and concluding by entreating the king to let search be made, "whether indeed it be so, that a decree was made of Cyrus the king, to build this house of God at Jerusalem, and let the king send his pleasure to us concerning this matter." It is clear from the words of this letter that some time had elapsed, and divers kings intervened since the decree of Cyrus; the tone is different to that in which Bishlam, Mithredath, and others addressed Smerdis—more conciliating and enquiring —not the determined opposition of the previous appeal. The letter, though written by their adversaries, served the Jews as fully as if they had appealed to the king themselves.

In the sixth chapter, we find that Darius did make the requisite search for the decree, which was found, and so fully confirmed the statement of the Jews, that Darius instantly promulgated another decree, not only confirming that of Cyrus, but commanding the adversaries of the Hebrews to let the work of this house of God alone, so that the Jews and their governors might build it in the place appointed: and to give them help in forwarding the work, and in all that they needed for sacrifice, etc. That he who hindered it should be hanged on timber taken from his dwelling, and his house be made a dunghill; "And the God that hath caused His name to dwell there, destroy all kings and people that shall put their hands to alter and destroy this house of God, which is in Jerusalem. I, Darius, have made a decree—let it be done with speed."

A decree peremptory as this was of course productive of good. The building progressed rapidly; the elders being still more encouraged by the prophesying of Haggai and Zechariah: —"And they builded and finished it according to the commandment of the God of Israel, and according to the decree of Cyrus and Darius, and Artaxerxes, kings of Persia." This Artaxerxes, though not reigning at the time of the event here recorded, is introduced by Ezra, the writer of the book, in compliment to the favour he ever showed the Hebrews; and this Artaxerxes it is, who is, in all probability, the Ahasuerus of the book of Esther.

The remainder of the sixth chapter is devoted to the rejoicing of the children of Israel, on occasion of the dedication of their temple, the building of which was completed in the sixth year of King Darius's reign; their offerings; the establishment of their priests, "as it is written in the book of Moses;" the solemn celebration of the Passover "seven days with joy"—for they had been purified from the filthiness of the heathen, and the "Lord had made them joyful, and turned the heart of the king of Assyria unto them, to strengthen their hands in the work of the house of God, the God of Israel."

So concludes the sixth chapter of the book of Ezra: and between that and the seventh, a period of some years must have elapsed. Darius reigned thirty-six years; Xerxes, who succeeded him, twelve; and it was not till the seventh year of Artaxerxes, consequently forty-nine after the completion of the building of the temple, that Ezra obtained permission from the king to go up to Jerusalem, armed with the royal repetition of a decree in favour of the Hebrews, and the rebuilding of the city, already promulgated by his predecessors Cyrus and Darius.

In this interval it appears then, most probable, that the events recorded in the book of Esther took place. Whether we believe the Ahasuerus so closely connected with her, to be the tyrant Xerxes, according to Milman's view of his character, or Artaxerxes Longimanus, according to Josephus and other commentators; still the period of these events remains, unalterably, between the six and seventh chapters of Ezra, as we have stated before.

ESTHER.

SUGGESTIONS AS TO THE IDENTITY OF THE AHASUERUS OF SCRIPTURE, AND DATE OF HIS ROYAL FEASTS, ETC.

ACCORDING to the events of profane history, a period of sixty-three years must have elapsed between the decree of Cyrus for the return of the Jews, and the accession of Artaxerxes Longimanus. In the Jewish calendar we find only six. How this disparity can ever be reconciled, we know not, and must leave it to wiser heads than our own; suffice it, that the events narrated in the first six chapters of Ezra must have covered a longer interval than six years; but on such a subject our readers must search and judge for themselves: we offer no opinion to be adopted as the right one, and will willingly and thankfully receive any communication likely to elucidate this difficult point.

That the events of Esther took place *after* the decree of Cyrus is, however, a truth on which there can be no dispute; and, whatever number of years may have elapsed since the permission to return to Jerusalem, it is equally clear that an immense number of the Hebrews yet remained scattered over the large dominions of Ahasuerus, which we are told " extended from India even unto Ethiopia, over a hundred and seven and twenty provinces," including, of course, Persia and Media.

Among these was a Jew of noble descent, Mordecai by name, a Benjamite by tribe; consequently, not one of the Ten Tribes; but of the two who had faithfully adhered to the royal house of Judah. In direct compliance with the law of Moses, which had expressly commended the fatherless to the care of their countrymen, Mordecai had brought up, as his own child, Esther, or Hadassah, the orphan daughter of his uncle, and resided with her in an establishment according to his rank in "Shushan the palace;" meaning the city which was the usual residence of the king.

In the third year of Ahasuerus, the city of Shushan was thrown into a ferment of excitement by the royal feasts given alike to princes and nobles, and to all the people, and lasting several months. The princes of the provinces were present, to whom, we are told, in the scriptural record, all the riches of his glorious kingdom, and the honour of his excellent majesty, were lavishly displayed. And this excitement was followed by another,—the banishment of Queen Vashti from her royal estate, and proclamation made throughout the provinces that all the fairest maidens were to be gathered together unto Shushan the palace, from whom the king might select a queen in the place of Vashti. The extreme beauty of Esther, whose very name, in Persian, signifies *a star*, of course attracted the attention of the king's officers, and she also " was brought unto the king's house, to the custody of Hegai, the keeper of the women."

That this distinction was more painful than pleasing, both to Mordecai and Esther, we cannot for a moment doubt : the former, whose unwavering faithfulness to his religion has marked him amongst the most deserving and distinguished of our ancestors, was not likely to have connived at a union for his adopted child which must prevent her strict adherence to her father's faith. That Esther herself was equally repugnant, we have the authority of the oldest Jewish writers ; if her prayer in the Apocrypha be written by them. That the Apocrypha is *not* divine, we are quite aware, but as the writers of the Talmud do not disdain to quote from the "Wisdom of Solomon," as a good moral essay, *not* as divine, we may perhaps be permitted to regard the remaining chapters of the book of Esther in the same light ; as an enlargement or commentary on the Bible-record of the same events ; not that Mordecai and Esther really did use the words of prayer which are there put into their mouths; but as a reflection of the opinions of our old writers on the subject.

To resist, or refuse compliance, would of course have been vain : and we find Esther winning such regard from Hegai, that he showed to her more kindness and respect than to any other of her companions. Beauty alone could not have done this: for to loveliness in all its varieties he had no doubt been accustomed. But the cultivated intellect, the spiritual graces, of the Hebrew woman, which so marked her superiority over the females of every other nation, gave to the mere perishable beauty of face and form, an interest and a charm unlike every other; and this it was which so powerfully attracted the regard of Hegai, and, in due time, the devoted love of the king.

Some time (probably two or three years) must have elapsed between Esther's being taken from her adopted father's care and her public proclamation as queen. It was in the third year of Ahasuerus that Vashti was dethroned, and not till the seventh that Esther was raised to the royal dignity in her stead. During this interval "Esther had not showed her people, nor her kindred; for Mordecai had charged her that she should not show it"—a charge which appears to us somewhat strange and irreconcilable with the constancy and dignity evinced by Mordecai, and at a time that, though captives in a strange land, concealment of their peculiar tenets was not necessary for their safety. But if this part of his conduct be incomprehensible, or, at least, unsatisfactory, not so is the paternal affection which is so forcibly betrayed in the simple words, "And Mordecai walked every day before the court of the women's house, to know how Esther did, and what would become of her." His child was removed from under his own eye, but his watchful love was with her; and Esther must have felt comforted in the consciousness that he was near her—his thoughts and affections with her still.

And could she need comfort, surrounded as she was with state and luxury? Alas! these are not the ingredients of happiness. Esther had been brought up with the greatest tenderness from her earliest years; from the situation of her people, perhaps, educated with even more than usual care in her father's faith. Her affections, habits, associations, all were confined to the house of her childhood—the father of her love. Was it nothing, then, to be torn from all these by an imperious mandate, and, at a moment's warning, debarred from the exercise of her faith, compelled to worship only in her own young heart, with no friend near to strengthen and to guide? Even the very idea of becoming queen, had she been one likely to be dazzled by so high a dignity, must have been fraught with terror when she recollected the fate of her predecessor.

z

Thoughts like these were quite sufficient to have clouded the heart and mind of Esther, and rendered the change in her earthly lot more sad than joyous. But, from the favour she received, it is evident that she did not allow herself to murmur: the buoyancy of youth too was her own, and the very respect and regard which she received from Hegai, must have strengthened her to continue the same course of meek submission and trusting hope.

Her unambitious spirit and modest gentleness, we infer from her asking nothing but what the chamberlain appointed. Yet "the king loved Esther above all the women, and she found grace and favour in his sight"; and "he set the royal crown upon her head, and made her queen instead of Vashti. Then the king made a great feast unto all his princes, and his servants, even Esther's feast; and he made a *release to the provinces*, and *gave gifts*, according to the state of the king."

This was in the seventh year of Ahasuerus, and it was in the seventh of Artaxerxes that Ezra obtained permission to go up from Babylon to Jerusalem with a new decree authorising the return of all the Jews who wished it, and granting greater privileges to them, and more lavish gifts than any king had yet bestowed.

Now, if this Artaxerxes of Ezra be the Ahasuerus of Esther, this event tallies exactly with the "release to the provinces, and the gifts made according to the state of the king," of which we have just read. Esther's parentage and faith were, indeed, not yet disclosed; therefore this favour to Ezra was not so much owing to her influence, as to the gracious mood and munificent rejoicing, with which the king greeted her accession as his queen.

The very words of Ezra, "Blessed be the Lord God of our Fathers, which has put such a thing as this into the king's heart, to beautify the house of the Lord which is in Jerusalem; and hath extended mercy unto me, before the king and his counsellors, and before all the king's mighty princes!" imply that his request was made, and permission accorded, during some great public rejoicing, and in presence of all the king's counsellors and mighty princes. And thus, it is in exact agreement with the feasts and rejoicing which Ahasuerus gave unto all his princes and servants, when Esther was acknowledged queen.*

* We read in Ezra, that it was in the first month Ezra commenced his

ESTHER. 339

It was during the rejoicings attending the choice of Esther as queen, that it appears most probable that Mordecai obtained that situation in the royal household, which is implied by his sitting at the king's gate. What office it was, does not appear. But he evidently had not occupied it before ; perferring to remain in dignified retirement, as enabling him more strictly to attend to the ordinances and requirements of his faith. Affection and anxiety for Esther, was without doubt the real incentive to this change in his life. We have already read of his

---

journey, and the fifth when he arrived in Jerusalem, " which was in the seventh year of the king ;" and in Esther, that it was the tenth month when Ahasuerus first made her queen, in the seventh year of his reign, but this does not prove that Ezra's return to Jerusalem took place *before* the events of Esther. We will endeavour to make our meaning more distinct : —Queen Victoria, we all know, ascended the throne of England in 1837, on the 20th of June, which is, counting by the solar months, the *sixth* month ; on the 20th of June, 1843, therefore, she entered the seventh year of her reign. In the tenth month, which is *October*, 1843, we read, that an insurrection took place in Barcelona. In the first month, coveal with *January*, 1844, the Spanish Cortes was dissolved ; and in the fifth month, which was *May*, 1844, another revolution at Barcelona. Now, all these events took place in the *seventh year* of Queen Victoria's reign ; but the events of the first and the fifth months, occurred *after that* of the *tenth :* and in exactly the same manner, Esther's accession as queen, and Ezra's migration, might both have taken place in the seventh year of Artaxerxes, and yet the event of the tenth month occur before that of the first and fifth. Tebeth was the tenth month : in the festive rejoicings which followed, lasting several weeks, as was the custom of Royal amusements, and in the presence of the princes and counsellors, Ezra made his request, encouraged by the release given to all the provinces. In Nisan, which is the first month, his preparations being completed, and the Jews wishing to depart collected together, he set off on his journey, and in the fifth month, which is Ab, he arrived in Judea ; and still it might be all in the seventh year of Artaxerxes, granting, which is most probable, that that monarch ascended the throne, either in the sixth, seventh, or eighth month. This is of course differing with the Jewish calendar, which makes seventeen years elapse between Esther's being made queen and the departure of Ezra ; but then, who is the Ahasuerus of Esther ? And who is the Artaxerxes of Ezra ? They cannot be the same persons. Josephus, again, makes Xerxes the Artaxerxes under whom Ezra and Nehemiah go to Jerusalem, and asserts that this migration took place *before* Esther : this appears not only historically but scripturally incorrect. But to reconcile all the differing opinions is impossible ; we must leave it, as we have said before, to our readers to judge for themselves, only stating that the opinion we have advanced is founded on a careful research of both *scriptural* and *ancient* history, an examination of all the opposing points, and the adoption of that which appears most reconcilable with the narrations of both Profane History and the Word of God.

z 2

walking every day before the court of the women's house to know how she did, and what would become of her; and his seeking an office in the king's household, evidently proceeded from the same affectionate cause.

There is a dignity about Mordecai, in the simple fact of his concealing his relationship with the petted and all-powerful queen of Ahasuerus—in his pursuing, undisturbedly, the calm and meditative tenor of a good man's way, which we cannot fail both to reverence and admire. It was enough for him that he was one of the children of God; what higher dignity could he have?

"Esther had not yet showed her kindred, nor her people, as Mordecai had charged her: for *Esther did the commandment of Mordecai, like as when she was brought up with him.*" How eloquently illustrative of her sweet and gentle character! She was of that tender age, when the mind and temper are more liable to take the impression of things and characters around them, than to remember and act upon the education and impressions of earlier years. She had been two or three years completely separated from personal intercourse with her adopted father. She had received nothing but indulgence; was translated from a lowly and retired home to be the sole possessor of a monarch's love, and the sharer of a mighty kingdom—surrounded by luxury and adulation: and yet, so unchanged was her gentle mind and loving heart, that, in her high estate, she did "the commandment of Mordecai, as she had done in her childhood and her youth." The faith of her fathers was the safeguard: for strangers and heathens were around her: the pleasures proffered were all tinctured with earth and time. In the spiritual, the deathless, part of her nature, the youthful Esther was alone. How perseveringly and religiously must Mordecai have trained her infant years, that even, in this utter loneliness, she could yet have steadfastly trodden the one straight path; and never wavered in her duty, either to her guardian or her God.

So some few years passed on, the exact number we cannot ascertain from the widely differing chronologists. During that interval, a conspiracy had been formed against the king by two of his chamberlains, which becoming known to Mordecai, he imparted it to Esther, and by her it was "certified to the king in Mordecai's name." Inquisition was made into the matter, and the facts being discovered, the plotters were hanged, and the account written in the chronicles of the Persian kings. The instrumentality of Mordecai appears, however, to have been entirely forgotten, though doubtless Esther's influence increased. Had he come forward himself with his important discovery, he would, no doubt, have at once received the honours afterwards bestowed; but he heeded them not, and the whole affair sunk into oblivion with regard to man, but not so in the Divine economy of God.

"After these things," we are told in Scripture, which is a term always signifying some lapse of time, the exaltation of Haman took place. Raised, through the favour of the king, above all the princes that were with him, the royal household vied with each other in doing him reverence, such being the command of the king; but "Mordecai bowed not, nor did him reverence." He who neither seeks nor cares for ambitious advancement and earthly honours himself, acknowledges them not in others. Haman, also, was an Agagite, or Amalekite, one of the idolatrous nations whose iniquities were such as to demand the signal punishment of the Eternal—an enemy from the first to His people: and, therefore, the very race of Haman would have been sufficient for Mordecai to refrain from noticing him. But even had he been of different lineage, the laws of the Hebrews strictly prohibited all unseemly veneration to mere mortal man, as unbefitting those whose adoration was to be paid to God alone. We do not, therefore, at all agree with Milman's supposition, that it was merely because they were rivals in earthly ambition, that Mordecai refused to do reverence to Haman. We have already seen that Mordecai had had opportunities enough already to aggrandise himself, but had neglected them all; and, in fact, the word of God itself favours the inference, that his reason for refusing to do Haman homage, simply was, because "he [Mordecai] was a Jew." The servants of the king spake daily to him, demanding, "Why transgressest thou the king's commandment?" and seeing that he "hearkened not to them, they told Haman, to see whether Mordecai's matters would stand, for *he had told them that he was a Jew.*" This was a bold and fearless statement, exactly in accordance with the character of Mordecai as already displayed. He had made no show of his religion when there was no necessity so to do; but his freely avowing it as his reason for refusing undue reverence to a man, and an Amalekite, ought to convince us that his desiring Esther to conceal her race and faith proceeded from no unworthy or cowardly motive—however we may fail to discover a satisfactory reason why he should have done so.

Haman, full of wrath that any one should dare to hold him in contempt—a wrath no doubt increased, when he heard that the bold man who did so was a Jew—one of a despised and captive people, determined on a signal revenge. That some connection existed between Mordecai and Esther, was no doubt, secretly suspected by him; to attack Mordecai alone, would therefore avail him little, as he would be protected by the queen. The destruction of the whole Jewish people, if he could but procure the king's consent, might involve Esther (of whose influence he was very probably jealous), as well as the hated Mordecai; and the mandate once gone forth, according to the laws of the Medes and Persians, was, he knew, unalterable.

That nothing might fail him, he cast lots, according to the superstition of his age and country, to discern what month would be most favourable for his project. The lot, guided by a merciful Providence, who was permitting the temporary ascendancy of evil only to bring forth permanent good, fell on Adar, the last month in the year. It was then Nisan, the first month, and therefore twelve months intervened; an interval doubtlessly hailed by Haman as allowing the entire destruction of the Jews, even of those situated in the remotest province of the empire; but which was in fact their salvation.

With consummate caution Haman proceeded. Working upon the usual jealousy of the royal prerogative, he alluded to a certain people, who, dispersed amongst all the king's provinces, followed a worship and laws of their own; that it was not to the king's profit they should do so; insinuating, no doubt, that they were likely, from their disloyal practices, to turn others also from their allegiance and their gods: it would be wise, therefore, to have them destroyed—and, that the king's coffers should not suffer, the wily minister concluded his counsel, by a promise of paying ten thousand talents of silver into the royal treasuries.

The instant accordance of Ahasuerus with this cruel counsel, by giving into Haman's hand his royal signet to do with the people as seemed good to him, certainly more resembles the character of the capricious Xerxes, than the mild and benevolent Artaxerxes Longimanus; but then, in the brief record of Scripture, we can hardly know all the subtle counsels of a minister already high in his master's favour. The noblest and best monarchs have, at one period or another, been liable to be led by evil ministers.*

Whoever the monarch, thus much is certain, the horrible decree went forth over the vast domains of Ahasuerus, and consternation and mourning took possession of the hapless people, who, men, women, and little children, the old and the young, were condemned to be destroyed on the thirteenth day of the twelfth month, and all their possessions to become the spoil of their destroyers. Can we imagine a situation more appalling? To know the fate impending—each day, each month to draw it nearer—and yet to have no power either to resist or fly; to feel themselves hemmed in by destined murderers—men whom, perchance, they were in the habit of meeting in terms of kindly fellowship, turned into ruthless destroyers, simply from a monarch's word? Yet such was once the awful condition of the Hebrew people; and it was the Eternal's will, that by a *woman's* instrumentality they should be saved.

"When Mordecai perceived all that was done, he rent his clothes, and put on sackcloth with ashes, and went out into the midst of the city, and cried with a loud and bitter cry; and came even before the king's gate: for none might enter clothed in sackcloth. And in every province, whithersoever the king's commandment and his decree came, there was great mourning among the Jews, fasting, and weeping, and wailing; and many lay in sackcloth and ashes."

Then was the time, had Mordecai been other than we assert he was, for him to have concealed his religion, not by his public mourning to proclaim that he, too, was one of the doomed. But such was not his conduct. When all was peace amongst his people, he was content to remain in seclusion, to practise and to love his faith, without obtruding it by outward appearance of sanctity and holiness. Many of his brethren might, perhaps, in secret, have condemned him as lukewarm to the interest of his nation, or he would long before have made use of Esther's influence for their peculiar benefit. They might, and probably did accuse him of scarcely belonging

* We need but instance Isabella of Spain, who, one of the most noble, most magnanimous, ay, and most humane, alike as a sovereign and a woman, was yet persuaded into the expulsion of six hundred thousand of her innocent subjects, as an act, not of policy, for that was against it, but of *religion.*

to them; but, in the hour of their affliction and danger, they learned differently. He was in very truth among, and of them; and the eyes of all turned to him alone for help and guidance.

Esther, meanwhile, had continued in the retirement of the king's palace; still his best beloved wife, yet retaining all the affection for her adopted father which had characterised her youth. That Mordecai was very closely connected with her must have been generally suspected, else we should not find her maids and her chamberlains coming hastily to inform her of his strange proceeding; but so ignorant were they of its cause, as to excite in us the supposition that his religion, and that of Esther also, was still not publicly known. They merely mentioned that Mordecai was clothed in sackcloth and ashes, as in deep affliction, but made no allusion to the decree.

"Esther was exceedingly grieved; and she sent raiment to clothe Mordecai, and to take away his slackcloth from him: but he received it not." Yet still he spoke not the cause of his grief; and Esther, unable to follow the dictates of her own heart, to go to him herself, sent Hatach again to him, with her royal command, to know what it was, and why it was; thus blending the dignity of the queen with the affection of the child, and compelling his reply.

His silence at first might have proceeded from the momentary hesitation, as to whether or not he should involve Esther in the danger of her people. Her race and faith were still unknown; why should he betray them at a time when their betrayal threatened death? The affection of a father might have struggled with the feelings of the patriot: but ere Hatach returned, his decision was made; and imparting the designs of Haman, and the decree which had thence proceeded, sent a copy of the writing to Esther; charging her to go in unto the king, and supplicate him for her people.

"*For her people*"—the fatal words were said, and her race revealed; he could not withdraw them, and the decree from that moment equally extended unto her, as to the humblest of her brethren. How fearful must this intelligence have been to the young queen; and yet more fearful, if possible, the alternative proposed. We see at once, that her feeling towards her husband was fear, not love; by her shrinking from his presence, unless expressly called. The favour with which she had been regarded from the first, would, had she been a woman of a bold, intriguing spirit, have given her such influence, as to obtain access to her husband whenever she willed it, regardless of all laws to the contrary: but even the impending and wide-spreading danger could not conquer Esther's natural terror. It seemed easier to let the decree proceed, and share the fate of her people, than call down the monarch's wrath by intrusion into his presence: and the very fear endears her to us, proving that it was no unnaturally endowed heroine, but a very woman of whom we read.

"Again Esther spake unto Hatach, and gave him commandment unto Mordecai: All the king's servants, and the people of the king's provinces, do know, that whosoever, whether man or woman, shall come unto the king into the inner court, who is not called, there is one law of his to put him to death, except such to whom the king shall hold out his golden sceptre, that he may live: but I have not been called into the king's presence these thirty days:" probably an unusual lapse of time, which, supposing a decrease of the royal favour, naturally increased Esther's shrinking repugnance from the task proposed.

But Mordecai's plan was already fixed; and this answer was instantly returned: "Think not to thyself that thou shalt escape in the king's house, more than all the Jews. For if thou altogether hold thy peace at this time, then shall enlargement and deliverance arise to the Jews from another place; but thou and thy father's house shall be destroyed: for who knoweth whether thou art come to the kingdom for such a time as this?"

These last words give us the solution of Mordecai's confidence, alike in the influence of Esther, and the eventual deliverance of the Jews. His heart, ever faithful to his father's God — ever watchful to trace the superintending Providence which guarded his people as the shepherd his flock, had solved, as by a flash of light, the mystery formerly surrounding him. He knew now why, in preference to every other maiden, his precious child had been called to that high estate which he had mourned, as uniting her with heathens, and dividing her seemingly for ever from her people and her faith. The Eternal, in His wisdom and His mercy, had placed her there, that she might be the chosen instrument, in His hand, for the preservation of His people. Convinced of this, despondency and doubt passed from the heart of Mordecai.

He felt almost with a prophet's certainty, that deliverance would come for his people; and, therefore, in words that sounded almost stern, in their total disregard of woman's feelings, he called upon her to perform the part for which she had been raised to the kingdom—to listen, not to the voice of fear, but to arise and speak, else would she herself be destroyed, ay, and her father's house (which included Mordecai himself), and deliverance arise for her people from another place.

It is evident that his confidence extended not to her, though with meek submissiveness she made no further resistance to her guardian's will. There is a deep and mournful meaning, breathing through her gentle answer—a hopelessness, yet self-devotion, which must twine her round our hearts, as one peculiarly unfitted for the terrible ordeal.

"Go, gather together all the Jews that are present in Shushan, and fast ye for me, and neither eat nor drink three days, night or day: I also and my maidens will fast likewise; and so will I go in unto the king, which is not according to the law: and *if I perish, I perish.*"

No undertaking, of whatever nature it might be, was ever commenced by the Hebrew nation without earnest prayer and fasting—not by the act of fasting to obtain favour in the sight of the Merciful Being who has no pleasure in the affliction of His creatures; but by abstinence from all corporeal enjoyments to give the spirit ascendancy over the clay, and better enable us to attain that perfect commune with our God, which, in periods of supplication, we so much need. Though in the Book of Esther only fasting is named, yet evidently prayer is understood, for to the Hebrews the first was wholly useless without the second; and in the beautiful prayer written by the author of the remaining chapters of Esther in the Apocrypha, we read in what light her character was regarded. We will transcribe it entire, entreating our readers at the same time to remember, that we do not regard it as inspired, and therefore as the *actual prayer* used by Esther on the occasion, but simply as a proof of the feeling with which she was considered by the ancient writers; and that they too supposed with us, that her queenly state was a matter far more of loathing and repugnance, than of pride and joy.

"And she prayed unto the Lord God of Israel, saying, O my Lord, thou only art our King. *Help me, desolate woman, which have no helper but Thee.* For my danger is in mine hand. From my youth up, I have heard in the tribe of my family, that Thou, O Lord, tookest Israel from among all people, and our fathers from all their predecessors, for a perpetual inheritance; and Thou hast performed whatsoever Thou dost promise them. And now we have sinned against Thee; therefore hast Thou given us into the hands of our enemies, because we worshipped their gods. O Lord, Thou art righteous. Nevertheless it satisfieth them not that we are in bitter captivity; but they have stricken hands with their idols, that they will abolish the thing that Thou with Thy mouth hast ordained, and destroy Thine inheritance, and stop the mouth of them that praise Thee, and quench the glory of Thine house, and of Thine altar; and open the mouths of the heathen to set forth the praises of the idols, and to magnify a fleshly king for ever. O Lord, give not thy sceptre unto them that be nothing; and let them not laugh at our fate, but turn their device upon themselves; and make him an example that hath begun this against us. Remember, O Lord, make Thyself known in time of our affliction; *give me boldness, O King of the nations, and Lord of all power. Give me eloquent speech in my mouth* before the lion: turn his heart to hate him that fighteth against us, that there may be an end of him, and all that are like-minded with him. But deliver us with Thine hand, *and help me that am desolate, which have no other help but Thee. Thou knowest all things, O Lord; Thou knowest that I hate the glory of the unrighteous, and abhor the bed of the uncircumcised and the heathen. Thou knowest my necessity; for I abhor the sign of my high estate which is upon my head,* and in the days wherein I show myself, that I abhor it, *and that I wear it not when I am private by myself. And that thine handmaid hath not eaten at Haman's table;* and that I have not greatly esteemed the king's feast, nor drunk the wine of drink offerings. *Neither had thine handmaid any joy since the day I was brought hither to the present, but in Thee, O Lord God* of Abraham. O thou Mighty God above all, *hear the voice of the forlorn,* and deliver us out of the hands of the mischievous, *and deliver me out of my fear.*"

Well, indeed, must the writer of the above prayer have been acquainted with the female heart, and consequently with all the secret suffering which Esther's exaltation occasioned her individually. No thought of her own influence—no recollection that the king loved her above all others, could give her confidence sufficient in herself. Taught from her youth up to recognise the God of Israel as the guardian of her fathers—as the only Being who could come forward to their help—to Him she looked alone—and she could look to Him with confidence; for in the years she had been compelled to hide her parentage, she had sought Him as her only pleasure and only consolation. She had worn her crown because it was His will; but it was but a weight and sadness; for in her private hours it was ever laid aside—she felt now, in her hour of intense supplication, the full comfort of previous and intimate commune with her God, and her trembling heart was strengthened.

Some natures could not have borne the delay of three days, in the full anticipation of a trial; they must have gone at once to the king, or failed in power to go at all. Yet such natures, in a mere casual view, would seem far stronger and bolder than Esther's; and therefore demand and obtain greater admiration. But it is the exquisitely *feminine* character of Esther that is to me her peculiar and touching charm; it is the still under-current of deep feeling, which betrays itself throughout her history, and which is so peculiarly woman's—the power of uncomplaining endurance—the firm reliance on a higher and all-merciful power for individual happiness—the absence of all trust in her own gifts of beauty and eloquence, unless so blessed by Him as to soften the heart of the king towards her—the courage, not *natural*, but acquired through prayer—the conquest of her own weak tremblings, and venture of her own life, for the welfare of her people—and this not the mere impulse of the moment, but pondered on through three days' incessant prayer; these are traits which surely must rivet our interest and our love.

Clothed in unwonted georgeousness, and radiant in her extraordinary beauty, but her heart, at that awful moment scarcely able to realise the holy strength and trust which prayer had wrought, on the third day Esther stood in the dreaded presence of the king: and though uncalled, and therefore disobedient to the law of the Persian kings, God gave her grace in the monarch's sight; and, instead of displaying anger, he held forth his sceptre towards her, and she drew near and touched it, in sign that she implored a boon. In the Apocrypha we are told that faintness overpowered her, a natural portraiture of feminine weakness, and depriving her at once of all those attributes of a heroine, which would divide her from our sympathy as a being differently endowed to ourselves. Prayer *had* given her strength, else had she not thus stood uncalled before Ahasuerus; but the mind, strong as it may be, cannot always bear up its mortal shrine: and by the description of the deadly terror, depriving Esther of sense and speech, given by our ancient fathers, we see at once the awful struggle she was enduring.

Her beauty, her very terror, all strongly excited the king's affection; and hastening towards her, he soothingly exclaimed, "What wilt thou, Queen Esther, and what is thy request? It shall be even given thee, to the half of the kingdom."

How blessedly must these words have fallen on Esther's still quivering heart! Yet, not at that moment, dared she utter her request, fearful lest its boldness and extent should change the royal mood. She, therefore, merely besought him, "If it seem good unto the king, let the king and Haman come this day unto the banquet that I have prepared for him." The invitation was accordingly transmitted to Haman, and he and the king went in unto the banquet which Esther had prepared.

It was a strange proceeding: this commencement—inviting the deadly enemy of her people to her private banquet—aggrandising him as it were still more—rendering her own task more fraught with danger—and filling the minds of her countrymen with doubts as to the purity of her intentions towards them. It has ever seemed to me that Esther's conduct, with regard to the two invitations, before her boon was spoken, proceeded not from previous design, but rather from *impulse*, which she followed as supposing it the inward direction of the Eternal: but which, when accepted, startled even herself. But to retract was impossible; and the daughter of Israel, radiant in her loveliness, entertained the king and his prime minister at her private table.

Again did the king reiterate his inquiry and his promise, "What is thy petition? and it shall be granted thee: and what is thy request? even to the half of my kingdom it shall be performed." And again did Esther fail in the necessary courage to give it words; and, instead of her weighty boon, we find her simply saying, "If I have found favour in the sight of the king, and if it please the king to grant my petition, and perform my request, let the king and Haman come to the banquet that I shall prepare for them, and I will do to-morrow as the king hath said."

Her concluding words betrayed that she had yet another boon; and her trembling spirit was probably reassured by the graciousness with which the invitation was accepted. Haman, too, left her presence rejoicing and triumphant. Little could the wily plotter dream that the God of her people was with Esther, inspiring the words of her mouth; and that this very exaltation was the forerunner of his fall. But yet, in the very midst of his triumph, as he left the palace, Mordecai, who still sate at the king's gate in his sackcloth, stood not up, nor moved for him; and Haman's indignant wrath caused the exclamation, that riches, prosperity, gratified ambition, regal favours, all availed him nothing, so long as he saw Mordecai the Jew sitting at the king's gate. To disperse these gloomy thoughts, he entered eagerly into the counsel of his wife and friends; and a gallows was erected fifty cubits high, while his blackened mind revolved some tale, the which to bring the king on the morrow, that his consent might be obtained for the instant execution of the man he abhorred.

But that same night others also were wakeful. Surely we may picture the young queen wrapt in earnest and fervid prayer, still for strength and grace for the pursuance of her entreaty: was she not a weak and trembling woman, whose only strength was PRAYER? Thousands were destined to the destroyer; if she held back, who would arise and save? And, in that nightly vigil, when fear and doubt are so often magnified and darkened, what could she rest on but her God?

Nor was she the only wakeful one in the royal palace. Even as she prayed, the Eternal answered; and His guiding mercy was at that very moment so ordering events as to prepare the way for her successful petition. Unable to sleep, Ahasuerus, towards morning, commanded the chronicles of the kingdom to be read before him, and it so happened that the roll opened on the conspiracy against himself, which Mordecai had discovered. Imparted to the king as it had been by Esther, the names and minute particulars had passed unnoticed, more especially as Mordecai had always so shrunk from public notice. But, read now from the records of the kingdom, the king's attention was irresistibly fixed; and he demanded "What honour and dignity had been done to Mordecai for this?"—
"Then said the king's servants that ministered unto him, There

is nothing done for him." The king, self-reproached at the neglect, and determined not to expose himself to forgetfulness again, inquired, "Who is in the court?" And on being told that Haman stood without, commanded his instant admittance. "What shall be done," he asked, when the minister appeared, "unto the man whom the king delighteth to honour?" And puffed up by his inordinate pride and vanity, Haman thought in his heart, "Who can the king delight to honour more than myself?" and advised a triumph, which would make him second only to the king. But when, elated with his own description, and convinced he was advising his own triumph, these words came—"Do even so to Mordecai the Jew, who sitteth at the king's gate: let nothing fail of all that thou hast spoken;" —how can we attempt to describe the fierce rage of vindictive passions which must have taken possession of Haman's heart? How attempt to portray the black emotions with which the baffled plotter must have walked beside the splendidly caparisoned charger, on which, robed in the king's apparel, sat his detested rival? And no comfort waited him when, mourning and enraged, he sought his home. "If Mordecai be of the seed of the Jews," they told him, "before whom thou hast begun to fall, thou shalt not prevail against him, but shalt surely fall before him," words which prove how forcibly the estimation in which the Jews, as the chosen and beloved people of God, were held by the nations around them, even by those who called them captives.

But little time had Haman to ponder on further schemes of vengeance. "While they were yet talking with him, came the king's chamberlains, and hasted to bring Haman to the banquet which Esther had prepared." Again had the queen assembled around her all of gorgeousness and festivity to gratify the luxurious taste of the Persian king. Her beauty, heightened by successful adornment, concealing under the graceful courtesy of the hostess the tremblings of the petitioner, —fear probably becoming more and more intense with every passing moment—longing, yet fearing for the king to speak those words which must impel reply. And at length they came, coupled as before with the royal promise of fulfilment for whatever she might ask, and she, who had fainted from very terror when first in presence of the king—who had felt so powerless to speak from the very magnitude of her boon— now boldly and firmly answered:—

"If I have found favour in thy sight, O king, and if it please the king, let my life be given to me at my petition, and my people at my request; for we are sold, I and my people, to be destroyed, to be slain, and to perish. But if we had been sold for bondmen and bondswomen, I had held my tongue, although the enemy could not countervail the king's damage." Few manifestations of self-devotion are more touching and complete than these simple words of Esther. We have seen and known the extent of her human fears—she might have worded her petition as in no point to include herself, but she scorned it; she might have been divided from her people in periods of prosperity and peace because such was the will of Mordecai, but not when danger and death threatened. Their fate should be her own; and fearlessly she included herself with them. Whether or not Ahasuerus at once associated this people for whom Esther implored, with those destined for death by the machinations of his minister, we cannot determine; but by his instant question—"Who is he, and where is he, that durst presume in his heart to do so?" we are induced to suppose that he did not, but imagined it simply some plot against the life and immediate kindred of his queen—a supposition likely enough to excite the fierce wrath which, when his long-favoured minister, Haman, was accused as the adversary and enemy, caused him to leave the banquet in much disorder, and pace the palace garden, endeavouring so to pacify his anger as calmly to decide. Haman, meanwhile, had fallen in deadly terror and agonised supplication on the couch where, in accordance with Persian fashion, Esther had reclined during the banquet—a posture of apparent familiarity, rousing the monarch to yet greater fury; and guided by his gestures even more than his words, the guards present seized Haman, and covered his face, an Eastern custom existing still, and signifying that the criminal is condemned to instant death. Harbonah, the chamberlain, at the same moment came forward with the information of the gallows prepared in Haman's house for Mordecai, who had acted so faithfully towards the king, and Ahasuerus, still more incensed, commanded him to hang Haman thereon. The royal command was instantly obeyed, and then only "was the king's wrath pacified."

This summary mode of proceeding may seem strange to modern notions and civilised customs, but it is in exact accordance with the despotic government of the East, not only in a time so long past, but even now, when the bowstring is the instant executor of punishment. Trial and witnesses for and against, the minute examination into facts, and the deliberate sentence of judgment, are all utterly unknown to this day in the East; and, therefore, the instant chastisement of Haman in no way marks the sovereign as the capricious tyrant, which, identifying him with Xerxes, some historians represent him. Egregiously deceived as he had been so long in his prime minister, who had dared, as he supposed, to compass the life of his dearly-beloved queen and her kindred, and who had secretly and vindictively prepared a gallows for the death of one who had saved the king's life—all these circumstances were quite sufficient to rouse an Eastern temper into such fury as could only be calmed by the death of the offender. Nor did the monarch stop here. He gave unto Esther the whole house (probably the rich possessions) of Haman, and then it was that the queen revealed her near relationship to Mordecai, and her faith; and Mordecai came before the king, and received from his hand the ring, or signet, which Ahasuerus had taken from Haman, as a symbol that he was now prime minister in his enemy's place. "And Esther set Mordecai over the house of Haman."

But personal safety and aggrandisement were not the intention of the noble Mordecai and his courageous child. Falling prostrate at the feet of her husband, Esther besought him with many tears to put away the mischief of Haman the Agagite, and his evil schemes against the Jews—imploring "If it please the king, and if I have found favour in his sight, and the thing seem right before the king, and I be pleasing in his eyes, let it be written to reverse the letters devised by Haman the Agagite, which he wrote to destroy the Jews which are in all the king's provinces : for how can I endure to see the evil that shall come unto my people? and how can I endure to see the destruction of my kindred?"

She could not have framed her petition in words more likely to reach the heart of the sovereign, than by making the cause of the Jews so completely her own. A mere entreaty for them as a people, unjustly sentenced to destruction, would not have been thus successful; but she identified them with HERSELF. In their low estate—in their impending danger, she appealed for them as *her* people, *her* immediate kindred, that life would be joyless were they descroyed; and her eloquent appeal was granted, for her beauty, her gentleness, her very deference and respect, had rendered her all-powerful with the king. Full permission was given to her and Mordecai to write as it pleased them; "for the writing which is written in the king's name, and sealed with the king's seal, might no man reverse." Scribes were accordingly summoned in all haste—scribes who could write in every language of the hundred and twenty-seven provinces, to the lieutenants, and the deputies, and the rulers: "Wherein the king granted the Jews which were in every city to gather themselves together, and to stand for their life, to destroy, to slay, and to cause to perish, all the power of the people and province that *would assault them*, little ones and women, and *to take the spoil of them for prey;*" and copies of these writings were forwarded by riders on mules, camels, and young dromedaries, being hastened and pressed on by the king's commandment.

Vindictive as, in a mere superficial view, this decree may appear, it was imperative, for the Jews could be saved by *no other* means; the writing that was once written in the king's name, and sealed with the king's ring, could never be reversed—the laws of the Medes and Persians, once passed were unalterable, however unjust or tyrannical they might be. Ahasuerus had commanded the entire destruction of the Jews; he could not *annul* that edict, and, consequently, was impelled to grant Esther's entreaty, by issuing another, desiring the Jews to defend themselves, even by the death of those who, in compliance with the previous decree, should assault them. A mode of proceeding very repugnant to present notions, but which can only be judged by the customs and laws of the past.

We find in Josephus another reason for this destruction of Ahasuerus' subjects. Alluding to some words in his letter to the governor, Josephus says in a note, "These words give an intimation, as if Artaxerxes suspected a deeper design in Haman than had openly appeared—that, knowing the Jews would be faithful to him, and that he could never transfer the crown to his own family, who were of the posterity of Agag, the old king of the Amalekites, while they were alive, and spread over all the Persian dominions, he endeavoured to destroy them. Nor is it to me improbable, that those of the Jews' enemies who were soon destroyed by the Jews, by permission of the king, were Amalekites, their old and hereditary enemies (Exod. xvii. 14, 15); and that thereby was fulfilled Balaam's prophecy, "Amalek was the first of the nations, but his latter end shall be, that he perish for ever' (Numb. xxiv. 20)."*

If this be well founded, it is a most agreeable solution to what appears, on a superficial reading, such indiscriminate slaughter on the part of the Jews. It was the fulfilment of Divine prophecy on a race whose exceeding wickedness had for so many centuries marked them out as objects of the Eternal's wrath; and His people were but instruments in His hands, instead of the fire or plague, with which, had it pleased Him, their destruction would equally have been brought about. But to return to Esther.

With what joy must she have beheld the termination of all her fears and inward struggles in the salvation and glory of her people. Her beloved guardian, Mordecai, was now acknowledged and honoured by prince and people, as his many years of unpresuming worth deserved. "He went out from the presence of the king in royal apparel of blue and white, with a great crown of gold, and with a garment of fine linen and purple: and the city of Shushan rejoiced and was glad. The Jews had light, and gladness, and joy, and honour. And in every province, and in every city, wheresoever the king's commandment and his decree came, the Jews had joy and gladness, a feast and a good day. And many of the people of the land became Jews; for the fear of the Jews fell upon them."

And this, under the God of her people, was a WOMAN'S work—wrought not by beauty, or power, or any of those arts which but too often guide the female favourites of monarchs, but solely by the STRENGTH of PRAYER. We have seen the tremblings of her gentle woman heart—that she had entered on the plan, with the conviction that she was risking her own life—that her own death for intruding upon the sovereign's presence was far more likely than the preservation of her people, else, wherefore the words, "And if I perish, I perish." All this we have seen; and can we hesitate a moment in the belief, that strength, eloquence, all she needed, were *infused* by the Hearer and the Answerer of prayer—that they were not of herself? How had she commenced this terrible under-

* Josephus, Book xi. chap. vi. note to p. 229 of second volume.

taking? By three days and nights passed in fasting and prayer, the long period proving in itself the extent of her shrinking fears, the magnitude of the task in which, simply in obedience to Mordecai, she had engaged; and when we remember how her work *commenced*, can we not rest satisfied as to the how it *concluded?* The sacred historian passes on to more eventful matters, to more public and national concerns; but we, lineal descendants of this fair and noble Jewess, shall not we accompany her to the same retirement, where she had fasted and prayed, and behold her again prostrate, not now in agonised supplication, but in glorified, rejoicing adoration!—tracing the hand of her God in all—hearing the answer to her fervent prayer in the shouts of joy and triumph which rose from the city without—in the honourable exaltation of Mordecai—in the pure delicious feeling that she was no longer lonely in her high estate; the Guardian of her infancy, second only to the king himself, would ever be beside her. Her faith known, and still herself beloved! O that in itself must have removed a mountain of lead from her bounding heart. Hundreds, ay, thousands of her people were saved in one brief day from death; and she had done this, her words—hers—weak trembling woman as she was! How might she bear the weight of joy—the magnitude of the success. Heavy to humanity as was the magnitude of the terror and the boon, no heart, moulded as was hers, could have contained it, save in prostration before Him whose sole work it was. The burden of joy, as the burden of grief, *must* find vent before our God—must pour back its gushing tide into the living fountain whence it sprung, or it will crush the heart which holds it; and can we doubt that these were Esther's feelings, because we find them not in written words? O let every right-feeling woman look within her own heart, and place herself in Esther's position, from the very beginning of her dreaded task to the completion, and then say how could such joy be borne, save as we have pictured it, in adoration of the Lord?

We have only one more public mention of Esther in the book bearing her name (except her writing to confirm the second letter of Purim), and that mention, according to the opinions of some, destroys the beauty of her character, and makes her appear in a vindictive and unfeminine light. We, ourselves, once shrunk from the verse, and wished it had not had existence; but a more matured consideration removes the objection, and completely exonerates Esther from the bloodthirsty vengeance with which she has by some historians been charged. Even Milman, usually so just and moderate, speaks of the barbarous execution of the ten sons of Haman as proceeding from her request, when in fact they were *already slain*. Verses 12, 13, of the ninth chapter of Esther, are those to which we allude.

In the Jewish law, the gallows was *not used*, as it is now. The criminal was always executed first, either by stoning or strangling, and only the dead body suspended upon it, as a further mark of guilt and ignominy; and also to deter others from following the sinful example. Esther's request that Haman's ten sons might be hanged on the gallows, had nothing whatever to do with a vindictive desire of vengeance upon them for their father's sin. They had been already slain amongst the enemies of the Jews in Shushan; slain most probably in their own assault, for the Jews were not to *attack*, but merely to *defend*. "They gathered together, we are told, to lay hand on *those that sought their hurt*." And the governors and rulers, lieutenants, and deputies of the king all helped the Jews. Consequently those who assaulted them were their determined and hereditary foes, resolved, from the great hatred they bore them, to act on the king's first edict, even if the second should cost them their lives. Amongst these, of course, were Haman's sons, who, Amalekites and Agagites like their father, were the Jews' most deadly foes; and the foremost in assault, falling in strife, and stricken by the God whom their iniquities had profaned, through the swords of His people. The 7th, 8th, 9th, and 10th verses of this same chapter (the ninth), specify them by name, amongst the slain, which is confirmed by the words of Ahasuerus himself in the 12th verse, "The Jews have destroyed five hundred men in Shusan the palace, and the *ten sons of Haman*," etc. And that Esther should have made her request, that her people should do on the morrow as they had done the preceding day—and that Haman's ten sons should be hanged upon the gallows, proceeded from no unfeminine or vindictive feeling; but simply from the wish, that the future safety of the Hebrews should be fully secured. As an individual, and judging by her previous truly feminine character, Esther would, without doubt, have shrunk from the awful retribution, which the plot against the Jews had wrought. But she was denied the privilege of thus judging and thus acting: on her depended the present honour and future security of a people, liable to be trodden under foot at every capricious change in the mood of her captors; not alone in her own time, but years after. Guided most probably by the counsels of Mordecai, Esther was compelled to resort to those measures, which were likely to deter their enemies from future attacks. The ignominious exposure of the dead bodies on the gallows—sons of the one-time mighty and all-powerful, all-ambitious Haman—would bring more forcibly than aught else to the minds of men, the palpable evidence that the Most High God still watched over His people; and turned every evil thought against them to the evil and the ruin of their connivers. And the request of the second day's defence is but a proof that the deadly haters of the Jews were not yet subdued, but were likely to spring up again more inveterate than before. Esther's words are, " Let it be granted to the Jews to do *to-morrow according unto this day's decree;* and that decree was to *defend,* not to revenge—to *protect themselves* against the assaults which by the previous edict would be made; not to slay and cause to perish, and take the spoil, as had been determined against *them.* Esther, therefore, issued no order of blood and vengeance, of which she is sometimes accused, nor were the Jews guided by any feeling but that of *self-defence;* else we should not read, more than once repeated, that even in the homes of their deadliest foes, and with the royal decree to appropriate all to themselves—" *On the spoil laid they not their hand.*" Not in Shushan alone, but in every province and every city where they gathered together and stood for their lives—where the richest and most tempting spoils must have offered themselves to their very grasp—still " *on the prey laid they not their hand.*"

Was this a war of revenge, of national aggrandisement? What could have prevented, had they so desired, the entire subjection of the whole Persian kingdom? What people, save the people of God, in those dark times, would have been satisfied merely to stand on their own defence, goaded, as they must have been, by the entire destruction and inveterate enmity working against themselves? But the wars of the Jews were never, from the first of their selection as the Eternal's chosen, actuated by either ambition or revenge.

A reference to the Third Period (Deborah) will give the causes and intentions of their first wars—the reduction of the Holy Land, *not* for personal aggrandisement, but in direct obedience to the direct command of the Eternal. In looking further on, through all the different phases of Jewish history, we find no mention of wars undertaken for aggrandisement or private revenge. Their wars were always defensive ; and, though richly gifted with all the noble and heroic qualities necessary to warriors and heroes, they were nationally a peaceable and pastoral people, satisfied with the lands assigned them, and with becoming wealthy through the direct blessing of their God. We never read, as is so often the case in the histories of contemporary nations, of acts of private revenge, or public dispute settled by the sword. No personal appropriation of acquired spoil—no inroads from one tribe to another, as, even in modern times, is so often the case with nations who are divided into clans or bodies. Whatever wars we read of, as undertaken by the Hebrews, are either by the direct command of their heavenly King, or in their own defence.

Glancing, then, back on the Bible history regarded in this light, from the selection of Abraham to the time of Esther, we cannot find one incident or trait to justify the idea, that the slaughter of Ahasuerus' subjects proceeded from any revengeful or vindictive motive, but was simply in *self-defence*. We cannot draw any inference contrary to the supposition, that it was the Eternal Himself who ordained and permitted this destruction, not alone because of their designs against His people, but because they were descendants of a most sinful race, and inheritors and promulgators of iniquities and abominations which the God of Truth and Love abhorred, and for which he had, from the very first, sentenced them to chastisement and wrath.

Looking upon it in this light, all over-refined notions must pass away. It is idle, in such an incident as this, to condemn our noble Ancestress as vindictive and revengeful, because her request shocks our individually sensitive notions. We must take a wide grasp of the whole character and bearing, not of Esther alone, nor of the Jews in Persia alone ; but of the general character of the nation in the *past*, and how their *present* danger was likely to affect them in the *future*. We must recollect that they were still captives—still liable to persecution and intolerance—to be attacked and slaughtered, at the very first caprice of the despotic monarchs under whom they lived.

Even as Ahasuerus had been persuaded by the specious reasoning of a favourite minister, so might be other monarchs. It was therefore the especial care of Mordecai and Esther to adopt every means for the *future* security of their people, not alone for their *present* safety; and in that barbarous age, and still more barbarous people, no measures were so likely to be efficient, as the public degradation of Haman's family, and the noble stand made by the Hebrews against their idolatrous oppressors. The Jews had probably been considered a poor-spirited, unnerved people, likely to bend beneath oppression, and to be easily subdued. Their spirited defence, however, taught their adversaries a very different lesson; not only that the God of Israel was with them still, but that they possessed within themselves all the attributes of an heroic nation, who would never fail in the assertion and protection of their rights; and who, were the necessary liberty of action allowed them, would never tamely submit to the insults and oppression which they had endured.

In reading and reflecting over this history, let us never forget the important truth so often repeated, that "on the spoil the Jews laid not their hand," because this one brief sentence is sufficient to convince us, that no revengeful or rapacious feelings actuated our ancestors. In the edict issued against *themselves*, not only their lives were to be destroyed without any regard to age, infancy, or sex, but their possessions were to have been confiscated to the king's treasury—they were to be spoiled as well as slain; and they might have retaliated. All which had been decreed against them, they were at perfect liberty to have turned upon their foes; but they scorned it. The same spirit which caused Abraham to refuse the gifts of the king of Sodom, lest he should say, "I have made Abraham rich," actuated them to touch not one item of the vast stores, which, from the awful amount of slaughter, might have been their own. Accused as we have so often been of love of gold above all other love—of seeking, by honorable or dishonorable means to increase our worldly stores—of grasping and rapacious dispositions—let us point to this simple line, "On the spoil laid they not their hand;" and the charge is at once proved false! Let us look back on this—on a hundred other similar traits in our history—and our national character will stand forward as free from such ignominious stain as any other nation in the world. What, if our modern history seem to contradict this, and the sneerer and scoffer point to the usurers of the middle ages, and, dilating on their wealth, their rapacity (so called), their grasping minds and hardened hearts, in such opprobrious colours portray the Jew? What, if they do this? They prove nothing—nothing to tarnish the national character of the Hebrew, as proved in the momentous records of the past, and confirmed by their giving up all of wealth and greatness, rather than their religion, in their expulsion from Spain,—but much, much against themselves, in the fearful effects of persecution and intolerance, which they have hurled upon the People of the Lord.

The Book of Esther concludes with the establishment of the festival of Purim, which, observed as it is by every class, and every denomination of the Jews throughout the world to the present day, is in itself a convincing evidence of the perfect truth of the whole history. The 14th and 15th days of Adar were ordained to be "remembered and kept throughout every generation, every family, every province, and every city; that these days of Purim should not fail from among the Jews, nor the memorial of them *perish from their seed*. Then Esther the queen, the daughter of Abihail, and Mordecai the Jew wrote with all authority, to confirm this second letter of Purim." And from that time it has been observed by every man, woman, or child, bearing the honoured name of Jew. Its ordinance and confirmation is the last mention which we have of Esther *by name;* and, therefore her after influence with respect to the favor shewn her people can only be conjecture. Yet if the Ahasuerus of Esther be indeed Artaxerxes Longimanus, the Artaxerxes of Ezra and Nehemiah, surely we may be justified in the theory (which we acknowledge to be a favourite one), that the ready granting of Nehemiah's petition, and the subsequent favourable edicts issued for Jerusalem and the Jews, originated in the love borne by Artaxerxes for his lovely Jewish queen. We are told, "that Mordecai the Jew was next unto King Ahasuerus, and great amongst the Jews, and accepted by the multitude of his brethren, seeking the wealth of his people, and speaking peace to all his seed." He no longer refused a situation of dignity and trust, because it was bestowed upon him as a *Jew*. He had no need either to deny or conceal the religion of his forefathers. He had been chosen to succeed Haman in dignity and favour with the king, because he was of Esther's kindred and Esther's faith: and, his duty marked out for him, as his pious mind must have felt, by God Himself, it would have been but mock modesty, to have shrunk from the high estate and honors with which its performance was associated.

The lofty beauty, and retiring dignity of his previous character, were not yet, in the smallest degree, infringed by his acceptance of the office proffered. The welfare of his people was ever the uppermost in his thoughts; and if he could serve them better in public than in private life, he would not shrink from the notoriety attendant on his doing so. We read, "that he was accepted by the multitude of his brethren," meaning that they regarded him with the same deep love and reverence which they had felt towards him in his low estate. No envy, none of those bitter feelings so often excited towards greatness, could actuate them towards him; for he sought but "the prosperity of his people, the peace of all his seed."

If Mordecai retained so much influence, years after the events which had occasioned his accession to greatness had faded into the past, it is not likely that Esther retained less. Her public and private positions must both have been very much happier than before. Her influence over the heart of her lordly husband had been acknowledged, by a concession, which, in a Persian Emperor, was as unprecedented as it was extraordinary. That it either created or heightened love towards him, we cannot doubt, for it is not in woman's nature to receive such manifestations of kindness and forbearance, without giving some warmth in return. Besides, he knew her faith, her race, and yet he continued, nay increased, his favour towards her: thus proving forgiveness of her previous silence on that important point. The beloved guardian of her youth was ever near her, second in rank to the king himself; her people honoured and protected; and many who had before been heathens, embracing the covenant of the Lord, and swelling the Hebrew ranks; and all this, under the blessing of the Eternal, had been achieved by her *conquest over herself*, and her influence with the king. Was it likely, with such memories, that Esther would sink into a mere nonentity in the Persian Court? That she would not, even as Mordecai, use all her influence for that holy people to whom her whole heart still clung? And when we think attentively over all this, her character, her eventful history, her power over her husband, may we not, in some degree, be justified in the supposition, that the Artaxerxes who permitted the departure of his favourite Jewish cupbearer, Nehemiah, and gave him letters to the keepers of the king's forests, and to the governors, etc., in furtherance of the rebuilding of Jerusalem, and to ensure the safety of the Jews in Judea, was the same monarch, who, under the name of Ahasuerus, had already so favored them in Persia?

The very fact of Nehemiah, a Jew, being the chosen cupbearer to the king, and evidently in such high favour, that the sadness of his countenance attracted even his royal master's notice; the remarkable coincidence that the king's court was still in Shushan the Palace, the very scene of Esther's request, and the favourite residence of Ahasuerus, when every other notice of the kings of Persia placed them in Babylon; the particulars mentioned, by Nehemiah, of the *queen being by the king's side,* when the petition was made; all confirms the above supposition, and gives rather a solid foundation to the conjecture of Esther's influence forwarding the suit of Nehemiah, which we have with all humility advanced.

The character of Esther, as an individual and a female, possesses many traits to call for admiration and love. She was not, indeed, a heroine; nor do we perceive in her, that peculiar energy and promptness under danger and trial which we have noticed in the characters of Abigail and the Shunammite; but the very want of this quality is consoling, proving, as it does, that the most timid, the most essentially feminine, may be permitted to accomplish great ends, and become instruments in the Eternal's hand for the welfare of His people. Energy of purpose and of action, though essentially woman's attribute, is yet a portion only for the few. There are more to resemble Esther than Abigail; and to those that are timid and fearful, and shrinking from an imperative duty, or some imposed task, —who would rather remain in sad quiescence than make one effort to conquer an imagined destiny—to them we would point the consoling moral of Esther's history, and beseech them, like her, to arm themselves with the arrows of fervent prayer, in the very face of inward tremblings and a failing frame, and to go forth and do, and leave in kinder hands the rest.

Esther's quiescence and obedience to her destiny was necessity. Chosen as the bride of a heathen monarch, desired by Mordecai not to show her people or her kindred, debarred from all her friends, and pleasures of her earlier and happier years, it was her duty to submit patiently and calmly; and her gentle and enduring character enabled her to do so less sufferingly than more energetic minds. But we see that to endure was less painful to her than to act, by her repugnance to go forward when the call of duty came. Her spirit, instead of being roused, by the extreme emergency of the case, shrunk back appalled: and to brave the king's anger, by venturing uncalled into his presence, seemed far more terrible than the danger threatening thousands. To *share* their fate appeared easier far than to court it; and even when, in obedience to Mordecai, she promised to seek the king, it is very evident that her anticipation was failure—and death. Had Abigail or Deborah been in her place, their different character would scarcely have required even the direction of Mordecai; their own energy would have urged them forward, and supported them by the inward promise of success.

But that Esther did not naturally possess this strength and firmness, renders her conduct yet more worthy of our grateful admiration. We see her displayed before us, in her woman's weakness, as, indeed, one of ourselves. We behold her in not one point, except in her surpassing loveliness, our superior; nay, to bring her closer to us still, she is a captive in a strange land, even as we are now; and yet was she, this weak trembling girl, the saviour, the benefactor of thousands; and her name has come down through a thousand ages, wreathed with the admiring love of that very people whose ancestors she saved.

To do as she did, to be exposed to the same awful ordeal—of a monarch's wrath, or a people's preservation—is, indeed, not ours; and we should be grateful that it is not; but how often will the annals of private life demand as mighty a conquest of self in woman. How often are we called upon to subdue, or, at least, entirely to disregard natural weakness and disinclination, and go forward, when we feel so wholly incapacitated from the task proposed, that we would more gladly sit down, and let the waves of care and sorrow roll over us, than make one effort to stem the rushing torrent, and make evident the supremacy of MIND OVER CIRCUMSTANCE, of the WILL over EVENTS. There are trials and exertions in private life demanding such courage and firmness to meet, that we often feel as if the frame must sink under them; but still, like Esther, let us go forward, feeling, it may be, with her, "If I perish, I perish," rather than draw back from the path of duty. Life and death are not with us, but with the Lord; and, in His hands, how often does anticipated death become rejoicing life : and the thunder-clouds, which we feared to meet, dissolve, when boldly fronted, into sunshine and bliss. Suffer, indeed, we *may* and *must*. Even the approval of conscience—the conviction that what we do is undoubtedly right, and a blessing will spring from it—will not shield us either from inward trembling or mental pain. Physical weakness itself will cloud and blacken our mental vision. The blood disturbed by unusual exertion will flow unequally; sometimes so sluggishly, that further efforts appear impossible, and mind and heart both feel stagnant; sometimes so wildly and hotly, that the whole frame feels one mass of *nerve* and irritation and ill-temper, even towards those we most love, impossible to be avoided. The very comfort, even the power of Prayer, is gone from us. But, in such times (for they *must* come), let us only remember that we are suffering *physically*, and nerve our minds to bear them; even as we would some bodily pain, or sickness, the source of which is so much more easy to be traced. Let us not shrink back, because we feel as if we were doing nothing ; as if our former fears told us right, and we are too weak, in constitution and in mind, to be anything but a burden, and had, therefore, better sit down, and *endure*, instead of rising up to *act*.

Had Esther, when overcome with natural terror she fainted in the presence of Ahasuerus, given up her purpose, because she felt so utterly incapacitated, both mentally and physically, from pursuing it—her people would have perished, and she herself have been either swallowed up in the universal destruction, or sunk into a mere soulless, spiritless nonentity : her whole life embittered by the consciousness of what she *might have done*, and what *she did not do*. But we have seen that she did not draw back; though the stoppage of every pulse, from pure terror, evinces the struggle with natural feeling,—which it was.

We do not find her deploring her constitutional timidity and wishing she possessed the energy of others. No ; the fount of living waters, whence Esther derived the strength and determination, which she so much needed, to go forward is open to us all. It was incessant and most fervent PRAYER. The God of compassion and love, who hearkened unto her, is still our God—and will grant us the same strength and firmness for our individual duties which He vouchsafed to her. Let us not suppose, for a single instant, that only in great emergencies He hears us. Esther prayed to Him, and conjured others to pray for her to Him, in this danger, only because she had known the efficacy of prayer in *little things*. "Neither had thine handmaid any joy since the day that I was brought hither, to this present, save in thee, O Lord God of Israel!" She had been accustomed from her youth upwards to look on Him, and pray to Him, as the Saviour and Father of her people and of herself; and, therefore, she knew and felt that now, in this great danger, and most repugnantly-accepted task, prayer only could be her strength.

And, without this infused strength, O what is woman!—a reed, liable to be turned by every passing wind, or crushed before the slightest storm; to bend to the soiling earth, and clogged with the particles of dust and taint, which, in its prostration, will cling to and deaden it, find it a weary, if not a hopeless task, to lift up its drooping head towards the pure heavens again.

But let us not imagine, because, mentally and physically we are weaker than others of our sex; because we have no energy, no firmness, no self-support (if we may be allowed the term), that we are to pass uselessly and wearily and despondingly through life—that the Bible gives no sympathy or encouragement to such as we—and, therefore, that nothing is expected from us! Nothing can be, when we are so different, so much weaker than our fellows. Alas! alas! for those who hug themselves in such comfortable belief; and when the day of reckoning comes, behold what they might have done—behold it and in the agony of remorse, yearn to do it, and yearn in *vain*. How know we, but our punishment after death, may be to look on all which in life we have neglected; to awaken, as by a flash from Heaven, to its awful consequences; and to know no rest, no sleep, in the wild yearning to perform it, and to feel we have no more the necessary power—and this through weary, weary time, which in Heaven has no measure, in eternity no end! It is an awful thought; one it would be well to ponder on ere it be too late.

That the Bible does give both sympathy and encouragement, even to the most constitutionally weak, is proved by the sweet, gentle, feminine character of Esther. Strength of herself, indeed, she had none; but it was asked, and granted, and so it will be unto all.

To the women of every faith, race, and land, then, her history is alike instructive and inexpressibly consoling; but it is in the hearts of her descendants, the women of Israel, she should be most closely shrined. By us, the festival of Purim should be hailed as something more than a mere rejoicing season, or even as the anniversary of a great redemption. Every woman should take it to her own heart, and remember, with holy joy and thankfulness, that the preservation of her people, which that day recalls, was, under the Eternal, the work of a woman not stronger, not more gifted, than herself. God might equally have worked by other means; but that He did choose so weak and frail an instrument, is right, indeed, to be a source alike of consolation and rejoicing unto us; and strengthen each and all of us in the hope that we, too, may become instruments in His hands for good.

It was not, that Esther was a free agent, or had powers more extended than our own. Though the wife of a mighty monarch, she was captive; and so too are we.

We, too, may individually be thrown into positions begirt with sadness, where the rights and ceremonies of our faith must be adhered to in the secrecy of our own hearths and hearts. Yet may we still be ready at the first call to identify ourselves with those who suffer for our faith—still be enabled to serve the good and holy cause. And those unshackled by peculiar positions, following so publicly and unquestioned the religion of Moses, that they are likely to forget they are the Lord's captives, because man makes them his equal—to whom life is such a quiet routine of uninterrupted employment, that the idea of individuals serving our nation is regarded as a tissue of folly and romance; yet even these can serve the cause of the Jews. We can, each and all, determine to honour our religion ourselves, and so make it honoured. We can introduce such seeds into the hearts of our sons, that Judaism may never want defenders, or such representatives as will raise it, even in its captive state, in the respect and consideration of the nations. Yes! though, through the infinite mercy of the Eternal, such intercession as Esther's is no longer needed, still let us emulate Esther in the elevation and the acknowledgment of our holy faith—in our individual adherence to its spirit and form, through every difficulty and through every woe. Let every returning festival of Purim find us as women, and in our own retired spheres, still loving, still knowing, still working for our holy religion, and determined, through social and domestic conduct, to make its glory, and its comfort, and its beauty, evident to all. We shall not see the fruit of this still and silent working; but we shall feel its efficacy in the calm and tranquil gladness of our hearts and homes.

REVIEW OF THE EVENTS NARRATED BY EZRA AND NEHEMIAH.

BEFORE we conclude this Fifth Period of our subject, we must take a brief review of the condition of our ancestors contemporary with the captives of Babylon; but who, under Ezra and Nehemiah, had returned to Jerusalem. The first captivity caused a complete revolution in the history of the Jews. Their very characteristics as a people, and as individuals, appeared to have undergone a change.

Adversity and captivity retained the Hebrews in that faith, and those forms, which, in their prosperity, they had neglected and despised. Men arose from their ranks gifted with such power as to lead the multitude as with a silken thread—to sever even the strongest and most endearing ties, because such was the word of the Lord, such the law He had ordained. Marriages with the heathen were not alone again forbidden, but actually dissolved. The Sabbath-day, cleansed from the profane employments of buying and selling which had before desecrated it, commanded to be kept holy; an ordinance established amongst the priests, "to charge themselves yearly with a half shekel for the service of the house of God, for the shew-bread, and the continual meat-offering, and the burnt-offering of the sabbaths and the new moons, for the set feasts, and for the holy things, and for the sin-offerings, to make atonement for Israel, and for all the work of the house of our God;" a covenant, entered into under "a curse and an oath to walk in God's law, which was given by Moses, the servant

of God; and to observe and to do all the commandments of
the Lord our God, and His judgments and His statutes."

Nor was this solemn covenant entered into by the *males* of
Israel alone. Their *wives* and their *daughters* are distinctly
and emphatically named (see Nehemiah x. 28), as amongst
those who had voluntarily separated themselves from the
people of the land unto the law of their God, "every one
having knowledge and understanding." And in chap. viii.,
which so impressively and affectingly describes the reading of
the law by Ezra, in the presence of the whole congregation of
Israel, the *women* are also expressly mentioned. "And Ezra
the priest brought the law before the congregation both of
men and *women*, and all that could hear with understanding,"
etc. "And he read therein before the street that was before
the water gate from the morning until midday, before the men
and *women*, and those that could understand; and the ears of
all the people were attentive unto the words of the law."

The scene must indeed have been of mournful interest.
The temple was still unbuilt; the city, by far the greater part,
in ruins. On a pulpit of wood, with the sad memorials of
Judah's departed glory all around him, stood Ezra, probably
now an aged man; for it was some years since he had left
Babylon. On his right and left hand were thronged his
brother Levites, who, voluntarily consecrated to the service
of their God, lent a dignity and solemnity to the proceedings,
reminding the populace of those days when they officiated in
the Temple, and the glory of the Lord was visibly revealed.
Below them, as far as the eye could reach, the people had
gathered themselves as one man, ardent and earnest to hear
once more the words of the Most High God. Men and women
indiscriminately blended, for the law appealed to *both*, and
not then had the blighting words been whispered, that woman
has no power to seek and know the Lord—that the study and
comprehension of the law are for man, not for her. We see
her hastening, even as man, to listen to the words of her God
—to accept, with the whole fervour of her ardent heart, His
covenant; and she is welcomed, not rebuked.

"And Ezra opened the book in the sight of all the people
(for he was above them); and when he opened it all the people stood up: and Ezra blessed the Lord, the great God.
And all the people answered, Amen, Amen, with lifting up
their hands; and they bowed their heads, and worshipped the

Lord with their faces to the ground." And then "the Levites caused the people to understand the law: and they read in the book of the law of God distinctly, and gave the sense, and caused the people to understand the reading." And when the people would have wept—for their own and their ancestor's sinful departure from the commands of the Lord, stood before them more vividly, more appalling, as they thus listened to the law—Nehemiah and Ezra forbade it, for they said, "The day was holy unto the Lord their God; mourn not, nor weep; but go your way, eat the fat, and drink the sweet, and send portions unto them for whom nothing is prepared; for this day is holy unto our Lord: neither be ye sorry; for the joy of the Lord is your strength."

Solemn rejoicing in consequence followed this public reading of the law. The Feast of Tabernacles was proclaimed throughout all the cities of Judea, and observed with such solemnity and gladness as had not been since the days of Joshua the son of Nun, and in exact accordance with the written law of Moses, keeping the feast seven days, and on the eighth day a solemn assembly. A general fast, confession of sins, repentance and prayer, with reading the law, and worshipping the Lord their God, soon after followed, the Levites rehearsing the many tokens of the Eternal's goodness, from the selection of Abraham unto the present time, and the awful wickedness of the people. Then followed the acceptance and sealing of the covenant by the men of Israel, their *wives*, sons, and *daughters* —the selection of the people—the rulers to dwell in Jerusalem —and the rest of the people, one in ten, to be chosen by lot to dwell in Jerusalem, and the other nine to dwell in other cities, and thus re-people the still beautiful, but mournfully desolate land. In the twelfth chapter, we find the selection of priests and officers for the service of the Temple, and the solemn dedication of the wall, "with gladness, and with thanksgiving, and with singing, with cymbals, psalteries, and harps. Also on that day they offered great sacrifices, and rejoiced: for God had made them rejoice with great joy: the *wives* and children rejoiced, so that the joy of Jerusalem was heard even afar off." Officers for the treasuries, offerings, firstfruits, tithes, singers, porters, all were appointed, exactly in accordance with the law of Moses, and "the commandment of David, and of Solomon his son."

The mixed multitude was also separated from the children

of Israel. Even Tobiah, the Ammonite, closely allied to Eliashib the priest, who had weakly allowed him, although an Ammonite, a chamber in the Temple, was cast forth with all his household stuff. No distinction of persons was made. All who had married strange wives, were they united even to the priest and highest officers, were, if they refused to separate from their unlawful connections, scouted from the congregation of the Lord. And thus, after a weary interval, faithfulness to the religion of Moses, and, in consequence, external and internal peace, seemed once more about to be the portion of Judea.

But let it not be imagined that this was either easily or satisfactorily accomplished; or that the noble exertions of Ezra and Nehemiah were productive of enjoyment, and, consequently, of earthly reward. So far from it, that if we read over the books of Ezra and Nehemiah attentively, we must be struck by the repeated mention of humiliation, fast, and prayer with which their efforts were attended—the constant struggle, constant disappointment—the hope roused by a seeming response to their own ardent aspirations, and crushed again by revolt and disobedience. We find both Ezra and Nehemiah repeatedly taking on themselves the burden of their brethren's guilt, and beseeching pardon, as if themselves were the offenders. The prayer of Ezra, in the ninth chapter of the book bearing his name, and that of Nehemiah in his first chapter, are the most exquisite illustrations of pure patriotism that can be found in any history, and should bid our hearts glow with love and veneration towards men who so toiled and suffered for their country and their God. Profane History can give us no nobler and purer patriots than Ezra and Nehemiah. They may tell of warlike deeds and glorious heroism; but it is a nobler heroism, a more exalted valour, which can struggle on to free their countrymen from self-inflicted slavery—from those shackles of the *spirit*, which are far more difficult to remove than the shackles of a tyrant. Ezra and Nehemiah had to work not only against the enslaver, but also against the enslaved, for men's evil passions and rebellious wills were the tyrants who held them chained, and these were to be subdued ere freedom could be achieved, and Judea liberated from the thraldom of her children's sins. Modern patriots in general read the full reward of their exciting enterprise in national prosperity and individual glory. The deaths of Ezra and Nehemiah are not specified; but their books reveal enough to convince us that they toiled unto the end—that personal aggrandisement, earthly distinctions, entered not their thoughts. They had indeed done much : but their lives probably closed ere half their patriotic wishes were accomplished, or their ceaseless exertions crowned with visible success.

And so it must be with all those who embark heart and soul in the glorious service of a people's good. There must be darkness and despondency but too often, even in the noble mind, which has cast behind it all thought of selfish enjoyment, who pines, seeks, aspires after but one glorious goal, the improvement, religious and intellectual, of his species. There must be sadness, there must be disappointment, for such minds look far beyond, into space and time, and hope to compass the advance of an *age* in the brief period of one human life. They feel, they know what should be; they thirst, they struggle after its attainment with a giant's strength, forgetful that in the individual minds of the vast mass of their fellows, there may be but one little grain of the immortal, the intellectual, which is so restlessly working in themselves ; and, therefore, that time only can behold the reception and acknowledgment of those important Ends and Truths, which they so vividly behold.

Those, then, who would serve their fellows, must be armed with patience, with perseverance, which will bid them work on, in the very face of disappointment, and an utter want of sympathy; with hope that will carry them on her angel wings, above the ruggedness and toil of mere earthly labour ; with faith that will look into the future, to behold there the fruition of those seeds which they have, perhaps, even unconsciously sown.

Would we, then, in truth, labour in the cause of God, by endeavouring to benefit our fellows, we must utterly annihilate the vain presumptuous dream that we shall behold our own work, and thus reap a reward which has never yet been found on earth. Why do we see so many turn their shoulders from the wheel at the very moment when they should persevere? Why do we see the best and noblest exertions often checked in their first vigour, and never resumed ? Why do we hear so many, whose words had once been so eloquent with hope of good, in a few brief years speak but of the prevalence of evil, the impossibility of achieving aught of lasting worth? Why? because they look to *present reward*—they expect to see the matured *fruit* before even the *seed* could have taken root; they provided not against disappointment; they studied not the rugged nature of man; they look not back into the past, and comparing it with the present, mark *what was*, and *what is*—and note the long years which intervened before improvements which we now feel so common, that they, are no longer improvements could be accepted and acknowledged. They forget that almost every national benefit conferred on man, was in its first projection deemed a very madness, and more than one of its hapless originators persecuted unto death. Yet the seeds which supposed maniacs planted, *never withered;* they lay in often uncongenial soil, proving their existence, and passing from one mind into another, perchance only by a breath which bore them unconscious of its burden, till in the proper time they burst into full blossom, were cherished, fostered, for men had advanced while that little seed lay in abeyance, and then ripened into fadeless fruit.

Irrelevant as these remarks may appear to our subject, yet a little consideration will prove their application.

In Judaism, as in every thing else, the present is an age of advancement—of improvement. The law, indeed, which God gave, remains pure, perfect, eternal as Himself, needing nought from man; but it is in the *observance* of that law, its *spiritual observance*, in which we remark *progression*, and hail it with glowing thankfulness, as seed, which, when ripened into fruit, will lead us once more to our own Holy Land, and to the restored favour of our God. But we are no enthusiasts to believe this will be either in our own time, or in that of some generations down. We do not suppose, because there is a stir in our ranks—an aspiration after holiness—a struggle with deep-rooted prejudices, — a desire to become purer, more spiritual, more enlightened,—that we shall look upon the *fruit* of such holy seed,—that twenty, fifty, ay, even a hundred years will complete the full perfection of the glorious End for which we aspire now. No! And we would conjure and beseech our brethren, in whose hearts lieth the ardent desire to accomplish national and individual good, to think with us —to despond not, if they behold nothing which would reveal that the holy seed has taken root, but much to make them tremble that it has faded into air. Let them but cease to hope to reap what they sow—let them but look far into Space and Time, and rest content that their labours will then bring forth fruit—only let them nerve themselves to work, without the faintest dream of earthly recompense or visible success, and labour on. They "will have cast their bread upon the waters, and they will find it after many days."

It is not, however, only in a generally national view that we have taken this rapid sketch of the books of Ezra and Nehemiah. They are particularly important to us as women of Israel, burdened as we are with the charge, that Judaism degrades and enslaves us. By the especial mention of *wives* and *women* in every ceremony and covenant with which Ezra and Nehemiah again organised the people, it is very evident that no written or even traditional law then existed to our disparagement. Neither had captivity, and a residence with a heathen people, altered the national equality of the sexes, which in every religious ordinance the Jewish law commanded. This is a very important truth; as the period of Ezra is many years removed from the direct interference of the Almighty with His people: and in such a time of confusion and departure from the pure law, had there been any traditional statute which could have allowed the degradation of the weaker sex, we should find it acting against them in full force. Had the women of Israel been accustomed to join in religious exercises, or to feel themselves of no importance in the congregation of the Lord, it is not likely, that after so long an interval of captivity, when the national ceremonies were compelled to be suspended, we should find them so eagerly flocking to listen to the reading of the law, bringing their children with them to join in the confession and humiliation for national sin, and to enter, heart and soul, into a covenant to walk in the law of Moses. They had no doubt seen enough in their captivity, of the women of other countries, to feel more gratefully than ever, their own superiority in station, intellect, and responsibility. Eagerly and joyfully then they resumed obedience to that law, which guided and protected them with such mild and gentle guardianship, lifting up their hearts to a Father in heaven, who so watched over and tended them, and compelled man to assign them that station of equality and respectful tenderness, which, without such law, would, if we judge of the manners and customs of other and cotemporary nations, have inevitably been refused them.

With this important fact, then, we close our present Period, and with it the records of our female ancestors, which are found in the Bible. Our succeeding Parts will contain notices of those exalted Hebrew females mentioned in Josephus —a brief review of Israel as she was after the erection of the second temple—and the effects of war, dispersion, and persecution, upon her now. We shall find, even there, enough to confirm us in the position we have advanced; but even had we not—even if the records of more modern Judaism presented nothing but a dark and awful picture of social and individual degradation—even if laws were promulgated by erring man, depriving us of our long-granted privileges, and debasing us in the scale of creation much below our brother man—still it would prove nothing but the fearful effects of superstition and intolerance on the human mind. It could not do away with the law which God Himself had given. It dare not term itself divine, if it contradict one item of that which the Bible holds up before us, alike in the precepts given by the voice of God, and in the history of His female children; and, therefore, as in not one precept, in not one mention of woman in the Word of God, can be discovered one evidence of her social or individual abasement, so must not only the Israelite, but his opponents be convinced, that the women of Israel needs no other law, no other faith but her own, to convince her of her immortal destiny and her earthly duties—to guard the hallowed circle of her home—or raise her, as an individual, to perfect equality with man.

SIXTH PERIOD.

Women of Israel during the Continuance of the Second Temple.

[As, in proceeding with her subject, the Author found many more interesting notices of the Women of Israel in Josephus than she at first anticipated, she has been compelled slightly to alter the plan of the Sixth Period from that laid down in the Introduction to the Work. See p. 10.]

REVIEW OF THE JEWISH NATION,

FROM THE RETURN FROM BABYLON TO THE APPEAL OF HYRCANUS AND ARISTOBULUS TO POMPEY.

WE are now to commence a period in the History of the Women of Israel, completely and even painfully distinct from any which had gone before it. Indeed, so complicated, so amalgamated with the histories of other nations, so little purely national is Israel, and so few and far between are the notices of women in the history of the nation from the death of Nehemiah to the dispersion—that there is very very little which we can claim our own, or from which we can glean the consolation and lessons for individual social guidance, which are presented in the word of God. So little is there, in fact, of woman, that we may be censured for dwelling so long on a period which has so little to do with a work entitled "The Women of Israel," as almost to contradict its name. Yet where there are so very few works relative to our history in the vernacular idiom, and still fewer in which the Hebrew himself comes forward with an attempt to fill up the void in national literature, and give the youth of his nation some assistance, distinct from the peculiar tenets which must pervade the writings of the most liberal of other creeds; *we* trust, that to linger a little while on our general history and thus explain away some of the errors and prejudices which have unconsciously gathered round us from *unanswered* accusations, may not be considered unnecessary, or even irrelevant to the subject on which we professed to treat

Where there is no allusion *to* the Women of Israel of the *past*, let it be remembered that we are writing *for* the Women of Israel of the *present*, and, therefore, that we do not depart from the profession of our title. To the men of Israel—the works of our own ancient writers are, or ought to be, open; and they, therefore, cannot need the feeble effort of a female pen: but woman does. She has neither the time nor privilege, nor, in fact, the capability of seeking and penetrating into the vast tomes of stupendous learning, the complicated and allegorical questions and replies, narratives and histories, contained in the works of our venerable teachers; but is she on that account to remain entirely ignorant of the history of her people, in which, whether in prosperity or adversity, in patriotism or persecution, she has ever borne a distinguished part? How is she ever to realise that spirit of nationality and holiness which should be so peculiarly her own, if she knows little of her national history, save from Gentile writers—how know what is demanded of her *now*, if she does not sometimes ponder on the *past*, remembering, while she shudders at the awful sufferings of her people, that what *has been, may again be?* And is she endowed with the same noble spirit which guided her hapless ancestors? Has she the same deep love of her God and His religion, which will keep her faithful in the midst of the horrors of persecution, or amidst the yet more dangerous ordeal of prosperity and peace? How is she to know this if she looks upon herself only as the child of the soil which has given her a home and all its attendant blessings? How is she to feel this if she looks on the history of her people as far too antiquated to concern her now, and lends but too ready an ear to the false tale that ancient and modern Judaism are totally distinct. How is she to reject prejudice, and to separate the true from the false, if all her information concerning the history of her people be derived from Gentile writers? It is expecting far too much from human nature to believe that we can *feel as Jews* only because we are *born such*—more particularly women, who, seeing so little different in the daily routine of their domestic lives from those around them, may be liable entirely to overlook their nationality, and imagine that a formal adherence to peculiar forms and ceremonies is sufficient for them; and, in consequence, know much less of their own history, teeming, as it does, with so much to interest and appal, than that of the country in which they dwell.

The scarcity of Jewish works by Jewish writers is the real cause of this much regretted evil. We have histories without number, and suited to every age and every taste, of other countries; but where shall we find one of the Jews which we can safely put into the hands of our children and youth?* The love of England, of France, of America, is imbibed with their growth, because they know and delight in every event of these their adopted countries; and they would feel the same towards their own land could they learn as much concerning it.

To provide for this want cannot be accomplished in a work like the present. The writer has only mentioned these things to explain why, instead of concluding where the biographies of the "Women of Israel" may appear to conclude, noticing only the few female characters which may be casually mentioned, from the erection of the Second Temple to the Dispersion, she prefers taking a rapid, but connected, survey of the history of her people during that period. Where notices of individuals are scarce, we must endeavour to defend our position from generalities. Analogies may be drawn from the histories of states as well as from the biographies of individuals; and, as we proceed, we shall find that much, which may appear from a mere superficial glance irrelevant to the *Women* of Israel *individually*, will yet so bear upon them *socially*, that our assertion of their non-degradation, their equality and elevation in the Jewish law and in Jewish history, will be strongly and unanswerably confirmed.

The return of the Jews from Babylon did not restore that nationality and exclusiveness which Ezra and Nehemiah hoped, and for which they laboured. With the Babylonish captivity had in truth ended the history of Judæa as a distinct nation. The very division of the tribes appears to have been lost; and instead of the patriarchal territories of Reuben, Simeon, Ephraim, etc., we only read of Samaria, Galilee, Perea, Idumea, and of Judæa as signifying a very trifling portion of what had once been comprised under that name. Two tribes only returned from captivity, and for them the province termed Judæa might have been sufficient; but how changed must

* Milman's is an exception. What we want, are those histories which we can put into young persons' hands; so written that they are read for pleasure, not as tasks.

they have felt was the aspect of their once beautiful land—
how vainly have yearned to behold their brethren occupying
the territories which had been assigned them by God Himself,
and thronging to His one Temple in the feasts He had
appointed? Not only were strangers and aliens within their
land, but ten tribes were lost; and they themselves, though
nominally free, in reality still under the yoke of the Persian
kings. Nor was Palestine any longer the *only* residence of the
children of God. Communities were forming in many parts
of the world, particularly in the many territories of Persia and
in Egypt; and thus, though outwardly bound by the same
religion, inwardly, interests could not fail to be divided,
according to the position which they occupied in connection
with foreign courts.

Of the constant rebellions against their Heavenly King, by
the recurrence of idolatry and those awful practices mentioned
in the previous periods of their history, we no longer hear; but
in their place we find assimilation and intimate connection
with the manners and customs of other nations. In fact, so
intimately blended with the histories of Persia, Macedon, Syria,
Egypt, Parthia, and, finally, Rome, is the history of Judæa
from the Babylonish Captivity to the War, that it is scarcely
possible to divide them, or find any national incidents of
sufficient note as to enable us to dwell upon them as we have
hitherto done. The Eternal had veiled His face from them.
Even in their return we find no evidence that He had restored
them the light of His presence, and acknowledged them once
more as a distinct and holy nation—governed by Himself.
The very religion, therefore, appears to have taken a different
aspect—the High Priest was still nominally the head of the
nation—the ceremonials of the law rigidly and perseveringly
observed—but its beautiful spirit of love, which had entered
into every household, blessing and guiding every domestic
relation, appears to have been entirely lost, from the national
assimilation with other countries. That there were still families
in whom this blessed spirit existed, true and faithful to every
spiritual as well as outward ordinance, cannot be doubted; but
in the darkness enveloping this part of our history, we can only
trace the general departure of nationality and prevalence of
public evil which so repeatedly exposed us to misery and wrath.
Before the Babylonish captivity, even the periods of most awful
iniquity were illuminated by rays from God Himself in the holy

men who, inspired by Him, stood up to threaten or console.
We were not left entirely to our own hearts—to sin, unrebuked; but on our return from Babylon this might no longer be—we *had indeed power* to *subdue sin* and *become holy*, fitted once again to occupy the promised land, and in the face of the whole earth stand forth the chosen people of the Lord; but this conquest was to be achieved by individual and national efforts. The Eternal had instructed us in those things, the observance of which would regain His favour. He left us to pursue our own paths.

During the wars of Alexander of Macedon, and the contests of his successors, Judea repeatedly changed masters—and we therefore perceive how little she can be considered as an independent state. So few claims had she to nationality, that we repeatedly read of the Hebrews joining voluntarily the ranks of their several masters—serving as faithful soldiers to the Greek or Egyptian, and, in consequence, imbibing interests and feelings totally distinct from the Hebrew warriors of the olden time. These soldiers seldom or never returned to their own land, but swelled the Jewish colonies of other states; and therefore, long before the general dispersion, we perceive the prophecy of Moses already in partial fulfilment—proving at once the utter fallacy of the argument entertained by some Gentiles, that the return from the Babylonish captivity is the fulfilment of those glorious and consoling promises contained in all the Prophets—and comforting us by the conviction, that these things are yet to be.

At length, however, the national spirit was aroused; and for a brief interval independence was secured. The awful cruelties of Antiochus Epiphanes, the universal suffering of the whole Jewish people, not only from bodily torment, but from the prohibition of their sacred law (which, of course on the instant became more dear), the desecration of their holy Temple—evils so terrible could no longer be endured; and under the heroic Maccabean brothers, the Jews threw off the yoke of slavery. It was a noble epoch in our history, as full of chivalric daring, of the purest patriotism, of the most heroic perseverance, as can be found in the pages of any history, ancient or modern. They fought for no personal aggrandisement—for no increase of territory—no dominion over their fellows—but simply to purify their land from the abominations which had desecrated its holy soil—to re-establish the religion of their God, and obtain the freedom of their persecuted brethren.

And all this they did. The plan of our present work forbids our lingering on this glorious epoch, and we are compelled to pass it by as briefly and unsatisfactorily as all our other historic notices; but what Hebrew of either sex can read this period of Jewish history, even in the narration of Gentile writers, without such emotions stirring within him as instinctively betray his near connection with the heroic spirits of whom he reads. Have we not patriots and heroes, on whom to dwell with that glowing admiration, so thrilling and so beneficial to our aspiring youth?—and shall we only associate our ideas of the Jewish nation with what she *is*, never casting a thought on what she *was?*

The independence wrought by the Asmonæans, or Maccabees, permitted Judea, for a brief interval, to take her position in the world as a sovereignty governed by her own kings. The gratitude of the people naturally led to the bestowal of the royal dignity on the family of their deliverers. Simon was the only one of the brothers remaining; and, in a general assembly held at Jerusalem, the people made both the High Priesthood and the office of Regent, or Prince of the Jews, hereditary in his family.

Aristobulus the First, the grandson of Simon, was the first who assumed the title of King. His father, John Hyrcanus, and his grandfather, Simon, having been satisfied with their dignity of High Priest, and being acknowledged by foreign potentates and their own people, as Princes of the Jews. The regal dignity lasted but a very brief interval: and those who possessed it, instead of strengthening and nationalising their *home* dominions, endeavouring to restore that ancient and exclusive kingdom which had once characterised Judea, were continually making alliances with the Romans, and other states; becoming, as it were, so blended with them, that it is difficult to regard Judea, even in her well-earned independence, as the holy and peculiar nation, which she had been, and was, in fact, commanded still to be. We find it difficult to recognise her as the same nation which had before occupied the land. Her frequent missions to other countries, her alliances and foreign friendships, could not fail to decrease her nationality, by the constant efflux of Jews to distant lands, where it was scarcely possible for them to adhere to their religion, and the repeated and invited admission of strangers within Judea. We can no longer recognise the High Priest of Moses' ordination, who was to bear on his breast and brow the solemn symbol of his inauguration; who was to minister in the holy of holies, till he seemed, in the eyes of the people, to stand on the very threshold of heaven and receive direct communications from the Most High. We cannot recognise this peaceful and sacred minister in the high priesthood of any who, after the Babylonish captivity, bore that solemn name. The service of the Temple could have been but secondary in the multitudinous affairs, foreign and domestic, which crowded round the Prince or sovereign of Judea. In the law of Moses, the offices were not to be united; because, in the first place, the tribe of Levi were devoted as the elected priests or servants of the Temple; and from them, therefore, no king could have been chosen. In the second, engaged, as a sovereign must be, in unavoidable wars, and other temporal concerns, Moses knew that it was impossible for him to devote himself to spiritual things, as the office of High Priest demanded; and in the third, no king, who, as the leader of armies, must have been a shedder of human blood, could ever have been sufficiently pure to have attended at the altar of the Most Holy. David was not even permitted to build a "House for the Lord"; how much less, then, could he have officiated as High Priest?

In the later kings, one prevention to their obtaining that solemn office, was evaded. They were descended from the priestly line of Joiarib; but that very circumstance proves how completely at an end was the division of land and service, which had formerly characterised Judea and her sons. We are told repeatedly, "unto the tribe of Levi Moses gave not any inheritance; the Lord God was their inheritance, as he said unto them." How then, if the division of the tribes had continued in force, could the office of High Priest and king have been united? How could a king's inheritance be the house of the Lord God alone, as it could and ought to be the priest's? We are particular on this point, because it is often asserted, and by some believed, that the temporary independence of Judea as a sovereignty fulfilled the prophecies; whereas the very fact of the royal family descending from Levi, not from *Judah*, and the complete amalgamation of the tribes, so that their division was impossible, is a sufficient evidence in itself, that the prophecies contained most forcibly in Ezekiel xxxvii. from verse 15 to the end, and in the whole of the forty-eighth chapter, were not, in any one single point fulfilled by our return from Babylon; and, therefore, must allude to a period centuries more distant from the term of the Prophet's life.

Simon, John Hyrcanus, Aristobulus the First, and Alexander Jannæus, reigned successively, uniting, as had been established by the people, the priesthood, with the royal purple. Alexander Jannæus left the crown to his wife Alexandra, and, in consequence, the high priesthood was severed from the crown and given to Hyrcanus, her eldest son. Had he succeeded his mother, as was anticipated, the offices would have probably been quietly re-united. But the daring and aspiring spirit of his younger brother, Aristobulus, by causing internal dissension, gave the first fatal blow to the tottering independence (so called) of Judea. On the death of Alexander, Hyrcanus was, indeed, nominated king, and the children of Aristobulus retained as hostages for their father's conduct; but a single battle between the brothers decided the point. Hyrcanus consented to retire to private life; and Aristobulus was acknowledged king. The high priesthood is not mentioned; and from the continued enmity manifested towards Aristobulus by the Pharisees, who were mostly priests and teachers, it almost appears as if he could not have occupied that station. Even had he been publicly acknowledged high priest, the office must have been merely nominal; for his constant foreign and civil wars would have allowed him but little time or inclination for attention to an office demanding such individual purity and domestic peace.

The independence of Judea (if indeed it can be so called), reckoning from the election of Simon, in 14 B.C. to the appeal of the brothers to Pompey, the great Roman general, in 63 B.C., had lasted eighty years—a period fraught with foreign war and civil dissension, cruelties and miseries; resembling indeed the histories of the nations around them, but utterly incompatible with the pure law, which had guided Judah before the captivity.

We read of Aristobulus the First shutting up his mother in prison, and starving her to death, because his father having left the crown to her, she naturally refused to relinquish her authority; and this man was termed a high priest of a people, whose beautiful law had commanded that even disrespect to a mother should be punished with death! We read of brothers arming against brothers, the most influential imprisoning and even murdering the others—of Jews rising against Jews, or compelled to fight against each other, by joining opposing armies, and adopting the interests of different states. We search in vain for that beautiful spirit, which, had the law been obeyed, would have quieted and hallowed the people. We glance over these sickening horrors, and ask, are these records of a people to whom God Himself spake in thunder from Mount Sinai, and deigned to give a law which all had the power to obey, and which, if obeyed, would have brought down the days of heaven upon earth? Can we marvel as we read the appalling history of the Jews, from their return from Babylon to the last war, at the awful punishments and miseries which have been their portion in every quarter of the globe? And yet, while other nations have passed away for ever, leaving not a trace, we still remain as witnesses of the awful effects of human sin; and more thrilling still, of that changeless truth which had said we should be a people before Him FOR EVER, and therefore we exist;—of that unfathomable mercy, which holds out promises of pardon, restoration, love, and therefore we may hope and pray, and cling to Him as our Rock of Refuge still.

Of our domestic history as a people during these eighty years, we can glean little, except that at the very time the law was so appallingly disobeyed and disregarded—there had arisen men, stern and exclusive adherents of both written and traditional laws. At the very time that in some points all nationality appeared entirely lost, and Judea only sought for temporal dominions, which might be secured and widened by hostile wars or peaceful alliances with other potentates, a spirit of exclusiveness, of rigid observance of some portions of the law had, as in direct contradiction, chained one body of Jews. We are told that "the law, which of old was perpetually violated, or almost forgotten, was now enforced by general consent, to its extreme point, or even beyond it. Prone before on every occasion to adopt the idolatrous practices of their neighbours, they now secluded themselves from the rest of the world, in proud assurance of their own religious superiority—their city, their native soil, their religion, became the objects of the most passionate attachment; the observance of the Sabbath, and even of the sabbatical year were enforced with rigour. In short, from this period (the return from captivity) commences that unsocial spirit—that hatred towards mankind—that want of humanity to all but their own kindred, with which they have been branded by all the Roman writers."*

This, though an eloquent passage, scarcely appears to have sufficient foundation, as actuating the *whole nation*. How could the whole law be rigidly enforced when we see Aristobulus the First acting as we have noticed? How could the laws, alluding to the extreme purity and sanctity of the high priest, have been obeyed, when that office was so often filled by a warrior? How could they be said to keep themselves secluded as a nation, when we see so many thousands fighting under the banner of foreign kings, and accepting offices and dignities at their hands? How could they demonstrate hatred to all mankind when foreign alliances were so often made? And we shall find Herod sending his own sons to Rome for their education, and forming intimate friendships with Anthony and other noble Romans. How could the manners and customs of their land and religion be said to claim their most passionate attachment, when we see kings and people so often sedulously cultivating the manners, arts, games, and vices, first of Greece and then of Rome!

As a people and a nation, whatever they might have *professed*, they *acted* contrary to the law of God, in plunging deeper and deeper into the dark abyss from which no arm either heavenly or earthly could be stretched forth to save them. To a certain body of the nation, the passage we have quoted may be applicable; and it is to them we allude, as in the midst of national anarchy and disobedience, even in the midst of their own too often mistaken zeal, the preservers of the religion and the law.

To obtain a just and impartial estimate of the real character, intentions, and bearings of this body, known as the Pharisees, is to the Hebrew of the present day almost impossible. The Jew, whose mind and heart have been guided by his Talmudical studies, cannot fail to regard them with the deepest veneration and love;—the Jew, who has known them only through the medium of Gentile writers, must unconsciously imbibe a portion of their feeling, and perhaps regard them only as superstitious zealots, following the letter of the law, but not

* Milman.

its spirit. The allusion to the Pharisees, in the book which Gentiles believe divine, and the subsequent explanations in their various commentaries, cannot fail to engender this spirit. But the Hebrew should guard against imbibing it, because the view is false in many of its bearings. It is very difficult, when we only possess histories written by Gentiles in a liberal and friendly spirit, and containing so much with which we can fully sympathise, to realise that on some points as Hebrews, our opinions must form themselves, and not be guided by those of the historian. The Pharisees is one of these—on which we must reflect and exercise our own judgment. The Rabbinical historian would unhesitatingly pronounce them saints, as little less holy or inspired than the prophets themselves;—the Gentiles, as cruel prejudiced bigots, hiding the most fearful vices under the mask of extremest sanctity. Both are probably wrong. The Pharisees were but men, liable to all the failings of humanity; but their religion, even if carried beyond the law, was honest and sincere. The laxity and indifference of the multitude compelled a greater degree of strictness; they were forced to raise around them a wall of exclusiveness, lest they too should fall. They beheld the awful evils creeping steadily amidst all ranks, and was it strange that they should have encouraged an unsocial spirit, and held themselves aloof? They beheld foreign manners and customs destroying the nationality of their people and land; that the law of their God, which they justly held supreme, was disregarded; and was it unnatural that they should seclude themselves, proud of their spiritual superiority—or that their attachment to their land and Temple should increase in passionate intensity, as they beheld it so often trampled upon and desecrated by foreigners? That a want of charity, of humility, of forbearance, marked their religion, might be; nay, in that terrible period it could scarcely be otherwise. Party spirit even then had dried up the channels of social affection, and the spirit of love and meekness which the religion of Moses taught, could not be realised in the popular tumults and crimes for ever raging round them. Individuals there were, no doubt, combining the pure spirit and loving mind with the outward ceremonial; but in this brief sketch we can only generalise. Still, spite of their faults—spite of the too rigid, too exclusive notions, which, if indeed they had existence, originated simply from the fear of being too lax, and sharing the indifference and infidelity of too many of their fellows, the Pharisees must be regarded with veneration as the preservers of the law.

Nor should the Zaddikim, or *righteous*, be passed unnoticed. Of these men we shall find no notice in the Talmudical writers, because they were opposed to much which that party considered of equal sanctity and obligation with the written law of God. But in an historical sketch, which to be correct and useful, must be perfectly impartial, untinged by any individual feeling, we cannot refrain from noticing them, and in a very different spirit, to the abhorrence with which they are generally regarded. However mistaken might have been some of their notions, however impossible to follow the law of the Eternal, without some regard to the useful practical explanations of the Elders; still that they were as sincere and zealous as their opponents, cannot be doubted. These differing views aided materially in the preservation of the law, although the dissensions appeared to, and in fact did, increase the internal miseries and quarrels of Judea.

Given up as they were to their own imaginations, their divine nature—apparently utterly lost in the dominion of evil passions—we seem to read but of anarchy and sin, more fearful than any which had come before, and increasing to a climax which *compelled* the chastisement so long deferred. But if with a faithful heart and unshrinking eye, we look *within* this rolling tumult—if we look *beneath* the stormy waves of dissension and hate and wrath—we trace in the very elements that increased our miseries, those of our final preservation. We behold but the workers of evil, for wickedness ever comes uppermost; but the faithful hearts, the enduring martyrs, the good, the true, are invisible in history, as in daily life, even as the still calm depths of the ocean, whose waves are in tumult and in storm. Never was the divinity of virtue entirely extinct, either in man or nations; and we may rest content and satisfied, that even in the midst of the blackened annals on which our eyes must rest, there was virtue and spirituality, and truth, sincerity, and zeal; and that there will be these to the end of time—invisible in history, invisible in life, but working on silently and unceasingly, even to themselves towards the purity and elevation, and preservation of the religion of the Lord. Nor are such workers confined to one party or one creed : outwardly, each will condemn each—but inwardly they work together.

FROM THE APPEAL TO POMPEY TO THE DEATH OF HEROD.

HYRCANUS' quiet surrender of his authority was not of long continuance. Urged on by Antipater, the father of Herod, he again took the field; and after various alternations of success and defeat, both brothers appealed to Pompey, the Roman general ;—first by commissioners, and then, by command, in person.

Each produced defenders; but many of the nation came to protest against both, as having illegally changed the form of government from the supremacy of the High Priest to that of king : a charge sufficient to confirm our idea that, from the death of Alexander, the former office had completely merged into the latter. The representatives of neither party, however, had much weight. Pompey decided as was best for his own and the Roman interest, only so far favouring Hyrcanus, to tempt Aristobulus to resume hostilities ; convinced that so doing would only prove his weakness, make him prisoner to Pompey, and eventually cause the whole nation to submit; and his prognostics were correct, with the sole exception of a remnant of Aristobulus's faction, who threw themselves into the Temple, valiantly resolved to defend it to the last.

After three months' struggle, during which the cessation of warfare on the Sabbath had given the Romans their only advantage, the Temple was taken, and twelve hundred of the Jews slain. Amongst them were several priests, who, engaged in sacrifices and other services of the Temple at the moment of the assault, never moved from the altar, nor faltered in the performance of a single rite, but fell murdered where they stood, firm and undaunted, and truly warriors of the Lord.

The faction of Hyrcanus were amongst the most furious in the massacre of their countrymen, painfully proving the fearful effects of party spirit, and how completely nationality must at this period have been lost. Hyrcanus was nominated High Priest and Prince of the country, on condition of his

RESTORATION OF HYRCANUS.

submitting to the Roman government, paying tribute, making no effort to increase his territories, and never to resume the crown. The dignity was thus merely nominal, the independence of the country at an end, and Judea little more than a province of Rome.

Aristobulus and his children, his sons and two daughters, were carried captives to Rome. Alexander, one of these sons (and afterwards the father of Mariamne and Aristobulus), escaped on the journey to Rome, and returned to Judea.

The desecration of the Temple by Pompey, in profaning its most sacred precincts, excited towards him the utmost hatred of the Jews—a hatred which caused them to behold his gradual decline with satisfaction, and wherever they were scattered, they simultaneously swelled the ranks of his rival Julius Cæsar.

From this period, in all the internal troubles of Judea, we read of her appealing to the Romans for assistance; the never-failing method of kingdoms being entirely subjected by the party to whom they appeal. Hyrcanus did not enjoy his authority in peace—Alexander, the elder son of Aristobulus, above alluded to, raised a considerable force, and made every preparation for reobtaining the possessions of his father. Gabinius, pro-consul of Syria, called in by Hyrcanus, made head against him, and compelled him to surrender his fortresses. Aristobulus himself, and his younger son, soon after escaped from Rome, and headed another revolt against Hyrcanus, but with worse fortune; the former, severely wounded, was sent back in chains to Rome—Antigonus, through the intercession of his mother, obtained his release.

The form of government was then altered by Gabinius, proving the very small portion of dignity or independence which the nominal prince retained. Hyrcanus had had nothing to do with the revolts; but we find him deprived entirely of the royal authority—and five senates, or sanhedrins, established at Jerusalem, Jericho, Gadara, Amatheus, and Sepphoris. This government continued till ten years afterwards, when Cæsar restored Hyrcanus to his former power.

Though his arms were defeated, the spirit of Alexander, in whom all the courage, enterprise, and chivalry of the Asmonæans appeared to have centred, was still unsubdued. The moment Gabinius had drawn off his forces, intent on the conquest of Egypt, Alexander re-appeared, drove the few remaining Romans into a strong position on Mount Gerizim, and there besieged them—courageously met Gabinius, who had returned on hearing of the revolt, valiantly gave him battle at the head of 80,000 men, and, though again defeated by the irresistible Roman arms, and compelled to take flight, bore with him his unconquered spirit still.

Both he and his father, however, fell victims to the Roman civil war. Cæsar had given Aristobulus his freedom, and commanded him to create a diversion in Palestine in his favour. The adherents of Pompey poisoned the unfortunate prince on his journey. Alexander, who was levying soldiers in Judea for the assistance of Cæsar, was seized at Antioch by Scipio, the friend of Pompey, and beheaded. Antigonus was, therefore, the only scion of the family of Aristobulus remaining. Hyrcanus retained the sovereignty in name, Antipater in power. Winning the favour of Cæsar in his Egyptian wars, Antipater, while he demanded, and received the re-establishment of the High Priesthood for Hyrcanus, obtained for himself all the rights of a Roman citizen, and the procuratorship of the whole of Judea. Soon after, presuming still more on the incapacity of the feeble prince whom he pretended to befriend, and on the friendship of the Romans, he made his eldest son, Phasael, governor of Jerusalem, and his younger, Herod, governor of Judea. This is the first mention of a character so intimately blended with the fortunes of the Jewish people. The brevity of our present sketch will not permit us even to attempt a delineation of the shrewd and sagacious policy, and unfailing enterprize with which this extraordinary man made his way through the most adverse factions, both Jewish and Roman, to the supremacy of Judea, and to the intimate friendship of all the contending heads of Rome. Julius Cæsar, Mark Antony, Lepidus, and, finally, Augustus Cæsar—men whose views were never the same, were yet brought over by Herod's indomitable will, to befriend and exalt him. Much of his public, and almost all his private history will be found in the memoir of Mariamne; and, therefore, needs no mention here. We will merely touch on those points important in a national view. Antigonus, the sole surviving son of Aristobulus, still struggled for the crown. He obtained the succour of the Parthians, who overran Syria and Asia Minor, while he himself, with a large native force, entered Jerusalem and took possession of the Temple; the Hyrcanians, under Herod and

Phasael, holding the palace. The Jews had, at this season, assembled from all quarters to celebrate the feast of Pentecost, and thus thronged the ranks of the contending factions. How little did this national assemblage fulfil the spirit of the beautiful law which had thus called them together! How appallingly they contradicted the spirit of the divine law and social unity; for the encouragement of both which this holy festival had been instituted! They celebrated the delivery of that holy Law which, in the very hour of its commemoration, they defiled!

The partial success of Antigonus in Jerusalem, through his Parthian allies, was more than balanced by the successful intrigues carried on by his rival Herod in Rome, to which city, after a multitude of adventures, he had safely escaped. His entreaty that the sovereignty of Judea might be conferred on the young son of Alexander gave the much coveted honour to himself; and, conducted to the Capitol by Antony and Octavius, he was there, in a *heathen city*, and with *idolatrous sacrifices*, anointed king over the holy people of a Most Holy God!* Will this fulfil the beautiful promises of the prophets —this prove the nationality of the Jewish people at that period? Alas! this was but the commencement of denationalisation!

But though nominally king, and aided by the all-powerful Roman influence, Herod was not universally received as sovereign by the Jewish people until some years afterwards, when Antigonus, entirely defeated, surrendered at discretion; and, in spite of his cowardly entreaties for life, was, at Herod's solicitation, condemned by Antony, and by the axe of a common lictor received his death.

Herod was now, indeed, sovereign of Judea. Never, before the Babylonish captivity, had the crown of Judah thus passed into the family of an alien, who dared not assert himself of royal blood, and whose very birth as a Jew is doubtful. Josephus tells us that Antipater was indeed said, by Nicholaus of Damascus, to be of the stock of the principal Jews who came out of Babylon; but "that assertion of his was to gratify Herod, who was his son, and who came afterwards, by certain revolutions of fortune, to be King of the Jews." It is evident, from this passage, that Josephus himself doubts Herod's Jewish descent; and so must every one who reflects on his

* Josephus; and Jahn's "History of the Hebrew Commonwealth."

character and life. He thought of and pursued his own aggrandisement alone. The kingdom of Judea was no more to him than any other territory; it was no longer a *holy* land —no longer the land of promise under the direct guardianship of the Most High. Where have we found, since the return from Babylon, that divine interference which, in the worst and darkest periods of the kingdom before the captivity, had been so distinctly visible? Where do we ever read of the throne of Judea being obtained by aid of *foreign powers?* the holy kingdom allied with, or subordinate to, the heathen and idolator? The word of the Lord had passed, that the line of David (and consequently the tribe of Judah), was the line of kings appointed, and the only line recognised by Him; and, therefore, every prophecy alluding to the restoration of the kingdom IS STILL TO BE FULFILLED. The very fate of the Asmonæans appears to evince the displeasure of the Eternal in their acceptance of the kingdom; for they were not of *His appointed race*. As deliverers of the heathen, as restorers of the Temple and the religion, they were accepted individually in His sight; but, from the very hour of their assumption of the royal dignity in the person of Aristobulus the First, only one who bore the Asmonæan name, Alexander Jannæus, died naturally in his bed. And not the guilty alone: the young and innocent—even those connected only by the mother's side with the Asmonæans, shared the same awful doom, which hemmed round, as by an impenetrable wall, the whole of that fated race.

Success the most brilliant crowned every foreign policy of Herod. His marvellous ability extricated him from every difficulty, and pushed forward his successes, till he became the terror of all the surrounding nations. The country was at peace, breathing, as it were, once again, from the dissensions and miseries which, till the accession of Herod, had deluged Judea with her own blood. But, though thus prosperous and at peace, it was the peace and prosperity of any of the heathen nations, not of the land of the Lord.

Herod, a very doubtful Jew himself, felt that the strong and exclusive principles of nationality were adverse alike to foreign ambition or domestic greatness. The law of Moses undoubtedly circumscribed the regal power. Nor were foreign conquests compatible with the exclusiveness of the Hebrew people. To remove this barrier, and gradually prepare the minds of his subjects for foreign usages, Herod introduced all the Grecian and Roman games. A theatre was built within, and an amphitheatre without, the walls of Jerusalem. Chariot-racing, boxing, the drama, even the gladiators and wild beasts were then introduced. The people submitted, but with silent abhorrence; for such sanguinary exhibitions as the two last mentioned were completely contrary to the mild and loving spirit of the Mosaic law.

Nor was this all. Building after building, all more or less associated with the Roman and Grecian, rose up at the bidding of Herod. His first magnificent enterprise was a superb palace on Mount Sion; his next was to rebuild and change into a strong fortress, the palace of Baris; to erect citadels at Gaba in Galilee, and at Heshbon in Peræa; and to rebuild Samaria on a scale of extraordinary magnificence, peopling it with his own soldiers, and the descendants of its former inhabitants. At a later period in his reign, he erected a sumptuous palace-fortress, in his usual style of architecture, on the spot where he had defeated Antigonus, seven miles from Jerusalem, round which a superb city speedily arose.

He spent twelve years in the erection and decoration of a maritime city, which he called Cæsarea, and almost entirely colonised with Greeks. It resembled in its sumptuous style of architecture, a city of gorgeous palaces. A great temple dedicated to Augustus, occupied the centre, with two colossal statues, one of Rome and the other of Cæsar; and, of course, possessing the necessary appendages to a Grecian city, the theatre and amphitheatre, in which the usual heathen games were quinquennially performed.

Was it strange then, as they beheld this increase of heathen temples with every newly erected city, that the Jews should forget the magnificence of their monarch in the terrible thought, that slowly, but surely, he was carrying out his design of heathenising their country and themselves? In some parts nationality was still awake, burning to throw off the yoke of one who had sunk them from their proud superiority as the Kingdom of God, to a level with the vassal-kings of Rome; but though their murmurs were loud and deep, though conspiracies were continually forming, Herod retained his power, continuing to support his double character of Jew and Roman to the last.

Hoping to ingratiate his people, and employ the disaffected, he determined to rebuild the Temple, which, from the lapse of

500 years, and its repeated sieges, had become, in some parts, dilapidated and ruinous. At first, the Jews feared that these professions did but conceal the intention of entirely destroying their solemn sanctuary; but the immense preparations before the work of demolition began, removed the apprehension; and with a delight and pride, which, for the time, almost gave Herod favour in their sight, the nation beheld a beautiful fabric crowning Mount Moriah with "masses of white marble and pinnacles of gold." But at the very time he was thus occupied as a Jewish king, he retained his character of a Roman vassal, by presiding at the Olympic games, making such magnificent donations for their support that he was elected their perpetual president; and this man has been denominated the last independent sovereign of Judea—and the hapless people, burdened with his idolatry and sins—as if he were one of them! Who that reflects upon his reign alone, can associate for one moment the blessed promises of the prophets with the kingdom of Judea between the return from captivity and their final dispersion?

The very sending his two sons to Rome for education was a measure directly contrary to the law of Moses. Nor did it proceed only from his anxious desire to conciliate the Romans. Herod was seldom actuated by but *one* motive. Looking upon the sons of Mariamne as his successors, he probably hoped that their Roman education would effectually remove all national prejudices, and render them able assistants in his ardent desire to Romanise his subjects, and gradually do away with all those remnants of that ancient superstition which excluded them from the conquests and ambition of other nations. The Jews, as a nation, were never in greater danger of becoming amalgamated with other countries, than in the reign of Herod; but still the God of their fathers watched over them, preserving them for the sake of His changeless word, as His chosen people still; interfering, not visibly, indeed, because of their awful crimes, but making even their threatening chastisement the means of their preservation.

The law issued by Herod, decreeing that thieves should be sold into slavery out of the country, is another manifestation of his anxiety to adopt every measure for the denationalising of Judea; and, from its direct disobedience to the law of Moses, it was so obnoxious to the Jews, as to annul their rising gratitude for the rebuilding of the Temple. Nor was his last public act, the placing a large golden eagle over the great gate of the Temple, less offensive. It was torn down by two valiant youths, who were unhappily apprehended, and fell victims to his revenge. The horrible disease under which he laboured increased his sanguinary propensities. Execution after execution followed, till scarcely a family was spared the agony of bereavement. His last barbarous order, that all the principal families of the nation should be seized, shut up in the Hippodrome, and murdered the instant of his own death, that he might insure a general mourning, was happily disregarded, and the victims spared.

And with such a command died Herod, misnamed the Great, in the second year of the Christian era, and after a reign of thirty-four years as undisputed monarch.

He has been termed the last independent sovereign of Judea: but even in this brief survey, we have seen enough to convince us that the Jewish people were never further from national independence than in his reign; that though a strong party of the people still remained zealous and earnest in the national cause, yet the extreme laxity of the Mosaic code, the fearful innovations adopted from heathen and foreign customs, the close intimacy with the Greeks and Romans, must have presented fearful temptations to the people generally, and hastened that day of destruction and dispersion which the eye of Omniscience saw, could alone preserve His holy law from annihilation, by its complete amalgamation with the surrounding nations.

FROM THE DEATH OF HEROD TO THE WAR UNDER FLORUS.

For nine years the throne of Judea was occupied by Archelaus, the son of Herod and his sixth wife, Malthæ, a Samaritan. Little of national interest occurred during that period except a constant reference to Rome, for the claims of Archelaus were disputed by his brother, Herod Antipas—repeated insurrections of the Jewish people, and, in consequence, numberless executions—and the increasing power of the Romans within Judea, who overspread the country, and ruled with such despotic hand, as to cause innumerable adventurers to spring up, collecting daring bands around them, who, either as robbers or fanatics, increased the wretchedness of the people. Archelaus appears to have neither possessed nor exercised any kingly power. In fact, we can scarcely regard him either as a Hebrew, or a Hebrew king. His marriage with Glaphyra, the widow of his brother Alexander, and the mother of children by him, was in direct disobedience to the law of Moses, and consequently very obnoxious to the people; and so completely were himself and his kingdom in the power of the Romans, that the emperor would not even allow him the title of king, recognising him simply as Ethnarch of Judea. In the tenth year of his reign, he was suddenly summoned to Rome, and thence banished to Vienne in Gaul, and all his estates confiscated. From that hour, though one or other noble Hebrew was continually rising, with claims to the sovereignty, Judea sunk into a Roman province dependent on the prefecture of Syria, with a subordinate administration of its own in a Roman governor, generally of the equestrian rank—and recognised in history as Procurator of Judæa.

Coponius, Marcus Ambivius, Valerius Gratus, and Pontius Pilate, successively enjoyed this office. During the reign of Caligula, we again read of the Jews being persecuted for their religion. That emperor, anxious to be universally acknowledged as a god, was furious that a nation of captives (for such the Jews actually were) should dare to worship other than himself, treated them with even more severity than any other of his subjects. In Rome, Syria, and Egypt, the nation felt the effects of the imperial tyranny; but its only effect was to draw them yet closer together, and increase the value of that sacred religion, which both foreign and native princes, seemed so determined to undermine.

In Alexandria, their sufferings equalled the previous cruelties of Antiochus Epiphanes. The Roman Prefect of the period was Flaccus Aquilius, whose tyrannical oppressions even surpassed those of the Emperor himself. He was the first to deny the Jews their rights of citizenship; and this without the smallest provocation on their part. Two quarters of the city were occupied by Jews, though many were also scattered about the other parts. Without any given reason, they were ordered to remove into a district so small, that they were compelled to spread along the sea-shore, and take refuge even in the cemeteries.* Their homes were pillaged, the contents of their magazines and shops publicly divided; pestilential disorders, from the heat and famine of their cooped-up abodes, broke out most fearfully; and, when rendered desperate by their condition, they left their assigned quarter, a general massacre ensued. The sword and club, fire, scourging, suffocation, all were employed against them. Neither man, woman, nor child escaped; and this continued, until, at length, the arrest of Flaccus, by order of the Emperor, put an end, in a measure to these atrocities. In Babylon also there were persecutions, whose origin our readers will find in the authorities so often quoted, Josephus and Milman. In Judea, images were raised all over the country, and an edict issued to place the statue of Caligula in the Temple of Jerusalem. Once more the national spirit was aroused. Thousands of the Hebrews of either sex, and every rank and age, unarmed, and clad in sackcloth and ashes, traversed the land, solemnly protesting their intention to sacrifice their lives rather than consent to this awful profanation of their Temple. Petronius, an upright and humane man, sought to dissuade them from their resolution, urging the power of the Emperor, the submission of other nations, and the horrors of war.

"We have no thoughts of war," was their unanimous reply; "but we will submit to be massacred rather than thus infringe our Law:" and they fell with their faces to the ground, boldly offering their throats to the sword.

The humanity of Petronius delayed the execution of the imperial mandate, on pretence of allowing time for the statue to be finished; but it was to a native prince, yet more than to Petronius, that the Israelites owed their security.

On the early and romantic history of Herod Agrippa, the son of Aristobulus and grandson of Mariamne, we cannot here be permitted to linger. He had been taken to Rome by his mother, Berenice, directly after his father's murder; and there, enjoying the favour and friendship of many noble Romans, had passed his youth. His varied fortunes might fill a volume. We can here only make such mention of him as is connected with this general sketch. Caligula had made him King of Gaulanitis, Batanea, and Trachonitis, and Tetrarch of Galilee and Peræa. Greater part of what had

* Will not this remind us of a modern persecution ? Alas ! the History of the Jews can scarcely ever be considered *Past*.

formerly been the Holy Land in consequence belonged to him;
but Judea was still possessed by Rome.

Though educated in the Roman capital, and continually
residing there, even after he was termed King of the Jews,
Agrippa appears to have retained that strong feeling of
nationality, and earnest love for his country and religion, so
peculiar to the valiant founders of the Asmonæan race.
On hearing of the disastrous alternative proposed to his countrymen in Judea—the desecration of their Temple or their
entire destruction, he invited Caligula to a banquet, and
treated him with such extraordinary splendour as to excite
the astonishment of even that luxurious sovereign, who, in
the moment of enjoyment, desired him to ask a boon, which
he swore to grant. The true Asmonæan blood flowed in the
veins of the grandson of Mariamne. It was easy to have
asked increase of dominion—of revenue—and thus have
aggrandised himself; but not such was his request! He
entreated the repeal of the fatal edict; and, after a struggle
between wounded pride and his attachment to the petitioner,
Caligula consented, and the decree was suspended.

The murder of Caligula followed. Agrippa alone paid him
the last honours. He could forget the vices of the man in
the attachment of the friend. The peaceful acknowledgment
of Claudius as emperor was mainly attributable to this Jewish
prince, and Claudius did not forget the obligation. The in-
vestiture of all the domains of the great Herod was conferred
on Agrippa; Judea and Samaria were once again united with
Galilee, Peræa and the provinces beyond Jordan—forming one
independent kingdom, which a public edict proclaimed as a
donation from the Emperor to Agrippa; between whom a
treaty was formally concluded.

Once more, then, for the brief interval of three years, did
the Hebrews breathe in religious and moral freedom. Once
more the reins of government were held by a native prince,
whose Asmonæan descent rendered him universally popular,
save to some stern zealots, whose factious spirits were ever on
the watch for turbulence and blood. Once more we seem to
associate with a people following the Law of God, ruled by a
prince whose most ardent desire appeared to follow the statutes
of Moses with the utmost exactness! Daily sacrifices were
offered, legal impurities strictly prohibited, taxes remitted, the
religion and comfort of his people made his first object; while

the munificence and splendour of his court, the sumptuous buildings he erected, surrounded him with all the pomp and power of an independent sovereign. His brief reign, marked as it is with such meek and gentle authority in the sovereign, such calm and peaceful nationality in the people, shines forth like a bright star amidst the troublous wars and stormy clouds of awful darkness which it followed and preceded. Its beams had power to disperse, for a brief interval, the dim shadows of the PAST; but the black wings of the FUTURE gathered round and shrouded up its mild light in such awful darkness that we almost forget it ever shone.

The death of Agrippa, while it occasioned the deepest grief amongst the Hebrews, excited the most brutal exultation amongst the Greek inhabitants of Cæsarea and Sebaste. The cause of this enmity appears an impenetrable mystery, Agrippa having treated them with unvarying kindness. Their insolent conduct occasioned Claudius to command the cohorts in their city to remove into Pontus, and their places to be filled with drafts from the legions in Syria. We are particular in mentioning this, because Josephus believes it to be the primary cause of the Jewish War. The mandate of the Emperor was not executed, but the disgrace was equally the same; and, rankling in the hearts of the troops, exasperated them yet more against the Hebrews, and incited those horrible acts of oppression and cruelty which at length goaded Judæa into a general revolt.

The son of Agrippa (who bore the same name) being considered too young to succeed him as sovereign, Judæa relapsed into a Roman province. Agrippa remained at the court of Claudius, imbibing Roman feelings and Roman principles so completely to the exclusion of nationality, as caused him, in the war which followed, basely to adhere to the Roman party, and to make no effort to ameliorate the condition of his countrymen. He appears to have lived occasionally at Jerusalem, at Alexandria, and at Rome, enjoying at the former city the title of King, and the power of appointing High-Priests; but otherwise his was a very empty dignity—the real government of the country resting in the hands of the Procurators. Rome, however, was his usual residence; its luxurious enjoyment being more according to his vitiated taste than the bold stand for independence which his unhappy countrymen were making. The term of his death is uncertain; but he died, as he had lived, forgetting the calamities and ruin of his country in the morally degraded, but physically secure condition of a Roman vassal. He was the last, either of the Asmonæan or Idumean race, who bore the title of King.

Meanwhile, Zadus, Tiberius (an apostate Egyptian Jew, and consequently, yet more odious to the people than the Romans themselves), Cumanus, Felix, Festus, Albinus, and Florus, had been successive Procurators of Judæa; occupying a period of rather more than twenty years—a term brief in itself, but fraught with increasing misery to the inhabitants of Palestine. Each Procurator appeared more oppressive, more exacting than the last. Insults from the Roman soldiery, constantly accompanying those religious forms and ceremonies, which, in consequence, had become yet dearer, were answered by fiery spirits ripe for vengeance; and this, of course, was followed by indiscriminate slaughter of the Jews. Massacres of hundreds, even of thousands, took place under every Procurator, not only in Judæa, but in Syria: and we are told that, after the defeat of the Romans under Cestus by the excited Hebrews, the citizens of Damascus massacred ten thousand of their Hebrew brethren, notwithstanding their own wives were all attached to Judaism.

Pillage and insult of course accompanied these fearful massacres. All legal authority was at an end. Though the high priesthood was retained, the temple worship continued, the outward ordinances of the feasts and the fasts were observed, yet the beautiful laws, guiding not only communities but households, were swallowed up in the vortex of oppression, insult, and misery which, under the administration of Florus, reached its crisis. The evil passions of man were alone visible. Robbers and assassins, the last blaspheming the mild law of Moses by pretending its authority for their deeds of blood—were amongst the Jews themselves—and devastated both province and city. Divided within themselves—so goaded by oppression that the dictates of humanity were unheard—party spirit utterly preventing that national union which alone could hope for success—without a leader—without a plan—for the most part regardless of the laws of either God or man; such was the condition of the country on the eve of its general revolt. Darkness, morally and mentally, had gathered round; and it was no marvel. The return from Babylon had been granted as a trial of their return to their God and the pure

DISTRACTED STATE OF JUDEA.

worship of their ancestors. He inspired a heathen sovereign to grant them liberty and independence. It was in their power then to have come back, heart and soul, to the pure and faithful observance of His law, to the making the Land of Promise once more a Holy Land—resting on the blessing, the guidance, the sovereignty of their God. He gave them free will to choose, and we have seen that choice:—a union from the first with surrounding nations, a lingering amidst the heathen lands, or invitations to the heathen within their own—adoption of heathen customs—faithful in the hour of persecution, only to relapse into indifference when the iron rod was withdrawn— the Priesthood, the Sovereignty stained with crimes, even to read which, causes the blood to curdle—alliance with the Heathen Mistress of the world, instead of that pure reliance on the Eternal to increase prosperity and dominion, which His law ordained—the holy religion He deigned to teach, so fitted for every class and condition of men, split into opposing factions, arming each against the other—statues and images desecrating the Temple and the land, erected indeed by the Romans, but originating primarily in the Jewish assimilation and alliance with that nation. Was it marvel that the Eternal, in His justice, should make the sin of their assimilation with other nations the very means of their punishment—and that the power they had courted, flattered, made voluntary submission to (because the Roman name was omnipotent in earthly glory, earthly greatness, forgetting that if they trusted in and served their God, His word had gone forth to make them greatest amongst the nations)—was it marvel that that power should be the instrument in the Eternal's hand to execute His wrath? We shudder at the horrible oppressions of which we read. Its *human* agency must excite our abhorrence, as it would the anger of the Lord; but on themselves the Jews had hurled it; they reaped the wretchedness their own hands had sown.

But let it not be supposed, in the fearful state to which the nation was reduced, that there were none to uphold the glory of the Lord, and be His witnesses on earth. In the tumultuous annals of the period—in the vast and whelming ocean of despair and misery and crime, how may the historian discern and bring forward those who were yet faithful and accepted servants of the most high God? Yet even as the Eternal promised that Israel should never cease from being a nation before Him, so has He equally promised that He would never be without His witnesses on earth; and, therefore, are we bound to believe that even in this awful epoch of Jewish history, ay, throughout its dark annals of previous years, there were yet, as there had been in the days of Elijah, "seven thousand who had not bowed the knee to Baal." In every faction, every party, there were noble and faithful spirits of either sex acting or enduring a martyr's part—leavening many a mass of otherwise foul iniquity, and as acceptable to the Almighty as the saints of old. We see them not; we know them not, for not on earth may we " discern between the righteous and the wicked "—not on earth may their fate be distinct—not in the threatened vengeance of the Eternal might a miracle interpose to protect His faithful from the destruction waiting the rebellious and the sinful, but in His heaven, the distinction between him that serveth Him and him that serveth Him not, was made. And therefore did He permit universal misery and destruction to whelm all on earth, as a warning to the nations, as a witness of His word, a fulfilment of His threatened wrath for disobedience; preparing for the "thousands that had not bowed the knee to Baal," such transcendant glory and unspeakable happiness with Him that the evils they had endured below seemed but as a "watch in the night,"—or as the transient pang of "yesterday when it is passed."

In this rapid and very imperfect sketch of the history of Judæa, from the return from Babylon to the commencement of the war under the administration of the odious Florus, A. C. 66, we have seen how little of rest or independence she enjoyed—that in fact massacre and persecution even for religion may be dated many years, even centuries, before the general dispersion—that the national divisions of tribes, both of land and people, were entirely lost—the throne not once occupied by that royal branch of David which the Eternal has so expressly promised—that the Jews had settled by their own will in various parts of the world besides Jerusalem. And, having seen all this, do we need more than a knowledge of our own history to refute the assertion of our adversaries that our return from Babylon fulfilled the prophecies? Shall we not rather, in deepest gratitude and consolation, take them to our hearts and believe in their fulfilment YET TO COME! rejoicing even as did the venerable Akiba, who laughed when his companions wept at beholding a fox run out from the place where the Holy of Holies once stood; and, being asked the reason of such

unseemly mirth, replied by inquiring wherefore they wept:
"Should we not weep," they answered, "when we see the curse
so clearly verified; 'for the mountain of Zion, foxes shall walk
upon it!'"

"And therefore do I laugh," replied the venerable man.
"Whilst the evil remained unaccomplished, there might have
been doubts entertained for the fulfilment of the good promised
by our prophets; but now, when we see the evil coming to pass,
can we possibly doubt the eventual fulfilment of the consolation
of Zion, and does not God rather reward than punish?" And
shall we not also rejoice; for Akiba's hope is ours!

THE MARTYR MOTHER.

IN a time so fraught with national confusion, foreign alliances,
treacherous peace, or destructive war, as the period which our
sketch comprises, history reveals but little to aid us in our
attempt to delineate the character and condition of our female
ancestors. Yet that little is most important, tending unanswerably to prove the exaltation of our social position, the
elevation of our individual character, and also to convince us
that there was not a single law then in force that could, either
morally, physically, or socially debase us. We shall find the
influence of woman actuating man, in more than one instance,
for the evil unhappily, also with the good; but the very power
of the evil is, as we have before said, an argument in favour
of our equality and freedom.

During the persecution under Antiochus Epiphanes, the sufferings of the women of Israel must have been as fearful, as
their constancy and fidelity were powerful proofs of the perfect
adaptation of the Law of the Eternal to their temporal and
spiritual wants. Never could a religion which made them
soulless slaves, have become so dear, so part of their very
hearts, that it was easier to endure torture and slavery and
death, rather than depart from it themselves or refuse its
privileges to their infant sons. Eighty thousand persons, men,
women, and children, slain in the forcible entrance of Antiochus within Jerusalem, and forty thousand of both sexes
sold into slavery, was the horrible preface to the misery which
followed. Every observance of the Law, from the keeping of

the Sabbath and the covenant of Abraham, to the minutest form, was made a capital offence. Yet, in spite of the scenes of horror so continually recurring, the very relation of which must now make every female heart shrink and quiver—yet were there female martyrs baring their breast to the murderous knife, rather than bow down to the idol, or touch forbidden food. Women, young, meek, tender, performed with their hands the Covenant of Abraham upon their sons, because none else would so dare the tyrant's wrath; and, with their infants (for whose immortal souls they had thus incurred the rage of man) suspended round their necks, received death by being flung from the the battlements of the Temple into the deep vale below; others were hung, and cruelties too awful to relate practised upon others. Yet no woman's spirit failed; and what must have been their attachment to their holy religion, what their sense of its responsibility, and its immortal reward, what their horror of abandoning it themselves and cutting off their sons from its sainted privileges, to incur martyrdoms like these? It is useless to argue that persecution always creates martyrs, as opposition kindles constancy. The religion degrading or brutalising woman never yet had martyrs. The Catholic, the Protestant have had their martyrs in young and feeble women equally with ourselves: because their religion, founded upon ours, shares its heavenly privileges and spiritual love, and twines itself so round woman's clinging breast, that it is far easier to die for it than live without it, by apostacy and falsehood. But where do we find a Mahommedan female enduring martyrdom rather than forsake the religion of the Prophet (so called)? History does not present us with one example; and why? The reply is easy. We will not say one word against the religion itself; because equally with the Nazarene, it is doing the work of the Eternal, and teaching many nations to worship the one sole God. But its doctrine degrades woman in very truth to be the slave of man—gives her neither temporal nor spiritual privileges—treats her, looks on her as being without soul, or, if possessing one, created even in Heaven only to minister to man's pleasures.* Is it marvel then, the Eastern women are now indeed degraded, or that amongst them we should never read of martyrs? But

* Such at least are its *reported* doctrines. We cannot vouch for their truth or falsehood, not knowing sufficient of the religion itself, or its followers.

not such were the women of the East when it was peopled by the nation of the Lord!

Where, in the vast tomes of history, sacred or profane, shall we find a deed more heroic, a fortitude more sublime, than is recorded of Hannah, the Hebrew mother, during the persecution of Antiochus? We read in the 2nd Maccabees, chap. vii. (confirmed also by all our Hebrew writers), that a mother and her seven sons were taken, and brought before the tyrant; who, in the wantonness of cruelty, commanded them to eat the forbidden meat, commencing first with the more moderate torment of whips and scourges, but heightening them gradually to torments, which we leave our readers to peruse in the chapter we have quoted; for the soul sickness so to dwell upon them, as deliberately to write them down: we will content ourselves with repeating the words they spake in the midst of those appalling sufferings; for surely they are in themselves witness of what the religion of the Eternal taught.

"What wouldst thou ask or learn of us?" the first said: "We are ready to die rather than transgress the law of our fathers." And as his brethren beheld his lingering torments, instead of failing, they exhorted one another, and their mother, to die manfully, saying thus, "The Lord God looketh upon us, and in truth hath comfort in us; as Moses, who in his song witnessed to their faces, declared: And he shall be comforted in his servants." To the second the question was put, "Wilt thou eat?" under threat of similar tortures, which he had witnessed but in vain. "Thou, like a fury, takest us out of this life," he said in the very agonies of death; "but the King of the World *shall raise us up*, who have died for his laws, *unto everlasting life*." The third himself stretched forth his limbs for the torture, saying, "These I had from Heaven, and for His Law I despise them, for *from him I expect to receive them again*." Inasmuch as the king and those that were with him, marvelled at the young man's courage, for that he nothing regarded his pains. The fourth then suffered; and he said, "It is good being put to death by man, to look for hope from God *to be raised up again for Him;* as for thee, thou shalt have no resurrection to life." And the fifth, in his dying agony, calmly looked upon the king, and said, "Thou hast power over men, but art corruptible; thou doest what thou wilt; but think not our nation is forsaken of God; but abide awhile, and behold His great power, how He will torment thee and thy seed." And the sixth being ready to die, emulating his brother's constancy, addressed the tyrant, " Be not deceived without cause : we suffer these things for ourselves, having sinned against God, therefore marvellous things are done unto us; but think not thou, who takest in hand to strive against God, that thou shalt escape unpunished."

Nor was it one alone who thus endured. The Hebrew mother witnessed these agonising tortures, done not unto one, but unto six of her cherished offspring. Yet how do our elders speak of her: " The mother was marvellous above all, and worthy of honourable memory; for when she saw her seven sons slain within the space of one day, *she bare it with a good courage, because of the hope that she had in the Lord.* Yes, she exhorted every one of them in her own language, filled with courageous spirit, and stirring up her womanish thoughts with a manly stomach, she said unto them, 'I cannot tell how ye came into my womb, for I neither gave you breath nor life; neither was it I who formed the members of every one of you; but, doubtless, the Creator of the world, who formed the generation of man, and found out the beginning of all things, will also, of His *own mercy, give you breath and life again*, as ye now regard not your own selves for His law's sake.'"

Quaint and terse as this language is, and devoid of all ornament, yet how emphatically it breathes of the extent of this mother's trial, the struggle with her "womanish" feelings, and her triumph over nature, over humanity, through that superhuman faith! Nor is the trial over. One still remained—her youngest born; probably still the tender and best-beloved of his mother—one round whom the bleeding tendrils of her lacerated heart must have clung in such unutterable love; her last, her loveliest; and, evidently, from the tyrant's own words, one in the first and freshest prime of youth, when life has so many rich enjoyments, it seems doubly hard to turn from them to the cold, dark grave ; and heaven's perfected happiness, to such ardent spirits, feels dim and distant, compared to the present joy of earth. We know he was of such age, and such aspirings, else the temptations of the tyrant would not have been couched in promises to make him a rich and happy man, and take him for his friend, and trust him with affairs, only on condition of his deserting the law of his fathers: and when the young man would not hearken to him, the king called upon the mother, and exhorted her with many words to counsel him to save his life. He believed nature, in such a case, must triumph; for he knew not the hope beyond the grave, which could still the throbbings of maternal love; and bid, even on earth, the Angel triumph over the Human—the Immortal shine above the Mortal!

Calmly she listened to the tyrant's "many words," and then bowing to him as about to obey, addressed her son in her own language, "O my son, have pity on me who love thee, and gave thee suck three years, and nourished thee, and brought thee up unto this age, and endured the troubles of education, I beseech thee, my son, look upon the heaven and upon the earth, and all that is therein, and consider that God made them of things that were not, and so was mankind also. Fear not this tormentor; but, being worthy of thy brethren, take thy death, *that I may receive thee again in mercy with thy brethren.*" And even while she was yet speaking, the young man said, "Whom wait ye for? I will not obey the king's commandment; but I will obey the commandment of the Law that was given unto our Fathers by Moses. And thou that hast been the author of all the mischief against the Hebrews, shalt not escape the hands of God; for we suffer because of our sins; and though the living God be angry with us a little while for our chastening and correction, yet He shall return, and be again with His servants. But thou, O most godless man, and of all others most wicked, be not lifted up without cause, nor puffed up with uncertain hopes, lifting up thy hand against the servants of God; for thou hast not yet escaped the judgment of Almighty God, who seeth all things. For our brethren who have now suffered a short pain, *are dead under God's covenant of everlasting life;* but thou, through the judgment of God, shalt receive just punishment for thy pride. But I, like my brethren, offer up my body and life for the laws of our Fathers, beseeching God that He would speedily be merciful unto our nation, and that thou, by torments and plagues, mayest confess that He alone is God, and that in me, and in my brethren, the wrath of the Almighty, which is justly brought upon all our nation, may cease." Then the king being in a rage handled him worse than all the rest, and took it grievously that He was mocked; so this man died undefiled *and put his whole trust in the Lord*. Last of all, after the sons, the mother died. "Let this be enough," the writer concludes, "now to have spoken concerning the idolatrous feasts, and the extreme tortures."

Enough? It is enough, indeed, for every Israelite to dwell upon, not with shuddering horror, not with that squeamish kind of affected feeling which pretends incapacity to look fearful truths in the face, but with emotions of intense thankfulness, that such a record has been left, bearing such faithful witness as it does to the true Israelite's belief. It is not merely a record of superhuman heroism, alike in male and female. It is not merely a proof of the little moment in which torture and death were held by the Hebrews, compared with which the far-famed firmness of Spartan and Roman mothers sinks into nothing. It is the *doctrines* betrayed throughout, which revealed at such a moment, must have impregnated the very existence of the Israelite; and these doctrines may be treasured up as invaluable evidences of all which was taught by our Holy Law, however some may disbelieve the actual Tale of Martyrdom in which they are disclosed. The books of the Maccabees in the Apocrypha are on all points the exact counterpart of the same history in Josephus, and also of Antiochus Epiphanes in Rollin.

There can be no doubt that the books were written by a *Hebrew* for his countrymen; and therefore the words put into the mouths of the sufferers, must have been the exact transcript of the Hebrew's true belief. If the doctrine of immortality—that hope beyond death and the grave—was, as it is reported, unknown and unrevealed to the Israelites, what could have inspired, not only the hope itself, but the expression of that hope, in the very midst of torture and anguish which human nature of itself could never have sustained. We have quoted the words of the sufferers at full length, only to illustrate this doctrine—to prove, that, all of immortality—of resurrection —of being with God in Heaven—of re-union there with our beloved ones—of the transientness of the severest agonies below compared to the permanency of bliss awaiting us above—that all was revealed to us, all was known to every Hebrew—male and female, childhood and age—believed in, acted upon, ages before the advent of that religion which was the first, her followers believe, to inculcate such doctrines. In a work like the present we may not dilate on this glorious subject as much as inclination prompts—but oh, let us not, by present indifference, by stagnant ignorance, or fearful shrinking from the idea of death, give our opponents only too much reason to believe, that to them alone has been revealed the consolation, the glory, the blessedness of the belief and hope in Immortality.

Great emergencies will often create great characters; but in the narrative which we have been considering, we read something more in the character of the Hebrew mother, than even the heroism which she displayed. By her close connection with her sons, in being brought before the tyrant, and condemned to share their fate; it is clear that though a woman in Israel, her influence must have been supposed of some consequence. That her sons owed their all to her, even to their education, and that her influence on them was very great, we read alike in her own words, and in the appeal of the king to her, to save by her exhortations her youngest born. There is no mention of a father; she had probably been from the infancy of her children, that especially beloved of the Eternal, a widow in Israel. And in the calm courage, the noble words of each of her sons, we learn the education she had given. They had probably been amongst the valiant, though unsuccessful defenders of their land; amongst the faithful few, who, in the very face of the persecutor, dared to obey the law of Moses, and refused every effort to turn them from their God. Would this patriotism, this devotedness, have come at the moment needed, had it not been taught, infused from earliest boyhood—by example as well as precept? A mother in Israel could be herself no warrior, but she could raise up warriors—she could be no priest, but she could create priests—she could not face the battle's front, or drive the idolatrous invader from God's Holy Land—she could not stem the torrent of persecution and of torture; but she could raise up those who would seek the one, and by unshrinking death, bear witness to the fruitless efforts of the other; and it was these things this heroic mother did. She had trained up her boys in that faithfulness, that constancy, which could only spring from virtue. She must have taught them, aye, infused it with her very milk, that the pains and troubles of this world are, in their sharpest agony, but of a moment's duration, compared with the everlasting blessedness awaiting them in Heaven. She must have taught them, that death itself was but a darkened portal, opening into an infinity of glory; that man, might indeed, have power over this present life; but over the future what mortal could have dominion? —that all they possessed, even to the members of the body, life itself they had had from God, to whom they were ready to resign them, knowing that from Him they would be received again—that even in that extremity of bodily torture, their lot was happier than that of their tormentor, for *their* heritage was everlasting, but *his* was corruptible, and vanishing with a breath. She must have taught them in the true spirit of the Law, that, however persecuted, however sinful in themselves, their nation would *never* be forsaken by God; yet, that it was for *their sins* they suffered, not to gratify the exulting tyranny of their persecutor, but for themselves, for the sins of their hapless countrymen. Their sufferings in the flesh were to make manifest to the whole world, God's judgment upon His children for their national sin; but that still to the virtuous, even such a death had no sting, for their earthly sufferings bore witness to the *justice;* and their Heavenly reward to the *mercy* of their God. She must have infused within them, that pure beautiful spirit of self-devotion, which is *woman's own*, and can only be imparted by woman to the more selfish, more calculating man, else we should not find the last and youngest martyr, beseeching God even at that terrible moment, to turn His just wrath from His people; and that the sacrifice of himself and his brethren for the laws of their fathers, might be so accepted as to cause the national misery to cease. All this (and in such doctrines, how much more is comprised than we can trace in a brief survey!) she must have taught her boys. We hear her herself refer to the labours of education, as an additional incentive to her sons' obedience; and we must be convinced, that all their heroism, firmness, self-devotedness, sprung from her, and had become part of their very being, years before such exalted principles were thus called upon to be displayed.

Will not this narrative then strongly confirm all that we have stated in the second chapter of our second period, as elevating the position and marking the duties of Jewish mothers? Will it not prove, that the mothers of Ancient Israel, were perfectly aware of all the responsibility attendant on them, in the education of their sons—and that they really were included in the charge of Moses, contained in Deut. vi. 20—25. The education given by this martyr mother to her sons, is an exact illustration of the manner in which these ordinances were obeyed, including also the instruction in the history, theocracy, and claims of Israel down to the times in which they lived. And how could this be, if the Jewish female were lowered by social treatment to the position of a slave or heathen, on whom no responsibility, no religious duty devolved. Be the narrative itself truth or tradition, it matters not; the ancient fathers would never have given woman that influence and elevation in *tradition*, which had not its foundation in truth—would never have made her occupy that position in tradition which the ordinances of the law forbade. This consideration is most important to us; for we are now rapidly advancing to the period, whence it is said modern Judaism, in contradiction to ancient Judaism, takes its rise. There will be many perhaps to agree with the theories formed on Scripture, already brought forward; but to declare it is modern, or what is termed Rabbinical Judaism, which they condemn. We hope to satisfy such enquirers, that even in rabbinical Judaism, there is no foundation whatever for the degradation of woman.

And what were the "wages" received by the martyr mother, for thus "nursing her boys for God?" Could it be their earthly tortures, their agonising deaths? Alas, what female heart, in its first natural weakness, will not shrink and quiver, and feel, if such must be her wages, how can she nurse her child for God? How may she instil such feelings, if torture and death must be their reward. Why are obedience, constancy, allegiance, virtue, said to be acceptable to the Most High, when such is their earthly end; and the sinful, the faithless, the apostate are spared and enjoy? Let us ponder on what was the support, the hope, ay even at that moment the triumph, of Hannah.* Did she feel as if that trial's intolerable agony, were indeed her "wages"? We know not how a frail weak woman could thus have looked on, and instead of unnerving them by cries and sobs, encouraged them to suffer still. God gave her power (it was not in humanity), and so increased the strength, the might, the vividness, of those hopes beyond the grave, which she had felt and realised so long, that the blessedness awaiting her children with their God, seemed palpably revealed. The veil of flesh, of corruption, was rent from her mortal eyes, and all which the Lord had prepared for those that love Him, unseen by human eye and unheard by human ear, was through her pure FAITH disclosed; nothing else could have so sustained her, or given the immortal spirit

* She is so called in Rollin, though I know not from what authority he takes the name.

such dominion. We are expressly told "she stirred up her womanly thoughts with a manly resolve." Consequently we know and feel, that she had all a woman's nature. "Take thy death," she bade her youngest born, "*that I may receive thee again in mercy with thy brethren.*" Had an angel from heaven spoken in her ear these words she could not have believed more strongly. "The Lord will of His own mercy give you life and breath again," she had before said; and if she had fear when she exhorted her youngest born, it was, not that he should pass away from her earthly love, but by his acceptance of the tyrant's proffers, be lost to her in Heaven; Faith, Trust, Hope, these then were her sustainers; she had brought up her children not for Earth, but for Heaven; not for Time, but for Eternity; and she knew that she should receive her wages, not from Earth but in His presence, for whom her boys were martyred; and can we doubt for a single moment that those "wages" *were* received—can we believe in the God of love, whom Pentateuch, Psalms, and Prophets, all reveal, and yet allow the faintest shadow of an unbelieving thought to come across our minds? Can we with a sceptic's fearful scorn, refuse faith in another purer lovelier world, where such noble and faithful spirits receive their promised recompense, because to the finite sight, hearing, and wisdom, of frail poor humanity, it has not been visibly or palpably revealed? No! No! stagnant and indifferent as Israel may sometimes appear, he never has thus fallen, never can reject that unutterably consoling revelation of immortality, which became his own glorious heritage, long long ages, before it was vouchsafed to the Gentile world.

By the words, "Last of all, after the sons, the mother died," and no mention of tortures, we may hope that, if the tyrant commanded her death, it was comparatively easy, or, which is our own belief, that the Eternal, in His infinite mercy, Himself called her to rejoin her sons, never, never more to be separated from them. The spirit might be supernaturally strengthened, to make manifest such firmness and faithfulness as would exalt the glory of the Lord; but the physical powers must have sunk beneath it. And if the tyrant did indeed put the seal to the work of butchery by slaying her, he did but forestal the death which would inevitably have come—and his cruelty in this instance was mercy.

It may be said, that striking as this narrative is, it cannot bear upon us now, either as guidance or example, and that, even if it could, it would be impossible for us to imitate the heroism of which we read. Earnestly we trust that such manifestations of faithfulness are indeed no longer needed.

Yet that mother's lessons may still be to us as guidance— may teach us how we should instruct our children, so as to provide them against the arrows of misfortune, which ere life close, may assail them, either through bodily affliction or mental woe. Religion, real spiritual religion, *will not* find resting in the human heart unless infused—unless made the first great object in childhood : not to affect with gloom, but inexpressibly to deepen the enjoyment and hilarity of youth. Affliction may do the work for us in riper years, and bring the soul to its God—because earth has become a void—its former pleasures dashed with poison ; but, oh ! it is a fearful thing, when we wait for affliction to teach us our God—when sorrow must be sent to bring us to Him. If the mother would but look forward—would but sometimes think that the sweet and smiling babe upon her lap, the laughing girl and merry boy now playing in such shadowless glee around her knee, may one day be bowed down in sorrow, exposed to bodily pain—to bereavement—to one or more of the numberless sorrows ever incidental to humanity ; nay, to privation of health, of sight, of use of limb—will they not, must they not seek to provide them with some unfailing refuge, some fadeless hope and inward consolation ? Why are they so anxious to provide for their temporal welfare, to secure provision for earthly wants, resources of education, enjoyment, ambition, wealth ?—Why fill the infant mind with every branch of learning, and train it to think, and calculate, and act ? Why be so careful of all these things, did not the thought of the *Future* guide the workings of the *Present*—did not love itself become ambition, and future hope inexpressibly heighten present enjoyment ? And these thoughts, these hopes, are natural, and right : but why provide only for a future of *Success* and of *Joy ?* These things may be. It may please our Father in Heaven to fulfil the mother's every wish, and make her child's future as smiling as its present ; but it may equally please Him to try that cherished darling in the ordeal of adversity ; and then, if he have only been provided for a future of prosperity, O what shall sustain him ? How may he bear up against the trials which may be his, as well as of thousands of his fellows? No! Mothers of Israel: let us ever train our children for a future, and strengthen them for sorrow as well as for joy. Should we think our duty done did we provide them only with summer clothing, and expose them unprotected to the wintry blast and howling storm? Might they not with justice reproach us in the first tempest, if we bade them thus set forth on the journey of life? However smiling as far as the eye can pierce, is not the horizon enveloped in such mists, that we know not whether it conceal sunshine or storm—and shall we send forth our beloved ones provided only for the one?

Let it not be thought that, to inculcate piety—that clinging love of and confidence in God, the only support in mental or bodily affliction—demands a relinquishment of the buoyant light-heartedness of childhood. Far from it. The peculiar susceptibility of childhood to emotions of gladness and love, renders the task easy and most blessed (if the right moment be seized) to lift up the young spirit to the kind and loving Father who has given so many things to love and to enjoy. And when the young mind has expanded to a consciousness of the temporal enjoyments it has received from God, let it rise still higher, in the tale of that world where there is no sin, no pain, no change, but where joy and love live for ever —where their souls will be with God and His angels, if they *seek* to live there, and in all they do, and think, and feel, pray and seek to love and serve the heavenly Father who is so good to them in this world, and has provided such a home for them with Him. Teach them that sorrow and pain are *not* proofs of their Father's *wrath*, but of His *love*—that all he does is love, however we may not understand it—that much, very much must puzzle us while we are on earth, but that we shall understand it all in Heaven, and till then, if we will but believe He loves us, and all He does is love, we may be sorrowful and sad for a time; but we know He will once more give us joy.

Lessons like these, united with a firm observance of the ordinances and commands of Judaism, will indeed be blessed to our children, even though we see not their fruit till long, long years after the first seeds were planted. Let us not suppose, because we can discern nothing in the heedlessness, the levity, the occasional faults, even the apparent indifference to spiritual things, in our offspring, that we have worked in vain.

Let sorrow, let sickness come, and our children will bless the parental love which, under God, has provided them with such hopes, such thoughts, that pain itself is comparatively easy to be borne, and sorrow is assuaged. Better, far better provide for adversity a hundred times, and the provision be not needed, than one case in which the sufferer shall need religious comfort, and in vain—and, in bitterness of anguish, exclaim, "Why was I not taught to know and love God?—Why not guided in my childhood to that holy consolation, of which I hear others speak, but which I cannot feel?" How in the midst of suffering can we teach that God is love? How can the bruised and broken spirit lift up its thought to heaven, when it has, until that moment, been chained to earth? If the soul, in health and joy, has not been taught that it has wings, wherewith, even in its earthly shell, to fly to heaven, how may we hope to use them when they lie crushed and broken beneath the heavy hand of woe? It is vain to hope it! Then, oh!—would we do our duty to our children—would we indeed provide for their future—would we have them recall us, with the tenderest love and deepest gratitude, long, long after we may have passed away from earth?—let us imitate the Martyr-Mother, and, clothing them for affliction as well as joy, nurse them from their infancy for God; and we shall indeed receive them once again in mercy from His hand—and in His presence for everlasting

---

MOTHER OF JOHN HYRCANUS.—WIFE OF JOHN HYRCANUS.—ALEXANDRA.

THE victim of Antiochus was not the only instance of singular heroism and self-devotedness amongst the Mothers in Israel. Her sacrifice of all natural feelings, which we have been regarding, originated in a faithfulness and constancy to a persecuted faith—a resolution to dare all the torture of Earth rather than, by disobedience and apostacy, lose the glories of Heaven. This was love of faith and race: we are now to behold patriotism as strong and fervid a feeling in the woman of Israel, as in the women of the Gentile nations, whose deeds are trumpeted by fame.

Simon, the last of the heroic Maccabæan brothers, and the

General and High Priest of Judea, was inveigled by his son-in-law Ptolemy, to the fortress of Jericho, and there, at a banquet, assassinated. His eldest son shared his fate; and efforts were made in the same treacherous spirit to capture John Hyrcanus, Simon's third son, at Gazara. The young man however, escaped the danger, and, appearing in Jerusalem, was universally acknowledged as the successor to his father, Prince, and High Priest of Judea. Burning with desire to avenge the death of Simon, he marched with his forces instantly to Jericho. Ptolemy had however obtained possession of the mother and the brethren of Hyrcanus, and with his captives shut himself up in a strong fortress in that town. Hyrcanus, instantly laid his plans for a close siege; but drew back appalled as he beheld his mother and brothers exposed on the walls, scourged and tortured before his eyes, with the threat if he did not instantly withdraw his forces, they should be put to death. Josephus expressly tells us, that the force of Hyrcanus was stronger than Ptolemy's "*but he was rendered weaker by the commiseration he had for his mother and brethren,*" a touching proof of his filial affection. He knew that Ptolemy, in conjunction with Antiochus Sidetis, king of Syria, was seeking to overthrow Judea, and therefore, danger to his country as well as a father's murder—called upon him to capture Ptolemy. But still he hesitated—would have withdrawn, had not his heroic mother stretched out her hands imploringly towards him, beseeching him to heed her not, but to revenge the cruel treachery done unto his father. Torture and death for herself and her children awaited her; but still, with noble and unshrinking courage, she called on Hyrcanus to renew the siege. While the spirit of son and warrior absolutely quailed before, only *witnessing* the sufferings of his mother, the mother and the woman failed not under their *infliction*. What was her life (she probably felt), and even the life of her two young sons, compared with those treacherously slain, and with the valiant and energetic warrior who still remained? Why should her sufferings so unnerve his stalwart arm, as to tempt him to raise the siege, and so perhaps expose him to the displeasure of the people, who though they had so lately made him Prince and Priest, might turn from him with a breath? The wife and mother of Asmonæans, she had imbibed their spirit, and displayed it when most needed. The captor flung indelible disgrace upon his manhood, by seeking terms with his foe, through the torture of a woman; but fearlessly she scorned alike the torturer and his tortures: she could not fear death, for she was a woman of Israel, whose sure and stedfast hope was fixed above.

Inspired by her heroic words, Hyrcanus recommenced the siege with vigour, but at every fresh cruelty offered to his mother he appears to have relaxed; and thus, according to Josephus, the siege was protracted to the sabbatic year, when all offensive warfare was forbidden; and in consequence he withdrew his forces; but his withdrawal did not save his mother; Ptolemy slew both her and her sons, and fled to Philadelphia; and history mentions him no more.

There is nothing in this anecdote to interest us as women in a domestic point of view. The mother of Hyrcanus is brought before us only as a noble-minded heroine, who cared not for personal suffering, so the murderer of her husband and son was brought to justice, and the country rid of his treacherous intrigues. We do not hold her up as an example to our young countrywomen, because we trust that they will never be exposed to such a trial, and we have not enough of her to know if her previous life were in accordance with the heroism displayed in peril. We must not allow admiration of *greatness* to usurp the place in our hearts due to the admiration of *goodness*, more especially as we are *always* called upon to cultivate and display the latter, and not once in a century, not one individual in a thousand, required to make manifest the former. Admiration of greatness, if too much encouraged, occasions a neglect of goodness: seeking for opportunities to make manifest the one, we overlook the innumerable opportunities in our daily life to prove the other. The one lives but in excitement, the other at home; and modern women must be content to change the one for the other, or their lives must be unhappy; for in these matter-of-fact prosaic days, where shall we find adventures to make us feel and act as heroines?

Not to call forth romantic admiration, have we brought this incident forward, but simply to prove that, in time of need, Israel as well as every other nation had her great and noble-minded heroines. Qualities such as the mother of Hyrcanus displayed, are the offspring of freedom only. The affection, the reverence borne her by her son, deprived him of his wonted energy, unnerved his heart, and bade his sword lie

powerless. This marks the distinction between a heroine of
Israel and a heroine of savages : even amongst the latter we
may find the heroism of endurance, but not the filial affection,
which would pause in the midst of a triumphant career,
appalled and powerless, because a mother suffered. The affection of Hyrcanus is even a more convincing proof of the
elevation to which the women of Israel could attain, than her
own fortitude; while her address, and its inspiring effect, must
convince us that the men of Israel disdained not to derive
increase of courage and of firmness from a woman's lips ; and
would this, could this be, if it were the mandate of their law
to degrade and to enslave her ?

A still more powerful proof of the perfect equality of the
women in Israel, in the eyes of their husbands, and of all the
people, is the curious and important fact, that more than one
sovereign of Israel left his kingdom to his WIFE. Now this is
a custom, or even an instance, found in the annals of no other
nation, except in the Semiramis of Babylon, and the Catharine
of Russia ; and these became queens less from the will of their
husbands than their own successful ambition. Whereas in
Israel, it never appeared to excite surprise, even though the
turbulence of the people or the rebellion of sons, prevented
the actual government of a queen, except in one instance.

That the wife of John Hyrcanus should have had such
a monster for her son as Aristobulus the First was her misfortune ; but his violently depriving her of the authority
which his father had left her, does not at all interfere with
the bequeathment itself, or lessen the importance of the facts
derived from that bequeathment. Josephus tells us, speaking
of Aristobulus, and of his ambitious design of changing the
government into a kingdom, "He also cast his mother into
prison, because she disputed the government with him; for
Hyrcanus *had left her to be mistress of all*. He also proceeded to that degree of barbarity, as to kill her in prison with
hunger." The extreme cruelty of his conduct, marks his fear
of her influence, and the people's support of her authority.
That Hyrcanus left her to be "mistress of all" very forcibly
proves the high esteem in which he must have held her, even
if that bequeathment devolved on her an office which it was
impossible for her sex to hold, that of High Priest. We are
rather to suppose that he left to her judgment, which he had
no doubt previously well proved, the choice of a successor for

that office from amongst his sons, and the rest of the administration to be retained by her. Had she been unfitted by insufficient mental ability, for the retention of this high and responsible office, Aristobulus need not have proceeded to extremities. Whereas we read her capability, influence, and authority, in the awful measures which this monster of barbarity adopted. Far happier would it have been for her to have occupied a domestic station in Israel ; but her story is a strong confirmation of all we have advanced.

Already had the opposing factions of traditionists and anti-traditionists appeared in Judea. The former, under the name of the Pharisees, insisted that the observances which they had handed down to the people, though not written in the Law of Moses, were equally obligatory. The latter, under the cognomen of Sadducees, rejected them as obligatory, and adhered only to the written Law. We only mention this important fact to add weight to our argument, that neither traditional nor written Judaism could authorise the abasement of women either socially or domestic, as we shall find the Pharisees giving all their powerful support to a female's authority, which could hardly have been if tradition forbade her to assume it.

The death of Aristobulus, who had succeeded in changing the government into a kingdom, left the nation without an acknowledged head. Antigonus, the next brother to Aristobulus, had been murdered by his orders, and his three other brothers retained in prison. One might suppose that the nobility of the nation would at once have proceeded to action in the choice of a sovereign ; but we find a *woman* acting for them. Salome, the wife of Aristobulus, instead of retaining the regal dignity herself, which it is very evident she might have done, chose the wiser course of acting. We do not read of her taking counsel with any one ; but, entirely by her own will and pleasure, and on her own authority, she released her husband's brethren from prison, and made Alexander Jannæus king. Her individual power and authority must undoubtedly have been great, or she could not have thus acted. Nor could she have been an ambitious woman : but we do not hold her forth as a good or amiable character, so little being reported of her ; and that little, if we are to believe the words of Josephus, not in her favour. Her independent authority and undisputed influence are all we need, as evidences of the freedom and equality of her social state.

The reign of Alexander Jannæus lasted twenty-seven years, varied by foreign wars and domestic seditions. A fearful vengeance on his disaffected subjects in Jerusalem, however, produced peace; and, for the remainder of his reign his iron rule retained them in subjection. His foreign policy had been equally successful; and many conquered provinces were added to his hereditary possessions. When, however, he was seized by a mortal malady, three years after his subjection of the insurgents, he trembled for the fate of his kingdom. A turbulent and angry people, and provinces so newly conquered, were little likely to submit to the rule of women and children. Yet still we do not perceive any change in his resolution, founded on the customs of his country, to leave his kingdom to his wife.

Instead of taking counsel, we find him summoning his wife Alexandra to his bedside, and giving such advice as forcibly manifests her power to follow it. Even granting that he did not say the exact words which Josephus puts into his mouth, yet the Hebrew woman must have been quite capable of undertaking the solemn responsibility, and of accomplishing all he desired, or Josephus himself, well acquainted with the customs and habits of the strict Jews, would not have had the veracity of his narrative doubted, by giving her instructions which a fettered position must have entirely prevented her fulfilling.

Fully aware of the desolate and painful position in which she and her children would be left by the death of her husband—" She came to him," as Josephus says, " weeping and lamenting;" but Alexander roused himself from the stupor of his mortal illness to give such advice as would secure the kingdom to her and tranquillity to the people. He bade her conceal his death from his soldiers, till the fortress (Ragabah, near Jordan), which he was besieging, had been subdued; and then to march to Jerusalem in triumph, place his body in the hands of the Pharisees, whom he had so mortally offended during his life, to do with as they pleased, and promise to conduct the affairs of government under their advice and approbation. " If thou dost but say this to them," Josephus makes him continue, " I shall have the honour of a more glorious funeral from them than thou couldst have made for me: and when it is in their power to abuse my dead body they will do it no injury at all, and thou wilt rule in safety."

And his wise policy was followed. That he should have given such to his wife must suppose a perfect conviction on his part that her sex would be no hinderance to its performance; and that he had perfect confidence in her abilities for the task. Surely, then, wives in Israel must have held a very distinguished position! We know that no statute in the written Law existed to their disadvantage; and we must be equally sure that there was none in the traditions, else surely Alexander would not have desired his wife to throw herself upon the mercy of a set of men who, if tradition contained a single statute confining her to an inferior and powerless position, rendering her a mere nonentity before God and man, would have been actually *compelled*, from their own guiding laws, to deprive her of all authority, refuse obedience to her husband's bequest, and drive her ignominiously from her inherited throne.

The Pharisees were strict orthodox, unyielding traditionists, enthusiasts, and zealots—often led on to mistaken violence by the excess of their zeal—exposing themselves a hundred times during the war to increase of misery and torture from their unshrinking adherence to the minutest point of traditional laws. Yet these very men not only permit a woman to ascend the throne of Judea, hold the reins of government, levy troops, have complete dominion over her sons, who were both of sufficient age to claim the crown themselves, but actually defend her upon it. And, even on her death-bed, demand her counsel, refusing to decide themselves while she was alive, however ill she might be. The anti-traditionist may persist in his belief that the woman of Israel *is* degraded, and bring forward detached sentences from our venerable teachers wherewith to prove it; but, with the history of the past so vividly before us, we heed them not at all.

Alexandra appears fully to have possessed the necessary qualities for the cautious mode of proceeding which her husband advised. Her very first action proves her capable of immense control and strong fortitude, else she could hardly have preserved the secret of her husband's death, and so pushed forward the siege as to succeed in conquering the fortress. She must have been well acquainted with the secrets of military command, of retaining a tumultuous soldiery in obedience: for all orders supposed to be sent from their dying king must have had their origin in herself alone. Had she had advisers, the secret of Alexander's death could not have been preserved, and its very first rumour would most probably have occasioned revolt. The brief notice of the historians— "So Alexandra, when she had taken the fortress, etc." "Alexandra followed the counsels of her husband," etc. "His widow Alexandra immediately adopted the policy," etc.—gives but a weak idea of the painful and difficult position in which she was placed.

A widow mourning for her husband with no common grief, for the emotions of Eastern women can scarcely be measured by those of the North, yet not daring either to evince her own natural sorrow, or give the dead its due respect; an army without a head, dependent entirely on herself for their present measures to end in victory or confusion; a kingdom still quivering and brawling in civil discord, ripe for insurrection, enraged with their monarch, yet standing in such awe of his terrible severity that, as long as they believed him still living, all thought of active rebellion was paralysed; this was no enviable position for a feeble woman, even though her fortitude and talents were adequate to the emergency. Did the secret of his death transpire *before* she could obtain the ear of the Pharisees, she knew that the flame of civil dissension would light up from one end of Judea to the other; and who might prophecy the end?

Nobly she must have averted this evil. The soldiers of Israel were not unaccustomed to female heroism. The chronicles of their ancestors told them of a Deborah, of the female saviour of the citizens of Abel, of Abigail, of Esther, and, in later times, of the martyr mother and the noble wife of Simon; and, therefore, that a woman should mingle in their ranks, and urge them on to victory, was no matter of astonishment. The fortress was gained, and a triumphant march brought them to Jerusalem, accompanied, as they still believed, by their dying king.

What then must have been their surprise, when summoning the heads of the Pharisees, Alexandra committed into their keeping the dead body of the king, and the soldiers learned that it was no commands of a warrior, but a woman's self who had thus led them on to victory. This action alone would have dazzled the eyes of the multitude, ever eager for excitement; and united as it was, with the popular measure of bringing the Pharisees into power and favour, and re-establishing the traditional forms and practices which had been abolished by John Hyrcanus and his sons, but which were greatly endeared to the people, secured her their love yet more. Her giving the body of her husband to his bitterest enemies was hailed as a proof that she had never approved of his conduct, and a very brief interval fixed her securely on her throne.

But though great authority was thus lodged in the hands of the Pharisees, the Queen was evidently a free agent in individual administration. She made her elder son Hyrcanus high priest, as a matter of course. Fortunately, for the peace of the kingdom, his indolent character prevented his meddling with the politics of the day; high priesthood and kingdom owned the same acquiescence with the measures of the Pharisees: but, while Hyrcanus permitted himself to be a *passive* agent in their hands, his more energetic and enterprising mother pursued her own active and independent course. Instead of sinking into a mere shadow of a sovereign, because her domestic government was so circumscribed, she newly organised and increased the power of her armies by levying large bodies of mercenary troops, and striking terror into the hearts of all the surrounding nations. Hostages were demanded and sent; so that the depredations and petty warfare, which had so often harassed the borders of Judea in the reign of Alexander, were effectually prevented, and the whole land was at peace. In all these foreign affairs, Alexandra acted alone. The Pharisees were much too busily employed in their home administration, and in their desire to obtain summary vengeance for all the insults which their body had received in the previous reign. More especially, they demanded justice on those who had assisted in the massacre of the eight hundred men who had fallen victims to the severe vengeance of Alexander four years previous. Aristobulus, the Queen's second son, who had long felt with secret indignation his exclusion from all power, seized the opportunity to put himself at the head of the oppressed party; and, seeking the presence of the Queen, appealed, not to her mercy alone, but to her justice, reproaching her with "ingratitude in thus abandoning the faithful adherents of her husband to the vengeance of their enemies."

It was a difficult position for the Queen, thus appealed to by both parties; but her extraordinary sagacity triumphed even over this. She saved them from the wrath of their enemies by permitting them to leave Jerusalem, enrolling them in the garrisons of the frontier cities, and gave Aristobulus, whose restless intrigues were likely to endanger the peace she had so laboured to attain, the command of a large army, nominally to check the depredations of the petty prince of Chalcis, but secretly to obtain possession of Damascus. The prince was successful in accomplishing both his mother's object and his own. Damascus was taken,* and the army, a very considerable one, was won over, and strongly united to his personal interests.

Alexandra reigned nine years, a breathing-time of peace for her distracted country, which only waited for her death to plunge again into all the miseries of civil discord, the issue of which was complete subjection to the power of Rome. The advice of Alexander regarding the Pharisees certainly aided domestic peace which lasted during the government of his wife; but a less enlightened, less energetic sovereign, could not have so triumphed over the difficulties of the age. There is no little wisdom in knowing when and how to submit when submission is required, and yet in so retaining individual dignity and self respect, that the station we occupy may continue its proper elevation in the minds of common men, who so often pay to *state* the homage they refuse to *worth*. Alexandra was more truly beloved and venerated by the multitude, than any of the sovereigns who preceded, or succeeded her; and this would not have been had she succumbed to the power of any party. She allowed the political administration to be carried on by the favourites of the people; but she was no idle cypher in their hands. She kept peace between the adverse bands by a measure which no weak or fearful disposition could have counselled. She guarded her kingdom from all foreign aggressions; and her people, both in her capital and in the provinces, were prosperous and happy. Even the turbulent and ambitious spirit of her younger son, did not dare display itself during the government of his mother; though, the very hour that the dangerous nature of her illness was rumoured, he stole away from Jerusalem, unknown

* According to Milman. Josephus says he did nothing considerable at Damascus; but, from the issue, we incline towards the opinion of Milman.

to all save his wife, to visit alternately the fortresses of his friends, and so secure their subjection and allegiance to himself.

Ill, and suffering from a mortal disease, the flight of Aristobulus at first occasioned the queen little uneasiness; but when many messengers came with the tidings that fortress after fortress had submitted to the prince, and he was, in fact, lord of almost all the strongholds of the country, his design became apparent both to the queen and to the nation. The latter, or, more properly speaking, the immediate followers of the Pharisaic administration, were struck with consternation, fearing the vengeance of Aristobulus for the insults offered both to his followers and house. From a careful consideration of the queen's conduct, and reply to the nobles and Hyrcanus, when they sought her on her death-bed, and demanded her final counsel, it appears to me that her own affections and wishes sided with her younger son. She must have intimately known the character of both. Her own experience had taught her that energy, firmness, activity, were all imperatively needed to secure the peace and prosperity of the kingdom, and to preserve the popular party at its proper distance from the throne. In these qualities she must have long known Hyrcanus was greatly deficient. His extreme inertness had been of little importance when merely High Priest; but would subject both himself and his people to the dominion of a party the moment he ascended the throne. Yet he was the elder, and was rightful heir. Aristobulus, it is true, had all the qualities necessary for a monarch of Judæa at that period; but he was not the heir according to seniority, and he was the known enemy to that party whose influence with the factious multitude had so long aided in preserving peace. To nominate Aristobulus was to wrong her first-born, and plunge the king into civil discord with her dying breath. To nominate Hyrcanus, was to behold the same evils, only at a greater distance; and in such a painful position, alike as a mother and a sovereign, her answer to the nobles was a wise one. They had demanded her counsel as to the present posture of affairs: "for that, in effect, Aristobulus was lord of almost all the kingdom, and that it was useless and absurd for them to take counsel by themselves while she was yet alive, how ill soever she might be;" words somewhat convincing how completely Alexandra had contrived to retain her own authority. Here are the elders of the nation, men grey in years and wisdom, acknowledging and obeying

both scriptural and traditional laws, coming to a weak and
dying woman, and demanding her counsel as their sole guidance
in a dangerous emergency. What would this prove regarding
the social position and mental education of the Hebrew women?

But with death and eternity so near, what had the Queen
of Judæa further to do with life and time? How could the
mother's heart, lingering with both her sons, wrong one at the
expense of the other? How could the amiable and peace-loving
sovereign send forth from her death-bed such decrees as would
wring tears of blood? Yet, how appear before her Maker if
her last words breathed such advice as her heart denied? It
could not be, and therefore "she bade them do what they
thought proper to be done—for they had many circumstances
still in their favour; a nation in good heart, an army, and
money in their several treasuries. For herself, she had small
concern about public affairs now, when the strength of mind
and body had already failed." Surely these were not the dying
words of either an ambitious, or an intriguing woman, but
simply of one glad to lay down the toils and cares of government, and seek that immortal peace and blessedness, which, as
a woman of Israel, she knew awaited her above. She died soon
afterwards at the age of seventy-three. She must, therefore,
have been sixty-four when she first ascended the throne, an
age which ought to increase our admiration of the courage and
energy which she then displayed. We can imagine a young
woman, or one even in the prime of life, nerving herself for
such a difficult task as the concealing a husband's death, and
carrying on a military enterprise with such skill that conquest
followed, but to a woman of sixty-four, from whom all the
glow, the romance of life, we imagine, has faded, the task must
have been more difficult still.

It proves that her youth had been one of energy, intellect,
and active usefulness, or age could not thus have displayed
them. That she had been accustomed to receive the confidence
as well as the affection of her husband; that he had associated
her in his civil and military government by confiding in her
bosom all his designs, else it would have been impossible for
her at the age of sixty-four to claim and to retain monarchical
power. The people must have known and loved her as a wife
in Israel, or, in her unprotected widowhood, they would never
have accepted her as their queen. Her sons must have been
taught her superiority in rank to themselves; been accustomed

from boyhood to regard her, if she survived, as the successor to their father before themselves, or they would have disputed her authority; the law and traditions must both have permitted the sovereign power to rest in the hands of a female, or all Israel would have risen up against it.

We are not now considering the subject in its political bearings as to whether such a system of monarchical succession be a wise one or not; but simply in a national view, as it marks the condition of woman in Israel, even at a period when national sin and civil bloodshed were desecrating the Holy Land of the Eternal, and the pure beautiful spirit of His Holy Law, was concealed beneath the tempest clouds of bigotry and superstition on the one side, and of laxity and indifference on the other; yet still, through the infinite mercy of God, shining forth upon some faithful hearts in the ranks of both.

The summing up of Alexandra's character and administration by Josephus, is one of the most extraordinary specimens of historical contradiction man ever compiled; we subjoin it in a note for the perusal of our readers, assuring them that if they can come to a satisfactory conclusion as to its real meaning, we shall feel really obliged to them, if they will impart it for our especial benefit.* Meanwhile, we will take leave, very humbly, to differ from the reverend historian, and regard her reign and character in a light which strikes us, as doing the most justice to its subject. In the first place, Josephus talks of her "ambition of governing," her obtaining the crown through hazards and misfortunes, and all out of a desire which does not belong to a woman; and we can discover nothing of

* "A woman she was, who shewed no signs of the weakness of her sex, for she was sagacious to the greatest degree in her ambition of governing." So far, leaving out ambition, he is correct, but here follows a most incomprehensible sentence: "She demonstrated by her doings at once, that her mind was fit for action; and that sometimes men themselves show the little understanding they have, by the frequent mistakes they make in forms of government; for she always preferred the present to futurity, and preferred the power of an imperious dominion of all things; and in comparison of that, had no regard to what was good, or what was right. However, she brought the affairs of her house to such an unfortunate condition, that she was the occasion of the taking away that authority from it; and that in no long time afterward, which she had obtained by a vast number of hazards and misfortunes. [What were they? Her husband's will!] And this out of a desire which does not belong to woman, and all by her compliance with those who bare ill-will to her family, and by leaving the administration destitute of a proper support of great men; and indeed, her management

the kind. She came to her husband weeping and lamenting
the desolation which would be hers on his death. Surely if she
had ambition (a desire which we quite agree with Josephus
does not belong to a woman), then was the time to display it,
and urge her husband to take measures for her succession.
She was not the first wife to whom the crown had been left,
though the only one permitted to reign ; but that there was a
precedent in the annals of her country, permitted her surely
to regard her right to the throne merely as a matter of course.
Then, again, the "hazards and misfortunes," which he tells us
she risked to gratify her desire of imperious dominion, what
were they? Simple and exact obedience to a husband's dying
counsel, his will confirmed, and her accession not even disputed
or occasioning a dissenting murmur. We can discover no trace
whatever of her neglecting the "right" and "good" to increase
a despotic power; and we rather think Josephus himself would
find it difficult to prove it from *his own account* of her. Her
preferring present peace and prosperity, and seeking to confirm
such blessings to her people, surely cannot be deemed a fault;
and how the miseries that followed her death can be imputed
to her, as the historian so sapiently seeks to prove, passes our
poor comprehension. Let us suppose a moment that she had
not succeeded her husband, and the crown had descended, as
in the right line of succession it must, to Hyrcanus, Alexander's
elder son. What would have followed? exactly the same evils
as took place after Alexandra's death; the quarrels of the
brothers, each supported by a powerful party, and final appeal
and subjection to Rome. The national sins and departure
from the Eternal, by amalgamation with foreign powers, were
rapidly advancing, Israel was hurrying forward his own fearful
destiny in exact accordance with the prophecies of God. He
was not only sinning against God sins by which no one was
injured but himself; but darkly, fearfully, terribly against
his *brother man*. The sins of Aristobulus the First, against
his mother and brother, were, unhappily, neither without precedent nor repetition. They were but the preface to others
quite as horrible and more extended. The nation was rapidly

---

during her administration, while yet alive, was such as filled the palace
after her death with calamities and disturbances. *However, though this had
been her manner of governing, she preserved the nation in peace.*" Most extraordinary how she could, if so many errors of character and government
could be laid to her charge !—See Josephus, vol. ii, p. 379.

approaching that fearful state pictured by the prophet when the Lord bade him "Make the heart of this people fat, and make their ears heavy, and shut their eyes, lest they see with their eyes, hear with their ears, and understand with their hearts, and convert, and be healed;" meaning, that the sins of the people were such, that they had turned away the mercy of God from them; and, refusing to bestow on them the softening spirit of repentance and amendment, because they neither prayed for nor sought it, he left them to their own impenitent and sinful inclinations ; and, in consequence, they hurried on their own awful destiny—the destruction of their Temple and city, the desolation of their land, and their dispersion over the whole world. And this fearful state of things had already commenced. The reign of Alexandra, instead of her mal-administration causing the "calamities and disturbances" of which Josephus so unjustly accuses her, actually *averted* the tempest for nine years. The Bible gives us more than one instance of the judgment of the Lord being turned aside for a certain period, even though it may not eventually be averted. The reign of Alexandra appears to us one of these breathing times; obtained History tells us not how; but reasoning, as the earnest study of God's Holy Word would bid us reason), it was permitted through His infinite mercy, from the intercession of those few noble and trusting hearts still faithful to Himself. How know we that Alexandra herself might not have been one of these? The scanty and contradictory records of the time will not permit our upholding such an idea as proven truth; but it is more accordant with the history of her administration and its issue, than the charge of Josephus "that the miseries which followed were attributable to her. Where were the great men whose assistance, we are to suppose from Josephus, she neglected? In placing part of the home administration in the hands of those who had borne ill-will to her family, we can simply trace the loving obedience of a faithful wife to her husband's dying counsel ; and her own anxious desire to secure the welfare of her people, even by the sacrifice of her prejudices. Surely such a course of acting is the wisdom of a sovereign. The conquest of our own prejudices, the acting exactly contrary to one's own will, is not less difficult for a monarch than for ourselves; nor less meritorious when achieved. Why then refuse her the admiration which, in this instance, is certainly her due? Yet, with all this unjust censure, and

charges which have no solid foundation, Josephus allows, "that
she showed no weakness of her sex, was sagacious in the greatest
degree in the power of governing, and preserved the nation in
peace." Now how could she possibly be sagacious in the power
of governing, if her mal-administration were the cause of all
her country's after misery? How could she have neglected all
that was right and good if, in such fearful times, she had yet
preserved the nation in peace? a measure which no *male*
sovereign had yet been able to accomplish. Surely we must
all feel that such contradictory assertions are of very little
worth; and our best means of coming to a just conclusion is to
ponder, not on what followed, or came before, but simply on
what she did, and on the *age in which she lived*.

To our own feelings, tinctured perhaps as they are with
national warmth, Alexandra appears far more worthy to occupy
a place in the annals of female sovereigns, than many who
have found eager hearts, and talented pens, to bring them forward. She achieved no great victories it is true—she enlarged
not the boundaries of her kingdom. We have read of no
dazzling connections with foreign potentates, which, though
throwing a lustre over the pages of history, were incompatible
with that obedience to the Law which was to make Judea a
land "holy unto the Lord." Like a true woman, on whom
the calm, sober wisdom of maturity has descended, she preferred
peace to conquest, and she obtained it.

It is an idle sophistry to attempt lessening the dignity and
firmness of her character, by the assertion that the peace of
the kingdom was owing to the supreme power having been
placed in the hands of the Pharisees. Her wisdom manifested
itself in the very bestowal of this power, and in yet so retaining her own independence as to be, in power as well as in name,
the head of the state—in so acting, so counselling, that the
Pharisees must have felt that all they did, though in strict
accordance with their own sentiments, was in reality mere
obedience to their sovereign. This consciousness it must have
been, which compelled their appeal to her on her death-bed.
"It was absurd for them to take counsel by themselves while
she was yet alive." Are these the words of men in whose
hands was the whole power of the kingdom, so that the regal
dignity was a mere cypher? No—though it was a woman
who swayed the Jewish sceptre, a woman who sat upon the
Jewish throne, and placed there by the suffrages of a whole

nation, obeying and acknowledging tradition as well as scripture—the sovereign dignity was never more nobly held. Man could scarcely have so triumphed over the age. His desire for absolute power, his ambition, restlessness, and his ungovernable pride, all would have made him regard concession as humiliation. The delicate manœuvres of leading, when the most trifling error would bring disaster—of commanding and enforcing obedience when we must otherwise obey—of retaining in subjection wills which the weight of a feather may turn to the overbalancing our own—these are politics too delicate for man, and not attainable to ordinary women.

But Alexandra was no ordinary woman. She united the masculine energy, the grasping intellect of man, to the delicate tact of her own sex, and, by the combination, exalted her sovereign power, and so triumphed over the difficulties of the age, that she is well deserving of the love and veneration of her descendants—well worthy of her own glorious descent.

It is greatly to be regretted, that in the records of historical personages, so little is given us of their domestic life. Too often history, though accurate, is the mere *surface* of things, and Truth we are told lies at the bottom of a well, not on its frothy surface. We ought, therefore, to accustom ourselves to *search deeply* for it, not to be content with receiving it merely *second hand*. Now, Truth is often elicited, by using not only our *intellectual* but our *imaginative* capacities. The first permits us to examine and compare; to reflect and condense: and to exclude the peculiar prejudices of the author whom we read, and, looking steadily on the bare fact, trace its *causes* and its *end*. And yet we shall not find this exercise of the intellect or reflective power, perfectly satisfactory, unless we can combine and unite all those distinct and separate thoughts into one perfect whole by the power of imagination, or creation. We are aware that imagination has been called a dangerous gift, as leading to folly and romance. Unite it with RELIGION and INTELLECT, REASON and TRUTH, and bless God for its bestowal, either on your children or yourselves! It will penetrate the imperfect records of the PAST. It will look calmly on the contending storms and dark pictures of the PRESENT, for through them it will trace the same calmly guiding hand, working the progression of mankind, to be visible only when the PRESENT becomes the PAST; and, piercing the impenetrable folds of the FUTURE, become almost a prophet in its pure faith of things which will be, human and divine. But deprive imagination of these glorious guardians—Religion, Intellect, Reason, and Truth—and then, indeed, exorcise it as you would a fiend!

Now, though history tells us nothing of Alexandra's domestic character, the exercise of Reason and Imagination may fill up the vacuum, and give us the information that we need. Let it be remembered, she was sixty-four when called upon to occupy a public station. Would her sons have submitted to her authority, even if the customs of the country authorised her succession, unless accustomed to that reverence and obedience, which if rendered to and deserved by a mother in Israel, as the law of God commanded, might easily be transferred from a mother to a sovereign? Josephus puts words in the mouth of Aristobulus which, as they are in direct contradiction to the will of his father, we do not believe he ever said; or, if he did, it is proved they were the mere impulse of momentary passion, by their having no effect in turning even his own party from their allegience.* Had it been mere ambition which placed his mother on the throne, as he dared to charge her, his was not the spirit to have submitted quietly. No; in the very postponement of his restless intrigues till her death, we read what power she must have exercised over him, both as his mother and his sovereign.

As there is no mention of Alexandra during the lifetime of her husband, the qualities she afterwards displayed must all have been cherished, cultivated, exercised in her *domestic sphere;* and in the respective duties of *wife* and *mother*. To the WOMEN in Israel was always entrusted the solemn responsibility of the education of MEN. We have already expressed our own conviction that mothers were associated with the fathers in the religious instruction of their sons, and innumerable precepts, in the valuable writings of our venerable fathers,† confirm this so strongly that no doubts can be entertained of their individual and social capabilities for the task; or of the consideration and reverence in which, as the accomplishers of such a mission, they must have been regarded by their countrymen. Again we repeat, we are no longer writing of

* Josephus' Histor. Antiq., book xiii. chap. 14.

† For this and other allusions henceforth to the Talmudic writings, the author is indebted to the valuable and imparted information of a gentleman well known by the initials T. T.

Bible times; but of Judaism nearing the advent of Christianity —that very epoch when it is stated, that Judaism had so fallen from the institution of the Eternal, that it was to pass away from Earth and give place to a new and reforming creed. With regard to woman's position, we see this charge is wholly false. The writers of the Talmud wrote of woman, her solemn mission, duties, and responsibilities as the Law of God commanded, and as they witnessed. And how could the education of the men of Israel have been intrusted to her, had she not been universally, and from the very first, recognised as mentally and spiritually on a perfect equality with man?

Having received their education, not only as boys, but in early manhood, from their mother, it was far more natural that Hyrcanus and Aristobulus should quietly yield allegiance to her as their sovereign, than, by demanding the regal authority during her life-time, sink her to a lower grade, and compel her submission to themselves. The exquisite beauty of the laws of Israel, guiding the conduct of children to their parents, would have been insulted by such proceedings. We can scarcely fail to be struck by their practical illustration of the law in the very customs of the country, that the wife of a *deceased* sovereign should reign before his sons. If she could educate them for the duties of a sovereign, she was certainly capable of governing in her own person; and this, then, reveals the secret of her wise administration. Whether or not a wife should outlive her husband, could only be known to God. The minds of the daughters and wives of royalty could never be cultivated only in the expectation of succeeding to the throne. No such ambition could have tarnished the lustre of the studies they pursued, or the acquirements they attained. They studied, thought, practised, that example as well as precept might aid them in their glorious task. Not for their own spiritual and temporal aggrandisement, but for their sons. In Israel it was not enough for mothers simply to give birth to men: it was theirs to train and create them! How different, how gloriously superior to the system of a contemporary nation,* where the boy was taken from his mother's arms at the tender age of seven, and deemed effeminate and weak if he ever sought her company again!

Minds accustomed to such exercise (for the education of

* Sparta.

men could be no light and merely feminine task), were of course capable of individual energy and exertion when called upon to make such qualities manifest. Alexandra had exerted energy too long and nobly in her domestic and maternal duties during her youth, for it to desert her in her age. There was no need for preparation to perform the monarchical duties; for, in preparing her sons for such destiny, she had prepared herself. That her sons did not reflect back her noble qualities, and failed alike in the unambitious patriotism and anxiety for her people's happiness which she so earnestly displayed, cannot and may not be traced to a defect in education. Very seldom is it that a mother's anxious work is so rewarded that her sons are exactly what she has prayed and striven that they should be. It is not the fault of the trainer but of the trained; the assumption of individual character, the budding forth of individual sin, which not the tenderest, the most careful education can ever entirely disperse. It will do much, very much; and though it may not expect always to be regarded upon earth, it is never wholly useless. How know we what the evil might have been, had we not sought at least in part to subdue it? The character of Hyrcanus and Aristobulus might have been very different had they lived in other times; but, in a period of such terrible social iniquity, the forbearance practised by Aristobulus alike towards his mother and brother in her life-time, is sufficient confirmation that, however she may have failed in making them all she wished for their *country*, she had at least impressed them with the strongest reverence and submission towards *herself*. In happier times the character of both brothers might have shone forth with untarnished lustre; as it was, they mingled with and were lost in the fearful vortex of the age. The nation was hastening on its own annihilation, and their unfortunate dispute, and its consequent reference to Pompey, hurried on the end.

We have lingered on the character of Alexandra, because it is a most important one, as concerns us nationally; although perhaps, as women in general, we may derive less instruction from it than from others. The characters of history, however, cannot be to us like characters of the Bible. We are no longer perusing inspired records, where example as well as precept can breathe the voice of God. Our aim now can be only a national one. To throw together every notice of the Hebrew women our history will present, which will prove their social and domestic positions, their mental capabilities, their responsibilities: all which will convince us that ancient and modern Judaism is the same. There is *not* the division which the caviller or the ignorant have raised up between them. Let us not then be charged with a change in our style and subject if the present notices read more like historical memoirs than the home-speaking essays of the characters of Scripture. We leave to our Seventh and Last period the conclusions to which the history of our Sixth will lead us—the moral and religious lesson which, even from History and its imperfectly sketched personages, may still be learned. Even did it give us no other mention of woman than the wife of Jannæus, we should possess enough to satisfy us, that we need no other than our own religion for our earthly elevation and our spiritual hope.

MARIAMNE.

The Idumæan dynasty was on the ascendant, the Asmonæan on the decline; yet the people still turned to the remaining scions of their native princes, with such constancy and affection, that Herod, though politically triumphant, felt that his claim to Judea would not be recognised by the multitude, unless he associated with him, one whose pure Asmonæan blood, enhanced by her engaging youth and extraordinary beauty, would win for him yet more strongly than his own power, the suffrages of the whole people of Judea.

In the person of the hapless Mariamne was represented, not the Asmonæan line alone, but the claims of both brothers, Hyrcanus and Aristobulus. Alexander, the son of the latter, married Alexandra, the daughter of the former; and their children, in consequence, inherited the claims and rights of both. But this was no longer the age for legal succession, or the recognition of native sovereigns. The people, indeed, still clung to the laws and prejudices of their fathers; and still loved the descendants of those valiant men who had once saved them from oppression—but Judea was no longer a kingdom—the Jews no longer a people. The divisions between brother and brother had opened a path to the all-conquering Romans. The line of David, in whom alone the promised monarchy could be restored, had long since passed away : and in this period of Jewish history, between the return from Babylon and the final captivity, we can but trace the gradual yet certain advancement in national iniquity, prophesied by Moses and every other ulterior prophet; when, notwithstanding the faithful obedience, spirituality, and love of individuals (ten, perhaps, in every thousand), God could not withdraw His avenging arm—leaving to that other and brighter world, in His presence to distinguish "between the righteous and the wicked; between him that serveth God, and him that serveth Him not."

The most powerful impetus to this progression in iniquity, originated in too close a connexion, and too blind an attachment in Hyrcanus for Antipater, an Idumæan by birth, and a Jew by adoption and semblance. Idumæa had only lately been united to Judea, and its inhabitants, by the representation of John Hyrcanus the First, won over as proselytes to Judaism. The family of Antipater, therefore, were *not* Hebrews. Herod, entitled the last king of the Jews, had no *national* right to the title; for he was a stranger and, by his actions, a very doubtful proselyte. There was, indeed, evil enough in Israel before the ascendancy of the Idumæan family; but not that utter disregard to nationality, that complete blending with Rome, that intimate association and adoption of its peculiar characteristics, as in the reign of Herod; whose insidious policy to lessen Jewish nationality—that no allegiance to the King of Heaven might interfere with the acknowledgment of his kingdom upon earth—opened the wide gate of utter destruction, for his hapless people. The web of misery flung by Vespasian and Titus over the miserable Jews, Herod's own hand originally wove.

The gallant son of Aristobulus, Alexander, had been murdered; and his widow and orphan children found protection with the powerful friend of Hyrcanus, the Idumæan Herod; whose father, Antipater, had fallen a victim to the hatred of the Jewish faction. Herod appears to have regarded Alexandra and her children only as the near relations of Hyrcanus, whose party he always pretended to befriend. As the widow and children of Alexander, the son of Aristobulus, whose claims and struggles for independent sovereignty the Idumæans had always so powerfully and perseveringly resisted, we might suppose they would be objects rather of enmity than of protection. Affection for the person, and gratitude for the favours of Hyrcanus, there could have been none in the hearts of either Antipater or Herod; they supported him simply because his indolent and confiding disposition placed all the actual power in their hands. With Aristobulus they knew this could not be; for he was, according to Josephus, "an active man, and one of a great and generous soul;" and the only means to *increase* their own power, they felt was to *decrease* his. When, however, Aristobulus and Alexander were both murdered, and the sole representative of that younger Asmonæan branch (except the children of Alexander) was Antigonus, who, notwithstanding his casual bravery and occasional success, appears to have possessed but little of the Asmonæan spirit, it became an act of policy to unite himself with the youthful representative of both the brothers; and Herod acted accordingly.

Mariamne could not have been, at this time, much above fourteen or fifteen years old, that is, granting that she was the senior of her brother Aristobulus, who, four years afterwards, is said to have only just completed his seventeenth year. The fierce and jealous passion which afterwards characterised Herod towards his young wife, does not appear to have been excited at the time of their betrothal. He might have been attracted by her exceeding beauty; but the character of the man allows the supposition, that at that period, when all his ambition was to aggrandise and secure his own power for the future, as well as for the present, he would equally have made this connection, had the granddaughter of Aristobulus and Hyrcanus been as ugly as sin, instead of lovely as virtue and innocence could make her. Happy indeed would it have been for her, had she not been thus lovely, and had the connection remained one of policy alone!

At the time of their betrothal, Mariamne knew little of Herod, save as one of the most gallant, most enterprising men of the day. She had been educated in perfect seclusion with her brother; kept apart as much as possible, from the fearful confusions and crimes of the state; and though she had not as yet been called upon to put away the thoughts and habits of youth, and come forward in all the early maturity of Eastern womanhood, still it was not unlikely that she was willing and contented to receive Herod as her destined husband. He could be as winning, as attractive, and as gentle as he could also be terrible in severity and rage. We read enough of his tastes for the arts, his expansive intellect, the magnificent scale of his architectural, and other civil improvements, to believe that he was not solely the monster of passion and cruelty which his later deeds pronounce him. His very intercourse with the luxurious Romans may have added a manly polish and graceful manner to the stern reserve of a Jewish warrior; and these were not qualities to pass unnoticed in that day. Mariamne supposed him the friend and protector of her grandfather and mother; and if he did seek at that time to win her affections, it was most likely she could bestow them willingly, and without repugance consider herself as his bride.

They were not, however, then together long enough, for that scarcely conscious preference to become real affection.

Awakened to a closely threatening danger, Herod fled with his family, including Mariamne as his bride, her mother, and brother, to Masada, a strong fortress on the Western shores of the Dead Sea, and near his paternal heritage, Idumæa. The journey was fatiguing, and so dangerous that Herod, in despair, had nearly attempted his own life; but his *temporal* good fortune did not desert him: he reached the fortress in safety, and was speedily reinforced by 800 native troops from Idumæa, under the command of his brother Joseph. This is the first mention history gives of Mariamne. Antigonus, whose connection with the Parthians occasioned this sudden flight, never appeared to remember even the existence of his brother's children; and, however the intriguing and ambitious Alexandra might have secretly hated the power of her son-in-law Herod, there was no eluding it, save by making it her own.

Four years elapsed ere Mariamne became the wife of Herod, and during that period her domestic life must have been far from happy. In fact, from her first connection with Herod, we may say her sorrows began; for their rapid flight to Masada, pursued so closely by the Parthian allies of Antigonus as repeatedly to meet in deadly fight, and encounter such dangers that Herod's own spirit quailed almost to despair, could have been but an interval of fearful terror, fatigue, and suffering to the young girl only just commencing life. If her affections had indeed been excited by Herod, the length of his absence, the dangers to which he was exposed, all must have weighed depressingly on a mind too young by many years for such heavy cares.

Alexandra and her children were not the only companions of Herod's hasty flight. He took with him his own mother Cypros, and his sister Salome; and it was at Masada, in consequence, that that fearful enmity between the female members of his family commenced, which was to dash his whole domestic life with woe. The extreme youth and purity of Mariamne, permits us the supposition that at the time she herself had little to do with the bickerings and petty provocations continually passing before her. But her position was a painful and a dangerous one; she had not one female friend who could be the guardian and guide which her youth and beauty so much needed. The character of her mother, as we see it afterwards revealed, was far more likely to infuse its own baleful influences within the young mind and heart in such perfect innocence looking up to her, than to strengthen and ennoble Mariamne's natural high qualities. Yet how was her child to discover this? How mistrust, and so turn from her only parent, nay, with the sole exception of her young brother, her only relative upon earth? Alexandra had intellect, policy, and wisdom, crooked as it was; and the reverence and love uniting the sons and daughters of Israel with their parents, must effectually have prevented Mariamne, at her tender age, from discovering aught which could frighten her from her mother's guardianship. How could she doubt the purity of her mother's love? How divide the true from the false? the judicious from the wary? A judicious parent would have taught and practised moderation and forbearance; would, if she had seen the necessity of uniting the pure high Asmonæan race with the degraded Idumæan, have bent at least to the necessity, and conciliated the family of her daughter's husband herself, and led her child to do so too. But this, to such a character as Alexandra, was impossible; her very subtlety in this instance succumbed to her over-bearing pride. The pure and beautiful spirit which, guiding the law of Moses, inspired the prophet to promise, in the name of the Lord, a place dearer than sons and daughters to the strangers who, turning from idolatry to Him, kept his covenants and sabbaths, had been lost in the dense cloud of sin and misery enveloping Judæa. Pride had folded up the Jewish heart, instead of the lucid robe of charity which the law commanded and infused; and from the insufferable haughtiness of Alexandra, we may trace all the misery which ended not even with the murder of her child.

To any disposition, the pride and haughty insolence of another, occasion a bitterness of feeling, a desire of retaliation, only to be conquered by a consciousness of one's position before God and our own souls, and of the absolute nothing, which such provocations are, in our strivings after eternity. But to feel thus needs an enlightened, a lowly, yet a noble mind; and not such was the disposition of either Salome or her mother. Of the latter, however, we read so little, except in conjunction with Salome, that we rather suppose her weak than wicked; too indolent herself to conspire against another, but willing enough to follow where a more energetic spirit would lead; and, in consequence, an equal accessory to evil deeds. To Salome, however, no negative terms need be applied; and the only relief we can discover in the perusal of her history, is that she was no woman of Israel. Even in that awful period of sin, the daughters of Israel had not thus fallen. Alexandra, indeed, was evil enough; but for her a train of fearful circumstances, a succession of misfortunes from treachery and cruelty may be some palliation. In her some womanly feelings once had existence; in Salome there were none. The petty vices and faults of woman were indeed the *foundation* of all her after-crimes; but in the overspreading poisoning torrent of her thoughts and deeds we can scarcely believe that its source lay in those small and often invisible springs of petty faults dwelling in every woman's breast.

The extreme beauty of her brother's bride would by such a disposition have been looked on as an unpardonable crime. Even ordinary attractions must have sunk to nothing before the sweet innocence and freshness of such loveliness as Mariamne's. Her pure Asmonæan blood, her lineage from a thousand priests, the ordained of God, and reverenced of His people, all was felt as a reproach to the haughty Idumæan, who, exalt herself as she might, could never boast such proud descent; and when to these sources of irritation was added the scorn and contempt of Mariamne's mother, and the daily provocations thence ensuing, heightened perhaps by the lofty bearing of the object of her hate herself, all recurring through successive weeks, months, and years, whilst they were thrown together in one home, which they dared not quit because of the dangers awaiting them without, and with no possibility at that period of evincing the hate consuming her, it became concentrated, defined, laid out in varied schemes, waiting but the opportunity to work, which, when it came, transformed her from the woman to the fiend.

That she imparted her machinations to her mother at that time is not likely. She was probably contented with infusing such hatred of Alexandra and her daughter as would secure her a willing agent in Cypros whenever she needed one. Provocations which the weak character of Cypros might have been too indolent even to remember, were recalled and magnified, till the sting of their recollection so rankled that even time could not remove it, and from them hatred sprung. Weak characters are quite as susceptible of the passions as strong ones; perhaps even more, for the latter can be guided by reason, the former cannot.

Amongst characters like these was the hapless Mariamne thrown without the power of escape, for those three or four years of her young existence, when the influences and impressions should be but virtue's own. At fourteen or fifteen what could she have known of life, except as imparted by her mother, her sole instructress? And in those three years' residence in Masada, what opportunity had she to weaken the maternal influence, by presenting to her notice, such noble and high specimens of her sex, as would cause her awakening mind to doubt and question; and without lessening the affection and duty of a child, yet bid her shrink from qualities and propensities which she could not love? Who was there to lead her to the pure unsullied fount of woman's virtue, and to bid her to conquer the trifling faults of her misguided education, so that not even hatred could fling its darts upon her, but enmity itself fall powerless, not from the utter absence of cause, for, alas! when did that ever quench hatred, but of opportunity for its display?

Such a guide she had not: and we can only marvel, that under such influences, such impressions, it is only "haughtiness," and a "want of moderation," of which the historian can accuse her. That she should have treated both Cypros and Salome with some haughtiness was only natural. Her mother's conduct must have guided hers; and the visible dislike with which she was regarded by the Idumæans, could but have fallen coldly and painfully on the eager heart of youth. In those three years, her brother was the being to whom, in all probability Mariamne clung with all the warm passionate emotions of her Eastern nature. Nearly the same age, equally lovely, equally gifted, the affections of the young Asmonæans became concentrated in each other. It was not to Alexandra, much, as no doubt, they loved her, that her children could reveal all the gushing tide of feeling, hope, joy, and awakening intellect which so characterises and blesses youth. The character which a careful study of the history marks as Alexandra's, could not have bent down to the freshness and artlessness of her children's. Wrapt in her own cares, for undoubtedly she had many, and sad ones—her own vindictive feelings towards the family of her son-in-law—the present and the future glooming darkly and terribly over her and hers—her aged father in the hands of his enemy, Antigonus, who, though his own nephew, scrupled not to deprive him for ever of the capacity for the high priesthood, by the mutilation of his ears—Masada itself continually liable to attack and seizure—and the safety of herself and children continually in jeopardy, for Antigonus was not likely to forget, if they were once in his power, that the youthful Aristobulus, as the son of his elder brother Alexander, had more claim to the sovereignty than himself. These were thoughts, all sufficient to render even a gentle and amiable character too full of painful anxiety, to enter into the hopeful buoyancy of youth.

Alexandra's haughty and intriguing spirit would bury it all deep in her own breast, and coldness, indifference, and pride mark her outward demeanour. Under such circumstances, the love between Mariamne and Aristobulus could not fail to grow stronger, more sustaining, and more consoling, every passing year. No affection is purer, stronger, more enduring, and lovely in its truth, than that subsisting between a brother and sister, when it *does* exist; perhaps, it is even stronger, when the sister is by one or two years the elder. It makes them more *twin* in age, capabilities, mutual appreciation, and comprehension of each other, than if the boy had the advance in years. It is a distinct, wholly distinct feeling, to that which actuates sister towards sister. There, pure and beautiful as such affection is, it is wholly *feminine*. In the other case, the highest and noblest qualities of the brother, insensibly infuse themselves into the sister, banishing in consequence all those petty failings and weaknesses which are natural to woman; and all the sister's purest, most spiritual, and unselfish influences, infuse themselves by the same process into the heart of the brother, and purifying it from its grosser and more worldly nature, make each more worthy, and more capable of entering into the other's feelings, and so twines them together, with a link strong as adamant, and pure as the crystal fount of love, whence all such affection comes. But this is no common emotion, or always existing when a sister and brother are of so near an age. Character and circumstance may both unite to *prevent* as well as to *create* it. Between Mariamne and Aristobulus, an earnest study of their characters and destiny seems to prove convincingly that it *had* existence. They had none other with whom to divide it; not even separated by education, or by Aristobulus being called to war, or to the priesthood, as might have been the case had their country been at peace, and the young scions of royalty occupying their natural position in their father's court. They shared one common danger, one common lot—were mutually the darlings of their people—mutually the objects of dread and hate to the opposing factions—mutually of consequence to Herod, whose ambition he knew would have no firm foundation, unless secured through them; all this combined to unite the natural links of affection (which assimilating characters had already so closely bound) with such strength and firmness, that their violent severing was in all probability the first and final cause of Mariamne's estrangement from her husband. Could it be otherwise?

We have lingered some time on this residence at Masada, which historians in general pass over in five or six lines, being too intent upon the manœuvres and actions of Herod, to examine deeper into the origin of those dark and terrible deeds, which afterwards so devastated his own household; but the object of our consideration is Mariamne, and not Herod; and therefore, we are anxious, by reflection on the early years of her life, on the circumstances which influenced her maturer character, and in fact, her destiny itself, to throw light on those darker portions of her history, which in general are touched upon alone. In a perusal of the historians open to us, we find ourselves scarcely knowing whether to blame or pity, and certainly quite unable to form a correct estimate of Mariamne's character. Her fearful trials, her early provocations, the dark influences which prevented the complete correction of her few natural faults; all these, in the bare recital of events, are impossible to be discovered, without that attentive study of *causes* as well as of *events*, of the *origin* as well as of the *end*, which in a more rapid perusal of History is not possible to be attained. We have excused our prolixity before, by assuring our readers, that our notices of individuals are far more suggestive than narrative, more essays than histories, and can only entreat them to bear with us still; the cLaracters of History demanding the same treatment as those of the Bible, still inculcating a moral, though not the same inspired lesson.

The three years passed at Masada, were not without frequent attacks from without, in addition to the annoyances within. The Parthian allies of Antigonus overran the country, and probably frequently threatened the fortress, though we do not hear of any direct siege, till that under Antigonus himself, which appears to have lasted several months, and to have exposed the garrison and inmates to dreadful suffering from the want of water. Meanwhile, Herod had arrived at Rome, and besought Augustus and Antony to confer the sovereignty of Judea on the young Aristobulus, who united in his own person the claims of both the contending sons of Alexander Jannæus, and grant him (Herod) the office of governor under him. The very nature of the request reveals the subtle policy of the man; no one can imagine, there was any further sincerity in his prosecution of Aristobulus' rightful claims, than the fear of grasping too much, by the actual demand of the crown for himself, and so losing all. Besides, had he done so, he would have lost at once all the confidence of Alexandra; whereas, by making her son's claims apparently his first object, he rivetted it on himself, as the only one likely to give her aid. That the Romans chose to confer the sovereignty on him instead of on Aristobulus, could not be attributed to any undue ambition on his part. That Alexandra was satisfied that he had at that time done all he could for her son, appears likely from her making no effort for him herself, until Herod's resolution to deny him any share in the government became more evident.

Seven days after his royal appointment, Herod left Rome, and three months afterwards was in Judea. Masada was of course his first object; the forces of Antigonus, aided by the want of water, had nearly reduced it, when a timely fall of heavy rain relieved the one, and Herod's impetuous attack removed the other. Mariamne had not, however, very long to renew her acquaintance with her betrothed husband. He appears only to have relieved Masada, and instantly departed with the intention of reducing Jerusalem; but was foiled by the treacherous desertion of his principal ally. Unable with his native forces, to subdue Judea, he fixed his head quarters at Samaria, and by his vigilant and energetic measures, freed the province of Galilee from the bands of robbers with which it had been infested. The following year he recommenced measures against Antigonus; but it was not till the spring of the next year that the siege of Jerusalem was regularly begun. During the siege Herod returned to Samaria, to complete his marriage with Mariamne, two years after he had been made king by the Romans, and consequently nearly five since their first betrothal. Where Mariamne, her mother and brother, had been since the siege was raised from Masada, history does not reveal. We rather suppose, that when Herod fixed his winter quarters at Samaria, all the females of his family joined him there. It appears strange that he did not solemnise his marriage then, instead of waiting to do so in the very midst of a most momentous siege. That ambition, not love, was the original incentive of his union with Mariamne, is proved at once by this proceeding. He feared that even the power of his arms would not have secured him the affections of the people of Judea, or reconciled them to his conquest of Antigonus, only that he might ascend the Asmonæan throne himself; and that this obstacle should be lessened, if it could not be entirely removed, occasioned his sudden resolution to leave the walls of Jerusalem, and at once unite himself with the Asmonæan princess. Once really his wife, he probably felt no chances could divide them, and so give her influence to another. The people would second him for *her* sake; and out of regard to his queen, forget he was that Idumæan alien, whom so many detested while they feared. The event proved the wisdom of his policy. At Samaria, the young and lovely Mariamne became indissolubly his wife, and many faithful partisans of her father instantly joined him with such reinforcements as enabled Herod to march with renewed spirit against Jerusalem. If Mariamne indeed loved Herod at that time, her life must have been a chaos of anxiety and fear. He never returned to remain with her, but left her again after a very brief interval, to encounter renewed dangers. Continually thrown amongst his relatives, whose envy and dislike were not likely to decrease now she was really his wife, she must, indeed, have rejoiced, when, after a protracted siege,

Jerusalem submitted, and Herod was acknowledged sovereign of Judea.

His endeavours to preserve the city from the vengeance of the Romans, his protection of holy places, and care of the religious prejudices of the people, were all actions likely to elevate his character in the mind of his young bride. Antigonus had received his death doom from the Romans, not from Herod. Compared with the awful iniquities of the time, his career had been unusually free from atrocity; and even the unsparing executions of the Antigonian faction, which followed his accession, his policy, no doubt, knew how to excuse, so as to appear actual necessity to his wife, and not the relentless cruelty which they seemed to us.

For a few, a very few months, Mariamne may have enjoyed some degree of happiness and peace. The mass of the people devotedly attached to the Asmonæan family, were stilled into some degree of submission, because she shared Herod's throne; but too soon even this transient calm was to pass away. Herod was sovereign of Judea, endured because of his connection with the Asmonæan line; but even this connection would not permit his assumption of the *priesthood*. He, an Idumæan, an alien—but a "half Jew," as the people called him—occupy that office of solemnity, the delegate of God himself! It was a thing unheard of, even in the most fearful annals of Jewish history, and impossible to be permitted. Herod always appeared aware of this; for at the commencement of his reign he made no attempt to assume it nominally, even though the measures he adopted, proved that he had resolved that all the actual power should be his own. Hyrcanus, the father of Alexandra, had been invited to Jerusalem, and treated with great apparent respect and regard by Herod, as the grandfather of his wife. The mutilation of his ears, however, disqualified him from again assuming the priesthood:* and neglecting not only the rightful heir to that solemn office, but many others of noble lineage and high qualities in Jerusalem, Herod sent for Ananel, an obscure individual, but of priestly descent from the Babylonian Jews, and appointed him High Priest.

This was an insult impossible to be borne with patience,

* This proves how faithfully, even at this period, some of the laws of Moses were still obeyed. "The priests were to be without blemish." Levit. xxi. 17—24.

either by Alexandra or the Asmonæan faction. The office of High Priest had been hereditary, from Aaron downwards. The law had made no condition for the exclusion of rightful heirs, save that of being "without blemish." Youth was no preventive; and while the young Aristobulus lived, and united in his own person not only the claims of his priestly race, but of two contending parties, to appoint another to the priesthood was an insult to the whole nation, impossible to be overlooked. The people were in a turmoil of indignation, but too much awed by the severity and power of Herod to attempt any popular disturbance; but all the mother's feelings were roused to more than passive indignation. She wrote to Cleopatra, beseeching her influence with Antony, to compel Herod's appointment of her son. Aided by a musician, her letters were conveyed to the far-famed queen of Egypt, who complied with the request; but Antony, unwilling to interfere with the civil government of the king he had himself created, hesitated and procrastinated, without coming to any decision. Meanwhile Dellius, a man infamous for his licentious conduct, and the friend and confident of Antony, visited Jerusalem. The extraordinary beauty of the brother and sister elicited his wondering admiration; and, in his secret conferences with Alexandra, he persuaded her to have their pictures taken, and sent to Antony, who would then be unable to refuse anything they asked. The horrible nature of this proposal would, we ought to imagine, have been rejected by a Jewish mother with indignation and abhorrence; but, worked on by her ambitious and intriguing spirit, even these revolting means were adopted, and the pictures sent: and to this woman had the tender years of Mariamne been entrusted! From a mind capable of such black, such unnatural horror, had the pure chaste mind of youth received its first impressions: and, knowing this, shall we not almost marvel at the stainless, shadowless purity, encircling the daughter of such a mother, almost like a halo, rendering her impalpable, and so transmitting every baleful arrow aimed against her, as would the atmosphere itself!

The honour of Mariamne was, however, in this instance safer with Antony than with Alexandra. The fiendish counsels of Dellius only prevailed upon him to send for Aristobulus; but Herod refused to obey, encouraged by the clause in Antony's letter, not to send the young man, "if he thought it hard upon him so to do." And no resentment followed. Aristobulus himself interfered not with the machinations working for and against him. His youth, his tastes, probably rendered him contented with the life of calm retirement which his exclusion from office permitted; but the love his sister bore him, her perfect consciousness of the rights and claims of her noble line, could not permit her to behold this indignity in silence. There is a calm dignity pervading the character of Mariamne, even in her youth, which almost unconsciously impresses us with a conviction of her own high sense of her priestly lineage, and its lofty claims, which no personal danger, no timid consideration, could ever remove. The wives and daughters of priestly lineage were looked upon, by their countrymen, from the very first delivery of the law, as sharing the sanctity of their fathers and husbands, and reverenced accordingly, as higher in station according to popular decision, as purer and holier in conduct than the wives and daughters of sovereigns. We read but too often of royal unions with the daughters of the heathen; but never save once of such abomination occurring in the households of the priests. Pride of birth, of descent, was almost the first impression on the hearts of the young daughters of the priests; that they might preserve both unsullied. And Mariamne was not likely to forget this precious heritage. It was not in accordance with a descendant of the Asmonæans to regard herself as queen merely as the wife of Herod. By right of heritage the kingdom was her brother's and her own; and though the arms of the Romans had conferred the crown on Herod, how might she behold the exclusion of her brother from his own hereditary honours, which it was in the power of her husband to grant or to refuse?

Mariamne ceased not her entreaties and expostulations till her boon was granted; still not so much for his love of her, to which passion Josephus imputes most of Herod's actions concerning his wife's family, but because he felt that, once established as High Priest, Aristobulus would have no temptation to leave the country, but would always remain in his power, to be removed whenever his unscrupulous cruelty deemed fitting. Assembling his friends, he told them that "Alexandra had conspired against his authority, seeking, by the aid of Cleopatra, to elevate her son to his throne—a proceeding doubly unjust, *as it would deprive her daughter of the dignity she now had*, and would bring disturbances into the kingdom. He had, therefore, in his anxiety to retain it, resolved to give the youth the high priesthood; and that he had, in fact, only set up Ananel, because Aristobulus was so young a child."

We have marked one line of this politic speech in italics, because it appears to us so convincing, that Herod himself was aware that his principal hold, as sovereign of the Jews, on the people, was his union with Mariamne. The depriving her of the dignity she now enjoyed, would have been of very little moment to him individually, if he had not strongly felt that her dignity supported his, and if one were shaken, so would be the other.

The appointment of Aristobulus reconciled the people, in a measure, to their king; and, for a brief interval, quieted the intriguing Alexandra. She professed, with many tears, "that she had never sought the kingdom for her son, nor would she accept it were it offered; having that confidence in Herod's capability of governing that would secure the safety of the remainder of her family; that she was satisfied, nay, overcome, by Herod's benefits, and thankfully accepted the honour shown by him to her son, praying him to excuse her if *the nobility of her family, and the freedom of acting which that nobility*, she thought allowed her, had made her act too precipitately and imprudently in this matter."

Josephus, who, in his own person, was a great stickler for woman's inferiority, would certainly not have put such words in Alexandra's mouth, if they had no foundation in the customs and characteristics of the Jewish people. He must have known that *freedom of acting* was perfectly compatible with the Hebrew woman's social position, or she could not have alluded to, and sought to excuse it. Nor would Herod, as we shall see in the sequel, have deprived her of liberty, had he not feared that she would again use it to the detriment of his interest. For a while peace seemed established between these two equally dark, and equally opposing spirits. Mariamne saw her beloved brother in his rightful position; and rejoiced that one subject of contention was thus removed. Her mind was too pure, too upright, to harbour suspicion of those around her. How could she penetrate the secret thoughts and wishes of her husband, or believe that, in the very fulfilment of her anxious wish, her brother's death-warrant was, in the tyrant's inmost heart, already sealed? Glad to escape from the pressure of care and sorrow which had darkened her early years, Mariamne probably gave herself up to the delight of her domestic affections, unconscious of the brooding passions in her mother's heart, or their provocation by her husband.

Fearful that Alexandra would renew her plots and innovations, Herod desired that she should dwell in the palace, his subtle policy most likely concealing the real reason of this command under the same show of reverence and honour with which he had welcomed Hyrcanus to the same dangerous precincts. But Alexandra's equally subtle penetration speedily discovered that her guard, appointed ostensibly in honour of her high rank, were creatures of Herod, restraining her liberty, and spies upon her most private hours, and most unguarded words. Burning with indignation, she wrote to Cleopatra, beseeching her assistance and advice, declaring that she would undergo any thing, rather than continue to live in this state of slavery. The very indignation which it caused her, proves how little accustomed were the women of Israel to the faintest semblance of restraint.

Cleopatra, who appears always to have befriended Alexandra (another proof in what light the Jewish female aristocracy were regarded by foreign nations), advised her to escape with her son into Egypt, where she promised them protection. Alexandra eagerly assented. She ordered two coffins to be made, as for two dead bodies. In these she intended to conceal herself and her son, desiring her servants, whom she could trust, to convey them away in the night time, and bear them to the sea-shore, where a ship would be waiting to take them to Egypt. The scheme promised fair, but was defeated, by its being spoken of to Sabion, one of her friends, under the impression that he was already in her confidence. This Sabion, believing its discovery would insure him favour, betrayed it to the king. Herod permitted the plan to go on, that he might be assured of its existence, and discovered the whole at the very moment Alexandra believed its success complete. Still no outward evidence of his anger appeared. He stood in too much dread of Cleopatra's influence with Antony, if exerted against himself, to adopt harsh measures against Alexandra. With every manifestation of generosity and kindness, more than likely to inspire the gratitude and affection of his young wife, he overlooked the offence; but his unhappy victim was marked for removal. It seems strange that Herod did not seek the destruction of Alexandra in the young man's stead, for there was nothing in his dawning character to arouse a tyrant's dread, except, indeed, those lofty virtues and outward attractions, which might mark him as a dangerous rival to the wily Idumæan. Still, though resolved in his diabolical purpose, he waited, lest a too summary removal might work against himself.

The Feast of Tabernacles approached; and the whole population of Judea flocked, in exact accordance with the Law, to Jerusalem. Festivity reigned throughout the city—the land was at rest from foreign oppressors—the spirit of faction itself seemed stilled—from palace to hut all was solemn rejoicing, and light-hearted merriment. On the holy days of convocation, the immense areas and courts of the temple were thronged with the dense multitudes, eager to receive the High Priest's triennial blessing. And there he stood, the youthful descendant of a thousand priests and warriors and kings, in the first bloom of graceful youth, clothed in the magnificent vestments of the solemn office, majestic in his bearing, so unusually tall and finely proportioned in his still boyish figure—his beautiful countenance, so radiant with the holy thoughts and feelings which his task called forth, that, as the multitudes gazed upon him standing at the high altar, gracefully and collectedly performing his priestly duties, themselves never witnessed (from their peculiar sanctity and holy associations) without emotion, enthusiasm, even at that holy moment, could not be restrained. Tears burst forth from young and old—the warrior, even as the woman, wept, thrilled to the very heart, at the beauty, innocence, and sanctity he beheld, though himself unconscious why he wept. Tears, blessings, prayers, swelling at length into shouts of joyous greeting, betrayed the zeal and love which burst irrepressibly from every heart. What was the sovereign himself, though present, compared with the High Priest—their own, not only in himself, but in his glorious race and family, the traits of whom he bore upon his features? And if such were the emotions of the multitude, what feelings must have swelled the hearts of the mother and sister? However ill-regulated ambition, and its awful train of evil passions, had marred the heart and mind of Alexandra, in all things relating to Aristobulus she felt as an anxious and affectionate mother; and some of the purest emotions which she had ever experienced, must have been excited in thus beholding him. And to his fond sister, what delicious emotions of love and admiration, aye, and reverence, for she knew him worthy of the solemn office, must have heightened and hallowed the deep affection she had ever borne him, as the hand-in-hand companion of her childhood and youth! Each quivering blessing, each ringing shout, found echo in her heart.

Darkly, and terribly in contrast with such emotions, did the storm of jealous hate rage in the bosom of Herod. He beheld, or fancied in the popular enthusiasm, rebellion against himself; in the grace and beauty of a boy, greater danger to his power and himself, than he had ever encountered, or feared from a thousand warriors, or from the wisdom and policy of a hundred veterans. But though the internal tempest could only be stilled by the victim's blood, Herod dissembled, and joined with apparent sincerity in the public rejoicing.

The festival passed: the multitude dispersed in quiet, from the capital to their respective homes. A hush of peace, foreign and domestic, seemed to have sunk on the troubled land; and Alexandra and her young son returned to the former's palace at Jericho. There, after a brief interval, they were joined by Herod and some of his court, no doubt including Mariamne; and a period of feasting and royal amusements followed. All enmity against Aristobulus had apparently subsided. Herod treated the young man with a semblance of caressing fondness, only too likely to remove suspicion both from Mariamne and her brother. Alexandra herself seems at that time to have suspected nothing evil. The skies over their head, and the distant horizon, all were smiling in cloudless blue and glowing sunshine, when the bolt fell with a shock and horror, as if indeed, nature had thundered from her very smiling calm, and hurled a death-bolt from her sunlit sky. The young prince had quitted the palace in company with the sovereign and their respective attendants; and wandered carelessly along the gardens and pastures, till they neared some spacious fishponds. The day was sultry, and many plunged into the refreshing waters, to indulge in the luxury (truly so, in the scorching East) of bathing. At first, the young prince had stood aloof, amused at the various manœuvres in the art of swimming, displayed by his attendants, but, instigated by Herod to try his skill also, willingly joined them. Twilight was advancing, but still the sports continued, till from the closing darkness a wild cry resounded, and then a suffocating moan, and then, a shout from many voices, "for help, the prince was drowning :" but it came too late. The measures of the tyrant and his fiendish helpers had been too well taken, and the hapless youth was conveyed home to his distracted relatives, a lifeless corpse, not three hours after he had quitted them, radiant in loveliness and life. A violent death is always fearful to the bereaved survivors; and how doubly aggravated, when traced to relentless murder! The actual cause of the young man's death must certainly have transpired, else Josephus, who generally tries to exonerate Herod, would not so decidedly have attributed this murder to him. As deep and universal as had been the love and sympathy which he had inspired at the altar, so deep and universal was the affliction at his loss. Every family, to use the (in this instance) expressive words of the historian, "looking on this calamity, not as it belonged to another, but *that one of themselves was slain.*" How inexpressible, how harrowing, must then have been the agony of his mother and sister; and in the latter how awfully heightened, by the scarcely restrained voice of public indignation, pointing to her husband, as his ruthless murderer. How many circumstances must, in those moments of agony, have returned to the heart of Mariamne, startlingly, appallingly convincing of the foundations for these rumours. Herod had in truth wept, in fearful agitation, as the body of the youth was exposed before him; but there are moments when the vision of the soul is clearer than heretofore—when human agony is such, that semblances which successfully deceived before, cast down their robes of falsehood, and appear naked in their own hideousness—and so it probably was with Mariamne. Tears and agitation, which a moment of less suffering might have so deceived, as to lead her to her husband's bosom for consolation, now spoke the language, not of grief for bereavement, but remorse and horror for the deed; revealed him not *mourner* but *murderer*. Where was she to turn in that deep agony; her mother had concealed her utter desolation, her passionate cravings for revenge, under an exterior of such chilling despair, that how might she give comfort? He, whom she had loved longest and best on earth, ay, even better than her husband; for Herod's was not a character so to concentrate all affection in himself, that the silver links of natural affection had been dulled before it; her brother in blood, in love, in the proud glories of their race and heritage, he lay in his cold grave; and dark suspicions filled her heart,

that the only other being in the wide world whom her young
spirit could have loved, was that brother's murderer! What
to her were the magnificent honours which were lavished on
his senseless remains, but as a mockery to the dead, and
triumph to the living, that the last obstacle to his ambition
was removed? If thus it was considered, even by the fickle
multitude, whose opinion magnificence and show generally
guide where a sovereign wills, can we doubt that it was thus
considered by the bereaved and agonised sister, to whom the
private character of Herod must have been more unguardedly
displayed? She had been too young, too innocent, too confiding, to become aware of it before ; but when awakened by
a flash of agony like this, how might the confidence, the
guileless trust of *youth* return. She had lived little more than
twenty years : but she was now ALONE, and in that word
dwells AGE.

Mariamne's deep affliction was visible only in her change of
bearing towards her husband, and the mournful ageing of
individual character. But Alexandra's anguish could have no
rest, no peace, till lost in the wild wish, and matured measures
for revenge. Till reason regained ascendancy, her agony was
such, that suicide seemed the only relief ; but then came the
desire to live, even to prolong life, till vengeance was accomplished : and so to prolong life demanded all possible care, by
neither word nor act, to offend Herod, whose unscrupulous
cruelty would not spare her, more than her son. To deceive
him, therefore, was that semblance of belief in his professed
grief assumed, which must so have chilled the heart of her
daughter—an apparent satisfaction from the honours awarded
to her boy in death—an impenetrable concealment of every
suspicion that murder, not accident, had deprived her of her
child, marked her outward conduct, while in secret she wrote
to Cleopatra, detailing the whole affair, and conjuring her
influence to bring Herod to justice.

With all her weaknesses, all her faults, the Egyptian queen
appears fully capable of woman's kindest feelings. Indignant
at the treacherous action, and sympathising deeply in the
mother's agony, Cleopatra never rested till she had prevailed on Antony to summon Herod before him, and defend
himself from an accusation so fraught with treachery and
horror. As this command was not, however, sent until Antony
was in Laodicea, the year following the murder, some months

must have elapsed, which probably removed all suspicion of Alexandra having been concerned in the charge. We only read of Herod being in great fear of the accusation, and of Cleopatra's known ill-will towards him. Had he suspected Alexandra as the originator, we cannot doubt but that her death, either by secret murder or public execution, would instantly have followed.

Finding it impossible to evade the summons, Herod left the charge of his kingdom to his uncle Joseph, as procurator of the government. With this public office he connected a private one; the extraordinary command that if Antony should condemn him to death, Joseph would instantly slay Mariamne, giving as his ostensible reason, that he had so tender an affection for his wife, that he could not bear the idea of her becoming, after his death, the wife of any other man. Joseph promised compliance, and Herod departed.

The historians of this period appear to believe in Herod's revealed reason for wishing the death of his wife, and lay great stress on the deep love he bore her. Love! Can it be possible that sober, reasoning men, looking back on these events, tracing the whole character of this man as on a map before them—beholding not one softening feeling, not one human emotion, not one pitying pause in his ruthless career— perceiving that his every aim, intent, desire, apart from individual aggrandisement, was the denationalisation of Judea —to incorporate it with the heathen kingdoms, and increasing his own power, exterminate its peculiar people from the face of the earth—can it be possible, we repeat, that thoughtful and reasoning men, who at this distance of time can look back with much clearer ken on the records of the past, than those historians but lately removed from the scenes, and personages of whom they write, can yet adopt the views of Josephus, simply because he wrote them, and believe that love could ever have actuated Herod in commanding the death of his wife, or have guided his intercourse with her while she lived? Jealousy and selfishness might, indeed, have appeared to his own heart like love, but the reality would have dictated differently. He might, indeed, in his selfish tyranny, have resolved that she should never give to, nor receive happiness from, any other man; but if we judge of him according to his character and acts, there was yet another and deeper reason. He could not bear the thought, that the Asmonæan faction, whom he so hated, so oppressed, so sought to exterminate in life, should obtain ascendancy on his downfall, and rule that land which he had destined for himself. Mariamne was now almost its sole representative, with the exception of the aged Hyrcanus, who, though unfitted for the office of high priest, might yet rule as sovereign—and his kinsmen, the sons of Babas. Of the existence of these last, Herod was ignorant, having years before commanded their death.

Herod could not have doubted, that on the event of his death, Mariamne would instantly be acknowledged sovereign. The customs of the country had already provided examples of a wife succeeding her husband; nor was it likely this rule would be waived, when, as in the case of Mariamne, it was the wife and not the husband who possessed legal, hereditary and national right to the government. When we reflect on the extreme jealousy which Herod bore towards all the Asmonæans —that he never permitted an opportunity to pass without cutting them off—we have surely some foundation for the belief, that the *jealousy of ambition*, quite as deeply as the *jealousy of love*, actuated Herod in his determination, that if he died, Mariamne should die with him. He *could not* conquer the hated thought of beholding her ruling over a loving and obedient people in his stead, courted, followed, perchance united to one of her own race, willing and eager to join her in every effort to elevate Judea to her own exclusive holiness and pristine glory.

This analysis of the motives of Herod's barbarous command is merely offered to our readers as a suggestion. Histories of the time are open to them; and far more improving and satisfactory is it for them to read, and to form their own conclusions, than adopt, without examination, those of another.

From the words used by Josephus, we are led to imagine that Mariamne had a share in the government, and was consulted by the regent Joseph on all occasions. "But as Joseph was ministering the *public affairs of the kingdom*, and *was for that reason* very frequently with Mariamne, both *because his business required it*, and because of the respect he sought to pay to the queen," etc. Now, if the position of the Hebrew females had been what we are generally inclined to suppose it, the same as that of the *present* Eastern females, we should not find this very important passage. The lines marked in italics demonstrate very forcibly, that Joseph was in the habit of consulting with the queen, on all matters of business; and he did so, not only because it was *the custom of the country*, but also from his great respect towards her, a respect which could not have been excited in the respective ages and relation of uncle and niece, if intellect, and wisdom, and dignity had not been added to, and enhanced the exceeding beauty and grace which she so eminently possessed.

Had any modern or European historian penned the sentence we have quoted, its importance would not have been so great; but coming from Josephus, intimately acquainted as he was, with the manners and customs of the Jews of that day, it is a powerful proof of the perfect equality of the Jewish female, both in her domestic and social position. Had it not been quite customary for such reference to the wife of the sovereign during his absence, the visits of Joseph must have excited, not only private, but public suspicion, and called for animadversions from the historian: instead of which he describes it quite naturally, as a usual and common occurrence: and furthermore, declares Salome's accusations to be a groundless calumny, whose only foundation was individual hate.

These facts, trifling as they seem, should be remembered, when we are told that the condition of the Jewish females was so degraded and enslaved. Josephus, individually, may have a mean opinion of the sex; but his whole history, by an almost remarkable triumph of *facts* over *prejudices*, contradicts himself, and supplies us with unanswerable evidences of the truth of our theory.

Apparently anxious to increase Mariamne's love for her husband, or rather, perhaps to remove the cold restraint which had marked her conduct towards him since her brother's death, Joseph never allowed an opportunity to pass without alluding to the strong affection Herod bore her. Mariamne herself appears to have listened to these professions in silence. That love was strange and doubtful, which only manifested itself in individual passion, wholly regardless of her feelings, as sister, daughter, and Asmonæan: but complaint of Herod never passed her lips. Hers was that true spiritual dignity, which never stoops to reveal to others her own sufferings, when the originator of these sufferings was her husband.

Alexandra, however, listened to these speeches in a very different spirit, and replied with such satirical scepticism, that Joseph, in his anxious desire to prove the depth and extent of his nephew's love, incautiously revealed his last command, as an unanswerable evidence how dear she was to him, that he could not bear to separate himself from her, even in death.

The effect of this communication on Alexandra may be imagined. To lose her only remaining child for the gratification of a tyrant, would have been, in itself, agonising enough; but Alexandra was never actuated by such feminine emotions alone; she hated Herod; as the murderer of her boy, it was not much wonder. She was enraged and indignant that he should possess the heritage of her children : her mind was never quiet, constantly scheming and intriguing for his downfall; and in so doing, almost always compassing the ruin of her own family in his stead; and this last command she probably conceived, as we have done, as instigated much more by his hatred of Mariamne's *race*, than his love for her as an *individual*.

But her endeavours to incite Mariamne to revenge upon her husband were useless. There is not a single portion in the life or character of the princess which can permit the supposition of any such emotion entering her mind, even for a moment. What she felt at this command, even as from every other action of her husband, she did not reveal : but how fearfully and coldly must its dark selfishness have sunk into her heart. Life, except for one sweet tie (she was a mother), was, indeed, a dream of anxiety and sorrow; but to be deprived of it by the mandate of cruelty and violence, was no thought of relief. Did no personal considerations mingle with it (and they must have done), her children called upon her to live for them; and by the sweet emotions they inspired, illumined the heavy darkness round her. How could she feel towards a husband, capable of issuing such a command? What must have been the terror and anxiety, her daily portion till she could receive tidings of Herod's fate? And yet we read of neither word nor act, even in that horrible position, derogatory to the beautiful enduring consistency, which, to the very last, her character displayed.

And even when the report came that Herod had been executed, the idea of seeking the protection of the Romans originated with Alexandra, not with the one most injured. That Mariamne should adopt the plan, was natural, for her children's sake as well as her own; for how might she bear the thought of leaving them to the care of Cypros and Salome, who would not scruple to gratify on them the hatred they bore herself? How else, in fact, was she to preserve her life? She needed not the motive attributed to her, in conjunction with her mother, to lead her to the Roman camp. Her own people would have been sufficient protection, could she have appealed to them: but how could that be, when she was surrounded, almost imprisoned, by the relatives and creatures of Herod, whose bidding to them was absolute, even in his death?

That Mariamne looked to her personal influence with the licentious Antony, to protection and benefit, is disproved by the whole tenor of her life. A single impure thought would have prevented that perfect defence from all calumnious charges, which so satisfied the jealous Herod, that even he demanded nothing further than her simple word. Not even the most prejudiced can fling a doubt upon her name.

That Alexandra urged her to seek the Roman camp, because she looked to her child's influence with Antony, we believe, though we shudder as we do so; for such a thought was in exact accordance with her previous unnatural proceeding, of forwarding to him the pictures of her children. But even from such an influence—a mother's influence—Mariamne's own purity and innocence was her invulnerable shield. Alexandra dared not, could not have breathed such a thought to her; and was, therefore, content to work in secret. But her plans were frustrated by news from Herod himself, contradicting the report of his death, and containing a flourishing account of his favour with Antony; who not only established his absolute authority, as sovereign of Judea, but reproved Cleopatra for her interference. No allusion to the murder of Aristobulus appears to have been made on either side; and terrible must have been the pang of such omission to Alexandra.

While these events were passing, Salome had not been inwardly idle, though compelled, outwardly, to be on terms of intimacy with her brother's wife. It was impossible for the lofty character of the Asmonæan princess to condescend to treat as an equal and friend, one whose real character her penetration had probably fully discovered, and whose dislike Salome had never taken any pains to conceal. Josephus tells us, Salome " had a long time borne her ill-will; for when they had discoursed with one another, Mariamne took great freedom, and reproached the rest for the meanness of their birth." The great freedom of such reproaches we must confess ourselves incapable of discovering. It had probably been during their mutual residence at Masada, as we before stated; when Mariamne was a mere girl, and worked upon by the example of her mother, and the prejudices of her own education, to look down somewhat scornfully on Idumæan proselytes. That Salome had a "*long time* borne her ill-will," evidently refers to that distant period, the stings of which still rankled, increased by the haughty reserve which had probably marked the queen's conduct towards her since. It was not to the sister of her husband, Mariamne could breathe the agonised suspicion of her brother's murderer; not to Salome she could reveal sorrows and emotions concealed from every other. We have no doubt her manner was cold, nay, even haughty to a fault; when it would have been more to her interest to have conciliated. But we are writing not of angelic, but of human nature; and that she did not conciliate either Salome or Herod, as Josephus evidently thinks she ought, is, to us, a convincing proof of the consistent uprightness of her conduct. We do not read of Alexandra inspiring such enmity in Cypros and Salome as Mariamne; because the former could *feign*, when she saw it was her interest, both forbearance and regard— the latter *could not*. That she thought somewhat too proudly of the "accident of birth" in herself, and too scornfully of it in others, was the fault of her education, not of herself.

An opportunity had now arrived for Salome's secret plans to ripen. Accompanied by her mother, who, in these schemes, always appears just that secondary tool, which an active vindictive spirit would make of a passive weak one, Salome met Herod on his return to Judea; and, informing him first of Alexandra's intentions to seek the protection of the Romans, artfully insinuated that Joseph would no doubt have aided the intention, followed by a direct charge of dishonourable conduct between him and Mariamne. The feelings of any man would have been roused by this calumny. With Herod, jealousy generally maddened him into a fiend. But in this instance he acted more nobly than he ever did before or after; and would almost persuade us, that *could* such a feeling be possible, he had moments of real love for Mariamne individually. He appealed to herself for the truth or falsehood of the calumny. How must even his fierce intriguing character have unconsciously acknowledged and loved the simple truth and purity of his wife, that even in such a moment he could have turned to her, and permitted the solemn assurance of innocence from her lips, to weigh against the accusations and proofs with which Salome and his mother sought to madden him against her.

The true dignity and natural amiability of Mariamne's character, are proved by her conduct in this interview. A really haughty, contentious, and scornful woman would have used reproaches, scarcely condescending to reply to such a charge, and instead of soothing, irritate still anew. Love her husband Mariamne could not, but she knew her duty as a wife. She could feel that, however he had injured her family and herself, in this instance he did her at least the justice to demand the truth or falsehood of the charge from her own lips, and with all a woman's quickness of feeling, have felt for his agony under such a suspicion, and at that moment felt she might love him yet again. Conquering all personal emotions, she so calmly, so fully exculpated herself, that Herod was not only convinced, but conjured her to pardon the momentary suspicion. Her truth, her purity, seemed for the moment to infuse themselves into him, and to arouse his better nature. Professing, and by caresses endeavouring to manifest unbounded affection and firm confidence in her fidelity, Josephus tells us, that he sought to "draw from her a like confidence in himself," words very convincing, that Mariamne, even while she vindicated herself, never lost that lofty bearing, and quiet, gentle dignity, which, from the hour of her brother's murder, had marked her conduct. Even to her husband she never stooped, as many women so situated would have done, to feign a love and confidence which she could not feel. She must have known that her life with him was in constant danger—a word might be her death-doom; but she feared him not. Strong in her own innocence and noble virtues, she walked on her way, acting as honesty dictated, without turning to this side or to that, or fearing any peril that straightforwardness might bring.

Exactly in accordance with the uncomplaining, but deeply feeling spirit, which would never breathe to any human ear the anguish and terror which Herod's command must have excited, was the noble remonstrance which bade her reply to his entreaties for her confidence and love, "If the command he had given, that if any harm had befallen him from Antony, she who had been no occasion of it should perish with him, were indeed a proof of his love for her?"

Even had she known the evils, which were to spring from this very simple question, Mariamne could not have permitted its recollection to rankle in her heart, and secretly poison every outward demonstration of Herod's love. Touched, in all probability, at his unwonted candour towards herself, her upright mind shrunk from concealing her knowledge of his secret command, and she appealed to him, in the same confiding spirit as he had appealed to her; but the effect was as different as their respective characters. Herod sprung from her side, in a burst of uncontrolled fury. Her truth, her purity, all passed away before a blaze of passion, appalling to witness, and terrible to feel. Madly believing, that nothing but improper intimacy with Joseph could have called for such a betrayal of a command imparted to his uncle in strictest confidence, he rushed upon Mariamne, with his drawn sword, and would have slain her on the spot, had not the calm and dignified composure, enhancing her extraordinary beauty, even at such a moment, disarmed him towards herself. His whole rage fell on Joseph and Alexandra; ordering the immediate execution of the former without permitting trial, or even defence, and imprisoning the latter with every mark of ignominy and insult.

Why his rage, on this occasion, should so have fallen on Alexandra, appears rather a problem. He seems entirely to have overlooked the charge against her, of seeking the protection of the Romans, and to have imprisoned her on this implied supposition of being accessory to the dishonour of his wife. We rather imagine that he was rejoiced at any opportunity to get her out of his way, without caring to give any reason for so doing. Nor does it appear quite clear to me, that *after* the first transports of his rage, and its gratification in the removal of two obnoxious individuals, that he ever seriously retained any idea of Mariamne's guilt. He evidently lived with her, and loved her (if he could love) as before, seeking to conciliate her at every opportunity; as thus tacitly allowing, that he had accused and condemned her wrongfully; and if he really had believed her guilty, this, even to Herod, would have been impossible.

But whatever were his secret feelings, they could have brought neither rest nor comfort to the deeply wounded spirit of his injured wife. She must have felt more and more convinced, that her life was not worth a day's purchase,—her honour constantly liable to be attacked, her innocence impossible to be proved, for neither law nor defence would be allowed her,—compelled to associate in daily intimacy with the man who had actually drawn his sword upon her, insulted, vilified, and then added to the horror with which she must have regarded him, by daring to profess love, and lavish caresses, from which she must have shrunk in utmost loathing,—her mother imprisoned, degraded; and though Mariamne was conscious of Alexandra's many faults, she was yet her mother: he worst qualities were hidden from her child;—the power of her race, the glory of her people passing away before the successful ambition of an Idumæan usurper; the laws and customs of her country wholly disregarded, that by a gradual, yet sure process, the manners and customs of heathen nations should take their place;—it was impossible, that to an Asmonæan, the last pure unmixed scion of that noble race, such feelings should be unknown: and what then must have been the harrowing trials of her inward and outward life? Yet we read of no manifestation of her intense suffering, no secret intrigues, no public appeals, no turning to equivocal sources of enjoyment, to banish the misery of home. No! Compared with the dark machinations, the subtle intrigues of Salome, Alexandra, and Cypros, she stands forth in untouched and untarnished lustre, as some pure spirit of truth and light, sent upon the earth to whisper that even in the blackest and most appalling periods of human depravity, the divine essence breathed within us by God himself still has existence; often, it may be invisible, but still there. Historians do Mariamne no justice. It is only by reflection and analogy, that we can penetrate the truth concerning her and other characters of the period; and doing so with one or two, bringing out the strong lights of individual *character* against the dark shadows of the tyrant *circumstance*,—comparing what *is*, with what *might be*,—it is thus, we relieve truth in its crystal purity from the web of prejudice and superficialism, and so learn the important lesson, that never yet was human nature wholly dark, or this earth left without some witnesses of the divinity within us. A mere glance over Josephus and other histories compiled from him, confounds Mariamne with the intriguing and subtle spirits, male and female, by whom she was surrounded; and thus it is, that we can so seldom discern the good from the bad, the divine from the earthly, and we condemn all as equally evil, equally retrograding. A careful study of history, not merely satisfied with the views of the writer, but using, freely and fearlessly, our own powers of reflection and analogy, would teach us much to fill our hearts with charity and hope, and inculcate the refreshing faith, that every IDEAL of the immortal mind, may find in the ACTUAL its origin and end.

For about four years, Mariamne lived so far in peace, that no attack from the calumny of female hate, or from the violence of jealous passion, reached her individually. Her trials were from the sources to which we have already alluded. How fondly in this interim must her desolate heart have clung to her children, four of whom now called her mother. The very names given to her sons, reveal the love borne by her to her own race and family. All Herod's other children had names relative to his Idumæan descent, or in compliment to his Roman allies. It was not likely that he would have chosen the name of Aristobulus for one of his sons, laden as it was with the recollection of his murdered victim; but we may well imagine the feelings with which Mariamne bestowed it on her first-born — how, clinging to the memory of a brother so beloved, she should seek to continue the name in her own family, and in the caresses of an infant Aristobulus, struggle for forgetfulness of the agony which still lingered round the memory of her brother. Her second son, she named Alexander, in respectful recollection of her father. Her daughters, born afterwards, Salampsio and Cypros, do not appear to possess the same dear associations,—she had no female relation to call for them; but we trace how her memory lingered with the dead, and how lonely she felt amid the living, in the simple fact of the names given to her sons.

The awakening intelligence, the infant caresses of her children, were Mariamne's only scources of joy. She probably looked to her boys, once more to raise the Asmonæan name, and renew the national glory of Judea; and had she lived to rear them from infancy to youth, to instil within them the nobility of race and faith, which she felt and manifested herself, Judea would have wept their deaths still more. As it is, though Aristobulus could have been little more than six when his mother died, we can trace in the after-history of both the young men, the lofty bearing and proud virtues hereditary to their mother's race—even though their Roman education must have deadened every infant impression of their peculiar religion and their holy land. Four years after

Herod's injurious conduct towards herself, Mariamne was called upon to mourn the death of her last male relative, the harmless and aged Hyrcanus. Whether or not Alexandra's intrigues had really urged the old man to such measures, as gave Herod a pretence for ordering his execution, or whether the plot were Herod's own, only to get rid of one whose claims to the crown he still seemed to fear, cannot now be correctly ascertained. The indolent character of Hyrcanus gives some colour to the latter supposition; the intrigues and restless spirit of Alexandra, authorise the former. From whatever cause, the loss to Mariamne was the same, and it widened the breach between her heart and her husband. The freedom enjoyed by Hyrcanus, and the respect, at his first accession, proffered to him by Herod, who gave him lodging at the palace, and board at the king's table, had probably given Mariamne many opportunities of enjoying the old man's society, and bound her to him still more closely than their consanguinity. She could not have believed the charges brought against him, nay, most probably, *knew* that they were false, and traced their contrivance to her ambitious and ever-scheming husband, beholding in them yet another proof of Herod's resolve to crush every remnant of her race. She had not, however, long to indulge in grief. Herod was at this period anxious to conciliate the youthful conqueror of Antony, Octavius Cæsar, who was then at Rhodes; and trembling, as usual, lest the popular love for the Asmonæans, should snatch the home goverment from his hands, and give it to Mariamne and her children, he resorted to the cruel expedient of separating his wife from her only treasures, placed them under the care of his own mother and sister, at Masada, and confined Mariamne and Alexandra in the fortress of Alexandrina, under charge of his treasurer Joseph, and Sohemus of Itruria, giving to the latter exactly the same selfish and brutal command, as he had given to his uncle Joseph five years previously, that if his death were the consequence of his dangerous expedition, not only Mariamne, but her mother, should die with him, and the kingdom proceed to his brother Pheoras, regent for his (Herod's) sons. This command at once proves that not love, but ambition and hatred of the Asmonæan race, were his real motives, not only at the second time, but at the first. There was now no Antony in such power, as to unite himself to the wife of his victim. Octavius Cæsar was no character for the terror of such an alternative. Besides, if it were only his love (so called), which could not bear its object to survive him, why command the death of Alexandra also? It is clear throughout this dark domestic history, that love for Mariamne *individually* and hatred of her as an Asmonæan, whose claims to the throne of her people were continually endangering his own, were ever at such fierce internal war, that he could never define from which of these contending passions, the motives of his actions sprung; and the historians are therefore equally obtuse, giving often to love of the woman, what was in fact nothing but hatred of the race.

There is no proof more convincing of her right to the throne which Herod occupied, than his determination that she should never survive him to enjoy it; love held his hand, while he could revel in her exceeding loveliness, but when she could no longer be his, she was to share the fate of all her race.

Josephus is amusingly astonished, that Mariamne could feel no affection for her husband; and quite blames her for not dissembling her dislike. We should feel very grateful to any one who would bring forward a single instance in Mariamne's hapless life, where love for Herod on her part was even possible, or what single proof he ever gave of his exceeding love for her. We will not again refer to sufferings on which we have already dilated; but ask, if separation from the only beings she had loved on earth, and such imprisonment in a well-garrisoned fortress, as utterly prevented all exercise of power, and privileges of rank, which she had enjoyed, were any striking proof of conjugal regard? In Herod's previous absence, he had had at least the grace to associate his wife with his uncle in the government. In this, Josephus expressly tells us, "that they had no power over anything, either of others or of their own affairs;" and this he need not have written, unless conscious that they both had the right and the will to execute authority.

To some characters, the injury of placing her children under any care but her own, would have swallowed up all other emotions. But Mariamne was no ordinary woman. To her heart it was not only maternal suffering: the cruel deprivation of her privileges was in direct disregard of the customs and habits of her people, who in every stage of their eventful history, gave to mothers, and mothers only, the education of both sons and daughters. It was an insult as well as a source of personal suffering, aggravating not lessening the degradation of imprisonment. Had her children been still with her, she would not have regarded her residence at Alexandrina as anything more than a measure of security. But when she felt herself deprived of a privilege granted to the meanest of her subjects, so watched and guarded, that she had scarcely the liberty of careless speech, was it marvel, was it out of nature, that her proud Asmonæan blood deepened the injured feelings of the wife and mother, and that from that hour she made no further efforts to love her husband?

Yet still, true to the beautiful dignity of her womanly character, Mariamne descended to neither intrigue nor revenge. Her winning beauty and graceful manner, so fascinated all who approached her, even her keepers, creatures strong in Herod's confidence and favour, that had she ever attempted to obtain her rights by an appeal to the people, there does not seem a doubt, that she would ultimately have obtained them; all Herod's magnificence in building, in connection with foreign potentates, had not made him popular. He was endured far more for his Asmonæan wife than for himself, and hundreds, aye thousands, amidst the Jewish people would have flocked round Mariamne, had she but uplifted her standard in opposition to the authority of Herod. But she was far too essentially and exquisitely feminine, to plunge the nation into renewed war and misery for her sake; far too truly noble, to make her private anguish a theme of publicity and blood, or reveal to others, save Herod's self, the loss of affection which his acts had caused. We never hear a syllable of complaint or reproach, save boldly and openly to himself. Her character changed not an atom of its gentle dignity, its forbearing endurance. Nought of irritation, sourness, or that *consciousness of injury*, which some women love to reveal, as proving them martyrs, marks her conduct. Sorrow could not make her selfish; painful as it is, when the heart is aching in its own unceasing anguish, to think of pleasing others even by daily words and common manner; yet even in this lowly duty she did not fail.

Sohemus, like her previous guardian Joseph, was unable to retain the cruel command of Herod, when in presence of its intended victim. Though at first stern, and resolved to remain faithful to his master, his determination faded away before the fascination of Mariamne, who, without any effort on her own part, won every heart that still retained the emotions of humanity. Even Josephus's prejudiced and contradictory account, absolves Mariamne from any undue influence over Sohemus. He was evidently at first led to shrink from obeying Herod's injunction, simply from the unfailing gentleness of her manner, in their daily intercourse. Then, imagining that Herod would not obtain the confirmation of his authority from Cæsar, he became anxious to conciliate the queen; convinced that if she did survive her husband, "she would give him abundant recompense" for his fidelity to herself—for she could not be overlooked in the settling of the government, *as she must either reign herself, or be very near those that reigned.* He hoped also, that his informing her of the charge entrusted to him, and of his determination at all hazards to disobey— would obtain him favour even if Herod did return, by Mariamne's influence obtaining for him some honourable post.

This conviction that Mariamne must reign herself in case of Herod's death, or be very near those that did, meaning her sons, in preference to their elder half-brother Antipater, proves in what light she was in reality regarded by the people in general, and confirms our supposition, that had she been constituted like her intriguing mother and so raised the banner of revenge and revolt, she would have found very many to support her cause. It tells us, too, that her being a female in no way interfered with her right of heritage in the estimation of her people; and this is an important evidence of woman's social position at that period.

The information of Sohemus could scarcely have been unexpected, though it could not fail to alienate Mariamne from Herod yet more. Her mother, too, was to share her fate: the tyrant was not content with one victim. How was it possible she could regard his professions of affection as meaning aught but hypocrisy and guile? How trust to them, when it was so clearly evident that he could never rest till every scion of her race had been cut off? How must her fond heart have clung to the recollection of her children, thus doomed to be snatched from them! And leaving them to such a father! If we reflect but deeply on her position, we surely cannot agree with Milman, as to the difficulty of deciding "what ought to have been her feelings and her conduct."

Herod returned—crowned with success. Octavius Cæsar had confirmed him in possession of Judea—accepted his

friendship, and dismissed him with distinguished honours.
The home affairs of Judea had prospered, and, seeking
Mariamne, he revealed his unexpected success with an exultation and rejoicing which could find little response in the
heart he addressed. She listened to him calmly, coldly—it
might be haughtily. The time had passed, when as in their
former interview, she could appeal to him, and inquire if the
order of her death in case of his, were indeed proof of love.
Those simple words had caused the death of one individual
whose only crime was fidelity to herself, and the imprisonment
of her mother, who, though generally intriguing, had in this
instance offended in nothing save in being the wife and mother
of Asmonæans. How might she speak them again? Yet how
could her noble spirit stoop to the semblance of interest and
affection, when Herod's own deeds had alienated both? It
was impossible—and with calm and proud indfference, she
received him; and so treated him thenceforward. That there
was imminent danger in this line of conduct, no doubt she
knew; but her mind was not one to stoop to deceit for preservation. Had she concealed her sentiments of dislike, she
would have failed in the beautiful truth which encircles her as
a halo. No conjugal duty could have demanded this concealment. There may be some to think that under all insult, all
oppression, all injustice, she should have remembered that she
was a wife, and in duty bound to submit to her husband. We
answer, that, as a wife, she never failed in duty; she could
have appealed to the Jewish law, and have demanded a
divorce; she could have returned his underhand measures
against her life and happiness, by equally undermining his,
both publicly and privately; she might have sought solace for
her domestic misery and personal gratification in pleasures of
doubtful tendency, which, in that dark stormy period, and
laxity of morals, would have passed unnoticed; but Mariamne
was a Jewish wife, a Jewish mother; and so, unsullied, by
even the passing breath of such dark thoughts. She failed
not either in fidelity or allegiance. She endured without one
murmur, one struggle to ameliorate her misery; but her truth
would have been sacrificed, had she treated the human author
of her trials as if she could give him love, or believe in his.

Her coldness roused Herod's contending passions of love and
hate almost to madness. The one repeatedly urged him to
violent measures against her; the other restrained him, fearing

by her death to inflict deeper misery upon himself than upon her. No profession, no effort on his part, could change her dignified and quiet manner, to the demonstration of love for which his strange spirit seemed to long. Her presence bowed him, monster as in reality he was, under the influence of overwhelming love for her individually; her absence changed this feeling into as overwhelming a hate for her as an Asmonæan, who dared insult him by an assumption both of dignity and coldness—the first of which his secret conscience admonished him was natural to her rank and race, and the latter deserved by his own deeds in the ruthless murder of her grandfather, father,* and brother.

Now, then, was the opportunity for which Salome had so long waited. Though foiled four years previous, her envy and hatred had not diminished, but, hoarded in her own evil heart, imparted only to her mother, who was her ready adjunct, were ready to pour forth as a poisonous torrent, the first moment that she could gain her brother's ear. Already half maddened by his contending passions, Herod listened eagerly, and heard such specious tales of calumny and shame, as excited his jealousy of herself, in addition to his hatred of her race. Still he could not proceed against her, though every lying tale in his distorted fancy was confirmed by her proud coldness towards him. Each week increased the evil. His ill-regulated fitful mind and temper—the fierce strife of opposing, but equally violent passions—the one inflamed to madness, from the malignant whisperings of his serpent sister—the other heightened, fired by the sight of that soul-subduing beauty, which shone forth in its cold resplendence, unwarmed by a single ray towards him—all raged within, and at length so furiously, that he was on the point of proceeding to extremities, to the gratification of Salome, when the evil was postponed.

No domestic passions ever seemed to interfere with his public ambition. Hearing that Antony and Cleopatra were both dead, and Cæsar conqueror of Egypt, he hastened to meet him there, leaving his family affairs in their present turbulent condition, and without, as usual, leaving any charge concerning his wife. It was when setting out on this journey, that Mariamne recommended Sohemus (no doubt at his own intreaty) to Herod, asking for him a place in the government,

* Though the father of Mariamne did not fall by Herod's own hand, or command, he was supposed to have had a principal share in his death.

which was granted. She could appeal for one who had acted faithfully towards herself and children, though she would ask no favour, no privilege for herself.

Nothing but prosperity awaited Herod in all his foreign concerns. Octavius Cæsar not only received him as a personal friend, but richly increased his monarchial dominions. The dominions of Gadara, Hyppos, and Samaria—the cities of Gaza, Anthedon, Joppa, and Strabo's Tower, all commanding extensive maritime commerce, were made over to him by the emperor; and after attending Cæsar as far as Antioch, Herod returned to his own capital, flushed with success, and more imperious than ever.

Still, though every throb of ambition seemed fulfilled, Herod could not be satisfied. While earnestly pursuing his career of individual power, all the inward torments of jealous hate and jealous love subsided, but were recalled with redoubled violence on his return. The emperor of the world called him friend, and treated him as such. Other foreign potentates courted, flattered, paid him homage. A monarchy larger, and more independent than had belonged to any of the former kings of Judea, acknowledged him as king; and its millions of inhabitants were obedient and peaceful through terror, if not through love. And still one woman-heart refused him the homage of love and reverence which he demanded—refused to disgrace and humble her own noble Asmonæan name by acknowledging him rightful sovereign of Judea. So at least, on mature reflection, it appears that Herod's own conscience regarded her conduct. Had she given him the love he demanded, he would have accepted it as a tacit acknowledgment of his supremacy; but the unwavering coldness of her manner, the noble bearing, throwing an air of princely dignity over her simplest action—the calm indifference with which she regarded his exaltation, all betrayed, that over her soul he could have no power, either by love or hate; and, therefore, the mortification of feeling himself, in spite of his power, his magnificence, his severity, actually despised by a weak and delicate female whom he would have crushed a hundred times, had not his consuming passion for her exceeding loveliness held his hand, heightened his jealous passion to a pitch of madness, which embittered every moment of his life.

Some months passed, nearly a year, from his last command which Sohemus had betrayed. Salome and Cypros continued their poisonous intrigues, their enmity receiving hot increase from its apparent utter impossibility to chafe the collected spirit of their victim. That her penetrative mind beheld their design is most probable, and also that holding them in most supreme contempt, her manner increased in haughtiness towards them. Mariamne had never been taught to conquer, or even to know, the natural failings of her race. If she had, she would not have *aggravated* enmity, though she might not have averted it. She would not have stooped to feign a friendship she could not feel; but she would have avoided all occasions to give offence. But to one educated as herself this was not easy. Her very hatred of the insidious conduct, unfailingly practised towards her by Cypros and Salome, naturally increased the contempt which their Idumæan birth had originally excited. She no doubt knew the danger which this enmity threatened ; but fear was as much unknown to females, as to the males of the Asmonæan line. That she treated them with undue haughtiness, and may even have spoken of them with the contempt she felt, is not unlikely. We have no wish to exalt our hapless ancestress into the paragon of perfection in which some writers create their heroines; but this we will assert, her failings were those of her education, her virtues intrinsically her own, and so far superior in number and in brightness to her faults, that combined as they were with her severe and unmerited sufferings, we can only think of them, and love her for their sakes. The fierce flames of hate which had been smothered so long at length burst forth. Every preparation, in case of such an opportunity, had long been made by Salome. The train, as it were, laid, only waiting for the kindling match.

In one of his paroxysms of love, Herod one day sent for Mariamne, and endeavoured by lavish caresses and passionate professions to draw from her a similar return: but he sought in vain. Roused at length from her wonted calm endurance, unable to restrain the agony of recollection, deepened as it was by such false professions of a love which his every act denied, she demanded, how she could love one whose ambition and reckless cruelty had caused alike her brother and her grandfather to be slain, and heaped misery and degradation upon her family and herself? Enraged beyond all forbearance, Herod would have committed personal violence on his wife, but appears to have been again restrained by her still subduing beauty. But his chafed spirit so raged and stormed, that

Salome paused no longer. Mariamne had scarcely left the apartment, before his cup-bearer entered, and with every appearance of agitation, informed him that the queen had bribed him with many presents to administer a love-potion, the composition of which he knew not, and fearing what its effects might be, had resolved, as the safest course, on communicating the whole to the king.

Already more than usually enraged, and glad of any charge wherewith to proceed against Mariamne, the king instantly commanded her most faithful eunuch to be seized and tortured, knowing that the queen could have done nothing without his aid. The man in his extremity of agony, never alluded to the charge for which he was tortured; but allowed, that so far as he knew, the dislike borne by his mistress to the king had been occasioned by something which, during Herod's absence, Sohemus had said to her. Again the same fearful belief of treachery and dishonour, which had actuated his conduct towards his uncle five years before, took possession of his heart and mind, and this time with still more fearful effects. Mariamne's petition for Sohemus probably heightened the conviction of her guilt, and prevented all delay. Sohemus was seized and slain without even being informed of his offence, or being enabled to exculpate the queen by his denial of the charge. Mariamne herself, summoned before judges of Herod's own selection, was tried on the accusation of her husband— some historians say of adultery; but the words of Josephus are these:—" He allowed his wife to take her trial, and *got together those that were most faithful to him*, and laid an *eloborate accusation against her* for *this love potion and composition*, which had been charged upon her by way of *calumny* only." Now this is convincing to me that he did *not* accuse her of adultery, knowing that if he did so, she might demand, and he dared not have refused, the trial of the waters of jealousy, expressly provided by the mercy of the Eternal for such emergencies. It was an unchanged statute of her people, as much her right then as it had been that of her ancestresses in centuries past. Again, the judges themselves, however terrified at the wrath of the king, dared not have pronounced her guilty of adultery, without positive proofs of her crime, at the mouth of more than one witness. The intemperate rage of Herod had so far acted against himself, that the death of Sohemus prevented his appearance in treachery and falsehood, if he had been so inclined, to inculpate the victim. For substantiating the charge of attempted assassination through the love-potion, however, Herod could easily obtain tools. The same heart and hand which had already kindled the brand, was still there to nurse it into a wide-spreading flame. The creatures of her scheme were ready to do the bidding of their sovereign. Once in Salome's power, it was easy to complete the deed. Herod's phrenzy prevented all correct judgment; and if for the words, "got together those that were most faithful to him," we read, "got together all those that were ready to swear away their own souls, if by so doing they could oblige their mistress Salome, and compass the death of Mariamne," we may chance to obtain the only correct rendering of the sentence.

Before such judges, and against such witnesses, what would innocence avail? Josephus does not give us the particulars of the trial; but from the queen's conduct on her way to execution, we may suppose her demeanour when in presence of her judges. A dignified composure, a calm denial of the charge, were the only words which probably passed those lips which falsehood had never tarnished. She was innocent—innocent alike of the charge accused and the charge implied; for, no doubt, though adultery was not made the reason of the trial for the reasons stated above, they sought to cover her with the implication of dishonour; and innocence in such awful hours, in truth, is strength. It will not always support us through lingering years of misery, of being shunned by our fellows, because accused of deeds we have no power to prove are false; but God Himself has mercy then, and when the frame dwindles from a breaking heart, takes us to His heaven, to enjoy an eternity of blessedness for a period of woe.

On the threshold of that eternity Mariamne stood; and no thought of the opinion of man could disturb the tranquillity with which innocence strengthened her to look on death. She must long have expected this. From the hour of her brother's murder, disclosing, as it did, the true character of Herod, and his fixed resolve to exterminate the Asmonæan line, she must have anticipated for herself a similar fate. She had faced it, as impending for five years; and the noble spirit which had enabled her, during that interval, so calmly to regard it as never to waver in the line of strict integrity, or even by word or sign to lower the dignity of her character and race, would not forsake her at its termination.

The mockery of justice enacted by that iniquitous trial Josephus himself proves. Creatures of Herod, his will was theirs, and their sentence his. "Accordingly, when the court was at length satisfied *that he was so resolved*, they passed the sentence of death upon her." There is not a syllable as to their own conviction, or their own judgment, nor the wherefore of their *sentence*, except the resolution of the king—not a word as to the guilt of the prisoner—still Herod shrunk in his selfish passion from losing her entirely. He remanded the sentence of death for one of perpetual imprisonment. But, dreading that, if permitted to live even now, every scheme for her destruction would fall to the ground, Salome and her party never rested till, by dint of alarming the *ambition* of the king, they obtained the order for her execution. Here, again, we penetrate the passion which divided Herod's heart with the opposing element of love. It was not by bringing forward the chances of her again dishonouring him, or her becoming the property of another, with which Salome now endeavoured to work upon her brother, but by artfully suggesting that, were she permitted to live, there was always danger of the multitudes revolting, releasing her from prison, and making her sovereign in his stead : for such is evidently the meaning of Josephus's words; and not, as a mere hasty reading might suppose, that the people were so enraged against her that they would be tumultuous if she were suffered to live. This is contrary to both history and reason. We know that Herod was not so much beloved that the multitudes should be enraged against an intending assassin, by the simple fact that conspiracies were continually forming against him—men forming in bodies by some means to compass his death. His very race, as well as his public measures and private character, were odious; whereas Mariamne was almost idolised, alike for herself and as being the last representative of a race so long beloved. A very little reflection on these facts will, I think, be convincing that the above analysis of Salome's arguments is founded on reason.

The order for the execution of the queen was at length issued, and Mariamne prepared for it with the same calm intrepidity as she had faced it years before. Yet who can refuse sympathy in this undeserved fate for one so innocent, so lovely, and still so young that she could barely have exceeded five and twenty years? Nor was she entirely without ties

binding her with silvery links to earth, fraught with anguish
and trial as it was. All whom she had loved with a girl's and
woman's fondness had either fallen in death, or by their dark
deeds annihilated every capability of affection; but others had
arisen, to concentrate on them a heart clinging in its desolation
to them even yet more closely, more devotedly than ordinary
love. How might she leave her infant children? Who on
earth was to care for them? Would not the same persevering
hatred poison their young existence, as it had her own? To
whom did she leave them, Herod, Salome, Cypros? Would
they supply her place? And her own mother? Alas! she
must have already learned that she, too, was not one on whom
her heart could rest, or to whom she could entrust treasures
far more precious than herself; and in the brief interval
stretching between her and death, she was to feel this yet more
agonisingly—the last drop of bitterness flung into her cup was
thrown by a mother's hand! It was not then the mere
separation by her own violent death from her beloved ones.
Thoughts of far deeper anguish must have occupied some of
her parting moments. Nor is this, as we shall, no doubt, be
accused, taking too great licence, and allowing imagination to
usurp the unvarnished tale of history. We never refuse the
meed of sympathy to Anne Boleyn, Lady Jane Grey, Mary
Queen of Scots, and other sufferers of more modern times; yet,
compared with the unsullied purity of Mariamne, the first of
these was irredeemably guilty, and the last burdened by many
historians with a charge (which, though we ourselves believe it
a false and most unproved one, still attaches itself to her name)
of a husband's murder. In point of innocence the second only
can be named with her; and sad as was her fate, it was little
removed from joy compared to the trials and death of Mariamne.
If we give these three our sympathy—if we teach the young
heart to feel for them—if the tale of Anne's parting from her
own Elizabeth, and remorse for her neglect of Mary excite our
sympathy—why shall we hurry over the memoirs of our own,
and refuse them the meed of admiration, love, and pity which,
if we reflect, even their brief unsatisfactory records in Jewish
history must excite? Let any wife and mother place herself
in idea in the position of the Asmonæan princess; or if this be
too fanciful for her imagination, let her suppose her nearest
and dearest relatives injured alike openly and secretly by the
man she has married, and whom she could have loved—herself

insulted, doubted—treated at one time with furious love, at others imprisoned and in danger of her life from the same being —and then accused, condemned, without hope of justice or relief—let her ponder on this; and if she be a mother, say where her last thoughts would rest, and then accuse us, if she can, of so infusing history with imagination as to render it impossible to divide the one from the other. Is human nature —human feeling—different now to what it was in former ages? Shall we deprive the characters of history of all power of emotion, only because they existed under a different modification of social customs? If so, and we are not to exercise either reflection, analysation, or intellect, history must remain the bare recital of events and dates, of which so many justly complain, and from which no lesson, no moral, can be deduced.

Josephus is silent both as to the period elapsing between Mariamne's trial and her death, and as to the manner of that execution. Stoning had originally been the Jewish penalty for all crimes; but the Roman punishment of decapitation had very probably taken its place, and by the axe, no doubt, the last of the Asmonæans fell.

Whatever the death, no doubt attends the last moments of the victim. Calmly, unflinchingly, we are told, she walked to the place of execution. No terror, no unseemly indignation at the injustice dealt her, marred the modest and tranquil dignity which had marked her life, and left her not in death. There she was, in her touching youth and exquisite beauty, accused of crimes which not one of those vast multitudes who looked on believed, though none dared tempt the tyrant's wrath, by rising in her cause. Not a sound broke the awful stillness—the very emissaries of Salome, scattered in large numbers amongst the crowds to silence the faintest semblance of murmuring or pity, appear to have been awed by the dignified composure of the prisoner, and horror-struck, even as the rest of the spectators, by the sudden appearance of Alexandra, not, as might be supposed, to lament and mourn over her child, but to heap upon her reproaches and abuse, declaring "that her punishment came justly upon her for her ingratitude to her husband, and her insolent behaviour in not making proper returns to him who had been their common benefactor." The motives of this fearful hypocrisy, terror for herself, and the consequent desire to avert all personal danger from Herod, by publicly condemning her child, whom she, above all persons, knew to be innocent, appear to have been penetrated, even at that moment, by the multitudes, and excited their loudest condemnation ; but no word of reproach, or suffering, escaped the lips of her whom a *mother* thus assailed. Yet how bitter must have been the pang of such unexpected conduct. How fearfully must the cold selfishness which could, at such a moment, seek personal security, by asserting belief in the guilt of her own child, whom she knew to be unstained, have sunk on the heart of the prisoner. But all human emotions had been stilled—she was standing on the threshold of that glorious eternity, which to her, as a woman of Israel, a descendant of priests, was revealed in all its fulness, all its bliss. A brief, brief pang, and she knew she should be with the idolised brother of her youth, whose angel spirit might even at that moment be hovering near her, to waft her released soul to the footstool of her God. For Israel death had no terror—immortality was to them revealed. They knew that with God was the fulness of joy, and at His right hand were everlasting pleasures. And in the calm fortitude, the meek endurance, yet lofty bearing of the Asmonæan princess, we read, not the stoicism of the Roman martyr, but the rejoicing faith, and unshrinking courage of the Hebrew believer, firm in the blessed consciousness of Immortality and Heaven !

One look of pitying forgiveness fell from the eyes of the injured, on her unnatural mother, and a few words addressed to those near her, expressed the deep concern for Alexandra's degradation. Not for its injury towards herself, but as it concerned her mother individually, exposing her, as it did, to the contempt of the populace, and little likely to conciliate the king. These appear to have been her last words ; " for herself," Josephus continues, " she went to death with an unshaken firmness of mind, and without *even changing* the colour *of her face*, and thereby discovered the nobility of her descent to the spectators, even in the last moments of her life."

We do not think that "nobility of descent" is or was the real lesson derived from such a death. It was the calm intrepidity of innocence—the composed and gentle firmness of a soul at peace with itself, and resting on its God. She had lived long enough to learn, and feel too sadly, that not in this world may we " distinguish between the righteous and the wicked, between him that serveth God, and him that serveth Him not;" and, the pangs of parting from her children once subdued, she gladly turned to that everlasting home where her innocence was known, where her wearied spirit would find its yearned-for rest, and her desolate heart, which earth had crushed, be filled with love infinite as perfect, bliss unending as complete.

We have endeavoured to make manifest throughout this eventful history, how mistaken and contradictory are the impressions with which Josephus would burden the character of Mariamne. Whereas Salome, whose actions it is utterly impossible to misunderstand, and whose dark thoughts and sinful machinations are distinctly visible, from the moment she appears on the theatre of life to the end of her existence, he dismisses without a shadow of blame, either written or implied. Thus leaving the idea, that trifling errors of education, the only faults which can be applied to Mariamne, are, because visited with suffering and death, infinitely more culpable and heinous than the palpable and uncalled-for crimes of calumny, false witness, murder, and a long list of atrocities, either actually performed by Salome herself, or planned and committed by her sole orders and persuasions, but whose blackness becomes white in the eyes of the historian, through the marvellous transformation of temporal elevation and success. Surely, we ought to be careful how we place such opinions in the hands of our children, and not rest contented with merely giving them history to peruse. As an author, Josephus is most valuable; we have no doubt of his accuracy with regard to events, but we cannot depend upon either his discrimination or impartiality in the delineation of *character*, or in the justice and entireness of his conclusions. We repeatedly find that his drawing up, as it were, of a character, is contradicted by the whole tenour of previous events, which being related by himself as facts, must guide us much more correctly than his own conclusions. We have seen this already in the life and character of Alexandra; and we shall perceive it as clearly in his winding up of the character of Mariamne, which we subjoin :—

"And thus died Mariamne; *a woman of excellent character both for chastity and greatness of soul;* but she wanted moderation, and had too much contention in her nature. Yet had she all that can be said, in the beauty of her body, *and her majestic appearance in conversation: and thence* arose the greatest part of the occasions, why she did not prove so agreeable to the king, nor live so pleasantly with him as she might otherwise have done, for while she *was most indulgently used by the king,* out of his fondness for her, and did not expect that he could do any hard thing to her, she took too unbounded a liberty. Moreover, that which afflicted her was, what he had done to her relations, and she ventured to speak of all they had suffered by him; and at last greatly provoked both the king's mother and sister, till they became enemies to her, and even he himself also did the same, on whom alone she depended for her expectations of escaping the last of punishments."

Now we would ask any casual reader, what would be the impression of this extraordinary passage? Would they not suppose, that Mariamne had not only drawn down her fate upon herself, but had actually deserved it? That she was the only one to blame, and Herod, Cypros, and Salome all alike were guiltless? And yet even, in leaving this most unfounded and most unjust impression, of what does he accuse her? Compelled (it would seem almost in spite of himself) to acknowlege her chastity and greatness of soul, all he can bring against her is, that her "majestic appearance in conversation" (meaning, we imagine, the calm dignity of her manner) rendered her less agreeable to the tyrant, than she would have been could she have resembled her mother, and condescended to deceive. We are told that "she was most indulgently used by the king, who out of his great fondness for her could do no hard thing to her, and that, therefore, she took too great a liberty, wanted moderation, and evinced too contentious a spirit." Where throughout her history, and we have given it at full length, can we find the foundation for either of these clauses? How did Herod demonstrate his deep love and great indulgence? By the murder of her brother and grandfather, the constant indignity offered to her mother, the death of all those who befriended, or were faithful to her; or by the continued insults offered to herself, in doubting her truth, commanding her imprisonment, and separation from her children, twice sentenced to death in case of Herod's death, and final execution on a false and unproved charge? Where can we find proofs of her want of moderation, etc.? In her calm endurance of her constant sufferings? In her breathing not

one syllable of complaint or injury, forming no plots, joining
no intrigues, passing through her brief life in such unstained,
unsullied purity and chastity, that not even the most prejudiced can dare fling a stigma on her noble name ; exposed
times out of number to temptation from the machinations of
an evil mother, and the insults of a frenzied husband, yet
eschewing all, and standing forth in her own brightness, before
which neither slander, hatred, nor calumny, could stand ? We
read how impossible Salome felt it to compass her death on the
plea of her dishonour, by the artifice of the love-potion, which
in the end she was compelled to adopt. In what can we discover too contentious a spirit ? In the high-minded uprightness
which revealed to the injurers, and to the injurers alone, her
consciousness of their evil intentions towards her ? In the
absence of all deceptive conciliation, and yet the avoidance of
all attempted vengeance ? In what took she so unbounded a
liberty ? We read of her asking no boon, save one, and that
was Sohemus' own seeking. If, indeed, Herod had so "indulgently used her," and she was of so rapacious a disposition, is
it not almost marvellous that history reveals not a single
instance in which this unbounded liberty was used; that
Mariamne should never have accused Salome and Cypros to
the king, and urged his interference to prevent the injurious
treatment of herself; that we do not read of her interfering
also in the government, in foreign and civil affairs, in which
other women, who really did take "too unbounded a liberty,"
were so often mischievously engaged? There was neither law
nor custom in her nation to prevent this interference, had she
been so inclined.

Again, was it so very remarkable that "what afflicted her
most, was Herod's conduct to her relations?" Yet Josephus
and even Milman, seem to imagime that because she was the
murderer's wife, she was not to feel these things. Was it in
human nature to retain affection or even esteem, for a man
"who had more or less concern in the murder of her grandfather, father, brother, and uncle,"[*] even could she forget and
forgive that twice he had commanded her death in case of his
own ? Was it a fault, that "she ventured to speak of all they
had suffered by him?" Or was it not rather a proof of a
noble spirit and courageous soul, which urged her to risk her
own life, rather than by silence and deceit tacitly acquiesce

[*] Milman.

in the *necessity* for their destruction ? We are told, too, that Mariamne "greatly provoked both the king's mother and sister ;" but of their hatred to her, and malignantly working enmity, Josephus takes no note, permitting us to suppose that it was *deserved*, and Mariamne not Salome was to blame. Haughtiness and reserve, then, according to this historian, are greater crimes than slander, false witness, and actual murder. Mariamne might have treated Salome and Cypros with undue haughtiness, but the fault originated in her education, not herself. Had she, as she might have done, sought to injure Salome with the king, or given evidence of her dislike by public insult or private annoyances, we might acknowledge that she was in error; but of such things we can discern no trace whatever. Mariamne's sole offence was having in her girlhood reproached Salome and Cypros with the meanness of their birth, urged on to do so most probably by her designing mother; and for this offence Salome pursued her with unrelenting hate, caring for neither falsehood nor murder, so she at length succeeded in removing her by death. We know that Mariamne's original offence must have been committed quite in her girlhood, for from the time of the death of Aristobulus, Salome commenced her machinations; and, aware of her hate and designs against her as she must have been, was it strange that Mariamne, shrinking from sight of falsehood even in manner, should treat Salome on all occasions with a reserve and dignity, which her seditious and violent spirit considered as haughtiness and insult impossible to be borne, and so aggravating her passionate desire for revenge?

Such is our dispassionate analysis of Josephus' complex winding up of the character of Mariamne. We can only entreat our readers, old and young, to refer to the history itself, and if our narratives of the same events be deemed erroneous, or prove to have no foundation in reflection and reason, to draw thence their own conclusions, and pronounce judgment on the character of our hapless ancestress accordingly. We wish merely to *suggest*, to *assist* in the perusal of history, not to push forward our individual opinions in opposition to existing authorities, or in contradiction of established theories; acknowledging at the same time boldly and freely, that having long thought that neither Jewish nor Gentile historians have done justice to the personal character and the painful position of the last proud scion of the Asmonæan line, we were glad of this opportunity, so to bring her forward, that our readers perceiving *little things* and *trifling events* more clearly before them than they can be found in a history of the time, may form their own conclusions.

Long as we have already lingered, our task were scarcely accomplished, did we not endeavour to "point a moral" in this eventful tale. Let not our young sisters turn from its perusal, in that sadness and sinking of the heart which must accompany the first conviction, that virtue and goodness and truth are *not* rewarded upon earth; that in Salome, they perceive guilt and crime triumphant, prosperous, rejoicing; in Mariamne, the virtuous falling a victim to the sinful—truth crushed by falsehood, innocence by guilt—Herod living out his days, surrounded by temporal prosperity, power, magnificence, conquering alike foes abroad and seditions at home—courted by foreign potentates—allied to the empress of the world—Aristobulus, the young, the innocent, the gifted, cut off by the dark deeds of this very man, in his first and loveliest youth. To the unenlightened and the sceptic, these are truths fraught with darkness and suffering, likely to lead to the fearful labyrinth of denial and atheism—necessity and nature. To the believer, be his actual creed what it may, so it be founded on the revelation of the Old Testament (which Christian as well as Hebrew is,) narratives like these are some of the very strongest, most unanswerable evidences of our immortality which history presents. In the history of Jeroboam, we find the foundation and commentary on this assertion. His young son Abijah fell sick, and Jeroboam desired his wife to take a present in her hand, and seek Ahijah the prophet, to implore his intercession for the restoration of the child. The aged prophet was blind, and though the wife of Jeroboam concealed her rank and name, and sought to pass herself for another woman, the Lord revealed her name and mission, and Ahijah after prophesying the awful calamities which would befall the house of Jeroboam for their iniquities, proceeded to pronounce these impressive and remarkable words, "Arise, thou, therefore, get thee to thine own home, and when thy feet enter into the city *the child shall die*. And all Israel shall mourn for him, and bury him, *for he only of Jeroboam shall come to the grave*, BECAUSE IN HIM THERE WAS FOUND SOME GOOD THING TOWARD THE LORD GOD OF ISRAEL, IN THE HOUSE OF JEROBOAM." If we would but remember this striking fact, revealed as it is in the inspired word of the Eternal, to be our consolation and instruction in those dark ages, when such direct communings with our Father in Heaven were to be at an end; even Profane History would strengthen us in our belief, and reveal many times the truth of our immortality.

We should cease to regard death with the horror which its very name often inspires, if we would but realise it, *not* as the cessation of existence, but as the revealed entrance into another and purer sphere, where every intellectual capacity, every capability of love and affection, every aspiring after the great and good, the beautiful and true, which has blessed us here, will find exercise and fulfilment, completion and perfection. If we believe in a God, and that he is, as He revealed Himself, a God of TRUTH, we *must* believe in our existence elsewhere, or this world is chaos—our God but a name, His word false. We could write more, much more on this argument but this is not the place. Writing for professed Israelites, we must suppose that their belief in immortality, in death, not as a cessation, but as a *change* of existence, is as fixed as their belief in their Father's God; and if it be, we shall find little difficulty in removing all impression of doubt and sadness from the history of Mariamne.

The iniquities of Judea and her children at the period of Herod, and some years before, far exceeded, in magnitude and variety, those of Israel in the time of Jeroboam. If we glance forward from the reign of Herod, we shall perceive misery increasing on every side—horrors multiplying—man rising against man, more appallingly, more terribly, than had ever before devastated this beautiful world. In addition to the tale of Jeroboam's son, we are told in the same Divine Book, "*The righteous is taken from the evil to come;*" and in the death of Aristobulus and Mariamne, both these Divine Truths are fulfilled. "There was good" found in Aristobulus; and God, in His mercy, over-ruled the wickedness of man, to the Eternal blessedness of the youth he loved. He took him, ere temptation and evil could sully the purity and virtue which his youth revealed. Every kind of death is suffering. It is the penalty we all pay for the sinful inclinations inherited from our first parents; but what was the agony of a violent death, granted it lasted an hour, compared with the eternity of bliss awaiting the released spirit with its pitying God? The sin of Herod was the same. That the eternal over-ruled his hate and persecution of the innocent to the endless joy and peace of his victim, in no way exonerated him from the blackness of the deed. Crime is crime. The worker of sin looks but to the triumph of his wickedness, and, as such, is responsible to his God; but his evil deeds, however they may seem to carry all before them while below, do but add a glory to the Divine economy above; and for those they seek to injure upon earth, provide yet deeper bliss in heaven.

As it was with Aristobulus, so it was with Mariamne. Her life was, indeed, one of far severer trials, far deeper agony than his; but God saw she needed them to fit her for heaven, or they would not have been sent. There might have been inclinations and whisperings of evil naturally in her heart, which, without the trial of suffering, might have made her another Alexandra, or Salome; but God loved her, and so He purified her in the ordeal of suffering, and then in His deep mercy took her to Himself ere the evil days came, in which she would have seen her beloved children tortured and condemned. If we look forward in the history of her family, we must feel that she was indeed removed from the "evil to come." The Eternal might, indeed, had He so willed, have "made bare His holy arm," and wrought salvation and delivery for her even on earth: but to make such a distinction between the righteous and the wicked in this world, would interfere with the free-will, to choose the good, and eschew the evil; or choose the evil and forsake the good, which God Himself bestowed on man. No; in this life, evil will often appear to be predominant; but we shall cease to murmur and despond that so it is, if we will but look up firmly and faithfully to that world, where all that is incomprehensible here will be made clear, and the injured and the innocent live for ever with their God, shining as the chosen "jewels" of His crown.

Do not then let us envy the prosperous, and believe ourselves forsaken, if our sojourn on earth be one of adversity and pain. We have still a Father who loveth those whom He chastises, for by chastisement and probation He prepares them for that eternal blessedness, which is denied to those who continue in their hardened course. In direct opposition to the comforting words we have quoted, we read in the same inspired Book, "When the wicked spring up like grass, and when all the workers of iniquity do flourish, *it is that they shall be destroyed for ever.*" And, again, "Fret not thyself because of evil-doers, neither be thou envious against the workers of iniquity, *for they shall soon be cut down like the grass*, and wither like the green herb." If we recollect these words, and those quoted before—if we believe, humbly and faithfully, that this world is actually to the righteous but the *threshold* of existence, and permit this belief to attend us, not only in every *event*, but in every *thought* of life, running through our studies from the severest to the lightest, history would not be the sad and unsatisfactory task which it but too often is. We should never feel saddened and depressed at the often apparent triumph of oppression and evil over the helpless and the good, for we should know this was but the surface, whose depths were in infinity; the beginning, whose end was immortality.

Which of our young readers would, if she could choose, exchange the trials and death of Mariamne for the prosperous and unchecked career of Salome? The inward answer contained in the *first* thought would reveal the real state of the heart and soul to their youthful owner. We ask not the reply, for none could truly give it. Those who know not, and have never *studied* humanity, would loudly condemn the very suspicion, that preference could be accorded to the *career* (remember we do not say the character) of Salome; but the earnest and heartfelt student of humanity, knows that the human heart, of *itself*, is but too often "deceitful above all things, and desperately wicked." And though religion and education, vitalised by the grace of God, can and will subdue these natural inclinations, still it is only inward questions such as these which will reveal whether, indeed, every seed of evil has been trampled down and rooted out. And, therefore, is it good so to cultivate self-knowledge, that even the characters of ages past may aid us on through the dark and dangerous paths of present life!

The sinfulness of Salome would warn us from such choice; but there may be many youthful hearts to think and feel, that to be prosperous is not always to be wicked—to pass through life without trial, does not always prove our non-acceptance with the Lord. And they are right: but our question condenses itself into simply this—would we choose a life of prosperity and joy *without* religion—*without* that internal communing with our Father in heaven which bids us think of, and fits us for heaven; or a life of trial *with it*, with that religion which not only *sustains* but *blesses*—which gives us joy in the very midst of grief, strength in the midst of weakness, hope beyond the grave, in the dark shadow of death—assurances of unending love in loneliness, of sympathy in misconception and suspicion, of One who will never leave us nor forsake, however every friend departs by change or death, of that realisation of immortality, which bids us walk this world as a bird that passeth, and in his very resting sees afar, and yearneth for his native clime. According to the inward answer, so are our hearts right or wrong, in their secret thoughts of God.

Such were the trials, and such the infused strength of Mariamne. As a woman of Israel—to whom these things were known and felt by the faithful, far more vividly then than now—we may rest assured that her pure chastity, her high sense of rectitude, her unvarying truth and collected dignity, in the very midst of trials and temptations, which in those dark times must have morally and spiritually lowered any ordinary woman, had their foundation and constancy in religion alone. Nothing else could have sustained her, or withheld her so completely from the committal of a single fault, or even venial error, which could throw a shadow on her name. To realise to the full the beauty of her character, we must think of the age in which she lived—the wickedness with which she was surrounded—the false notions of right and wrong with which her own mother sought to mislead her unguarded youth—the laxity of morals, even in Judea, from the amalgamation of its people with the heathen nations—and the intensity of suffering to which as a wife and sister, queen and mother, she was so constantly and cruelly exposed—these considerations, added to her extreme youth, must excite our love and admiration yet more than our pity, for we know that her death was not only the cessation of sorrow, but the commencement of an eternity of bliss. "To believe in the heroic makes heroes," we have lately read; and there is a world of solid truth in those brief words; and even so to *admire* virtue with the pure fresh feelings of the unsophisticated heart, will *excite* to virtuous deeds. The trials of the wife of Herod are no longer ours to encounter; but without trial who may pass through life? And oh, however deceived, insulted, wearied, let us never stoop to use the weapons of revenge, but calmly and steadily pursue our suffering course, as purely, as truly, as nobly, as Mariamne!

Before entirely leaving this subject, we will take a hasty glance over the fate of the characters so intimately connected with the history of Mariamne.

Herod's after career will be found in the historians of the times—suffice it to state here, that if ever retribution were permitted to be visible in this world, we can trace it in the tortures, physical and mental, which afflicted him from the moment of his wife's murder to his own death, not only as concerned him individually, but in the continual plots and misery which, through the fiendish machinations of Salome, devastated his household.

A pestilential disease breaking out just after Mariamne's murder, and carrying off immense numbers, appears to have been so universally felt as Divine vengeance and wrath for the iniquitous deed, that her innocence, if it had ever been doubted, must from that moment have been publicly acknowledged, and Herod regarded with increased loathing as her unjustifiable murderer. Overpowered by mental agony, he went from place to place, from solitude to solitude, in the vain search for peace. The body succumbed to the torture of the mind; and a fierce incurable disease seizing him while at Samaria, confined him there for several months, and without any intermission of pain.

The mother who could insult her innocent and only child on her way to death—who could at such a moment think only of endeavouring to preserve her own life, and seek to do so by false accusations of her own offspring—was not likely to be much affected by her loss. No misfortune, no bereavement, no personal imprisonment, appears to have had any effect in decreasing that fearful thirst for ambition which was the secret origin of all Alexandra's own crimes, and much of her children's misery. Hearing of Herod's incurable distemper at Samaria, she commenced her machinations by endeavouring to obtain possession of the fortifications of Jerusalem, in which place she resided. One of these commanded the Temple; and she knew if this were obtained the whole nation would be in her power, for without the Temple there could be no sacrifices; and without these daily holocausts, universal rebellion would inevitably ensue. These strongholds she demanded in the name of Mariamne's sons, on the plea of guarding them for the young princes in case of their father's death. The link, however, which had in former times united the populace to Alexandra, had been snapped asunder by the death of Mariamne. There could be no belief in her fidelity to the interests of her grandsons when her unnatural conduct to her own child was remembered, and she was now yet more an object of popular hate and indignation than Herod himself. Her schemes were all frustrated; first by the positive refusal of the governor of the fortifications to take any step till the actual death of the king; and, secondly, and still more effectually, by the betrayal of her machinations: and Herod, though scarcely able to move or breathe from physical torture, gave instant orders for her execution.

The fate of Alexandra was, then, the same as Mariamne's; but how differently do we regard it. Her restless intrigues, caring for neither sin nor shame in their accomplishment; her fearful ambition, always ending in destruction to the innocent, as well as to herself; her entire want of all human feelings, save in her grief for Aristobulus, and those, too, her after-conduct bids us trace more to the agony of mortified ambition than of maternal bereavement, all compel us actually to recoil from the contemplation of her character and deprive us of all sympathy in her fate.

Had she been other than she was; had she taught her proud spirit submission, and sought to conciliate, not offend, the female members of Herod's family, much of misery both for Mariamne and herself might have been averted. We can derive no individual lesson from her history, save of warning, lest the temptations of this world, luxury and worldliness, the petty ambition of rivalry in riches and appearance, prejudice and envy, should distort the fair, sweet colouring of humanity, and close up our hearts in the icy mail of selfishness and pride. Alexandra was not, by nature and constitution, different from other women; but the seeds of sin, of which circumstances and education prevent our very consciousness, in her obtained ascendancy, and crushed all of human feeling and womanly tenderness beneath their poisonous and over-spreading weeds.

Her intrigues and ambition, however, are strong confirmatory proofs of the social position of the Women of Israel in her time. We see she had full liberty to scheme and act, and endeavour in more than one instance to put herself forward in actual opposition to the mighty and magnificent Herod, powerful as he was in himself, and courted by all foreign states. That she never succeeded showed indeed the weakness of her cause, but not the debasement of her social condition. There could have been no law existing, either written or oral, to the disparagement of women at the time, or her natural position would have rendered her too powerless and insignificant even for the formation of intrigues, much less to permit their importance in the eyes of Herod, and consequent persecution of herself.

The mother of Herod is mentioned no more in history, and, not being a woman of Israel, we are not even bound to follow Salome's sinful course any further; but for the completion of the history we will sketch, briefly as may be, the continuance of her career. Her first public act after the death of her victim, for such, undoubtedly, Mariamne was, was, in defiance of all Jewish law and womanly delicacy, to send a bill of divorce to her husband, Costabarus, with whom she had quarrelled, excusing the deed to Herod by telling him that it was for his sake she had thus acted, having discovered that Costabarus had joined in a conspiracy against him, and had also preserved alive, in direct contradiction to Herod's orders (issued twelve years before), the sons of Babas, men of the Asmonæan line, and in great favour with the multitude. Being found in the place designated by Salome, they were all slain; and Costabarus, with four other of Herod's intimate friends, executed on Salome's charge. The sons of Babas were the last even distantly connected with the Maccabæan line; and Herod now reigned unencumbered, without a single remaining family of sufficient rank and dignity to interfere with or prevent his denationalisation of Judæa.

Sixteen or eighteen years passed, and we read nothing of Salome; but from the moment of Alexander's and Aristobulus' return to Judæa, her hatred against Mariamne seemed re-kindled towards her sons, and her machinations recommenced. The young princes had been educated at Rome, and were received by the Jewish population with such enthusiastic delight as appears to have re-awakened the old hatred of the Asmonæan line. The princes bore in their majestic mien and noble features, all the characteristics of their mother's race. The intervening years seem to have had as little power to deaden the people's love for their native princes, as to diminish Salome's hate. They could scarcely have arrived at Jerusalem ere the calumnies and suspicions against them commenced, not, indeed, as yet conveyed to Herod by his sister; but reports raised abroad that they had been heard to speak reproachfully against their father as their mother's murderer, and boldly to assert their own belief in her innocence and virtue. These rumours of course reached Herod's ear, and, reviving all the thoughts and tortures of previous years, shook the affection he was beginning to feel towards his sons, and his naturally jealous and suspicious temper regained ascendancy.

Still, though shaken, he pursued his more kindly intention towards his sons, marrying both with great splendour to wives o their own rank: Alexander, to Glaphyra, daughter of Archelaus, king of Cappadocia, a union which, if approved of by the people, clearly demonstrates how completely the Laws of Moses were put aside or observed, according to the caprice of the king, and how little that power can be supposed to realise the promises of the prophets; Aristobulus to Berenice, the daughter of Salome. That she should consent to give her daughter to a man she hated, and whose destruction she had resolved to compass, may excite some surprise, but is fully explained by the issue. Whether the princess Berenice's affections were excited towards her husband, or not, we know not; but, even had they been, Salome herself was too completely void of any human or womanly feeling to permit such affection to interfere with her designs, or care for the suffering which in that case she inflicted on her child. She permitted, nay, probably, proposed the union, to obtain a spy on Aristobulus' most private moments and most unguarded words; and that Berenice could be *persuaded*, as Josephus tells us, into "ill-nature" against her husband, and to "gratify *her mother*," forge the most improbable tales concerning her husband's private speeches, argues but too painfully that the character of Salome found its reflection in her daughter; and Berenice married Aristobulus not from affection, but only to aid her mother's plans.

We have no space, nor is this the work to dilate on all the fearful machinations pursued by Salome and her party, against these ill-fated young men. The unsuspicious candour, the open independence, and courageous assertion of their mother's honour, against all who purposely assailed it, were no match for the fiendish subtlety which marked every word and movement of Salome. They actually regarded her as their best friend, at the very period that her every energy was used in maddening the king against them, till he himself urged on their destruction with the violence and hatred of a demon.

The Law of Moses, totally disregarded in the condemnation of Mariamne, and the marriage of Alexander with a heathen, was now used by the infatuated father, as a reason for his demanding the execution of his sons.* For five or seven years these machinations worked, ere their end was accomplished by the actual destruction of the victims; and during that interval, the most awful state of suspicion from one man to another, obtained possession not of the court alone, but of the whole population. Executions were constantly occurring. Men accused, however innocent, and tortured into confessions of guilt, which included many others—dark doubts of friend against friend—brother against brother—till all of nature itself and human affections appeared to succumb beneath the baleful influence of suspicion and distrust; and all this was a woman's work, and originated in a woman's hate, called forth by the petty feelings of jealousy and envy.

In Josephus we find an elaborate, in Milman, a clear, succinct, account of this fearful period of Herod's reign. To these we refer our readers: suffice it here to state, that Salome's hate was gratified. The gifted and accomplished sons of Mariamne shared their mother's fate: and though the dark deed recoiled with horror and murder on many of its perpetrators, Salome herself remained uninjured by the shock, spared to work out her own destiny, and in another world receive its recompense.

But let it not be imagined that hate and its concomitant desire of injury were the only characteristics of Salome: her life was one continued course of intrigue, alike political and personal. We do not linger on them, for there can be neither profit nor pleasure in so doing. Her treatment of Costabarus we already know; and before she was married to Alexas, some years afterwards, her conduct had been such as to excite the shame and abhorrence of even those licentious times. Her third husband was Alexas, one of Herod's favourites, and with him she appears to have lived more peacefully and honourably than with his predecessors. That, with all her fearful deeds and thoughts, she was a woman of masculine intellect and immense capability, is proved by the consummate skill and talent with which she always contrived and carried out her nefarious plans. Often in danger, but never outwitted, she repeatedly saw her companions in iniquity fall victims to their own arts against others, while she herself remained untouched and un-

* Josephus, Antiquities, book xvi. chap. xi.

suspected. None but a clever woman could so nave intrigued and kept up such a continued course of fraud, deceit, and falsehood, without ever injuring herself. But how fearfully do these very talents and capabilities increase her responsibility and her guilt.

The only act recorded of her of a somewhat superior nature, to those we have touched upon, was her releasing from the Hippodrome all those Jewish nobles and elders whom Herod had collected there, commanding them to be slain the moment of his own death, that there might be a general mourning in Judea. Before the king's death was publicly known, Salome and Alexas gave them freedom, desiring them, in Herod's name, to return to their own lands. Remembering the character of Salome, we must believe this action, like all the rest, had its origin in policy, not in goodness. Had obedience to Herod's command been equally politic, we should undoubtedly have read of their execution instead of their release.

So skilfully had she contrived to retain her brother's affections, that, though it was to her machinations alone he actually owed all his domestic, and consequent mental misery, Herod remembered her largely in his will, leaving her the cities of Jamnia, Ashdod, and Phasaelis, with five hundred thousand drachmæ in silver. To her too was entrusted his letter to the soldiery, thanking them for her fidelity to himself, and exhorting them to grant the same to his son, Archelaus, whom he had appointed king. Salome read it herself to the soldiery, whom her commands had mustered in the amphitheatre, and the appointment was received with acclamations.

But her intrigues were not yet over. A sedition in Jerusalem, soon after the accession of Archelaus, though subdued and punished, urged the young monarch to journey to Rome, there to defend his conduct, and obtain the confirmation of his father's will. Thither Salome and her whole family accompanied him, ostensibly, to use her influence with Augustus in his favour; secretly, to work against him, by encouraging Antipas, another of Herod's sons, to come to Rome, and promising him her aid with the emperor to displace his brother. False charges were accordingly brought against Archelaus by a son of Salome, as subtle and intriguing as his mother; and, after a variety of delays and pleadings, Archelaus was appointed by the emperor ethnarch over half the territory left him by Herod (a poor substitute for the title and power of king), and the remainder divided between two of his brothers, Philip and Antipas. Here again we trace the workings of Salome's intrigues, paving the way for the complete reduction to a Roman province of that beautiful land which her brother had so strenuously sought to denationalise. With herself, all prospered. Besides confirming to her the legacy of her brother, Augustus conferred the royal residence of Askelon; and alternately here and at Rome she seems to have passed the remaining years of her existence.

As we do not read any further record of her interference in the goverment, we are to suppose that she confined her subtilty to more private life. She lived long enough to behold the transient kingdom of Herod swallowed up in the dominion of the Romans: her nationality, her glory, her laws, all trampled under foot by the heathen power that over-ran the land. But to Salome this must have been rather a source of rejoicing than of grief. Judging by her acts, she never loved Judea, nay, had shared her brother's resolution to hurl it from its proud supremacy as the chosen kingdom of the Lord—and this was done. The banishment of Archelaus gave the government into the hands of Roman procurators; and two years afterwards Salome closed her iniquitous career, leaving all her cities to the empress Julia, thus confirming our assertion, that neither by birth nor adoption, character nor feeling, was she a daughter of Jerusalem.

Glad to quit such a subject of dissatisfaction and pain, we leave to our readers' own minds all reflections on the character of Salome, bidding them only remember, that, awful as is the picture of female depravity, it is *truth* not *fiction*, and therefore demands our serious consideration as to the origin of these over-spreading crimes. The seeds of wickedness are so small as to be invisible, religion only can destroy them ere they are discovered; and Salome knew not GOD.

HELENA, QUEEN OF ADIABENE, AND BERENICE.

THIRTY years passed: the miseries of Judea and her hapless people increased. The Law of Moses was still, indeed, the religion of the country; in some hearts pure and spiritual as it had been given, in others, burdened with superstition, violence, and minutiæ, wholly foreign to its beautiful consistency : in others fast giving place to the customs and habits of the Romans. Darkness—moral, intellectual, and spiritual—had gathered over the nation as a whole. God had left them in His wrath to pursue their own hardened course; but even at this period, when the true religion seemed fast fading from the earth, a ray of reviving lustre beamed exactly in confirmation of the consoling theory, that God never leaves Himself without witnesses upon earth.

Helena, queen of Adiabene, a district beyond the Tigris, had embraced Judaism. An independent sovereign, whose dominion over her own subjects was absolute, and whose actions owned no supremacy but her own will, this act must have been both voluntary and from conviction. It could have had no ulterior motive in ambition, for Judea was not only under iron subjection to the Romans, but devastated by famine and disease. Izates, the son of Helena, had been sent by his father, Monobazus, to be educated at the court of Abenerig, king of Characene, a district on the Persian Gulf. While there, he became acquainted with Ananias, a Hebrew merchant, who, in his commercial character, had frequent access to the women's apartments, and never lost an opportunity of inculcating the tenets of his faith. Izates, who had married the daughter of Abenerig, appears to have been present at these conferences, and also became a convert, by a curious coincidence, at the very time that his mother, Helena, embraced the religion also. So earnest was Izates in the cause, that, on his return to his country, and accession, after his father's death, he insisted on being received into the covenant of Abraham, against the advice of his mother, and even Ananias, who appears to have accompanied the young monarch as his chosen counsellor and friend. Izates had not the right of primogeniture to his father's crown ; and knowing that he had very many enemies in the partizans of his brothers, Helena, though an earnest convert herself, feared that such a public departure from the religion of his country would create sedition and rebellion in his people. Izates at first yielded to her counsel ; but his inclinations receiving fresh incentive from the representations of Eleazer, a learned Galilæan Jew, and his own impressions of a frequent and earnest study of the Law of Moses, he was received into the covenant of Abraham, and no evils followed ; for, to use here the words of Josephus, "it was God who hindered what they feared from taking effect, and preserved both Izates himself and his sons from many dangers, and procured their deliverance when it seemed impossible, demonstrating thereby, that the fruit of piety does not perish, for those who have regard for Him, and for their faith upon Him only."*

But Helena's conversion is of more importance to our present subject than than of Izates. Her zeal was so earnest, her faith so heartfelt, that, when her natural anxiety was calmed by the peace and prosperity which followed her son's profession of Judaism, she requested his permission to make a journey to Jerusalem, and worship at the holy temple there. This was, at that time, no trifling undertaking. Travelling was dangerous and fatiguing: Judea in constant petty warfare, and almost exhausted by a severe and long-continued famine. But Helena, who appears a woman of great energy, did not hesitate to incur all these evils, so that she could but offer her sacrifice of thanksgiving in the chosen house of God. Izates readily acceded, making lavish preparations for her journey according to her rank, bestowing on her large sums of money; and, in the true spirit of the religion they had both professed, which so inculcated filial respect and love, he himself accompanied her great part of her journey.

The famine raging in Jerusalem would have terrified away any less zealous convert; but Helena quietly took up her abode in the distressed city, making it her business to relieve the sufferers by munificent gifts both of food and money. She despatched some of her household to Alexandria, to purchase large quantities of corn, and others to Cyprus, for a cargo of dried figs; and both missions accomplished with unusual promptness, and relief most judiciously bestowed, the memory of Queen Helena long lingered with the oppressed people; and her acts are recorded by Josephus with a feeling and impressiveness which are not often found in his details. Izates, too, on being informed of the famine, sent large sums to the principal men in Jerusalem. Both himself and his mother appeared eager to demonstrate the truth and sincerity of their conversion by their earnest endeavours for the good of the Jewish people; a striking contrast to the conduct of those Idumæan proselytes, whose only desire had been to Romanise

---

* Josephus, Ant. xx. 2.

the people, and amalgamate with the heathen, both their religion and their land.

How long Helena dwelt in Jerusalem does not appear; but, from the good she accomplished, and the magnificent tombs, or pyramids, which she erected about three furlongs from Jerusalem, we are led to suppose that she had adopted the country as well as the religion for her own, and dwelt there the greater portion of the remainder of her life. Her strong affection for Izates demanded a powerful incentive to her living apart from him, and that incentive appears to have been the delight of worshipping the Eternal in his temple; the privileges of obeying every tittle of his law more faithfully, fully, and precisely than she could have done in her own land, and the constant kindness and good works to the Hebrew people, with which she proved her piety and zeal. The death of Izates, after a prosperous reign of twenty-four years, caused the deepest affliction to his mother, for not only were they bound together by the adoption of the same creed, which drew the human affections still closer than merely natural ties, but Josephus alludes to him as a most dutiful and affectionate son. One consolation, however, she had; the privileges and principles of Judaism were not all lost to her country by the death of Izates. The crown of Adiabene went to Monobazus, her eldest son, who had also embraced Judaism; and Helena, though aged and infirm, and bowed down by her sad bereavement, hastened to Adiabene, to congratulate and bless him on his accession. Izates had left the crown to his brother, instead of to either of his own sons, in gratitude for the fidelity and affection, which although put aside for the accession of a younger brother, Monobazus had always proved. Helena, however, did not long survive Izates; she died at Adiabene. And Monobazus, in dutiful obedience to the last wishes of his mother and brother, had their remains transported to Jerusalem, where they were interred in the splendid mausoleum erected by Helena no doubt with that intent.

The history of Helena, is a refreshing picture of feminine gentleness and family love, after the fearful deeds and characters we have of late perused. There is a gentle womanly disposition, apparent even in her appeal to the people after her husband's death, a horror of violence and severity, peculiarly consistent with her true feminine qualities: "I believe you are not unaquainted that my husband was desirous that Izates should succeed him in the government, and thought him not unworthy so to do," was her calm address, whose only eloquence was sincerity and truth. "However, I wait your determination; for happy is he who receives a kingdom not from a single person only, but from the willing suffrages of a great many."

When the *amour propre* of a nation is thus conciliated, their decision is generally sure to be the decision desired. Unanimously they pressed forward to pay homage to their queen, and confirm their late king's resolution, advising at the same time the death of all the brethren and kinsmen of Izates, to secure him on the throne. But Helena's gentle spirit shrunk from so fearful a deed, though of Izates' brethren only one was her son. She calmed the popular excitement by thanking them for their zeal, but desiring them to postpone such violent measures till Izates returned, and should himself think them expedient. The multitude consented, only exhorting her to restrain them in bonds for their own security, till the arrival of Izates, and to set up some one in whom she could place perfect trust, as regent of the kingdom in the meantime. Had Helena been an ambitious, or a politic and suspicious woman, it would have been very easy for her to have retained the regency herself; and had she not had perfect trust in the honour and affection of her eldest son, both for herself and Izates, she could not have confided the kingly power to his keeping, even placing the diadem upon his head, and the signet on his hand, endowing him with full powers as sovereign till Izates' return. Few characters could have sustained this ordeal, and resigned a power, the sweets of which had been fully tasted, to a younger brother; yet Monobazus did so: and in this very deed, and in the confidence and affection existing uninterruptedly between the brothers throughout their lives, as in the beauty and unselfish honesty of their mutual characters, we read a still clearer commentary on the true character of their mother, than in her own acts, gentle and full of beauty as they were.

None but a mother's judicious training and impartial love, could so have united her sons, that the elder could submit to the superiority of the younger without jealousy and resistance. Milman, indeed, attributes to the sedition of Monobazus, the attacks of the Arabian and Parthian kings; but as Josephus, who might have been living at the very time of these events, does not give us any warrant for the surmise, we reject it altogether. According to him it was the desire of Monobazus and other of the king's kindred, to become Jews, which roused the Adiabenians to revolt, and to invite foreign potentates against their king. In fact, every war in which Izates was engaged, originated in the annoyance of his subjects at his embracing Judaism; but he remained firm and unshaken in the religion, embraced not from ambition but conviction, and he triumphed over both foreign and domestic foes.

The character of Helena would have ornamented any religion; but we can discern throughout it the pure spirituality at that period only discoverable in the religion of the Lord. Her disposition naturally clinging and gentle, her heart capable of the strongest emotions, her mind constantly urging to the good, could not rest satisfied with Heathen worship. She was instructed in the Jewish tenets; their spirituality, their temporal consolation, their eternal hope, and infinite love, their vast capabilities for exercising the intellect and heart, filled up the void which heathenism could not; and Helena believed; and she bore witness throughout the whole tenour of her after life, to the sincerity and purity of that belief.

Now would this, could this conversion have taken place, if the Jewish religion degraded women to the rank of slaves and and heathens? This single story would be sufficient to prove the groundless falsity of the charge. Helena was a powerful and respected queen and mother in her own nation, accustomed to receive homage, to be consulted, to make use of her intellect and political sagacity, to take, in fact, a higher and more esteemed grade than was the general condition of heathen women; and is it likely she would sacrifice all these privileges of sex and station, by the adoption of a religion which deprived her of both? What would have been the use of her conversion, if there were any ground for the false assertion, that women have no souls, and neither the form nor the spirit of religion is incumbent upon them? Had her conversion taken place when Israel was at the height of its temporal and spiritual glory, when a world acknowledged its holy supremacy, and sought its friendship, as a land divinely favoured, there might have been a doubt allowable, as to whether Helena sought the safety and increase of her temporal dominions in the public profession of Judaism; but no such doubt can attach itself to the purity of her motives, when we reflect on the then position of Judea. There could be neither glory nor satisfaction in uniting herself with a nation sunk to the very lowest ebb of degradation, hovering, as it were, on the very brink of annihilation. But one motive could have actuated her : and that was the natural craving for a revealed religion, peculiar to dispositions such as hers. But Judaism would not have satisfied those cravings, if it really were the stern, harsh, exclusive superstition which it is by some proclaimed ; if its ordinances were for man, and woman were a mere cypher in its laws. But such Judaism was unknown, till the slanders of modern times so reported it. Helena read in the Law of Moses the tender pitying care of woman, in all her varying relations and positions of life, as we have endeavoured to display it in our Second Period. She read that a Father had promised a place in His house, dearer even than sons and daughters, to all who kept His sabbaths and embraced His covenants, and therefore it was she believed ; and in her earnest zeal parted from her beloved children, left a home of peace and luxury, where she was known, respected, loved, to journey many toilsome and weary leagues, only for the happiness of sacrificing offerings of thanksgiving to the Lord of Hosts, who had in His mercy given her the knowledge of Himself. Famine and misery were around her in Jerusalem ; she must have seen many painful evidences, that the holy religion she had embraced was desecrated by its own offspring; that social iniquities and individual apostasies were throwing a dark barrier between the Jew and his God ; yet she never wavered, devoting her fortune and her energies to deeds of kindness, charity, and love ; thus proving how completely she had become one with the people whose religion she professed.

If woman were prohibited the privilege of sacrifice, etc., is it likely we should find Josephus recording the visit of a female proselyte to Jerusalem for that sole purpose? or Helena herself so anxious to obey the ordinances of the Law ? It is needless to continue the argument, the fact contains in itself the strongest refutation of the charge levelled by the ignorant against us. The prejudices of education may endear even superstition or heathenism to its votaries themselves ; but we may rest assured that no woman, respected and elevated by the customs and habits of her original creed and native subjects, would *voluntarily* adopt another tending to enslave and to debase her. Helena's virtue and intellect had raised her above her nation and her age, occasioning a void and loneliness, which urged her to seek and find repose in unusual studies. To define the void might have been even to herself impossible, until the word of God, explained by an earnest and pious Israelite, at once revealed and filled it; and in its inexhaustible fulness, satisfied her woman heart on earth, and pointed with an angel-finger to another world, where all the pantings of intellect and affection would find sufficiency and rest; and hope, yet dearer, where she and her beloved ones would meet again, and be with Israel's God for ever! To some women (Salome and Alexandra for instance), these considerations would be of little value; but to characters such as Helena of Adiabene, they would mark their immortal truth, in the glow of joy and blissful calm inseparable from real religious faith, pervading for the first time an awakened human heart.

The first year of the Jewish war, 66 of the Christian Era, presents us with a striking illustration of the Hebrew female's capability and freedom, to make and to fulfil singular vows. The fact is briefly recorded and trifling in itself, but important, as the only instance of the kind mentioned in our history. That there were many others, is more than likely. No law was instituted by our great lawgiver, which had not its practical illustration in the history of his people. Nor would the law of vows of either kind, "singular or Nazarite," have formed part of the given code, if their necessity had not been visible in the wants and customs of the multitude. That we have only one recorded instance of its obedience by a woman of Israel, does not prove its previous disuse, but that those who had occasion to make and fulfil singular vows, were in too domestic and retired a position, to obtain the notice of the historian. The manner in which Josephus alludes to it, marks it of frequent, not of singular occurrence, a custom in fact of the nation, in case of distempers or other distresses."*

The subject of this "singular vow," is one that we may perhaps be blamed for introducing into our pages, her character, according to some of the Latin historians, being of doubtful reputation. As, however, this calumny cannot be proved,— as, being a woman of Israel by birth and creed, she was an object of prejudice and aversion to the Romans; and as the

Josephus' Wars, book ii. ch. 15.

satirists then, as now, hesitated not to calumniate innocence and blacken reputation, only to provide themselves with a jest, —we are not bound to credit the assertions of either class of writers. A glance over the appendix to the fifth book of Tacitus' History will show the unfavourable light in which his nation was accustomed to regard the belief, customs, and ordinances of Judaism; and, therefore, it is more than likely that the very fact of Berenice, being a Jewish woman, unusually beautiful and gifted, admired by Vespasian, and actually beloved and nearly wedded by Titus, should have excited the extreme jealousy of the Romans, from which calumny and suspicion, however base and unfounded, are sure to proceed.

Josephus, whose history favours the Romans, and adopts their views as much as possible, of course insinuates the same scandal, which, however, he never attempts to *prove;* and the only instance in which he does bring Berenice forward, is not only in a womanly and amiable, but in a religious and patriotic light. Had this not been the case, we should have left her to the general historian; but as that void in our records is rapidly advancing, where there is scarcely any mention of individuals, male or female, and the history of the women of Israel is lost in the fearful vortex of national misery and subsequent dispersion, we are glad to seize the faintest and most unfinished notice, which can in any point confirm our theory and illustrate our laws.

One fact, also, our readers must bear in mind: the period in which the object of our present notice existed was one of the grossest immorality. Custom authorised, in many nations actually *legalised*, marriages, which, in the earlier stages of the world, and when the law of God was established and followed, had been regarded, as they would be now, most unlawful and impure. The religion of the Hebrews existed but in name. From the reign of Herod the denationalisation commenced. After his death, Roman procurators governed and Roman soldiers overran the land; and such an awful spirit of party divided the Jews who yet remained, that the neutrals believed the dominion of the Romans far less evil than the divisions and seditions of their own. At such an epoch all statutes, human and divine, were set aside; a man did as his neighbour did, and custom alone was law. The pure, beautiful ordinances, prohibiting too near consanguinity in the marriage ties, were completely laid aside by the once holy nation for whom they

were framed; and the family of Herod appeared resolved on
assisting their father's plans for Romanising the Jewish people
by emulating all the heathen nations in their utter indifference
to the laws of marriages, and framing unions regardless of the
ties of relationship formerly restraining them.* The union of
brother and sister, horrible as it reads to us, was then in constant practice amongst the Egyptians, Syrians, Parthians, and,
occasionally, amongst the more refined and polished Romans
themselves. *Nationally*, this was an awful state of society,
calling down always the visible wrath and chastisement of the
Eternal in the annihilation of the sinning nations. *Individually*, the crime was of far less magnitude; for many sinned
unconsciously, and the horror and loathing with which we look
upon these things, could not have been felt by those to whom
custom was authority,—example, law.

We do not write this to excuse Israel's sinful departure from
the law of Moses: we know the awful magnitude of their
iniquities by the appalling nature of their chastisement. We
simply mention the fact to remove what would now appear the
extreme sinfulness of Berenice if the reports against her had
foundation; which foundation, search history as we may, we
cannot find. Nay, in the extreme laxity of morals and multitude of impure connections, we read the probable rise and only
source of the rumours. Neither satirists nor prejudiced historians were likely to draw a line between unproved rumour and
proved reality; and it was enough for them that Berenice was
a beautiful Jewess, to burden her with charges, frivolous and
light to them, but throwing a stain upon her reputation, the
blackness of which could scarcely be known till discovered by
the reading of modern times.

The records of the great-granddaughter of Mariamne are so
brief and so little satisfactory, that all we can give is a simple
statement of what is not very generally known concerning her,
her parentage and connections; making the link uniting her
with Jewish and Roman history more distinct than can be the
case with mere general researches; and then revert to the
circumstance which is the occasion of this notice.

We have already alluded to the two sons of Mariamne—
Aristobulus and Alexander—and to their marriages: the former
with his cousin Berenice, Salome's daughter; the latter with
Glaphyra of Cappadocia. Aristobulus left five children; two

* Josephus' Antiq., book xviii. ch. 5 and note.

of whom were—Agrippa, afterwards king of Judea, and Herod king of Chalcis. Agrippa, himself a grandson of Mariamne married Cypros, a granddaughter of the same princess by her daughter Salampsio. By this Cypros, King Agrippa had five children—two sons, one of whom, Drusus, died young; the other, known as the young Agrippa, was the last of the Idumæans who, even nominally, was king of the Jews; and three daughters—Berenice, the object of our sketch, Mariamne, and Drusilla. Berenice was, then, great granddaughter to Mariamne by both her parents, and seems to have inherited all the grace and beauty of the Asmonæan family. In Jewish households there never was any distinction made between the education of sons and daughters; both equally shared the care and instructions of their mother, who, were she a " Woman of Israel," was always, or ought to have been, perfectly competent to the task. We find in the Talmud repeated ordinances to this effect, even so far as to say—" that if a man marries a woman without education, and only for her money, he will not have children according to his wishes,"—thus giving an illustration of the laws which we insisted upon in our Second Period, as including mothers equally with fathers in the education of their children.

The close connection of brother and sister we have already seen in our notice of Aristobulus and Mariamne, and also, though in a very opposite light, of Herod and Salome, and some other instances. Sisters were never nonentities in the Jewish state; they always shared, not the affection alone, but the rank and influence of their brothers, and were looked on by the multitude in a much superior light to the female scions of royalty in modern times. From the extreme care of woman in the Jewish laws, the celebrated characters which, as women, had swelled their history, the custom for females to inherit when there were no males—the succession of a wife to the crown in preference to the sons—all elevated the position of royal females to a perfect equality, socially considered, with their husbands and brothers, and brought them more forward in the history of their people than is generally believed.

We are anxious to mark this important fact, because it will throw light on the true position of Berenice, which, from being misunderstood by the mere chronicler of the age, is, of course, misrepresented, and so mystifies his readers equally with himself.

There scarcely appears a year's difference in the ages of

Herod Agrippa's elder children—the young Agrippa and Berenice,* and they were, therefore, thrown together as intimately and fondly as Aristobulus and Mariamne, probably accompanying their father and mother in all their wanderings, sharing their vicissitudes, and educated together in Rome. There were six years between Berenice and her next sister, Mariamne, and four between Mariamne and Drusilla; consequently Berenice could have had no companion in her own family except her brother, with whom Agrippa the elder appears always to have associated her. We suppose this from a sentence in Josephus,† which we transcribe. Alluding to a slave, from whom Agrippa had received a trifling kindness, he says, "When, afterwards, Agrippa was come to the kingdom, he took particular care of Thaumastus, and got him his liberty from Caius, and made him his steward over his own estates; and when he died *he left him to Agrippa, his son, and to Berenice, his daughter, to minister to them* in the same capacity.

Now, unless Berenice had been, by her father's will, associated with her brother in the possession and government of these estates, there would have been no need to mention her name in conjunction with Agrippa's in so simple a thing as the retaining a faithful servant in his post. In reading the unsatisfactory annals of the general historians, we must reason by analogy, or be for ever groping in the dark, searching for minute but important facts, and never successful in the search. It must have been a habit and a common judgment with the father to associate his elder children, as mutually and equally concerned in his public and private affairs, or this charge would not have been so naturally left. We have the confirmation of this suggestion in later notices of Berenice; but the historians of that period forget the sentence we have quoted, though that in itself is sufficient to account for her influence with Agrippa in the government, and needs no supposition whatever of a nearer connexion between them.

The first person to whom Berenice appears to have been betrothed was Marcus, according to Josephus, a son of Alexander Lysimachus, an alabarch who had been imprisoned by Caligula, and set at liberty and restored to all his former honours by Claudius, whose intimate friend he was. As Berenice was, however, only fifteen, if so much, when her father gave

* Josephus' Antiq., book xix. ch. 9.
† Ibid. book xviii. ch. 6.

her in marriage to her uncle, Herod of Chalcis, this could not have been more than a betrothal entered into while they were children, as was frequently the custom, but which Marcus did not live to complete. The intended union, however, is sufficient proof how little nationality existed in the heart of Agrippa at that period. His varied life had naturally occasioned this, though he appears to have governed his kingdom during his brief reign with all the feelings of a Hebrew, and to have inculcated the same in the hearts of his children.

Berenice was the second wife of Herod, whom Agrippa's influence with Claudius had, before he gave him his daughter, made king of Chalcis. His first had been Mariamne, granddaughter of Herod the Great and his Samaritan wife, Malthæa. Berenice appears to have enjoyed six years of a happy, though uneventful, wedded life with Herod, becoming the mother of two sons, Berenicianus and Hyrcanus. Her residence seems, however, to have been more in the dominions of her father in Judea, than at Chalcis. Josephus repeatedly alludes to Herod of Chalcis, as if he were a constant attendant at Agrippa's court, which accounts for Berenice's interest in the people of Judea, and being, in fact, more intimately known to them than her brother Agrippa, who, for the last three years, had been finishing his education under Claudius Cæsar. Herod Agrippa died in 45; Berenice was then sixteen; and Herod of Chalcis, dying in 50, left her a young and beautiful widow of twenty-one. For fifteen or seventeen years she remained a widow, residing alternately at Rome and in Jerusalem. Her father's long residence in the former place, and intimate friendship and connexion with the highest Romans, of course made Rome her second country, and caused her to be as well known there as in Jerusalem. In 66 we find her in Jerusalem, in pursuance of her singular vow, and exposed to great danger from the infuriated Roman soldiery (to both of which circumstances we will refer at the conclusion of our sketch). Between 66 and 69 she must have become queen of Pontus, by her marriage with Polemo, king of that country, an engagement entered into to silence the tongue of falsehood, which had dared charge her with an improper connexion with her brother. Before, however, she consented to the union, Polemo embraced Judaism, and was received into the covenant, a proof that even in that dark period of national apostacy, some regard to religious decency was observed. In 69 we find her, as queen of Pontus, embracing the cause of Vespasian against his rival, Vitellius,* whom the Roman legions were endeavouring to elect emperor in Vespasian's stead, joining the confederacy in the latter's favour, and levying troops for his assistance.

Her marriage with Polemo, however, was not of long continuance. Entered into without love on either side, by her to prove the utter falsity of a scandalous rumour, by him to obtain possession of her riches, it was soon dissolved by mutual consent. Polemo repudiated his Judaism, only embraced for Berenice's gold; and Berenice returned to her life of freedom. Then it was she must have attracted the love of Titus; for it was in 73† that he would have married her, had he not feared the violent opposition of the Roman people, then more than usually incensed against the Jews, from the vast numbers of Romans who had perished in the Jewish war, and the daring and noble opposition to the imperial arms, which the miserable people had so very lately made.

Instead of marrying her (a dazzling destiny, which, to one educated in the Roman school, as had been Berenice, would have been difficult, if not impossible, to refuse, simply from national motives), Titus separated from her, and Berenice's life closed in retirement. Her name is not again mentioned in history, not even her subsequent residence, nor what was her final lot: this last female representative of the Idumæan and Asmonæan lines, is lost to her posterity. We know that Agrippa lived and died the contented vassal of Rome; but of his sister, so nearly raised to become even empress of the world, this scanty detail is refused us; and we look in vain for her slightest mention. This is disappointing; for, in the desolate condition of the Jews, their miseries, martyrdoms, massacres, and dispersions, we cannot form even an idea of her future destiny. Milman says, that "She returned some years afterwards to Rome, but never regained her former favour." In that case, her residence was probably again with the beloved brother of her youth; and on this idea we can rest more satisfied, than did we think of her homeless and wandering like the remainder of her wretched nation.

The sketch we have given is all that history, either Jewish or Roman, records in any connected point of view. Of her character we can learn little; but she appears to have been

* Tacitus, Hist book v sect. 81.
† 73 according to Tacitus—79 according to Goldsmith.

endowed with those superior qualities, which gave her position and influence both with Jews and Romans. The occasion of her making the vow which she went to Jerusalem to perform, history does not mention. But that she did perform it, offering sacrifices for thirty days, is sufficient for us: by its strong confirmation of our assertion, that the Jewish religion elevated woman in all her religious duties and responsibilities to a perfect equality with man. Berenice, too, lived at the very time, in which our opponents declare the religion of God had been so changed and abused by mistaken zealots, as imperatively to need reform and extermination, which Jesus was sent to accomplish. Whatever these zealots might have done, they certainly could not have deprived woman of her spiritual privileges, and denied her the power of either performing her vow or offering sacrifices, or Berenice would not have come to Jerusalem, then in a most awful state of misery and constant murders, expressly for the observance of the forms necessary to its fulfilment; nay, she could not have made the vow at all, if she had not had perfect liberty, spiritual and temporal, so to do.

This fact, then, is very important in our history, as women of Israel, and has nothing whatever to do with the private character of Berenice (which, however, we will endeavour to clear from the misrepresentations of historians). The fact, that the vow was taken by a widow in Israel, and observed in Jerusalem with all the attendant ceremonies enjoined by the priests, is enough in itself to prove that such vows *were* customary, and woman, as well as man, had the power to make and to fulfil them.

Nor in the thirty days' sacrifice, and going barefoot, which appears to have been the case with Berenice, can we discover what Whiston, in his note to this chapter of Josephus, supposes—the extreme rigour of Pharisaic ordinances. The permission to make vows, and the care lest females should be carried away by ill-regulated enthusiasm, is all that was ordained in the law of Moses—the *manner* of performing that vow, and the service or penance which its performance included, was left to the will of the subject, or, at his or her discretion, to the guidance of the priest. It was for this very reason, that the making and manner of fulfilling vows were to be entirely voluntary, that woman was compelled to have the sanction of father or husband. Such a vow for instance, as Berenice's, would have been incompatible with the duty of a wife or daughter, and therefore probably not have received the necessary sanction of man, though the enthusiasm of the woman might have urged her to make it. Had the *manner* of performing vows been laid down by our great lawgiver, there would have been no need for him to have burdened woman's observance of them with a proviso, for the service or penance would have been ordained according to her *power* of obedience: but this would have interfered too closely with domestic and social freedom; and she was, therefore, permitted to make vows of service or penance, according to her own inclination, subservient only to the superior wisdom and calmer reasoning of her husband or father.

Berenice, at the time of her vow, was six-and-thirty years of age, a widow, and perfectly independent, both of will and action. She had neither father nor husband to interfere with her intentions—was of sufficient age to know well what she was about—of sufficient mental qualifications, and having been educated in Rome, without any of the exclusiveness of her own people, of sufficient freedom of thought in religious matters, not blindly to follow the instructions of priests, if they interfered with her own ideas; and, therefore, it is more than probable, that the sacrifices and going barefoot, were no orders of the priest, but Berenice's own voluntary adoption, the *manner* in which she chose to perform her "singular vow," and with which the priests interfered not, save in their sacred functions, to aid her in its performance. The riches of Berenice are more than once alluded to; and, therefore, the thirty day' sacrifice, although expensive, was quite within her power; and the going barefoot, though revolting to our ideas of the religion of Moses, which ordained *loving obedience*, not *personal penance*, was then probably considered a mark of humility, and as revealing to the nation, that rank and station were not to interfere with the personal devotion to the Eternal, comprised in the making and observance of singular vows.

So much for Berenice's vow, as regards us nationally. As it regards her individually, it proves that, even while giving them what, in those times, was considered the advantages of a Roman education, Herod Agrippa must have taught them the religion of the Hebrews—made it a point with them—

else we should never hear of Berenice deeming this singular vow was needed, or that it was absolutely necessary for Polemo, king of Pontus, to become a Jew before she married him. Nor, had she been educated in Roman principles only, would she have felt and acted as she did for her hapless people during her residence in Jerusalem. Florus was then procurator of Judea, and governing with a mercilessness and ferocity, that at length caused the already full cup of Jewish forbearance and Jewish misery to run over. Imprisonments, scourgings, crucifixions, and massacres by wholesale, ceased not during the whole period of his authority. In one day, 3,600 men, women, and children fell unresisting victims: and neither rank, nor worth, nor even Roman citizenship—for some of the distinguished Jews had obtained equestrian rank—were spared; the highest suffering with the meanest, the worthy with the base.

Repeatedly had Berenice sent messengers—the most distinguished of her household to intercede with Florus for her miserable countrymen: but high as was her rank, influential as she was with his Roman masters, the monster heeded her not; not even when, in her penitential attire, she herself stood before his tribunal, and sought by her own pleadings to check the torrent of his cruelty. Her hapless countrymen were hewn down before her very eyes; old age and helpless infancy—the delicate female—all perished; and she herself was in such imminent danger from the infuriate soldiery, as to be compelled to fly to the palace, and collect her guards around, to shield herself from insult, as well as death. Yet she made no effort to quit Jerusalem, which she could have done with the greatest ease. Rather than fail in the performance of her vow, she shared the dangers of her countrymen; living in daily dread of her own death, and in daily sight of misery and murder. Nor was she merely a passive witness; she wrote the most touching accounts of the cruelty and rapacity of Florus, to his superior officer, Cestius Gallus, entreating his interference in behalf of her oppressed people, and when Agrippa returned, joined with him in every effort to reconcile the Jews and Romans, and so obtain for the former security and peace. She sat beside her brother during his memorable address, by her tears and silent eloquence betraying that her heart also was in his words; and even when, indignant at their ungrateful conduct to himself,

Agrippa left the miserable city to itself, and returned to his own kingdom of Chalcis,* Berenice still seems to have lingered. Nor did she leave the country until her vow was fully performed, and Jerusalem in too fearful a state to admit of any hope of achieving or administering good.

Surely these are characteristics of an energetic, yet gentle, feeling woman. We can trace nothing, in this lowly adherence to a penitential vow, and devotion to the interests of a miserable people, resembling the gay life, and pleasure-loving propensities of a professed and alluring beauty. Josephus, indeed, accuses her of the unamiable qualities of annoying and ill-treating her youngest sister, Drusilla, on account of her extraordinary beauty; but that this charge must have been made without either foundation or reflection on the part of the historian, is very clear from his own recital. The beauty and influence of Berenice had been long known and widely acknowledged. She had neither occasion, nor probably inclination, to envy her sister the gifts she herself possessed. But the very manner in which Josephus writes the charge, shows its fallacy. Drusilla was already married to Aziz, king of Emesa, who had consented to embrace the Jewish religion to obtain her. When Felix was procurator of Judea, he saw Drusilla, and fell madly in love with her. Through the means of a Cypriot Jew, he persuaded her to forsake her husband Aziz, and marry him. "Accordingly, she acted ill; and because she was desirous to avoid her sister Berenice's envy,—for she was very ill-treated by her on account of her beauty—was prevailed upon to transgress the laws of her country, and marry Felix." Now, it appears to me, that Berenice's envy (even granted she had to encounter it) had nothing whatever to do with this decision. The representations of the Cypriot, the seductive persuasions of Felix, and her own inclinations were the sole incentives: for she certainly was not a whit more protected from her sister's envy as the wife of Felix, than she had been as the wife of Aziz: nay, scarcely as much; for, when united to Felix, she was continually liable to be thrown in Berenice's way, both in Jerusalem and Rome; and this could not have been the case when residing in her first husband's kingdom of Emesa. This charge, then, against Berenice has no foundation in reason; but most probably originated in

---

* After the death of his brother-in-law, and also uncle, Herod of Chalcis, the kingdom of Chalcis was given to Agrippa.

Josephus's great wish to conciliate the Romans, even while he appeared to be writing an impartial history of his own country. Had he been straightforward, we should have found some condemnation of Drusilla for marrying a heathen, and forsaking, without any just cause, her former husband. But as the heathen was a Roman, he passes over the transgression very lightly ; and, instead of blaming Drusilla for conduct which was undoubtedly evil, absolves her at the expense of her sister, who had probably no more to do with it than he had himself. And this is the justice of historians ! Surely we should examine well, ere we permit the youthful mind to embrace their views as infallible ; and rather encourage them to reflect, and have an opinion of their own, instead of blindly swallowing the food which historians provide.

That Berenice should sometimes be regarded as the sister, and sometimes as the wife of Agrippa, does not at all surprise us, for some historians actually call her his wife.* What foundation they have for this assertion, however, we should be glad to know. Certainly, Josephus must be to them an unknown authority ; for he shows her parentage and connections somewhat too clearly for this idea to originate with him. The mistake of the moderns, and the false scandalous reports of the ancients, may however arise from the same causes. We have already shewn the close tie uniting Jewish brothers and sisters of nearly the same age; that Agrippa and Berenice were always associated in the thoughts, and even the will of their father. As Herod's wife, and queen of Chalcis, Berenice was more continually in Jerusalem, and learning lessons of government rather from her father than her brother, who was then at Rome. Herod, though king of Chalcis, almost continually resided in Jerusalem ; and during the minority of the young Agrippa, obtained the sovereignty over the Temple, and the privilege of nominating the high priest. Berenice was, therefore, actually queen over the Jews at that time, as well as of Chalcis ; and the former people were accustomed to regard and feel towards her, as, with her husband, the representative of royalty.

When Herod died, his kingdom of Chalcis, over which Berenice was still queen, was given to Agrippa, and the brother and sister were, in consequence, again thrown so closely together, that as Agrippa had no wife, they were always alluded

* Jahn's Hebrew Commonwealth.

to, and spoken of as king and queen. As the daughter, sister, and widow of kings acccustomed, too, to share in the government, and influence the people, she was always spoken of as Queen Berenice, and queen of Chalcis, over which country Agrippa was also king. And mere casual readers are therefore likely to consider her as the *wife* of the king, not knowing how, as his sister, she could have any right to the title. Acting in concert with Agrippa, as their early education had accustomed them to, we see her, as in the affair of Florus and Agrippa's address to the people, occupying that position which not generally devolving on sisters of royalty, confirms the supposition of a nearer connection. But the supposition falls to the ground before the simple facts we have brought forward. Berenice was, in fact, a more independent sovereign of Judea, or rather of a remnant of the Jewish people, than her brother; for him the Romans feared, lest by placing regal power in his hands, their own power over Judea would be diminished. Berenice as a woman, and the wife of a king of Chalcis, was to them a mere cypher with regard to the state, however admired as a beautiful woman in Rome; but the interest she really did take in the affairs of the people, we perceive by her conduct during the administration of Florus.

We have read and reflected on the subject deeply; but though we see much which might be perverted into the rumour to which we have alluded, a consideration of facts proves its utter want of solid foundation. Our authorities are, however, open to all readers, and they are at liberty to adopt their own opinions. We would only entreat them to reflect on the facts here brought forward under their view, as likely to assist them in their decision—to accustom themselves to *reason from analogy*, as well as to exercise understanding, which is too often thought sufficient in itself for the comprehension of history. We are too far removed from the time in which Berenice lived, to pronounce judgment decidedly for or against her; but when not a single instance is brought forward to make manifest impropriety of conduct, and all that is clearly related of her proves a religious, national, and feeling character—when her defamers are *Roman* satirists, and *Roman* historians, for whose dislike it was enough that she was a Jewess—when the pages of her own historian are but too often tarnished with crooked views, partial representation, and Roman feelings, why should we not be permitted to judge charitably, as well as harshly?

to doubt as well as believe? Her character is, indeed, not written with sufficient clearness for us to draw thence a lesson: but our history of the Women of Israel would scarcely have been complete had we omitted her, more especially as her history practically illustrates a law of our state, and demonstrates convincingly that even in that period of spiritual and moral darkness, not a statute existed which could contradict the written law of Moses, by a refusal to women of those spiritual privileges, and that solemn responsibility, therein so forcibly inculcated.

GENERAL HISTORY, AND CONCLUSIONS THENCE ELICITED.

In the fearful epochs of misery and war which followed, we find no further mention of woman individually; but, as an important evidence of the care which the Jewish religion took of females, we find Josephus in his character of general (which he filled infinitely better than that of historian), labouring with zeal and earnestness to protect the females from insult or outrage. In lawless nations, in times of such terrible evil, this would not have been thought of; whereas with the Hebrew patriot, surrounded as he was with many heavy cares and imminent dangers, it was the first consideration, and was never lost sight of throughout the whole of his career.

In glancing back over the period which has detained us much longer than we anticipated, from the return from Babylon to the war, we cannot find a single evidence of the veracity or foundation of the charge of Jewish female degradation, nor in fact the workings of a single statute contradictory to the beautiful spirit of the law of Moses. All we have read, every female character brought forward, marks the superior social elevation and individual intellect of the Hebrew females, to the women of any of the surrounding nations. Nay, we see them occupying positions as *wives* and *sisters*—of kings, higher and far more influential than they ever did, or do, in any Gentile land. Instead of being sunk into mere nonentities, as, were they refused all spiritual privileges and temporal freedom, they must have been, we behold their influence, either for good or bad, as great and far-spreading as female influence ever was in any other either ancient or modern land. We cannot discern a trace of that social or domestic abasement which, had any either divine or human statute existed, *must* have been visible at a time when human nature was sunk to the lowest ebb. It is no longer Bible-times, or inspired characters which we are considering. The nation was a holy nation no longer, having departed through her iniquities from the Lord. He had left her children to their own hearts; but in the midst of evil, still the law and its beautiful ordinances lived and breathed in many noble hearts, and its *atmosphere* was still inhaled by the people, though its reviving *sunlight* had departed. Not in such a period could woman have taken her natural position, if any law had once existed to her abasement; but she simply *retained* that which she had always *possessed*, and this at the advent of Christianity.

Nor can we discern the faintest evidence of polygamy at this period. If we glance back to the return from Babylon, we must remark that every king and priest and prince is recorded as possessing but one wife. Simon, John Hyrcanus, Aristobulus I., Alexander Jannæus—both his sons, Aristobulus and Hyrcanus—Alexander, the father of Mariamne, her own two sons, and the other descendants of Herod, the wives of all of whom are mentioned, confirm both the legality and the custom of but one wife, at the very era when our opponents declare the religion of Jesus was absolutely needed to reform the abuses in the married state. "Herod had ten wives," there will be many to exclaim, and bring history forward as their authority. With all due deference to them, we assert, ay, and will prove, that Herod had but *three legal wives*, and that just in the same way as adversaries of Christianity *might*, if they chose, declare that Charles II. had ten or twenty wives, and so believe Christianity permitted polygamy; so with an equal share of justice may the opponents of Judaism bring forward Herod as an evidence of the degradation of the Jewish religion, and its sanction of polygamy. The personal character of Herod, as well as his magnificence, indeed, much more strongly resembled the character of Henry VIII.: the similarity, in fact, between them on many points being so curious, that it might make an interesting historical parallel, though, in the violence of passion and power of remorse, Herod had the advantage; but we mention Charles II., simply to state, that he might just as well be looked upon as the representative of Christianity, as Herod of Judaism.

But now to prove that only three of his wives can be considered as legally wedded :—Before he married Mariamne, or even made overtures for her hand, *Herod divorced his first wife Doris*, though she had already given him a son, and he had nothing to allege against her but his own desire to forward his ambition, by a union with the Asmonæan line. Now if polygamy were the law and the *custom* of the land, why need he have taken the trouble of divorcing Doris? Mariamne would equally have been his legal wife, her children equally his heirs, and though Doris might be the less beloved, the law provided for her, even under such an emergency. But, nothwithstanding all this, *he divorced her before he married Mariamne;* and surely this alone would prove, that man had already, in some degree, made the advance contemplated, when the law interfered not with his private habits, and *custom* had already rendered the remission needless, although the laws for the offspring of divorced wives still rendered their births legal, and gave them their share of the inheritance. It is, in fact, from this, that Herod in his own person appears to have practised polygamy; but that only one wife had become the custom of the country is further proved by the historian, who mentions but one other *public union*. Two years after the execution of the Asmonæan princess, during which time he was too much tormented by mental remorse and physical disease to think of taking another wife, Herod married another Mariamne, the daughter of Simon, an obscure individual, but of princely descent, and she enjoyed that dignity, such as it was, for twenty years, till, supposing her to be an accomplice in the conspiracy of Antipater against himself, he divorced her in the last year of his life and reign. Now of this second Mariamne, Josephus makes particular mention in his Antiquities (book xv. ch. 9, sect. 3), that to enable him to make her his wife, he elevated the rank of her father, thinking if he did not legally wed her, he would be stigmatised with cruelty and tyranny, qualities the *semblance* of which he wished to avoid.

There is no mention of his thus wedding any of his other (so called) wives; and, therefore, that he had them, and that their children were all considered legitimate, is not any proof of polygamy being then a national custom: for even granting Herod had publicly married the whole nine, it would not have weighed a single grain against the fact, that every other king, priest, or prince, mentioned since the return from Babylon, had but one. He was one who in every single act, set law, especially the Jewish law, at defiance. According to Gibbon, the wise and good emperor Charlemagne had also nine wives, but we do not therefore accuse Christians of favouring that doctrine; then why should we lay Herod's licentiousness, granting he proved it, which history denies rather than confirms, to the score of the holy religion which, though he *professed* he certainly never *practised?*

In a careful and critical survey of the manners and customs of the Jews, between the return from Babylon and their final dispersion, we find nothing whatever, differing from the precepts of the early Christians. The apostles were themselves Jews, who wrote for the Gentiles, and condensed and simplified for them, the sublime morality of the Mosaic code. They do not preach a single precept, they do not proclaim a single truth, they do not give a single rule for social and domestic guidance, which we Hebrews had not known, and practised ages before they wrote—and wrote, in fact, from their own experience of Jewish manners and customs. The reverend collector of the " Old Paths " could have known very little of Jewish history, or wilfully misinterpreted that which he did know, to make the extraordinary assertion that the introduction of monogamy belongs to Christianity alone. With very few exceptions, the actors of the New Testament are all Jews; and the domestic life there recorded of course reflects the Jewish life of those days: and had polygamy then existed, would it not have been one of the most important points for the Apostles of the new creed, to exalt the new moral law above the old ? But we do not find this :—exactly in accordance (in this instance) with the Old Testament, *the New Testament nowhere ordains monogamy and prohibits polygamy.* Impartial men allow this, and Dr. Channing, who, though no Protestant, must surely be considered a Christian, writes concerning Milton's opinion of polygamy, " Finding no prohibition of polygamy in the New Testament, he believed that not only holy men would be traduced, but Scripture dishonoured by pronouncing it morally evil:" and again, "We believe it to be an undisputed fact, that although Christianity was first preached in Asia, which had been from the earliest ages the seat of polygamy, the Apostles never denounced it as a crime and never required their converts to put away all wives but one."* Surely this is an important confirmation of our assertion, that we did not require the preaching of the Apostles to teach us that refinement and elevation of the social system which, with the advancement of humanity, time would procure us, and which was in fact obtained at the very era, in which we are told it was *first* offered us, by the adoption of a superior moral code.

The text to which Christians appeal as the prohibition of polygamy, is one from which a very different conclusion might be drawn—" Whoso shall put away his wife (except for adultery) and shall marry another, committeth adultery, and whoso marrieth her which is put away doth commit adultery." Surely this can only mean, that a man is forbidden unlawfully to put away one wife, and marry another in her stead, not to keep the first, and add another to his household: and the spirit of this precept we have already had in the Mosaic law; but, even granting that it does prohibit polygamy, we, too, have a prohibition of equal, if not superior, force, and written much about the same time by the venerable Rabbi Arni: " I say, that any man who marries a second wife, must *fully have repudiated his first;*"† a precept on which Herod appears to have originally acted, by his divorcing Doris before he married Mariamne. That he took Doris back again after the first Mariamne's death, proves nothing. The Jewish law forbade such an act; but we have seen that he cared nothing for the laws; but that Mariamne was his sole wife while she lived, is sufficient for our purpose.

There may, perhaps, be some who think these remarks irrelevant to our subject; but if they aid, as they must do, our assertion, that the Jewish religion is enough for her female votaries, that we need no other to elevate and secure our natural position, we earnestly trust that they will not need be dismissed unread. We mean no disrespect to other creeds: we shrink from following the example of some, who endeavour to exalt their own faith by debasing and throwing contempt upon another. We would only prove, that the imperfection

* Channing's Works, People's Edition, vol. i. page 26.

† Yebamoth, fol. 65, col. a. For this and many of the preceding remarks on polygamy and the Christian and Jewish discussions on the point, I am indebted to the kind suggestions and valuable information of Mr. Theodores, of Manchester.

(if the non-prohibiting of polygamy be such) of our moral code, exists equally in the other; and that it is the gradual, but sure advancement of the human species, which is the refiner and elevator of domestic and social life—not solely the ordinances of any particular laws. The first idea of polygamy being allowed, supposes a degraded position for women; but we have seen, that even at the period of its practice in Judaism, women were *not* degraded, for the law provided against its abuse: and even then, with very few exceptions, the chosen servants of the Eternal proved, in their own persons, the advance beyond their age in the practice of monogamy.

The captivity in Babylon had been an era in Jewish history. The partial return to Jerusalem, and dispersion over other lands, had occasioned very many changes. Man, even in the midst of apparently increasing evil and darkening morality, had yet, in actual fact, made a stride in advance, and much which had polluted the nation before, in the worshipping and sacrificing to idols, the fearful abuse of the gracious non-interference with Eastern customs and long endeared habits, and other crimes coeval with man's least refined state of existence—all had given way and been trampled on in the terrible revolution which, through the Babylonish power, had overwhelmed the land. Sins of equal magnitude, and demanding yet more fearful retribution, from the neglect and heedlessness of former chastisement, indeed, desecrated Judea; but, in the very different nature of the evil, the very sins themselves, we see, as it were, the advancement in human powers. The good in human nature will not make advance alone. Good and evil passions mutually sway the heart of man; and, according as the one or the other gains the ascendancy, so will be the increased good or increased evil in the appearance of the world. But having an equally increased power of good, the evil is only *visibly* evil; the under-current is still working, though *invisibly*, far more powerfully and beneficially, than in those periods when the capabilities of good and of evil were less than they are now. The conflicting powers could not produce the same end; but as the Divinity in the good advances, the evil will, in the end, be both visibly and invisibly subdued; and man, through the grace of God, attain that perfection for which he was originally framed.

We see the prophecy of this in the sublime fact, that there is never evil without its being the parent of good. No national revolution ever yet took place without being followed

by a rapid stride in human nature, and as strikingly visible as
far-spreading good : yet during the continuance of those
revolutions, what can we trace or feel, but the supremacy of
evil, in the war, famine, misery in a thousand shapes, which
devastate mankind ? Still good is working, and we know and
see it when the darkened torrent has rolled back, and the clear
crystal waters, reflecting the blue azure of the eternal heavens,
are seen beneath.

Thus good sprung for Israel from the captivity of Babylon,
working even in the midst of the crime and sin, in which its
visible form was but too soon swallowed up. The minds of
men had advanced ; but, left to their own hardened hearts
to obey or disobey the laws of their God, and so *prove*
themselves worthy of the mercies proffered *if* they obeyed,
they chose the evil, and so by their increased capabilities for
its accomplishment, drew down the most awful chastisement
on their own heads, and on their holy land, sweeping in one
fearful vortex the innocent and the guilty, the pious and the
blasphemer, the obedient and disobedient ; for in this world
no distinction might be made. The King of heaven waited
till they appeared before His throne, to pronounce sentence
according to their *hearts* yet more than according to their
deeds.

But humanity itself had not gone back, though all on earth
seemed dark and terrible. Good worked even there. The
Divine part of our mingled nature was visible in those
instances of patriotism, martyrdom, earnestness, and spirituality, which our history records of man and woman, old age
and youth, even in the blackest tempest of the war, and
surrounded as they were with men, who, given up to their
own passions and inclinations, so succumbed to the evil as to
appear incarnate fiends. And good sprung from this ; ay,
not only from the evil of the war, but from the untold-of,
incalculable, indescribable wretchedness of dispersion and
persecution. It brought, nay, it is still bringing Israel once
more, in loving faith and unquestioning obedience, to his God,
and hastening on that day, when the evil shall be entirely
subdued, and the good reign triumphant.

With these reflections, we will conclude the Sixth Period of
our history, leaving to the Seventh a glance over our dispersion,
and its effects on the present condition of our nation, male
and female. Brought down, as the history of the women of
Israel now is, to nearly seventy years after the advent of

Christianity, the proofs of our non-abasement and degradation become yet more important; for there are many to assert, that in the Bible-times the Hebrew females shared the holy privileges of the males, but that it was the falling-off from this spiritual Judaism, the mingling human with Divine authority, which so degraded and blinded the Hebrews after the Babylonish captivity, as absolutely to demand for our salvation the belief in the atonement of Jesus, and adoption of the new creed which his apostles preached.

We trust that we have convincingly proved to our own nation, and from our own history, that this was *not* the case—that no human additions to the pure law had, between the first and second captivity, lowered the position, or interfered with the spiritual privileges of the Women of Israel. The conversion and earnest zeal of Helena of Adiabene would be in itself sufficient to controvert this charge: and we have, in addition, alike the story of the martyr-mother—the independent sovereignty of Alexandra, wife of Alexander Jannæus—the influence of Mariamne, as sole representative of the Asmonæans—and of Salome, in the pursuit of her fiendlike machinations—of Berenice, in the performance of her singular vow, and her rank and power as the *sister* and *widow* of kings, to convince us still more unanswerably, that the woman of Israel enjoyed a temporal power, and privileges peculiarly her own; and was debarred in not a single instance, of the spiritual privileges and solemn responsibilities which had been bestowed on her by the law of God, and which the manners and customs of her country at the advent of Christianity undeniably confirmed. This, then, is enough for us. There is no trace *before* the dispersion of that mingling of human with Divine ordinances with which we are charged; and therefore we cannot allow, that for *us* the moral preaching of the Christian apostles was needed. If such, indeed, took place *after* the dispersion, it was from the care of holy men to keep pure and holy the jewel of their faith, which was threatened to be buried, alas! beneath the bloody ashes of constant persecution; and how might we accept as saving, purifying, and reforming, the creed of those very men, whose cruel oppression occasioned the very evil from which they bid us turn. No! even in the midst of anarchy, misery, and blood, the religion of God shone forth DIVINE. It was sufficient for us *then;* and O doubly dearer, holier, more precious is it to us now!

SEVENTH PERIOD.

The Women of Israel as influenced by their Dispersion and by the History of the Past.

THE WAR.

ITS HORRORS.—ORIGIN AND END.—FULFILMENT OF PROPHECY.—REAL CAUSE OF JEWISH CHASTISEMENT.—DISPERSION.—THOUGHTS ON THE TALMUD.

It is with emotions of actual relief and gladness, that we leave to other works the details of that awful war, during the continuance of which 1,356,460 of our hapless countrymen perished, and 101,700 graced as prisoners the triumph of the Roman emperor and his son; and this calculation relates only to the period of the destruction of Jerusalem: the thousands and thousands of men, women and children, who fell victims to after massacres, are not included.

As a History of the Women of Israel, we need not linger on details which our own historian, Josephus, and, yet more powerfully, in all the eloquence of modern writing, Milman, has brought so vividly before us, save to give one shuddering glance on what must have been the anguish, the tortures, of the female children of the Lord at that awful period. Every social tie—mother, daughter, sister, wife—must every hour have been subject to the agony of such bereavement as we can but faintly imagine now. We see, by both Isaiah and Ezekiel, that the sins of the women had added to the weight of national iniquity; but still all were not sinful, all were not rebellious. Countless thousands of those that fell were true to their God and His law. The service of the Temple, the daily offerings, were continued in the very midst of the most horrible internal dissensions and outward siege; and not only men armed for battle, but the aged and the feeble, the loveliest and the most unprotected female, the stripling youth and the tender child, sought the temple-courts to worship, and often by the very altar found their deaths. What, in this dark epoch, would have supported the Hebrew female and given her strength to witness misery, suffer torture, and then die—what but an assurance of that immortality, wherein the distinction between the righteous and the wicked should be discerned, and all of this world's agony be swallowed up in an eternity of bliss?

In shrinking from the pages of horror which relate the Jewish war, we sometimes forget to bring forward in its deserved light the noble and exalted patriotism from which the awful struggle sprang. In our last period we have endeavoured to give some idea of the enslaving and savage nature of the Roman government over the provinces of Judæa. A reference to the historians of the period will make it clearer still. From Herod, falsely called the Great, originated, as we have seen, the Roman subjection of Judæa, and the denationalising of the Jewish people. But all of nationality, all of patriotism, had not merged into the slavish subjection which the persecuting cruelty of the Roman governors seemed determined to enforce. In the very face of crushing tyranny and inward depression, the Hebrew people rose as one man to throw off the yoke of Rome —Rome, the mistress of the world, empress of a thousand cities, of a hundred provinces, each one larger and more mighty than the unprotected land whose daring sons held forth the banner of rebellion, and dared to strike for freedom! It was not Rome who commenced the struggle. She would have laughed to scorn the very idea that Judæa could lead armies to subject her, when her officers and troops already held the land. No, it was the Jews themselves. And who, after this, shall accuse us of tacit submission, of being wanting in courage, patriotism, spirit, all that makes the warrior? Had we succeeded, we, too, should have been held up as examples of man in his noblest nature, even like the Swiss under Tell, the Scotch under Wallace and Bruce, and the Americans of a later day; for, when compared with the Hebrews' struggles for liberty and soil, how faint and feeble were the efforts of these modern lands. But the exalted *origin* of the Jewish war is lost in its awful close. We could not succeed; for it was the Lord who fought against us through the Roman swords in just chastisement for national iniquity, and in fulfilment of His prophecy by Moses. Still, let not our sons forget that their ancestors alone dared brave the mighty force of imperial Rome —their ancestors alone so fought for freedom that mightier armies than were needed for the reduction of any other province were summoned against them. Ay, and that, had not the wrath of the Eternal worked against them, in the division of themselves, and in the awful fulfilment of the threatenings which they had disregarded, Judæa would have been unconquered still.

One important fact it is necessary to notice here. Our young sisters, no doubt, have often read and heard (for it is impossible to peruse Gentile historians of the time without such impressions) that the awful occurrences of the war, the destruction of our glorious Temple, and banishment from our Holy Land, all were occasioned, not by our departure from the law of God, and manifold national transgressions, but from our obstinate rejection of Jesus when he came for our salvation. Now, without an intimate knowledge of our history during the continuance of the Second Temple, this might be a startling argument. We see that we are dispersed; we read of all the miseries and massacres which have befallen us; of the omens and prodigies that preceded the destruction of the Temple. We are told by eager Gentile acquaintance, or read in their books, that so Jesus prophesied, and that he wept when he looked on Jerusalem, foreseeing all the calamities about to ensue *because the people rejected him;* and unless we know another cause for all these things, how are we to answer?

And yet how easy is the true reply! A very cursory glance over our history from the return from the Babylonish Captivity, even if we go no farther than the death of Herod, will bring glaringly before us the awful sins for which we are thus punished. Even in the brief sketch which we have given at the commencement of our Sixth Period, we surely must trace the national departure from the pure law of Moses, the assimilation with other nations, the entire forgetfulnesss that we were to be a "nation of priests, holy unto the Lord," the awful deeds of parricide and massacre, devastating the houses of those very princes chosen as the Lord's anointed priests: and even had we but the reign of Herod, we read of a sufficiency of sin to hurl down on us the threatened chastisement of the Eternal. The period between the first and second Captivity was granted us as a period of trial whether or not we would return with our whole hearts unto the Lord. The twenty-eighth chapter of

Deuteronomy, with its sublime and startling prophecy, was ours *then*, even as it is *now*. We had already felt the wrath of the Lord; and the power to return to Him and to His law, or to reject them, His mercy had planted in our hearts. If man had no power of himself to keep the law of God, as the Gentiles teach, then, indeed, would the law have been instituted in mockery, not in love—to destroy, not to save; and there could have been no need for that sublime prophecy of Moses. This is not the work to dilate on the twenty-eighth chapter of Deuteronomy, as inclination might prompt. We can only beseech our readers to turn to it themselves—to observe the blessings promised for obedience—the curses threatened on the disobedient—to compare the history of Israel during the continuance of the Temple, with the first fourteen verses of the chapter, and reflect if such blessings could be ours; and then from the fifteenth to the end of the chapter; and do we need more to instruct us in the nature of our sins—and the wherefore they were punished?

"But it shall come to pass, if *thou wilt not* hearken unto the voice of the Lord thy God, to observe to do all His commandments and His statutes which I command thee this day, that all these curses shall come upon thee and overtake thee." This single verse is all-sufficient to overturn every Gentile argument. The prophecy which it precedes is so exact a description of all that took place in Jerusalem *before* its siege by the Romans, *during* the siege, and, *afterwards*, in the various lands where we were scattered, that it would seem as if it must have been written by an eye-witness, or *after* those events took place—not by a historian living hundreds and thousands of years before. This single chapter is sufficient to prove the truth of the Bible, Judaism, and God. The description of the siege may in a slight degree be applicable either to the first or second destruction of the Temple; but, as a whole, it refers *only* and *solely* to the destruction of Jerusalem by Titus, and the final dispersion of the Jews.

Let not, then, the impressions derived from Gentile historians, so confine the youthful Hebrew mind, as to conceal for a single instant the real reason for our past miseries and present dispersion. We *were*, we *are*, chastised, not for rejecting Jesus, but for long long years of disobedience to our law. We are chastised for those national and individual crimes and sins, recorded in our history during the continuance of our Second Temple—not for refusing belief in Jesus. If omens and prodigies did precede the destruction of the Temple, might not Nature have been equally moved with horror for the fate threatening the Jewish people for their *manifold sins*, as for a single one. Jesus wept when he thought on the calamities of Jerusalem; but this only proves, that, like every *Jew*, he was well acquainted with the prophecy of Moses, and, in the supremacy of national sin, beheld its near fulfilment— wholly and entirely distinct from their treatment of himself.

Surely, then, the Gentile arguments, as to the cause of our dispersion, must fall harmless to the ground. A knowledge of our own history being all that is required to supply us with defence.*

The war itself lasted but five years: but the miseries and massacres of the Jews, commenced almost from the death of Herod, and continued, with little cessation, long after Jerusalem was destroyed. In every Roman province where they took refuge, they were almost universally massacred, either from some fancied insult, or revolt among themselves, or from the determination of the Romans to sweep them from the earth. The Greeks joined in this universal persecution—their only point of cordial union with the Romans seeming, in fact, to be their detestation of and cruelty towards the exiles of the Lord. The reign of Adrian threatened them with almost as complete an extermination as their expulsion from their land. Yet still they lived on, endowed, it seems, with an undying vitality, which neither cruelty, nor suffering, nor death in its most awful shape, could extinguish. Nor was it the *race* only, which was preserved, but the *religion*. Wherever they were, in whatever circumstances, either of prosperity or

* Our opponents will, no doubt, urge, that it was to redeem us from those very sins, dilated on above, that Jesus came; and had we accepted him, our punishment, in the destruction of our beautiful city, and banishment from our Holy Land, would have been averted. This sounds well: but as no such condition whatever was annexed, as a saving clause, to the prophetic threatenings of Moses, in chapter twenty-eight of Deuteronomy, we can neither accept or allow it. Had the Eternal ordained and required this acceptance of Jesus, He would have inspired Moses to insert, at the end of verse fifteen, chapter twenty-eight, " But it shall come to pass, if thou wilt not hearken, etc.—*nor accept the salvation that I offer through the atonement* of the Saviour whom I will send." But as there are *no* such conditions, the cause of all that has befallen us originates in the awful disobedience to the " voice of the Lord our God," and disobedience to the law, which he gave through Moses.

adversity, oppression or partial freedom, still they were Jews—more earnest, more hearty, more resolute followers of their law, than they had been when outward circumstances might have permitted its strictest observances.

It was not till the reign of Antoninus Pius, that the miseries of the Hebrews subsided into a partial calm, and privileges were granted them throughout Italy and the various provinces of Rome, which enabled the patriarch of Tiberias to obtain such freedom and power in the observance of his religion, as to be recognised by the whole Jewish nation, wherever scattered, as their supreme head and spiritual sovereign.

It was under his mild jurisdiction, that the rabbins or learned men crept from their hiding-places, and resumed the study of the law. From them, at various times, emanated many of the minor ordinances, and learned explanations of the written word, which were afterwards collected and compiled under the different names of Gemara, Mishna, and later, the Talmud. The synagogues may also be said to have arisen from this period. Wherever there were ten Jews, there was a synagogue, with its books of the written law, and teachers; and its galleries for the accommodation of the Hebrew females, that they too might partake of the spiritual instruction and privileges offered to their brethren.

Over all the provinces of the great Empire, the Hebrew race extended; and from them penetrated all over Europe, and into the far-off countries of China, Malabar, other parts of the East Indies, the Coast of Africa, and places equally remote, where their very origin is plunged in mystery. In China, their synagogue we are told much more resembles the ancient Temple, than any of those in Europe. In Malabar there are both black and white Jews, the former most probably either the descendants of black slaves or converts. In Bokhara and Persia, particularly in the cities of Ispaham and Shiraz, Rashan and Yezd—in Mesopotamia, Assyria, Damascus, Arabia, Egypt, Cairo, the borders of Abyssinia, Morocco;—in all these places the Hebrews found a resting, precarious and uncertain indeed; but there they still continue to exist. In all the different kingdoms of Europe (except Norway, in which country we never remember seeing them mentioned), they have lived, flourished, been persecuted and expelled, recalled and protected. In Spain alone, the edict of expulsion never appears to have been recalled; but, as if in direct manifestation of the protecting arm of that gracious Providence, who had ordained the eternal existence of His people, the very year of their banishment from Spain, Christopher Columbus discovered that new continent, which was to be to them a home of more perfect freedom and peace than they had enjoyed since their dispersion. In America, persecution never assailed—expulsion never banished. In Spain, they had acquired a greater degree of learning, influence, and power, than in any other European nation; and such they might equally obtain in that land, which appeared to be called from the deep, at the voice of the Creator, to provide them a home where neither oppression nor even civil disabilities can check the same advance of mind and species, to which in Spain, and in Spain alone, they had attained. Surely, this consideration ought to weigh deeply in the minds of our brethren across the Atlantic, and, inciting them to rise superior to the worldly dreams and time-seeking pursuits of the age, urge them to make manifest to the world what freedom and equality will make the Jew.

It would be an interesting and curious study, to endeavour to trace the first colonies of the Hebrews in all these varied lands; though, from the utter absence of all authentic documents, we fear the task, however interesting, would be impossible. We seem only to know, that in every quarter of the globe, God has placed witnesses in simple fulfilment of His unalterable word. In the North, and in the South, in the East and in the West, there we are, and there we shall be, until that glorious day, when the same mighty word which sent us forth will recall us to the land of our fathers—when, for our path, the mountains shall be laid low and the valleys exalted, and the tongue of the Red Sea shall be dried up, and the crooked shall be made straight, and the rough places plain, and in Jerusalem the glorious Temple be upraised from the dust, as the visioned eye of Ezekiel saw and prophesied, in the sublime description contained in the last eight chapters of his book.

We cannot doubt that these things WILL BE, when we behold, by our residence in every land, what HAS BEEN and WHAT IS, and remember, that the same word which prophesied the PAST, whose fulfilment we have seen, hath prophesied the FUTURE, whose fulfilment we must equally behold, and *believe* even while it is deferred.

The history of the Jews, as a body, however, enters not into the plan of the present work; nor shall we even dwell upon it as long as we did in our previous Period. From the siege of Jerusalem, our history is very much more generally known, than during the period between the return from Babylon and the final dispersion. We still trace the effects of the one in our present condition, and in the frequent mention of us in modern history, the other is but too often entirely forgotten, or only thought of as blended with the records of Syria, Greece, Rome, and the final siege.

Our task rests with the Women of Israel; and of them we have unhappily so little mention, either as individuals or as a body, in modern times, that we can add but little to our previous pages. Yet that little, trifling as it may seem, on a superficial consideration, is of real importance to the confirmation of our asserted point, the perfect freedom and equality of the Hebrew female.

We shall not find her wanting in any single point which constitutes the fit recipient and promulgator of a persecuted creed, or shrinking, as her physical weakness might portend, from any suffering, even that most agonising—the bereavement of her children, by her own or their father's hand, could they thus only be saved from the denial of her God. Could any woman have done this, have looked on the pitiless murderers of all she loved, and then by cruel tortures calmly shared their fate; had she been deprived, as our opponents in their ignorance declare, of the belief in, and hope of, the bliss and rest of immortality.

Before, however, we bring forward instances of female martyrdom, there is one subject which, though we approach it with reluctance, from the opposition and wilful misconception which it is likely to produce, we desire to bring most strongly before our readers. It is the supposition of many amongst the Gentiles, and we fear amongst some few of ourselves, that it is the Talmud which, promoting the spirit of the Mosaic law, authorises, nay commands, the degradation and enslaving of the Jewish female. In confirmation of this theory, there are many zealous conversionists who bring forward, as translations from the Talmud, detached verses and portions, which appear so strongly to support their assertion, as to prevent all reply. Now it should be well remembered, both by ourselves and our opponents, that much which is called the Talmud, and supposed to be coeval with its original venerable compilers, are the speculations, inquiries, and even ordinances of much later writers, whose opinions were no doubt often biassed (though unconsciously) by the habits and customs of their own darkened age. Let us first consider the origin and real intent of these most venerable and often falsely abused forms. Divine, they are not. There are, we think, comparatively but few now, who will place them, in point of divinity and dignity, with the written oracles of God; for if they are, why do we not see the same honour and reverence paid to them, as to the sacred rolls, whose dwelling is the House of God; and whose appearance and elevation in the sight of the assembled multitude, cause the congregation simultaneously to rise in silent homage to their inspired author?

When expelled from their own land—banished into every quarter of the globe—the temple service, and worship, exactly as Moses had ordained, was impossible.* The sacrifices were compelled to cease; for the fire from heaven consumed them no longer as in the First Temple; nor as in the Second, were there courts and altars for the sacrifices; nor flocks and herds in possession of the Israelites to offer up. The multitudes, more eager than ever, from their state of adversity and trial, to return to the Lord their God, and once more obey that holy law, which, when it was in their power to obey, they had totally disregarded, beheld the opportunity so to do gone from them. Morning and evening, sabbaths and holidays, they had been accustomed to offer sacrifice and prayer. In case of singular vows, of thanksgiving, or penance, in every circumstance of life, they had a high priest to whom to resort, a Temple where to come, offerings ordained by Moses, and laws and statutes entering into every man's household, and guiding not only his spiritual and social but his domestic life. But these laws and ordinances were from Israel when an independent state, subjects of God alone, and in possession of lands and their produce—flocks, herds—all of which were absolutely necessary for exact obedience to the law. In their banishment how could they be guided in exact accordance with the pure law of Moses? At first perusal, they must have been almost appalled at the many ordinances which they could not observe; yet, on a second study of the holy books of Moses, and comparing them with the prophets, they must have seen, that

* For these remarks on the Talmud, and supposition of its use and intent, the author alone is answerable.

obedience, as far as lay in their power, in their several lands of exile, was imperatively demanded from them ; that their only hope of restoration and salvation was in a faithful adherence to the God and law of their fathers, and a firm faith in His promised mercy, to strengthen and purify man's feeble efforts, and render them acceptable unto him.

But how were they to obey? Eager and earnest in their repentance and desire to return to their God, now that the long-threatened chastisement had fallen, they welcomed with rejoicing the efforts of holy and good men to lay down a path of obedience which, even in their exile and in the midst of persecution, they might tread. Hence arose those ordinances which are accused of clogging with dead and soulless weight the pure and spiritual Law of God; but which, in those fearful eras of exile and persecution, bound Jew to Jew, and with God's protecting blessing, saved his religion from amalgamation with other nations, and all adoption of the Gentile creeds. But the holy men who originally raised the protecting casket around the beautiful jewel of their faith, never either preached or intended that their ordinances were to be considered divine or spiritual. It was to *preserve* the purity, the spiritual purity, of their Law unsullied, when circumstances must otherwise have crushed it (we are writing humanly, not alluding to the Divine Guardian, who would always have preserved us from annihilation), *not* to take its place and be considered in the same unalterable and changeless light with which we look on the Law of God. Circumstances might demand the modification, even the alteration, of some of these Rabbinical statutes; and could their wise and pious originators have been consulted on the subject, they would have unhesitatingly adopted those measures most likely to advance and aid spiritual improvement, even if to do so demanded a modification of some of their previously instituted statutes. We have but to glance over the life and writings of the great Maimonides to prove this assertion.

To the speculative theorists, students, and additional compilers of the middle ages, be it remembered, we do not allude. The great mischief which has befallen our people, in the supposed superiority of form over spirit—the ordinances of the Talmud over those given by Moses, and explained by the prophets—originates not in the first venerable compilers of the Talmud at the time of our dispersion, but in the writers of the middle ages, whose minds were darkened by the bloody ashes of persecution, who beheld all of spirituality apparently about to succumb before the awful darkness and abasement in which misery had plunged the mass; and who, in consequence, multiplied forms to guard them still more strictly from assimilation with their persecutors. And all those laws, in which the fierce exclusiveness, so contrary to the spirit of love pervading the law of God, is founded, owe their origin to the same source. Opponents would do well to remember this, and, when they point to vows and laws, which *appear* to contradict the law of God, apply them to their only source, not the disobedience of the Jew, but the persecution of the Gentile, and the darkening misery thence ensuing.

But in our first dispersion, eagerly and rejoicingly the people listened to and observed the mild protecting ordinances of their spiritual teachers. In their banishment and misery they beheld the awful fulfilment of the Eternal's word; and, remembering the beneficent mercy and forbearance which they had scorned, turned in deep repentance once more to their God. Their conscience, their earnest longings, to prove repentance by obedience, found rest and peace in the steady observance of ordinances which in their captive state they could obey, and which brought down the spiritual religion of their own bright land, to the homes and synagogues of their captivity. These ordinances, and the spiritual supremacy of the Rabbins, became even the more necessary, as the Christian and then the Mahomedan religions spread. It was comparatively easy to separate themselves from the idolatrous abominations of the Heathen; but when they were thrown, sometimes amongst the followers of the Nazarene, acknowledging the same God and the same moral law—at others, with the followers of Mahomed, proclaiming the unity of God, observing the same covenant of Abraham, having some belief in Moses, and refusing the same interdicted food—the necessity of increased exclusiveness and care of the great mass of the people, who were in much too degraded and enslaved a position to realise the superior spirituality of truth of their own religion, became more and more evident, and gave our wise men still greater power and authority than they had originally sought. The multitudes scattered in every land, and liable to every insult and persecution, had neither the opportunity nor the mind to study for themselves, and were glad to follow unquestioningly in the path laid down.

If we impartially consider our position in the long centuries of persecution, we cannot surely wonder even if inward spirituality did in some degree give place to outward form. To realise the former as our God demands, requires a position of comparative freedom—a breathing space, as it were—to cultivate all those refining and elevating emotions which enlarge and spiritualise the soul. In many countries, the Hebrew was sunk to a lower and more degraded position, than even (we will not say the slaves) the very beasts of the soil. If, in those eras, they had not had some ordinances which they could obey, without even caring to know the wherefore, how could their religion have been preserved? We allude merely to those brief calms in their lives, when the sword of slaughter, though hovering over them, was still sheathed. At those times, the mass might have appeared only to possess and value the casket, not the jewel; but where the hovering sword fell, and multitudes were doomed to the dread alternative of death, or denial of their God, then did the immortal glory of the jewel flash through the encircling casket, and endow them with the pure spirit of hope and faith which gave them strength to die! Mere blind adherence to instituted forms could never have done this. The spirit of their holy religion was breathed into every breast, invisible and unfelt in the sluggish depths of daily misery and constant fear, but bursting into life at the first call, and endowing with that firm belief in immortality which alone creates the martyr.

Those periods, then, in our history, in which the spirit of the Mosaic laws seems lost in multiplied and weighty forms, cannot be charged to the ordinances of our ancient fathers, but to the still sluggish indifference which ever follows extreme excitement. Accustomed through so many centuries to anticipate and endure only persecution and slavery, it required a very long interval for the Israelites even to *realise* the belief that there were actually some countries in which they might live in perfect freedom and equality with their Gentile neighbours, and, consequently, that something more was demanded from them, than mere adherence to instituted forms because so did their fathers. No longer called upon to *suffer*, the spirit within them so slept, that they became, at length, almost unconscious of its existence; and if asked wherefore they observed such forms, and what was the origin of their belief, they might have found it difficult to reply. From this unnatural stagnation, many Christians formed the opinion that the religion of the Jews was a mere spiritual formula, unenlightened by a single ray of immortal hope or spiritual faith, forgetting that the very evil they condemn, originated in the persecution of their own ancestors, *not* in the religion of the Jews.

The period of this stagnation is now, however, almost extinct. It had but its appointed time; and though, in some lands, it still too oppressively exists, yet wherever the Hebrew is FREE, a new spirit is awakening, giving precious promise of that time when spirit and form shall be re-united, as the God of Love ordained, the one aiding the other, till that perfection is attained, which, with the purifying blessing of the Lord, will lead us to our own dear land, and permit us once more to be His own.

ORDINANCES AND TALES OF THE TALMUD,

RELATING TO THE WOMEN OF ISRAEL.

HAVING thus briefly glanced over the real origin, intent and meaning of the Talmudical Ordinances, we will return to the point whence we started, and ascertain whether or not our venerable sages so completely contradicted the spirit of the law of Moses, as to hint, countenance, or ordain the degradation of the Hebrew female. For this purpose we will transcribe a few of the rabbinical maxims, with which we have been favoured by the kindness of the friend already referred to, whose sound knowledge of the Hebrew, both Biblical and Talmudical, and deep research, render his information on the subject indeed invaluable. The Hebrew Review, and one or two other casual notices in divine history, have also enabled us to form an opinion; but the Talmud itself should be its foundation; and from that we, as a female, are unhappily debarred.

We must refer once more, though unwillingly, to the Nazarenes' assertion, that their religion was the first, and is the only one which provides for woman. "*For woman never would, and never could have risen to her present station in the social system, had it not been for the dignity, with which*

Christianity invested those qualities, peculiarly her own,"* etc. We can quite understand and sympathise in the Christian woman's love for her own faith, and heartfelt eloquence in the privileges it assures her. We can quite understand—when she compares her lot with that of the Heathen and Mahomedan, and remembers, that had it not been for the wider spread of Christianity, her fate would still have been the same—the glow of mind and heart, which must infuse her whole being, and naturally be reflected in her writing; but then, in her eloquent appeal to her young country-women to remember what they owe to Christianity, let her not be so unjust as to count the Jewish religion amongst those in which woman, in her clinging and truly feminine character, is uncared for and unvalued. The moral laws to which she owes her privileges came from US, and US alone. Who were the apostles and preachers? Who went about, giving the Heathen a knowledge of Israel's God, though they disregarded the ceremonial law? Who but the HEBREWS, whose whole minds and hearts were imbued, *not* with new doctrines, but with the Hebrew moral law, which they disseminated in their wanderings, in such simple language as was best fitted for the long-darkened understandings of the Heathen whom they addressed? Jesus himself was a Jew, and every word which he preached, or said in regard to morality, even his parables themselves, have their foundation in the commentaries of the Jewish elders on the written law. We cannot trace a single moral statute throughout the New Testament, which is new, or even simplified to us. What may seem obscure, from the pure spirituality of the

* Woman's Mission, page 140. We should not lay so much stress upon this point, were such observations as those quoted above confined to *conversation*. But when we see such sentiments as are contained in pages 140, 141, and 142, of a work, which, from its deserved popularity, is disseminated, not only over our England, but, no doubt, over many other countries, how can we pass such charges by? Did the authoress not allude to the Jews, we should not feel the necessity of noticing it so imperatively; but when even the religion of the people of God is included in such false and sweeping assertions (see page 142), we should be failing in either respect or love for our own holy faith, did we not endeavor to remove the impression. Many of our young sisters are acquainted with the really excellent little work in question, and unless well guarded, by finding all that the authoress urges in support of Christianity in their *own* holy faith, are likely to be startled and annoyed by what appears so plausible; the more so from the justice and moderation and truth of the previous chapters. In writing for our own sex, we are not authorised in refusing to notice such mistaken charges.

words of Moses, our venerable sages explain in language so simple and expressive, that the most obtuse could not fail to understand. While, then, we willingly acknowledge that every *Gentile* nation, under the mild equitable influence of Christianity, has every reason to love and venerate the religion it upholds, and that every Christian woman would be wanting alike in honesty and enthusiasm, did she not consider her lot as blessed above that of every other Gentile land, let her not throw a slur upon the females of that holy faith, from whose privileges *her own have sprung*, and for whose safety, protection, guidance, and elevation for the obtaining and encouraging all the loveliest and most *feminine* attributes of her sex, the Most High Himself deigned to lay down laws, disregard to which was disobedience to Himself.

This argument we have already treated at length in our Second Period, where we brought forward every statute relative to the Hebrew female, which our great law-giver wrote down. In the succeeding Periods, even after we left the records of the Bible for the later history of Josephus, we have shown, and we believe somewhat satisfactorily, how those laws were followed by the influence and treatment of the females of Judea, even when the pure law was almost lost in the national anarchy reigning, with little intermission, during the continuation of the Second Temple.

Surely this ought to be sufficient, even for those who declare that modern Judaism is distinct from, and even opposed to, the Judaism of the Bible, and that the Talmud is the cause. We do not think that the New Testament itself can bring forward a more touching and beautiful ordinance than the following :—" Make allowance for the weakness of thy wife ; and if thou canst not raise her to thee, do thou stoop, and speak encouragingly to her "—or. " If thy wife be of small stature, stoop, and speak gently to her." Again, " Ever be zealous for the honour of thy wife ; for there is no blessing found in a man's house, which comes not through his wife."

To love their wives was natural; therefore love is not so much insisted upon as honour and respect. "Hold your wives in *high respect*, and you will be *rich indeed ;*" but how could a man respect his wife, if her domestic and social position were degraded and enslaved ? Again, " A man should *honour* his wife *more* than himself, and *love* her as he does *his own* person." Here love is valued less than honour, because we may *love* an *inferior* being. We can only *respect* and *honour* superior virtue and elevated qualities; and this statute could never have proceeded from men accustomed to look on their wives in the light of inferiors, or in any single point but on an equality with themselves.

"Whoever marries a woman *for money* alone, will not have children according to his wishes," because the ancient fathers looked on "woman's mission" to be principally the education of her family, an idea borne out by the whole history of the Jews, in the particular mention of the mothers of kings, and other exalted persons. "A man should beware of marrying the daughter of an uneducated man; for should he die, or be banished, his children must remain uneducated, their mother being unacquainted with the glory of education." An equal care is taken for the comfort and respect due to an educated wife. "A man should give his daughter to an educated man, for no disgrace or strife enters the house of a man of education." Now, were the Hebrew wife a mere cypher in the household, what could it signify on whom she was bestowed? Exactly in accordance with the spirit of the Mosaic Law, the duties prescribed by the Talmud towards mothers are of equal weight and force as towards the fathers: even more, for if a son see his mother and father either imprisoned or in danger, he is bound to save his *mother* even before his father—a natural and an affecting ordinance; for the latter is supposed, from greater physical strength and mental energy, to be more easily enabled to save himself, while the weakness and delicacy of the mother rendered her entirely dependent on her son. The Law of God commanded the same honour to be paid the mother as the father (see Second Period—laws for mothers), and the venerable compilers of the Talmud, departed not one item from its spirit; thus upholding the moral and social dignity of women, even had there been no other law. That the *mother* as well as the children, were to honour the father of a family, surely cannot be twisted into a degrading ordinance. Unhappy, indeed, is the woman of any creed, rank, or country, who cannot, with her whole heart, mind, and soul, honour the father of her children—the husband of her choice!

The laws for the widows and the fatherless also, on which we laid so much stress, as marking the care for woman by the Mosaic law, in our Second Period, we find commented upon by our ancient fathers, so exactly in the pure spirit of the Divine ordinance, that we cannot resist transcribing the whole passage.

"Be very careful in the treatment of widows, and orphans, not merely if they be poor; but because *their spirit be broken*, though they be ever so rich. Even the widow of a king, and his orphans, demand that carefulness. For it is said, 'All widows and orphans shall ye not oppress.' Let the manner of addressing them be kind : do not burthen them with labour or oppress them with harsh words. Let their property be more precious to thee than thine own ; for he that offends or oppresses them, and injures their property, is an evil-doer, and his punishment is expressed in the law : ' And my anger shall break out against you,' etc. (Exodus xxii. 24). The Holy One, blessed be he, has vouchsafed to grant them a particular covenant, that when they invoke Him against their oppressors, they shall be heard, as it is said, 'When they call up to me I will hear them, for I am merciful'" (Ex. xx. 23).

The prohibition to offend them is, however, only in cases where it may cause them injury ; but when it is for their good, as for instance, where a teacher is to instruct them in the law or in his trade, it is a duty to reprove them ; nevertheless, a distinction ought to be made in their favour, and they should be treated with greater forbearance than other pupils, so as to instruct them mildly, with great patience and attention; for it is said, "the Lord will defend their cause," etc. (Psalm cxl. 12). Whether the child have lost father or mother, it is alike called an orphan, until it attain an age to protect itself.*
And this at once proves that the Hebrew mother was even on a more acknowledged equality with the father than in any other nation ; for we believe that orphans in general mean those who have lost *both parents*, or a *father* only.

We think, if we look the world over, and examine every religious or moral code, we shall fail to find any laws to surpass these ; not only in humanity, but in most exquisite tenderness to that bruised and broken reed, a widow of any rank or class, from the relict of a sovereign to the relict of a slave (so called), guiding not alone *conduct* towards her, but actually words and the *manner* of address.

Again, we find peculiar regard paid by the Talmudists to the laws instituted by Moses for females of every denomination,

* Extracted from the Hebrew Review, pp. 60 and 61. Thence taken from Morality of the Talmud. Hilchoth Deoth (Ethic Precepts), Div. vi. sect. 10.

as is proved by such laws as the following : "The woman *takes precedence* of the male in being fed, clad, and freed from captivity." Repeatedly recommending us to afford protection and relief to the *female first*, and then to the male, in strong figures, which are so common to Eastern idiom, it commands, "Let thy table be considerably *within* thy means; thy dress and appearance *according* to thy means; but the comforts of thy *wife* and children *beyond* thy means."

We have already noticed the humane statutes in our law for the protection and comfort of the maid-servants, or female slaves in Israel (see Second Period); and that it was illegal for a man to transfer his Hebrew maid-servant to another master. In exact accordance with the spirit of this beautiful ordinance, Tradition (or the Talmud) tells us: The male servant became free on his master's death, *provided* there was no male heir; but for the *female* servant's release there was no such condition." Her master's dying hour was the moment of her manumission, expressed in the Talmudic simple brevity by the words, "The Hebrew maid-servant serves neither son nor daughter."

Here, then, even in these few and trifling extracts, we find that, instead of contradicting, every statute given by Moses relative to mothers, wives, daughters, widows, and maid-servants in Israel, is *confirmed* by the Talmudic precepts, and so simplified that it is impossible even for wilful misconception to mistake their meaning. There may be many turns and points in the writings of our ancient sages seeming to contradict them, more especially in the light in which our opponents, to serve their own purposes, bring them forward : but with such laws as we have quoted, all else is of little moment. We *know* that they must have been written by men well versed, not only in the ordinances, but in the *spirit* of the law written by Moses, simply because of their exact accordance; that at the time such precepts were collected and written, the social or domestic position of woman *could not* have been the degraded and frivolous one assigned in general to the females of the East. That the Talmud *must* have regarded them as companions and friends to their husbands—educators of their children—mistresses of their household; and possessing, from their physical weakness and delicacy, such claims on the protection, tenderness, and kindness, not of their relatives alone, but of their *nation* in general, which are not to be found in the moral code of any other people.

What later Jewish writers, therefore, may urge upon the subject, if it contradict this spirit, by assigning either position, duties, or employments, derogatory to her as a female, a recipient and promulgator of the law of God, or debarring her from those religious and social principles which were granted her from the delivery of the law, and proved her own by the history of every Jewish female mentioned in the Bible—those laws, statutes, ordinances, precepts, or even allusions, can be now *nothing worth whatever*, for not only (if there be such) do they contradict the law, but the traditions; not only disregard Moses, but the venerable fathers; and, therefore, need neither notice nor denial. However wise and learned may be their writers, however gravely they may be weighed and given, if in one single instance they contradict the law of God and the traditions of the fathers quoted above, we reject them altogether as neither guiding nor binding laws. Speculative theories they may be, probably originating from an intimate association with the Moors of Spain and other nations of Eastern origin and Moslem faith, or even the Nazarenes themselves; for, in the middle ages, under the darkened sway of Catholicism, we certainly can trace very little of the humanising and elevating effect of Christianity on her female votaries, to which the authoress of "Woman's Mission" so eloquently reverts. But speculative theories have nothing to do with a guiding law. The middle ages teemed with suggestive and inquiring spirits amongst the Jews. The Bible became almost a sealed book, from the extreme danger attendant on public perusal and public explanation. Debarred alike from social intercourse or means of gratifying individual ambition, the study of the Talmud was their only resource; the hyperbolic and orient figures, which were mingled with beautiful parables and simple precepts, became to the uninitiated significant of meanings never contemplated by the writers themselves. On these they raised their own theories and speculations—some reasonable, some fanciful, but none gifted with authority to contradict, or take the place of previous laws. They swelled the multitude of volumes already known as the Talmud; and, therefore, when one word or precept is discovered which can be twisted into Jewish contempt of woman, not only the whole work, but the religion itself is contemned; such contemners entirely forgetting that the mighty work they quote is the reflection not of one, but of *very many* differing minds, and that the opinions are either merely individual or national, according as they contradict or uphold, not only the ordinances but the *spirit* of the law of Moses.

Thus, then, even granting the existence of some portions in our Talmud *apparently* derogatory to women, they are of no importance, and never guided our social system : but often those very portions, on which our opponents argue most eloquently, have nothing to do with the contempt towards females with which they are charged. We will bring forward one instance to explain our meaning.

Amongst the Hebrews no capital punishment could be inflicted on the testimony of a woman : now this is, of course, twisted by mistaken men into an idea that it proceeded from a contemptuous notion of woman's judgment, an utter mistrust of her veracity, and a supposition that she was not even considered of sufficient consequence to take an oath, or otherwise share in solemn public proceedings.

A brief glance back on the respect paid to Miriam, Deborah, and Huldah, must at once overthrow this idea. It would certainly be an inconsistency not at all according to the stern simplicity of the Jewish character, to allow the mothers and wives in Israel " the high prerogative of speaking in the name of the Eternal, obey their behests, and yet to refuse them the common justice of being believed." But eager zeal to promote the all-important object of our conversion, does not venture quite so deeply. Happily we can reply by facts as strongly as by suggestions: " It was the awful duty of the witness to bear out the truth of his deposition by the *execution of the verdict;* and it was this part of the functions of a witness which the law nobly declared the female citizen to be unable to perform. Instead of being a stigma upon the character of the nation generally, and of their female population especially, it must, on the contrary, inspire us with admiration of the delicacy of feeling displayed in that enactment."* And when we compare this delicacy with the manners and customs of contemporary nations, the superior elevation and advancement of the people of God must strike us very forcibly. The Hebrew female was debarred by a most just and humane ordinance from even *witnessing* the shedding of human blood. Surely this is a forcible proof of the care taken in the Talmud to

* Hebrew Review, vol. iii. p. 22, from an article entitled "On the Administration of Justice among the Hebrews."

preserve her *feminine* nature in all its original gentleness and
purity ; even if the restriction should be thought a harsh one
by those females who, in civilised countries, may still be found
accompanying the criminal to the place of execution, not to
bear witness against him, but simply to satisfy their own will
and pleasure by the sight of death. In those horrible combats
between the hapless gladiators and the wild beasts, in polished,
though heathen, Rome, women thronged the amphitheatre.
In later days, when Catholicism usurped the place of
Heathenism, bull-fights arose, in which not only was an
innocent animal tortured, but many human beings exposed to
death, and yet the beauties of Spain would have felt it a hard
restriction had they been prohibited from witnessing the sports.
The tournaments themselves, if we examine them, we must
confess to be scarcely fit scenes for women; though we ourselves
feel that, in their *age*, they must have been fraught with an
excitement and a chivalry from which, in the position the
higher females then occupied, it might have seemed hard
for them to be debarred. But in Judæa, in the Hebrew
commonwealth at least, we never find mention of such things.
War, with its concomitants, was to them a necessity, not a
pastime. The introduction of the Greek and Roman games
was a source of the deepest national affliction, as a departure
from the holy purity and refined simplicity inseparable from a
strict adherence to the laws of Moses.

It is impossible to compare the social system of the Jews
even with the refined notions of other nations of our own day,
and yet not to perceive its superiority at once. Even plays
were unknown. Actors, ballet-dancers, buffoons were meaningless terms. The holy people would surely have thought
themselves degraded by the very admission of such characters.
Yet the arts and sciences were cultivated by them to a pitch
of learning, glory, and perfection, unsurpassed, if even equalled,
by either Greece or Rome. Music and poetry were to them the
atmosphere they breathed; architecture, engraving, embroidery,
cunning work in every metal and in every precious stone, rose
to a height in their One Temple, and in their palaces, and even
houses, which modern times vainly strive to outvie. Painting
and sculpture, as the arts we now esteem them, were not so
much known, from the care taken to prevent the smallest assimilation to the idolatrous worship of the neighbouring
nations, by, either in paint, wood, or stone, making the likeness

of anything that is in heaven above, or the earth beneath, or the waters under the earth, although the cherubim which adorned the Ark, and the brazen bulls of the Temple, proved that even sculpture must have been an art well known. Dancing, usually common to barbarous nations, we have seen, was not *such* to us, but usually made the constant accompaniment of national and holy rejoicings; and therefore not regarded in Israel merely as a frivolous pastime; but as the natural recreation of the young and happy, considered as an acceptable and pleasing offering of loving hearts to their holy and gracious King.

In a nation then so peculiarly and especially spiritualised and refined, if there should be some social laws respecting their female population which appear to give them less freedom than the females of other nations, it was simply to render them more and more worthy of sustaining that two-fold most holy character—*mothers* of *Israel*, and *daughters of the Lord*. We can find nothing either in the Law or its commentaries, by our *really* ancient fathers, to permit the supposition that either in the religious, moral, social, or domestic system, we were to be regarded as of less importance, less responsible, and of less value in the sight of our God, and of the state than our brother Man. We were—we are—equals in every spiritual privilege, and every social and domestic law. Man could neither degrade us individually, nor deprive us generally, of any privilege or promise given unto Israel. That he never attempted to do so during the continuance of Israel as a nation, we have seen; and therefore, whatever statutes from the Talmud may be brought forward to startle us by their seeming to enslave us—we may rest quietly assured, first, that they might be explained away were the whole examined, with the same ease, as those prohibiting female witnesses, which we have noticed; secondly, that they were probably absolutely necessary at the time they were given, to preserve the feminine purity, gentleness, and modesty of the women of Israel unsullied; and lastly, if they will not abide either of these tests, and are absolutely and unanswerably enslaving, heathenising, and degrading, that they have foundation in neither law nor tradition, and consequently possess no authority, and demand no obedience—their own incongruity with both the history, as well as the law of Israel, being quite sufficient for their entire rejection, and utter condemnation, alike by the Hebrew state as by individuals.

Precepts to insure the elevated position of the women of Israel were not in themselves sufficient to satisfy our ancient fathers. Besides the historical evidence that widows of kings could reign in their own right in Israel, we find many most beautiful allusions to woman in narrations, which, even granting they be but tradition, could only have sprung from the generally received idea of woman's dignity, gentleness, and influence, and also her vast capabilities of acquiring, and opportunities of using, the most erudite readings of the Law. We are told that the wisdom and learning of Beruria, the wife of R. Meir, were received with even more deference than those of Meir himself. She not only understood the written word, but left three hundred traditions, and is placed amongst the Tanaites, or expositors of the Mishna. Now, how could such an assurance be found in Talmud, if religious knowledge and opportunities of deep and severe study were, either by a law of the state or public opinion, denied to woman? It is folly to suppose it, even for a moment. If some *modern* Jewish opinions, concerning the impossibility of woman comprehending the Law, or the presumption and folly of her attempting to make religion her study, had had existence then, why poor Beruria might have shared the fate of some of the hapless learned of the middle ages, who were persecuted and burned, simply because their minds outstripped their age. But the memorable chroniclers of Beruria knew too well both the position and the capabilities of their countrywomen to refuse their appreciation and reverence when called upon to give them. Their affection for her memory is proved by the touching apologues in which she is brought forward, in a character so essentially feminine, that it is clear how completely they believed in the perfect compatibility of learning with every womanly feeling and attribute. To our countrywomen the brief notices are so well known, that it would be needless to repeat them, did we not hope that they would bring the Talmudic notices of woman in a somewhat novel light to our Christian friends.

Rabbi Meir appears to have been as impetuous and rash as his wife was gentle and judicious. Irritated at persecuting insults, which he had received from some sinful men in his neighbourhood, he uttered an imprecation against them in the words of David: "Let the sinners be consumed out of the earth, and let the wicked be no more." "You are wrong, my husband—such was not King David's meaning," was the soothing reply. "He prayed that *sin* might be consumed from off the earth; for then the wicked would be no more. He sought the destruction of *sin*, not of the sinners;" and, perfectly aware that the Hebrew quite authorised such rendering of the verse, the Rabbi acknowledged the justice of his wife's rebuke.

The other apologue of the same gentle feeling woman is more generally known through the medium of Coleridge's "Friend." It was the custom of Rabbi Meir to attend the school and synagogue for several hours consecutively, often during the whole day—and, during one of these long absences from home, his sons, boys of great promise and beauty, both died. Conquering the anguish of a mother in the strong affection of a wife, who knew the passionate love borne by the father for his offspring, and dreading the effect of sudden grief, she met her husband at supper with her usual calm and tranquil mien. He naturally inquired for his sons, but she skilfully evaded the question; and, at the conclusion of the meal, stated that she had an important question to ask him, the answer to which had much troubled her. The rabbi encouraged her to speak; and she related, "that a neighbour had lent her some jewels of inestimable value, and now required them to be returned. Ought she to give them back?" Surprised, the rabbi replied, "that surely his wife needed not even to ask the question, the answer was so self-evident." Without rejoinder, she led him into the room where the bodies lay, and, removing the white cloth which concealed them, revealed their loss. She permitted the first burst of agonised grief; and then, soothingly recalling his own verdict, touchingly repeated, "The Lord gave, and the Lord hath taken away; blessed be the name of the Lord!"

Can any thing be more beautifully true to woman's nature than these brief tales? Even granting they cannot be proved as true, but are merely traditionary, what a high and beautiful sense of the female Israelite's capability and characteristics, must the ancient fathers have entertained! How contradictory to the modern assertion—that they degrade and enslave us, and so regard us with contempt! Accustomed to associate with such characters as Hannah, Abigail, Huldah, the Shunammite, and Esther, the sages knew, that to be highly gifted, learned and wise, in a far nobler sense than the modern acceptation of the terms, and withal to be truly and exquisitely *feminine*, essentially the *woman*, was not the apocryphal combination, which it is at present considered. The Talmudic writers *must* have thought highly and nobly of women, or such traits as we have brought forward, and those found in Hurwitz's Hebrew Tales, would never have been admitted within their volumes. Their minds were much too solemn, and too fond of weighty research, to allow such flights as romantic descriptions of woman's excellence; which, if only accustomed to regard their mothers, wives, and sisters in a degraded light, these notices and even laws would be.

Surely then, even this brief and imperfect reference to the venerable volumes which—as reflections of some of the highest and the purest, the noblest and the holiest minds, who ever laboured for the good of man, and lived but to know and prove the glory of the Lord—we value from our very heart; even this may be permitted to remove some prejudice, and convince our opponents and ourselves, that not a thought so contrary to the spirit of the law as the degrading of woman either socially or individually, or even the non-caring for her weakness and her gentle nature, the refusing of all regard to her peculiarly feminine characteristics, ever entered the hearts or minds of our sages: their aim was to obey the law of God, and to provide for and protect her as *woman*. The very laws that, on a mere hasty reading, might seem in their strictness to interefere with her perfect freedom of act and will, are only evidences of their desire to preserve the feminine beauty and modesty of her character unsullied, and were probably instituted at those times when the extreme laxity and rudeness of the nations around rendered them absolutely necessary, to keep the "Women of Israel" apart, that their holiness might never be profaned, even by casual association.

O that we had but eloquence and influence sufficient to urge our brethren to engage in the glorious task of removing the dust and rubbish, which persecution, prejudice, and ignorance have gathered round the pure and simple lessons, the exquisite allegories, and glowing diction of our ancient fathers, and to publish in the vernacular idiom of every land, the wisdom which those mighty tomes conceal! Give us our own! Compel us not, out of pure thirst, to seek the works of Gentile writers for commentators on the word of our God— for sympathy in our aspiring thoughts, for rest to our wearied souls, unable yet to understand the full beauty of the Bible, without some simple explanation, which would flash light over the ins ired pages, and so enable us to take them to our heart and fin consolation. Compel us not to turn to the Gentile works for these! Unseal the fountains of pure waters which our aged seers provided; give us their renderings of the moral law; their spirit and aphorisms: their orient imagery, which in its power and imagination will outvie every other. Give us their detail of Jewish History; do not compel us to abide by the details of those whose faith is opposed to our own, who believe us blinded and degraded, and whose peculiar views must inspire their pages. The Hebrew who would do this, however gradually, who would provide our youth with orks from our own writers, simplified, if needed, to their comprehension, and selected as would best meet the spirit of the age, would, indeed, rank among the first and noblest benefactors of his kind, and would prove the love which, as an Israelite, should be borne in his heart towards Israel's sons and Israel's God.

EFFECTS OF DISPERSION AND PERSECUTION.

GENERAL REMARKS.

It would be irrelevant to our present task, besides extending our work to much too great a length, to attempt any detailed account of the Hebrew nation, from their dispersion to the present time; the third volume of Milman's History, and an admirable American work, History of the Jews, by Hannah Adams, commencing from the destruction of Jerusalem, and accompanying us through our varied destinies till some fifty years ago; besides many other works in the modern languages, which no doubt exist, though to us they may not be known, will give all the needful information of us, as a people.

One trifling incident we will, however, mention, ere we leave the history of the past; and conclude our work by a brief survey of the present. In the reign of the emperor Julian, an edict was issued for the re-erection of the Temple of Jerusalem on Mount Moriah, and the "restoration of the Jewish worship in all its splendour."

The commotion which this edict occasioned to the Jews in

every quarter of the empire may be imagined. They crowded in vast numbers to Palestine, and their wealth poured forth in such lavish profusion, that even the tools they used were to be sanctified to the service by being made of the most costly materials—the *women* seconded their brethren, giving up every personal ornament and hoarded jewel to forward the glorious work. The prophets allude to the pride and folly of the women of Judea, loving their ornaments more than the law, as one of the iniquities from which Judea was to be purged; and it would seem by this mention, as if the propensity had been indeed crushed from the hearts of the women of Israel, and that even, as in the time of Moses, when to adorn the tabernacle, they brought all their ornaments and the work of their hands till more than enough was given,—so now they were equally earnest and enthusiastic in the holy cause. The work was indeed frustrated; for the word of the Lord had passed, and the land was to enjoy her sabbaths and the temple remain unbuilt till, the term of exile past, repentant Israel might be recalled; but the mention of the eager zeal of the women of Israel marks how dear and precious to them, as well as to their brother men, was the religion of Jerusalem; that they must have known and felt that their temple service, and the law it included, gave them, as women, higher and nobler privileges than any other, or they could not have been so eager for its restoration.

Throughout our history, in all those horrible epochs of persecution, we can find not a single trace of the love of the Lord, and of his Holy Faith, burning with stronger and more enduring light, in man's heart than in woman's. The female Hebrew never shrunk from any alternation, however awful, which could save her, or her children from the denial of their faith. Death of the most horrible kind was welcome, not only for themselves, but (a trial far more awful) for their children, rather than the forcible baptism to which they were repeatedly exposed. No faith can bring forward a longer or more noble list of willing female martyrs: and what motive could have inspired this devotion? What could have so triumphed over the emotions of humanity—the tremblings of the mortal frame—but the deepest love of their holy religion, the firmest conviction of its immutable truth, and an unwavering belief in the immortality which it was the first to teach, and which could alone have endowed weak clinging woman with the noble strength and constancy which taught her how to die? Let those who, in their utter ignorance of the spirit and the tenets of the Jewish religion, dare to assert that we have no belief in the immortality of the soul, that it was neither taught by Moses and the prophets, nor preached and simplified by our ancient sages—let those, if they cannot read our venerable fathers, just glance back on the history of our people, and answer—What was it caused so many millions, women as well as men, to die rather than desert their faith? What availed such sacrifice, if they believed this earth were all? What mattered their creed in this life, if death was annihilation? No: our martyrs are our witnesses; and we need little other proof of the universality of the Jewish belief in immortality, than the countless numbers who have sealed its mighty truth in their own blood.

As our martyrs are witnesses of such belief, so are our existence and preservation, of the Truth of the Revelation, of the perpetuity of that holy faith which God Himself proclaimed should last for ever. Where now are the mighty nations of Babylon and Rome, before whose conquering arms Judea lay prostrate, and her children fell mingling dust with dust, or were scattered to every quarter of the globe like chaff before the wind? *Where* are the mighty conquerors? Lost amid the dim shadows of the past: and *what* are they but names which *once* were great? But *where* are the conquered? Ask of every land and every age; and they will point to them as a people still, for ever PRESENT, never PAST: and *what* are they? God's people still—His witnesses, whom nought of earth and earthly change can touch. Nations and dynasties, conquerors and conquered, are swept from the face of the earth, leaving not a trace; but the persecuted, the oppressed, the tortured, the only nation which has seen millions and millions fall by the destroying sword, and in later times, beheld but too many lost by smoother, but even more dangerous means;—that nation still lives, breathes unchanged, its ranks undiminished, its undying vitality seeming to receive increase of strength and firmness from every blow that seeks its downfall. Cemented by the blood of noble martyrs, supported by the pillars of divine truth, and wisdom and love, it rears its head in every land, as a temple that will never fall; and all—man, woman, and child—who seek to love and obey the Lord according to his law vouchsafed to Moses, add to its solidity and beauty, and bear witness to its truth.

Our existence is in itself a miracle: nought but the providence of God could have thus preserved us; a nation so completely apart, that, though for more than eighteen centuries scattered over the whole world, and found in every land, our identity has never been lost, our race has never mingled, our religion has never changed. Our most vehement opposers grant us this; but they tell us, that we worship not now as Moses taught; that we are guided by the Talmud, not by God. We could reply, that if the one dared to contradict the other, no Jew would acknowledge its legality, or obey its dictates; but we wish to prove, that if our manners and customs do in some instances appear to differ from the spirit inculcated by our inspired law-giver, it is the necessary consequence of our captivity, foreseen by God Himself, and provided for by the principle statutes contained in Levit. xxvi. ver. 39 to the end, and Deut. xxx., which, in clear and emphatic terms, laid down all that was necessary for our acceptance.

Our law was given to a holy people, framed for a government and a nation which, in its domestic and political bearings, was to stand alone. When the sins and manifold rebellions of the children of Israel, compelled their expulsion from the Holy Land, lost them the direct interference of their God, both by the Shechinah and by His prophets, and scattered them all over the whole world, it was part of their awful chastisement, that, while the word of the Eternal preserved their *faith* and its holy ordinances unchanged, their *social, domestic,* and *individual* position should be guided no longer by the pure spirit of the law, but by the spirit of the nations amongst whom they were thrown. Thus we always perceive that the Jews are in a measure civilised or barbarised, according as civilisation or barbarism pervade the people amongst whom they dwell. How was it possible for them to retain the social and mental elevation, the pure spiritual religion, the loveliness of home which had marked them in their own land, when subjected to the oppression, the slavery, the cruelty, with which the history of the middle ages teems; when moral and mental darkness was all around them, seeking also to crush them under the fierce persecutions, which from such mental and moral darkness sprung; how could the mass retain the spirituality, the elevation of their ancestors? Individuals there were, no doubt, who were Israelites indeed, spiritually and mentally, as well as rigid adherents to every form; but the mass must of necessity have shared the darkness of the oppressors under whom they groaned. Spiritually and mentally, social and domestic elevation demands, and imperatively needs, an atmosphere of equality and freedom, or they must either droop and die, or be shrouded in such secresy, and so closely next the heart, as to be entirely invisible in history.

This is proved by our history, in what is aptly termed by Milman, the "Golden Age of Judaism." It was, indeed, of very short duration; but during its continuance, we find "the Jews not only pursuing unmolested their lucrative and enterprising traffic, not merely merchants of splendour and opulence, but suddenly emerging to offices of dignity and trust, administering the finances of Christian and Mahomedan kingdoms, and travelling as ambassadors between mighty sovereigns."* In France, during the reign of Charlemagne, "From the ports of Marseilles and Narbonne, their vessels kept up a constant communication with the East." In Narbonne, of the two prefects (or mayors of the city) one was always a Jew; and the most regular and stately part of the city of Lyons was always the Jewish quarter. The superior intelligence and education of the Jews, during a period when nobles and kings, and even the clergy, could not always write their names, pointed them out for offices of trust. They were the physicians and the ministers of finance to nobles and to monarchs. And in the reign of Charlemagne, "Europe and Asia beheld the extraordinary spectacle of a Jew named Isaac, setting forth with two Christian counts, one of whom died on the road, as ambassador from Charlemagne to Haroun Al Raschid, and conducting the political correspondence between the courts of Aix-la-Chapelle and Bagdad."†

In Spain, both under the influence of Moorish and Christian sovereigns, the golden age of Judaism endured the longest, to set in the deepest darkness. The long line of literary men, who swelled the Jewish ranks during that epoch, sufficiently mark the influence of freedom and prosperity upon the *mind*— while the writings of Maimonides are pretty certain evidence of their effect upon the *spirit*. In the calm and dignified repose of the social position which that golden age allowed him, Maimonides advanced so much beyond his times and country that, like all benefactors of their kind, he was neither under-

* Milman, vol. iii. p. 369.
† Milman's Hist., vol. iii. p. 280—281.

stood nor appreciated by his cotemporaries. But the more enlightened our nation has become, the more have his profound wisdom and spiritual revelations of the wisdom and goodness of the Deity, as displayed in the Law of Moses, been valued and appreciated, and the more they will be as the Jewish mind advances.

The iron age, *preceding* the golden one, had originally cramped the intellectual and spiritual powers of the mass. They had been content and glad to tread the path laid down for them by their teachers, without inquiring *wherefore* they thus worshipped. Even their teachers, except a select and holy few, had accustomed themselves to regard the magnificent fabric of the Mosaic Law with silent adoration and admiring wonder; but Maimonides, in his daring and all-conquering wisdom, looked on it with the searching light of reason, as well as the living orb of faith: and *how* he was spiritually rewarded, let his beautiful writings testify. His cotemporaries were dazzled by the lustre he flung upon the meaning and intentions of the holy Law, and feared to approve it; but his labour was not lost. The flash, too bright to illuminate his own age, * penetrated the folds of the far future, and spreading gradually, found souls prepared to meet and welcome it, and shrine in their heart of hearts the glorious mind whose wisdom had kindled it to life.

But for many, many terrible years, even the memory of the golden age was buried under the dense pall of misery and oppression which gathered round the hapless Israelites in every land, and so crushed all mental and social elevation, so confined the sphere of action and employment, so banished all religious instruction, except such as could be imparted in the deepest secrecy, that the word "Jew" became and has continued synonymous with all that is debased—with a bowed, and bowing servility, with exacting usury, with hard exclusiveness, and with a merciless hatred of all mankind, and a detestation of every religion but his own. Ay, even now, to those who have never associated with us, whose only knowledge is drawn from books—whose authors, with but two noble exceptions,† seem to delight in fabling us as the Shylock of Shake-

* Wisdom like his becomes to the unenlightened "dark from excess of light."

† Sir Walter Scott, in his exquisite delineation of Rebecca and her father; and Mrs. S. C. Hall, in her breathing portrait of Manaseh Ben Israel, in

speare, the old clothesman of nursery tales (noticed thus even by Miss Edgeworth), or as the money-lenders, interest-exactors and dishonorable adepts in all the grades of usury which abound in fashionable novels. And little, perhaps, do their writers know that their fictions demonstrate far more clearly the consequences of persecution, which their ancestors have hurled upon us, than the real character of the Jew, or the true spirit of his creed. Writers who know us not, depict us, not what we *are*, but what lingering prejudice creates us, entirely forgetting the *real cause* of our fallen state—the impossibility of our attaining to that elevated social state which freedom and peace have granted to other lands, while bent to the very earth, and for ever liable, even at this very present, to insult, ignominy, and such oppressions as even slavery does not know. The mischief which is done by such false pictures of the Jewish character in social and domestic life is incalculable. It not only fosters prejudice and confirms ignorance in our opponents, but actually causes many Jews themselves to tremble at the term, and to endeavour to conceal a faith and descent which should be their glory. Even those domestic narrations which portray some members of a Jewish family in a favourable light, that they may conclude by making them Christians, and the other members as so stern, harsh, and oppressive, that they bear no resemblance whatever to any Israelite, except the Israelite of a Gentile's imagination—do but swell the catalogue of dangerous because false works; and never fail to impress the minds of Christian readers with the unalterable conviction, that whenever spirituality, amiability and gentleness, kindliness and love, are inmates of a Hebrew heart, it is an unanswerable proof that that heart is verging on Christianity, and will very speedily embrace that faith. Nay, mental endowments themselves are welcomed as an earnest that their possessors must quickly desert the Jewish creed; such supposers entirely forgetting that mental acquirements, the most profound and searching wisdom, the most vivid and beautiful

---

the "Buccaneer," where she has so beautifully and skilfully blended all the characteristics of the Talmudic Israelite, with the emotion and virtues of a father and a man—a union which most authors appear to imagine incompatible. The character of Sidonia, in "Coningsby," is not a being of flesh and blood, but a type of a class; and therefore we do not include him, though the author has done us justice as a nation.

imagination, the most elegant accomplishments, have been the heir-loom of the Jewish nation, from their very first selection as the chosen of the Lord ; and that, instead of losing these endowments in their dispersion, all of mind and talent in the whole European and Asiatic world was possessed by them ; and that Gentiles of every denomination and every creed came with humility and deference to them, glad to learn from the *oppressed* those glorious gifts of mind which to the *oppressors* were denied.

It is not from the present state of the Hebrews, that the true spirit of their creed and their characteristics as a nation can be discovered. They have, indeed, retained all that marks them as a distinct people, and prevents amalgamation with the children of the soil in which they are but sojourners; but their social and domestic habits are now so completely one with the the manners and customs of the land in which they are scattered, that there is nothing to distinguish them from their Gentile brethren ; and this it is which often causes the false portraits of Jewish character, when introduced in tales of the present day. They think a Jew must be different to his fellows, and so call him from the Past when oppression forced upon him a particular character, and place him in the Present, where he looks about as much out of place, as a mail-clad baron and his rude-mannered suite would seem in the luxurious and refined assemblage of England's present peers. As a people—as the chosen witnesses—the first-born sons of the Most High God, they will ever remain a distinct nation over the whole world. They will ever be preserved from annihilation —ever be kept from all assimilation with the Gentiles ; even as the river, which is said to retain its peculiar taste and colouring in the very lakes through which it passes. But the Jews in captivity are not what they *have been*, or what they *will be*. Even while they remain a distinct race, they have unconsciously imbibed many of the characteristics of the people amongst whom they dwell. The indomitable pride, the haughty air of superiority, which (not fifty years since) characterised the Spanish and Portuguese Jew, were of Spain and Portugal, not of Judea : and if we examine the condition of the poorest classes of that congregation, and compare them with the same ranks in Spain and Portugal, we shall find them so exactly similar, that the pride, indolence, dirt,[*] and poverty

[*] Of course there are exceptions. We allude but to some of the very

from dislike to labour, are the remnants of their assimilation
with the manners and customs of the above-named countries;
not the characteristics of Judaism, which especially commands
honest labour and most scrupulous cleanliness. The active
business habits, and rather a want than a superfluity of pride,
in the German Jew, mark their assimilation in domestic and
social habits with the Gentile inhabitants of Germany and
Holland; the distinction between them and their (so-called)
Spanish and Portuguese brethren, which was very much more
marked fifty years ago than it is now, originates not at all in
Judaism, whose beautiful unity ought to banish all such con-
ventional terms, but simply in the distinction which exists
between the characteristics of the different countries in which
they dwelt. Observe the Spaniard and Portuguese, and then
look on the German and the Dutchman; their characteristics
are so totally distinct, that it is impossible to mistake them;
and the Jewish inmates of these diverse lands naturally shared
the distinction, even while their holy law was the undying link
which bound them together, and separated them from the
religion of every other land. Fifty years ago, the Sephardim
congregation* was considered so superior to the Ashkenazim,†
as to be universally acknowledged as the aristocracy of the
nation; but this supposition had nothing to do with Israelitish
notions. It was, in fact, contrary to the spirit of the Jewish
law, which, except in the beautiful organisation of ranks in
the state, looked on all Jews as equal, and on the whole nation
as the aristocracy of the Lord. The modern distinction simply
arose from the fact, that in Spain and Portugal the Jews had
held the highest stations in the court and camp and council;
that even after their expulsion, they existed apparently as
Christians, but in reality most faithful Jews, amongst the very
nobles and princes in both countries; or as merchants and
doctors, not only in medicine, but in various branches of
learning: and so wealthy as always to take their places
amongst the aristocracy of the land. Germany has indeed
ennobled a Jew; and latterly our most learned men have
sprung from German schools. But *contemporary* with the

---

lowest of our nation, yet unhappily plunged in ignorance and superstition,
the still remaining results of the persecution and slavery of Spain and
Portugal.

* Spanish and Portuguese. † German.

Jewish aristocracy of Spain and Portugal, the Jews in Germany were so oppressed and enslaved, as never to rise above those confining and debasing employments which must ever be the consequence of persecution; and therefore when the two parties met on equal ground, the free and blessed soil of England, the haughty pride of the *Spaniard* (not of the *Jew*, for that would have counselled differently) caused that exclusiveness even from his German brother, which formerly had existence, but which happily is now fading rapidly into the past. England offers a rest and home of perfect freedom to the exile and oppressed : and if she welcomes all, will Israel continue that mistaken distinction which only circumstances wrought? That there is still a difference in the characteristics of German and Portuguese, we allow; and very probably, so constitutional is prejudice in favour of one's own, that neither would change with the other; but the difference and the prejudice are alike foreign to *Judaism*. These are the effects of our dispersion; of sixteen or seventeen centuries of assimilation with the manners and customs of Germany and of Spain, which unconsciously makes us feel so completely as children of the soil, that we forget the national unity which our holy religion so imperatively demands and which will be gradually attained; but it requires time. Enthusiasm may believe it is only to be wished, to be accomplished; but reason tells us, that *two* centuries in England is not quite sufficient to banish the prejudices of *fifteen* centuries spent in other lands. We have neither of us yet become English in feeling: nay, very many take pleasure in fostering as a heritage the remnant of Spanish feelings, forgetting that such characteristics have nothing to do with Judaism : and till we are really English Jews, the distinction which has existed so many centuries will never be entirely lost. The Germans will much more easily become English than the Spanish, simply because the national characteristics between England and Germany are less distinct and palpable than those between England and Spain.

In exactly the same manner, the Jews, wherever they are scattered, have imbibed prejudices, customs, and even the sentiments which belong—not to their religion, but to the lands of their captivity and compelled adoption. The very prejudice, to remove which this book has been written—the Jewish degradation of woman, her abasement in the social system, as a non-partaker of religious responsibility and immortality—if traced to its source, will be found to have originated in the blinded notions of the Jews of Barbary, and other Eastern countries; infused unconsciously, by the contempt for the sex, peculiar to the Mahomedan inhabitants of those lands. Other prejudices and superstitions, supposed by the unobservant to be part of Judaism, proceed from exactly the same reason, and have nothing whatever to do with the religion of God.

The travellers in the Crimea speak of the filth and rapacity, and occasional dishonesty of the Jews dwelling in that quarter, as the necessary consequence of their blinded religion, quite forgetting that they are but the characteristics of the Russian and Cossack inhabitants of the same land, and imbibed by the Jews as the necessary consequence of such long and close association, but utterly repugnant to the spirit of their creed.

The Polish Jews, again, are different from the German and Dutch, much more resembling the Spanish and Portuguese, because their *social position* was more like the latter than the former. Whilst Poland was an independent kingdom, the Jews formed the only middle order. Their privileges had been secured by Casimir the Great, from the affection felt by him towards a beautiful Jewess. They were the corn-merchants, shop-keepers, inn-keepers, in fact, almost every branch of traffic was confined to them; they formed the principal population of towns, and some villages were exclusively peopled by them. This social freedom accounts for the dignified bearing and general lofty character of the Polish Jew, at once distinguishing him from his cowed and oppressed brethren of Germany. Even now Poland is the principal seat of rabbinical authority. The religion, from the supremacy of forms and minute ordinances, occasions a greater degree of rigidity and exclusiveness than is the case elsewhere, where the spirit of the Mosaic Law is more freely awaking. Since the partition of Poland, however, the condition of the Jewish population is as oppressed and lowered as their brethren under the Russian, Prussian, and Austrian Governments. But still the Polish Jew, like the Spanish and Portuguese, retains the peculiar characteristic of his former more elevated position.

The French and Italian Jews have equally the peculiar characteristics of their adopted lands; but they are less marked than those of Germany and Spain, the above-named lands not having been their residence for such a long continuance. But wherever we are scattered, still the truth is evident that, though our law and its beautiful forms remain unchangeable, immutable as their divine ordinance, our social and domestic customs are modified and characterised, according to the manners and customs of the lands of our exile. We are still captives of our God, though His mercy grants us a social freedom and relief from persecution; and, in captivity, how might we hope that the spirit of our holy law could be permitted to pervade our households? The consequence of transgression was to expel us from our own lovely land, to raise a barrier between us and the direct interference of the Lord, to scatter us as by a whirlwind over the known world, and there so to degrade us from our high estate, from being subject to the Most High God alone, that the guiding spirit of our homesteads was lost in the darkened barbarism of the Gentile world.

And so it is with the Jews of the present day. English writers, when they introduce the nation, overlook the Jewish inmates of their own land, and delineate either the Spanish, or the German, or the Polish, or the Russian Jews; and as the picture they draw is necessarily quite distinct from their own manners and customs, they believe themselves, and make others believe, that it is a perfect portrait of the Jew, whereas it is in fact nothing more or less than a delineation of the Spaniard, or Pole, or German, who might just as correctly be of the Gentile as of the Jewish creed.* To draw the Jew correctly, then, not his present condition, but the annals of the past, must provide materials. For the spirit and ordinances of his beautiful faith, let the word of the Lord be consulted; and the most simple mind must understand what and why the Jew believes, and the forms that he obeys. Where modern Judaism, so called, differs from that standard, it is not the religion which has changed, but circumstances which have occasioned the Jews unconsciously to adopt the feelings, super-

* This extraordinary misconception of their own subject, was never more clearly marked than in the works entitled "Sophia and Emma de Lissau, a fiction of the Jews, of the nineteenth century;" where, placing the scene in *England*, and in the present era, the author gives an imaginary picture of the *Polish* Jews, at least one or two centuries back, and containing not the very smallest resemblance to *English Jewish* life at any time; in fact, there is nothing to write concerning Anglo-Jewish life in the present age. With the sole exception of the ordinances of their creed, their households and families are conducted exactly on the same principles as English households of the same standing.

stitions, and sentiments, the offspring of that darkness which is the atmosphere of persecution, or of that prosperity which has infused the sentiments and superstitions of the Gentiles, with whom they live in reality in close association, while in appearance their differing creeds keep them widely apart. Let it be remembered, we allude not to the *religion*—that never has and never will amalgamate—that will ever be a thing sacred and apart, will never change, nor modify, nor alter; God hath said it shall last for ever, that its children will never cease from being a nation before Him for EVER—and so IT WILL BE. The assimilation in social, domestic, and individual life of the Jew and Gentile, touches not their respective creeds. Wherever he is, in whatever land, whatever company, whatever position, a Hebrew is known as a Hebrew—and he should glory in that distinction, ordained by God Himself to keep His people apart—should use his utmost endeavour to preserve that distinction—and neither be ashamed of it himself, nor occasion others to look down upon him with contempt. He can retain all the characteristics of his race and creed, and yet, in social, domestic, and individual position, be one with the children of that land which has received the exiles to her fostering breast, and extended the right hand of fellowship to all. Let us be English men and English women, even while we still glory in being Hebrews. The union is perfectly compatible, and it would tend to our social happiness and the consolidation of our national unity. Would it not render us a firmer, nobler, because a more consolidated mass, if we could forget the distinctions of German and Spanish, and Polish and Dutch, and only vie with each other to be a noble body of English Jews, and mark our pre-eminence in the land where we are FREE? Why should there be German and Spanish charities? Is not benevolence open-handed, universal, wide-spreading, scorning earthly distinctions, and only seeking whom it can befriend? Is not a Hebrew a Hebrew in the sight of God and man—and why then should we not be brothers? Why will not the German imitate the Spaniard in some things, and the Spaniard the German in others, and so forget the idle distinctions of our captivity, and only strive to become Hebrews as our Bibles teach, and Englishmen, as a love for our adopted country would dictate. How glorious would be that consolidation, that unity, which, the moment a Jew of any land sets foot in England there to make his home, would hail him brother, and open to him at once our synagogues and our charities without one question as to what congregation he belonged. Hebrews and Englishmen—we may look round the world, but what prouder titles can be our own!

This may seem digression; but as we proceed we shall find it not so wholly unconnected with our main subject as it may appear. Not only are our social and domestic habits infused with the manners and customs of the lands of our captivity; but our mental and spiritual attainments are in some degree advanced or retrograded, according to the measure of mental and spiritual attainments in our Gentile brethren. This is easily explained by comparing our positions in Italy, in Russia, in parts of Germany and in the East; with our position in England, in America, in France, and in Belgium.

Italy is still plunged in moral and mental darkness. The word of God, revealed only to priests, to whom the consciences of the multitude are entrusted, is unknown, and, in consequence, edicts are still at work against us, as oppressive and degrading as in the middle ages. Russia, under a despot-sovereign, and unenlightened by the religion of the Protestant, which, from considering the Old Testament divine, and permitting its perusal by the mass, cannot fail greatly to benefit the Jew, entirely prevents, by a precarious and degraded position, all power of elevation in its Hebrew subjects; and on the least, even imaginary offences, issues edicts against us as horrible as any of less enlightened times.[*] Austria, under Catholic dominion, by a most extraordinary contradiction, grants a barony to a Jewish family; and yet, if we are to believe contemporary travellers, so degrades the Jews as a class, that their condition is little removed from most abject slavery.

In the East, under the superstitious, and oppressive sway of Mahomedanism, they are still constantly liable to persecution,[†] and cruelty too horrible to relate. And what then is the condition of our hapless brethren in these oppressing lands? Still faithful Hebrews indeed, willing to die, or worse, to suffer such horrible mental and physical tortures that death were bliss, rather than give up one item of their treasured faith; but the mind is cramped, the spirit fettered, the soul cannot spring upward, in that mental and spiritual communing, only to be

---

[*] The late Ukase.
[†] The Damascus Cruelties of 1840.

found amongst the free; and God, more merciful than man, demands not what His omniscience knows cannot be given. Enough, they are true to Him, they worship, they love Him. The power to spiritualise and enlighen that worship by rays of mind, will be granted when His will removes the yoke, now bowing them to the earth.

In Germany, the state of the religion seems strangely contradictory. Our most learned men come from that land. The spirit of their faith, in some few quarters, appears awaking, or we could not have such preachers as Gotthold Solomon, Phillipson, Hirsch, and others; and yet how appalling is the indifferentism, the rationalism, which seems to compass, as a thick mist, the greater portion. But this is not Judaism : it has its origin, exactly as we have stated, in the spirit of the land where the Hebrews are sojourners. What is the real religion of Germany? Ask the enlightened Protestant, and he will tell you; but too often rank infidelism, indifference, or that religion which seeks to do away with revelation, and rest on nature (alas for such delusion!); and fearful is this association for the Jew, just beginning to breathe from the oppressive horrors of persecution. Better, far, even occasional oppression, so it will but burst the bonds of that deadening stagnation; better the complete and visible distinction of creeds, than that fearful indifference of all, which appears to characterise religion in Germany. But let not the Gentile seek to burden *Judaism* with the indifference of the Jews in Germany, or the Hebrew may, with equal justice, burden Christianity with the indifference and infidelism of Christians in the same land.

In France, the Jews are free, enlightened, earnest Israelites, and faithful citizens; and yet, if the writer of the review of the "Spirit of Judaism" in the "Archives," of March, 184 spoke the sentiments of all his countrymen, we should fear that equality was, in some degree, deadening the national spirit of religious exclusiveness, which should ever mark the Jew.* We should, indeed, feel and act the part of faithful

* The following is the passage in question :—" Mais Miss Aguilar dépasse peut-être le but, et dans son zèle ardent pour le maintien de l'esprit de Judaism, elle néglige parfois trop l'esprit du siècle. Les Juifs, à ses yeux, forment non seulement une *secte* à part ; ils forment aussi une nation à part, une nation captive, et dans l'attente de son Messiah ou libérateur... *La Nationalité Juive n'existe plus.* Partout, et même dans les contrées où on leur conteste encore les droits de l'homme et du citoyen, les Juifs

citizens where such privileges are allowed us; but we are not to consider ourselves so completely children of the soil, as to forget we are children of the Lord. That privilege can never belong to the history of the past, as the writer seems, in some degree, to suppose. We can never be other than a distinct nation—His chosen people; and so, be favoured above every nation and every religion of the world. Surely we can unite this belief with the feelings of a French or English citizen. We do not require the sacrifice of the one to fit us for the other; for the more we felt that, as Hebrews, we are cherished, equalised, honoured, the more ardent would become our love for the land granting us these things, the more earnest our desire to serve her, and her children, with heart and hand.

But this absence of perfect nationality, if, indeed it do exist, is attributable, not to imperfection in Judaism, but to intimate association with a people, whose characteristic is lighthearted gaiety, and whose very religion is devoid of the solemnity of form, and sacredness of restriction, peculiar to Protestant lands. The French, as a nation, are *spirituelle*, but not *spiritual*. The freedom and equality enjoyed by the French Jews, have, to judge by their literature, decidedly advanced the latter quality. Mind and spirit are both unshackled; but it is neither unlikely nor unnatural, that they should in some degree imbibe the light spirit of their Gentile brethren, and so appear to divest their faith of a portion of its more solemn and exclusive attributes, though in reality they are earnest and faithful Israelites still.

But it is in the country of the *true*, not of the *nominal* Protestant that the Hebrew is at rest, and where his religion will attain to greater vitality and strength and spirituality than in any other land. The reason for this is obvious; not only because in real Protestant countries persecution of the Jew is a thing unheard of, and never has existed from the time it gained ascendancy, but because the Protestant religion, in its morality, its reverence for the Old Testament, its acknowledgment of the Jews as the chosen people of the Lord, its spirituality, its abhorrence of all image-worship, comes nearer the *spirit* of the Jewish religion than any other creed; even whilst in its actual doctrines, that of a trinity, a dying

---

s'efforcent à prouver qu'ils sont de la même nation que ceux, dont ils partagent le sol, et ne *sont Juifs que devant Dieu.*"

Saviour, an infinite atonement, and original sin, it is most *widely opposed;* but actual *creed,* absolute doctrines of belief, are of far less moment in a multitude, than the *spirit* of a faith. If we present the Athanasian creed to fifty individuals, taken from mixed ranks, it is a question whether ten out of the fifty will tell you that they believe it as it stands, or whether they have not modified it, according to the temperaments of individual minds and the reasoning of individual studies; and yet, they would shrink in horror from being considered any thing but earnest Protestants and faithful Christians. Actual belief is *individual,* but the spirit of a faith is *universal,* and therefore, in relation to the position of the Jews, the latter is of infinitely more consequence than the former. When we know and perceive that the whole moral and spiritual system of the Protestant faith, is literally grafted on the moral and spiritual (not the ceremonial) revelation vouchsafed to Moses, and, as in the latter days, simplified to the meanest understanding by our elders; we must feel satisfied that our position must be infinitely securer and happier, than where the spirit of a religion is concealed from the mass, and confined to their (so called) spiritual teachers, or in those lands where the moral laws are totally distinct from our own. Let me repeat, and enforce this repetition, that by the spiritual system common to the Protestants and Jews, I do not in the very least allude to doctrinal points, for in our *articles* of creed we are *utterly, entirely,* and *necessarily* opposed; but simply to the mutual belief of immortality, and that heaven is infinitely preferable to earth; to our mutually binding laws, "Thou shalt love the Lord thy God, with all thy soul, and all thy might; and thou shalt love thy neighbour as thyself;" to both being commanded to practise charity, modesty, humility, brotherly love, forgiveness of injuries, unquestioning faith, and child-like obedience. It would detain us too long to dilate on all the points on which we agree; points, it would be well for both parties to ponder on more frequently, but which too often become invisible, from the too often haughty arrogance of the Christian, refusing to us the very privileges, spiritual and moral, which he has derived from us alone; and from the more charitable, but equally mistaken, seeking our conversion, as the only means of our salvation and of our attaining a true knowledge of God, when, from us, and us alone, their knowledge of the Eternal, and their hopes of heaven are derived.

But while, from the spirit pervading Protestant laws (a spirit springing from the simple, but important fact, that the BIBLE, the WHOLE BIBLE, is open to rich and poor, prince and peasant, man, woman, and child), our social position is secure, and we assimilate more closely to our Gentile brother—let it not be forgotten, that our spiritual position is begirt with more danger than when the differences between our holy religion and that of other nations were more strongly marked. Would we be Israelites indeed, we must study the *doctrines* and adhere to the *forms* as well as be infused with the *spirit* of our faith. We must learn in what we differ so widely from our Gentile brother, that, while we acknowledge the same moral law, and experience the same spiritual aspirations, there should be such an impassable barrier between us, that we must ever keep apart, guarded as by invulnerable mail from the constant attempts to lure us from our creed. The more closely we examine and study our own faith, and in riper years the more we look into the religion of other creeds, the more clearly shall we understand the vital points of difference, and the very many of agreement, and we shall rise from such study with love tenfold increased towards our own faith, and charity redoubled towards our Gentile brethren.

If then, as all will agree, the cause of the superior enlightenment, freedom, morality, and charity of Protestant lands, originates in the fact of their possessing and believing and preaching the spirit of the WHOLE BIBLE—ours as well as theirs—it is clearly evident why the Hebrew in such lands can become more spiritual, more earnest, and more exalted mentally and individually. In the first place he is FREE! and the mind and spirit, released from the shackles of darkness and persecution, can once more resume the native dignity and mental superiority, and spiritual aspirations, peculiar to his race and creed, and which through long ages of oppression were invisible indeed, but never lost. In the next, he mingles with the people, free, enlightened, spiritual, moral, benevolent, become so, from the spirit of the same *moral* law as guides himself; and the atmosphere, congenial to his native tastes and native feelings, inspires him with a spirit of nationality and elevation, which circumstances have long denied him, but to which he returns with zest and earnestness, glad to burst from the stagnating indifference which is the unavoidable successor of brutalising persecution.

If then, as we have endeavoured to show, the social and domestic habits, nay, the very character of the Hebrews, must, during their captivity, in some degree, be modified, altered, infused, according to the manners, customs and characteristics of the nations in which we are captives, even while our faith and its holy ordinances still mark us as a people apart, a distinct and never assimilating nation; it is forcibly evident, that the Israelites in England have greater advantages, and more, therefore, is demanded from them, than in any other land (America, perhaps, alone excepted). Of America, as a nation, we know not enough to attempt discussion on her domestic character and habits, and how such may improve the character of her adopted children. The Hebrew's advantages in that land, more numerous even than in England, consist in perfect freedom, so that neither civil, military, nor naval disabilities, interfere with his elevation in any art, science, or profession to which his talents point; thus neither persecution nor interference can prevent his guiding, not only his public adherence to his religion, but the sanctity of his house, according to the domestic, as well as social and ceremonial laws of Moses; and he is free to become mentally and spiritually elevated, and to raise the name of Israelite by deed as well as faith—these are his advantages in America: and fearful is his responsibility, if he passes them by unused.

But on the character of the English there is no darkness in our mind—integrity—honour—solidity—reserve, which only renders his friendship when given more worthy—a lofty spirit of independence and consciousness of his own position, as distinct from the radical contemner of differing ranks as respect is from servility—benevolence—domestic virtue, which, in either man or woman, must make home happy—intellect and genius, which can only breathe in freedom—such are the characteristics of the English; and if they fail in the sparkling vivacity and apparent warmth of the French, the artistic genius and strong passions of the Italians, the music and metaphysics of the Germans, surely they have qualities sufficient of their own, to make us truly love the land, and thank God that He has granted His captives so secure and bles ed a rest. Nobly, then, in England may Judaism make manifest her spiritual, her elevating influence on the characters of her children; for the manners and customs of her Gentile brethren in this blessed land, instead of infusing characteristics foreign to the Jew, will but forward his advance in the scale of being, recall every minor moral law, which oppression had banished, and encourage every elevating, humanising, and intellectual power, which, in the eras of persecution and darkness, seemed to have departed. The son of Israel may now cultivate the intellect and genius natural to his distinguished race. He can now prove, that if ever he were debased, it was not his religion, but the slavery of oppression, which was at fault; if ever spirituality seemed to have departed, torture had banished it from his heart—but that once free, it was the life, the breath, the glory of his faith; that without it Judaism was not Judaism, but a lifeless worship, only rendered acceptable by obedience in the midst of woe. And what may not the Women of Israel become in this thrice blessed land? Much, much to recall what they have been, and to shadow forth what they will be!

At length we have reached the point at which, throughout this concluding period, we have aimed, and towards which all our remarks have tended. In every other country but England and America, still lingering restrictions, or characteristics peculiar to the children of the soil, may prevent or retard the spiritual and domestic graces which are the woman of Israel's own—and of which, however deadened by circumstances, nothing can deprive her; but in England and America these can be cultivated, fostered, and so displayed, as to mark to the whole Gentile world our national privileges, our sacred duties, and our immortal hope. We have seen, from the very commencing of our creation, the natural position of the granted gifts, and inherited failings of our sex. We have looked with an unshrinking gaze on every mention of woman in the word of our God, from the mother of the whole human race, and the ancestresses of Israel, to the females under the law, and the beautiful captive, by whom a nation was preserved from death; we have gone still further from the records of Josephus, to draw forth every mention of our noble ancestors, that we might learn their domestic and social position at a time when inspired historians were silent; we have scanned every statute, every law, alike in the words of Moses, and in their simplifying commentary by our elders; and the result of such examination has been, we trust, to convince every woman of Israel of her immortal destiny, her solemn responsibility, and her elevated position, alike by the command of

God, and the willing acquiescence of her brother man. That IF any laws derogatory and contradictory to the station assigned her before God and man, by the merciful providence of our Father in Heaven, *have* sullied our homesteads, they come from the darkened ages of barbarism and persecution, the spirit of which naturally biassed the minds of the captives, as well as of the captors—and have neither authority nor weight. They have, indeed, ever been but words; for if we scan the Jewish households, in every age, we shall find the mothers, and wives, and daughters of Israel treated with such unfailing respect, tenderness, and consideration, as would shame the homes of many a Gentile land. We can find not the very faintest evidence of debasing or restricting laws: and once convinced, as surely we must be, that in the sight of God the women of Israel are cherished, loved, provided for, as He provided for none other; and in the sight of man are elevated, respected, and fostered in every relation of life; must we not think earnestly and deeply how best to make manifest our own conviction of our spiritual, social, and domestic responsibilities; and by our superiority in holiness, and in every virtue that makes home happy, and our sex beloved, prove, far more forcibly than the most eloquent words, the utter falsity of the charge against us, and that Judaism, indeed, gives us all we need.

According to our ancient fathers, whose opinion is evidently founded on our holy law, the mission of the women of Israel is education; and this, even as in olden times, we can still accomplish. We have written so much on this all-important point in our notice of Jochebed, and again in the "Martyr Mother," that little is needed in addition now: but earnestly we would entreat our sisters in Israel to compare their lot with that of those hapless wives and mothers, who, in the middle ages, continually beheld their sons and daughters snatched from them and forcibly baptised, or murdered before their very eyes; and, somewhat later, were compelled to send them to convents and monastic schools for education, implanting, as they could, the religion of their fathers. At the time of their expulsion from Spain, and when reaching the town of Fez, they hoped their sufferings were coming to a close, a pirate lured 150 Jewish youths on board his ship, and in the very sight of the distracted parents set sail, and sold them as slaves in some distant port. In Portugal the youths were baptised by force, and drafted off to the unwholesome island of St. Thomas; and in the reign of Emanuel, son-in-law of Ferdinand and Isabella, the Jews were not only ordered to quit the kingdom generally by a certain day, but a secret edict issued, that all the children under fourteen years of age should be torn from the arms of their parents, and dispersed through the kingdom, to be baptised and brought up as Christians. The awful secret transpired, and lest it should be frustrated, was instantly put into execution. What woman of Israel, be she mother, sister, or childless wife, can imagine the terror of this awful edict—can portray, in her fancy, not only the hapless children, torn from their mothers by brutal savages, but their mothers themselves, rendered desperate by the agonising alternative, throwing their offspring into wells and rivers, destroying them with their own hands, and yet not feel her whole being quiver with the burst of thanksgiving, that in some lands these awful days are past. Ever and anon, indeed, comes, even now, the low groan of Jewish suffering from distant shores. Damascus, Russia, Mogadore, within the last seven years, have vied with the oppressive cruelties of long-past days — cruelties at which every mother's heart must quake, and which bid every woman of Israel cling closer and closer yet to those nobler lands that give her a peaceful home, and so grant the sweet charities of life, and to the affections vitality and joy.

Even where the tempest-clouds of persecution have passed away, the spiritual atmosphere for the Jewish captives is deadened and stagnated by restricting clauses, which, directly contradictory to the spirit of Judaism, must have originated in former oppressive decrees, although, as the decrees themselves have been removed (though not their consequences,) the religion is falsely supposed itself to be the cause. In some parts of Germany, for instance, young unmarried females are forbidden to worship in the synagogues—it being considered indecorous to make their appearance there, unless engaged or wedded. There may be other customs equally enslaving; but we are cautious in repeating any but those we know to be true. We see they are the remnants of oppression, not the ordinances of the religion, by the simple fact, that where we are free, the women of Israel take, unquestioned, the place both in the synagogue and in the household, assigned them by our law.

When, therefore, we reflect on these things, and then on the spirit awakening in England, America, the Colonies, France, and no doubt in many parts of other lands (though, working secretly and almost unconsciously, as all improvements do at first, we see it not so broadly flashing as in the above-named lands); shall we not as a body do all we can to forward and confirm the advantages proffered? Fifty years ago, from the still lingering dread of exposing our peculiar tenets to members of other creeds, Judaism, though faithfully followed, and all its ordinances obeyed, never found voice in our households, much less in more public places of worship; we dared not speak or write of it, lest unwittingly we should offend, and so be exposed again to the horrors of persecution. Was it marvel, then, that we were Jews only because our fathers were, and that the vital spirit of piety seemed dead within us? Judging from us at that time, we do not wonder, that some more enlightened of the Gentiles should pronounce the Jewish religion to be void of all spirituality, and so a lifeless worship. They could know nothing of us but what they saw; and they were not likely to look so deep as to behold the origin of this stagnation, in the stupifying terror and ever present dread of oppressive persecution. But now, if we do not labour heart and soul to make manifest that our religion is the most spiritual, most life-breathing, comfort-giving religion of any, over the known world, the fault is with us and us alone. We need no longer be Jews, because our fathers were. In the synagogue our religion is taught; in our households the Bible is our companion; our daughters as well as our sons are instructed as our Great Lawgiver himself commanded.

In France, in some parts of Germany, in some of the Colonies, and in one synagogue of England, girls, as well as boys, are examined in their faith, and admitted to the beautiful rite of confirmation; and this we foresee will gradually extend over all our congregations. The Hebrew language is now taught, studied, known as any other modern tongue. The time may, nay it WILL come, though it seems a wild dream now, when it shall again be the language of the Israelites, not alone wherein to pray, but to converse, and write, as the vernacular idiom of the lands in which we are sojourners. Our girls, equally with our boys, are attaining real grammatical knowledge of this most glorious language, and in their youth are thus imbibing treasures, which, when, in their turn, they become mothers, will be imparted to their children, and so mark them from their earliest infancy Hebrew, as well as English, French, or German. To our daughters, as to our sons, the Bible is unsealed; and its explanation is fearlessly given by many a Jewish preacher. Books of Jewish sacred literature are rising in the vernacular of the many lands of our captivity, and the time is gone by when man might fear to call himself a Jew. In the countries so often quoted, the more a Hebrew respects his creed, the more he is respected; the more spiritually enlightened he is in the doctrines, the ordinances, the commands of his own religion, the more will he find himself appreciated and valued by the spiritual-minded of even opposing creeds; and the more universal will be his brotherly love, for the less dangerous will be social intercourse.

Will not then the women of Israel do all they can to prove how deeply and earnestly they feel these things? They are free now, not only to believe and obey, but to study and speak of their glorious faith. To look themselves within their Bibles, and read there the foundation for all which we have sought humbly, yet most heartfully, to bring before them. To find in that ceaseless fountain of living waters, not alone their privileges as women of Israel, but all of strength, comfort, peace, immortal hope, and earthly guidance, which as weak frail women, they so imperatively need. Will they not then come there, and beholding not only their responsibilities and their duties, but, in the prophets, their sins in the Past and their destiny in the Future, do all they can to break from the one and forward the other? To cultivate with heart, soul, and might, all those spiritual, mental, and accomplished graces which should be every woman's, and yet more strikingly every woman's who calls herself of Israel?

In very many lands of their captivity, it is fully in their power so to do, even if it were possible, yet more so than men: for the ordinances and commands of our holy faith interfere much less with woman's retired path of domestic pursuits and pleasures, than with the more public and more ambitious career of man. Her duty is to make home happy; her mission, to *influence* man, alike in the relative duties of mother to her son, wife to her husband, sister to her brother, and, in her own person, to upraise the holy cause of a religion, which, from its pure spirituality and long concealment, is by the multitude misunderstood, vilified, and charged with such false accusations as only *acts* can remove. Something more is needed for the elevation of our faith, than even making it known through books (though that may accomplish much). We must prove the superiority of our guiding law, by the superiority of our own conduct, as women of Israel, in our own houses.

To obtain this superiority, is to become more SPIRITUAL; for in that single word every feminine grace and Jewish requisite is comprised. Let a woman truly and sincerely love her God, feel that His image is in her heart, that she can bring Him so close to her, that her every thought, her every aspiration, her every joy, as well as every prayer and sorrow, can be traced up to Him, and we need not fear that she will ever fail in her duties either to Him or to man, in His service or in her home. Once this spiritual love obtained, and a halo is thrown over her whole life, be it one of sorrow or of joy. His Law becomes part of her very being; she could not disobey it, without disobeying the gracious Father and Lord whom she loves better than herself. She will love all mankind, think evil of none (without mighty cause), for they are His children, created in His image. She will love the ties of home, her parents, husband, children, brothers and sisters, with intensest and most endearing love, for He has granted them, and filled her glowing heart with the sweet emotions which *love in Him* creates. She will regard death for herself as yet more happy than life, for then she will be with her God, and her beloved ones, for evermore undisturbed by sin or doubt, or fear or woe; and for those she loves, with human suffering indeed, for such we are permitted and encouraged to feel, but still with the firm conviction that for them all must be joy, for they are with God, and in spirit with her still. She will think less of the Grave on Earth, than of the Soul in Heaven. She will feel indeed the blank within her home, but she will realise in her heart of hearts the blessed conviction, that if Earth has one less, Heaven has one more, and becomes with each that departs, a dearer, more longed-for home. She will look on the meanest flower, the humblest bird, even as on the loftiest things of nature, with that peculiar feeling which the poet describes in those exquisite lines,

> "Thanks to the human heart by which we live,
> Thanks to its tenderness, its joys and fears.
> To me, the meanest flower which blows, can bring
> Thoughts that do often lie too deep for tears;"—
> WORDSWORTH.

because she feels them the work of her Father in heaven, created as much for her individual joy and thanksgiving, as for the multitudes, who in the Past and the Present and Future have gazed, and will still gaze upon the same.

This is to be spiritual—this is to be an Israelite—this is to be WOMAN! We are quite aware that many of our English readers will exclaim, "Why, this is to be Christian!" and refuse to believe that such emotions can have existence in a Jewish heart. While our Jewish readers will, in consequence, refuse to seek its attainment, because, if it resembles Christianity, it cannot be Jewish; both parties choosing to forget that the SPIRIT of their widely differing creeds has exactly the same origin, the word of God; whence all of Christianity, save its doctrine of belief, originally came.

Let those who deny spirituality to Israel, and declare that it is only from association with the Christian, and reading Christian books, that we think of spirituality at all, read the morality of the Talmud, even if they can only procure those extracts in the Hebrew Review; and unless resolved to retain their opinion in the very face of conviction, they must acknowledge that from us all their spirituality came, and that if we are re-awakening to its sublime call, it is not from association with them, but from peace and freedom, permitting us once more to honour the Lord as our God, and giving us those extracts from our venerable teachers, which show us in what light they regard the ordinances of the Lord. We will quote one passage, even at the risk of being thought tedious, merely to prove our assertion, that spirituality was the very breath of our religion; and how, in fact, could it be otherwise, when it came direct from the revelation of the Lord?

"Man is to impress his mind, *that whatever he does, is to be with the intention to glorify his Creator.* His rising, his walking, his speech, and all his occupations, are to have that aim. When eating, drinking, indulging in affection, his purpose is not to be the mere gratification of his desires. His food is merely to be wholesome and nourishing, far removed from luxury. In love he is to recollect its end and aim. Even when he lies down to sleep, it is to be with the intention to arise cheerful and refreshed for the service of his Creator, and thus, even the act of sleep will be an act of worship to his Creator, for our rabbies say, *Let the aim of all thou undertakest be the glory of the Deity.* And thus Solomon says, *In all thy*

ways acknowledge Him, and He shall direct thy paths."*
Again, we are commanded to associate with the pious and wise, in order to learn their ways; as it is said in the Law, ye shall attach yourselves to Him, you shall *attach yourself to everything that leads to Him, sanctity and perfection*. And again, after most minute directions, as to the forgiveness of injuries, and banishment of inward resentment, even to its being sinful for man, when he does a kind action to an injured, to say, "Take it, I will not do to thee as thou didst to me," for it is transgressing the command, "Thou shalt not resent," it continues, "*a man is entirely to dismiss every feeling of ill-will from his heart and mind, as the law not only extends to the actual deed, but likewise to the inward sentiments; and, therefore, the mind must be pure, so that the actions must flow from a worthy source.*"†

With such writings *our own*, and ours from centuries long past, do we need the works of Christian divines to make Israel spiritual? Oh shame! shame on those sons of Israel, who, from pure ignorance, deny spirituality to their beautiful creed, and report that we are not a spiritual people! If we have not been, oppressive slavery is the cause. If we are not now, in those nations where we are FREE, the heart shudders at the sin we are incurring: and, oh, fearful is it, if the Women of Israel neglect the opportunities now their own, and refuse to become the pure spiritual beings, which not only their religion, but their sex so imperatively demands. We fear, that with all our efforts to explain our meaning, we shall still by several not be understood; for spirituality is so exquisite and refined, so subtle an essence, that to describe, or explain, or teach it, is impossible. It can only be infused by the earnest desire to possess it, and by the grace of God. It is so peculiarly woman's attribute, that without it her loveliest charms, her highest intellect, appears imperfect. By man it is unattainable to the same extent, unattainable, in fact, at all, unless infused by the influence of woman—and therefore do we so earnestly beseech our sisters in Israel to invite, cultivate, cherish it till it so become a part of themselves, as to pervade their every word, thought, and private deed, the domestic worship of *act* and *love*, and the public service of prayer and praise, and thus it be infused into their sons with the very nourishment they give,

* Selected from Morality of the Talmud. Hebrew Review, page 29.
† Morality of the Talmud. Hebrew Review, pp. 59 and 62.

the caresses of their infancy, the education of their boyhood. Then, indeed, might man become spiritual, and in all things fitted for the first-born of the Lord.

To explain our meaning as to this spiritual essence, which should be indivisible from the woman of Israel, we will refer our young readers to some probably favourite authors. Every single line written by Mrs. S. C. Hall, whether it be a story for a little child, or a three volume novel, a tale for Chambers' Journal, or a sketch of Irish character, is so essentially SPIRITUAL, that without a single syllable unduly introduced of religion, we know it must be the religion of God's word which is the mainspring of her being. Mrs. Hemans, Mrs. Howitt, Mrs. Southey (Caroline Bowles), Joanna Baillie, are all of the same beautiful class. On the other hand, Miss Edgeworth and Miss Austin, two first-rate female writers, are *moral, not spiritual*, in their works. Among male writers—Howitt, Wilson (whether in prose or verse), James Montgomery, Wordsworth, are spiritual writers: Scott, Campbell, Rogers, and many others, are not, and yet their writings are as moral and pure as their more spiritualised brethren's. We are not alluding to either class of writers as elevating one above the other, but simply to endeavour by such reference to make our own feeling of spirituality more clearly understood.

If, then, spirituality is so essentially the vital breath of the Jewish religion and of woman's loveliest nature, will not every woman of Israel seek and strive, and pray to make it her own, now that freedom and peace are hers; and her home, though it be but of the exile, is not exposed to the awful trials of the Past, and of the Present in very many lands? If she looks into the records of her ancestors—if she remembers Leah, Deborah, Naomi, Hannah, Abigail, the Shunammite, Huldah, and Esther—must she not feel that spirituality *was* the natural attribute of the Women of Israel in the PAST? and, if she carefully studies the prophets, she will find that such *will be* their attribute in FUTURE; and there she will read that, until it is attained by man as well as woman, Israel must remain exiled and captive, far from Jerusalem and Jerusalem's God.

We have heard that censures have been passed upon our work, professing to illustrate the future destiny, as well as past history and present duties of the Hebrew females, as a presumptuous allusion to what we can know nothing about. Now, with all due deference to such critiques, we would say that unless we disbelieve the prophets, our Future Destiny is quite as clearly traced out as our own past history. To quote all the eloquent passages, prophesying not only our restoration to Jerusalem, but the circumcision of the heart, and awakening of that spiritual religion which will unite us, even on earth, with God, would be useless here. We can only refer our readers to the prophets themselves, and, as briefly as may be, condense and indite what appears to us to be their meaning.

When restored to Jerusalem, sin will be purified from the human heart; all of stagnation, of hardness, of unbelief, will have vanished; we shall not have to struggle with those imperfections and failings which come between the heart and its God, and deaden all spiritual worship. We shall all know Him then, from the smallest to the greatest of us; there will be no occasion to say to one another, "Know ye the Lord?" Our burnt-offerings and sacrifices will be again acceptable; the temple of the Lord will be re-established on His holy mountain; and not only will it be sought by the remnant of Israel, gathered from the North and from the South, and from the East and from the West, but *strangers* will join themselves to Israel, and *all nations* will flow unto it, and never more walk in the imagination of their own hearts. The Ten Tribes will be discovered, and Israel and Judah once again made one. Disease and suffering will pass away; even death itself be swallowed up for ever. Our nobles shall be of ourselves, our governors spring from the midst of us, and the Lord himself God over all the families *of Israel*. Pastors and shepherds will be granted us according to the spirit of the Lord, and they will fill us with knowledge and understanding. Not only will the law and its everlasting ordinances be restored; but it will so be written in our hearts that we shall never more disobey or fail in its spiritual observance. There will be no more vain yearnings in the soul, seeking to spring from its earthly prison to obtain more earnest communion with its God; for every soul will be satisfied with His goodness; the heavy and the sorrowful will be so filled with His love, that weariness and sorrow will alike flee away, and be but names belonging to the Past. And this spiritual restoration will not be distinct from a return to Jewish ordinances and Jewish ceremonies, as our opponents believe. I know not how any reasoning and believing mind, be his creed what it may, can peruse the prophet Ezekiel, from the 40th chapter to the end, without being almost startled at its close resemblance to the Hebrew religion ordained by God through His servant Moses. More extended, indeed, alike in the size of the Temple and the Holy Land, as *must be*, for the reception of the multitude, not only of Israel, but of the nations who will universally flow thither, till the earth overflows with righteousness. But, however extended, we must perceive that the prophet divides the land once more into the inheritance of the *twelve* tribes; that the gates of the Holy City all bear the names of Jacob's sons. The heritage of the sons of Levi is again to have the service of the Lord. The altars, and courts, and fountains, are all prepared for the restoration of the holy sacrifices and offerings, which, in our captivity, God ordained to cease; nay, the very number and species of animals for the offerings are named, the feasts and fasts referred to: and how, then, can our opponents attempt to persuade us that the sacrifices, and offerings, and festivals, are all but types of another dispensation, and done away with now for ever? What, then, is the meaning of this sublime prophecy, if the religion of the Lord revealed by Moses, *ceremonial* as well as spiritual and moral, is never to be restored? The merit of sacrifices and offerings consisted, not in themselves, but in OBEDIENCE, and that obedience, in our restoration, will again be tried, and never more found to fail, for God Himself has promised to remove the stony heart from our breasts, and encase it with the heart of flesh, on which love for Him and His ordinances will be impressed for everlasting.

Faint and feeble is this attempt to portray the destiny awaiting Israel in his own bright land, and earnestly, entreatingly, we beseech our readers to turn to the prophecies themselves, and, tracing it there, remember that every consoling promise, every spiritual joy, every forgiveness of sin, is promised to *all Israel*, woman as well as man. Who that believes in the prophecies can continue to say that the future destiny of the Hebrew females is a subject unknown, and that, therefore, it is presumptuous to allude to it? To be restored to our own land, and to the religion of God, as Moses taught it, undimmed, untarnished by a single breath of man; to love the Lord, indeed, with heart, and soul, and might, and our neighbours as ourselves; to feel no shade, no doubt, creep over our minds, and deaden all of spiritual joy; no human imperfections steal between loving hearts, and bid discord reign where God ordained all peace—to feel no weariness, no sadness—but every yearning filled; to be exposed no more to war, be it of sword or word; to become sisters, wives, mothers of men, who, as the first-born of the Lord, in whatever social rank they occupy, be it prince or peasant, noble or servant, priest or herdsman, will yet, in the sight of all the nation, uphold and show forth the glory, and the majesty, and the mercy of the Lord. This is our future destiny—this the goal to which, as women of Israel, we must press forward, heart and soul; for no little towards its eventual attainment depends on *us*, weak, frail, insignificant in seeming as we are.

It is, we believe, the supposition of some, that as God had ordained these things, nothing depends on man; we have only to wait His time. A long and careful study of His word, will, however, convince that merely to *wait* is not enough: our own exertions, our own ceaseless prayers, must hasten the day of our restoration, or still it will be postponed. We must return to the Lord in our captivity, or how will He hear us? "If they shall confess their iniquity, and the iniquity of their fathers, with their trespass which they have trespassed against me, and that also they have walked contrary to me; and that I also have walked contrary unto them, and have brought them into the land of their enemies; *if then* their uncircumcised heart be humbled, and they then accept of the punishment of their iniquity, *then* will I remember my covenant with Jacob, and also my covenant with Isaac: and also my covenant with Abraham will I remember; and I will also remember their land."*
And that covenant was, that as the stars of heaven and the sand of the sea-shore, so should be his seed, and in that seed all the nations of the earth should be blessed, whilst before the Lord it was a nation for everlasting and he would be their God. And again still more forcibly, "And it shall come to pass when all these things are come upon thee, the blessing and the curse, which I have set before thee, *and thou shalt call them to mind amongst all the nations, whither the Lord thy God hath driven thee*, and *shalt return unto the Lord thy God, and shalt obey his voice, according to all that I command thee this day, thou and thy children with all thine heart, and with all thy soul,* THAT THEN the Lord thy God will turn thy captivity and have compassion on thee, and will return and gather thee *from all the nations whither the Lord thy God hath scattered thee; and thy Lord thy God will circumcise thy heart and the heart of*

* Levit. xxvi. 40—42.

thy seed, to love the Lord thy God with all thine heart, and with all thy soul, THAT THOU MAYST LIVE."*

With these eloquent words of Moses before us, confirmed as they are throughout every prophet, can we doubt a single moment, that the Eternal waits to return unto us till we return unto Him, to release us from captivity, till we acknowledge its justice, by deploring, confessing, and conquering our sins? We must know and feel it relates to *us now*, and not to our first captivity; for then, Babylon alone was the scene of our exile, and now it is *over all* the nations that we are scattered. And what is the first gracious promise proffered to win us to return? "That our stony hearts shall be circumcised, that we may *love the Lord our God with all our heart and soul,* and so that we may *live,* not only on earth, but *in heaven,*" for such is the true meaning of Moses' words; and will not this prove to us, that to *love* GOD stands first of every duty and hallows every form, which, without such love, is mere mockery to Him, and lifelessness to us? And to love God thus, is to attain that spirituality which we so earnestly conjure every woman of Israel to seek; for unless she attain it, there is little hope for man, and without it, O when will Israel be restored—when will our captivity be at an end? We appeal not to our sisters in Israel merely *as women*, though that is in itself sufficient need for the comfort, the blessedness, of a spiritual worship; but as, under God, the influencers of *man*. Compare the boy whose tender years have been passed with a spiritual, a gentle mother, to him who from his earliest infancy has been thrown on the rude influences of man's guidance in a public school; follow these boys to manhood, and there will be little doubt who will most maintain the spiritual, as well as the ceremonial worship of his fathers, or tend most to uphold the glory of his God. Oh, as we would hasten our glorious destiny, let us ponder well our own responsibilities, and, becoming more spiritual ourselves, infuse the same immortal essence into man! If we do this, shall we say we have done nothing? Shall we not uphold the dignity, the beauty, the holiness, of our privileges as women of Israel, if we so infuse, so guide, as mothers, that man, uplifted from his grosser self, shall unite the spiritual with the worldly, the love of God with the dreams of earth, that without neglecting or despising a single earthly duty, or human feeling, he may forward the

* Deut. xxx. 1—6.

glorious cause of God, and, in the sight of the whole Gentile world, stand forth an Israelite indeed? And not as mothers only may we do this: let but the women of Israel cast aside the frivolous occupations, the petty failings, the love of mere pleasure, which are sometimes the characteristics of her sex, and remembering she is a woman of Israel, a daughter of the Lord, cultivate and love the higher and nobler attributes of heart and spirit; let her prove, by the whole aspect of her life, be she young or old, married or single, the cherished member of a family, or lonely upon earth, yet let her prove that she is spiritual, alike in the cloudless happiness, the elastic enjoyments of the young girl, and in the quieter pleasures of the matron, the peaceful calm of the more aged; that there is a deeper source than meets the eye; that all man sees and feels so loveable is formed from that close communion with her God—called spirituality;—and without one serious word, without one reference to the subject blended with her being, yet will woman influence man, and, raising her in his estimation, bid him reverence whilst he loves, and so gradually become infused with the same loftiness of thought, and holiness of deed, inseparable from spiritualised woman. His superior reason, his mightier power, his cooler and more penetrating judgment, will dictate the just medium how to make these noble qualities, imbibed from woman, most useful to his fellows, most serviceable in the cause of God; but not the less will he love and value that weaker sex from whom they are derived.

To the women of Israel, then, is entrusted the noble privilege of hastening "the great and glorious day of the Lord," by the instruction they bestow upon their sons, and the spiritual elevation to which they may attain in social intercourse, and yet more in domestic life. O that we might hope that we have not entirely worked in vain! but that, becoming, through these lowly pages, more sensible of their privileges as Women of Israel—feeling that for them, and them alone, the Most High God deigned Himself to provide a law, and take them in their weakness, their liability to suffering and oppression, under His own especial care—that (instead of degrading and enslaving) the Mosaic religion (as Moses taught, and as the elders commented upon, and the people practised) cared for woman as none other did: else others, too, would have produced their prophetesses;—that to them is entrusted the regeneration of Israel, and from their instructions, their influence, there must arise men, spiritualised and gifted for the service of Israel, and his God, and also women, fit helpmates for such men;—that on them, in their homes, and in their world, depends the manifestation of that spiritual, mental and lofty superiority which their whole history marks their own; —that *they* must prove the falsity of those charges hinted by the ignorant against their religion and themselves;—that, feeling to their heart's core these things, they would break from the long years of slavery and woe, unshackle the spirit from the heavy chains of indifference, which a cessation from oppression originally wove, burst from the prejudices of darkened years, and stand forth, in the face of their nation and the whole world, the ministering spirits of love, and thoughtfulness, and worth, companions of man's intellect and need; yet seeking not, dreaming not to vie with him; beautifiers of home, spiritualisers of earth, even as at their creation, and in the revelation of his law, the God of Israel ordained! And if we can attain to this, shall we fail? O let us press forward in this glorious path! Let us on, heeding not disappointment, difficulty, or depression! Man cannot deny us our privileges, cannot banish us from the heritage of the children of the Lord—for from everlasting will Israel endure. "Thus saith the Lord, which giveth the sun for a light by day, and the ordinances of the moon and the stars for a light by night, which divideth the sea when the waves thereof roar—the Lord of Hosts is His name. If these ordinances depart from before me, saith the Lord, *then* the seed of Israel shall cease from being a nation before me for ever. Thus saith the Lord, If heaven above can be measured, and the foundations of the earth searched out beneath, I will cast off the seed of Israel for all that they have done, saith the Lord." And if we are daughters and sisters, wives and mothers, of a people so beloved, O what does not devolve on us to forward and proclaim the glory, and the mercy, and the wisdom, and the love of Israel's Almighty God!

THE END.

www.ingramcontent.com/pod-product-compliance
Lightning Source LLC
Chambersburg PA
CBHW011743220426
43666CB00017B/2879